THE PROSE READER

THE PROSE READER

Essays for Thinking, Reading, and Writing

EIGHTH EDITION

Kim Flachmann

Michael Flachmann

California State University
Bakersfield

PEARSON
Prentice
Hall

Upper Saddle River, New Jersey 07458

Library of Congress Cataloging-in-Publication Data

The prose reader : essays for thinking, reading, and writing / [compiled by] Kim Flachmann, Michael Flachmann. — 8th ed.

    p. cm.

    Includes index.

    ISBN 0-13-157754-9

1. College readers.   2. English language—Rhetoric—Problems, exercises, etc.   3. Report writing—Problems, exercises, etc.   I. Flachmann, Kim.   II. Flachmann, Michael.

    PE1417.P847 2007

    808′.0427—dc22

                                                   2006101528

Editorial Director: Leah Jewell
Senior Acquisitions Editor: Brad Potthoff
Senior Marketing Manager: Windley Morley
Marketing Assistant: Kim Caldwell
Director of Marketing: Brandy Dawson
Executive Managing Editor: Ann Marie McCarthy
Editorial Assistant: Megan Dubrowski
Production Liaison: Fran Russello
Permissions Specialist: Lisa Black
Manufacturing Buyer: Mary Ann Gloriande
Cover Design: Kiwi Design
Cover Illustration/Photo: Brightly-Colored Woven Hats/Corbis RF
Photo Researcher: Julie Tesser
Image Permission Coordinator: Craig Jones
Composition/Full-Service Project Management: Pine Tree Composition, Inc.
Printer/Binder: The Courier Companies
Cover Printer: Coral Graphics

For permission to use copyrighted material, grateful acknowledgment is made to the copyright holders on pages 655 through 658, which are hereby made part of this copyright page.

Pearson Education LTD., London
Pearson Education Singapore, Pte. Ltd
Pearson Education Canada, Ltd.
Pearson Education—Japan
Pearson Education Australia PTY, Limited

Pearson Education North Asia Ltd
Pearson Educación de Mexico, S.A. de C.V.
Pearson Education Malaysia, Pte. Ltd
Pearson Education, Upper Saddle River,
   New Jersey

10 9 8 7 6 5 4 3 2 1
ISBN-13: 978-0-13-157754-1
ISBN-10: 0-13-157754-9

For Our Students

RHETORICAL TABLE OF CONTENTS

Introduction: *Thinking, Reading, and Writing* 1

1   Description: *Exploring through the Senses* 31

The description of a simple, comforting ritual—the putting up of a front-porch swing in early summer—confirms the value of ceremony in the life of a small town.

Have you ever wondered what being in prison is like? Kimberly Wozencraft takes us for a no-nonsense tour of the "correctional institution" in Kentucky that was her home for over a year.

---

2 Narration: *Telling a Story*   91

3 Example: *Illustrating Ideas* 141

Why do people have children? Comedian Bill Cosby presents several hilarious and ironic reasons in this truthful look at the effects kids have on our lives.

Do you speak the same language in public that you do in private with your family and friends? Richard Rodriguez argues for the importance of both forms of communication.

How should we treat the handicapped? Blind author Harold Krents gives us a few lessons in judging people on their abilities rather than their disabilities.

In this provocative and intriguing essay, author Amy Tan examines the relationship between her mother's "fractured" English and her own talent as a writer.

Brent Staples's horrifying description of his brother's inner city killing lays bare the decay of urban America and its effect on the young African-America men who are imprisoned there.

4 Process Analysis: *Explaining Step by Step* 188

Feeling frantic and disorganized? Time-management expert Edwin Bliss reveals secrets of organization that will make your life much easier.

---

5 Division/Classification: *Finding Categories*   245

10 The Research Paper: *Reading and Writing from Sources*   545

BARBARA EHRENREICH   *The Ecstasy of War*   **561**

Do men and women possess a natural "warrior instinct" that enables them to kill their enemies during battle? Not so, claims Barbara Ehrenreich, though many social and cultural rituals help transform ordinary people into effective soldiers.

NANCY NADOLSKI   *Getting a Good Night's Sleep: Diagnosing and Treating Insomnia*   **570**

When was the last time you got a really great night's sleep? Nurse practitioner Nancy Nadolski says you need one every night, and she tells you how to get it.

EDWARD AYERS   *The American Civil War, Emancipation, and Reconstruction on the World Stage*   **585**

Award-winning professor and author Edward L. Ayers explains the mysteries of the American Civil War in this beautifully written documented essay.

Chapter Writing Assignments   600

11 Further Thinking, Reading, and Writing: *Combining Rhetorical Modes*   601

Essays

ROGER ROSENBLATT   *"I Am Writing Blindly"*   **603**

What is the basic, primal urge that drives us to communicate with each other? In this brief yet brilliant essay, Roger Rosenblatt examines the reasons why we write "blindly" to the world around us.

RITA MAE BROWN   *Writing as a Moral Act*   **605**

Novelist Rita Mae Brown argues persuasively that good writers should always tell the truth. "If you aren't reading books that challenge you, you're reading the wrong books," she claims.

Fiction

RICHARD WRIGHT   *The Library Card*   **611**

Set in the segregationist South, Wright's short story illustrates the triumph of one brave man's lust for learning over a society that seeks to keep him "in his place."

THEMATIC
TABLE OF CONTENTS

PREFACE
TO THE INSTRUCTOR

The Prose Reader is based on the assumption that lucid writing follows lucid thinking, whereas poor written work is almost inevitably the product of foggy, irrational thought processes. As a result, our primary purpose in this book, as in the first seven editions, is to help students *think* more clearly and logically—both in their minds and on paper.

Furthermore, we believe that college students should be able to think, read, and write on three increasingly difficult levels:

1. *Literal—characterized by a basic understanding of words and their meanings;*
2. *Interpretive—consisting of a knowledge of linear connections between ideas and an ability to make valid inferences based on those ideas; and*
3. *Critical—the highest level, distinguished by the systematic investigation of complex ideas and by the analysis of their relationship to the world around us.*

To demonstrate the vital interrelationship between reader and writer, our text provides students with prose models intended to inspire their own thinking and writing. Although studying rhetorical strategies is certainly not the only way to approach writing, it is a productive means of helping students become better writers. These essays are intended to encourage your students to improve their writing through a partnership with some of the best examples of professional prose available today. Just as musicians and athletes richly benefit from studying the techniques of the foremost people in their fields, your students will grow in spirit and language use from their collaborative work with the excellent writers in this collection.

HOW THE TEXT WORKS

Each chapter of *The Prose Reader* begins with an explanation of a single rhetorical technique as a means of processing information. These explanations are divided into six sections that progress from the effect of this technique on our daily lives to its integral role in the writing process. Also in each introduction, we include a student paragraph and a student essay featuring each rhetorical strategy under discussion. The essay is annotated to illustrate how to write that type of essay and to help bridge the gap between student writing and the professional selections that follow. After each student essay, the writer has drafted a personal note with some useful advice for other student writers.

The essays that follow each chapter introduction are selected from a wide variety of well-known contemporary authors. Although each essay in this collection focuses on a single rhetorical mode as its primary strategy, other strategies are always simultaneously at work. These selections concentrate on one primary technique at a time in much the same way a well-arranged photograph highlights a certain visual detail, though many other elements function in the background to make the picture an organic whole.

Before each reading selection, we offer some material to focus your students' attention on a particular writer and topic before they begin reading the essay. This "prereading" segment begins with biographical information about the author and ends with a number of questions to whet the reader's appetite for the essay that follows, including an Internet exercise with a companion writing assignment after the professional essay. This section is intended to help your students discover interesting relationships among ideas in their reading and then anticipate various ways of analyzing the essay. The prereading questions forecast not only the content of the essay, but also the questions and writing assignments that follow.

The questions after each reading selection are designed as guides for thinking about the essay. These questions are at the heart of the relationship represented in this book among thinking, reading, and writing. They are divided into four interrelated sections that shepherd your students smoothly from a literal understanding of what they have just read, to interpretation, and finally to analysis.

After your students have studied the different techniques at work in a reading selection, specific essay assignments let them practice all these skills in unison and encourage them to discover even more secrets about the intricate and exciting details of effective communication. Four "Ideas for Discussion/Writing" topics (one based on the prereading Internet exercise) are preceded by "prewriting" questions to help your students generate new ideas. Most of these topics specify a purpose and an audience so your students can focus their writing as precisely as possible.

The word *essay* (which comes from the Old French *essai,* meaning a "try" or an "attempt") is an appropriate label for these writing assignments, because they all ask your students to wrestle with an idea or problem and then *attempt* to give shape to their conclusions in some effective manner. Such "exercises" can be equated with the development of athletic ability: The essay itself demonstrates that your students can put together all the various skills they have learned; it proves they can actually play the "sport" of writing.

At the end of every chapter is a collection of essay assignments that ask your students to choose a topic in one of three categories: Practicing a particular rhetorical mode, Exploring Ideas, or Analyzing Visual Images. Each of these groups of assignments has a slightly different focus so students can choose the prompts that bring out their strengths.

WHAT REMAINS THE SAME

Logical Organization

The Prose Reader is still organized according to the belief that our mental abilities are logically sequential. In other words, students cannot read or write analytically before they are able to perform well on the literal and interpretive levels. Accordingly, the book progresses from selections that require predominantly literal skills (*Description, Narration,* and *Example*) through readings involving more interpretation (*Process Analysis, Division/Classification, Comparison/Contrast,* and *Definition*) to essays that demand a high degree of analytical thought (*Cause/Effect* and *Argument/Persuasion*). Depending on your curriculum and the caliber of your students, these rhetorical modes can, of course, be studied in any order.

Two Tables of Contents

The Prose Reader provides two Tables of Contents: Rhetorical and Thematic. First, the book contains a Rhetorical Table of Contents, which includes a one- or two-sentence synopsis of each selection so you can peruse the list quickly and decide which essays to assign. An alternate Thematic Table of Contents lists selections by academic discipline for the instructor who likes to teach essays in thematic clusters.

Useful Rhetorical Introductions

The chapter introductions are filled with a variety of useful information about each rhetorical mode. Each of the nine rhetorical divisions in the text is introduced by an explanation of how to think, read, and write in that particular mode. Although each chapter focuses on one rhetorical strategy, students are continually encouraged to examine ways in which other modes help support each essay's main intentions.

Two Student Writing Samples in Each Chapter

Two separate student writing samples are featured for each rhetorical mode. The chapter introductions contain a sample student paragraph and a complete student essay that illustrate each rhetorical pattern.

After each essay is the student writer's analysis of the most enjoyable, exasperating, or noteworthy aspects of writing that particular essay. We have found that this combination of student essays and commentaries makes the professional selections easier for students to read and more accessible as models of thinking and writing.

Reading and Writing Checklists for Each Rhetorical Mode

This edition still includes user-friendly checklists for reading and writing at the end of each chapter introduction. These checklists summarize the information in the chapter introduction and serve as references for the students in their own reading and writing tasks. Students should be directed to these lists as early in the course as possible.

Thorough Biographies

Each reading selection is preceded by thorough biographical information on the author and provocative prereading questions on the subject of the essay. Because our own experience suggests that students often produce their best writing when they are personally involved in the topics of the essays they read and in the human drama surrounding the creation of those essays, the biographies explain the real experiences from which each essay emerged, and the prereading questions ("Preparing to Read") help students focus on the purpose, audience, and subject of the essay. The prereading material also foreshadows the questions and writing assignments that follow each selection. Personalizing this preliminary material encourages students to identify with both the author of an essay and its subject matter, thereby engaging the students' attention and energizing their responses to the selections they read.

Companion Internet Exercises

We have continued the Internet exercises for each essay. The prereading material before each essay contains an Internet exercise that will allow your students to explore some aspect of the topic on the Internet before reading the essay. The exercises offer the students guidance in going to specific sites. Following the essays, these tasks are then linked to a writing assignment that draws on the Internet as well.

Wide Range of Essay Topics

The essays in *The Prose Reader* continue to represent a wide range of topics. As in the past, the essays in this edition were selected on the basis

Preface to the Instructor

of five important criteria: (1) high interest level, (2) currency in the field, (3) moderate length, (4) readability, and (5) broad subject variety. Together, they portray the universality of human experience as expressed through the viewpoints of men and women, many different ethnic and racial groups, and a variety of ages and social classes. The essay topics in this volume include such provocative subjects as discrimination, ethnic identity, job opportunities, aging, war, DNA testing, women's roles, prison life, time management, travel, risk-taking, sports, the Patriot Act, family values, immigration, physical handicaps, reading, and the writing process itself.

Strong Commitment to Cultural and Gender Diversity

This edition continues its strong commitment to cultural and gender diversity. Although multicultural and women's issues have always been well represented in *The Prose Reader,* this edition includes even more essays by women and ethnic minority authors, among them Linda Hogan, Richard Rodriguez, Malcolm X, Stephanie Ericsson, Lyn Mikel Brown, Meda Chesney-Lind, Barbara Kingsolver, Kim Severson, and Nancy Nadolski.

Other Select Literature

Following a request by an overwhelming majority, we have retained the collection of literature in our "Thinking, Reading, and Writing" section (Chapter 11). This chapter includes two essays, two short stories, two poems, and a brief play—all on the topics of thinking, reading, or writing. In addition to demonstrating all the rhetorical modes at work, these selections provide a strong conclusion to the theoretical framework of this text by focusing intently on the interrelationships among thinking, reading, and writing.

Four Progressively More Sophisticated Types of Questions

This edition offers four progressively more sophisticated types of questions at the end of each selection. These questions are designed to help students move sequentially from various literal-level responses to interpretation and analysis; they also help reveal both the form and content of the essays so your students can cultivate a similar balance in their own writing.

1. *Understanding Details—questions that test the students' literal and interpretive understanding of what they have read;*

2. *Thinking Critically*—*questions that require students to analyze various aspects of the essay;*

3. *Discovering Rhetorical Strategies*—*questions that investigate the author's rhetorical strategies in constructing the essay;*

4. *Making Connections*—*questions that ask students to find thematic and rhetorical connections among essays they have read.*

Prewriting Prompts

The writing assignments ("Ideas for Discussion/Writing") are preceded by Preparing to Write questions. These questions are designed to encourage students to express their feelings, thoughts, observations, and opinions on various topics related to their reading. Questions about their own ideas and experiences help students produce strong convictions that they can then mold into compelling essays.

Realistic Writing Assignments

The writing assignments after each essay seek to involve students in realistic situations. For instructors who like to use role-playing in their teaching, many writing assignments provide a specific purpose and audience in the essay topics. In this manner, student writers are drawn into rhetorical scenes that carefully focus their responses to a variety of questions or problems. These assignments are designed for use inside or outside the classroom.

Glossary of Composition Terms and an Index

The book concludes with a glossary of composition terms and an index of authors and titles. The glossary provides not only definitions of composition terms but also examples of these terms from essays in this book, including specific page numbers. The index lists the author and title of each reading in the book to assist you if you are searching for a particular selection. Both the glossary and the index serve as excellent reference tools for your students as they progress through the material in the text.

WHAT IS NEW

We have made several changes in the eighth edition of *The Prose Reader* that represent the responses of instructors from many different types of colleges and universities throughout the United States.

Thinking/Reading/Writing Triangles

Special triangles throughout the text mark the discussion of critical thinking, reading, and writing. In each chapter, the points of these triangles feature a brief checklist of highlights in that particular section. These lists serve as summaries of the material in that section. These highlights are then incorporated into the more complete reading and writing checklists at the end of each chapter introduction.

Twenty New Essays

The eighth edition of *The Prose Reader* contains twenty new essays, including an interesting and provocative photo essay. We have updated some of the essays, added new authors, and introduced many new topics, such as committing to a place, language acquisition, learning to read, the theory of evolution, girl-fighting, bingeing on college campuses, violence in the United States, gay marriage, graffiti, DNA testing, the Patriot Act, insomnia, and the American Civil War.

Seventeen New Photographs

In addition to the nine photos we included in the critical thinking section of each chapter introduction in the last edition, we have added sixteen more pictures to this edition. Since most students have grown up accustomed to visual stimulation from television and video games, they have the natural ability to "read" pictures. But they need to learn how to analyze them, just as they analyze words and ideas. As a result, we have added one black-and-white photograph to the writing assignments at the end of each chapter and seven color photos as an essay in Chapter 9. Finally, two additional critical-thinking assignments now appear in the margins of the book in case your students need more practice in a particular mode.

Interactive Critical Thinking Questions

Introduced in this edition is a new set of questions that will help students interact critically with their reading as they prepare for the assignments after each essay. These questions appear at the bottom of the pages of the essays and are designed to provide a "bridge" between the personal prereading questions and the more broad-based academic questions and assignments that follow each essay. Through these queries, students will understand their reading on a deeper level by filtering the content of each essay through their own experience. The questions are marked both in the essays and at the bottom of the pages by numbers within diamonds.

Completely New Argument/Persuasion Chapter

The Argument/Persuasion section (Chapter 9) now includes five essays on a variety of topics, one photo essay, and three sets of opposing-viewpoint essays (with a total of eight essays). These essays in Chapter 9 are particularly useful for helping students refine their critical thinking skills in preparation for longer, more sustained papers on a single topic. The first five essays in this chapter encourage students to grapple with provocative issues that make a crucial difference in how we all live, such as disciplining children, binge drinking, the value of life, violence and TV, and gay marriage. The photo essay asks students to participate in an ongoing conversation on graffiti in American cities. Then the three sets of opposing-viewpoint essays will help your students see coherent arguments at work from several different perspectives on a single issue. These final essays cover such timely topics as immigration, postconviction DNA testing, and the Patriot Act.

Revised Research Paper Chapter (Chapter 10)

"The Research Paper: Reading and Writing from Sources" (Chapter 10) features a new student essay and some up-to-the-minute information on citing sources in three different documentation styles. The essays in this chapter now demonstrate documentation in Modern Language Association (MLA), American Psychological Association (APA), and the Chicago Manual of Style (CM). By including term papers, we intend to clarify some of the mysteries connected with research and documentation and to provide interesting material for creating longer and more elaborate writing assignments. These essays cover the history of war, insomnia, and the American Civil War. We offer a full range of apparatus for these selections, and at the end of each selection we provide a list of Further Reading on each subject and suggested topics for longer, more sophisticated essays and research papers.

New Set of Writing Assignments

This edition offers a new set of writing assignments at the end of each chapter based on pictures. The assignments at the end of each chapter are now divided into three categories, offering (1) more practice in a specific rhetorical mode, (2) a focus on interesting contemporary themes regardless of rhetorical mode, and (3) an opportunity to analyze and respond to a provocative photograph. This new feature gives you even more prompts to choose from if you want your students to have further writing practice at any time.

WHAT SUPPLEMENTS ARE AVAILABLE?

Available with *The Prose Reader* is an extensive ***Annotated Instructor's Edition*** designed to help make your life in the classroom a little easier. We have filled the margins of the ***AIE*** with many different kinds of supplementary material, including instructor comments on teaching the different rhetorical modes, provocative quotations, background information on each essay, definitions of terms that may be unfamiliar to your students, a list of related readings from this text that can be taught together, innovative teaching ideas, detailed answers to the questions that follow each selection, additional essay topics, and various revising strategies.

In addition to the *Annotated Instructor's Edition,* we have also created the ***Instructor's Resource Manual with Quiz Book.*** In it, we identify and discuss some of the most widely used theoretical approaches to the teaching of composition; we then offer innovative options for organizing your course, specific suggestions for the first day of class, a summary of the advantages and disadvantages of using different teaching strategies, and several successful techniques for responding to student writing. Next, we provide two objective quizzes for each essay to help you monitor your students' mastery of each selection's vocabulary and content. This supplement ends with three additional professional essays (two opposing-viewpoint essays and one documented essay), a series of student essays (one for each rhetorical strategy featured in the text) followed by the student writer's comments, and an annotated bibliography of books and articles about thinking, reading, and writing.

Also available with *The Prose Reader* is a Companion Website™ (**www.prenhall.com/flachmann**) that offers an extensive collection of additional resources for both the student and the instructor for every essay in the text. This Web site allows students to get additional reinforcement for the text material and provides an easy way for the instructors to integrate the World Wide Web into their courses. The site includes

▶ *author biographies with contextual links;*

▶ *online vocabulary comprehension quizzes for every selection, with instant scoring;*

▶ *prereading and postreading assignments that foster critical thinking for every essay;*

▶ *dynamic Web links that provide a valuable source of additional information about the essay topics;*

- *communication tools such as chat rooms and message boards to facilitate online collaboration and communication;*

- *built-in routing that gives students the ability to forward essay responses and graded quizzes to their instructors; and*

- *a faculty module that includes an* Instructor's Resource Manual *with additional quizzes.*

This entire instructional package is intended to help your students discover what they want to say and to assist them in shaping their ideas into a coherent form, thereby encouraging their intelligent involvement in the complex and exciting world around them.

ACKNOWLEDGMENTS

We are pleased to acknowledge the kind assistance and support of a number of people who have helped us put together this eighth edition of *The Prose Reader.* For creative encouragement and editorial guidance at Prentice Hall, we thank Yolanda De Rooy, President of Humanities and Social Sciences; Leah Jewell, AVP/Editorial Director; Brad Potthoff, Senior Acquisitions Editor; Megan Dubrowski, Editorial Assistant; Brandy Dawson, Director of Marketing; Windley Morley, Senior Marketing Manager; Kim Caldwell, Marketing Assistant; Ann Marie McCarthy, Executive Managing Editor; Fran Russello, Production Liaison; and Karen Berry, Pine Tree Composition, Project Manager.

For the insightful reviews directly leading to this eighth edition, we are grateful to Amy Lawlor, Pasadena City College; Bill Day, Carl Albert State College; Hal Crimmel, Weber State University; M. Susan Schmidt, Carteret Community College; Melanie Whitebread, Luzerne County Community College; Ollie Oviedo, Eastern New Mexico University; Donna Smith, Odessa College; Michael W. Donaghe, Eastern New Mexico University; John Ziebell, Community College of Southern Nevada; Nelda Sellers, Jackson State Community College; Melissa Richardson, Central Texas College; Beth Maxfield, Blinn College; Marie T. Cox, Stark State College; Diana Nystedt, Palo Alto College; Mechel Camp, Jackson State Community College; Lorena Horton, San Jacinto College North; and Marlene Martin, Monterey Peninsula College.

For the many reviews of previous editions whose valuable contributions have guided *The Prose Reader* through many successful editions, we wish to thank Janice Jones, Kent State University; Lyle W. Morgan II, Pittsburgh State University; Carolyn D. Coward, Shelby State Community College; Teresa

Purvis, Lansing Community College; Gena E. Christopher, Jacksonville State University; Donnie Yeilding, Central Texas College; Steve Katz, State Technical Institute; Craig Howard White, University of Houston; Judith Dan, Boston University; Arlie R. Peck, University of Rio Grande; Barbara Smith, Iona College; Vermell Blanding, Hostos Community College; Nancy G. Wright, Austin Peay State University; Paula Miller, Azusa Pacific University; Paul Kistel, Pierce College; Christopher Belcher, Community College of Allegheny County; Helen F. Maxon, Southwestern Oklahoma State University; Geoffrey C. Goodale, University of Massachusetts at Boston; Martha Bergeron, Vance-Granville Community College; Jan LaFever, Friends University; Virginia Leonard, West Liberty State College; Melissa A. Bruner, Southwestern Oklahoma State University; James Zarzana, Southwest State University; Terrence Burke, Cuyahoga Community College; Ellen Dugan-Barrette, Brescia College; Lewis Emond, Dean Junior College; Jay Jernigan, Eastern Michigan University; Nellie McCrory, Gaston College; Leslie Shipp, Clark County Community College; William F. Sutlife, Community College of Allegheny County; Maureen Aitkn, University of Michigan; Mickie R. Braswell, Lenoir Community College; Judith Burnham, Tulsa Community College; Charles H. Cole, Carl Albert State College; Todd Lieber, Simpson College; Bill Marsh, National University; Felicia S. Pattison, Sterling College; Dianne Peich, Delaware County Community College; K. Siobhan Wright, Carroll Community College; Melody Ziff, Northern Virginia Community College–Annandale; Robin Morris Hardin, Cape Fear Community College; Matthew Stiffler, Utah State University; Melanie Whitebread, Luzerne County Community College; June Farmer, Southern Union State Community College; Martha R. Bachman, Camden County College; Arnold Bradford, Northern Virginia Community College, Loudoun Campus; Nate Gordeon, Kiswaukee College; Alice Sink, High Point University; Bill Clemente, Peru State College; Stella Shepard, Henderson State University; Rosie Soy, Hudson County Community College; Kevin Nebergall, Kirkwood Community College; Dr. Marcia Shams, Gwinnett Technical College, Arts & Sciences Division.

Several writing instructors across the United States have been kind enough to help shape *The Prose Reader* over the course of its development by responding to specific questions about their teaching experiences with the book: Charles Bordogna, Bergen Community College; Mary G. Marshall and Eileen M. Ward, College of DuPage; Michael J. Huntington and Judith C. Kohl, Dutchess Community College; Ted Johnston, El Paso County Community College; Koala C. Hartnett, Rick James Mazza, and William H. Sherman, Fairmont State College; Miriam Dick and Betty Krasne, Mercy

College; Elvis Clark, Mineral Area College; Dayna Spencer, Pittsburg State University; James A. Zarzana, Southwest State University; Susan Reinhart Schneling and Trudy Vanderback, Vincennes University; Carmen Wong, Virginia Commonwealth University; John W. Hattman and Virginia E. Leonard, West Liberty State College; Jonathan Alexander, Widener University; Jo Ann Pevoto, College of the Mainland; Anita Pandey, University of Illinois at Urbana-Champaign; Leaf Seligman, University of New Hampshire; Arminta Baldwin, West Virginia Wesleyan College; Joaquim Mendes, New York Institute of Technology; and Sandra R. Woods, Fairmont State College.

For student essays and writing samples, we thank Rosa Marie Augustine, Donel Crow, Dawn Dobie, Gloria Dumler, Jeff Hicks, Julie Anne Judd, Judi Koch, Dawn McKee, Paul Newberry, Joanne Silva-Newberry, JoAnn Slate, Peggy Stuckey, and Jan Titus.

We also want to thank two incredibly talented colleagues for helping us with some of the new features in this edition: Monica Bulger and Anne Elrod. We are grateful to two other colleagues who served as research assistants throughout the creation of this edition: Laura Peet and Randi Brummett, who also revised the *Instructor's Resource Manual*. We also greatly appreciate the special talents of Tara Polhamus and Noel Guaglianone.

In preparing the text and the *Annotated Instructor's Edition,* we owe special gratitude to the following writing instructors who have contributed their favorite techniques for teaching various rhetorical strategies: Mary P. Boyles, Pembroke State University; Terrence W. Burke, Cuyahoga Community College; Mary Lou Conlin, Cuyahoga Community College; Ellen Dugan-Barrette, Brescia College; Janet Eber, County College of Morris; Louis Emond, Dean Junior College; Peter Harris, West Virginia Institute of Technology, Montgomery; Jay Jernigan, Eastern Michigan University; Judith C. Kohl, Dutchess Community College; Joanne H. McCarthy, Tacoma Community College; Anthony McCrann, Peru State College; Nellie McCrory, Gaston College; Alan Price, Pennsylvania State University–Hazelton; Patricia A. Ross, Moorpark College; Leslie Shipp, Clark County Community College; Rodney Simard (deceased), California State University, San Bernardino; Elizabeth Wahlquist, Brigham Young University; John White, California State University, Fullerton; and Ted Wise, Porterville College.

This book also benefits from the amazing insights and consummate teaching of Kathryn Benander (Porterville College) and Cheryl Smith (California State University, Bakersfield), who served as editorial consultants throughout the entire project. Their work and opinions were invaluable.

Our final and most important debt is to our children, Christopher and Laura, who have inspired us to be good teachers since the day they were born.

THE PROSE READER

INTRODUCTION
Thinking, Reading, and Writing

Have you ever had trouble expressing your thoughts? If so, you're not alone. Many people have this difficulty—especially when they are asked to write their thoughts down. The good news is that this "ailment" can be cured. We've learned over the years that the more clearly students think about the world around them, the more easily they can express their ideas through written and spoken language. As a result, this textbook intends to improve your writing by helping you think clearly, logically, and critically about important ideas and issues that exist in our world today. You will learn to reason, read, and write about your environment in increasingly complex ways, moving steadily from a simple, literal understanding of topics to interpretation and analysis.

Part of becoming a better writer involves understanding that reading and writing are companion activities that engage people in the creation of thought and meaning—either as readers interpreting a text or as writers constructing one. Clear thinking, then, is the pivotal point that joins together these two efforts. The traditional rhetorical strategies are presented in this text as thinking techniques or ways of processing information that you can use in other academic tasks. We feature one strategy at a time in each chapter so you can understand how it works before you combine it with other strategies, thus providing you with a systematic means of improving your ability to think, read, and write critically.

Inspired by the well-crafted prose models in this text and guided by carefully worded questions, you can actually raise the level of your thinking skills while improving your reading and writing abilities on three progressively more difficult levels:

1. *The literal level* is the foundation of all human understanding; it entails knowing the meanings of words—individually and in relation to one another. In order for someone to comprehend the sentence "You must exercise your brain to reach your full mental potential" on the literal level, for example, that person would have to know the definitions of all the words in the sentence and understand the way those words work together to make meaning.

2. *Interpretation* requires the ability to make associations between details, draw inferences from pieces of information, and reach conclusions about the material. An interpretive understanding of the sample sentence in level 1 might be translated into the following thoughts: "Exercising the brain sounds a bit like exercising the body. I wonder if there's any correlation between the two. If the brain must be exercised, it is probably made up of muscles, much like the body is." None of these particular thoughts is made explicit in the sentence, but each is suggested in one way or another.

3. *Thinking, reading, and writing critically,* the most sophisticated form of rational abilities, involves a type of mental activity that is crucial for successful academic and professional work. A critical analysis of our sample sentence might proceed in the following way: "This sentence is talking to me. It actually addresses me with the word *you.* I wonder what my mental potential is. Will I be able to reach it? Will I know when I attain it? Will I be comfortable with it? I certainly want to reach this potential, whatever it is. Reaching it will undoubtedly help me succeed scholastically and professionally. The brain is obviously an important tool for helping me achieve my goals in life, so I want to take every opportunity I have to develop and maintain this part of my body." Students who can disassemble an issue or idea in this fashion and understand its various components more thoroughly after reassembling them are rewarded intrinsically with a clearer knowledge of life's complexities and the ability to generate creative, useful ideas. They are also rewarded extrinsically with good grades and are more likely to earn responsible jobs with higher pay because they are able to apply this understanding effectively to their professional and personal lives.

In this textbook, you will learn to think critically by reading essays written by intelligent, interesting authors and by writing your own essays on a wide range of topics. The next several pages offer guidelines for approaching the thinking, reading, and writing assignments in this book. These suggestions should also be useful to you in your other courses.

THINKING CRITICALLY

Reading ———— Writing

Recent psychological studies have shown that thinking and feeling are complementary operations. All of us have feelings that are automatic and instinctive. To feel pride after winning first place at a track meet, for example, or to feel anger at a spiteful friend is not behavior we have to study and master; such emotions come naturally to all of us. Thinking, on the other hand, is much less spontaneous than feeling; research suggests that study and practice are required for sustained mental development.

Thinking critically involves grappling with ideas, issues, and problems that surround you in your immediate environment and in the world at large. It does not necessarily entail finding fault, which you might naturally associate with the word *critical,* but rather suggests continually questioning and analyzing the world around you. Thinking critically is the highest form of mental activity that human beings engage in; it is the source of success in college and in our professional and personal lives. Fortunately, all of us can learn how to think more critically.

Critical thinking means taking apart an issue, examining its various parts, and reassembling the topic with a more complete understanding of its intricacies. Implied in this explanation is the ability to see the topic from one or more new perspectives. Using your mind in this way will help you find solutions to difficult problems, design creative plans of action, and ultimately live a life consistent with your opinions on important issues that we all must confront daily.

Since critical or analytical thinking is one of the highest forms of mental activity, it requires a great deal of concentration and practice. Once you have actually felt how your mind processes information at this level, however, re-creating the experience is somewhat like riding a bicycle: You will be able to do it naturally, easily, and skillfully whenever you choose.

Our initial goal, then, is to help you think critically when you are required to do so in school, on the job, or in any other area of your life. If this form of thinking becomes part of your daily routine, you will quite naturally be able to call upon it whenever you need it.

Working with the rhetorical modes is an effective way to achieve this goal. With some guidance, each rhetorical pattern can give you a mental workout that prepares you for writing and critical thinking in the same way that physical exercises warm you up for various sports. Just as in the rest of the body, the more exercise the brain gets, the more flexible it becomes and the higher levels of thought it can attain. Through these various guided thinking exercises, you can systematically strengthen your ability to think analytically.

As you move through the following chapters, we will ask you to isolate each rhetorical mode—much like isolating your abs, thighs, and biceps in a weight-lifting workout—so that you can concentrate on these thinking patterns one at a time. Each rhetorical pattern you study will suggest slightly different ways of seeing the world, processing information, and solving problems. Each offers important ways of making sense of your immediate environment and the larger world around you. Looking closely at rhetorical modes or specific patterns of thought will allow you to discover how your mind works in that mode. In the same fashion, becoming more intricately aware of your thought patterns will help you improve your basic thinking skills as well as your reading and writing abilities. Thinking critically enables you to identify fresh insights in old ideas, generate new thoughts, and see connections between related issues. It is an energizing mental activity that puts you in control of your life and your environment rather than leaving you at the mercy of your surroundings.

Each chapter introduction provides three exercises—one of which is based on a photograph—specifically designed to help you focus in isolation on a particular pattern of thought. While you are attempting to learn what each pattern feels like in your head, use your imagination to play with these exercises on as many different levels as possible.

When you practice each of the rhetorical patterns of thought, you should be aware of building on your previous thinking skills. As the book progresses, the rhetorical modes become more complex and require a higher degree of concentration and effort. Throughout the book, therefore, you should keep in mind that ultimately you want to let these skills accumulate into a full-powered, well-developed ability to process the world around you—including reading, writing, seeing, and feeling—on the most advanced analytical level you can master.

READING CRITICALLY

Reading critically begins with developing a natural curiosity about an essay and nurturing that curiosity throughout the reading process. To learn as much as you can from an essay, you should first study any preliminary material you can find, then read the essay to get a general overview of its main ideas, and finally read the selection again to achieve a deeper understanding of its content. The three phases of the reading process explained next—preparing to read, reading, and rereading—will help you develop this natural curiosity so you can approach any reading assignment with an active, inquiring mind.

Preparing to Read

Focusing your attention is an important first stage in both the reading and the writing processes. In fact, learning as much as you can about an essay and its context (the circumstances surrounding its development) before you begin reading can help you move through the essay with an energetic, active mind and then reach some degree of analysis before writing on the assigned topics. In particular, knowing where an essay was first published, studying the writer's background, and doing some preliminary thinking on the subject of a reading selection will help you understand the writer's ideas and form some valid opinions of your own.

As you approach any essay, you should concentrate on four specific areas that will begin to give you an overview of the material you are about to read. We will use an essay by Lewis Thomas to demonstrate these techniques.

1. *Title.* A close look at the title will usually provide important clues about the author's attitude toward the topic, his or her stand on an issue, or the mood of an essay. It can also furnish you with a sense of audience and purpose.

To Err Is Human

From this title, for example, we might infer that the author will discuss errors, human nature, and the extent to which mistakes influence human behavior. The title is half of a well-known proverbial quotation written by Alexander Pope ("To err is human, to forgive, divine"), so we might speculate further that the author has written an essay intended for a well-read audience interested in the relationship between errors and humanity. After reading only four words of the essay—its title—you already have a good deal of information about the subject, its audience, and the author's attitude toward both.

2. *Synopsis.* The Rhetorical Table of Contents in this text contains a synopsis of each essay, very much like the following, so that you can find out more specific details about its contents before you begin reading.

> Physician Lewis Thomas explains how we can profit from our mistakes—especially if we trust human nature. Perhaps someday, he says, we can apply this same principle to the computer and magnify the advantages of these errors.

From this synopsis, we learn that Thomas's essay will be an analysis of human errors and of the way we can benefit from those errors. The synopsis also tells us the computer has the potential to magnify the value of our errors.

3. *Biography.* Learning as much as you can about the author of an essay will generally stimulate your interest in the material and help you achieve a deeper understanding of the issues to be discussed. From the biographies in this book, you can learn, for example, whether a writer is young or old, conservative or liberal, open- or close-minded. You might also discover if the essay was written at the beginning, middle, or end of the author's career or how well versed the writer is on the topic. Such information will invariably help you reach a more thorough understanding of a selection's ideas, audience, and logical structure.

LEWIS THOMAS   (1913–1993)

Lewis Thomas was a physician who, until his death in 1993, was president emeritus of the Sloan-Kettering Cancer Center and scholar-in-residence at the Cornell University Medical Center in New York City. A graduate of Princeton University and Harvard Medical School, he was formerly head of pathology and dean of the New York University–Bellevue Medical Center and dean of the Yale Medical School. In addition to having written over two hundred scientific papers on virology and immunology, he authored many popular scientific essays, some of which have been collected in *Lives of a Cell* (1974), *The Medusa and the Snail* (1979), *Late Night Thoughts on Listening to Mahler's Ninth Symphony* (1983), *Etcetera, Etcetera* (1990), and *The Fragile Species* (1992). The memoirs of his distinguished career have been published in *The Youngest Science: Notes of a Medicine Watcher* (1983). Thomas liked to refer to his essays as "experiments in thought": "Although I usually think I know what I'm going to be writing about, what I'm going to say, most of the time it doesn't happen that way at all. At some point, I get misled down a garden path. I get surprised by an idea that I hadn't anticipated getting, which is a little bit like being in a laboratory."

As this information indicates, Thomas was a prominent physician who published widely on scientific topics. We know that he considered his essays "experiments in thought," which makes us expect a relaxed, spontaneous treatment of his subjects. From this biography, we can also infer that he was a leader in the medical world and that, because of the positions he has held, he was well respected in his professional life. Last, we can speculate that he had a clear sense of his audience because he was able to present difficult concepts in clear, everyday language.

4. **Questions.** One other type of preliminary material will broaden your overview of the topic and enable you to approach the essay with an active, thoughtful mind. The "Preparing to Read" questions following the biographies are intended to focus your attention and stimulate your curiosity before you begin the essay. They will also get you ready to form your own opinions on the essay and its topic as you read. Keeping a journal to respond to these questions is an excellent idea, because you will then have a record of your thoughts on various topics related to the reading selection that follows.

Preparing to Read

The following essay, which originally appeared in the *New England Journal of Medicine* (January 1976), illustrates the clarity and ease with which Thomas explains complex scientific topics.

Exploring Experience: As you prepare to read this essay, take a few moments to think about the role mistakes play in our lives: What are some memorable mistakes you have made? Did you learn anything important from any of these errors? Do you make more or fewer mistakes than other people you know? Do you see any advantages to making mistakes? Any disadvantages?

Learning Online: Most computers have games included in their operating systems. Find a game on your computer, and play it for a while. Who won? What types of mistakes did the computer make? What types of mistakes did you make? Consider your experience while reading Thomas's essay.

Learning where, why, and how an essay was first written will provide you with a context for the material you are about to read: Why did the author write this selection? Where was it first published? Who was the author's original audience? This type of information enables you to understand the circumstances surrounding the development of the selection and to identify any topical or historical references the author makes. All the selections in this textbook were published elsewhere first—in another book, a journal, or a magazine. The author's original audience, therefore, consisted of the readers of that particular publication.

Then two types of questions focus the readers' attention for the first reading. The first type (Exploring Experience) asks you to begin drawing on your prior knowledge in reference to this particular topic; they ask pointed questions about your previous life experiences in preparation for this reading assignment. The second set guides you to some Internet activity that will prepare you for your reading; this activity is then linked to the final writing assignment at the end of the essay.

From the sample "Preparing to Read" material, we learn that Thomas's essay "To Err Is Human" was originally published in the *New England Journal of Medicine,* a prestigious periodical read principally by members of the scientific community. Written in 1976, the article plays upon its audience's growing fascination with computers and with the limits of artificial intelligence—subjects just as timely today as they were in the mid-1970s.

The Exploring Experience questions here prompt you to consider your own ideas, opinions, or activities in order to help you generate thoughts on the topic of errors in our lives. The Internet exercise is designed to stimulate your thinking and expand your knowledge on this and related subjects. These queries are, ideally, the last step in preparing yourself for the active role you should play as a reader.

Reading

People read essays in books, newspapers, magazines, and journals for a great variety of reasons. One reader may want to be stimulated intellectually, whereas another seeks relaxation; one person reads to keep up with the latest developments in his or her profession, whereas the next wants to learn why a certain event happened or how something can be done; some people read in order to be challenged by new ideas, whereas others find comfort principally in printed material that supports their own moral, social, or political opinions. The essays in this textbook fulfill all these expectations in different ways. They have been chosen, however, not only for these reasons, but for an additional, broader purpose: Reading them can help make you a better writer.

Every time you read an essay in this book, you will also be preparing to write your own essay concentrating on the same rhetorical pattern. For this reason, as you read you should pay careful attention to both the content (subject matter) and the form (language, sentence structure, organization, and development of ideas) of each essay. You will also see how effectively experienced writers use particular rhetorical modes or patterns of thought to organize and communicate their ideas. Each essay in this collection features one dominant pattern that is generally supported by several others. In fact, the more aware you are of each author's writing techniques, the more rapidly your own writing process will mature and improve.

The questions before and after each essay teach you a way of reading that can help you discover the relationship of a writer's ideas to one another as well as to your own ideas. These questions can also help clarify for you the connection between the writer's topic, his or her style or manner of expression, and your own composing process. In other words, the questions are designed to help you understand and generate ideas, then discover various choices the writers made in composing their essays, and finally realize the freedom you have to make related choices in your own writing. Such an approach to the process of reading takes some of the mystery out of reading and writing and makes them manageable tasks at which anyone can become proficient.

Within each essay, at the bottom of the pages, are questions designed specifically to raise your level of thinking as you read. They provide a "bridge" between the personal prereading questions and the more broad-based academic questions and assignments that follow each essay. In other words, the questions within each essay prepare you for the thinking and processing you will be asked to do at the end of a reading assignment. The bridge questions actually teach you how to interact critically with your reading material, guiding you through the text as you become partners with the essay to create meaning. As you move further into the text, these questions help you understand each essay on a deeper level by filtering the context through your own experience. They invite you to engage fully with your reading and bring it into your life so you understand it both instinctively and intellectually. If you take the time to produce a written response to these questions, you will quite naturally form your own opinions and arguments in preparation for the assignments that follow each essay.

To understand your reading material on the critical level, you should be prepared to read each essay at least three times. The first reading is an overview, during which you want to get a general sense of the essay in relation to its title, purpose, audience, and publication information. You should annotate the essay with your personal reactions and make sure you understand all the author's vocabulary.

To illustrate this process, on the following pages is the Thomas essay with a student's comments in the margins, showing how she reacted to the essay while reading it for the first time. The student also circled words she didn't know and put the definitions in the margins.

LEWIS THOMAS   (1913–1993)

To Err Is Human

Boy is this true

Everyone must have had at least one personal experi- 1
ence with a computer error by this time. Bank balances are suddenly reported to have jumped from $379
into the millions, appeals for charitable contributions
are mailed over and over to people with crazy sound-
ing names at your address, <u>department stores send the</u> *Last spring*
<u>wrong bills</u>, utility companies write that they're turn- *this*
ing everything off, that sort of thing. If you manage to *happened*
get in touch with someone and complain, you then *to me*
get instantaneously typed, guilty letters from the same
exactly computer, saying, "Our computer was in error, and an
adjustment is being made in your account."

These are supposed to be the sheerest, blindest ac- 2
cidents. Mistakes are not believed to be part of the
normal behavior of a good machine. If things go
How can wrong, it must be a personal, human error, the result
this be? of fingering, tampering, a button getting stuck, someone hitting the wrong key. The computer, at its
(perfect) normal best, is (infallible).

I wonder whether this can be true. After all, the 3
whole point of computers is that they represent an
extension of the human brain, vastly improved upon
but nonetheless human, <u>superhuman</u> maybe.[1] A good *In what*
computer can think clearly and quickly enough to *way?*
beat you at chess, and some of them have even been
programmed to write obscure verse. They can do any- *Can this be*
thing we can do, and more besides. *proven?*

I expected It is not yet known whether a computer has its own 4
this essay consciousness, and it would be hard to find out about
to be so this. When you walk into one of those great halls now
much more built for the huge machines, and stand listening, it is
stuffy than easy to imagine that the faint, distant noises are the
it is. I can sound of thinking, and the turning of the spools gives
even under- them the look of wild creatures rolling their eyes in
stand it.

Reading Critically

[1] To what extent do you feel computers "extend" the human brain? Can humans do anything that computers can't do? If so, what?

the effort to concentrate, choking with information. *In what*
But real thinking, and dreaming, are other matters. *way?*

On the other hand, the evidences of something like 5
an unconscious, equivalent to ours, are all around, in
every mail. As extensions of the human brain, they *good, clear*
have been constructed with the same property of *comparison*
error, spontaneous, uncontrolled, and rich in possibil- *for the gen-*
ities.[2] *eral reader*

so true   Mistakes are at the very base of human thought, 6
embedded there, feeding the structure like root nod- *great image*
I don't { ules. If we were not provided with the knack of being
understand { wrong, we could never get anything useful done.
this   We think our way along by choosing between right⎫
and wrong alternatives, and the wrong choices have to⎬ *I agree!*
be made as frequently as the right ones. We get along⎪ *This is how*
in life this way. We are built to make mistakes, coded⎪ *we learn*
for error.[3]

??   We learn, as we say, by "trial and error." Why do we 7
always say that? Why not "trial and rightness" or "trial
and triumph"? The old phrase puts it that way because that is, in real life, the way it is done.

Another   A good laboratory, like a good bank or a corpora- 8
effective   tion or government, has to run like a computer. Al-
comparison most everything is done flawlessly, by the book, and all
for the   the numbers add up to the predicted sums. The days *Isn't this a*
general   go by. And then, if it is a lucky day, and a lucky labo- *contradic-*
reader   ratory, somebody makes a mistake: the wrong buffer *tion?*
something in one of the blanks, a decimal misplaced
in reading counts, the warm room off by a degree and *storage*
a half, a mouse out of his box, or just a misreading of *area for*
plan   the day's protocol. Whatever, when the results come in, *data being*
something is obviously screwed up, and then the ac- *transferred*
tion can begin.   *What?*

aha!   The misreading is not the important error; it opens 9
the way. The next step is the crucial one. If the investigator can bring himself to say, "But even so, look at
that!" then the new finding, whatever it is, is ready for
snatching. What is needed, for progress to be made, is
the move based on error.

Reading Critically
[2] How could computer errors be "rich in possibilities"?
[3] Have you ever made an error that turned out to be beneficial? What happened?

Whenever new kinds of thinking are about to be   10
accomplished, or new varieties of music, there has to
be an argument beforehand. With two sides debating
arguing in the same mind, (haranguing,) there is an amiable understanding that one is right and the other wrong.
Sooner or later the thing is settled, but there can be no   *I believe*
action at all if there are not the two sides and the ar-   *Thomas*
interesting gument. The hope is in the faculty of wrongness, the   *here be-*
idea tendency toward error. The capacity to leap across   *cause of his*
mountains of information and land lightly on the   *background*
wrong side represents the highest of human endow-
ments.

Could this It may be that this is a uniquely human gift, perhaps   11
be related even stipulated in our genetic instructions.[4] Other
to the creatures do not seem to have DNA sequences for
human abil- making mistakes as a routine part of daily living, cer-
ity to think tainly not for programmed error as a guide for action.
critically?

We are at our human finest, dancing with our   12
minds, when there are more choices than two. Some-   *nice mental*
Yes, but times there are ten, even twenty different ways to go,   *image*
this is so all but one bound to be wrong, and the richness of se-
frustrating lection in such situations can lift us onto totally new
ground. This process is called exploration and is based
(imperfection) on human (fallibility). If we had only a single center in
our brains, capable of responding only when a cor-   *This is a*
rect decision was to be made, instead of the jumble   *great*
(gullible) of different, (credulous), easily (conned) clusters of neu-   *sentence—*
(fooled) rons that provide for being flung off into blind alleys,   *it has a lot*
up trees, down dead ends, out into blue sky, along   *of feeling*
wrong turnings, around bends, we could only stay the
way we are today, stuck fast.

I love the The lower animals do not have this splendid free-   13
phrase dom. They are limited, most of them, to absolute   *See ¶ 11*
"splendid (infallibility). Cats, for all their good side, never make
freedom" mistakes. I have never seen a (maladroit), clumsy, or   *look up*
blundering cat. Dogs are sometimes fallible, occasion-   *"maladroit"*
(perfection) ally able to make charming minor mistakes, but they   *(awkward)*
get this way by trying to mimic their masters. Fish are   *I like this*
flawless in everything they do. Individual cells in a tis-   *idea*

Reading Critically

[4] Do you agree with Thomas that we are genetically programmed to make mistakes in our
lives? Explain your answer.

I never thought of mistakes this way

sue are mindless machines, perfect in their performance, as absolutely inhuman as bees.

We should have this in mind as we become dependent on more complex computers for the arrangement of our affairs. Give the computers their heads, I say; let them go their way. If we can learn to do this, turning our heads to one side and wincing while the work proceeds, the possibilities for the future of mankind, and computerkind, are limitless. <u>Your aver-</u>

14

so true

Thomas makes our technology sound really exciting

<u>age good computer can make calculations in an instant</u> <u>which would take a lifetime of slide rules for any of</u> us. Think of what we could gain from the near infinity of precise, machine-made (miscomputation) which is now so easily within our grasp. We would begin the solving of some of our hardest problems. How, for instance, should we go about organizing ourselves for social living on a planetary scale, now that we have become, as a plain fact of life, a single community? We can assume, as a working hypothesis, that all the right ways of doing this are unworkable. What we need, then, for moving ahead, is a set of wrong alternatives much longer and more interesting than the short list of mistaken courses that any of us can think up right

error or mistake

yes

We need to program computers to make deliberate mistakes so they can help our natural human ten-dency to learn thru error

So mistakes have value!

Not a contradiction after all

now. We need, in fact, an infinite list, and when it is printed out we need the computer to turn itself on and select, at random, the next way to go. If it is a big enough mistake, we could find ourselves on a new level, stunned, out in the clear, ready to move again.[5]

After you have read the essay for the first time, summarize its main ideas in some fashion. The form of this task might be anything from a drawing of the main ideas as they connect with one another to a succinct written summary. You could draw a graph or map of the topics in the essay (in much the same way that a person would draw a map of an area for someone unfamiliar with a particular route); outline the ideas to get an overview of the piece; or summarize the ideas to check your understanding of the main points of the selection. Any of these tasks can be completed from your original notes and underlining. Each will give you a slightly more thorough understanding of what you have read.

Reading Critically

[5] What do the author's final words mean to you: "stunned, out in the clear, ready to move again"?

Finally, read the questions and assignments following the essay to help focus your thinking for the second reading. Don't answer the questions at this time; just read them to make sure you are picking up the main ideas from the selection and thinking about relevant connections among those ideas.

Rereading

The second and third readings will dramatically increase your understanding of each essay in this book. The temptation to skip these last two stages of the reading process is often powerful, but these readings are crucial to your development as a critical reader in all of your courses. Rereading can be compared to seeing a good movie for the second or third time: The first viewing provides you with a general understanding of the plot, the characters, the setting, and the overall artistic accomplishment of the director; during the second viewing, however, you would undoubtedly notice many more details and see their specific contributions to the artistic whole. Similarly, the second and third readings of an essay provide for a much deeper understanding of the essay and prepare you to analyze the writer's ideas.

During your second reading, you should answer the questions at the bottom of the pages of the essay (the "bridge" questions). These questions are marked throughout the text both in the essay and at the bottom of the pages by numbers within diamonds. Then, you might ask some additional questions of your own. You will get the most out of this process if you respond in writing. Keeping a journal to collect these responses is especially effective as you work to make this essay your own. Here are some sample student responses to the bridge questions accompanying the Thomas essay.

1. Sample response: Computers usually supply us with more memory than we could ever have. Perhaps we even rely on them too much for this service. On the other hand, I think we can reason on more complex levels than the computer can.

2. Sample response: Errors on the computer, like errors in humans, might lead to new discoveries or new insights into old theories and observations.

3. Sample response: I have made several mistakes that turned out to be beneficial: I dated a guy who turned out to be a negative force in my life, which helped me understand what it means to be happy; I followed a lead on the Internet that taught me an important lesson; and I learned a lot about myself when I discovered a mistake I made on a math test.

4. Sample response: Compared to cats and dogs, we are definitely programmed to make mistakes. We are not meant to do everything perfectly, and we learn from our mistakes—in both positive and negative ways.

5. Sample response: My guess is that Thomas means we will be stunned by our new discoveries and ready to break into the clear—like a football player running with the ball.

During your third reading, you should also be prepared to do some detective work and look closely at the assumptions on which the essay is based: For example, how does the writer move from idea to idea? What hidden assertions lie behind these ideas? Do you agree or disagree with these assertions? Your assessment of these unspoken assumptions will often play a major role in your critical response to an essay. In the case of Thomas's essay, do you accept the unspoken connection he makes between the workings of the human brain and the computer? What parts of the essay hinge upon your acceptance of this connection? What other assumptions are fundamental to Thomas's reasoning? If you accept his thinking along the way, you are more likely to agree with the general flow of Thomas's essay. If you discover a flaw in his premises or assumptions, your acceptance of his argument will start to break down.

Next, answer the questions that follow the essay. The "Understanding Details" questions will help you understand and remember what you have read on both the literal and the interpretive levels. Some of the questions ask you to restate various important points the author makes (literal); others help you see relationships among the different ideas presented (interpretive).

Understanding Details

Literal	1. According to Thomas, in what ways are computers and humans similar? How are they different?
Lit/Interp	2. How do we learn by "trial and error"? Why is this a useful way to learn?
Interpretive	3. What does Thomas mean by the statement, "If we were not provided with the knack of being wrong, we could never get anything useful done" (paragraph 6)?
Interpretive	4. According to Thomas, in what important ways do humans and "lower" animals differ? What does this comparison have to do with Thomas's main line of reasoning?

The "Thinking Critically" questions require you to analyze and evaluate some of the writer's ideas in order to form valid opinions of your own. These questions demand a higher level of thought than the previous set and help you prepare more specifically for the discussion/writing assignments that follow the questions.

Thinking Critically

Analytical   1. What is Thomas's main point in this essay? How do the references to computers help him make this case?

Analytical   2. In paragraph 10, Thomas explains that an argument must precede the beginning of something new and different. Do you think this is an accurate observation? Explain your answer.

Analytical   3. Why does Thomas perceive human error as such a positive quality? What does "exploration" have to do with this quality (paragraph 12)?

Analytical   4. What could we gain from "the near infinity of precise, machine-made miscomputation" (paragraph 14)? In what ways would our civilization advance?

The "Discovering Rhetorical Strategies" questions ask you to look closely at what strategies the writer uses to develop his or her thesis and how those strategies work. The questions address important features of the writer's composing process, such as word choice, use of detail, transitions, statement of purpose, organization of ideas, sentence structure, and paragraph development.

Discovering Rhetorical Strategies

1. Thomas begins his essay with a list of experiences most of us have had at one time or another. Do you find this an effective beginning? Why or why not?

2. Which main points in his essay does Thomas develop in most detail? Why do you think he chooses to develop these points so thoroughly?

3. Explain the simile Thomas uses in paragraph 6: "Mistakes are at the very base of human thought, embedded there, feeding the structure like root nodules." Is this comparison between mistakes and root nodules useful in this context? Why or why not? Find another simile or metaphor in this essay, and explain how it works.

4. What principal rhetorical strategies does Thomas use to make his point? Give examples of each from the essay.

The intent of these questions is to raise various elements of the composing process to the conscious level so you can use them in creating your own essays. If you are able to understand and describe what choices a writer makes to create certain effects in his or her prose, you are more likely to be able to discover the range of choices available to you as you write, and you will also become more aware of your ability to control your readers' thoughts and feelings.

A final set of questions, "Making Connections," asks you to consider the essay you have just read in reference to other essays in the book you have encountered. The questions are written so you can focus on what you have read in your responses. The questions may have you compare the writers' treatment of an idea, the authors' style of writing, the difference in their opinions, or the similarities between their views of the world. Such questions will help you see connections in your own life—not only in your reading and your immediate environment, but also in the larger world around you. These questions, in particular, encourage you to move from specific references in the selections to a broader range of issues and circumstances that affect your daily life.

Making Connections

1. Kimberly Wozencraft ("Notes from the Country Club") and Judith Wallerstein and Sandra Blakeslee ("Second Chances for Children of Divorce") refer both directly and indirectly to learning from mistakes. Would Lewis Thomas agree with either of their approaches to this topic? In what ways do these authors think alike about the benefits of making errors? In what ways do they differ on the topic? Explain your answer.

2. Lewis Thomas, Jessica Mitford ("Behind the Formaldehyde Curtain"), and Michael Dorris ("The Broken Cord") all write about the intersection of science and humanity. Which of these authors, from what you have read, is most intrigued by the human aspect of this equation? Explain your answer.

3. According to Thomas, humans are complex organisms with a great deal of untapped potential. Maya Angelou ("New Directions") and Barbara Ehrenreich ("The Ecstasy of War") also comment on the uniqueness of human beings. In what ways do these three writers agree or disagree with each other on the intelligence and resourcefulness of humans? To what extent would each author argue that we use our mental capacities wisely and completely? Explain your answer.

WRITING CRITICALLY

The last stage of responding to the reading selections in this text offers you various "Ideas for Discussion/Writing" that will allow you to demonstrate the different skills you have learned in each chapter. This material includes questions to consider as you prepare to write and the writing topics themselves. You will be most successful if you envision each writing experience as an organic process that follows a natural, recursive cycle of prewriting, writing, and rewriting.

Ideas for Discussion/Writing

Preparing to Write

Write freely about an important mistake you have made: How did the mistake make you feel? What (if anything) did you learn from this mistake? What did you fail to learn that you should have learned? Did this mistake have any positive impact on your life? What were its negative consequences? How crucial are mistakes in our lives?

Choosing a Topic

1. You have decided to write an editorial for your local newspaper concerning the impact of computers on our lives. Cite specific experiences you have had with computers to help make your main point.

2. You have been invited back to your high school to make a speech to a senior English class about how people can learn from their mistakes. Write your speech in the form of an essay explaining what you learned from a crucial mistake you have made. Use examples to show these students that mistakes can be positive factors in their lives.

3. In an essay for your writing class, explain one specific human quality. Use Thomas's essay as a model. Cite examples to support your explanation.

4. If you could repair a single mistake with an e-mail, what mistake would you fix? Who would you send the e-mail to? What would you say? Write an e-mail in which you reflect on this mistake and offer an explanation of its consequences and outcomes.

Preparing to Write

The prewriting phase involves exploring a subject, generating ideas, selecting and narrowing a topic, analyzing an audience, and developing a purpose. Preceding the writing assignments are "Preparing to Write" questions you should respond to before trying to structure your thoughts into a coherent essay. These questions will assist you in generating new thoughts on the topics that follow and may even stimulate new approaches to old ideas. Keeping a journal to respond to these questions is an excellent technique because you will then have a record of your opinions on various subjects related to the writing assignments. No matter what format you use to answer these questions, the activity of prewriting generally continues in various forms throughout the writing process.

Responses to the prewriting questions above can be prompted by a number of different "invention" techniques and carried out by individuals, in pairs, in small groups, or as a class project. Invention strategies can help you generate responses to these questions and discover related ideas through the various stages of writing your papers. Because you will undoubtedly vary your approach to different assignments, you should be familiar with the following choices available to you.

Brainstorming.   The basis of brainstorming is free association. Ideally, you should get a group of students together and bounce ideas, words, and thoughts off one another until they begin to cluster around related topics. If you don't have a group of students handy, brainstorm by yourself or with a friend. In a group of students or with a friend, the exchange of thoughts usually starts orally but should transfer to paper when your ideas begin to fall into related categories. When you brainstorm by yourself, however, you should write down everything that comes to mind. The act of recording your ideas in this case becomes a catalyst for other thoughts; you are essentially setting up a dialogue with yourself on paper. Then, keep writing down words and phrases that occur to you until they begin to fall into logical subdivisions or until your new ideas come to an end.

Freewriting.   Freewriting means writing to discover what you want to say. Set a time limit of about ten minutes, and just write by free association. Write about what you are seeing, feeling, touching, thinking; write about having nothing to say; recopy the sentence you just wrote—anything. Just keep writing on paper or on a computer. After you have generated some material, locate an idea that is central to your writing assignment, put it at the top of another page, and start freewriting again, letting your thoughts take shape around this central idea. This second type of preparation is called *focused freewriting* and is especially valuable when you already have a specific topic.

Journal Entries.   Journal entries are much like freewriting, except you have some sense of an audience—probably either your instructor or yourself. In a journal, anything goes. You can respond to the "Preparing to Write" questions, jot down thoughts, paste up articles that spark your interest, write sections of dialogue, draft letters (the kind you never send), record dreams, or make lists. The possibilities are endless. An excellent way of practicing writing, the process of keeping a journal is also a wonderful means of dealing with new ideas—a way of fixing them in your mind and making them yours.

Direct Questions.   This technique involves asking a series of questions useful in any writing situation to generate ideas, arrange thoughts, or revise prose. One example of this strategy is to use the inquiries journalists rely on to check the coverage in their articles:

Who:	*Who played the game?*
	Who won the game?
What:	*What kind of game was it?*
	What happened in the game?
Why:	*Why was the game played?*
Where:	*Where was the game played?*
When:	*When was the game played?*
How:	*How was the game played?*

If you ask yourself questions of this type on a specific topic, you will begin to produce thoughts and details that will undoubtedly be useful to you in the writing assignments that follow.

Clustering.   Clustering is a method of drawing or mapping your ideas as fast as they come into your mind. Put a word, phrase, or sentence in a circle in the center of a blank page. Then put every new idea that comes to you in a circle and show its relationship to a previous thought by drawing a line to the circle containing the original thought. You will probably reach a natural stopping point for this exercise in two to three minutes.

Although you can generate ideas in a number of different ways, the main principle behind the "Preparing to Write" questions in this text is to encourage you to do what is called *expressive writing* before you tackle any writing assignment. This is writing based on your feelings, thoughts, experiences, observations, and opinions. The process of answering questions about your own ideas and experiences makes you "think on paper," enabling you to surround yourself with your own thoughts and opinions. From this reservoir, you can then choose the ideas you want to develop into an essay and begin writing about them one at a time.

As you use various prewriting techniques to generate responses to the "Preparing to Write" questions, you should know that these responses can (and probably will) appear in many different forms. You can express yourself in lists, outlines, random notes, sentences and paragraphs, charts, graphs, or pictures—whatever keeps the thoughts flowing smoothly and productively. One of our students used a combination of brainstorming and clustering to generate the following thoughts in response to the prewriting exercise for the Thomas essay:

Brainstorming

Mistakes:

happen when I'm in a hurry	*getting back on track*
make me feel stupid	*parents*
love	*corrections*
relationships	*learning from mistakes*
trip back East	*I am a better person*
pride	*my values are clear*
going in circles	*mistakes help us change*
Bob	*painful*
learned a lot about people	*helpful*
people aren't what they seem	*valuable*

Clustering

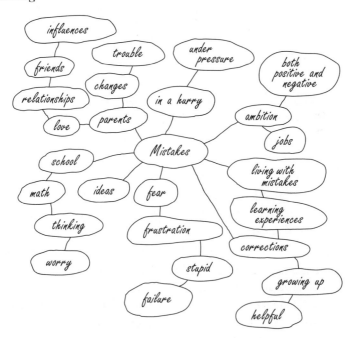

From the free-flowing thoughts you generate, you need to decide what to write about and how to limit your subject to a manageable length. Our student writer chose topic 2 from the "Choosing a Topic" list after the essay (see page 18). Her initial responses to the prewriting questions helped her decide to write on "A Time I Got Lost." She then generated more focused ideas and opinions in the form of a journal entry. It is printed here just as she wrote it, errors and all.

Journal Entry

The craziest mistake I think I ever made was on a trip I took recently—I was heading to the east coast from California and reached Durham, North Carolina. I was so excited because I was going to get to see the Atlantic Ocean for the first time in my life and Durham was one of my last landmarks before I reached the sea. In Durham I was going to have to change from a northeast direction to due east.

When I got there the highway was under construction. I took the detour, but got all skrewed up till I realized that I had gone the wrong direction. By this time I was lost somewhere in downtown Durham and didn't know which way was east. I stoped and asked a guy at a gas station and he explained how to get back on the east-bound highway. The way was through the middle of town. By the time I got to where I was supposed to turn right I could only turn left. So I started left and then realized I couldn't turn back the other way! I made a couple of other stops after that, and one jerk told me I "just couldn't get there from here." Eventually I found a truck driver heading toward the same eastbound highway, and he told me to follow him. An hour and forty minutes after reaching Durham's city limits I finally managed to leave going east. I felt as if I had spent an entire month there!

The thing I learned from this was just how egocentric I am. I would not have made this error if I had not been so damn cocky about my sense of direction. My mistake was made worse because I got flustered and didn't listen to the directions clearly. I find that the reason I most often make a mistake is because I don't listen carefully to instructions. This has been a problem all my life.

After I got over feeling really dum I decided this kind of thing was not going to happen again. It was too much a waste of time and gas, so I was going to be more careful of road signs and directions.

This all turned out to be a positive experience though. I learned that there are lots of friendly, helpful people. It was kind of reassuring to know that other folks would help you if you just asked.

I feel this and other mistakes are crucial not only to my life but to my personal growth in general. It is the making of mistakes that helps people learn where they are misdirecting their energies. I think mistakes can help all of us learn to be more careful about some part of our lives. This is why mistakes are crucial. Otherwise, we would continue in the same old rut and never improve.

This entry served as the foundation upon which the student built her essay. Her next step was to consider *audience* and *purpose* (which are often written into the writing assignments in this text). The first of these features identifies the person or group of people you will address in your essay. The second is a declaration of your principal reason for writing the essay, which usually takes the form of a thesis statement (the statement of purpose or the controlling idea of an essay). Together these pieces of information consciously or subconsciously help you make most of the decisions you are faced with as you write: what words to choose, what sentence structures to use, what order to present ideas in, which topics to develop, and which to summarize. Without a doubt, the more you know about your audience (age, educational background, likes, dislikes, biases, political persuasion, and social status) and your purpose (to inform, persuade, and/or entertain), the easier the writing task will be. In the rough draft and final draft of the essay in the section that follows, the student knew she was writing to a senior English class at her old high school in order to convince them that mistakes can be positive factors in their lives. This clear sense of audience and purpose helped her realize she should use fairly advanced vocabulary, call upon a variety of sentence structures, and organize her ideas chronologically to make her point most effectively to her intended audience.

At this stage of the writing process, some people benefit from assembling their ideas in the form of an outline. Others use an outline as a check on their logic and organization after the first draft has been written. Whether your outlines are informal (a simple list) or more structured, they can help you visualize the logical relationship of your ideas to each other. We recommend using a rough outline throughout the prewriting and writing stages to ensure that your work is carefully and tightly organized. Your outline, however, should be adjusted to your draft as it develops.

Writing

The writing stage asks you to draft an essay based on the prewriting material you have assembled. Because you have already made the important preliminary decisions regarding your topic, your audience, and your purpose, the task of actually writing the essay should follow naturally. (Notice we did not say this task should necessarily be easy—just natural.) At this stage, you ought to look upon your essay as a way of solving a problem or answering a question: The problem/question is posed in your writing assignment, and the solution/answer is your essay.

The four "Choosing a Topic" assignments that follow the prewriting questions throughout the text invite you to consider issues related to the essay you just read. Although they typically ask you to focus on one rhetorical pattern, they draw on many rhetorical strategies (as do all writing assignments in the text) and require you to support your statements with concrete examples. The assignments for the Lewis Thomas essay (Choosing a Topic, p. 18) emphasize the use of example, his dominant rhetorical strategy.

The following essay is our student's first-draft response to topic 2. After writing her journal entry, the student drafted a tentative thesis statement: "I know there are positive changes that can come from making a mistake because I recently had an opportunity to learn some valuable lessons from one of my errors." This statement helped the student writer further develop and organize her ideas as she focused finally on one well-chosen example to illustrate her thesis. At this point, the thesis is simply the controlling idea around which the other topics take shape; it is often revised several times before the final draft.

First Draft: A Time I Got Lost

Parents and teachers frequently pressure us to avoid committing errors. Meanwhile, our friends laugh at us when we make mistakes. With all these different messages, it is hard for us to think of mistakes as positive events. But if any of you take the time to think about what you have learned from mistakes, I bet you will realize all the good things that have come from these events. I know there are positive changes that can come from making a mistake because I recently had an opportunity to learn some valuable lessons in this way.

While traveling back east this last summer, I made the mistake of turning west on an interstate detour in order to reach the Atlantic Ocean. The adventure took me into the heart of Durham, North Carolina, where I got totally lost. I had to get directions several times until two hours later I was going in the right direction. As I was driving out of town, I realized that although I had made a dumb mistake, I had learned a great deal. Overall, the detour was actually a positive experience.

The first thing I remember thinking after I had gotten my wits together was that I had definitely learned something from making the mistake. I had the opportunity to see a new city, filled with new people—3,000 miles from my own hometown, but very much like it. I also became aware that the beach is not always toward the west, as it is in California. The entire experience was like getting a geography lesson firsthand.

As this pleasant feeling began to grow, I came to another realization. I was aware of how important other people can be in making a mistake into a positive experience. My first reaction was "Oh no, someone is going to know I made a mistake!" But the amazing part about this mistake was how supportive everyone was. The townspeople had been entirely willing to help someone they did not know. This mistake helped me learn that people tend to be nicer than I had imagined.

The final lesson I learned from getting lost in Durham was how to be more cautious about my actions so as not to repeat the same mistake. It was this internalization of all the information I gleaned from making the mistake that I see as the most positive part of the experience. I realized that in order to avoid such situations in the future I would have to be less egocentric in my decisions and more willing to listen to directions from other people. I needed to learn that my set way of doing things was not always the best way. If I had not made the mistake, I would not have been aware of my other options.

By making this mistake I learned that there is a more comprehensive manner of looking at the world. In the future, if we could all stop after making a mistake and ask ourselves, "What can I learn from this?" we would be less critical of ourselves and have a great many more positive experiences. If I were not able to make mistakes, I would probably not be able to expand my knowledge of my environment, my sense of others, and my understanding of myself.

Rewriting

The rewriting stage includes revising, editing, and proofreading. The first of these activities, *revising,* actually takes place during the entire writing process as you change words, recast sentences, and move whole paragraphs from one place to another. Making these linguistic and organizational choices means you will also be constantly adjusting your content to your purpose (what you want to accomplish) and your audience (the readers) in much the same way you alter your speech to communicate more effectively in response to the gestures, eye movements, or facial expressions of your listeners. Revising is literally the act of "re-seeing" your essay, looking at it through your readers' eyes to determine whether or not it achieves its purpose. As you revise, you should consider matters of both content and form. *In content,* do you have an interesting, thought-provoking title for your essay? Do you think your thesis statement will be clear to your audience? Does your introduction capture the readers' attention? Is your treatment of your topic consistent throughout the essay? Do you support your assertions with specific examples? Does your conclusion sum up your main points? *In form,* is your essay organized effectively? Do you use a variety of rhetorical strategies? Are your sentence structure and vocabulary varied and interesting?

If you compose on a computer, you will certainly reap the benefits as you revise. Computers remove much of the drudgery of rewriting your drafts. Computers allow you to move paragraphs or whole sections of your paper from one position to another by pressing a few keys. As a result, you can immediately see if the new organization will improve the logic and coherence of your paper. You may then remove repetitions or insert words and sentences that will serve as the transitions between sections. If you write out your drafts, you may not make as many major revisions as necessary because of the length of time needed to rewrite the material.

You should also consider the value of the graphic design options available on computer software, because the way you present your papers generally affects how your instructor evaluates them. If they are clearly laid out without coffee stains or paw prints from your dog, you have a better chance of being taken seriously than if they are sloppily done. A computer can help in this regard, giving you access to boldface type, italics, boxes, bullets, and graphs of all sorts and letting you make a new copy if you do have an unexpected encounter with a coffee cup or a frisky dog.

Editing entails correcting mistakes in your writing so that your final draft conforms to the conventions of standard written English. Correct punctuation, spelling, and mechanics will help you make your points and will encourage your readers to move smoothly through your essay from topic to topic. At this stage, you should be concerned about such matters as whether your sentences are complete, whether your punctuation is correct and effective, whether you have followed conventional rules for using mechanics, and whether the words in your essay are spelled correctly.

Proofreading involves reading over your entire essay, slowly and carefully, to make certain you have not allowed any errors to slip into your draft. (Most college instructors don't look upon errors as kindly as Thomas does.) In general, good writers try to let some time elapse between writing the final draft and proofreading it (at least a few hours, or even a day or so). Otherwise, they find themselves proofreading their thoughts rather than their words. Some writers even profit from proofreading their papers backward—a technique that allows them to focus on individual words and phrases rather than on entire sentences.

Following is the student's revised draft of her essay on making mistakes in life. The final draft of this typical freshman essay (written to high school seniors, as the assignment specifies) represents the entire writing process at work. We have made notes in the margin to highlight various effective elements in her essay, some of which we have underlined for emphasis. The various rhetorical modes she draws on are listed in the margins in brackets.

Mistakes and Maturity

Catchy title; good change from first draft

Rapport with audience and point of view established

Parents and teachers frequently harp on us to correct our errors. Meanwhile, our friends laugh at us when we make mistakes. With all these negative messages, most of us have a hard time believing that problems can be positive experiences. But if we take the time to think about what we have learned from var-

Clear, stimulating introduction for high school seniors

Good brief summary of complex experience (see notes from Preparing to Write)

First topic (topics are in chronological order)

[Examples]

Nice close to this paragraph

Second topic

[Examples]

Good summary statement

ious blunders, we will realize all the good that has come from these events. <u>I know that making mistakes can have positive results because I recently learned several valuable lessons from one unforgettable experience.</u>

<u>While I was traveling on the East Coast last summer</u>, I made the mistake of turning west on an interstate detour in an attempt to reach the Atlantic Ocean. This adventure took me into the center of Durham, North Carolina, where I became totally lost, bewildered, and angry at myself. I had to ask for directions several times until two hours later, when I finally found the correct highway toward the ocean. As I was driving out of town, I realized that although I had made a "dumb" mistake, I had actually learned a great deal. Overall, my adventure had been quite positive.

The first insight I remember having after my wits returned was that <u>I had definitely learned more about United States geography from making this mistake.</u> I had become intimately acquainted with a town 3,000 miles from home that greatly resembled my own city, and I had become aware that the beach is not always toward the west, as it is in California. I had also met some pleasant strangers. <u>Looking at my confusion as a learning experience encouraged me to have positive feelings about the mistake</u>.

As I relaxed and let this happy feeling grow, I came to another realization. <u>I became aware of how important other people can be in turning a mistake into a positive event.</u> Although my first reaction had been "Oh, no! Someone is going to know I'm lost," I was amazed by how supportive other people were during my panic and embarrassment. From an old man swinging on his front porch to an elementary school boy crossing the street with his bright blue backpack, I found that the townspeople of Durham were entirely willing to help someone they did not even know. <u>I realized that people in general are nicer than I had previously thought</u>.

The final lesson I learned from making this mistake was <u>how to be more cautious about my future decisions</u>. This insight was, in fact, the most positive

Revised thesis statement

Background information

Good details

[Narration]

Adequate number of examples

[Cause/ Effect]

Clear explanation with details

[Description]

Third topic

Specific details — part of the entire experience. What I realized I must do to prevent similar errors in the future was to relax, not be so bullheaded in my decisions, and be more willing to listen to directions from other people. I might never have had these positive realizations if I had not made this mistake. — [Process Analysis] [Cause/Effect] Good summary statement

Clear transition statement — Thus, by driving in circles for two hours, I developed a more comprehensive way of looking at the world. If I were unable to make mistakes, I probably [Cause/Effect] would not have had this chance to learn about my environment, improve my impressions of strangers, and reconsider the egocentric way in which I act in certain situations. Perhaps there's a lesson here for all of us. Instead of criticizing ourselves unduly, if each Concluding statement one of us could pause after we make an error and ask, applicable to all "How can I profit from this?," we would realize that readers mistakes can often be turned into positive events that will help us become more confident and mature. — Good summary of three topics without being repetitive [Process Analysis] Nicely focused concluding remark

As these various drafts of the student paper indicate, the essay assignments in this book encourage you to transfer to your own writing your understanding of how form and content work together. If you use the short-answer questions after each reading selection as a guide, the writing assignments will help you learn how to give shape to your own ideas and how to gain control of your readers' thoughts and feelings. In essence, they help you recognize the power you have through language over your life and your environment.

CONCLUSION

As you approach the essays in this text, remember that both reading and writing function most efficiently as processes of discovery. Through these skills, you educate and expand your own mind and the minds of your readers. They can provide a powerful means of discovering new information or clarifying what you already know. Reading and writing lead to understanding. And just as you can discover how to read through writing, so too can you become more aware of the details of the writing process through reading. We hope your time spent with this book is both pleasant and profitable as you refine your ability to discover and express effectively the good ideas within yourself.

THE READING AND WRITING PROCESSES

Because checklists can provide a helpful method of reviewing important information, we offer here a series of questions that represent the reading and writing processes. All these guidelines can be generalized into a checklist for reading any academic assignment in any discipline.

READING INVENTORY

Preparing to Read

Title

✓ What can you infer from the title of the essay?

✓ Who do you think is the author's audience? What is the principal purpose of the essay?

Synopsis

✓ What is the general subject of the essay?

✓ What is the author's approach to the subject?

Biography

✓ What do you know about the author's age, political stance, general beliefs?

✓ How qualified is the author to write on this subject?

✓ When did the author write the essay? Under what conditions? In what context?

Content

✓ Where was the essay first published?

✓ What would you like to learn about this topic?

✓ What are some of my opinions on this subject?

Reading

✓ What are your initial reactions to the ideas in this essay?

✓ What words do you need to look up?

✓ What are the essay's main ideas?

Rereading

✓ What assumptions underlie the author's reasoning?

✓ How does the author achieve his or her purpose in this essay?

✓ Do I have a solid interpretive understanding of this essay? Do I understand the relationship among ideas? What conclusions can I draw from this essay?

✓ Do I have an accurate analytical understanding of this essay? Which ideas can I take apart, examine, and put back together again? What is my evaluation of this material?

✓ Do I understand the rhetorical strategies the writer uses and the way they work? Can I explain the effects of these strategies?

WRITING INVENTORY

Preparing to Write

✓ Do you understand your assignment?

✓ Have you narrowed your topic adequately?

✓ Who is your audience (Their likes/dislikes? Their educational level? Their knowledge of the subject?)

✓ What is your purpose?

Writing

✓ Can you express your thesis as a problem or question?

✓ Is your essay a solution or an answer to that problem or question?

Rewriting

Revising the Content

✓ Does your essay have a clear, interesting title?

✓ Will your statement of purpose (or thesis) be clear to your audience?

✓ Will the introduction make your audience want to read the rest of your essay?

✓ Have you included enough details to prove your main points?

✓ Does your conclusion sum up your central points?

✓ Will you accomplish your purpose with your audience?

Revising the Form

✓ Have you organized your ideas as effectively as possible for your audience?

✓ Do you use appropriate rhetorical strategies to support your main points?

✓ Is your sentence structure varied and interesting?

✓ Is your vocabulary appropriate for your topic, your purpose, and your audience?

Editing and Proofreading

✓ Have you written complete sentences throughout your essay?

✓ Have you used punctuation correctly and effectively (check especially the use of commas, apostrophes, colons, and semicolons)?

✓ Have you followed conventional rules for mechanics (capitalization, underlining or italics, abbreviations, and numbers)?

✓ Are all the words in your essay spelled correctly? (Use a dictionary or a spell-checker when in doubt.)

Chapter 1

DESCRIPTION
Exploring through the Senses

All of us use description in our daily lives. We might, for example, try to convey the horrors of a recent history exam to our parents, help a friend visualize someone we met on vacation, or describe an automobile accident for a police report. Whatever our specific purpose, description is a fundamental part of communication: We give and receive descriptions constantly, and our lives are continually affected by this simple yet important rhetorical technique.

DEFINING DESCRIPTION

Description may be defined as the act of capturing people, places, events, objects, and feelings in words so that a reader (or listener) can visualize and respond to them. Unlike narration, which traditionally presents events in a clear time sequence, description essentially suspends its objects in time, making them exempt from the limits of chronology. Narration tells a story, while pure description contains no action or time. Description is one of our primary forms of self-expression; it paints a verbal picture that helps the reader understand or share a sensory experience through the process of *showing* rather than *telling*. *Telling* your friends, for example, that "the campgrounds were filled with friendly, happy activities" is not as engaging as *showing* them by saying, "The campgrounds were alive with the smell of spicy baked beans,

31

the sound of high-pitched laughter, and the sight of happy families sharing the warmth of a fire." Showing your readers helps them understand your experience through as many senses as possible.

Descriptions fall somewhere between two extremes: (1) totally objective reports (with no trace of opinions or feelings), such as we might find in a dictionary or an encyclopedia; and (2) very subjective accounts, which focus almost exclusively on personal impressions. The same horse, for instance, might be described by one writer as "a large, solid-hoofed herbivorous mammal having a long mane and a tail" (objective) and by another as "a magnificent and spirited beast flaring its nostrils in search of adventure" (subjective). Most descriptive writing, however, falls somewhere between these two extremes: "a large, four-legged beast in search of adventure."

Objective description is principally characterized by its impartial, precise, and emotionless tone. Found most prominently in technical and scientific writing, such accounts might include a description of equipment to be used in a chemistry experiment, the results of a market survey for a particular consumer product, or a medical appraisal of a heart patient's physical symptoms. In situations like these, accurate, unbiased, and easily understandable accounts are of the utmost importance.

Subjective description, in contrast, is intentionally created to produce a particular response in the reader or listener. Focusing on feelings rather than on raw data, it tries to activate as many senses as possible, thereby leading the audience to a specific conclusion or state of mind. Examples of subjective descriptions are a parent's disapproving comments about one of your friends, a professor's glowing analysis of your most recent "A" paper, or a basketball coach's critique of the team's losing effort in last night's big game.

In most situations, the degree of subjectivity or objectivity in a descriptive passage depends to a large extent on the writer's purpose and intended audience. In the case of the heart patient mentioned above, the person's physician might present the case in a formal, scientific way to a group of medical colleagues; in a personal, sympathetic way to the invalid's spouse; and in financial terms to a number of potential contributors in order to solicit funds for heart disease research.

The following paragraph describes one student's fond memories of visiting a farm. As you read it, notice the writer's use of subjective description to communicate to her readers the multitude of contradictory feelings she connects with this rural retreat.

The shrill scream of the alarm shatters a dream. This is the last day of my visit to the place I call "the farm," an old ramshackle house in the country owned by one of my aunts. I want to go out once more in the peace of the early morning, walk in the crisp and chilly fields, and breathe the sweet air. My body feels jarred as my feet hit the hard-packed clay dirt. I tune out my stiff muscles and cold arms and legs and instead focus on two herons playing hopscotch on the canal bank: Every few yards I walk toward them, they fly one over the other an almost equal distance away from me. A killdeer with its piercing crystalline cry dips its body as it flies low over the water, the tip of its wing leaving a ring to reverberate outward. The damp earth has a strong, rich, musky scent. To the east, dust rises, and for the first time I hear the clanking and straining of a tractor as it harrows smooth the soil before planting. A crop duster rises close by just as it cuts off its release of spray, the acrid taste of chemicals filtering down through the air. As the birds chatter and peck at the fields, I reluctantly return to my life in the city.

THINKING CRITICALLY THROUGH DESCRIPTION

- Activate your imagination.
- Use your senses.
- Think about details.

Each rhetorical mode in this book gives us new insights into the process of thinking by providing different options for arranging our thoughts and our experiences. The more we know about these options, the more conscious we become of how our minds operate and the better chance we have to improve and refine our communication skills.

As you examine description as a way of thinking, consider it in isolation for a moment—away from the other rhetorical modes. Think of it as a muscle you can isolate and strengthen on its own in a weight-training program before you ask it to perform together with other muscles. By isolating description, you will learn more readily what it entails and how it functions as a critical-thinking tool. In the process, you will also strengthen your knowledge of how to recognize and use description more effectively in your reading, in your writing, and in your daily life.

Just as you exercise to strengthen muscles, so too will you benefit from doing exercises to improve your skill in using descriptive techniques. As you have learned, description depends to a great extent on the keenness of your senses. So as you prepare to read and write descriptive essays, do the following tasks so that you can first learn what the process of description feels like in your own head. Really use your imagination to play with these exercises on as many different levels as possible. Also write when you are asked to do so. The combination of thinking and writing is often especially useful when you practice your thinking skills.

1. Imagine what you might smell, taste, hear, feel, or see in the following photograph taken by Gerry Gavigan. Then, using words that will create

© Gerry Gavigan/Growbag.

these sensory details, write a few sentences that might accompany this photograph if it were published in a newspaper or travel magazine.

2. Make a list of five descriptive words you would use to trigger each of the following senses: taste, sight, hearing, touch, and smell.

3. Choose an unusual object, and brainstorm about its physical characteristics. Then brainstorm about the emotions this object evokes. Why is this object so unusual or special? Compare your two brainstorming results, and draw some conclusions about their differences.

Reading and Writing Descriptive Essays

All good descriptions share four fundamental qualities: (1) an accurate sense of audience (who the readers are) and purpose (why the essay was written), (2) a clear vision of the object being described, (3) a careful selection of details that help communicate the author's vision, and (4) a consistent point of view or perspective from which a writer composes. The dominant impression or main effect the writer wishes to leave with a specific audience dictates virtually all of the verbal choices in a descriptive essay. Although description is featured in this chapter, you should also pay close attention to how other rhetorical strategies (such as example, division/classification, and cause/effect) can best support an essay's dominant impression.

READING DESCRIPTIVE ESSAYS

- What is the essay's dominant impression?
- Is the essay mainly objective or subjective?
- What senses does the author engage?

Preparing to Read.   As you approach the reading selections in this chapter, you should focus first on the author's title and try to make some initial assumptions about the essay that follows: Does Ray Bradbury reveal his attitude toward his subject in the title "Summer Rituals"? Can you guess what the general mood of Kimberly Wozencraft's "Notes from the Country Club" will be? Then scan the essay to discover its audience and purpose: What do you think John McPhee's purpose is in "The Pines"? Whom is Malcolm Cowley addressing in "The View from 80"? Why does Linda Hogan write an essay about "dwellings"? You should also read the synopsis of each essay in the Rhetorical Table of Contents (on pages vii–xvi); these brief summaries will provide you with helpful information at this point in the reading process.

Next, learn as much as you can about the author and the conditions under which the essay was composed, information that is provided in the biographical statement before each essay. For a descriptive essay, the conditions under which the author wrote the essay, coupled with his or her purpose, can be very revealing: When and under what conditions did Kimberly Wozencraft write "Notes from the Country Club"? What was her intention in writing the essay? Can you determine when Malcolm Cowley's piece was written? Does it describe the author's life now or in the past? Learning where the essay was first published will also give you valuable information about its audience.

Last, before you begin to read, try to do some brainstorming on the essay's title. In this chapter, respond to the Preparing to Read questions before each essay, which ask you to begin thinking and writing about the topic under consideration. At the same time, take advantage of the Internet prompt to help you find more information on the topic you are about to consider. Then pose your own questions: What are some of the most important rituals in your life (Bradbury)? What would you like to learn from Cowley about the joys and frustrations of being eighty years old? What is one of your favorite places (Hogan)?

Reading.   As you read each essay for the first time, jot down your initial reactions to it, and try to make connections and see relationships among the author's biography; the essay's title, purpose, and audience; and the synopsis. In this way, you will create a context or framework for your reading. See if you can figure out, for example, what Bradbury is implying about rituals in general in his essay "Summer Rituals" or why Wozencraft wrote an essay about her experiences in prison. Try to discover what the relationship is between purpose, audience, and publication information in Cowley's essay.

Also determine at this point if the author's treatment of his or her subject is predominantly objective (generally free of emotion) or subjective (heavily charged with emotion). Or perhaps the essay falls somewhere between these two extremes.

In addition, make sure you have a general sense of the dominant impression each author is trying to convey. Such an initial approach to reading these descriptive selections will give you a foundation upon which to analyze the material during your second, more in-depth reading.

To help you develop the ability to read critically, a set of questions at the bottom of the essays' pages will prompt you to make connections between ideas, apply the material to your own experiences, and draw analytical conclusions that prepare you to answer the questions after each essay and ultimately write an essay on a related topic. These questions extend the mental exercises you complete before you read each essay to the deeper thinking you must do in the activities at the end of the essays. Responding to these questions in writing is the best way to discover new, innovative ideas about your reading on any subject.

Finally, at the end of your first reading, take a look at the questions after each essay to make certain you can answer them. This material will guide your rereading.

Rereading.   As you reread these descriptive essays, notice each author's careful selection of details that support his or her dominant impression. Also try to determine how certain details add to and detract from that dominant impression and how the writer's point of view affects it. Finally, get a sense of which senses the author is engaging to create this impression: How does Cowley enable us to identify with his experiences if we have never been 80 years old? How does Hogan create a sense of wonder in "Dwellings"?

Try to find during this reading other rhetorical modes that support the description. Although the essays in this chapter describe various persons, places, or objects, all of the authors call upon other rhetorical strategies (especially example and comparison/contrast) to communicate their descriptions. How do these various rhetorical strategies work together in each essay to create a coherent whole? In addition, the authors all attempt to get you to see their view of the world.

Finally, answering the questions after each essay will check your understanding of the author's main points and help you think critically about the essay in preparing for the discussion/writing assignments that follow.

For an inventory of the reading process, you may want to review the checklists on page 29 of the Introduction.

WRITING DESCRIPTIVE ESSAYS

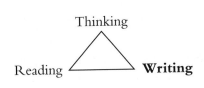

- Choose a dominant impression as your thesis.
- Find details that support your thesis.
- Engage all five senses.
- Choose a point of view.
- *Show* rather than *tell*.

Preparing to Write.   Before you choose a writing assignment, use the prewriting questions that follow each essay to help you discover your own ideas and opinions about the general topic of the essay. Next, choose an assignment or read the one assigned to you. Then, just as you do when you read an essay, you should determine the audience and purpose for your description (if these are not specified for you in the assignment). To whom are you writing? And why? Will an impartial, objective report be appropriate, or should you present a more emotional, subjective account to accomplish your task? In assessing your audience, you need to determine what they do and do not know about your topic. This information will help you make decisions about what you are going to say and how you will say it. Your purpose will be defined by what you intend your audience to know, think, or believe after they have read your descriptive essay. Do you want them to make up their own minds about summer rituals or old age, for example, based on an objective presentation of data, or do you hope to sway their opinions through a more subjective display of information? Or perhaps you will decide to blend the two techniques, combining facts and opinions in order to achieve the impression of personal certainty based on objective evidence. What dominant impression do you want to leave with your audience? As you might suspect, decisions regarding audience and purpose are as important to writing descriptions as they are to reading descriptions and will shape your descriptive essay from start to finish.

The second quality of good description concerns the object of your analysis and the clarity with which you present it to the reader. Whenever possible, you should thoroughly investigate the person, place, moment, or feeling you wish to describe, paying particular attention to its effect upon each of your five senses. What can you see, smell, hear, taste, and touch as you examine it? If you want to describe your house, for example, begin by asking yourself a series of pertinent questions: How big is the house? What color is it?

How many exterior doors does the house have? How many interior doors? Are any of the rooms wallpapered? If so, what are the colors and textures of that wallpaper? How many different shades of paint cover the walls? Which rooms have constant noises (from clocks and other mechanical devices)? Are the kitchen appliances hot or cold to the touch? What is the quietest room in the house? The noisiest? What smells do you notice in the laundry? In the kitchen? In the basement? Most important, do any of these sensory questions trigger particular childhood memories? Although you will probably not use all of these details in your descriptive essay, the process of generating and answering such detailed questions will help reacquaint you with the object of your description as it also assists you in designing and focusing your paper.

To help you generate some of these ideas, you may want to review the prewriting techniques introduced on pages 19-21.

Writing.   As you write, you must select details for your description with great care and precision so that you leave your reader with a specific impression. Pay special attention to the way you engage all five senses in your description. If, for instance, you want your audience to feel the warmth and comfort of your home, you might concentrate on describing the plush carpets, the big upholstered chairs, the inviting scent of hot apple cider, and the crackling fire. If, on the other hand, you want to gain your audience's sympathy, you might prefer to focus on the sparse austerity of your home environment: the bare walls, the quietness, the lack of color and decoration, the dim lighting, and the frigid temperature. You also want to make sure you omit unrelated ideas, such as a conversation between your parents you accidentally overheard. Your careful choice of details will help control your audience's reaction.

The next important quality of an effective descriptive essay is point of view, your physical perspective on your subject. Because the organization of your essay depends on your point of view, you need to choose a specific angle from which to approach your description. If you verbally jump around your home, referring first to a picture on the wall in your bedroom, next to the microwave in the kitchen, and then to the quilt on your bed, no reasonable audience will be able to follow your description. Nor will they want to. If, however, you move from room to room in some logical, sequential way, always focusing on the details you want your readers to know, you will be helping your audience form a clear, memorable impression of your home. Your vision will become their vision. In other words, your point of view plays a part in determining the organization of your description. Working spatially, you could move from side to side (from one wall to another in the rooms we have discussed), from top to bottom (from ceiling to floor), or from far to near (from the farthest to the closest point in a room), or you might progress from large to small objects, from uninteresting to interesting, or from funny to serious. Whatever plan you choose should help you accomplish your purpose with your particular audience.

To make your impression even more vivid, you might use figurative language to fill out your descriptions. Using words figuratively means using them imaginatively rather than literally. The two most popular forms of figurative language are *simile* and *metaphor*. A *simile* is a comparison between two dissimilar objects or ideas introduced by *like* or *as:* "The rocking chairs sounded like crickets" (Bradbury). A *metaphor* is an implied comparison between two dissimilar objects or ideas that is not introduced by *like* or *as:* "Life for younger persons is still a battle royal of each against each" (Cowley). Besides enlivening your writing, figurative language helps your readers understand objects, feelings, and ideas that are complex or obscure by comparing them to those that are more familiar.

Rewriting. As you reread each of your descriptive essays, play the role of your audience and try to determine what dominant impression you receive by the end of your reading.

- Do you communicate the dominant impression you want to convey?
- Do your details support your dominant impression?
- Which senses do you stimulate?
- Do you have a clear, consistent point of view toward your subject?
- Are you showing rather than telling in your description?
- Do you use similes or metaphors when appropriate?

For additional suggestions on the writing process, you may want to consult the checklists on page 30 of the Introduction.

STUDENT ESSAY: DESCRIPTION AT WORK

In the following essay, a student relives some of her childhood memories through a subjective description of her grandmother's house. As you read it, pay particular attention to the different types of sensual details the student writer chooses to communicate her dominant impression of her grandmother's home. Notice also her use of carefully chosen details to *show* rather than *tell* us about her childhood reminiscences, especially her comparisons, which make the memory as vivid for the reader as it is for the writer.

Grandma's House

Writer's point of view or perspective   <u>My most vivid childhood memories</u> are set in my Grandma Goodlink's house, a curious blend of familiar and mysterious treasures. Grandma lived at the end of a dead-end street, in the same house she had lived   Dominant impression in since the first day of her marriage. That was half a century and thirteen children ago. A set of crumbly steps made of concrete mixed with gravel led up to her front door. I remember a big gap between the house and the steps, <u>as if someone had not pushed them up close enough to the house.</u> Anyone who looked into the gap <u>could see old toys and books</u> that had fallen into the crack behind the steps and had remained there, forever irretrievable.

Comparison (simile) — right of "as if someone had not pushed them up"

Sight — left of "the gap could see old toys and books"

Only a hook-type lock on the front door protected Grandma's many beautiful antiques. Her living room was set up <u>like a church or schoolroom,</u> with an <u>old purple velvet couch</u> against the far wall and two chairs immediately in front of the couch facing the same direction. <u>One-half of the couch was always buried in old clothes, magazines, and newspapers, and a lone shoe sat on top of the pile, a finishing touch to some bizarre modern sculpture.</u> To one side was an aged and <u>tuneless</u> upright piano with <u>yellowed keys.</u> The ivory overlay was missing so that <u>the wood underneath showed through,</u> and many of the keys made only a <u>muffled and frustrating thump,</u> no matter how hard I pressed them. On the wall facing the piano was the room's only window, draped with <u>yellowed lace curtains.</u> Grandma always left that window open. I remember sitting near it, <u>smelling the rain</u> while the curtains <u>tickled my face.</u>

Comparison (simile) — left of "like a church or schoolroom"

Sight — right of "old purple velvet couch"

Sight — right of "One-half of the couch was always buried in old clothes, magazines, and newspapers, and a lone"

Comparison (metaphor) — left of "shoe sat on top of the pile, a finishing touch to some bizarre modern sculpture."

Sound — left of "tuneless"

Sight — right of "yellowed keys"

Sight — left of "showed through"

Sound — left of "muffled and frustrating thump"

Sight — right of "yellowed lace curtains"

Smell — left of "smelling the rain"

Touch — left of "tickled my face."

For no apparent reason, <u>an old curtain</u> hung in the door between the kitchen and the living room. In the kitchen, a large Formica-topped table always held at least a half-dozen varieties of <u>homemade jelly, as well as a loaf of bread, gooseberry pies or cherry pies with the pits left in, boxes of cereal,</u> and anything else not requiring refrigeration, <u>as if the table served as a small, portable pantry.</u> Grandma's kitchen always <u>smelled of toast,</u> and I often wondered—and still do—if she lived entirely on toast. <u>A hole had eaten through the kitchen floor,</u> not just the warped yellow linoleum, but all the way through the floor itself. My sisters and I never wanted to take a bath at Grandma's house, because we discovered that anyone who lay on the floor face down and put one eye to the hole <u>could see the bathtub,</u>

Sight — right of "an old curtain"

Taste — right of "homemade jelly, as well"

Comparison (simile) — left of "requiring refrigeration, as if the table served as a small, portable pantry."

Smell — right of "smelled of toast"

Sight — right of "A hole had eaten through the kitchen floor"

Sight — right of "could see the bathtub,"

which was kept in the <u>musty</u> basement because the Smell
upstairs bathroom was too small.

The back bedroom was near the kitchen and adjacent to the basement stairs. I once heard one of my
aunts call that room a firetrap, and indeed it was. The
Sight room was <u>wallpapered with the old newspapers</u>
Grandma liked to collect, and the bed was stacked
Sight high with <u>my mother's and aunts' old clothes</u>. There
was no space between the furniture in that room, only
a narrow path against one wall leading to the bed. A
sideboard was shoved against the opposite wall; a
sewing table was pushed up against the sideboard; a
short chest of drawers lay against the sewing table; and Sight
so on. But no one could identify these pieces of forgotten furniture without digging through the sewing
patterns, half-made dresses, dishes, and books. Any outsider would just think this was a part of the room
where the floor had been raised to about waist level,
so thoroughly was the mass of furniture hidden.

Stepping off Grandma's sloping back porch was <u>like</u> Comparison (simile)
<u>stepping into an enchanted forest</u>. The grass and weeds
were hip level, with a tiny dirt path leading to
Comparison (simile) nowhere, <u>as if it had lost its way in the jungle</u>. <u>A fancy</u> Sight
<u>white fence</u>, courtesy of the neighbors, bordered the
yard in back and vainly attempted to hold in the
Sight <u>gooseberries, raspberries, and blackberries</u> that grew
wildly along the side of Grandma's yard. Huge
Sight <u>crabapple, cherry, and walnut trees</u> shaded the house
and hid the sky. I used to stand under them and look
up, pretending to be deep in a magic forest. The
ground was <u>cool and damp</u> under my bare feet, even Touch
in the middle of the day, and my head would fill with
Smell the <u>sweet fragrance of mixed spring flowers</u> and <u>the</u>
Sound <u>throaty cooing of doves</u> I could never find but could
always hear. But, before long, the wind would shift,
Smell and the <u>musty aroma of petroleum</u> from a nearby re-
finery would jerk me back to reality.

Grandma's house is indeed a place of wonderful
memories. Just as her decaying concrete steps store
the treasures of many lost childhoods, <u>her house still</u> Dominant impression rephrased
<u>stands, guarding the memories of generations of chil-</u>
<u>dren and grandchildren</u>.

Student Writer's Comments

Writing this descriptive essay was easy and enjoyable for me—once I got started. I decided to write about my grandmother's house because I knew it so well, but I had trouble coming up with the impression I wanted to convey to my readers. I have so many recollections of this place I didn't know which set of memories would be most interesting to others. So I began by brainstorming, forcing myself to think of images from all five senses.

After I had accumulated plenty of images, which triggered other memories I had completely forgotten, I began to write. I organized my essay spatially as if I were walking through Grandma's house room by room. But I let my senses lead the way. Before I started writing, I had no idea how many paragraphs I would have, but as I meandered through the house recording my memories of sights, smells, sounds, tastes, and textures, I ended up writing one paragraph on each room, plus one for the yard. For this assignment, I wrote the three paragraphs about the inside of the house first; then, the introduction started to take shape in my head, so I got it down; and last, I wrote the paragraph on the backyard and my conclusion. Finally, my "dominant impression" came to me: This is a house that guards the memories of many generations. My grandmother has always lived in this house, and my mother has her own set of memories associated with this place too.

This focus for my paper made the revising process fairly easy, as I worked on the entire essay with a specific purpose in mind. Previously, my biggest problem had been that I had too many scattered memories and realized I had to be more selective. Once I had my dominant impression, I knew which images to keep and which to drop from my draft. Also, as I reworked my essay, I looked for ways to make my description more exciting and vivid for the reader—as if he or she were right there with me. To accomplish this, I explained some special features of my grandma's house by comparing them with items the reader would most likely be familiar with. I also worked, at this point, on making one paragraph flow into another by adding transitions that would move the reader smoothly from one group of ideas to the next. "Only a hook-type lock on the front door" got my readers into the living room. The old curtain between the kitchen and the living room moved my essay out of the living room and into the kitchen. I started my third paragraph about the indoors by saying "The back bedroom was near the kitchen and adjacent to the basement stairs" so my readers could get their bearings in relation to other parts of the house they had already been introduced to. Finally, I was satisfied that my essay was a clear, accurate description of my view of my grandma's house. My brother might have a completely different set of memories, but this was my version of a single generation of impressions organized, finally, into one coherent essay.

SOME FINAL THOUGHTS ON DESCRIPTION

Because description is one of the most basic forms of verbal communication, you will find descriptive passages in most of the reading selections throughout this textbook. Description provides us with the means to capture our audience's attention and clarify certain points in all of our writing. The examples chosen for the following section, however, are predominantly descriptive—the main purpose in each being to involve the readers' senses as vividly as possible. As you read through each of these essays, try to determine its intended audience and purpose, the object of the description, the extent to which details are included or excluded, and the author's point of view. Equipped with these four areas of reference, you can become an increasingly sophisticated reader and writer of descriptive prose.

DESCRIPTION IN REVIEW

Reading Descriptive Essays

Preparing to Read

✓ What assumptions can you make from the essay's title?

✓ Can you guess what the general mood of the essay is?

✓ What is the essay's purpose and audience?

✓ What does the synopsis tell you about the essay?

✓ What can you learn from the author's biography?

✓ Can you predict the author's point of view toward the subject?

Reading

✓ What is the essay's dominant impression?

✓ Is the essay predominantly objective or subjective?

✓ What senses does the author engage?

Rereading

✓ What details support the essay's dominant impression?

✓ What other rhetorical modes does the author use?

Writing Descriptive Essays

Preparing to Write

✓ What is your purpose?

✓ Will you be primarily objective or subjective?

✓ Who is your audience?

✓ What is the dominant impression you want to convey?

Writing

✓ Do you have a dominant impression for your thesis?

✓ Did you select details that support your dominant impression?

✓ Did you engage all five senses?

✓ What is your point of view toward your subject (objective or subjective)?

✓ Do you *show* rather than *tell* your narrative?

Rewriting

✓ Do you communicate the dominant impression you want to convey?

✓ Do your details support your dominant impression?

✓ Which senses do you stimulate?

✓ Do you have a clear, consistent point of view toward your subject?

✓ Are you showing rather than telling in your description?

✓ Do you use similes or metaphors when appropriate?

RAY BRADBURY   (1920–   )

Summer Rituals

Ray Bradbury is one of America's best-known and most loved writers of science fiction. His extensive publications include such popular novels as *The Martian Chronicles* (1950), *The Illustrated Man* (1951), *Fahrenheit 451* (1953), *Dandelion Wine* (1957), and *Something Wicked This Way Comes* (1962). He has also written dozens of short stories, poems, essays, plays, and radio and movie scripts (including the screenplay of John Huston's film version of *Moby Dick*). As a child, he escaped his strict Baptist upbringing through a steady diet of Jules Verne, H. G. Wells, and Edgar Rice Burroughs, along with Buck Rogers and Prince Valiant comic books: "I was a sucker for lies, beautiful, fabulous lies, which instruct us to better our lives as a result, but which don't tell the truth." A frequent theme in his many novels is the impact of science on humanity: "My stories are intended," he claims, "as much to forecast how to prevent dooms, as to predict them." Bradbury's more recent publications include *The Last Circus* (1981), *The Complete Poems of Ray Bradbury* (1982), *The Love Affair* (1983), *Dinosaur Tales* (1983), *A Memory for Murder* (1984), *Forever and the Earth* (1984), *Death Is a Lonely Business* (1985), *The Toynbee Convector* (1989), *A Day in the Life of Hollywood* (1992), *Quicker Than the Eye* (1996), *Driving Blind* (1998), *From the Dust Returned* (2000), *Let's All Kill Constance* (2003), and *Bradbury Speaks: Too Soon from the Cave, Too Far From the Stars* (2005). The author lives in Cheviot Hills, California, where he enjoys painting and making ceramics.

Preparing to Read

"Summer Rituals," an excerpt from *Dandelion Wine*, describes the comfortable ceremony of putting up a front-porch swing in early summer. Focusing on the perceptions of Douglas, a young boy, the essay clearly sets forth the familiar yet deeply significant rhythms of life in a small town.

Exploring Experience: Before you read this selection, take a few moments to consider the value of ritual in your own life: Can you think of any activities that you and your family have elevated to the level of ceremonial importance? What about holidays? Birthdays? Sporting events? Spring cleaning? When do these activities take place? Do the same people participate in them every year? Why do you repeat these rituals? What purpose do they have for you? For others whom you know? For society in general?

Learning Online: Go to http://www.naturephotographs.com, and look at pictures in the "Summer" section. Find a picture that represents summer to you. Study the picture, and think about how you would describe the location or moment in time.

Yes, summer was rituals, each with its natural time and place. The rit-   1
ual of lemonade or ice-tea making, the ritual of wine, shoes, or no
shoes, and at last, swiftly following the others, with quiet dignity, the
ritual of the front-porch swing. ◆1

On the third day of summer in the late afternoon Grandfather reappeared   2
from the front door to gaze serenely at the two empty eye rings in the ceiling of the porch. Moving to the geranium-pot-lined rail like Ahab surveying the mild day and the mild-looking sky, he wet his finger to test the wind,
and shucked his coat to see how shirt sleeves felt in the westering hours. He
acknowledged the salutes of other captains on yet other flowered porches,
out themselves to discern the gentle ground swell of weather, oblivious to
their wives chirping or snapping like fuzzball hand dogs hidden behind black
porch screens.

"All right, Douglas, let's set it up."   3

In the garage they found, dusted, and carried forth the howdah, as it were,   4
for the quiet summer-night festivals, the swing chair which Grandpa chained
to the porch-ceiling eyelets.

Douglas, being lighter, was first to sit in the swing. Then, after a moment,   5
Grandfather gingerly settled his pontifical weight beside the boy. Thus they
sat, smiling at each other, nodding, as they swung silently back and forth, back
and forth.

Ten minutes later Grandma appeared with water buckets and brooms to   6
wash down and sweep off the porch. Other chairs, rockers and straight-backs,
were summoned from the house.

"Always like to start sitting early in the season," said Grandpa, "before the   7
mosquitoes thicken."

About seven o'clock you could hear the chairs scraping back from the ta-   8
bles, someone experimenting with a yellow-toothed piano, if you stood outside the dining-room window and listened. Matches being struck, the first
dishes bubbling in the suds and tinkling on the wall racks, somewhere, faintly,
a phonograph playing. And then as the evening changed the hour, at house
after house on the twilight streets, under the immense oaks and elms, on
shady porches, people would begin to appear, like those figures who tell
good or bad weather in rain-or-shine clocks. ◆2

Uncle Bert, perhaps Grandfather, then Father, and some of the cousins; the   9
men all coming out first into the syrupy evening, blowing smoke, leaving the

---

Reading Critically

◆1 How can rituals bring dignity to our lives?

◆2 How does Bradbury speed up and slow down time? Mark all the time references you can
find, and examine them after you finish the essay.

women's voices behind in the cooling-warm kitchen to set their universe aright. Then the first male voices under the porch brim, the feet up, the boys fringed on the worn steps or wooden rails where sometime during the evening something, a boy or a geranium pot, would fall off.

At last, like ghosts hovering momentarily behind the door screen, 10 Grandma, Great-grandma, and Mother would appear, and the men would shift, move, and offer seats. The women carried varieties of fans with them, folded newspapers, bamboo whisks, or perfumed kerchiefs, to start the air moving about their faces as they talked.

What they talked of all evening long, no one remembered next day. It 11 wasn't important to anyone what the adults talked about; it was only important that the sounds came and went over the delicate ferns that bordered the porch on three sides; it was only important that the darkness filled the town like black water being poured over the houses and that the cigars glowed and that the conversations went on and on. The female gossip moved out, disturbing the first mosquitoes so they danced in frenzies on the air. The male voices invaded the old house timbers; if you closed your eyes and put your head down against the floor boards you could hear the men's voices rumbling like a distant, political earthquake, constant, unceasing, rising or falling a pitch. ❸

Douglas sprawled back on the dry porch planks, completely contented and 12 reassured by these voices, which would speak on through eternity, flow in a stream of murmurings over his body, over his closed eyelids, into his drowsy ears, for all time. The rocking chairs sounded like crickets, the crickets sounded like rocking chairs, and the moss-covered rain barrel by the dining-room window produced another generation of mosquitoes to provide a topic of conversation through endless summers ahead.

Sitting on the summer-night porch was so good, so easy and so reassur- 13 ing that it could never be done away with. These were rituals that were right and lasting; the lighting of pipes, the pale hands that moved knitting needles in the dimness, the eating of foil-wrapped, chill Eskimo Pies, the coming and going of all the people. For at some time or other during the evening, everyone visited here; the neighbors down the way, the people across the street; Miss Fern and Miss Roberta humming by in their electric runabout, giving Tom or Douglas a ride around the block and then coming up to sit down and fan away the fever in their cheeks; or Mr. Jonas, the junkman, having left his horse and wagon hidden in the alley, and ripe to bursting

---

Reading Critically

❸ How many different sound images can you find in the essay? How do these images help characterize Douglas, the young narrator? Which specific sounds are most memorable for him?

with words, would come up the steps looking as fresh as if his talk had never been said before, and somehow it never had. And last of all, the children, who had been off squinting their way through a last hide-and-seek or kick-the-can, panting, glowing, would sickle quietly back like boomerangs along the soundless lawn, to sink beneath the talking talking talking of the porch voices which would weigh and gentle them down. . . . ◀④

Oh, the luxury of lying in the fern night and the grass night and the night   14
of susurrant, slumbrous voices weaving the dark together. The grownups had forgotten he was there, so still, so quiet Douglas lay, noting the plans they were making for his and their own futures. And the voices chanted, drifted, in moonlit clouds of cigarette smoke while the moths, like late appleblossoms come alive, tapped faintly about the far street lights, and the voices moved on into the coming years. . . .

UNDERSTANDING DETAILS

1. What are the main similarities and differences between Douglas and Grandfather in this essay? How are their views of the world the same? How are their views different?
2. From the scattered details you have read in this essay, describe Douglas's house. How large do you think the front porch is? What color is the house? How many trees and shrubs surround it? What part of your description is based on facts in the essay? What part comes from inferences you have made on your own?
3. How do the men differ from the women in this excerpt? Divide a piece of paper into two columns; then list as many qualities of each gender as you can find. (For example, the narrator hears the men's voices "rumbling" like an "earthquake"; in contrast, the women move like "ghosts," their gossip "disturbing the . . . mosquitoes.") What other descriptive differences can you find between the men and women? What conclusions can you draw from these differences?
4. How did the conversation blend with the surroundings in Bradbury's description?

THINKING CRITICALLY

5. A "ritual" may be briefly defined as "a customarily repeated act that expresses a system of values." Using this definition, explain why the ritual of the front-porch swing is important to Douglas's family. What feelings or implicit values lie behind this particular ritual?

Reading Critically

④ What is the relationship between the children's games and the adult rituals mentioned by Bradbury? In what way can children's games be called "rituals"?

6. What other rituals are mentioned in this essay? How are they related to the front-porch swing? To summer? To Douglas and his family?

7. Bradbury helps us feel the comfort, warmth, and familiarity of the scene depicted in this essay through the use of a number of original descriptive details: for example, "summer-night festivals," "yellow-toothed piano," "rain-or-shine clocks," "syrupy evening," and "foil-wrapped, chill Eskimo Pies." Find at least five other descriptive words or phrases, and explain how each enables us to identify with the characters and situations in this story. Which of the five senses does each of these details arouse in the reader?

8. In what ways do you think Douglas was "completely contented and reassured" (paragraph 12) by the voices around him? Why did Douglas feel this contentment would last "for all time" (paragraph 12)?

DISCOVERING RHETORICAL STRATEGIES

9. Some of the author's sentences are very long and involved, whereas others are quite short. What effects do these changes in sentence length have on you as a reader? Give a specific example of a shift in length from one sentence to another and explain its effect.

10. This descriptive essay is filled with many interesting similes (comparisons using the words *like* or *as*) and metaphors (comparisons without *like* or *as*). For example, Grandfather standing on the front porch looks *like* Ahab, the possessed sea captain from Herman Melville's epic novel *Moby Dick* (paragraph 2). Later, Bradbury uses a metaphor to focus his readers on "the night of susurrant, slumbrous voices weaving the dark together" (paragraph 14). Find at least one other comparison, either a simile or a metaphor, and explain how it works within the context of its sentence or paragraph. What type of comparison is being made (a simile or a metaphor)? What do we learn about the object being described (for example, Grandfather or the night) through its association with the other reference (Ahab or voices weaving the dark together)?

11. What is the point of view of the author in this selection? Would the essay be more effective if it were reported from the standpoint of Douglas? Of Grandfather? Of the women? Why or why not? How does the author's point of view help Bradbury organize his description? Should the fact that Bradbury's middle name is Douglas have any bearing on our interpretation of this story?

12. Although Bradbury draws mainly on description to write this essay, what other rhetorical strategies work together to help the reader grasp the full effect of "Summer Rituals"? Give examples of each strategy.

MAKING CONNECTIONS

13. For Douglas, hanging the porch swing was an important yearly ritual. What rituals can you find in the family backgrounds of Russell Baker ("The Saturday Evening Post") and/or Michael Dorris ("The Broken Cord")? What specific meanings did these rituals have within each author's family?

14. Compare and contrast Bradbury's neighborhood with that of Robert Ramirez ("The Barrio"). Which neighborhood would you feel more comfortable in? Why would you feel comfortable there?

15. Which author's relationship with his/her parents was most like your own: Ray Bradbury's, Russell Baker's ("The Saturday Evening Post"), or Sandra Cisneros's ("Only daughter")? How did each of these children relate differently to his or her parents?

IDEAS FOR DISCUSSION/WRITING

Preparing to Write

List some of the most important rituals in your life: How many times a year do these rituals occur? What purpose do they serve? How do rituals help create a strong social framework in your life? In your friends' lives? In society in general?

Choosing a Topic

1. Write a descriptive essay about a ritual that is significant in your life, addressing it to someone who has never experienced that particular activity. Include the people involved and the setting. Try to use all five senses in your description.

2. Choose a ritual that is part of your family life, and write an essay describing your feelings about this ceremonial event. Address it to someone outside your family. Use similes and metaphors to make your description as vivid as possible.

3. Explain to someone visiting the United States for the first time the value of a particular tradition in American society. Then help this person understand the importance of that tradition in your life.

4. Bradbury's descriptions develop his narrative by providing concrete and consistent details. Using either a photo that has special meaning for you or an interesting image from the Internet, write an essay describing a moment or place suspended in time.

Before beginning your essay, you might want to consult the checklists on page 44.

KIMBERLY WOZENCRAFT   (1954–   )

Notes from the Country Club

Kimberly Wozencraft grew up in Dallas, Texas, and dropped out of college when she was twenty-one to become a police officer. Her first assignment, prior to training at the police academy, was a street-level undercover narcotics investigation. Like many narcotics agents, Wozencraft became addicted to drugs, which impaired her judgment and resulted in a 1981 conviction for violating the civil rights of a reputed child pornographer. After serving an eighteen-month sentence in the Federal Correctional Institution at Lexington, Kentucky, she moved to New York City, where she now lives with her husband and three children. She holds a master of fine arts degree from Columbia University, and her essays, poems, and short stories have appeared in a variety of publications, including *Northwest Review, Quarto, Big Wednesday, Witness, Texas Monthly, New York Newsday,* and the *Los Angeles Times.* Her first novel, *Rush,* was made into a movie in 1991. In 1998, she completed two more books, *The Catch* and *Slam* (with Richard Stratton). Her most recent novel, *The Devil's Backbone,* was just published in 2006.

Preparing to Read

Originally published in *Witness,* "Notes from the Country Club" was selected for inclusion in *The Best American Essays of 1988,* edited by Annie Dillard. Through carefully constructed prose, the author describes her prison environment and the anxiety caused by living for more than a year in such an alien, difficult place.

Exploring Experience: As you prepare to read this essay, take a moment to think about your own behavior in difficult situations: What kind of person do you become? How do you act toward other people? How is this behavior different from the way you usually act? How do you know when you're in a difficult situation? What do you generally do to relieve the tension? How successful are your solutions?

Learning Online: Wozencraft's description of her experience as an undercover narcotics agent was made into a movie entitled *Rush.* To better understand her experience, go to http://www.mgm.com. Conduct a keyword search for "Rush." Click on the "multimedia" link to view photos and clips from the film.

They had the Haitians up the hill, in the "camp" section where they   1
used to keep the minimum security cases.◆ The authorities were
concerned that some of the Haitians might be diseased, so they kept
them isolated from the main coed prison population by lodging them in
the big square brick building surrounded by eight-foot chain-link with concertina wire on top. We were not yet familiar with the acronym AIDS.

One or two of the Haitians had drums, and in the evenings when the rest   2
of us were in the Big Yard, the drum rhythms carried over the bluegrass to
where we were playing gin or tennis or softball or just hanging out waiting
for dark. When they really got going some of them would dance and sing.
Their music was rhythmic and beautiful, and it made me think of freedom.

There were Cubans loose in the population, spattering their guttural Span-   3
ish in streams around the rectangular courtyard, called Central Park, at the
center of the prison compound. These were Castro's Boat People, guilty of
no crime in this country, but requiring sponsors before they could walk the
streets as free people.

Walking around the perimeter of Central Park was like taking a trip in mi-   4
crocosm across the United States. Moving leftward from the main entrance,
strolling along under the archway that covers the wide sidewalk, you passed
the doorway to the Women's Unit, where I lived, and it was how I imagined
Harlem to be. There was a white face here and there, but by far most of
them were black. Ghetto blasters thunked out rhythms in the sticky evening
air, and folks leaned against the window sills, smoking, drinking Cokes, slink-
ing, and nodding. Every once in a while a joint was passed around, and always there was somebody pinning, checking for hacks on patrol.

Past Women's Unit was the metal door to the Big Yard, the main recre-   5
ation area of three or four acres, two sides blocked by the building, two sides
fenced in the usual way—chain-link and concertina wire. ◆

Past the Big Yard you entered the Blue Ridge Mountains, a sloping grassy   6
area on the edge of Central Park, where the locals, people from Kentucky,
Tennessee, and the surrounding environs, sat around playing guitars and
singing, and every once in a while passing around a quart of hooch. They
make it from grapefruit juice and a bit of yeast smuggled out of the kitchen.
Some of the inmates who worked in Cable would bring out pieces of a
black foam rubber substance and wrap it around empty Cremora jars to
make thermos jugs of sorts. They would mix the grapefruit juice and yeast
in the containers and stash them in some out-of-the-way spot for a few

---

Reading Critically

◆ Does the first sentence catch your attention? Why or why not? How soon do you know
what kind of place the author is describing?

◆ Why do you think the prison has two different types of fences?

weeks until presto! you had hooch, bitter and tart and sweet all at once, only mildly alcoholic, but entirely suitable for evening cocktails in Central Park.

Next, at the corner, was the Commissary, a tiny store tucked inside the en- 7 trance to Veritas, the second women's unit. It wasn't much more than a few shelves behind a wall of Plexiglas, with a constant line of inmates spilling out of the doorway. They sold packaged chips, cookies, pens and writing paper, toiletries, some fresh fruit, and the ever-popular ice cream, sold only in pints. You had to eat the entire pint as soon as you bought it, or else watch it melt, because there weren't any refrigerators. Inmates were assigned one shopping night per week, allowed to buy no more than seventy-five dollars' worth of goods per month, and were permitted to pick up a ten-dollar roll of quarters if they had enough money in their prison account. Quarters were the basic spending unit in the prison; possession of paper money was a ship-pable offense.[3] There were vending machines stocked with junk food and soda, and they were supposedly what the quarters were to be used for. But we gambled, we bought salami or fried chicken sneaked out by the food service workers, and of course people sold booze and drugs. The beggars stood just outside the Commissary door. Mostly they were Cubans, saying, "Oyez! Mira! Mira! Hey, Poppy, one quarter for me. One cigarette for me, Poppy?"

There was one Cuban whom I was specially fond of. His name was Shorty. 8 The name said it. He was only about five-two, and he looked just like Mick Jagger. I met him in Segregation, an isolated section of tiny cells where pris-oners were locked up for having violated some institutional rule or another. They tossed me in there the day I arrived; again the authorities were con-cerned, supposedly for my safety. I was a police woman before I became a convict, and they weren't too sure that the other inmates would like that. Shorty saved me a lot of grief when I went into Seg. It didn't matter if you were male or female there, you got stripped and handed a tee shirt, a pair of boxer shorts and a set of Peter Pans—green canvas shoes with thin rubber soles designed to prevent you from running away. As if you could get past three steel doors and a couple of hacks just to start with. When I was marched down the hall between the cells, the guys started whistling and hooting, and they didn't shut up even after I was locked down. They kept right on scream-ing until finally I yelled out, "Yo no comprendo!" and they all moaned and said, "Another . . . Cuban," and finally got quiet. Shorty was directly across from me, I could see his eyes through the rectangular slot in my cell door. He rattled off a paragraph or two of Spanish, all of which was lost on me, and I said quietly, "Yo no comprendo bien español. Yo soy de Texas, yo hablo

---

Reading Critically

[3] How do you feel about these prison rules? How restrictive would you find them if you were incarcerated?

inglés?" I could tell he was smiling by the squint of his eyes, and he just said, "Bueno." When the hacks came around to take us out for our mandatory hour of recreation, which consisted of standing around in the Rec area while two guys shot a game of pool on the balcony above the gym, Shorty slipped his hand into mine and smiled up at me until the hack told him to cut it out. He knew enough English to tell the others in Seg⁴ that I was not really Spanish, but he kept quiet about it, and they left me alone.

Beyond the Commissary, near the door to the dining hall, was East St.   9
Louis. The prison had a big portable stereo system which they rolled out a few times a week so that an inmate could play at being a disc jockey. They had a good-sized collection of albums, and there was usually some decent jazz blasting out of there. Sometimes people danced, unless there were uptight hacks on duty to tell them not to.⁵

California was next. It was a laid back kind of corner near the doors to   10
two of the men's units. People stood around and smoked hash or grass or did whatever drugs happened to be available and there was sometimes a sort of slow-motion game of handball going on. If you wanted drugs, this was the place to come.

If you kept walking, you would arrive at the Power Station, the other   11
southern corner where the politicos-gone-wrong congregated. It might seem odd at first to see these middle-aged government mavens standing around in their Lacoste sport shirts and Sans-a-belt slacks, smoking pipes or cigars and waving their arms to emphasize some point or other. They kept pretty much to themselves and ate together at the big round tables in the cafeteria, sipping cherry Kool-Aid and pretending it was Cabernet Sauvignon.

That's something else you had to deal with—the food. It was worse than   12
elementary school steam table fare. By the time they finished cooking it, it was tasteless, colorless, and nutritionless. The first meal I took in the dining room was lunch. As I walked toward the entry, a tubby fellow was walking out, staggering really, rolling his eyes as though he were dizzy. He stopped and leaned over, and I heard someone yell, "Watch out, he's gonna puke!" I ducked inside so as to miss the spectacle. They were serving some rubbery, faint pink slabs that were supposed to be ham, but I didn't even bother to taste mine. I just slapped at it a few times to watch the fork bounce off and then ate my potatoes and went back to the unit.

Shortly after that I claimed that I was Jewish, having gotten the word   13
from a friendly New York lawyer who was in for faking some of his clients' immigration papers. The kosher line was the only way to get a decent meal

---

Reading Critically

④ What does the word "Seg" mean? What other prison slang can you find in the essay?
⑤ To what extent does each location in the prison have its own ethnic identity?

in there. In fact, for a long time they had a Jewish baker from Philadelphia locked up, and he made some truly delicious cream puffs for dessert. They sold for seventy-five cents on the black market, but once I had established myself in the Jewish community, I got them as part of my regular fare. They fed us a great deal of peanut butter on the kosher line; every time the "goyim" got meat, we got peanut butter, but that was all right with me. Eventually I was asked to light the candles at the Friday evening services, since none of the real Jewish women bothered to attend. I have to admit that most of the members of our little prison congregation were *genuine alter kokers,* but some of them were amusing. And I enjoyed learning first hand about Judaism. The services were usually very quiet, and the music, the ancient intoning songs, fortified me against the screeching pop-rock vocal assaults that were a constant in the Women's Unit. I learned to think of myself as the *shabot shiksa,*[6] and before my time was up, even the rabbi seemed to accept me.

I suppose it was quite natural that the Italians assembled just "down the   14
street" from the offending ex-senators, judges, and power brokers. Just to the left of the main entrance. The first night I made the tour, a guy came out of the shadows near the building and whispered to me. "What do you need, sweetheart? What do you want, I can get it. My friend Ahmad over there, he's very rich, and he wants to buy you things. What'll it be, you want some smoke, a few ludes, vodka, cigarettes, maybe some kosher salami fresh from the kitchen? What would you like?" I just stared at him. The only thing I wanted at that moment was out, and even Ahmad's millions, if they existed at all, couldn't do that. The truth is, every guy I met in there claimed to be wealthy, to have been locked up for some major financial crime. Had I taken all of them up on their offers of limousines to pick me up at the front gate when I was released and take me to the airport for a ride home in a private Lear jet, I would have needed my own personal cop out front just to direct traffic.

Ahmad's Italian promoter eventually got popped for zinging the cooking   15
teacher one afternoon on the counter in the home economics classroom, right next to the new Cuisinart. The assistant warden walked in on the young lovebirds, and before the week was up, even the Cubans were walking around singing about it. They had a whole song down, to the tune of "Borracho Me Acosté a Noche."

At the end of the tour, you would find the jaded New Yorkers,[7] sitting   16
at a picnic table or two in the middle of the park, playing gin or poker and

---

Reading Critically

[6] How does the use of foreign language here and elsewhere contribute to the tone of the essay?

[7] Why do you think the New Yorkers are "jaded"?

bragging about their days on Madison Avenue and Wall Street, lamenting the scarcity of good deli, even on the kosher line, and planning where they would take their first real meal upon release.

If you think federal correctional institutions are about the business of re-   17
habilitation, drop by for an orientation session one day. There at the front of the classroom, confronting rows of mostly black faces, will be the warden, or the assistant warden, or the prison shrink, pacing back and forth in front of the blackboard and asking the class, "Why do you think you're here?" This gets a general grumble, a few short, choked laughs. Some well-meaning soul always says it—rehabilitation.

"Nonsense!" the lecturer will say. "There are several reasons for locking   18
people up. Number one is incapacitation. If you're in here, you can't be out there doing crime. Secondly, there is deterrence. Other people who are thinking about doing crime see that we lock people up for it and maybe they think twice. But the real reason you are here is to be punished. Plain and simple. You done wrong, now you got to pay for it. Rehabilitation ain't even part of the picture.[8] So don't be looking to us to rehabilitate you. Only person can rehabilitate you is you. If you feel like it, go for it, but leave us out. We don't want to play that game."

So that's it. You're there to do time. I have no misgivings about why I   19
went to prison. I deserved it. I was a cop; I got strung out on cocaine; I violated the rights of a pornographer. My own drug use as an undercover narcotics agent was a significant factor in my crime. But I did it, and I deserved to be punished. Most of the people I met in Lexington, though, were in for drugs, and the majority of them hadn't done anything more than sell an ounce of cocaine or a pound of pot to some apostle of the law.

It seems lately that almost every time I look at the *New York Times* op-ed   20
page, there is something about the drug problem. I have arrested people for drugs, and I have had a drug problem myself. I have seen how at least one federal correctional institution functions. It does not appear that the practice of locking people up for possession or distribution of an insignificant quantity of a controlled substance makes any difference at all in the amount of drug use that occurs in the United States. The drug laws are merely another convenient source of political rhetoric for aspiring officeholders. Politicians know that an antidrug stance is an easy way to get votes from parents who are terrified that their children might wind up as addicts. I do not advocate drug use. Yet, having seen the criminal justice system from several angles, as a police officer, a court bailiff, a defendant, and a prisoner, I am convinced that prison is not the answer to the drug problem, or for that matter to many

---

Reading Critically

[8] Do you believe prison rehabilitates its inmates? Why or why not?

other white-collar crimes. If the taxpayers knew how their dollars were being spent inside some prisons, they might actually scream out loud. [9]

There were roughly 1,800 men and women locked up in Lex, at a ratio   21
of approximately three men to every woman, and it did get warm in the summertime. To keep us tranquil they devised some rather peculiar little amusements. One evening I heard a commotion on the steps at the edge of Central Park and looked over to see a rec specialist with three big cardboard boxes set up on the plaza, marked 1, 2, and 3. There were a couple of hundred inmates sitting at the bottom of the steps. Dennis, the rec specialist, was conducting his own version of the television game show *Let's Make a Deal!* Under one of the boxes was a case of soda, under another was a racquetball glove, and under the third was a fly swatter. The captive contestant picked door number 2, which turned out to contain the fly swatter, to my way of thinking the best prize there. Fly swatters were virtually impossible to get through approved channels, and therefore cost as much as two packs of cigarettes on the black market.

Then there was the Annual Fashion Show, where ten or twenty inmates   22
had special packages of clothing sent in, only for the one evening, and modeled them on stage while the baddest drag queen in the compound moderated and everyone else ooohed and aahhed. They looked good up there on stage in Christian Dior and Ralph Lauren instead of the usual fatigue pants and white tee shirts. And if such activities did little to prepare inmates for a productive return to society, well, at least they contributed to the fantasyland aura that made Lexington such an unusual place.

I worked in Landscape, exiting the rear gate of the compound each week-   23
day morning at about nine after getting a half-hearted frisk from one of the hacks on duty. I would climb on my tractor to drive to the staff apartment complex and pull weeds or mow the lawn. Landscape had its prerogatives. [10] We raided the gardens regularly and at least got to taste fresh vegetables from time to time. I had never eaten raw corn before, but it could not have tasted better. We also brought in a goodly supply of real vodka, and a bit of hash now and then, for parties in our rooms after lights out. One guy strapped a six-pack of Budweiser to his arms with masking tape and then put on his prison-issue Army field jacket. When he got to the rear gate, he raised his arms straight out at shoulder level, per instructions, and the hack patted down his torso and legs, never bothering to check his arms. The inmate had been counting on that. He smiled at the hack and walked back to his room, a six-pack richer.

Reading Critically

[9] Do you think Wozencraft's opinions about the penalties for drug abuse have anything to do with the fact that she was a former drug addict?

[10] Why did most prisoners like Landscape duty?

I was fortunate to be working Landscape at the same time as Horace, a   24
fellow who had actually lived in the city of Lexington before he was locked
up. His friends made regular deliveries of assorted contraband, which they
would stash near a huge elm tree near the outer stone fence of the reservation. Horace would drive his tractor over, make the pickup, and the rest of
us would carry it, concealed, through the back gate when we went back inside for lunch or at the end of the day. "Contraband" included everything
from drugs to blue eye shadow. The assistant warden believed that female
inmates should wear no cosmetics other than what she herself used—a bit
of mascara and a light shade of lipstick. I have never been a plaything of
Fashion, but I did what I could to help the other women prisoners in their
never-ending quest for that Cover Girl look.

You could depend on the fact that most of the hacks would rather have   25
been somewhere else, and most of them really didn't care *what* the inmates
did, as long as it didn't cause any commotion. Of course, there were a few
you had to look out for. The captain in charge of security was one of them.
We tried a little experiment once, after having observed that any time he saw
someone laughing, he took immediate steps to make the inmate and everyone around him acutely miserable. Whenever we saw him in the area, we immediately assumed expressions of intense unhappiness, even of despair. Seeing
no chance to make anyone more miserable than they already appeared to be,
the captain left us alone.

Almost all of the female hacks, and a good number of the males, had out-   26
rageously large derrières, a condition we inmates referred to as "the federal
ass."⑪ This condition may have resulted from the fact that most of them appeared, as one inmate succinctly described it, simply to be "putting in their
forty a week to stay on the government teat." Employment was not an easy
thing to find in Kentucky.

Despite the fact that Lexington is known as a "country club" prison, I   27
must admit that I counted days. From the first moment that I was in, I kept
track of how many more times I would have to watch the sun sink behind
eight feet of chain-link, of how many more days I would have to spend eating, working, playing, and sleeping according to the dictates of a "higher authority." I don't think I can claim that I was rehabilitated. If anything I
underwent a process of dehabilitation. What I learned was what Jessica Mitford tried to tell people many years ago in her book *Kind and Usual Punishment*. Prison is a business,⑫ no different from manufacturing tires or selling

---

Reading Critically

⑪ What does the author mean by the term "the federal ass"?
⑫ In what way is prison a "business"?

real estate. It keeps people employed, and it provides cheap labor for NASA, the U.S. Postal Service, and other governmental or quasi-governmental agencies. For a short time, before I was employed in Landscape, I worked as a finisher of canvas mailbags, lacing white rope through metal eyelets around the top of the bags and attaching clamps to the ropes. I made one dollar and fourteen cents for every one hundred that I did. If I worked very hard, I could do almost two hundred a day.

It's not about justice. If you think it's about justice, look at the newspapers and notice who walks. Not the little guys, the guys doing a tiny bit of dealing or sniggling a little on their income tax, or the woman who pulls a stunt with welfare checks because her husband has skipped out and she has no other way to feed her kids. I do not say that these things are right. But the process of selective prosecution, the "making" of cases by D.A.s and police departments, and the presence of some largely unenforceable statutes currently on the books (it is the reality of "compliance": no law can be forced on a public which chooses to ignore it; hence, selective prosecution) make for a criminal justice system which cannot realistically function in a fair and equitable manner. Criminal justice—I cannot decide if it is the ultimate oxymoron or a truly accurate description of the law enforcement process in America. 28

In my police undercover capacity, I have sat across the table from an armed robber who said, "My philosophy of life is slit thy neighbor's throat and pimp his kids." I believe that the human animals who maim and kill people should be dealt with, as they say, swiftly and surely. But this business of locking people up, at enormous cost, for minor, nonviolent offenses does not truly or effectively serve the interest of the people. It serves only to promote the wasteful aspects of the federal prison system, a system that gulps down tax dollars and spews up *Let's Make a Deal!* 29

I think about Lexington almost daily. I will be walking up Broadway to shop for groceries, or maybe riding my bike in the original Central Park, and suddenly I'm wondering who's in there now, at this very moment, and for what inane violations, and what they are doing. Is it chow time, is the Big Yard open, is some inmate on stage in the auditorium singing "As Time Goes By" in a talent show? It is not a fond reminiscence or a desire to be back in the Land of No Decisions.[13] It is an awareness of the waste. The waste of tax dollars, yes, but taxpayers are used to that. It is the unnecessary trashing of lives that leaves me uneasy. The splitting of families, the enforced monotony, the programs which purport to prepare an inmate for re-entry into society but which actually succeed only in occupying a few more hours 30

Reading Critically

[13] Why does the author refer to prison as "the Land of No Decisions"?

of the inmate's time behind the walls. The nonviolent offenders, such as small-time drug dealers and the economically deprived who were driven to crime out of desperation, could remain in society under less costly supervision, still undergoing "punishment" for their crime, but at least contributing to rather than draining the resources of society.

Horace, who was not a subtle sort of fellow, had some tee shirts made up. 31
They were delivered by our usual supplier out in Landscape, and we wore them back in over our regular clothes. The hacks tilted their heads when they noticed, but said nothing. On the front of each shirt was an outline of the state of Kentucky, and above the northwest corner of the state were the words "Visit Beautiful Kentucky!" Inside the state boundary were:

- Free Accommodations
- Complimentary Meals
- Management Holds Calls
- Recreational Exercise

In small letters just outside the southwest corner of the state was: "Length of Stay Requirement."[14] And in big letters across the bottom:

Take Time to Do Time
F.C.I. Lexington

I gave mine away on the day I finished my sentence. It is a time-honored 32
tradition to leave some of your belongings to friends who have to stay behind when you are released. But you must never leave shoes. Legend has it that if you do, you will come back to wear them again.

UNDERSTANDING DETAILS

1. Draw Lexington prison, and put the names on the sections of the facility. Then describe each section in your own words.
2. Why was walking around the outside of Central Park "like taking a trip in microcosm across the United States" (paragraph 4)? Give examples to explain your answer.
3. Why was Wozencraft especially fond of Shorty? What secret did they share at the beginning of the author's prison term?
4. Does the author feel she had been unfairly punished by being sent to prison? What had she done wrong?

Reading Critically

[14] In what ways do you think a sense of humor would be helpful to inmates doing time in prison?

THINKING CRITICALLY

5. What was Wozencraft's attitude toward other people in Lexington prison? Why do you think she felt this way? What types of relationships did she have with inmates and staff members?

6. Why does the author say, "If the taxpayers knew how their dollars were being spent inside some prisons, they might actually scream out loud" (paragraph 20)? What exactly is she referring to? What is she implying? Give some examples.

7. Why do you think Lexington is known as a "country club" prison? What features of the prison might have brought about its nickname?

8. Wozencraft feels strongly that people who perform minor, nonviolent crimes should not be put in prison. Why does she feel this way? Who should be locked up according to the author? From her point of view, how does rehabilitation take place?

DISCOVERING RHETORICAL STRATEGIES

9. This essay is organized predominantly as a clockwise tour of Lexington prison. How and when does Wozencraft introduce the facts about her own imprisonment and her opinions about the current American system of justice? Explain in as much detail as you can the effect of integrating the guided tour and the related facts and opinions.

10. Wozencraft uses specific prison jargon throughout this essay. In what way does this jargon add to or detract from the essay? What effect would the essay have without this jargon?

11. Wozencraft ends her essay with an explanation of "a time-honored tradition." Is this an effective ending for the piece? Why or why not?

12. Though spatial description is the dominant rhetorical strategy the author uses in this essay to accomplish her purpose, what other strategies help make the essay effective? Give examples of these strategies.

MAKING CONNECTIONS

13. If Kimberly Wozencraft, Scott Russell Sanders ("Homeplace"), Robert Ramirez ("The Barrio"), and/or Mary Pipher ("Beliefs About Families") were discussing the importance of belonging to a "community," which of the authors would argue most strongly that community is a positive force in our lives? Explain your answer.

14. Malcolm Cowley ("The View from 80"), Harold Krents ("Darkness at Noon"), and Malcolm X ("Learning to Read") have all felt imprisoned in much the same way Wozencraft does in her essay. In what way is each of these authors "confined"? Have you ever felt imprisoned for any reason? Why? How did you escape?

15. What would Wozencraft, William Ouchi ("Japanese and American Workers: Two Casts of Mind"), and/or Robert Ramirez ("The Barrio") have to say about the importance of relying on other people to help endure difficult or

challenging situations? How much do you rely on friends and relatives in your own life? How comfortable are you with these relationships?

IDEAS FOR DISCUSSION/WRITING

Preparing to Write

Write freely about your memories of a recent difficult or awkward situation in your life: What were the circumstances? What did you do? What did others do? How did you relate to others in this situation? Why was the situation so difficult? How did you get out of it?

Choosing a Topic

1. Write an essay describing for your peers a difficult or awkward situation you have been in recently. Why was it awkward? Explain the specific circumstances so that your classmates can clearly imagine the setting and the difficulty or problem. Then discuss your reaction to the situation.

2. A friend of yours has just been sentenced to prison for one year. Write a letter to this person describing what you think his or her biggest adjustments will be.

3. Wozencraft describes many problems within the prison system. With these problems in mind, write a letter to the editor of your local newspaper discussing whether prisons actually rehabilitate criminals. Use examples from Wozencraft's essay to help make your point.

4. Wozencraft develops a descriptive narrative from personal experience. She "shows" rather than "tells" her readers about Lexington prison's attitude toward rehabilitation. Compose an e-mail written to a friend not attending college that describes your current educational experience. Try to show, rather than tell your observations, achievements, frustrations, and unique experiences. Remember to organize your descriptions to convey a clear and consistent message.

Before beginning your essay, you might want to consult the checklists on page 44.

JOHN MCPHEE   (1931–   )

The Pines

The range of subjects investigated by author John McPhee is quite astounding. In his twenty books and numerous articles, he has written about sports, food, art, geology, geography, science, history, education, and a variety of other topics. One of the most famous of these "non-fictional, book-length narratives," as he calls them, is *A Sense of Where You Are* (1965), a study of former basketball great Bill Bradley; another is *Levels of the Game* (1969), a chronicle of the epic 1968 U.S. Open semifinal tennis match between Arthur Ashe and Clark Graebner. Most of McPhee's essays have appeared first in the *New Yorker*, a prestigious literary magazine for which he has been a staff writer since 1965. His more recent publications include *The Ransom of Russian Art* (1994), *The Second John McPhee Reader* (1996), *Irons in the Fire* (1997), *Annals of the Former World* (1998) (which was awarded the Pulitzer Prize in 1999), and *The Founding Fish* (2002). "What all these pieces of writing have in common," according to the author, "is that they are about real people and real places. All the different topics are just milieus in which to sketch people and places." McPhee lives in New Jersey near Princeton University, where he teaches a seminar entitled "The Literature of Fact." His hobbies include going on long bike rides, fishing for shad and pickerel, and skiing.

Preparing to Read

The following essay, "The Pines," is a small section from a longer piece called *The Pine Barrens* (1968), which describes a remote wilderness in southern New Jersey. Like many of McPhee's narrative essays, "The Pines" is structured around colorful characters—in this case, Fred Brown and Bill Wasovwich, who worry openly in this essay about the encroaching civilization that threatens their unique way of life.

Exploring Experience: As you prepare to read this essay, think for a moment about the different types of people you know: Do you have talkative friends? Quiet friends? Which type of person is most appealing to you? Which type are you? Have you ever lived in the woods? What are the advantages of living in a rural environment instead of a big city? What are the disadvantages?

Learning Online: Using Google's search engine (http://www. google.com), click on the "Images" tab to conduct a picture search for the term "cranberry bog." Take a few minutes to consider how you would describe this particular area. What is unique about this place, and what seems familiar?

F red Brown's house is on an unpaved road that curves along the edge   1
of a wide cranberry bog. What attracted me to it was the pump that
stands in his yard. It was something of a wonder that I noticed the
pump, because there were, among other things, eight automobiles in the
yard, two of them on their sides and one of them upside down, all ten years
old or older. Around the cars were old refrigerators, vacuum cleaners, partly
dismantled radios, cathode-ray tubes, a short wooden ski, a large wooden
mallet, dozens of cranberry picker's boxes, many tires, an orange crate dated
1946, a cord or so of firewood, mandolins, engine heads, and maybe a thousand other things. The house itself, two stories high, was covered with tarpa-
per that was peeling away in some places, revealing its original shingles, made
of Atlantic white cedar from the stream courses of the surrounding forest. **❶**
I called out to ask if anyone was home, and a voice inside called back, "Come
in. Come in. Come on the hell in."

I walked through a vestibule that had a dirt floor, stepped up into a kitchen,   2
and went on into another room that had several overstuffed chairs in it and
a porcelain-topped table, where Fred Brown was seated, eating a pork chop.
He was dressed in a white sleeveless shirt, ankle-top shoes, and undershorts.
He gave me a cheerful greeting and, without asking why I had come or
what I wanted, picked up a pair of khaki trousers that had been tossed onto
one of the overstuffed chairs and asked me to sit down. He set the trousers
on another chair, and he apologized for being in the middle of his breakfast,
explaining that he seldom drank much but the night before he had had a few
drinks and this had caused his day to start slowly. "I don't know what's the
matter with me, but there's got to be something the matter with me, because drink don't agree with me anymore," he said. He had a raw onion in
one hand, and while he talked he shaved slices from the onion and ate them
between bites of the chop. He was a muscular and well-built man, with short,
bristly white hair, and he had bright, fast-moving eyes in a wide-open face.
His legs were trim and strong, with large muscles in the calves. I guessed
that he was about sixty, and for a man of sixty he seemed to be in remarkably good shape. He was actually seventy-nine. "My rule is: Never eat except
when you're hungry," he said, and he ate another slice of the onion. **❷**

In a straight-backed chair near the doorway to the kitchen sat a young man   3
with long black hair, who wore a visored red leather cap that had darkened

---

Reading Critically

❶ What do the descriptive details in the first paragraph imply about the trustworthiness of
the author?

❷ Do you think this is a sensible rule for good health?

with age. His shirt was coarse-woven and had eyelets down a V neck that was laced with a thong. His trousers were made of canvas, and he was wearing gum boots. His arms were folded, his legs were stretched out, he had one ankle over the other, and as he sat there he appeared to be sighting carefully past his feet, as if his toes were the outer frame of a gunsight and he could see some sort of target in the floor. When I had entered, I had said hello to him, and he had nodded without looking up. He had a long, straight nose and high cheekbones, in a deeply tanned face that was, somehow, gaunt. I had no idea whether he was shy or hostile. Eventually, when I came to know him, I found him to be as shy a person as I have ever had a chance to know. His name is Bill Wasovwich, and he lives alone in a cabin about half a mile from Fred. First his father, then his mother left him when he was a young boy, and he grew up depending on the help of various people in the pines. One of them, a cranberry grower, employs him and has given him some acreage, in which Bill is building a small cranberry bog of his own, "turfing it out" by hand. When he is not working in the bogs, he goes roaming, as he puts it, setting out cross-country on long, looping journeys, hiking about thirty miles in a typical day, in search of what he calls "events"—surprising a buck, or a gray fox, or perhaps a poacher or a man with a still. Almost no one who is not native to the pines could do this, for the woods have an undulating sameness, and the understory—huckleberries, sheep laurel, sweet fern, high-bush blueberry—is often so dense that a wanderer can walk in a fairly tight circle and think that he is moving in a straight line. State forest rangers spend a good part of their time finding hikers and hunters, some of whom have vanished for days. In his long, pathless journeys, Bill always emerges from the woods near his cabin—and about when he plans to. [3] In the fall, when thousands of hunters come into the pines, he sometimes works as a guide. In the evenings, or in the daytime when he is not working or roaming, he goes to Fred Brown's house and sits there for hours. The old man is a widower whose seven children are long since gone from Hog Wallow, and he is as expansively talkative and worldly as the young one is withdrawn and wild. Although there are fifty-three years between their ages, it is obviously fortunate for each of them to be the other's neighbor.

That first morning, while Bill went on looking at his outstretched toes, [4] Fred got up from the table, put on his pants, and said he was going to cook

---

Reading Critically

[3] What does Bill's impeccable sense of direction suggest about his moral and ethical "compass" in life?

me a pork chop, because I looked hungry and ought to eat something. It was about noon, and I was even hungrier than I may have looked, so I gratefully accepted his offer, which was a considerable one. There are two or three small general stores in the pines, but for anything as fragile as a fresh pork chop it is necessary to make a round trip from Fred's place of about fifty miles. Fred went into the kitchen and dropped a chop into a frying pan that was crackling with hot grease. He has a fairly new four-burner stove that uses bottled gas. He keeps water in a large bowl on a table in the kitchen and ladles some when he wants it. While he cooked the meat, he looked out a window through a stand of pitch pines and into the cranberry bog. "I saw a big buck out here last night with velvet on his horns," he said. "Them horns is soft when they're in velvet." On a nail high on one wall of the room that Bill and I were sitting in was a large meat cleaver. Next to it was a billy club. The wall itself was papered in a flower pattern, and the wallpaper continued out across the ceiling and down the three other walls, lending the room something of the appearance of the inside of a gift box. [4] In some parts of the ceiling, the paper had come loose. "I didn't paper this year," Fred said. "For the last couple months, I've had sinus." The floor was covered with old rugs. They had been put down in random pieces, and in some places as many as six layers were stacked up. In winter, when the temperature approaches zero, the worst cold comes through the floor. The only source of heat in the house is a wood-burning stove in the main room. There were seven calendars on the walls, all current and none with pictures of nudes. Fading into pastel on one wall was a rotogravure photograph of President and Mrs. Eisenhower. A framed poem read:

> God hath not promised
> Sun without rain
> Joy without sorrow
> Peace without pain. [5]

Noticing my interest in all this, Fred reached into a drawer and showed me what appeared to be a postcard. On it was a photograph of a woman, and Fred said with a straight face that she was his present girl, adding that he meets her regularly under a juniper tree on a road farther south in the pines. The woman, whose appearance suggested strongly that she had never been within a great many miles of the Pine Barrens, was wearing nothing at all.

Reading Critically

[4] How is meeting Fred a "gift" for the narrator and for the readers of his essay?
[5] How does this short poem help us understand the essay?

I asked Fred what all those cars were doing in his yard, and he said that 6
one of them was in running condition and the rest were its predecessors. The
working vehicle was a 1956 Mercury. Each of the seven others had at one
time or another been his best car, and each, in turn, had lain down like a sick
animal and had died right there in the yard, unless it had been towed home
after a mishap elsewhere in the pines. Fred recited, with affection, the history of each car. Of one old Ford, for example, he said, "I upset that up to
Speedwell in the creek." And of an even older car, a station wagon, he said,
"I busted that one up in the snow. I met a car on a little hill, and hit the brake,
and hit a tree." One of the cars had met its end at a narrow bridge about four
miles from Hog Wallow, where Fred had hit a state trooper, head on.

The pork was delicious and almost crisp. Fred gave me a potato with it 7
and a pitcher of melted grease from the frying pan to pour over the potato.
He also handed me a loaf of bread and a dish of margarine, saying, "Here's
your bread. You can have one piece or two. Whatever you want."

Fred apologized for not having a phone, after I asked where I would have 8
to go to make a call, later on. He said, "I don't have no phone because I
don't have no electric. If I had electric, I would have had a phone in here a
long time ago." He uses a kerosene lamp, a propane lamp, and two flashlights.

He asked where I was going, and I said that I had no particular destina- 9
tion, explaining that I was in the pines because I found it hard to believe that
so much unbroken forest could still exist so near the big Eastern cities, and
I wanted to see it while it was still there. "Is that so?" he said, three times.
Like many people in the pines, he often says things three times. "Is that so?
Is that so?"

I asked him what he thought of a plan that has been developed by Burling- 10
ton and Ocean Counties to create a supersonic jetport in the pines, connected
by a spur of the Garden State Parkway to a new city of two hundred and fifty
thousand people, also in the pines.

"They've been talking about that for three years, and they've never given 11
up," Fred said.

"It'd be the end of these woods," Bill said. This was the first time I heard 12
Bill speak. I had been there for an hour, and he had not said a word. Without looking up, he said again, "It'd be the end of these woods, I can tell you
that." 6

Reading Critically

6 In what ways have you experienced the conflict between nature and civilization in your
own life?

Fred said, "They could build ten jetports around me. I wouldn't give a   13
damn."

"You ain't going to be around very long," Bill said to him. "It would be   14
the end of these woods."

Fred took that as a fact, and not as an insult. "Yes, it would be the end of   15
these woods," he said. "But there'd be people here you could do business
with."

Bill said, "There ain't no place like this left in the country, I don't be-   16
lieve—and I travelled around a little bit, too."

Eventually, I made the request I had intended to make when I walked in   17
the door. "Could I have some water?" I said to Fred. "I have a jerry can, and
I'd like to fill it at the pump."

"Hell, yes," he said. "That isn't my water. That's God's water. That right,   18
Bill?"

"I *guess* so," Bill said, without looking up. "It's good water, I can tell you   19
that."

"That's God's water," Fred said again. "Take all you want."   20

UNDERSTANDING DETAILS

1. What attracted McPhee to Fred Brown's house? In what ways is this object
   representative of Fred's yard? Of Fred's life?
2. What other things are in Fred's front yard? What does this collection of junk
   say about Fred and his lifestyle?
3. In paragraph 3, McPhee comments that, despite the wide difference in age between Fred and Bill, "it is obviously fortunate for each of them to be the other's
   neighbor." In what ways do the two characters need each other?
4. Describe in your own words the inside of Fred's house. Which details does McPhee
   stress in his description? Why does he focus on these and not on others?

THINKING CRITICALLY

5. Why is McPhee visiting "the pines"? What do you think his opinion of "the
   pines" is? What specific references reveal his opinions?
6. Why does Bill go "roaming"? What do you think the purpose of these journeys
   is?
7. Why does Bill believe a jetport would be "the end of these woods" (paragraph
   12)? Why do you think these were the first words Bill had spoken since the author arrived? Explain your answer.
8. Why do you think McPhee ends this piece with several references to God?
   How does the dialogue about "God's water" help us understand Fred and Bill
   even more specifically?

DISCOVERING RHETORICAL STRATEGIES

9. Which senses does McPhee concentrate on most in this description? Choose one paragraph to analyze. In one column, write down all the senses the description arouses; in another, record the words and phrases that activate these senses.

10. What "tone" or "mood" is McPhee trying to create in this excerpt? Is he successful? Explain your answer.

11. What is the author's point of view in this essay? How would the method of description change if the story were told from Fred's vantage point? From Bill's? How does this particular point of view help the author organize his description?

12. McPhee relies heavily on description to make his point. What other rhetorical modes support this narrative essay? Give examples of each of these modes from the essay.

MAKING CONNECTIONS

13. How does the friendship between Fred and Bill described in McPhee's essay differ from friendships in Kimberly Wozencraft's "Notes from the Country Club" and/or Robert Ramirez's "The Barrio"? Which friendships are stronger in your opinion? Explain your answer.

14. Compare and contrast McPhee's concern about preserving the environment with comparable feelings by Linda Hogan ("Dwellings"). How are they similar? How are they different?

15. In McPhee's essay, how does Fred Brown feel about the uses and abuses of technology? Would Jessica Mitford ("Behind the Formaldehyde Curtain") and/or Dave Grossman ("We Are Training Our Kids to Kill") agree with him? Explain your answer.

IDEAS FOR DISCUSSION/WRITING

Preparing to Write

Write freely about someone you know who represents a specific personality "type": What distinguishes this type from other types you know? What do people of this type have in common? What are their looks, values, needs, desires, living conditions, and so on? What do you have in common with the type of person you have just described? How are you different?

Choosing a Topic

1. Give a name (either real or fictitious) to the person you have just described in the prewriting exercise, and write an essay depicting the house, apartment, or room in which this person lives. Try to make your description as vivid and as well organized as McPhee's portrait of Fred Brown. Imagine that the audience for your description is someone who has never met this person and has never seen where the person lives.

2. Write an essay describing for your classmates some of the "junk" you have collected over the years. Why are certain items junk to some people and treasures
   to others? What makes the things you are describing special to you?

3. Describe the inside of your house, apartment, or room, explaining to your class
   what the decorations say about you as a person. If someone in your class were
   to see where you live, could he or she make any accurate deductions about
   your political, social, or moral values based on the contents and arrangement of
   the place you call "home"?

4. What is the dominant impression of McPhee's article? Using McPhee's example, write a description of a significant moment suspended in time. Use description to convey the significance of this moment to your reader. If you need
   inspiration, conduct an online image search.

Before beginning your essay, you might want to consult the checklists on page 44.

MALCOLM COWLEY   (1898–1989)

The View from 80

Malcolm Cowley had a long and distinguished career as a literary historian, critic, editor, and poet. After receiving his bachelor's degree at Harvard, he served in the American Ambulance Corps during World War I, then pursued graduate studies in literature at the University of Montpellier in France. In 1929, he became associate editor of *The New Republic,* presiding over the magazine's literary department for the next fifteen years. Perhaps his most important book of literary criticism is *Exile's Return* (1934), a study of the "lost generation" of expatriate Americans living in Paris in the 1920s, which included Ernest Hemingway, Ezra Pound, F. Scott Fitzgerald, and Hart Crane. Cowley returned to the same topic in 1973 with *A Second Flowering: Works and Days of the Lost Generation.* He also published editions of such authors as Hemingway, William Faulkner, Nathaniel Hawthorne, Walt Whitman, and Fitzgerald; two collections of his own poetry, *Blue Juniata* (1929) and *The Dry Season* (1941); and numerous other translations, editions, and books of criticism. His most recent publications include *The Flower and the Leaf: A Contemporary Record of American Writing Since 1941* (1985) and *Conversations with Malcolm Cowley* (1986). Asked the secret of his amazing productivity, Cowley replied: "Writers often speak of 'saving their energy,' as if each man were given a nickel's worth of it, which he is at liberty to spend. To me, the mind of the poet resembles Fortunatus' purse: The more spent, the more it supplies."

Preparing to Read

The following essay was originally commissioned by *Life* magazine (1978) for inclusion in a series of articles on aging. Cowley later converted the piece into the first chapter of a book with the same title: *The View from 80* (1980). Through a combination of vivid personal experience and research, the author crafted an essay that helps us experience what life is like for an eighty year old.

Exploring Experience: As you prepare to read Cowley's description of "the country of age," take some time to think about age in general: How many people over the age of sixty do you know? Over the age of seventy? How do they behave? Do you think these older people see themselves in the same way you see them? Do you think they consider themselves "old"? What clues remind them of their advancing age? What events and attitudes remind you of your age? In what ways will you be different than you are now when you reach the age of eighty?

Learning Online: Visit the Web site of the American Association of Retired Persons (http://www.aarp.org), and read about some of the issues affecting the elderly. Keep these in mind while reading Cowley's observations about aging.

They gave me a party on my 80th birthday in August 1978. First there   1
were cards, letters, telegrams, even a cable of congratulation or con-
dolence; then there were gifts, mostly bottles; there was catered food
and finally a big cake with, for some reason, two candles (had I gone back
to very early childhood?). I blew the candles out a little unsteadily. Amid the
applause and clatter I thought about a former custom of the Northern
Ojibwas when they lived on the shores of Lake Winnipeg. They were kind
to their old people, who remembered and enforced the ancient customs of
the tribe, but when an old person became decrepit, it was time for him to
go. Sometimes he was simply abandoned, with a little food, on an island in
the lake. If he deserved special honor, they held a tribal feast for him. The old
man sang a death song and danced, if he could. While he was still singing,
his son came from behind and brained him with a tomahawk. 🔸

That was quick, it was dignified, and I wonder whether it was any more   2
cruel, essentially, than some of our civilized customs or inadvertencies in dis-
posing of the aged. I believe in rites and ceremonies. I believe in big parties
for special occasions such as an 80th birthday. It is a sort of belated bar mitz-
vah, since the 80-year-old, like a Jewish adolescent, is entering a new stage
of life; let him (or her) undergo a *rite de passage,* with toasts and a cantor.
Seventy-year-olds, or septuas, have the illusion of being middle-aged, even
if they have been pushed back on a shelf. The 80-year-old, the octo, looks
at the double-dumpling figure and admits that he is old. The last act has
begun, and it will be the test of the play.

To enter the country of age is a new experience, different from what you   3
supposed it to be. Nobody, man or woman, knows the country until he has
lived in it and has taken out his citizenship papers. Here is my own report,
submitted as a road map and guide to some of the principal monuments.

The new octogenarian feels as strong as ever when he is sitting back in a   4
comfortable chair. He ruminates, he dreams, he remembers. He doesn't want
to be disturbed by others. It seems to him that old age is only a costume assumed for those others; the true, the essential self is ageless. In a moment he
will rise and go for a ramble in the woods, taking a gun along, or a fishing
rod, if it is spring. Then he creaks to his feet, bending forward to keep his balance, and realizes that he will do nothing of the sort. The body and its surroundings have their messages for him, or only one message: "You are old."
Here are some of the occasions on which he receives the message:

Reading Critically

🔸 How do you feel about the Ojibwa custom described by Cowley? Do you agree with the
author that it conferred a "quick" and "dignified" death on decrepit older members of the
tribe?

- when it becomes an achievement to do thoughtfully, step by step, what he once did instinctively
- when his bones ache
- when there are more and more little bottles in the medicine cabinet, with instructions for taking four times a day
- when he fumbles and drops his toothbrush (butterfingers)
- when his face has bumps and wrinkles, so that he cuts himself while shaving (blood on the towel)
- when year by year his feet seem farther from his hands
- when he can't stand on one leg and has trouble pulling on his pants
- when he hesitates on the landing before walking down a flight of stairs
- when he spends more time looking for things misplaced than he spends using them after he (or more often his wife) has found them
- when he falls asleep in the afternoon
- when it becomes harder to bear in mind two things at once
- when a pretty girl passes him in the street and he doesn't turn his head
- when he forgets names, even of people he saw last month ("Now I'm beginning to forget nouns," the poet Conrad Aiken said at 80)
- when he listens hard to jokes and catches everything but the snapper
- when he decides not to drive at night anymore
- when everything takes longer to do—bathing, shaving, getting dressed or undressed—but when time passes quickly, as if he were gathering speed while coasting downhill. The year from 79 to 80 is like a week when he was a boy. ❷

Those are some of the intimate messages. "Put cotton in your ears and   5 pebbles in your shoes," said a gerontologist, a member of that new profession dedicated to alleviating all maladies of old people except the passage of years. "Pull on rubber gloves. Smear Vaseline over your glasses, and there you have it: instant aging." Not quite. His formula omits the messages from the social world, which are louder, in most cases, than those from within. We start by growing old in other people's eyes, then slowly we come to share their judgment.

Reading Critically

❷ List five ways you know how old you are.

I remember a morning many years ago when I was backing out of the 6
parking lot near the railroad station in Brewster, New York. There was a near
collision. The driver of the other car jumped out and started to abuse me;
he had his fists ready. Then he looked hard at me and said, "Why, you're an
old man." He got back into his car, slammed the door, and drove away, while
I stood there fuming. "I'm only 65," I thought. "He wasn't driving carefully.
I can still take care of myself in a car, or in a fight, for that matter."

My hair was whiter—it may have been in 1974—when a young woman 7
rose and offered me her seat in a Madison Avenue bus. That message was
kind and also devastating. "Can't I even stand up?" I thought as I thanked her
and declined the seat. But the same thing happened twice the following year,
and the second time I gratefully accepted the offer, though with a sense of
having diminished myself.[3] "People are right about me," I thought while
wondering why all those kind gestures were made by women. Do men now
regard themselves as the weaker sex, not called upon to show consideration?
All the same it was a relief to sit down and relax.

A few days later I wrote a poem, "The Red Wagon," that belongs in the 8
record of aging:

> For his birthday they gave him a red express wagon
> with a driver's high seat and a handle that steered.
> His mother pulled him around the yard.
> "Giddyap," he said, but she laughed and went off
> to wash the breakfast dishes.
>
> "I wanta ride too," his sister said,
> and he pulled her to the edge of a hill.
> "Now, sister, go home and wait for me,
> but first give a push to the wagon."
> He climbed again to the high seat,
> this time grasping that handle-that-steered.
>
> The red wagon rolled slowly down the slope,
> then faster as it passed the schoolhouse
> and faster as it passed the store,
> the road still dropping away.
> Oh, it was fun.
> But would it ever stop?
> Would the road always go downhill?
> The red wagon rolled faster.
> Now it was in strange country.
> It passed a white house he must have dreamed about,

Reading Critically

[3] Why do you think the author felt "diminished" by accepting someone else's seat on the bus?

deep woods he had never seen,
a graveyard where, something told him, his sister
was buried.

Far below
the sun was sinking into a broad plain.

The red wagon rolled faster.
Now he was clutching the seat, not even trying to steer.
Sweat clouded his heavy spectacles.
His white hair streamed in the wind.

Even before he or she is 80, the aging person may undergo another iden-   9
tity crisis like that of adolescence.[4] Perhaps there had also been a middle-
aged crisis, the male or the female menopause, but the rest of adult life he
had taken himself for granted, with his capabilities and failings. Now, when
he looks in the mirror, he asks himself, "Is this really me?"—or he avoids the
mirror out of distress at what it reveals, those bags and wrinkles. In his new
makeup he is called upon to play a new role in a play that must be impro-
vised. André Gide, that long-lived man of letters, wrote in his journal, "My
heart has remained so young that I have the continual feeling of playing a
part, the part of the 70-year-old that I certainly am; and the infirmities and
weaknesses that remind me of my age act like a prompter, reminding me of
my lines when I tend to stray. Then, like the good actor I want to be, I go
back into my role, and I pride myself on playing it well."

In his new role the old person will find that he is tempted by new vices,   10
that he receives new compensations (not so widely known), and that he may
possibly achieve new virtues. Chief among these is the heroic or merely ob-
stinate refusal to surrender in the face of time. One admires the ships that go
down with all flags flying and the captain on the bridge.

Among the vices of age[5] are avarice, untidiness, and vanity, which last   11
takes the form of a craving to be loved or simply admired. Avarice is the worst
of those three. Why do so many old persons, men and women alike, insist on
hoarding money when they have no prospect of using it and even when they
have no heirs? They eat the cheapest food, buy no clothes, and live in a single
room when they could afford better lodging. It may be that they regard money
as a form of power; there is a comfort in watching it accumulate while other
powers are dwindling away. How often we read of an old person found dead
in a hovel, on a mattress partly stuffed with bankbooks and stock certificates!
The bankbook syndrome, we call it in our family, which has never succumbed.

Reading Critically

[4] What does Cowley mean by the "identity crisis" of old age?

[5] What do you think are the worst "vices" of people who are twenty years old? Forty years old?

Untidiness we call the Langley Collyer syndrome. To explain, Langley   12
Collyer was a former concert pianist who lived alone with his 70-year-old
brother in a brownstone house on upper Fifth Avenue. The once fashionable
neighborhood had become part of Harlem. Homer, the brother, had been an
admiralty lawyer, but was now blind and partly paralyzed; Langley played for
him and fed him on buns and oranges, which he thought would restore
Homer's sight. He never threw away a daily paper because Homer, he said,
might want to read them all. He saved other things as well and the house became filled with rubbish from roof to basement. The halls were lined on
both sides with bundled newspapers, leaving narrow passageways in which
Langley had devised booby traps to catch intruders.

On March 21, 1947, some unnamed person telephoned the police to re-   13
port that there was a dead body in the Collyer house. The police broke down
the front door and found the hall impassable; then they hoisted a ladder to
a second-story window. Behind it Homer was lying on the floor in a
bathrobe; he had starved to death. Langley had disappeared. After some delay,
the police broke into the basement, chopped a hole in the roof, and began
throwing junk out of the house, top and bottom. It was 18 days before they
found Langley's body, gnawed by rats. Caught in one of his own booby traps,
he had died in a hallway just outside Homer's door. By that time the police
had collected, and the Department of Sanitation had hauled away, 120 tons
of rubbish, including, besides the newspapers, 14 grand pianos and the parts
of a dismantled Model T Ford.[6]

Why do so many old people accumulate junk, not on the scale of Lang-   14
ley Collyer, but still in a dismaying fashion? Their tables are piled high with
it, their bureau drawers are stuffed with it, their closet rods bend with the
weight of clothes not worn for years. I suppose that the piling up is partly
from lethargy and partly from feeling that everything once useful, including
their own bodies, should be preserved. Others, though not so many, have
such a fear of becoming Langley Collyers that they strive to be painfully
neat. Every tool they own is in its place, though it will never be used again;
every scrap of paper is filed away in alphabetical order. At last their immod-
erate neatness becomes another vice of age, if a milder one.

The vanity of older people is an easier weakness to explain, and to con-   15
done.[7] With less to look forward to, they yearn for recognition of what
they have been: the reigning beauty, the athlete, the soldier, the scholar. It is
the beauties who have the hardest time. A portrait of themselves at twenty

Reading Critically

[6] Why do you think some people accumulate junk? Do you feel that older folks collect it
more often than younger ones?

[7] What kinds of "vanity" do older people have?

hangs on the wall, and they try to resemble it by making an extravagant use of creams, powder, and dyes. Being young at heart, they think they are merely revealing their essential persons. The athletes find shelves for their silver trophies, which are polished once a year. Perhaps a letter sweater lies wrapped in a bureau drawer. I remember one evening when a no-longer athlete had guests for dinner and tried to find his sweater. "Oh, that old thing," his wife said. "The moths got into it, and I threw it away." The athlete sulked, and his guests went home early.

But there are also pleasures of the body, or the mind, that are enjoyed by a greater number of older persons. Those pleasures include some that younger people find hard to appreciate. One of them is simply sitting still, like a snake on a sunwarmed stone, with a delicious feeling of indolence that was seldom attained in earlier years. A leaf flutters down; a cloud moves by inches across the horizon. At such moments the older person, completely relaxed, has become a part of nature—and a living part, with blood coursing through his veins. The future does not exist for him. He thinks, if he thinks at all, that life for younger persons is still a battle royal of each against each, but that now he has nothing more to win or lose. He is not so much above as outside the battle, as if he had assumed the uniform of some small neutral country, perhaps Liechtenstein or Andorra. From a distance he notes that some of the combatants, men or women, are jostling ahead—but why do they fight so hard when the most they can hope for is a longer obituary? He can watch the scrounging and gouging, he can hear the shouts of exultation, the moans of the gravely wounded, and meanwhile he feels secure; nobody will attack him from ambush. 16

Age has other physical compensations besides the nirvana of dozing in the sun. A few of the simplest needs become a pleasure to satisfy. When an old woman in a nursing home was asked what she really liked to do she answered in one word: "Eat." She might have been speaking for many of her fellows. Meals in a nursing home, however badly cooked, serve as climactic moments of the day. The physical essence of the pensioners is being renewed at an appointed hour; [8] now they can go back to meditating or to watching TV while looking forward to the next meal. They can also look forward to sleep, which has become a definite pleasure, not the mere interruption it once had been. 17

Here I am thinking of old persons under nursing care. Others ferociously guard their independence, and some of them suffer less than one might expect from being lonely and impoverished. They can be rejoiced by visits and 18

Reading Critically

[8] How is "the physical essence of pensioners . . . renewed" during mealtime in retirement homes?

meetings, but they also have company inside their heads. Some of them are busiest when their hands are still. What passes through the minds of many is a stream of persons, images, phrases, and familiar tunes. For some that stream has continued since childhood, but now it is deeper; it is their present and their past combined. At times they conduct silent dialogues with a vanished friend, and these are less tiring—often more rewarding—than spoken conversations. If inner resources are lacking, old persons living alone may seek comfort and a kind of companionship in the bottle. I should judge from the gossip of various neighborhoods that the outer suburbs from Boston to San Diego are full of secretly alcoholic widows. One of those widows, an old friend, was moved from her apartment into a retirement home. She left behind her a closet in which the floor was covered wall to wall with whiskey bottles. "Oh, those empty bottles!" she explained. "They were left by a former tenant."

Not whiskey or cooking sherry but simply giving up is the greatest temptation of age. It is something different from a stoical acceptance of infirmities, which is something to be admired. 19

The givers-up see no reason for working. Sometimes they lie in bed all day when moving about would still be possible, if difficult. I had a friend, a distinguished poet, who surrendered in that fashion. The doctors tried to stir him to action, but he refused to leave his room. Another friend, once a successful artist, stopped painting when his eyes began to fail. His doctor made the mistake of telling him that he suffered from a fatal disease. He then lost interest in everything except the splendid Rolls-Royce, acquired in his prosperous days, that stood in the garage. Daily he wiped the dust from its hood. He couldn't drive it on the road any longer, but he used to sit in the driver's seat, start the motor, then back the Rolls out of the garage and drive it in again, back twenty feet and forward twenty feet; that was his only distraction.[9] 20

I haven't the right to blame those who surrender, not being able to put myself inside their minds or bodies. Often they must have compelling reasons, physical or moral. Not only do they suffer from a variety of ailments, but also they are made to feel that they no longer have a function in the community. Their families and neighbors don't ask them for advice, don't really listen when they speak, don't call on them for efforts. One notes that there are not a few recoveries from apparent senility when that situation changes. If it doesn't change, old persons may decide that efforts are useless. I sympa- 21

Reading Critically

[9] The image of Cowley's friend who drove his Rolls Royce in and out of the garage every day is a metaphor for the stagnation of old age. What other metaphors in the essay seem particularly vivid to you?

thize with their problems, but the men and women I envy are those who accept old age as a series of challenges.

For such persons, every new infirmity is an enemy to be outwitted, an ob-   22
stacle to be overcome by force of will.[10] They enjoy each little victory over
themselves, and sometimes they win a major success. Renoir was one of
them. He continued painting, and magnificently, for years after he was crip-
pled by arthritis; the brush had to be strapped to his arm. "You don't need
your hand to paint," he said. Goya was another of the unvanquished. At 72
he retired as an official painter of the Spanish court and decided to work only
for himself. His later years were those of the famous "black paintings" in
which he let his imagination run (and also of the lithographs, then a new
technique). At 78 he escaped a reign of terror in Spain by fleeing to Bordeaux.
He was deaf, and his eyes were failing; in order to work he had to wear several pairs of spectacles, one over another, and then use a magnifying glass; but
he was producing splendid work in a totally new style. At 80 he drew an ancient man propped on two sticks, with a mass of white hair and beard hiding his face and with the inscription "I am still learning."

"Eighty years old!" the great Catholic poet Paul Claudel wrote in his   23
journal. "No eyes left, no ears, no teeth, no legs, no wind! And when all is
said and done, how astonishingly well one does without them!"

UNDERSTANDING DETAILS

1. Name five ways, according to Cowley, that people begin to realize they are
   "old." How did Cowley himself learn that he was old?
2. List three vices of old age, and explain them as Cowley sees them.
3. What are three compensations of advancing age? In what ways are these activities pleasurable?
4. What does Cowley mean in paragraph 15 by "the vanity of older people"?
   How do older people manifest this vanity?

THINKING CRITICALLY

5. What does the wagon symbolize in the author's poem about aging (paragraph
   8)? What purpose does this poem serve in the essay?
6. For older people, what is the value of the conversations, images, friends, relatives, and melodies that pass through their minds? How might the elderly use
   these distractions constructively?
7. According to this essay, what qualities characterize those people who "surrender" (paragraph 21) to old age and those who "accept old age as a series of

---

Reading Critically

[10] Which physical infirmities have you "outwitted" recently?

challenges" (paragraph 21)? Why do you think Cowley has more respect for the latter group?

8. What is Cowley's general attitude toward "the country of age" (paragraph 3)? Why does he feel that way about this stage of life?

DISCOVERING RHETORICAL STRATEGIES

9. After reading this essay, try to summarize in a single word or phrase Cowley's impressions of old age. How does this dominant impression help the author organize the many different details presented in his essay?

10. Why did Cowley include the reference to the Ojibwas at the end of the first paragraph? What effect does that anecdote have on our sympathies as readers?

11. Cowley uses a number of distinct metaphors in describing old age. He equates being old, for example, with acting out a certain "role" in life. He also portrays aging as a "rite of passage," a "challenge," and an "unfamiliar country" through which we must travel. In what sense is each of these metaphors appropriate? How does each help us understand the process of growing old?

12. Cowley uses language to describe a state of being that most of us are not familiar with yet. What other rhetorical strategies does he call upon to make his descriptive essay effective? Give examples of each.

MAKING CONNECTIONS

13. What are the primary differences among the "ageism" recounted by Malcolm Cowley, the racism explained by Lewis Sawaquat ("For My Indian Daughter"), and/or the sexism described by Sandra Cisneros ("Only daughter")? Is one of these "isms" more dangerous than the others? Have you ever experienced any of these types of prejudice?

14. Compare and contrast the weaknesses of old age depicted in Cowley's essay with those portrayed by the grandfather in Ray Bradbury's "Summer Rituals" and/or by Fred Brown in John McPhee's "The Pines." Do you know anyone in his or her eighties? How does that person act? How do you think you will behave when you are that old?

15. How is Cowley's description of the "identity crisis" many older people go through similar to the identity crisis Lewis Sawaquat ("For My Indian Daughter") suffered when he discovered his Native American heritage and Malcolm X ("Learning to Read") discovered when he became more aware of his ethnic and racial heritage? Have you ever gone through an identity crisis? How did you resolve it? Was your crisis like those described by Cowley, Sawaquat, or Malcolm X in any way?

IDEAS FOR DISCUSSION/WRITING

Preparing to Write

Write freely about your impressions of one or more older people in your life: Who are they? What characteristics do they share? How are they different from each other? Different from you? Similar to you? How do you know they are "old"?

Choosing a Topic

1. Cowley explains at the outset of his essay that "the country of age is a new experience, different from what you supposed it to be. Nobody, man or woman, knows the country until he has lived in it and has taken out his citizenship papers" (paragraph 3). Interview an older person to discover his or her view of "the country of age." Then write an essay for your peers describing that person's opinions.

2. In his essay, Cowley describes the signals he receives from his body and his environment that tell him he is "old." What messages did you receive when you were young that indicated you were a "child"? What messages do you receive now that remind you of your present age? How are these messages different from those you received when you were a child? Describe these signals in a well-developed essay addressed to your classmates.

3. Do you think that Americans treat their aged with enough respect? Explain your answer in detail to an older person. Describe various situations that support your opinion.

4. In this essay, Cowley details many of the surprises and realities of aging. What "surprises and realities" have you encountered at your current age? Write an e-mail to your future retired self, titled "The View from _____" [insert your age], describing these observations and experiences.

Before beginning your essay, you might want to consult the checklists on page 44.

LINDA HOGAN   (1947–   )

Dwellings

Born in Denver, Linda Hogan is a Chickasaw Indian poet, novelist, essayist, and playwright whose many publications center on the theme that all of life is interconnected. Because her father was in the army while she was growing up, she and her family transferred to many different locations. She has always considered Oklahoma her home, however, because her father grew up there. Her first volume of poetry, *Calling Myself Home* (1978), celebrates the rich oral traditions of her Chickasaw language and heritage in this area of the country. This book of poems was soon followed by many others, including *A Piece of Moon* (1981), *Daughters, I Love You* (1981), *Seeing Through the Sun* (1985), and *Savings* (1988). Hogan next turned to fiction with her first novel, *Mean Spirit* (1990), which was an "ethnohistory" of the Osage oil boom in 1920s Oklahoma. Two other novels, *Solar Storm* (1995) and *Power* (1998), followed, along with another volume of poetry, *Book of Medicines* (1993), and a collection of essays entitled *Dwellings* (1995). Her most recent books are *The Sweet Breathing of Plants: Women and the Green World* (2000), *The Woman Who Watches Over the World: A Native Memoir* (2001), and *Sightings: The Gray Whales' Mysterious Journey* (2002). Currently a professor at the University of Colorado at Boulder, Hogan has explained that she has a natural calling to write: "Something about the process of doing that writing tapped into my own life in a way I wouldn't have done without the writing."

Preparing to Read

This essay was originally published in 1995 in Hogan's book of nonfiction entitled *Dwellings: A Spiritual History of the Living World*. In it, she considers how we reflect the natural world around us based on the places we choose to "dwell."

Exploring Experience: Nature is a place of peace and solitude for many of us, a retreat from our daily routine: How do you escape from the pressures of everyday life? Do you have ways of getting away both physically and mentally? How are these forms of escape different from each other?

Learning Online: Visit the photo gallery on the Hooked on Golf Blog Web site (http://www.hookedongolfblog.com/wp-gallery2.php), and click on the album with pictures of a beautiful beach-front house that was rumored to belong to Tiger Woods. Whether or not this home actually belonged to Tiger Woods, it has the style and atmosphere we associate with the rich and famous. Keep these images in mind as you read Linda Hogan's essay about dwellings.

Not far from where I live is a hill that was cut into by the moving   1
water of a creek. Eroded this way, all that's left of it is a broken wall
of earth that contains old roots and pebbles woven together and exposed. Seen from a distance, it is only a rise of raw earth. But up close it is
something wonderful, a small cliff dwelling that looks almost as intricate and
well made as those the Anasazi left behind when they vanished mysteriously
centuries ago. This hill is a place that could be the starry skies at night turned
inward into the thousand round holes where solitary bees have lived and
died. It is a hill of tunneling rooms. At the mouths of some of the excava-
tions, half-circles of clay beetle out like awnings shading a doorway. It is
earth that was turned to clay in the mouths of the bees and spit out as they
mined deeper into their dwelling places.

This place is where the bees reside at an angle safe from rain. It faces the   2
southern sun. It is a warm and intelligent architecture of memory[1] learned
by whatever memory lives in the blood. Many of the holes still contain gold
husks of dead bees, their faces dry and gone, their flat eyes gazing out from
death's land toward the other uninhabited half of the hill that is across the
creek from the catacombs.

The first time I found the residence of the bees, it was dusty summer.   3
The sun was hot, and land was the dry color of rust. Now and then a car
rumbled along the dirt road and dust rose up behind it before settling back
down on older dust. In the silence, the bees made a soft droning hum. They
were alive then, and working the hill, going out and returning with pollen,
in and out through the holes, back and forth between daylight and the cooler,
darker regions of the inner earth. They were flying an invisible map through
air, a map charted by landmarks, the slant of light, and a circling story they
told one another about the direction of food held inside the center of yellow flowers.

Sitting in the hot sun, watching the small bees fly in and out around the   4
hill, hearing the summer birds, the light breeze, I felt right in the world. I belonged there. I thought of my own dwelling places, those real and those
imagined.[2] Once I lived in a town called Manitou, which means "Great
Spirit," and where hot mineral springwater gurgled beneath the streets and
rose into open wells. I felt safe there. With the underground movement of
water and heat a constant reminder of other life, of what lives beneath us, it
seemed to be the center of the world.

Reading Critically

[1] What do you think Hogan means by the phrase "a warm and intelligent architecture of memory"?

[2] How does the residence of the bees remind the author of her own dwelling places?

A few years after that, I wanted silence. My daydreams were full of places   5
I longed to be, shelters and solitudes. I wanted a room apart from others, a
hidden cabin to rest in. I wanted to be in a redwood forest with trees so tall
the owls called out in the daytime. I daydreamed of living in a vapor cave a
few hours away from here. Underground, warm, and moist, I thought it
would be the perfect world for staying out of cold winter, for escaping the
noise of living.

And how often I've wanted to escape to a wilderness where a human   6
hand has not been in everything. But those were only dreams of peace, of
comfort, of a nest inside stone or woods, a sanctuary where a dream or life
wouldn't be invaded.

Years ago, in the next canyon west of here, there was a man who followed   7
one of those dreams and moved into a cave that could only be reached by
climbing down a rope. For years he lived there in comfort, like a troglodite.
The inner weather was stable, never too hot, too cold, too wet, or too dry.
But then he felt lonely. His utopia needed a woman. He went to town until
he found a wife. For a while after the marriage, his wife climbed down the
rope along with him, but before long she didn't want the mice scurrying
about in the cave, or the untidy bats that wanted to hang from the stones of
the ceiling. So they built a door. Because of the closed entryway, the temperature changed. They had to put in heat. Then the inner moisture of earth
warped the door, so they had to have air-conditioning, and after that the earth
wanted to go about life in its own way and it didn't give in to the people. ❸

In other days and places, people paid more attention to the strong-headed   8
will of earth. Once homes were built of wood that had been felled from a
single region in a forest. That way, it was thought, the house would hold together more harmoniously, and the family of walls would not fall or lend
themselves to the unhappiness or arguments of the inhabitants.

An Italian immigrant to Chicago, Aldo Piacenzi, built bird-houses that   9
were dwellings of harmony and peace. They were the incredible spired shapes
of cathedrals in Italy. They housed not only the birds, but also his memories,
his own past. He painted them the watery blue of his Mediterranean, the wild
rose of flowers in a summer field. Inside them was straw and the droppings
of lives that layed eggs, fledglings who grew there. What places to inhabit, the
bright and sunny birdhouses in dreary alleyways of the city.

One beautiful afternoon, cool and moist, with the kind of yellow light that   10
falls on earth in these arid regions, I waited for barn swallows to return from
their daily work of food gathering. Inside the tunnel where they live, hun-

---

Reading Critically

❸ What is the meaning of the following clause: "the earth wanted to go about life in its
own way"?

dreds of swallows had mixed their saliva with mud and clay, much like the solitary bees, and formed nests that were perfect as a potter's bowl. At five in the evening, they returned all at once, a dark, flying shadow. Despite their enormous numbers and the crowding together of nests, they didn't pause for even a moment before entering the nests, nor did they crowd one another. Instantly they vanished into the nests. The tunnel went silent. It held no outward signs of life.

But I knew they were there, filled with the fire of living. And what a marriage of elements was in those nests. Not only mud's earth and water, the fire of sun and dry air, but even the elements contained one another. The bodies of prophets and crazy men were broken down in that soil.   11

I've noticed often how when a house is abandoned, it begins to sag. Without a tenant, it has no need to go on. If it were a person, we'd say it is depressed or lonely. The roof settles in, the paint cracks, the walls and floorboards warp and slope downward in their own natural ways, telling us that life must stay in everything as the world whirls and tills and moves through boundless space.   12

One summer day, cleaning up after long-eared owls where I work at a rehabilitation facility for birds of prey, I was raking the gravel floor of a flight cage. Down on the ground, something looked like it was moving. I bent over to look into the pile of bones and pellets I'd just raked together. There, close to the ground, were two fetal mice. They were new to the planet, pink and hairless. They were so tenderly young. Their faces had swollen blue-veined eyes. They were nestled in a mound of feathers, soft as velvet, each one curled up smaller than an infant's ear, listening to the first sounds of earth. But the ants were biting them. They turned in agony, unable to pull away, not yet having the arms or legs to move, but feeling, twisting away from, the pain of the bites. I was horrified to see them bitten out of life that way. I dipped them in water, as if to take away the sting, and let the ants fall in the bucket. Then I held the tiny mice in the palm of my hand. Some of the ants were drowning in the water. I was trading one life for another, exchanging the lives of the ants for those of mice, but I hated their suffering, and hated even more that they had not yet grown to a life, and already they inhabited the miserable world of pain. Death and life feed each other. I know that.◆   13

Inside these rooms where birds are healed, there are other lives besides those of mice. There are fine gray globes the wasps have woven together, the white cocoons of spiders in a corner, the downward tunneling anthills. All these dwellings are inside one small walled space, but I think most about the mice. Sometimes the downy nests fall out of the walls where their mothers   14

Reading Critically

◆ How do "death and life feed each other"?

have placed them out of the way of their enemies. When one of the nests falls, they are so well made and soft, woven mostly from the chest feathers of birds. Sometimes the leg of a small quail holds the nest together like a slender cornerstone with dry, bent claws. The mice have adapted to life in the presence of their enemies, adapted to living in the thin wall between beak and beak, claw and claw. They move their nests often, as if a new rafter or wall will protect them from the inevitable fate of all our returns home to the deeper, wider nests of earth that houses us all.

One August at Zia Pueblo during the corn dance I noticed tourists picking up shards of all the old pottery that had been made and broken there. The residents of Zia know not to take the bowls and pots left behind by the older ones. They know that the fragments of those earlier lives need to be smoothed back to earth, but younger nations, travelers from continents across the world who have come to inhabit this land, have little of their own to grow on. The pieces of earth that were formed into bowls, even on their way home to dust, provide the new people a lifeline to an unknown land, help them remember that they live in the old nest of earth.   15

It was in early February, during the mating season of the great horned owl. It was dusk, and I hiked up the back of a mountain to where I'd heard the owls a year before. I wanted to hear them again, the voices so tender, so deep, like a memory of comfort. I was halfway up the trail when I found a soft, round nest. It had fallen from one of the bare-branched trees. It was a delicate nest, woven together of feathers, sage, and strands of wild grass. Holding it in my hand in the rosy twilight, I noticed that a blue thread was entwined with the other gatherings there. I pulled at the thread a little, and then I recognized it. It was a thread from one of my skirts. It was blue cotton. It was the unmistakable color and shape of a pattern I knew. I liked it, that a thread of my life was in an abandoned nest, one that had held eggs and new life. ◈⁵ I took the nest home. At home, I held it to the light and looked more closely. There, to my surprise, nestled into the gray-green sage, was a gnarl of black hair. It was also unmistakable. It was my daughter's hair, cleaned from a brush and picked up out in the sun beneath the maple tree, or the pit cherry where the birds eat from the overladen, fertile branches until only the seeds remain on the trees.   16

I didn't know what kind of nest it was, or who had lived there. It didn't matter. I thought of the remnants of our lives carried up the hill that way and turned into shelter. That night, resting inside the walls of our home, the   17

Reading Critically

◈⁵ How does the author feel about finding the blue thread from one of her skirts embedded in a bird's nest?

world outside weighed so heavily against the thin wood of the house. The sloped roof was the only thing between us and the universe. Everything outside of our wooden boundaries seemed so large. Filled with the night's citizens, it all came alive. The world opened in the thickets of the dark. The wild grapes would soon ripen on the vines. The burrowing ones were emerging. Horned owls sat in treetops. Mice scurried here and there. Skunks, fox, the slow and holy porcupine, all were passing by this way. The young of the solitary bees were feeding on the pollen in the dark. The whole world was a nest on its humble tilt, in the maze of the universe, holding us. ⬥6

UNDERSTANDING DETAILS

1. What does the "broken wall of earth" (paragraph 1) consist of? Why is it fascinating to her?
2. What is the "marriage of elements" Hogan refers to in paragraph 11?
3. What does Hogan mean by "a warm and intelligent architecture of memory" in paragraph 2?
4. To what does "the strong-headed will of earth" (paragraph 8) refer? How can the earth be "strong-headed"?

THINKING CRITICALLY

5. Why did the town of Manitou seem to be "the center of the world" (paragraph 4) to Hogan?
6. In what ways do "death and life feed each other" (paragraph 13)?
7. How do our dwellings represent us and our view of the world?
8. In what ways are humans like the bees that Hogan describes at the beginning of this essay?

DISCOVERING RHETORICAL STRATEGIES

9. Why does Hogan include the story about the man in a cave (paragraph 7)? What does it add to the essay?
10. Explain the image that the author creates when she says, "The whole world was a nest on its humble tilt, in the maze of the universe, holding us" (paragraph 17).
11. This essay is divided by spaces into nine sections. What does each section represent? What effect do these divisions have in the essay?
12. What is the significance of the "remnants of our lives" (paragraph 17) that Hogan found in the abandoned nest she discovered? In what way does the scene capture the main theme of the entire essay?

Reading Critically

⬥6 How do you feel about the author's concluding sentence, in which she compares the whole earth to a "nest" holding us all?

MAKING CONNECTIONS

13. Compare and contrast Linda Hogan's sense of place with that described by
    Kimberly Wozencraft ("Notes from the Country Club"), Robert Ramirez
    ("The Barrio"), and/or Edward Ayers ("The American Civil War, Emancipa-
    tion, and Reconstruction on the World Stage"). In which essay is the devotion
    to a particular place most vivid and compelling? Why?
14. Hogan's reverence for nature is echoed in John McPhee's "The Pines" and Gar-
    rison Keillor's "How the Crab Apple Grew." Which essay attaches the most
    religious significance to its natural world? Why do you think this is so?
15. How are the various "dwellings" described by Hogan different from those men-
    tioned in Ray Bradbury's "Summer Rituals," Kimberly Wozencraft's "Notes
    from the Country Club," Sandra Cisneros's "Only daughter," and/or Richard
    Rodriguez' "Public and Private Language"?

IDEAS FOR DISCUSSION/WRITING

Preparing to Write

Write freely about the importance of escape in contemporary society: Why do
people feel the need to escape or retreat? What are they escaping from? What pressures cause us to look for methods of escape? What are these methods? How are they
different from one another? In what ways do these strategies bring relief?

Choosing a Topic

1. You have been asked to write an article for your high school newspaper on
   safe, healthy methods of escape from the pressures that confront teens today.
   Explore your thoughts on this topic; then write an essay that will appeal to the
   values and concerns of today's high school students.
2. Why do we need various forms of escape? Is this need a positive or negative
   force? Analyze our need to escape, including both the reasons for it and its consequences.
3. Hogan indirectly compares some inhabitants in the wild with humans. Think
   of another comparison with humans that teaches us important truths about
   ourselves, and, using Hogan's essay as a model, write an essay that explores this
   comparison and leads us to new insights about the human race.
4. Picture the home you grew up in (or the home you remember most vividly).
   Now picture the "dream home" in which you want to retire and grow old.
   What are the similarities and differences between these two homes? Is your
   "dream home" luxurious like the home from the Hooked on Golf Web site,
   or does it have a more casual feel? Considering the images you have in your
   mind, write an essay describing what your basic requirements are in a home

Before beginning your essay, you might want to consult the checklists on page 44.

Chapter Writing Assignments

Practicing Description

1. Write a spatial description of your home by exploring its basic sections or rooms. What does your home reveal about you as a person? About your family?

2. Think about the extent to which influences such as family, education, and community have contributed to the person you are today. Describe the kind of person you are and the sources of a few of your most important qualities.

3. Consider the health of the environment in your immediate community (air, noise, landscape). Describe an environmental problem you have observed. Be sure to provide examples of the problem you are describing.

Exploring Ideas

4. Discuss a cultural icon (such as a rock star or a prominent building) and what it represents about the culture you are describing. How did this person or object become an icon in its culture? What biases or ideals does it express? How do people outside this culture view it?

5. Think about the ways people's physical surroundings (office, weather, house, apartment) affect them. Discuss one important way these surroundings have influenced someone's behavior. Provide examples in your discussion that explore the relationship between various features in your surroundings and the manner in which people react to them.

6. In your opinion, how well are elderly people treated in America? Write an essay describing the level of respect older people get in American society. Use examples of people you know to support your ideas.

Analyzing Visual Images

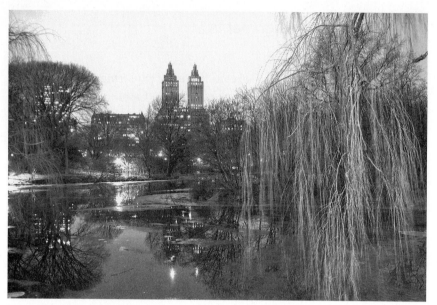

Dave Beckerman Photography.

7. Look at the detail in this picture, and try to imagine what smells, tastes, sounds, textures, and sights you might experience while standing in this setting. Write a description of this scene for someone who has never been here, including all the senses that this scene evokes.

8. Look at the photograph by Gerry Gavigan on page 34 at the beginning of this chapter. Choose a sense besides sight (smell, hear, taste, or feel), and explain why this sense is dominant in this picture.

Chapter 2

NARRATION
Telling a Story

A good story is a powerful method of getting someone's attention. The excitement that accompanies a suspenseful ghost story, a lively anecdote, or a vivid joke easily attests to this fact. In reality, narration is one of the earliest verbal skills we all learn as children, providing us with a convenient, logical, and easily understood means of sharing our thoughts with other people. Storytelling is powerful because it offers us a way of dramatizing our ideas so that others can identify with them.

DEFINING NARRATION

Narration involves telling a story that is often based on personal experience. Stories can be oral or written, real or imaginary, short or long. A good story, however, always has a point or purpose. Narration can be the dominant mode (as in a novel or short story), supported by other rhetorical strategies, or it can serve the purpose of another rhetorical mode (as in a persuasive essay, a historical survey, or a scientific report).

In its subordinate role, narration can provide examples or explain ideas. If asked why you are attending college, for instance, you might turn to narration to make your answer clear, beginning with a story about your family's hardships in the past. The purpose of telling such a story would be to show your listeners how important higher education is to you by encouraging them to understand and identify with your family history.

Unlike description, which generally portrays people, places, and objects in *space*, narration asks the reader to follow a series of actions through a particular *time* sequence. Description, however, often complements the movement of narration. People must be depicted, for instance, along with their relationships to one another, before their actions can have any real meaning for us; similarly, places must be described so that we can picture the setting and understand the activities in a specific scene. The organization of the action and the time spent on each episode in a story should be based principally on a writer's analysis of the interests and needs of his or her audience.

To be most effective, narration should prolong the exciting parts of a story and shorten the routine facts that simply move the reader from one episode to another. If you were robbed on your way to work, for example, a good narrative describing the incident would concentrate on the traumatic event itself rather than on such mundane and boring details as what you had for breakfast and what chores you did prior to the attack. Finally, just like description, narration *shows* rather than *tells* its purpose to the audience. The factual statement "I was robbed this morning" could be made much more vivid and dramatic through the addition of some simple narration: "As I was walking to work at 7:30 A.M., a huge and angry-looking man ran up to me, thrust a gun into the middle of my stomach, and took my money, my new wristwatch, all my credit cards, and my pants—leaving me penniless and embarrassed."

The following paragraph written by a student recounts a recent parachuting experience. As you read this narrative, notice especially the writer's use of vivid detail to *show* rather than *tell* her message to the readers.

> I have always needed occasional "fixes" of excitement in my life, so when I realized one spring day that I was more than ordinarily bored, I made up my mind to take more than ordinary steps to relieve that boredom. I decided to go parachuting. The next thing I knew, I was stuffed into a claustrophobically small plane with five other terrified people, rolling down a bumpy, rural runway, droning my way to 3,500 feet and an exhilarating experience. Once over the jump area, I waited my turn, stepped onto the strut, held my breath, and then kicked off into the cold, rushing air as my heart pounded heavily. All I could think was, "I hope this damn parachute opens!" The sensation of falling backward through space was unfamiliar and disconcerting till my chute opened with a loud "pop," momentarily pulling me upward toward the distant sky. After several minutes of floating downward, I landed rudely on the hard ground. Life, I remembered happily, could be awfully exciting, and a month later, when my tailbone had stopped throbbing, I still felt that way.

THINKING CRITICALLY THROUGH NARRATION

- Use your memory.
- Make chronological lists.
- Fill in details.

Rhetorical modes offer us different ways of perceiving reality. Narration is an especially useful tool for sequencing or putting details and information in some kind of logical order, usually chronological. Practicing exercises in narrative techniques can help you see clear patterns in topics you are writing about.

Although narration is usually used in conjunction with other rhetorical modes, we are going to isolate it here so you can appreciate its specific mechanics separate from other mental activities. If you feel the process of narration in your head, you are more likely to understand exactly what it entails and therefore use it more effectively in reading essays and in organizing and writing your own essays.

For the best results, we will once again do some warm-up exercises to make your sequencing perceptions as accurate and successful as possible. In this way, you will actually learn to feel how your mind works in this particular mode and then be more aware of the thinking strategies available to you in your own reading and writing. As you become more conscious of the mechanics of the individual rhetorical modes, you will naturally become more adept at combining them to accomplish the specific purpose and the related effect you want to create.

Scott Alberts.

The following exercises, which require a combination of thinking and writing skills, will help you practice this particular strategy in isolation. Just as in a physical workout, we will warm up your mental capabilities one by one as if they were muscles that can be developed individually before being used together in harmony.

1. Write or tell the story that goes with the Scott Alberts photo on the previous page. Make this scene the beginning of your story, and then create the remainder of the plot.
2. Make a chronological list of the different activities you did yesterday, from waking in the morning to sleeping at night. Randomly pick two events from your day, and treat them as the highlights of your day. Now write freely for five minutes, explaining the story of your day and emphasizing the importance of these two highlights.
3. Recall an important event that happened to you between the ages of five and ten. Brainstorm about how this event made you feel at the time it happened. Then brainstorm about how this event makes you feel now. What changes have you discovered in your view of this event?

Reading and Writing Narrative Essays

Making meaning in reading and writing is a fairly straightforward process with the narrative mode. To read a narrative essay most effectively, you should spend your time concentrating on the writer's main story line and use of details. Together, these tasks will help you make meaning as you read. To create an effective story, you have some important decisions to make before you write and certain variables to control as you actually draft your narrative. During the prewriting stage, you need to generate ideas and choose a point of view through which your story will be presented. Then, as you write, the preliminary decisions you have made regarding the selection and arrangement of your details (especially important in a narrative) will allow your story to flow more easily. Carefully controlled organization, along with appropriate timing and pacing, can influence your audience's reactions in very powerful ways.

READING NARRATIVE ESSAYS

- What is the story's context?
- What is the essay's story line?
- What is the author's purpose?

Preparing to Read.   As you prepare to read the narratives in this chapter, try to guess what each title tells you about its essay's topic and about the author's attitude toward that topic: Can you guess, for example, how Lewis Sawaquat feels about his daughter from his title "For My Indian Daughter" or what Maya Angelou's attitude is toward the events described in "New Directions"? Also, scan the essay and read its synopsis in the Rhetorical Table of Contents to help you anticipate as much as you can about the author's purpose and audience.

Next, the more you learn from the biography about the author and the circumstances surrounding the composition of a particular essay, the better prepared you will be to read the essay. For a narrative essay, the writer's point of view or perspective toward the story and its characters is especially significant. From the biographies, can you determine Maya Angelou's attitude toward Annie Johnson's energy and determination in "New Directions" or Russell Baker's opinion of his mother in "The Saturday Evening Post"? Also, what is Sandra Cisneros's reason for writing "Only daughter"?

Last, before you begin to read, answer the Preparing to Read questions, and then try to generate some of your own inquiries on the general subject of the essay: What do you want to know about being a Native American (Sawaquat)? What childhood experience greatly affected your life (Baker)? What do you think of children in general (Cisneros)?

Reading.   As you read a narrative essay for the first time, simply follow the story line, and try to get a general sense of the narrative and of the author's general purpose. Is Baker trying to encourage us all to be writers or simply to help us understand why he writes? Record your initial reactions to each essay as they occur to you. Is Keillor's purpose to make us feel sympathetic or antagonistic toward his childhood memories?

At the bottom of the pages of these essays are questions that will help you think analytically about the topic of the essay and related subjects. They are designed to provide a "bridge" between the questions at the beginning of the essay and the more complex questions at the end. Thinking critically is a skill that can be learned if you practice it, which is what these prompts intend to help you do. If you take time to consider and respond to each inquiry, you will be ready to write in depth on the questions and writing assignments that follow each essay.

Based on the biographical information preceding the essay and on the essay's tone, purpose, and audience, try to create a context for the narrative as you read. How do such details help you understand your reading material more thoroughly? A first reading of this sort, along with a survey of the questions that follow the essay, will help prepare you for a critical understanding of the material when you read it for the second time.

Rereading. As you reread these narrative essays, notice the author's selection and arrangement of details. Why does Angelou organize her story one way and Cisneros another? What effect does their organization create?

Also, pay attention to the timing and the pacing of the story line. What do the long descriptions of Annie's plans add to Angelou's "New Directions"? What does the quick pace of Keillor's narrative communicate?

In addition, consider at this point what other rhetorical strategies the authors use to support their narratives. Which writers use examples to supplement their stories? Which use definitions? Which use comparisons? Why do they use these strategies?

Finally, when you answer the questions after each essay, you can check your understanding of the material on different levels before you tackle the discussion/writing topics that follow.

For a general checklist of reading guidelines, please see page 29 of the Introduction.

WRITING NARRATIVE ESSAYS

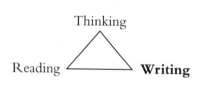

Thinking

Reading   **Writing**

- Decide on your thesis.
- Choose details to support your thesis.
- Arrange your details for a specific effect.
- Follow a time sequence.
- *Show* rather than *tell*.

Preparing to Write. First, you should answer the prewriting questions to help you generate thoughts on the subject at hand. Next, as in all writing, you should explore your subject matter and discover as many specific details as possible. (See pages 19–21 of the Introduction for a discussion of prewriting techniques.) Some writers rely on the familiar journalistic checklist of *who, what, when, where, why,* and *how* to make sure they cover all aspects of their narrative. If you were using the story of a basketball game at your college to demonstrate the team spirit of your school, for example, you might want to consider telling your readers *who* played in the game and/or *who* attended; *what* happened before, during, and after the game; *when* and *where* it took place; *why* it was being played (or *why* these particular teams were playing each other or *why* the game was especially important); and *how* the winning basket was shot. Freewriting or a combination of freewriting and the journalistic questions is another effective way of getting ideas and story details on paper for use in a first draft.

Once you have generated these ideas, you should always let your purpose and audience ultimately guide your selection of details, but the process of gathering such journalistic information gives you some material from which to choose. You will also need to decide whether to include dialogue in your narrative. Again, the difference here is between *showing* and *telling:* Will your audience benefit from reading what was actually said, word for word, during a discussion, or will a brief description of the conversation be sufficiently effective? In fact, all the choices you make at this stage of the composing process will give you material with which to create emphasis, suspense, conflict, and interest in your subject.

Next, you must decide on the point of view that will most readily help you achieve your purpose with your specific audience. Point of view includes the (1) person, (2) vantage point, and (3) attitude of your narrator. *Person* refers to who will tell the story: an uninvolved observer, a character in the narrative, or an omniscient (all-seeing) narrator. This initial decision will guide your thoughts on *vantage point,* which is the frame of reference of the narrator: close to the action, far from the action, looking back on the past, or reporting on the present. Finally, your narrator will naturally have an *attitude,* or *personal feeling,* about the subject: accepting, hostile, sarcastic, indifferent, angry, pleased, or any number of similar emotions. Once you adopt a certain perspective in a story, you should follow it for the duration of the narrative. This consistency will bring focus and coherence to your essay.

Writing.   After you have explored your topic and adopted a particular point of view, you need to write a thesis statement and to select and arrange the details of your story coherently so that the narrative has a clear beginning, middle, and end. The most natural way to organize the events of a narrative, of course, is chronologically. In your story about the school basketball game, you would probably narrate the relevant details in the order they occurred (i.e., sequentially, from the beginning of the game to its conclusion). More experienced writers may elect to use flashbacks: An athlete might recall a significant event that happened during the game, or a coach might recollect the contest's turning point. Your most important consideration is that the elements of a narrative essay follow some sort of time sequence, aided by the use of clear and logical transitions (e.g., *then, next, at this point, suddenly*) that help the reader move smoothly from one event to the next.

In addition to organization, the development of your essay with enough details is important. In this way, the details that you choose should *show* rather than *tell* your story. This approach will help your essay become interesting and believable to your readers. Furthermore, the point of view of your narrator should remain consistent throughout your essay, which will give the essay a high degree of credibility.

Rewriting.   As you reread the narrative you have written, pretend you are a reader (instead of the writer) and make sure you have told the story from the most effective point of view, considering both your purpose and your audience:

• Is your purpose (or thesis) clearly stated?

• Does your narrator help you achieve your purpose?

Further, as you reread, make certain you can follow the events of the story as they are related:

• Does one event lead naturally to the next?

• Are all the details relevant to your purpose?

• Do you *show* rather than *tell* your message?

For more advice on writing and editing, see page 30.

STUDENT ESSAY: NARRATION AT WORK

The following student essay characterizes the writer's mother by telling a story about an unusual family vacation. As you read it, notice that the student writer states her purpose clearly and succinctly in the first paragraph. She then becomes an integral part of her story as she carefully selects examples and details that help convey her thesis.

A Vacation with My Mother

First-person narrator   I had an interesting childhood—not because of ^{General subject} where I grew up and not because I ever did anything particularly adventuresome or thrilling. In fact, I don't think my life seemed especially interesting to me at the time. But now, telling friends about my supposedly ordinary childhood, I notice an array of responses ranging from astonishment to hilarity. The source of ^{Specific subject} their surprise and amusement is my mother—gracious, charming, sweet, and totally out of synchronization with the rest of the world. One strange family ^{Thesis statement} trip we took when I was eleven captures the essence of her zaniness.

My two sets of grandparents lived in Colorado and North Dakota, and my parents decided we would spend a few weeks driving to those states and seeing all the sights along the relaxed and rambling way. ^{Narrator's attitude} My eight-year-old brother, David, and I had some serious reservations. If Dad had ever had Mom drive him to school, we reasoned, he'd never even consider letting her help drive us anywhere out of town, let alone out of California. If we weren't paying attention, we were as likely to end up at her office or the Examples golf course as we were to arrive at school. Sometimes she'd drop us off at a friend's house to play and then forget where she'd left us. The notion of going on a long trip with her was really unnerving.

Transition   How can I explain my mother to a stranger? Have you ever watched reruns of the old *I Love Lucy* with Lucille Ball? I did as a child, and I thought Lucy Ricardo was normal. I lived with somebody a lot like her. Now, Mom wasn't a redhead (not usually, anyway), and Dad wasn't a Cuban nightclub owner, but Narrator's vantage point at home we had the same situation of a loving but bemused husband trying to deal with the off-the-wall logic and enthusiasm of a frequently exasperating wife. We all adored her, but we had to admit it: Mom was a flaky, absent-minded, genuine eccentric.

Transition   As the first day of our trip approached, David and I reluctantly said good-bye to all of our friends. Who knew if we'd ever see any of them again? Finally, the moment of our departure arrived, and we loaded suit– Careful selection of details cases, books, games, camping gear, and a tent into the car and bravely drove off. We bravely drove off again two hours later after we'd returned home to get the purse and traveler's checks that Mom had forgotten.

David and I were always a little nervous when using gas station bathrooms if Mom was driving while Dad Use of dialogue napped: "You stand outside the door and play lookout while I go, and I'll stand outside the door and play lookout while you go." I had terrible visions: "Honey, where are the kids?" "What?! Oh, gosh . . . I thought Examples they were being awfully quiet. Uh . . . Idaho?" We were never actually abandoned in a strange city, but we weren't about to take any chances.

Transition   On the fourth or fifth night of the trip, we had Passage of time trouble finding a motel with a vacancy. After driving futilely for an hour, Mom suddenly had a great idea: Why didn't we find a house with a likely-looking Example backyard and ask if we could pitch our tent there? To her, the scheme was eminently reasonable. Vowing quietly to each other to hide in the back seat if she did it, David and I groaned in anticipated mortification. To our profound relief, Dad vetoed the idea. Mom never could understand our objections. If a strange family showed up on her front doorstep, Mom would have been delighted. She thinks everyone in the world is as nice as she is. We finally found a vacancy in the next town. David and I were thrilled—the place featured bungalows in the shape of Native-American tepees.

<u>The Native-American motif must have reminded my parents that we had not yet used the brand-new tent, Coleman stove, portable mattress, and other camping gear we had brought.</u> We headed to a national park the next day and found a campsite by a lake. It took hours to figure out how to set up the tent: It was one of those deluxe models with mosquito-net windows, canvas floors, and enough room for three large families to sleep in. It was after dark before we finally got it erected, and the night had turned quite cold. We fixed a hurried campfire dinner (chicken burned on the outside and raw in the middle) and prepared to go to sleep. That was when we realized that Mom had forgotten to bring along some important pieces of equipment—our sleeping bags. The four of us huddled together on our thin mattresses borrowed from our station-wagon floor. That ended our camping days. Give me a stucco tepee any time.

We drove through several states and saw lots of great sights along the way: the Grand Canyon, Carlsbad Caverns, caves, mountains, waterfalls, and even a haunted house. David and I were excited and amazed at all the wonders we found, and Mom was just as enthralled as we were. Her constant pleasure and sense of the world as a beautiful, magical place was infectious. I never realized until I grew up how really childlike—in the best sense of the word—my mother actually is. She is innocent, optimistic, and always ready to be entertained.

Margin annotations:

Transition

Chronological order

Careful selection of details

Examples (spatial order)

Transition   <u>Looking back on that long-past family vacation</u>, I
now realize that my childhood was more special be-   Narrator's
cause I grew up with a mother who wasn't afraid to   attitude
try anything and who taught me to look at the world
as a series of marvelous opportunities to be explored.
What did it matter that she thought England was bordered by Germany? We were never going to try to   Examples
drive there. So what if she was always leaving her car
keys in the refrigerator or some other equally inex-
plicable place? <u>In the end, we always got where we
were going</u>—and we generally had a grand time along
Concluding   <u>the way</u>.
remark

Student Writer's Comments

I enjoyed writing about this childhood vacation because of all the memories it brought back. I knew I wanted to write a narrative to explain my
mother, and the word *zany* immediately popped into my mind. So I knew
what my focus was going to be from the outset. My prewriting started spon-
taneously as soon as I found this angle. So many thoughts and memories
rushed into my head that I couldn't even get to a piece of paper to write them
down before I lost some of them. But there were way too many to put into
one essay. The hardest part of writing this narrative was trying to decide
what material to use and what to leave out. Spending a little more time before writing my first draft proved to be a good investment in this case. I got
a clean piece of paper and began freewriting, trying to mold some of my scattered ideas from brainstorming into a coherent, readable form. During this
second stage of prewriting, I remembered one special vacation we took that
I thought might capture the essence of my mother—and also of my family.

My first draft was about three times the length of this one. My point of
view was the innocent participant/observer who came to know and love
her mother or her absent-mindedness. I had really developed my thesis from
the time I got this writing assignment. And I told my story chronologically
except for looking back in the last paragraph when I attempted to analyze
the entire experience. I had no trouble *showing* rather than *telling* because all
of the details were so vivid to me—as if they had happened yesterday. But
that was my downfall. I soon realized that I could not possibly include everything that was on the pages of my first draft.

The process of cranking out my rough draft made my point of view toward life with my mother very clear to me and helped me face the cutting
that was ahead of me. I took the raw material of a very lengthy first draft and

forced myself to choose the details and examples that best characterized my mother and what life was like growing up under the care of such a lovely but daffy individual. The sense of her being both "lovely" and "daffy" was the insight that helped me the most in revising the content of my essay. I made myself ruthlessly eliminate anything that interfered with the overall effect I was trying to create—from extraneous images and details to words and phrases that didn't contribute to this specific view of my mom.

The final result, according to my classmates, communicated my message clearly and efficiently. The main criticism I got from my class was that I might have cut too much from my first draft. But I think this focused picture with a few highlights conveys my meaning in the best possible way. I offered enough details to *show* rather than *tell* my readers what living with my mother was like, but not too many to bore them. I was also able to take the time in my essay to be humorous now and then ("David and I reluctantly said good-bye to all of our friends. Who knew if we'd ever see any of them again?" and "Give me a stucco tepee any time."), as well as pensive and serious ("I now realize that my childhood was more special because I grew up with a mother who wasn't afraid to try anything and who taught me to look at the world as a series of marvelous opportunities to be explored."). Even though in looking at the essay now I would tamper with a few things, I am generally happy with the final draft. It captures the essence of my mother from my point of view, and it also gave my class a few laughs. Aren't the readers' reactions the ultimate test of a good story?

SOME FINAL THOUGHTS ON NARRATION

Just as with other modes of writing, all decisions regarding narration should be made with a specific purpose and an intended audience constantly in mind. As you will see, each narrative in this section is directed at a clearly defined audience. Notice, as you read, how each writer manipulates the various features of narration so that the readers are simultaneously caught up in the plot and deeply moved to feel, act, think, and believe the writer's personal opinions.

NARRATION IN REVIEW

Reading Narrative Essays

Preparing to Read

✓ What assumptions can you make from the essay's title?

✓ Can you guess what the author's mood is?

✓ What is the essay's purpose and audience?

✓ What does the synopsis tell you about the essay?

✓ What can you learn from the author's biography?

✓ Can you predict the author's point of view toward the subject?

Reading

✓ What is the story's context?

✓ What is the essay's story line?

✓ What is the author's purpose?

Rereading

✓ What details did the author choose and how are they arranged?

✓ How does the author control the pace of the story?

✓ What other rhetorical modes does the author use?

Writing Narrative Essays

Preparing to Write

✓ What is your purpose?

✓ Who is your audience?

✓ What is your narrator's point of view—including person, vantage point, and attitude toward the subject?

Writing

✓ What is your thesis?

✓ What details will best support this thesis?

✓ How can you arrange these details to create a certain effect?

✓ Does your narrative essay follow a well-paced time sequence?

✓ Do you *show* rather than *tell* your story?

Rewriting

✓ Is your purpose (or thesis) clearly stated?

✓ Does your narrator help you achieve your purpose?

✓ Does one event lead naturally to the next?

✓ Are all the details relevant to your purpose?

✓ Do you *show* rather than *tell* your message?

For My Indian Daughter

Lewis Sawaquat is a Native American who is now retired from his thirty-year job as a surveyor for the Soil Conservation Service of the United States Department of Agriculture. He was born in Harbor Springs, Michigan, where his great-great-grandfather was the last official "chief" of the region. After finishing high school, Sawaquat entered the army, graduated from Army Survey School, and then completed a tour of duty in Korea. Upon returning to America, he enrolled in the Art Institute of Chicago to study commercial art. Sawaquat now lives on a revervation in Peshawbestown, Michigan, where his hobbies include gardening, swimming, walking in the woods, reading, and playing with his cat. He serves as a pipe carrier and cultural/spiritual adviser to his Ottawa tribe. Recently, he started a consulting firm and travels around the country speaking on Native-American issues. He also hopes to write a book entitled *Dreams: The Universal Language,* which will investigate the Native-American approach to dream interpretation. His daughter, Gaia, who is described in the following essay, recently graduated from Yale University. His advice to students using *The Prose Reader* is to "pay attention to life; there's nothing more important to becoming a writer."

Preparing to Read

"For My Indian Daughter" originally appeared in the "My Turn" column of *Newsweek* magazine (September 5, 1983) under the author's former name, Lewis Johnson. In his article, the author speaks eloquently about prejudice, ethnic pride, and growing cultural awareness, which are timely topics for all of us.

Exploring Experience: Before reading this selection, think for a few minutes about your own heritage: What is your ethnic identity? Are you content with this background? Have you ever gone through an identity crisis? Do you anticipate facing any problems because of your ancestry? If so, what do you think these problems will be? How will you handle them when they occur?

Learning Online: To understand the context in which Sawaquat is writing, visit the Smithsonian Web site (http://www.si.edu), and type "American Indian Art and Design" into the search field. View the online exhibits of Native-American culture, past and present.

My little girl is singing herself to sleep upstairs, her voice mingling 1
with the sounds of the birds outside in the old maple trees. She is
two, and I am nearly 50, and I am very taken with her. She came
along late in my life, unexpected and unbidden, a startling gift.

Today at the beach my chubby-legged, brown-skinned daughter ran laugh- 2
ing into the water as fast as she could. My wife and I laughed watching her,
until we heard behind us a low guttural curse and then an unpleasant voice
raised in an imitation war whoop.

I turned to see a fat man in a bathing suit, white and soft as a grub, as he 3
covered his mouth and prepared to make the Indian war cry again. He was
middle-aged, younger than I, and had three little children lined up next to
him, grinning foolishly. My wife suggested we leave the beach, and I agreed.

I knew the man was not unusual in his feelings against Indians. His beach 4
behavior might have been socially unacceptable to more civilized whites,
but his basic view of Indians is expressed daily in our small town, frequently
on the editorial pages of the county newspaper, as white people speak out
against Indian fishing rights and land rights, saying in essence, "Those Indians are taking our fish, our land." It doesn't matter to them that we were
here first, that the U.S. Supreme Court has ruled in our favor. It matters to
them that we have something they want, and they hate us for it. Backlash is
the common explanation of the attacks on Indians, the bumper stickers that
say, "Spear an Indian, Save a Fish," but I know better. The hatred of Indians
goes back to the beginning when white people came to this country. For me
it goes back to my childhood in Harbor Springs, Mich.

Theft.   Harbor Springs is now a summer resort for the very affluent, but 5
a hundred years ago it was the Indian village of my Ottawa ancestors. My
grandmother, Anna Showanessy, and other Indians like her, had their land
there taken by treaty, by fraud, by violence, by theft. They remembered how
whites had burned down the village at Burt Lake in 1900 and pushed the
Indians out. These were the stories in my family.

When I was a boy, my mother told me to walk down the alleys in Har- 6
bor Springs and not to wear my orange football sweater out of the house.
This way I would not stand out, not be noticed, and not be a target.

I wore my orange sweater anyway and deliberately avoided the alleys. I 7
was the biggest person I knew and wasn't really afraid. But I met my come-
uppance when I enlisted in the U.S. Army. One night all the men in my bar-
racks gathered together and, gang-fashion, pulled me into the shower and
scrubbed me down with rough brushes used for floors, saying, "We won't

---

Reading Critically

How does Sawaquat's description of the "fat man" who was "soft as a grub" betray the author's feelings about the confrontation on the beach?

have any dirty Indians in our outfit." It is a point of irony that I was cleaner than any of them. Later in Korea I learned how to kill, how to bully, how to hate Koreans. I came out of the war tougher than ever and, strangely, white. ❷

I went to college, got married, lived in La Porte, Ind., worked as a surveyor   8
and raised three boys. I headed Boy Scout groups, never thinking it odd when the Scouts did imitation Indian dances, imitation Indian lore.

One day when I was 35 or thereabouts I heard about an Indian powwow.   9
My father used to attend them and so with great curiosity and a strange joy at discovering a part of my heritage, I decided the thing to do to get ready for this big event was to have my friend make me a spear in his forge. The steel was fine and blue and iridescent. The feathers on the shaft were bright and proud.

In a dusty state fairground in southern Indiana, I found white people   10
dressed as Indians. I learned they were "hobbyists," that is, it was their hobby and leisure pastime to masquerade as Indians on weekends. I felt ridiculous with my spear, and I left.

It was years before I could tell anyone of the embarrassment of this week-   11
end and see any humor in it. But in a way it was that weekend, for all its silli-ness, that was my awakening. I realized I didn't know who I was. I didn't have an Indian name. I didn't speak the Indian language. I didn't know the Indian customs. Dimly I remembered the Ottawa word for dog, but it was a baby word, *kahgee,* not the full word, *muhkahgee,* which I was later to learn. Even more hazily I remembered a naming ceremony (my own). I remembered legs dancing around me, dust. Where had that been? Who had I been? "Sawaquat," my mother told me when I asked, "where the tree begins to grow." ❸

That was 1968, and I was not the only Indian in the country who was feel-   12
ing the need to remember who he or she was. There were others. They had powwows, real ones, and eventually I found them. Together we researched our past, a search that for me culminated in the Longest Walk, a march on Washington in 1978. Maybe because I now know what it means to be In-dian, it surprises me that others don't. Of course there aren't very many of us left. The chances of an average person knowing an average Indian in an average lifetime are pretty slim.

Circle.   Still, I was amused one day when my small, four-year-old neigh-   13
bor looked at me as I was hoeing in my garden and said, "You aren't a real Indian, are you?" Scotty is little, talkative, likable. Finally I said, "I'm a real

---

Reading Critically

❷ How and when did the author first acquire prejudice?

❸ What is the meaning of the Indian word "sawaquat," and how does it help characterize the author's increasing familiarity with his ethnic heritage?

Indian." He looked at me for a moment and then said, squinting into the sun, "Then where's your horse and feathers?" The child was simply a smaller, whiter version of my own ignorant self years before.[4] We'd both seen too much TV, that's all. He was not to be blamed. And so, in a way, the moronic man on the beach today is blameless. We come full circle to realize other people are like ourselves, as discomfiting as that may be sometimes.

As I sit in my old chair on my porch, in a light that is fading so the leaves are barely distinguishable against the sky, I can picture my girl asleep upstairs. I would like to prepare her for what's to come, take her each step of the way saying, there's a place to avoid, here's what I know about this, but much of what's before her she must go through alone. She must pass through pain and joy and solitude and community to discover her own inner self that is unlike any other and come through that passage to the place where she sees all people are one, and in so seeing may live her life in a brighter future. 14

UNDERSTANDING DETAILS

1. What is the principal point of this essay by Sawaquat? How many different stories does the author tell to make this point?
2. What does Sawaquat see as the origin of the hatred of Native Americans in the United States?
3. What does Sawaquat learn from his first powwow (paragraphs 9 and 10)?
4. How does Sawaquat discover his original identity? In what way does this knowledge change him?

THINKING CRITICALLY

5. Why does Sawaquat begin this essay with the story about his daughter on the beach? How does the story make you feel?
6. Why do thoughts about his daughter prompt Sawaquat's memories of his own identity crisis? What does the author's identity have to do with his daughter?
7. The author calls paragraphs 5–12 "Theft" and paragraphs 13–14 "Circle." Explain these two subtitles from the author's point of view.
8. Why do you think Sawaquat says that his daughter "must pass through pain and joy and solitude and community to discover her own inner self" (paragraph 14)? To what extent do we all need to do this in our lives?

DISCOVERING RHETORICAL STRATEGIES

9. Sawaquat occasionally uses dialogue to help make his points. What does the dialogue add to the various narratives he cites here?

Reading Critically

[4] What important truths did the author learn about himself during this major transition in his life?

10. Describe as thoroughly as possible the point of view of Sawaquat's narrator. Include in your answer a discussion of person, vantage point, and attitude.

11. Why do you think Sawaquat divides his essay into three sections? Why do you think he spends most of his time on the second section?

12. Although Sawaquat uses primarily narration to advance his point of view, which other rhetorical strategies help support his essay? Give examples of each.

MAKING CONNECTIONS

13. Compare the concern Lewis Sawaquat has for his daughter with that displayed for Russell Baker ("The Saturday Evening Post") by his mother and/or that for Amy Tan ("Mother Tongue") by her mother. Which parent do you think loves his or her child most? On what do you base this conclusion?

14. How strong is Sawaquat's attachment to his Native-American culture? Contrast the passion of his ethnic identity with that demonstrated by Malcolm X ("Learning to Read"), Alice Walker ("Beauty: When the Other Dancer Is the Self"), Sandra Cisneros ("Only daughter"), and/or Robert Ramirez ("The Barrio").

15. What responsibilities, according to Sawaquat, should parents accept regarding the eventual happiness of their children? Would Bill Cosby ("The Baffling Question") or Michael Dorris ("The Broken Cord") agree with him? Why or why not? To what extent do you agree with Sawaquat?

IDEAS FOR DISCUSSION/WRITING

Preparing to Write

Write freely about your own identity: What is your cultural heritage? How do you fit into your immediate environment? Has your attitude about yourself and your identity changed over the years? Do you know your own inner self? How do you plan to continue learning about yourself?

Choosing a Topic

1. Write a narrative essay that uses one or more stories from your past in order to describe to a group of friends the main features of your identity.

2. Explain to your children (whether real or imaginary) in narrative form some simple but important truths about your heritage. Take care to select your details well, choose an appropriate point of view, and arrange your essay logically so that you keep your readers' interest throughout the essay.

3. Have you recently experienced any social traumas in your life that you would like to prepare someone else for? Write a letter to the person you would like to warn. Use narration to explain the situation, and suggest ways to avoid the negative aspects you encountered.

4. Anyone can be an author on the Internet. If you owned a Web site that was a forum for your ideas, what topics would you want to write about and publish?

How have you experienced ignorance? Perhaps you have experienced prejudice based on your age, appearance, ethnicity, or abilities. Write a narrative for your personal Web site in which you share your experiences with prejudice. Using Sawaquat's essay as a model, describe specific incidents and the way they affected you.

Before beginning your essay, you might want to consult the checklists on page 103.

MAYA ANGELOU   (1928–   )

New Directions

Maya Angelou was born Marguerite Johnson on April 4, 1928, in St. Louis, Missouri. Nicknamed "Maya" by her brother, she moved with her family to California; then, at age three, she was sent to live with her grandmother in Stamps, Arkansas, where she spent the childhood years later recorded in her autobiographical novel *I Know Why the Caged Bird Sings* (1970). After a brief marriage, she embarked upon an amazingly prolific career in dance, drama, and writing. During the past forty years, Angelou has been at various times a nightclub performer specializing in calypso songs and dances, an actress, a playwright, a civil-rights activist, a newspaper editor, a television writer and producer, a poet, and a screenwriter. She has also written several television specials, including *Three Way Choice* (a five-part miniseries) and *Afro-Americans in the Arts,* both for PBS. Her most recent work includes five novels: *I Shall Not Be Moved* (1990), *Lessons in Living* (1993), *Wouldn't Take Nothing for My Journey Now* (1993), *A Brave and Startling Truth* (1995), and *Phenomenal Woman* (2000). In addition, she won the Presidential Medal of Arts in 2000, published *A Song Flung Up to Heaven* (2002) and *Hallelujah! The Welcome Table* (2004), and was given a Grammy Award in 2003 for her recorded reading of *A Song Flung Up to Heaven*. A tall, graceful, and imposing woman, Angelou was once described as conveying "pride without arrogance, self-esteem without smugness."

Preparing to Read

Taken from Angelou's book *Wouldn't Take Nothing for My Journey Now,* the following essay describes how Annie Johnson, a strong and determined woman, found "a new path" in her life.

Exploring Experience: Before you read this essay, take a moment to think about a time you changed directions: What were the circumstances surrounding this change? Why did you make the change? What did you learn from the experience? What alterations would you make if you followed this path again?

Learning Online: Maya Angelou has some strong opinions on the topic of courage. To get a sense of Angelou's thoughts on this subject, go to http://www.oprah.com/omagazine, and type "Oprah's cut with Maya Angelou" into the search field. Select the link titled "Oprah's Cut with Maya Angelou." Click the "watch" button. Then watch the flash movie entitled "Your life is defined by principles." As you read Angelou's article, consider how her attitudes toward courage and self-identity are evident in Annie Johnson's character.

In 1903 the late Mrs. Annie Johnson of Arkansas found herself with two   1
toddling sons, very little money, a slight ability to read and add simple
numbers. To this picture add a disastrous marriage and the burdensome
fact that Mrs. Johnson was a Negro. ❶

When she told her husband, Mr. William Johnson, of her dissatisfaction   2
with their marriage, he conceded that he too found it to be less than he expected and had been secretly hoping to leave and study religion. He added
that he thought God was calling him not only to preach but to do so in
Enid, Oklahoma. He did not tell her that he knew a minister in Enid with
whom he could study and who had a friendly, unmarried daughter. They
parted amicably, Annie keeping the one-room house and William taking
most of the cash to carry himself to Oklahoma.

Annie, over six feet tall, big-boned, decided that she would not go to   3
work as a domestic and leave her "precious babes" to anyone else's care.
There was no possibility of being hired at the town's cotton gin or lumber
mill, but maybe there was a way to make the two factories work for her. In
her words, "I looked up the road I was going and back the way I come, and
since I wasn't satisfied, I decided to step off the road and cut me a new path."
She told herself that she wasn't a fancy cook but that she could "mix groceries well enough to scare hunger away from a starving man."

She made her plans meticulously and in secret. One early evening to see   4
if she was ready, she placed stones in two five-gallon pails and carried them
three miles to the cotton gin. She rested a little, and then, discarding some
rocks, she walked in the darkness to the saw mill five miles farther along the
dirt road. On her way back to her little house and her babies, she dumped
the remaining rocks along the path.

That same night she worked into the early hours boiling chicken and fry-   5
ing ham. She made dough and filled the rolled-out pastry with meat. At last
she went to sleep. ❷

The next morning she left her house carrying the meat pies, lard, an iron   6
brazier, and coals for a fire. Just before lunch she appeared in an empty lot
behind the cotton gin. As the dinner noon bell rang, she dropped the savors
into boiling fat, and the aroma rose and floated over to the workers who
spilled out of the gin, covered with white lint, looking like specters.

Most workers had brought their lunches of pinto beans and biscuits or   7
crackers, onions and cans of sardines, but they were tempted by the hot meat

---

Reading Critically
❶ Why does Angelou describe Annie Johnson's ethnicity as "burdensome"?
❷ What specific details does the author include to indicate how hard Annie worked for success?

pies which Annie ladled out of the fat. She wrapped them in newspapers, which soaked up the grease, and offered them for sale at a nickel each. Although business was slow, those first days Annie was determined. She balanced her appearances between the two hours of activity.

So, on Monday if she offered hot fresh pies at the cotton gin and sold the remaining cooled-down pies at the lumber mill for three cents, then on Tuesday she went first to the lumber mill presenting fresh, just-cooked pies as the lumbermen covered in sawdust emerged from the mill.   8

For the next few years, on balmy spring days, blistering summer noons, and cold, wet, and wintry middays, Annie never disappointed her customers, who could count on seeing the tall, brown-skin woman bent over her brazier, carefully turning the meat pies. When she felt certain that the workers had become dependent on her, she built a stall between the two hives of industry and let the men run to her for their lunchtime provisions.   9

She had indeed stepped from the road which seemed to have been chosen for her and cut herself a brand-new path. In years that stall became a store where customers could buy cheese, meal, syrup, cookies, candy, writing tablets, pickles, canned goods, fresh fruit, soft drinks, coal, oil, and leather soles for worn-out shoes.   10

Each of us has the right and the responsibility to assess the roads which lie ahead, and those over which we have traveled, and if the future road looms ominous or unpromising, and the roads back uninviting, then we need to gather our resolve and, carrying only the necessary baggage, step off that road into another direction. ③ If the new choice is also unpalatable, without embarrassment, we must be ready to change that as well.   11

UNDERSTANDING DETAILS

1. What path is Annie Johnson following that she dislikes? How does she change this path?
2. Describe Annie physically and mentally in your own words. Use as much detail as possible.
3. Why does Annie carry stones in two five-gallon pails for three miles? What is she trying to accomplish?
4. In what ways does Annie's business grow? How does Annie's personality make this growth possible?

Reading Critically

③ Can you think of a recent time when you "changed direction" in your life? Has the change been good for you? Why or why not?

THINKING CRITICALLY

5. Why do you think Annie succeeds in her business? What are the main ingredients of her success?

6. In what ways are the details at the beginning of this narrative essay typical of the year 1903?

7. What does Angelou mean when she says, "Each of us has the right and the responsibility to assess the roads which lie ahead, and those over which we have traveled" (paragraph 11)? In what way is this message basic to an understanding of the essay?

8. Explain the title of the essay. Cite specific details from the essay in your explanation.

DISCOVERING RHETORICAL STRATEGIES

9. Angelou writes this narrative essay in a fairly formal style, using multisyllable words (*concede* rather than *yield* or *let*) and the characters' title and names (Mrs. Annie Johnson instead of Annie Johnson). Why do you think Angelou presents her essay in this way? Describe the tone she maintains throughout the essay.

10. The author uses the metaphor of taking a "new road" to describe Annie Johnson's decision. Is this metaphor effective in your opinion? Why or why not?

11. Over what period of time do you think this story took place? How does the author show her readers that time is passing in this narrative essay?

12. Angelou often ends her essays with lessons that she wants the readers to understand. How does her lesson in the last paragraph of this narrative essay affect the story? Does the story itself go with the lesson? How did you respond to having the author tell you what to think at the end of the story?

MAKING CONNECTIONS

13. In Angelou's essay, Annie Johnson cuts "a new path" for herself by selling food to factory workers. Contrast this sudden change in the direction of her life with similar "new paths" taken by Bill Cosby ("The Baffling Question"), by Brent Staples in "A Brother's Murder," and/or by female weightlifters in Gloria Steinem's "The Politics of Muscle." Who do you think had the most difficult transition to make? Explain your answer.

14. If Angelou, Russell Baker ("The Saturday Evening Post"), Sandra Cisneros ("Only daughter"), and/or Harold Krents ("Darkness at Noon") were discussing the value of persistence and determination in life, which author would argue most strongly for the importance of that quality? Why? Would you agree?

15. Food is an important ingredient not only in Angelou's essay, but also in those written by Ray Bradbury ("Summer Rituals"), Kimberly Wozencraft ("Notes From the Country Club"), and Garrison Keillor ("How the Crab Apple Grew").

Which of these most involves the topic of food? Which the least? Which authors use food as a structuring device in their essays?

IDEAS FOR DISCUSSION/WRITING

Preparing to Write

Write freely about all the major changes you have made in your life: Were most of these changes for the best? How did they benefit you? How did they benefit others? Did they hurt anyone? Do you think most people have trouble changing directions in their lives? Why or why not? How might we all improve our attitudes about change?

Choosing a Topic

1. The editor of your school newspaper has asked you to write a narrative essay about an important change you made in your life. The newspaper is running a series of essays about changing directions in life, and the staff has heard that you have a story to tell. Tell your story in essay form to be printed in the school newspaper.
2. Why are major changes so difficult for us to make? Write a narrative essay for your peers to respond to this question. Use characters to dramatize your answer.
3. Decide on an important truth about life, and then write a narrative essay to support that truth. Make the details as vivid as possible.
4. Go online and find an entrepreneur who inspires you. Possible examples include Shawn Fanning (Napster), Ben Cohen and Jerry Greenfield (Ben & Jerry's Ice Cream), Masaru Ibuka and Akio Morita (Sony), Walt Disney (Disneyland, Walt Disney Pictures), Anita Roddick (The Body Shop), Bill Gates (Microsoft), Oprah Winfrey (Oprah, O, HARPO), Ted Turner (Cable News Network, Turner Network Television), or Martha Stewart (Martha Stewart Omnimedia). Gather enough details about this person's life to write a narrative. Using Angelou's narrative style as a model, organize your story around a central theme or message.

Before beginning your essay, you might want to consult the checklists on page 103.

RUSSELL BAKER   (1925–   )

The Saturday Evening Post

Russell Baker is one of America's foremost satirists and humorists. Born in Virginia, he grew up in New Jersey and Maryland, graduated from Johns Hopkins University, and then served for two years as a pilot in the U.S. Navy. Following the service, he became a newspaper reporter for the *Baltimore Sun,* which sent him to England as its London correspondent. He subsequently joined the staff of the *New York Times* as a member of its Washington bureau. From 1962 to 1998, he wrote his widely syndicated "Observer" column in the *Times,* which blended wry humor, a keen interest in language, and biting social commentary about the Washington scene. His books include *An American in Washington* (1961), *No Cause for Panic* (1964), and *Poor Russell's Almanac* (1972), plus two collections of early essays, *So This Is Depravity* (1980) and *The Rescue of Miss Yaskell and Other Pipe Dreams* (1983). *Growing Up* (1982), a best-seller vividly recounting his own childhood, earned him the 1983 Pulitzer Prize for biography. His more recent publications include *The Good Times* (1989), which continues his life story from approximately age twenty until he began working for the *New York Times* in the early 1960s; *There's a Country in My Cellar: The Best of Russell Baker* (1990), a collection of his newspaper columns; *Inventing the Truth: The Art and Craft of Memoir* (1995, with William Zinsser), and *Looking Back,* a compilation of some of his articles written for *The New York Review of Books* (2002).

Preparing to Read

The following skillfully written essay is an excerpt from Baker's autobiography, *Growing Up.* In it, the author recalls enduring memories from his youth that clearly project the experiences and emotions of his coming of age in 1920s rural Virginia.

Exploring Experience: As you prepare to read this selection, think for a moment about some of your own childhood memories: What were your strengths as a child? Your weaknesses? Have these character traits changed as you've matured? How are you like or unlike various members of your family? How do you react to these similarities and/or differences? What are your main goals in life? How do your character traits affect these goals?

Learning Online: Explore the Norman Rockwell Museum Web site (http://www.nrm.org) to see online exhibits of *Saturday Evening Post* covers and other artistic representations of the 1930s and 1940s. These images represent the time period that Russell Baker describes. How do these pictures differ from your childhood images?

I began working in journalism when I was eight years old. It was my   1
mother's idea. She wanted me to "make something" of myself and, after
a levelheaded appraisal of my strengths, decided I had better start young
if I was to have any chance of keeping up with the competition. ❶

The flaw in my character which she had already spotted was lack of   2
"gumption." My idea of a perfect afternoon was lying in front of the radio
rereading my favorite Big Little Book, *Dick Tracy Meets Stooge Viller.* My
mother despised inactivity. Seeing me having a good time in repose, she was
powerless to hide her disgust. "You've got no more gumption than a bump
on a log," she said. "Get out in the kitchen and help Doris do those dirty
dishes."

My sister Doris, though two years younger than I, had enough gumption   3
for a dozen people. ❷ She positively enjoyed washing dishes, making beds,
and cleaning the house. When she was only seven, she could carry a piece
of short-weighted cheese back to the A&P, threaten the manager with legal
action, and come back triumphantly with the full quarter-pound we'd paid
for and a few ounces extra thrown in for forgiveness. Doris could have made
something of herself if she hadn't been a girl. Because of this defect, however, the best she could hope for was a career as a nurse or schoolteacher, the
only work that capable females were considered up to in those days.

This must have saddened my mother, this twist of fate that had allocated   4
all the gumption to the daughter and left her with a son who was content
with Dick Tracy and Stooge Viller. If disappointed, though, she wasted no energy on self-pity. She would make me make something of myself whether I
wanted to or not. "The Lord helps those who help themselves," she said.
That was the way her mind worked.

She was realistic about the difficulty. Having sized up the material the   5
Lord had given her to mold, she didn't overestimate what she could do with
it. She didn't insist that I grow up to be President of the United States.

Fifty years ago parents still asked boys if they wanted to grow up to be   6
President, and asked it not jokingly but seriously. Many parents who were
hardly more than paupers still believed their sons could do it. Abraham Lincoln had done it. We were only sixty-five years from Lincoln. Many a grandfather who walked among us could remember Lincoln's time. Men of
grandfatherly age were the worst for asking if you wanted to grow up to be
President. A surprising number of little boys said yes and meant it.

I was asked many times myself. No, I would say, I didn't want to grow up   7
to be President. My mother was present during one of these interrogations.

Reading Critically

❶ What does the first paragraph of the essay imply about Baker's opinion of his mother?

❷ What proof does the author offer that his sister Doris had "gumption"?

An elderly uncle, having posed the usual question and exposed my lack of interest in the Presidency, asked, "Well, what *do* you want to be when you grow up?"

I loved to pick through trash piles and collect empty bottles, tin cans with pretty labels, and discarded magazines. The most desirable job on earth sprang instantly to mind. "I want to be a garbage man," I said.   8

My uncle smiled, but my mother had seen the first distressing evidence of a bump budding on a log. "Have a little gumption, Russell," she said. Her calling me Russell was a signal of unhappiness. When she approved of me, I was always "Buddy."   9

When I turned eight years old she decided that the job of starting me on the road toward making something of myself could no longer be safely delayed. "Buddy," she said one day, "I want you to come home right after school this afternoon. Somebody's coming, and I want you to meet him."   10

When I burst in that afternoon, she was in conference in the parlor with an executive ❸ of the Curtis Publishing Company. She introduced me. He bent low from the waist and shook my hand. Was it true as my mother had told him, he asked, that I longed for the opportunity to conquer the world of business?   11

My mother replied that I was blessed with a rare determination to make something of myself.   12

"That's right," I whispered.   13

"But have you got the grit, the character, the never-say-quit spirit it takes to succeed in business?"   14

My mother said I certainly did.   15

"That's right," I said.   16

He eyed me silently for a long pause, as though weighing whether I could be trusted to keep his confidence, then spoke man-to-man. Before taking a crucial step, he said, he wanted to advise me that working for the Curtis Publishing Company placed enormous responsibility on a young man. It was one of the great companies of America. Perhaps the greatest publishing house in the world. I had heard, no doubt, of the *Saturday Evening Post*?   17

Heard of it? My mother said that everyone in our house had heard of the *Saturday Post* and that I, in fact, read it with religious devotion. ❹   18

Then doubtless, he said, we were also familiar with those two monthly pillars of the magazine world, the *Ladies Home Journal* and the *Country Gentleman*.   19

Reading Critically

❸ Do you think the man introduced to Russell is really an "executive" of the Curtis Publishing Company? How does this word betray his mother's manipulative nature?

❹ What does Baker's mother mean when she claims that everyone in her household reads the *Saturday Evening Post* "with religious devotion"?

Indeed we were familiar with them, said my mother.   20

Representing the *Saturday Evening Post* was one of the weightiest honors   21
that could be bestowed in the world of business, he said. He was personally
proud of being a part of the great corporation.

My mother said he had every right to be.   22

Again he studied me as though debating whether I was worthy of a   23
knighthood. Finally: "Are you trustworthy?"

My mother said I was the soul of honesty.   24

"That's right," I said.   25

The caller smiled for the first time. He told me I was a lucky young man.   26
He admired my spunk. Too many young men thought life was all play. Those
young men would not go far in this world. Only a young man willing to
work and save and keep his face washed and his hair neatly combed could
hope to come out on top in a world such as ours. ⑤ Did I truly and sincerely
believe that I was such a young man?

"He certainly does," said my mother.   27

"That's right," I said.   28

He said he had been so impressed by what he had seen of me that he was   29
going to make me a representative of the Curtis Publishing Company. On
the following Tuesday, he said, thirty freshly printed copies of the *Saturday
Evening Post* would be delivered at our door. I would place these magazines,
still damp with the ink of the presses, in a handsome canvas bag, sling it over
my shoulder, and set forth through the streets to bring the best in journalism, fiction, and cartoons to the American public.

He had brought the canvas bag with him. He presented it with reverence   30
fit for a chasuble. He showed me how to drape the sling over my left shoulder and across the chest so that the pouch lay easily accessible to my right
hand, allowing the best in journalism, fiction, and cartoons to be swiftly ex-
tracted and sold to a citizenry whose happiness and security depended upon
us soldiers of the free press.

The following Tuesday I raced home from school, put the canvas bag over   31
my shoulder, dumped the magazines in, and, tilting to the left to balance
their weight on my right hip, embarked on the highway of journalism.

We lived in Belleville, New Jersey, a commuter town at the northern   32
fringe of Newark. It was 1932, the bleakest year of the Depression. ⑥ My father had died two years before, leaving us with a few pieces of Sears, Roebuck furniture and not much else, and my mother had taken Doris and me
to live with one of her younger brothers. This was my Uncle Allen. Uncle
Allen had made something of himself by 1932. As salesman for a soft-drink

---

Reading Critically

⑤ Is this still good advice today? What is your advice for success?
⑥ How many signs of the depression can you find in this essay?

bottler in Newark, he had an income of $30 a week; wore pearl-gray spats, detachable collars, and a three-piece suit; was happily married; and took in threadbare relatives.

With my load of magazines I headed toward Belleville Avenue. That's 33 where the people were. There were two filling stations at the intersection with Union Avenue, as well as an A&P, a fruit stand, a bakery, a barber shop, Zuccarelli's drugstore, and a diner shaped like a railroad car. For several hours I made myself highly visible, shifting position now and then from corner to corner, from shop window to shop window, to make sure everyone could see the heavy black lettering on the canvas bag that said THE SATURDAY EVENING POST. When the angle of the light indicated it was suppertime, I walked back to the house.

"How many did you sell, Buddy?" my mother asked.   34

"None."   35

"Where did you go?"   36

"The corner of Belleville and Union Avenues."   37

"What did you do?"   38

"Stood on the corner waiting for somebody to buy a *Saturday Evening Post*."   39

"You just stood there?"   40

"Didn't sell a single one."   41

"For God's sake, Russell!"   42

Uncle Allen intervened. "I've been thinking about it for some time," he 43 said, "and I've about decided to take the *Post* regularly. Put me down as a regular customer." I handed him a magazine, and he paid me a nickel. It was the first nickel I earned.

Afterwards my mother instructed me in salesmanship. I would have to 44 ring doorbells, address adults with charming self-confidence, and break down resistance with a sales talk pointing out that no one, no matter how poor, could afford to be without the *Saturday Evening Post* in the home.

I told my mother I'd changed my mind about wanting to succeed in the 45 magazine business.

"If you think I'm going to raise a good-for-nothing," she replied, "you've 46 got another think coming." She told me to hit the streets with the canvas bag and start ringing doorbells the instant school was out next day. When I objected that I didn't feel any aptitude for salesmanship, she asked how I'd like to lend her my leather belt so she could whack some sense into me. I bowed to superior will [7] and entered journalism with a heavy heart.

Reading Critically

[7] When Baker admits that he "bowed to superior will," he is clearly being ironic since his mother has threatened to whack him with a belt if he doesn't begin selling the magazine. What other examples of irony can you find in the essay?

My mother and I had fought this battle almost as long as I could re-   47
member. It probably started even before memory began, when I was a country child in northern Virginia and my mother, dissatisfied with my father's
plain workman's life, determined that I would not grow up like him and his
people, with calluses on their hands, overalls on their backs, and fourth-grade
educations in their heads. She had fancier ideas of life's possibilities. Introducing me to the *Saturday Evening Post,* she was trying to wean me as early
as possible from my father's world where men left with their lunch pails at
sunup, worked with their hands until the grime ate into the pores, and died
with a few sticks of mail-order furniture as their legacy. In my mother's vision of the better life there were desks and white collars, well-pressed suits,
evenings of reading and lively talk, and perhaps—if a man were very, very
lucky and hit the jackpot, really made something important of himself—
perhaps there might be a fantastic salary of $5,000 a year to support a big
house and a Buick with a rumble seat and a vacation in Atlantic City.

And so I set forth with my sack of magazines. I was afraid of the dogs that   48
snarled behind the doors of potential buyers. I was timid about ringing the
doorbells of strangers, relieved when no one came to the door, and scared
when someone did. Despite my mother's instructions, I could not deliver an
engaging sales pitch. When a door opened I simply asked, "Want to buy a
Saturday Evening Post?" In Belleville few persons did. It was a town of 30,000
people, and most weeks I rang a fair majority of its doorbells. But I rarely sold
my thirty copies. Some weeks I canvassed the entire town for six days and
still had four or five unsold magazines on Monday evening; then I dreaded
the coming of Tuesday morning, when a batch of thirty fresh *Saturday Evening
Posts* was due at the front door. **8**

"Better get out there and sell the rest of those magazines tonight," my   49
mother would say.

I usually posted myself then at a busy intersection where a traffic light   50
controlled commuter flow from Newark. When the light turned red, I stood
on the curb and shouted my sales pitch at the motorists.

"Want to buy a *Saturday Evening Post?*"   51

One rainy night when car windows were sealed against me, I came back   52
soaked and with not a single sale to report. My mother beckoned to Doris.

"Go back down there with Buddy and show him how to sell these mag-   53
azines," she said.

Brimming with zest, Doris, who was then seven years old, returned with   54
me to the corner. She took a magazine from the bag, and when the light
turned red, she strode to the nearest car and banged her small fist against the

---

Reading Critically

8 How do you think selling is like writing?

closed window. The driver, probably startled at what he took to be a midget assaulting his car, ⁹ lowered the window to stare, and Doris thrust a *Saturday Evening Post* at him.

"You need this magazine," she piped, "and it only costs a nickel."   55

Her salesmanship was irresistible. Before the light changed half a dozen   56
times, she disposed of the entire batch. I didn't feel humiliated. To the contrary. I was so happy I decided to give her a treat. Leading her to the vegetable store on Belleville Avenue, I bought three apples, which cost a nickel, and gave her one.

"You shouldn't waste money," she said.   57

"Eat your apple." I bit into mine.   58

"You shouldn't eat before supper," she said. "It'll spoil your appetite." ¹⁰   59

Back at the house that evening, she dutifully reported me for wasting a   60
nickel. Instead of a scolding, I was rewarded with a pat on the back for having the good sense to buy fruit instead of candy. My mother reached into her bottomless supply of maxims and told Doris, "An apple a day keeps the doctor away."

By the time I was ten I had learned all my mother's maxims by heart.   61
Asking to stay up past normal bedtime, I knew that a refusal would be explained with, "Early to bed and early to rise, makes a man healthy, wealthy, and wise." If I whimpered about having to get up early in the morning, I could depend on her to say, "The early bird gets the worm."

The one I most despised was, "If at first you don't succeed, try, try again."   62
This was the battle cry with which she constantly sent me back into the hopeless struggle whenever I moaned that I had rung every doorbell in town and knew there wasn't a single potential buyer left in Belleville that week. After listening to my explanation, she handed me the canvas bag and said, "If at first you don't succeed . . ."

Three years in that job, which I would gladly have quit after the first day   63
except for her insistence, produced at least one valuable result. My mother finally concluded that I would never make something of myself by pursuing a life in business and started considering careers that demanded less competitive zeal.

One evening when I was eleven, I brought home a short "composition"   64
on my summer vacation which the teacher had graded with an A. Reading it with her own schoolteacher's eye, my mother agreed that it was top-drawer seventh grade prose and complimented me. Nothing more was said about it

---

Reading Critically

⁹ The description of Doris assaulting the car like a "midget" is one among many examples of humor in the essay. Can you find three other humorous images?

¹⁰ Can you find any signs that Doris is growing up to be a carbon copy of her mother?

immediately, but a new idea had taken life in her mind. Halfway through supper she suddenly interrupted the conversation.

"Buddy," she said, "maybe you could be a writer." 65

I clasped the idea to my heart. I had never met a writer, had shown no previous urge to write, and hadn't a notion how to become a writer, but I loved stories and thought that making up stories must surely be almost as much fun as reading them. Best of all, though, and what really gladdened my heart, was the ease of the writer's life.◆ Writers did not have to trudge through the town peddling from canvas bags, defending themselves against angry dogs, being rejected by surly strangers. Writers did not have to ring doorbells. So far as I could make out, what writers did couldn't even be classified as work. 66

I was enchanted. Writers didn't have to have any gumption at all. I did not dare tell anybody for fear of being laughed at in the schoolyard, but secretly I decided that what I'd like to be when I grew up was a writer. 67

UNDERSTANDING DETAILS

1. How does Baker's ideal day differ from that of his sister?
2. According to the author's mother, what is the main flaw in his character? How does this flaw eventually affect his choice of a career?
3. Why does Baker feel he has no "aptitude for salesmanship" (paragraph 46)? What has led him to this conclusion?
4. Which of his mother's maxims does the author dislike the most? Explain his reaction.

THINKING CRITICALLY

5. Why does Baker begin this selection with a comparison of his personality and his sister's? What does this comparison have to do with the rest of the essay?
6. Why does the author's mother insist that he work for the *Saturday Evening Post*? What does she think he will gain from the experience? What does he actually learn?
7. What "battle" (paragraph 47) have the author and his mother been fighting for as long as he can remember? Who finally wins this battle?
8. Why is Baker so delighted with the idea of becoming a writer when he grows up? How is this notion compatible with his personality?

DISCOVERING RHETORICAL STRATEGIES

9. How does Baker arrange the details in this excerpt? Why do you think he organizes them in this way? How would a different arrangement have changed the essay?

Reading Critically

◆ Do you think a writer's life is "easy"? Why or why not?

10. Who do you think is Baker's intended audience? Describe them in detail. How did you come to this conclusion?

11. What is the climax of Baker's narrative? How does he lead up to and develop this climactic moment? What stylistic traits tell us that this is the most exciting point in the story?

12. Besides narration, what other rhetorical strategies does Baker draw on to develop his thesis? Give examples of each of these strategies.

MAKING CONNECTIONS

13. Baker insists on the importance of dedicating oneself to a career. Compare and contrast his feelings on this subject with similar sentiments found in essays by Sandra Cisneros ("Only daughter"), William Ouchi ("Japanese and American Workers: Two Casts of Mind"), and/or Gloria Steinem ("The Politics of Muscle"). How dedicated do you intend to be to your own future career?

14. How is young Russell Baker's naive conception of a writer's "easy" life different from the views on writing expressed by Sandra Cisneros ("Only daughter"), Amy Tan ("Mother Tongue"), and/or Sherman Alexie ("The Joy of Reading and Writing: Superman and Me")? Which of these authors would argue most fervently that writing is "hard" work? How do you feel about the process of writing? Is it easy or difficult for you? Explain your answer.

15. Russell Baker's mother had a strong influence over him as he grew up. Imagine a conversation among Baker, Bill Cosby ("The Baffling Question"), Judith Wallerstein and Sandra Blakeslee ("Second Chances for Children of Divorce"), and/or Mary Pipher ("Beliefs About Families") concerning the importance of proper parental guidance as a child matures. Which author would be most adamant about the importance of the role of parents in a child's upbringing? Explain your answer.

IDEAS FOR DISCUSSION/WRITING

Preparing to Write

Write freely about yourself in relation to your aspirations: What type of person are you? What do you think about? What are your ideals? Your hopes? Your dreams? Your fears? What do you enjoy doing in your spare time? How are you different from other members of your family? Is anyone in your family a model for you? How have members of your immediate family affected your daily life—past and present? Your career goals? How do you anticipate your family will affect your future?

Choosing a Topic

1. Write a narrative essay introducing yourself to your English class. To explain and define your identity, include descriptions of family members whenever appropriate.

2. Write a narrative that helps explain to a friend how you got involved in a current interest. To expand upon your narrative, refer whenever possible to your long-term goals and aspirations.

3. Ten years from now, your local newspaper decides to devote an entire section to people getting started in careers. You are asked to submit the story of how you got involved in your profession (whatever it may be). Write a narrative that might appear in your hometown newspaper ten years from now; be sure to give the article a catchy headline.
4. Reflect on your worst memory of working at a particular job or chore. Write a narrative e-mail to Baker in which you explain how an experience that seemed horrible at the time actually had positive results. Following Baker's example, establish a strong sense of time and place in your narrative.

Before beginning your essay, you might want to consult the checklists on page 103.

SANDRA CISNEROS   (1954–   )

Only daughter

Born in Chicago, Sandra Cisneros was the Only daughter raised in a family with six brothers. She moved frequently during her childhood, eventually earning a B.A. in English from Loyola University and an M.F.A. in creative writing from the University of Iowa, where she developed her unique voice of a strong and independent working-class, Mexican-American woman. Her first book, *The House on Mango Street* (1984), is a loosely structured series of vignettes focusing upon the isolation and cultural conflicts endured by Latina women in America. Later publications include *My Wicked, Wicked Ways* (1987), *Woman Hollering Creek* (1991), *The Future Is Mestizo: Life Where Cultures Meet* (2000), and *Caramelo* (2002). Critics have described her works of fiction as "poetic": "nearly every sentence contains an explosive sensory image. She gives us unforgettable characters that we want to lift off the page and hang out with for a while." Asked to analyze her writing style, Cisneros has explained that "I am a woman, and I am a Latina. Those are the things that make my writing distinctive. Those are the things that give my writing power. They are the things that give it *sabor* (flavor), that give it *picante* (spice)." She currently lives in a bright purple house in San Antonio with five cats, three dogs, and two parrots.

Preparing to Read

"Only daughter," an essay first published in *Glamour*, chronicles one of the author's most memorable experiences on a visit to her parents' home in Chicago. Full of family history, the story uses the reunion as a focus for Cisneros's memories and observations about life in a Mexican family.

Exploring Experience: As you prepare to read this essay, take a few moments to consider the many social and cultural influences that shape your life: What is your family like? What activities do you enjoy? Have you ever felt that your family didn't accept these activities? Have you ever been angry at the extent to which social or cultural pressures have governed your life? How did you react to these forces? Can you think of a specific situation in which you overcame social or cultural differences? What were the circumstances? What was the result?

Learning Online: Explore the PBS "American Family" Web site (http://www.pbs.org/americanfamily) for a dynamic look into the Latino culture. While reading Cisneros's narrative, consider how her experience relates to the accounts on the Web site.

Once, several years ago, when I was just starting out my writing ca-   1
reer, I was asked to write my own contributor's note for an anthology. I wrote: "I am the only daughter in a family of six sons. *That*
explains everything."

Well, I've thought that ever since, and yes, it explains a lot to me, but for   2
the reader's sake I should have written: "I am the only daughter in a *Mexican*
family of six sons." Or even: "I am the only daughter of a Mexican father and
a Mexican-American mother." Or: "I am the only daughter of a working-
class family of nine." All of these had everything to do with who I am today.

I was/am the only daughter and *only* a daughter. Being an only daughter   3
in a family of six sons forced me by circumstance to spend a lot of time by
myself because my brothers felt it beneath them to play with a *girl* in public. But that aloneness, that loneliness, was good for a would-be writer—it
allowed me time to think and think, to imagine, to read and prepare myself.

Being only a daughter for my father meant my destiny would lead me to be-   4
come someone's wife. That's what he believed. But when I was in the fifth grade
and shared my plans for college with him, I was sure he understood. I remember my father saying, "*Que bueno, mi'ja,* that's good." That meant a lot to me, especially since my brothers thought the idea hilarious. What I didn't realize was
that my father thought college was good for girls—good for finding a husband.
After four years in college and two more in graduate school, and still no husband,
my father shakes his head even now and says I wasted all that education. ◆ 1

In retrospect, I'm lucky my father believed daughters were meant for hus-   5
bands. It meant it didn't matter if I majored in something silly like English.
After all, I'd find a nice professional eventually, right? This allowed me the liberty to putter about embroidering my little poems and stories without my
father interrupting with so much as a "What's that you're writing?"

But the truth is, I wanted him to interrupt. I wanted my father to   6
understand what it was I was scribbling, to introduce me as "My only daughter, the writer." Not as "This is my only daughter. She teaches." *Es maestra*—
teacher. Not even *profesora.*

In a sense, everything I have ever written has been for him, to win his ap-   7
proval even though I know my father can't read English words, even though
my father's only reading includes the brown-ink *Esto* sports magazines from
Mexico City and the bloody *¡Alarma!* magazines that feature yet another
sighting of *La Virgen de Guadalupe* on a tortilla or a wife's revenge on her phi-
landering husband by bashing his skull in with a *molcajete* (a kitchen mortar
made of volcanic rock). Or the *fotonovelas,* the little picture paperbacks with
tragedy and trauma erupting from the characters' mouths in bubbles.

Reading Critically
◆ Which type of discrimination is worst: gender, ethnic, or religious? Why do you think so?

A father represents, then, the public majority. A public who is disinterested   8
in reading, and yet one whom I am writing about and for, and privately trying to woo.

When we were growing up in Chicago, we moved a lot because of my   9
father. He suffered bouts of nostalgia. Then we'd have to let go of our flat,
store the furniture with mother's relatives, load the station wagon with baggage and bologna sandwiches and head south. To Mexico City.

We came back, of course. To yet another Chicago flat, another Chicago   10
neighborhood, another Catholic school. Each time, my father would seek out
the parish priest in order to get a tuition break, and complain or boast: "I have
seven sons." ❷

He meant *siete hijos,* seven children, but he translated it as "sons." "I have   11
seven sons." To anyone who would listen. The Sears Roebuck employee
who sold us the washing machine. The short-order cook where my father
ate his ham-and-eggs breakfasts. "I have seven sons." As if he deserved a medal
from the state.

My papa. He didn't mean anything by the mistranslation, I'm sure. But   12
somehow I could feel myself being erased. I'd tug my father's sleeve and
whisper: "Not seven sons. Six! and one *daughter.*"

When my oldest brother graduated from medical school, he fulfilled my   13
father's dream that we study hard and use this—our heads, instead of this—
our hands. Even now my father's hands are thick and yellow, stubbed by a history of hammer and nails and twine and coils and springs. "Use this," my
father said, tapping his head, "and not this," showing us those hands. He always looked tired when he said it.

Wasn't college an investment? And hadn't I spent all those years in college?   14
And if I didn't marry, what was it all for? Why would anyone go to college and
then choose to be poor? ❸ Especially someone who has always been poor.

Last year, after ten years of writing professionally, the financial rewards   15
started to trickle in. My second National Endowment for the Arts Fellowship. A guest professorship at the University of California, Berkeley. My book,
which sold to a major New York publishing house.

At Christmas, I flew home to Chicago. The house was throbbing, same as   16
always; hot *tamales* and sweet *tamales* hissing in my mother's pressure cooker,
and everybody—my mother, six brothers, wives, babies, aunts, cousins—talking too loud and at the same time, like in a Fellini film, because that's just
how we are.

Reading Critically

❷ What are the principal differences between Cisneros and her father?

❸ What do you believe is the relationship between attending college and the salary you will
earn after graduation?

I went upstairs to my father's room. One of my stories had just been trans-   17
lated into Spanish and published in an anthology of Chicano writing, and I
wanted to show it to him. Ever since he recovered from a stroke two years ago,
my father likes to spend his leisure hours horizontally. And that's how I found
him, watching a Pedro Infante movie on Galavision and eating rice pudding.

There was a glass filmed with milk on the bedside table. There were sev-   18
eral vials of pills and balled Kleenex. And on the floor, one black sock and a
plastic urinal that I didn't want to look at but looked at anyway. Pedro Infante was about to burst into song, and my father was laughing. 4

I'm not sure if it was because my story was translated into Spanish, or be-   19
cause it was published in Mexico, or perhaps because the story dealt with Te-
peyac, the *colonia* my father was raised in and the house he grew up in, but
at any rate, my father punched the mute button on his remote control and
read my story.

I sat on the bed next to my father and waited. He read it very slowly. As   20
if he were reading each line over and over. He laughed at all the right places
and read lines he liked out loud. He pointed and asked questions: "Is this So-
and-so?" "Yes," I said. He kept reading.

When he was finally finished, after what seemed like hours, my father   21
looked up and asked: "Where can we get more copies of this for the relatives?"

Of all the wonderful things that happened to me last year, that was the   22
most wonderful.

UNDERSTANDING DETAILS

1. How many children are in Cisneros's family? How many are boys?
2. Why does Cisneros's father always say he has seven sons? Why is this detail significant?
3. Why did Cisneros's father let her go to college? Explain your answer.
4. What are the differences in the way the author's father views his sons and his
   daughter?

THINKING CRITICALLY

5. What does Cisneros mean when she says, "I am the only daughter and *only* a
   daughter" (paragraph 3)?
6. What does her cultural heritage have to do with the fact that she is the only
   daughter?
7. Why does Cisneros write for her father even though he can't read English?
8. Why was her father's reaction to her story published in Spanish "the most wonderful" (paragraph 22) thing that happened to her last year? Why is her father's
   opinion so important to her?

Reading Critically

4 What would your parents' TV viewing habits tell others about them?

DISCOVERING RHETORICAL STRATEGIES

9. From what point of view does Cisneros write this narrative essay? How does this particular point of view help us understand her attitude toward the experience?

10. In writing this essay, Cisneros is making a comment about families in general and Mexican families in particular. What is her ultimate message? What details help you understand this message? Does the fact that she doesn't capitalize "daughter" in her title have anything to do with this message?

11. How does Cisneros organize the details of this narrative? Is this the most effective order for what she is trying to say?

12. Although Cisneros's essay is primarily narrative, what other rhetorical strategies does she use to make her point? Give examples of each.

MAKING CONNECTIONS

13. In "Only daughter," Sandra Cisneros describes the importance of her father's support of and appreciation for her writing career. Compare and contrast the theme of family support described by Sandra Cisneros, Russell Baker ("The Saturday Evening Post"), and/or Mary Pipher ("Beliefs about Families"). Which author would argue that support from one's family is most crucial to our development as a person? Why?

14. Both Sandra Cisneros and Amy Tan ("Mother Tongue") became extremely successful writers in English although they spoke another language at home as they grew up. Can you find any other common denominators in the experiences of these two authors that account for their current skill in using the English language?

15. Compare and contrast the use of examples in the essays by Sandra Cisneros, Harold Krentz ("Darkness at Noon"), and/or Brent Staples ("A Brother's Murder"). Which essay is most densely packed with examples? Which uses example most effectively? Which least effectively? Why?

IDEAS FOR DISCUSSION/WRITING

Preparing to Write

Write freely about a time in your life when you did not fit in with your own family: What were the circumstances? How did you feel? What were your alternatives? Did you take any action? What were the motivating forces for this action? Were you satisfied with the outcome? How do you feel about this experience now?

Choosing a Topic

1. Write a narrative essay telling your classmates about a time you did not fit in. Make a special effort to communicate your feelings regarding this experience. Remember to choose your details and point of view with an overall purpose in mind.

2. What is America's system of social classes? Where do you fit into the structure? Does our system allow for much mobility between classes? Write a narrative

essay for your classmates explaining your understanding of the American class system. Use yourself and/or a friend as an example.

3. Explain in a coherent essay written for the general public why you think we are all sometimes motivated by cultural or personal influences beyond our control. Refer to the Cisneros essay or to experiences of your own to support your explanation.

4. Cisneros shares personal details about her family while recounting her struggle to gain recognition from her father. Consider a time when you attempted to receive recognition from a family member. Using Cisneros's narrative style as a model, write an essay describing your experience. Imagine that your essay will be published as part of PBS's "American Family" online collection.

Before beginning your essay, you might want to consult the checklists on page 103.

GARRISON KEILLOR   (1942–   )

How the Crab Apple Grew

Best known for his creation of the Peabody Award–winning radio program *A Prairie Home Companion,* Garrison Keillor, a native of Anoka, Minnesota, began his career as a radio announcer and producer during his student days at the University of Minnesota. His show features an eclectic mix of traditional jazz and folk music, supplemented by Keillor's rambling, nostalgic, and often hilarious anecdotes about the zany inhabitants of the fictitious small town of Lake Wobegon, Minnesota. Chief among its residents are Father Emil, the local priest who blesses small animals on the lawn of Our Lady of Perpetual Responsibility Church; Dorothy, the garrulous owner of the Chatterbox Cafe; and Dr. Nute, a retired dentist who coaxes trout toward his fishing lure by intoning, "Open wide . . . this may sting a bit." Keillor—a tall, soft-spoken man who often performs in a tuxedo, high-top sneakers, red socks, and red suspenders—even has a pseudosponsor for the show: Powdermilk Biscuits, "a whole-wheat treat that gives shy people the strength to do what has to be done." Thus far, Keillor's monologues have spawned a number of short stories published in the *New Yorker* and several books, including *Happy to Be Here: Stories and Comic Pieces* (1982), *Lake Wobegon Days* (1985), *Leaving Home* (1987), *We Are Still Married* (1989), *WLT: A Radio Romance* (1992), *The Book of Guys* (1993), *Wobegon Boy* (1997), *Me: By Jimmy "Big Boy" Valente as Told to Garrison Keillor* (1999), *Lake Wobegon Summer 1956* (2001), and *Good Poems* (2002).

Preparing to Read

Taken from *Leaving Home,* this graceful and humorous story is a masterful demonstration by Keillor of how to write a narrative essay. In response to an English assignment, Keillor takes his main character through a series of memories that helps her understand her life a little better.

Exploring Experience: As you prepare to read this selection, take a few minutes to think about various items in your life (in your backyard, in your house, at school, at a friend's) that have special meaning to you: What are these items? Why is each of them significant? How do other people relate to these items? In what ways do your surroundings tell different stories about you? What items in your life bring complete stories to your mind? What are some of these stories?

Learning Online: Using Google's search engine (http://www. google.com), click on the "Images" tab to conduct a picture search for the term "crab apple tree." What stories come to mind when viewing these photos? Consider how you could develop a narrative around one of these images.

It has been a quiet week in Lake Wobegon. It was warm and sunny on 1
Sunday, and on Monday the flowering crab in the Dieners' backyard
burst into blossom. Suddenly, in the morning, when everyone turned
their backs for a minute, the tree threw off its bathrobe and stood trembling,
purple, naked, revealing all its innermost flowers. When you saw it standing
where weeks before had been a bare stick stuck in the dirt, you had to stop;
it made your head spin.

Becky Diener sat upstairs in her bedroom and looked at the tree. She was 2
stuck on an assignment from Miss Melrose for English, a 750-word personal
essay, "Describe your backyard as if you were seeing it for the first time."
After an hour she had thirty-nine words, which she figured would mean
she'd finish at 1:45 P.M. Tuesday, four hours late, and therefore would get an
F even if the essay was great, which it certainly wasn't. ❶

How can you describe your backyard as if you'd never seen it? If you'd 3
never seen it, you'd have grown up someplace else, and wouldn't be yourself; you'd be someone else entirely, and how are you supposed to know what
that person would think?

She imagined seeing the backyard in 1996, returning home from Holly- 4
wood. "Welcome Becky!" said the big white banner across McKinley Street
as the pink convertible drove slowly along, everyone clapping and cheering
as she cruised by, Becky Belafonte the movie star, and got off at her old
house. "Here," she said to the reporters, "is where I sat as a child and dreamed
my dreams, under this beautiful flowering crab. I dreamed I was a Chinese
princess." Then a reporter asked, "Which of your teachers was the most important to you, encouraging you and inspiring you?" And just then she saw
an old woman's face in the crowd, Miss Melrose pleading, whispering, "Say
me, oh please, say me," and Becky looked straight at her as she said, "Oh, there
were so many, I couldn't pick out one, they were all about the same, you
know. But perhaps Miss—Miss—oh, I can't remember her name—she taught
English, I think—Miss Milross? She was one of them. But there were so
many."

She looked at her essay. "In my backyard is a tree that has always been ex- 5
tremely important to me since I was six years old when my dad came home
one evening with this bag in the trunk and he said, 'Come here and help me
plant this'—" ❷

She crumpled the sheet of paper and started again. 6

Reading Critically

❶ What was the topic of the toughest essay you ever had to write? How did you finally
complete it?

❷ Why is each of these introductory sentences a bad start to Becky's essay?

"One evening when I was six years old, my father arrived home as he cus-   7
tomarily did around 5:30 or 6:00 P.M. except this evening he had a wonderful
surprise for me, he said, as he led me toward the car.

"My father is not the sort of person who does surprising things very often   8
so naturally I was excited that evening when he said he had something for
me in the car, having just come home from work where he had been. I was
six years old at the time."

She took out a fresh sheet. "Six years old was a very special age for me and   9
one thing that made it special was when my dad and I planted a tree together
in our backyard. Now it is grown and every spring it gives off large purple
blossoms . . ."

The tree was planted by her dad, Harold, in 1976, ten years after he mar-   10
ried her mother, Marlys. They grew up on Taft Street, across from each other,
a block from the ballfield. They liked each other tremendously, and then they
were in love, as much as you can be when you're so young. Thirteen and fourteen years old and sixteen and seventeen: they looked at each other a lot. She
came and sat in his backyard to talk with his mother and help her shell peas
but really to look at Harold as he mowed the lawn, and then he disappeared
into the house and she sat waiting for him, and of course he was in the
kitchen looking out at her. It's how we all began, when our parents looked
at each other, as we say, "when you were just a gleam in your father's eye,"
or your mother's, depending on who saw who first.

Marlys was long-legged, lanky, had short black hair and sharp eyes that   11
didn't miss anything. She came over to visit the Dieners every chance she
got. ❸ Her father was a lost cause, like the Confederacy, like the search for
the Northwest Passage. He'd been prayed for and suffered for and fought for
and spoken for, by people who loved him dearly, and when all was said and
done, he just reached for the gin bottle and said, "I don't know what you're
talking about," and he didn't. He was a sore embarrassment to Marlys, a
clown, a joke, and she watched Harold for evidence that he wasn't similar.
One night she dropped in at the Dieners' and came upon a party where
Harold, now nineteen, and his friends were drinking beer by the pail. Harold
flopped down on his back and put his legs in the air and a pal put a lit match
up to Harold's rear end and blue flame came out like a blowtorch, and Marlys
went home disgusted and didn't speak to him for two years.

Harold went crazy. She graduated from high school and started attending   12
dances with a geography teacher named Stu Jasperson, who was tall and
dark-haired, a subscriber to *Time* magazine, educated at Saint Cloud Normal School, and who flew a red Piper Cub airplane. Lake Wobegon had no

---

Reading Critically
❸ Why do you think Marlys visited the Dieners' house so frequently?

airstrip except for Tollerud's pasture, so Stu kept his plane in Saint Cloud. When he was en route to and from the plane was almost the only time Harold got to see Marlys and try to talk sense into her. But she was crazy about Stu the aviator, not Harold the hardware clerk, and in an hour Stu came buzzing overhead doing loops and dives and dipping his wings. Harold prayed for him to crash. Marlys thought Stu was the sun and the moon; all Harold could do was sit and watch her, in the backyard, staring up, her hand shielding her eyes, saying, "Oh, isn't he marvelous?" as Stu performed aerial feats and then shut off the throttle and glided overhead singing "Vaya con Dios" to her. "Yes, he is marvelous," said Harold, thinking, "DIE DIE DIE." ◆**4**

That spring, Marlys was in charge of the Sweethearts Banquet at the   **13** Lutheran church. Irene Holm had put on a fancy winter Sweethearts Banquet with roast lamb, and Marlys wanted to top her and serve roast beef with morel mushrooms, a first for a church supper in Lake Wobegon. Once Irene had referred to Marlys's dad as a lush.

Morel mushrooms are a great delicacy. They are found in the wild by peo-   **14** ple who walk fifteen miles through the woods to get ten of them and then never tell the location to a soul, not even on their deathbeds to a priest. So Marlys's serving them at the banquet would be like putting out emeralds for party favors. It would blow Irene Holm out of the water and show people that even if Marlys's dad was a lush, she was still someone to be reckoned with. ◆**5**

Two men felt the call to go and search for morels: Harold put on his Red   **15** Wing boots and knapsack and headed out one evening with a flashlight. He was in the woods all night. Morels are found near the base of the trunk of a dead elm that's been dead three years, which you can see by the way moonlight doesn't shine on it, and he thought he knew where some were, but around midnight he spotted a bunch of flashlights behind him, a posse of morelists bobbing along on his trail, so he veered off and hiked five miles in the wrong direction to confuse them, and by then the sun was coming up so he went home to sleep. He woke at 2:00 P.M., hearing Stu flying overhead, and in an instant he knew. Dead elms! Of course! Stu could spot them from the air, send his ground crew to collect them for Marlys, and the Sweethearts Banquet would be their engagement dinner.

Stu might have done just that, but he wanted to put on a show and land   **16** the Cub in Lake Wobegon. He circled around and around, and came in low to the west of town, disappearing behind the trees. "He's going to crash!" cried Marlys, and they all jumped in their cars and tore out, expecting to find the young hero lying bloody and torn in the dewy grass, with a dying poem

---

Reading Critically

◆**4** Describe Stu in your own words.

◆**5** How does the narrator's occasional use of clichés help characterize him?

on his lips. But there he was standing tall beside the craft, having landed successfully in a field of spring wheat. They all mobbed around him, and he told how he was going up to find the morels and bring them back for Marlys.

There were about forty people there. They seemed to enjoy it, so he drew   17
out his speech, talking about the lure of aviation and his boyhood and various things so serious that he didn't notice Harold behind him by the plane or notice the people who noticed what Harold was doing and laughed. ❻ Stu was too inspired to pay attention to the laughter. He talked about how he once wanted to fly to see the world but once you get up in the air you can see that Lake Wobegon is the most beautiful place of all, a lot of warm horse manure like that, and then he gave them a big manly smile and donned his flying cap and scarf and favored them with a second and third smile and a wave, and he turned and there was Harold to help him into the cockpit.

"Well, thanks," said Stu, "mighty kind, mighty kind." Harold jumped to   18
the propeller and threw it once and twice, and the third time the engine fired, and Stu adjusted the throttle, checked the gauges, flapped the flaps, fit his goggles, and never noticed the ground was wet and his wheels were sunk in. He'd parked in a wet spot, and then during his address someone had gone around and made it wetter, so when Stu pulled back on the throttle the Cub just sat, and he gave it more juice and she creaked a little, and he gave it more and the plane stood on its head with its tail in the air and dug in.

It pitched forward like the *Titanic,* ❼ and the propeller in the mud sounded   19
like he'd eaten too many green apples. The door opened and Stu climbed out, trying to look dignified and studious as he tilted eastward and spun, and Harold said, "Stu, we didn't say we wanted those mushrooms sliced."

Harold went out that afternoon and collected five hundred morel mush-   20
rooms around one dead elm tree. Marlys made her mark at the Sweethearts dinner, amazing Irene Holm, who had thought Marlys was common. Harold also brought out of the woods a bouquet of flowering crab apple and asked her to marry him, and eventually she decided to.

The tree in the backyard came about a few years afterward. They'd been   21
married awhile, had two kids, and some of the gloss had worn off their life, and one afternoon, Harold, trying to impress his kids and make his wife laugh, jumped off the garage roof, pretending he could fly, and landed wrong, twisting his ankle. He lay in pain, his eyes full of tears, and his kids said, "Oh poor Daddy, poor Daddy," and Marlys said, "You're not funny, you're ridiculous."

Reading Critically

❻ What do you think Harold was doing behind Stu's plane?

❼ How does this reference to the sinking of the Titanic help predict what will happen between Stu and Marlys?

He got up on his bum ankle and went in the woods and got her a pint   22
of morels and a branch from the flowering crab apple. He cut a root from
another crab apple and planted the root in the ground. "Look, kids," he said.
He sharpened the branch with his hatchet and split the root open and stuck
the branch in and wrapped a cloth around it and said, "Now, there, that will
be a tree." They said, "Daddy, will that really be a tree?" He said, "Yes." Marlys
said, "Don't be ridiculous."

He watered it and tended it and, more than that, he came out late at night   23
and bent down and said, "GROW. GROW. GROW." The graft held, it grew, and
one year it was interesting, and the next it was impressive and then wonderful,
and finally it was magnificent. It's the most magnificent thing in the Dieners'
backyard. Becky finished writing 750 words late that night and lay down to
sleep. A backyard is a novel about us, and when we sit there on a summer day,
we hear the dialogue and see the characters.

UNDERSTANDING DETAILS

1. Where does this narrative essay take place? Describe this particular place in detail. What one word might characterize this setting?
2. Why is Becky worried about this particular assignment?
3. How many false starts does Becky make when she is trying to write this essay?
   What causes those false starts?
4. Explain the rivalry between Harold and Stu. What do they both want?

THINKING CRITICALLY

5. How are the tree and Becky's writing assignment related?
6. Why does Marlys finally marry Harold?
7. What can you learn about writing from Becky's approach to this essay? How
   does she finally get started? How does she keep her essay going? How does she
   keep it focused? What truths from this experience can you apply to your own
   writing?
8. What does Keillor mean when he says, "A backyard is a novel about us, and
   when we sit there on a summer day, we hear the dialogue and see the characters" (paragraph 23)?

DISCOVERING RHETORICAL STRATEGIES

9. Keillor starts many of his narratives with "It has been a quiet week in Lake
   Wobegon." What effect does this beginning have on the rest of the essay?
10. What metaphor or comparison does Keillor use to explain in the beginning of
    his essay that the tree has bloomed? How effective is this opening? Explain your
    answer.

11. What does this particular crab apple symbolize? Explain your answer in detail.
12. How appropriate is the title of this essay? What are some other possible titles?

MAKING CONNECTIONS

13. Imagine that Mary Pipher ("Beliefs About Families") and Judith Wallerstein and Sandra Blakeslee ("Second Chances for Children of Divorce") have just read Keillor's essay about the courtship of Harold and Marlys Diener. According to these authors, how successful will the marriage between Harold and Marlys probably be?

14. Compare and contrast Keillor's technique of recalling the past in this essay with similar recollections in Ray Bradbury's "Summer Rituals," Russell Baker's "The Saturday Evening Post," and/or Phyllis Schneider's "Memory: Tips You'll Never Forget." Which author's technique of historical reporting seems most vivid and convincing to you? Explain why.

15. Throughout his essay, Keillor mentions a number of details that will strike most readers as funny. How is Keillor's use of humor different from that of Bill Cosby ("The Baffling Question"), Jessica Mitford ("Behind the Formaldehyde Curtain"), and/or Mary Roach ("Meet the Bickersons")? Which of these essays do you find most entertaining? Explain your answer.

IDEAS FOR DISCUSSION/WRITING

Preparing to Write

Write freely about various symbols in your life or your family's life: What are these symbols? What do they represent? Which of the symbols remind you of various relationships within your family? Which of these symbols are positive? Which are negative? Which symbols remind you of important stories about yourself or other family members? Why are these stories important? What makes specific family stories so important?

Choosing a Topic

1. Write a narrative essay introducing yourself to your English class through a special item in your life. To explain and define your identity, include your relationship to this item in your essay.

2. Write a narrative essay that explains how your parents met. What were the highlights of this meeting? Where did it lead? What is their relationship like now?

3. Your school newspaper is running a series of articles on symbols in our lives. You have been asked to submit a narrative essay on the item that best represents you as a student in college. What is this item? How does it represent you? Shape your answers to these questions into a narrative essay.

4. Return to Google's image search (http://www.google.com) and click on the "Images" tab. Enter "family" as your search term. Select a family photo from the

listings, and tell their story. Create a narrative that centers on an important event in this family's imagined life. Be sure to use specific details, as Keillor does, to provide a setting and purpose for your narrative.

Before beginning your essay, you might want to consult the checklists on page 103.

Chapter Writing Assignments

Practicing Narration

1. Think of a story that is often repeated by your family members because of its special significance or its humor. Retell the story to an audience who does not know your family, and explain to your readers the story's significance.
2. What has been the most challenging and life-changing event in your life? Remember this event as clearly as you can by noting special details on scratch paper. Write an essay that describes what led up to this event, what happened, and how you reacted to the event. Explain why this experience was so challenging and/or life-changing.
3. Think of a time when you received a very special gift. Tell the story of how you received this gift, who gave it to you, and why it was memorable. For a more sophisticated approach, try to think of gifts that are not material or tangible objects, but rather intangible qualities or concepts (such as love, life, and happiness).

Exploring Ideas

4. Write an essay that identifies the most important qualities in a friend. Explain how each quality is important to a meaningful and fulfilling friendship.
5. Cut an advertisement out of a magazine or newspaper. Examine its "story" and the way the advertiser is selling the product. Write an essay that discusses the effect of advertising on individuals and on American society. How honest or believable should advertising be? What are our expectations for advertising?
6. Describe a time when you quit a job or hobby that others thought you should continue. Discuss the principal features of this activity, your frustration with them, and the main aspects of the job or hobby that others valued. In retrospect, do you think you made a wise decision?

Analyzing Visual Images

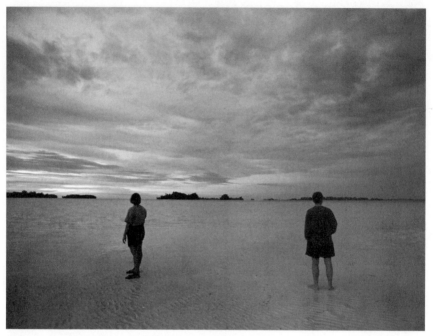

Photo © www.danheller.com/Dan Heller Photography.

7. Think of a time when you went to the beach. Tell a story based on your trip. What was most memorable? What simple pleasures pleased you most? Why was this particular trip to the beach important or noteworthy?

8. Reflect on the picture on page 93 at the beginning of this chapter. Develop the story that might lead up to this picture as its conclusion.

Chapter 3

EXAMPLE
Illustrating Ideas

Citing an example to help make a point is one of the most instinctive techniques we use in communication. If, for instance, you state that being an internationally ranked tennis player requires constant practice, a friend might challenge that assertion and ask what you mean by "constant practice." When you respond "at least three hours a day," your friend might ask for more specific proof. At this stage in the discussion, you could offer the following illustrations to support your statement: When not on tour, Andy Roddick practices three hours per day; Maria Sharapova, four hours; and Roger Federer, five hours. Your friend's doubt will have been answered through your use of examples.

DEFINING EXAMPLES

Well-chosen examples and illustrations are an essay's building blocks. They are drawn from your experience, your observations, and your reading. They help you *show* rather than *tell* what you mean, usually by supplying concrete details (references to what we can see, smell, taste, hear, or touch) to support abstract ideas (such as faith, hope, understanding, and love), by providing specifics ("I like chocolate") to explain generalizations ("I like sweets"), and by giving definite references ("Turn left at the second stoplight") to clarify vague statements ("Turn in a few blocks"). Though illustrations take many forms, writers often find themselves indebted to description or narration (or some combination of the two) in order to supply enough relevant examples to achieve their rhetorical intent.

As you might suspect, examples are important ingredients in producing exciting, vivid prose. Just as crucial is the fact that carefully chosen examples often encourage your readers to feel one way or another about an issue being discussed. If you tell your parents, for instance, that living in a college dormitory is not conducive to academic success, they may doubt your word, perhaps thinking that you are simply attempting to coerce money out of them for an apartment. You can help dispel this notion, however, by giving them specific examples of the chaotic nature of dorm life: the party down the hall that broke up at 2:00 A.M. when you had a chemistry exam that same morning at 8 o'clock; the stereo next door that seems to be stuck on its highest decibel level at all hours of the day and night; and the new "friend" you recently acquired who thinks you are the best listener in the world—especially when everyone else has the good sense to be asleep. After such a detailed and well-documented explanation, your parents could hardly deny the strain of this difficult environment on your studies. Examples can be very persuasive.

The following paragraphs written by a student use examples to explain how the writer reacts to boredom in his life. As you read this excerpt, notice how the writer shows rather than tells the readers how he copes with boredom by providing exciting details that are concrete, specific, and definite.

We all deal with boredom in our own ways. Unfortunately, most of us have to deal with it far too often. Some people actually seek boredom. Being bored means that they are not required to do anything; being boring means that no one wants anything from them. In short, these people equate boredom with peace and relaxation. But for the rest of us, boredom is not peaceful. It produces anxiety.

Most people deal with boredom by trying to distract themselves from boring circumstances. Myself, I'm a reader. At the breakfast table over a boring bowl of cereal, I read the cereal box, the milk carton, the wrapper on the bread. (Have you ever noticed how many of those ingredients are unpronounceable?) Waiting in a doctor's office, I will gladly read weekly news magazines of three years ago, a book for five-year-olds, advertisements for drugs, and even the physician's odd-looking diplomas on the walls. Have you ever been so bored you were reduced to reading through all the business cards in your wallet? Searching for names similar to yours in the phone book? Browsing through the National Enquirer while waiting in the grocery line? At any rate, that's my recipe for beating boredom. What's yours?

THINKING CRITICALLY THROUGH EXAMPLES

- Play with details.
- Let patterns emerge from details.
- Think logically.

Example   143

Working with examples gives you yet another powerful way of processing your immediate environment and the larger world around you. It involves a manner of thinking that is completely different from description and narration. Using examples to think critically means seeing a definite order in a series of specific, concrete illustrations related in some way that may or may not be immediately obvious to your readers.

Isolating this rhetorical mode involves playing with related details in such a way that they create various patterns that relay different messages to the reader. Often, the simple act of arranging examples helps both the reader and the writer make sense of an experience or idea. In fact, ordering examples and illustrations in a certain way may give one distinct impression, while ordering them in another way may send a completely different message. Each pattern creates a different meaning and, as a result, an entirely new effect.

With examples, more than with description and narration, patterns need to be discovered in the context of the topic, the writer's purpose, and the writer's ultimate message. Writers and readers of example essays must make a shift from chronological to logical thinking. A writer discussing variations in faces, for example, would be working with assorted memories of people, incidents, and age differences. All of these details will eventually take shape in some sort of statement about faces, but these observations would probably not follow a strictly chronological sequence.

Dr. Naseeb Baroody.

The exercises here will help you experience the mental differences among the rhetorical modes we have studied so far and will also prepare you to make sense of details and examples through careful arrangement and re-arrangement of them in your essay. In addition, these exercises will continue to give you more information about your mind's abilities and range.

1. In the photograph on the previous page by Naseeb Baroody, what kinds of examples do you see? Is this an example of simplicity or complexity? Good photography or bad photography? Make a list of at least five other ways this photograph could serve as an example.
2. For each sentence below, provide two to three examples that would illustrate the generalization:
   a. I really liked (disliked) some of the movies released this year.
   b. Many career opportunities await a college graduate.
   c. Some companies make large sums of money by selling products with the names of professional sports teams on them.
3. Jot down five examples of a single problem on campus that bothers you. First, arrange these examples in an order that would convince the president of your school that making some changes in this area would create a more positive learning environment. Second, organize your five examples in such a way that they would convince your parents that the learning environment at your current school cannot be salvaged and you should immediately transfer to another school.

Reading and Writing Example Essays

A common criticism of college-level writers is that they often base their essays on unsupported generalizations, such as "All sports cars are unreliable." The guidelines discussed in this introduction will help you avoid this problem and use examples effectively to support your ideas.

As you read the essays in this chapter, take time to notice the degree of specificity the writers use to make various points. To a certain extent, the more examples you use in your essays, the clearer your ideas will be and the more your readers will understand and be interested in what you are saying.

Notice also that these writers know when to stop—when "more" becomes too much and boredom sets in for the reader. Most college students err by using too few examples, however, so we suggest that, when in doubt about whether or not to include another illustration, you should go ahead and add one.

Example   145

READING EXAMPLE ESSAYS

- What is the essay's context?
- What is the writer's main message?
- How do examples communicate this message?

Preparing to Read.   Before you begin reading the essays in this chapter, take some time to think about each author's title: What can you infer about Bill Cosby's attitude toward having children from his title "The Baffling Question"? What do you think is Richard Rodriguez's view of his past? In addition, try to discover the writer's audience and purpose at this point in the reading process; scanning the essay and surveying its synopsis in the Rhetorical Table of Contents will provide you with useful information for this task.

Also important as you prepare to read is information about the author and about how a particular essay was written. Most of this material is furnished for you in the biography preceding each essay. From it, you might learn why Harold Krents is qualified to write about blindness or why Brent Staples published "A Brother's Murder."

Finally, before you begin to read, take time to answer the Preparing to Read questions and to make some associations with the general subject of the essay: What do you know about your cultural and ethnic heritage (Richard Rodriguez)? What are some of your thoughts on bilingualism (Amy Tan)?

Reading.   As you first read these essays, record any ideas that come to mind. Make associations freely with the content of each essay, its purpose, its audience, and the facts about its publication. For example, try to learn why Cosby writes about having children or why Krents titles his essay "Darkness at Noon." At this point, you will probably be able to make some pretty accurate guesses about the audience each author is addressing. Creating a context for your reading—including the writer's qualifications; the essay's tone, purpose, and audience; and the publication data—is an important first step toward being able to analyze your reading material in any mode.

Each essay also contains questions at the bottom of the pages that guide you to think critically about the essay's subject and the claims the author is making about that topic. Answering these questions as you read will help you develop the skills to read critically and succeed in your other classes. Your responses will also help you generate ideas to build on as you continue to read. Ultimately, they help you build a bridge between your prereading thoughts and the exercises and writing assignments at the end of each essay.

Finally, after you have read an essay in this section once, preview the questions after the selection before you read it again. Let these questions focus your attention for your second reading.

Rereading.   As you read the essays in this chapter for a second time, focus on the examples each writer uses to make his or her point: How relevant are these examples to the thesis and purpose of each essay? How many examples do the writers use? Do they vary the length of these examples to achieve different goals? Do the authors use examples their readers can easily identify with and understand? How are these examples organized in each case? Does this arrangement support each writer's purpose? For example, how relevant are Cosby's examples to his central idea? How many examples does Richard Rodriguez use to make each point? Does Krents vary the length of each of his examples to accomplish different purposes? How does Tan organize her examples? Does this arrangement help her accomplish her purpose? In what way? Does Staples use examples that everyone can identify with? How effective are his examples?

As you read, consider also how other rhetorical modes help each writer accomplish his or her purpose. What are these modes? How do they work along with examples to help create a coherent essay?

Last, answering the questions after each essay will help you check your grasp of its main points and will lead you from the literal to the analytical level in preparation for the discussion/writing assignments that follow.

For a thorough summary of reading tasks, you might want to consult the checklists on page 29 of the Introduction.

WRITING EXAMPLE ESSAYS

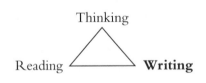

- Draft a thesis statement.
- Choose relevant examples to support your thesis.
- Arrange your examples to prove your main point.

Preparing to Write.   Before you can use examples in an essay, you must first think of some. One good way to generate ideas is to use some of the prewriting techniques explained in the Introduction (pages 19–21) as you respond to the Preparing to Write questions that appear before the writing assignments for each essay. You should then consider these thoughts in conjunction with the purpose and audience specified in your chosen writ-

Example   147

ing assignments. Out of these questions should come a number of good examples for your essay.

Writing.   In an example essay, a thesis statement or controlling idea will help you begin to organize your paper. (See page 24 for more information on thesis statements.) Examples become the primary method of organizing an essay when they actually guide the readers from point to point in reference to the writer's thesis statement. The examples you use should always be relevant to the thesis and purpose of your essay. If, for instance, the person talking about tennis players cited the practice schedules of only unknown players, her friend certainly would not be convinced of the truth of her statement about how hard internationally ranked athletes work at their game. To develop a topic principally with examples, you can use one extended example or several shorter examples, depending on the nature and purpose of your assertion. If you are attempting to prove that Americans are more health conscious now than they were twenty years ago, citing a few examples from your own neighborhood will not provide enough evidence to be convincing. If, however, you are simply commenting on a neighborhood health trend, you can legitimately refer to these local cases. Furthermore, always try to find examples with which your audience can identify so that they can follow your line of reasoning. If you want your parents to help finance an apartment, citing instances from the lives of current rock stars will probably not prove your point because your parents may not sympathize with these particular role models.

The examples you choose must also be arranged as effectively as possible to encourage audience interest and identification. If you are using examples to explain the imaginative quality of Disneyland, for instance, the most logical approach would probably be to organize your essay by degrees (i.e., from least to most imaginative or from most to least original). But if your essay uses examples to help readers visualize your bedroom, a spatial arrangement of the details (moving from one item to the next) might be easiest for your readers to follow. If the subject is a series of important events, like graduation weekend, the illustrations might most effectively be organized chronologically. As you will learn from reading the selections that follow, the careful organization of examples leads quite easily to unity and coherence in your essays. *Unity* is a sense of wholeness and interrelatedness that writers achieve by making sure all their sentences are related to the essay's main idea; *coherence* refers to logical development in an essay, with special attention to how well ideas grow out of one another as the essay develops. Unity and coherence produce good writing—and that, of course, helps foster confidence and accomplishment in school and in your professional life.

Rewriting. As you reread your example essays, look closely at the choice and arrangement of details in relation to your purpose and audience:

- Have you included enough examples to develop each of your topics adequately?
- Are the examples you have chosen relevant to your thesis?
- Have you arranged these examples in a logical manner that your audience can follow?

For more detailed information on writing, see the checklists on page 30 of the Introduction.

STUDENT ESSAY: EXAMPLES AT WORK

In the following essay, a student uses examples to explain and analyze her parents' behavior as they prepare for and enjoy their grandchildren during the Christmas holidays. As you read it, study the various examples the student writer uses to convince us that her parents truly undergo a transformation each winter.

Mom and Dad's Holiday Disappearing Act

General topic → Often during the winter holidays, people find surprises: Children discover the secret contents of brightly wrapped packages that have teased them for weeks; cooks are astonished by the wealth of smells and memories their busy kitchens can bring about; workaholics stumble upon the true joy of a few days' rest. My surprise over the past few winters has been the personality transformation my parents go through around mid-December as they change from Dad and Mom into Poppa and Granny. Yes, they become grandparents and are completely different from the people I know the other eleven and a half months of the year.

← Details to capture holiday spirit

Background information →

← Thesis statement

The first sign of my parents' metamorphosis is the delight they take in visiting toy and children's clothing stores. These two people, who usually despise anything having to do with shopping malls, become crazed consumers. While they tell me to budget my money and shop wisely, they are buying every doll, dump truck, and velvet outfit in sight. And this is only the beginning of the holidays!

← First point

Examples relevant to thesis →

Example   149

When my brother's children arrive, Poppa and Granny come into full form. First they throw out all ideas about a balanced diet for the grandkids. While we were raised in a house where everyone had to take two bites of broccoli, beets, or liver (foods that appeared quite often on our table despite constant groaning), the grandchildren never have to eat anything that does not appeal to them. Granny carries marshmallows in her pockets to bribe the littlest ones into following her around the house, while Poppa offers "surprises" of candy and cake to them all day long. Boxes of chocolate-covered cherries disappear while the bran muffins get hard and stale. The kids love all the sweets, and when the sugar revs up their energy levels, Granny and Poppa can always leave and do a bit more shopping or go to bed while my brother and sister-in-law try to deal with their supercharged, hyperactive kids.

Once the grandchildren have arrived, Granny and Poppa also seem to forget all of the responsibility lectures I so often hear in my daily life. If little Tommy throws a fit at a friend's house, he is "overwhelmed by the number of adults"; if Mickey screams at his sister during dinner, he is "developing his own personality"; if Nancy breaks Granny's vanity mirror (after being told twice to put it down), she is "just a curious child." But if I track mud into the house while helping to unload groceries, I become "careless"; if I scold one of the grandkids for tearing pages out of my calculus book, I am "impatient." If a grandchild talks back to her mother, Granny and Poppa chuckle at her spirit. If I mumble one word about all of this doting, Mom and Dad have a talk with me about petty jealousies.

When my nieces and nephews first started appearing at our home for the holidays a few years ago, I probably was jealous, and I complained a lot. But now I spend more time simply sitting back and watching Mom and Dad change into what we call the "Incredible Huggers." They enjoy their time with these grandchildren so much that I easily forgive them their Granny and Poppa faults.

Margin annotations:
- Transition
- Second point
- Humorous examples (organized from particular to general)
- Transition
- Third point
- Examples in the form of comparison
- Transition to conclusion
- Writer's attitude

Writer's analysis of situation — <u>I believe their personality change is due to the lack of responsibility they feel for the grandkids:</u> In their role as grandparents, they don't have to worry about sugar causing cavities or temporary failures of self-discipline turning into lifetime faults. Those problems are up to my brother and sister-in-law. All Granny and Poppa have to do is enjoy and love their grandchildren. They have all the fun of being parents without any of the attendant obligations. And you know what? Specific reference to introduction

Concluding remark — <u>I think they've earned the right to make this transformation—at least once a year.</u>

Student Writer's Comments

To begin this essay, I listed examples of my parents' antics during the Christmas holidays as parents and as grandparents and then tried to figure out how these examples illustrated patterns of behavior. Next, I scratched out an outline pairing my parents' actions with what I thought were the causes of those actions. But once I sat down to write, I was completely stumped. I had lots of isolated ideas and saw a few patterns, but I had no notion of where this essay was going.

I thought I might put the theory that writing is discovery to the ultimate test and sit down to write out a very rough first draft. I wanted the introduction to be humorous, but I also wanted to maintain a dignified tone (so I wouldn't sound like a whiny kid!). I was really having trouble getting started. I decided to write down *anything* and then come back to the beginning later on. All of the examples and anecdotes were swimming around in my head wanting to be committed to paper. But I couldn't make sense of many of them, and I still couldn't see where I was headed. I found I needed my thesaurus and dictionary from the very beginning; they helped take the pressure off me to come up with the perfect word every time I was stuck. As I neared the middle of the paper, the introduction popped into my head, so I jotted down my thoughts and continued with the flow of ideas I needed for the body of my essay.

Writing my conclusion forced me to put my experiences with my parents into perspective and gave me an angle for revising the body of my essay. But my focus didn't come to me until I began to revise my entire paper. At that point, I realized I had never really tried to analyze how I felt toward my parents' actions or why they acted as they do during the Christmas holidays. I opened the conclusion with "I believe their [my parents'] personality change is due to" and sat in one place until I finished the statement with a reason

Example   151

that made sense out of all these years of frustration. It finally came to me: They act the way they do during the holidays because they don't have primary responsibility for their grandkids. It's a role they have never played before, and they are loving it. (Never mind how it is affecting me!) This basic realization led me to new insights about the major changes they go through during the holidays and ended up giving me a renewed appreciation of their behavior. I couldn't believe the sentence I wrote to close the essay: "I think they've earned the right to make this transformation—at least once a year." Holy cow! Writing this essay actually brought me to a new understanding of my parents.

Revising was a breeze. I felt as if I had just been through a completely draining therapy session, but I now knew what I thought of this topic and where my essay was headed. I dropped irrelevant examples, reorganized other details, and tightened up some of the explanations so they set up my conclusion more clearly. Both my parents and I were delighted with the results.

SOME FINAL THOUGHTS ON EXAMPLES

Although examples are often used to supplement and support other methods of development—such as cause/effect, comparison/contrast, and process analysis—the essays in this section focus principally on examples. A main idea is expressed in the introduction of each, and the rest of the essay provides examples to bolster that contention. As you read these essays, pay close attention to each author's choice and arrangement of examples; then try to determine which organizational techniques are most persuasive for each specific audience.

EXAMPLE IN REVIEW

Reading Example Essays

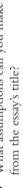

Preparing to Read

✓ What assumptions can you make from the essay's title?

✓ Can you guess what the general mood of the essay is?

✓ What is the essay's purpose and audience?

✓ What does the synopsis tell you about the essay?

✓ What can you learn from the author's biography?

✓ Can you predict the author's point of view toward the subject?

Reading

✓ What is the essay's context?

✓ What is the writer's main message?

✓ How do examples communicate this message?

Rereading

✓ What examples help the author communicate the essay's message?

✓ How are these examples organized?

✓ What other rhetorical modes does the author use?

Writing Example Essays

Preparing to Write

✓ What is your purpose?

✓ Who is your audience?

✓ What is the message you want to convey?

Writing

✓ What is your thesis or controlling idea?

✓ Do the examples you are choosing support this thesis?

✓ Are these examples arranged as effectively as possible?

Rewriting

✓ Have you included enough examples to develop each of your topics adequately?

✓ Are the examples you have chosen relevant to your thesis?

✓ Have you arranged these examples in a logical manner that your audience can follow?

BILL COSBY   (1937–   )

The Baffling Question

Comedian, actor, recording artist, and author Bill Cosby is undoubtedly one
of America's best-loved entertainers. From his beginnings on the *I Spy*
television series through his *Fat Albert* years and his work on *Sesame Street,* his
eight Grammy awards for comedy albums, his commercials for everything
from Kodak film to Jell-O pudding, and his portrayal of the affable obstetrician
Cliff Huxtable on his immensely popular *Cosby Show,* he has retained his
public persona of an honest and trustworthy storyteller intrigued by the ironies
in our everyday lives. "When I was a kid," he has explained, "I always used to
pay attention to things that other people didn't even think about. I'd remember
funny happenings, just little trivial things, and then tell stories about them
later. I found I could make people laugh, and I enjoyed doing it because it gave
me a sense of security. I thought that if people laughed at what you said, that
meant they liked you." After a series of hit movies in the 1970s, Cosby decided
to return to prime-time television in 1984: "I got tired of seeing TV shows
that consisted of a car crash, a gunman, and a hooker talking to a Black pimp.
It was cheaper to do a series than to throw out my family's six television sets."
At the peak of its success, *The Cosby Show* was seen weekly by over sixty
million viewers. Cosby's publications include *You Are Somebody Special* (1978),
Fatherhood (1986), *Time Flies* (1988), *Love and Marriage* (1989), and a children's
book entitled *Friends of a Feather* (illustrated by his daughter, Erika Cosby,
2003). He lives with his wife, Camille, in Los Angeles, where he relaxes by
playing an occasional game of tennis.

Preparing to Read

The following selection is from *Fatherhood,* which details the joys and
frustrations of raising children. In this essay, he puts a comic spin on several
serious issues connected with parenthood.

Exploring Experience: Before reading this piece, pause to consider the effect
parenthood has had or might have on your life: How did/would you make the
decision whether to have children? What variables were/would be involved
in this decision? What are/would be some of the difficulties involved in raising
children? Some of the joys? What memories do you have of your own
childhood?

Learning Online: Visit the United States Department of Health and
Human Safety Web site located at http://www.hhs.gov, and select an article
related to children or new parents. What types of examples do the writers use
to support their main claims? While reading "The Baffling Question," consider
how these examples differ from the types of examples used by Bill Cosby.

So you've decided to have a child. You've decided to give up quiet   1
evenings with good books and lazy weekends with good music, intimate meals during which you finish whole sentences, sweet private
times when you've savored the thought that just the two of you and your love
are all you will ever need. You've decided to turn your sofas into trampolines
and to abandon the joys of leisurely contemplating reproductions of great art
for the joys of frantically coping with reproductions of yourselves. ◆

Why?   2

Poets have said the reason to have children is to give yourself immortal-   3
ity; and I must admit I did ask God to give me a son because I wanted someone to carry on the family name. Well, God did just that, and I now confess
that there have been times when I've told my son not to reveal who he is.

"You make up a name," I've said. "Just don't tell anybody who you are."   4

Immortality? Now that I have had five children, my only hope is that   5
they all are out of the house before I die.

No, immortality was not the reason why my wife and I produced these   6
beloved sources of dirty laundry and ceaseless noise. And we also did not
have them because we thought it would be fun to see one of them sit in a
chair and stick out his leg so that another one of them running by was
launched like Explorer I. After which I said to the child who was the launch-
ing pad, "Why did you do that?"

"Do what?" he replied.   7

"Stick out your leg."   8

"Dad, I didn't know my leg was going out. My leg, it does that a lot."   9

If you cannot function in a world where things like this are said, then you   10
better forget about raising children and go for daffodils.

My wife and I also did not have children so they could yell at each other   11
all over the house, moving me to say, "What's the problem?"

"She's waving her foot in my room," my daughter replied.   12

"And something like that *bothers* you?"   13

"Yes, I don't *want* her foot in my room."   14

"Well," I said, dipping into my storehouse of paternal wisdom, ◆ "why   15
don't you just close the door?"

"Then I can't see what she's doing!"   16

Furthermore, we did not have the children because we thought it would   17
be rewarding to watch them do things that should be studied by the Men-
ninger Clinic.

Reading Critically

◆ What would you say are the top five reasons most people want to have children?

◆ What does Cosby mean by the phrase "my storehouse of paternal wisdom"? In what way
are these words ironic in this context?

"Okay," I said to all five one day, "go get into the car."   18

All five then ran to the same car door, grabbed the same handle, and spent   19
the next few minutes beating each other up. Not one of them had the intelligence to say, "Hey, *look*. There are three more doors." The dog, however,
was already inside.

And we did not have the children to help my wife develop new lines for   20
her face or because she had always had a desire to talk out loud to herself:
"Don't tell *me* you're *not* going to do something when I tell you to move!"
And we didn't have children so I could always be saying to someone,
"Where's my change?"

Like so many young couples, my wife and I simply were unable to pro-   21
ject.❸ In restaurants we did not see the small children who were casting
their bread on the water in the glasses the waiter had brought; and we did
not see the mother who was fasting because she was both cutting the food
for one child while pulling another from the floor to a chair that he would
use for slipping to the floor again. And we did not project beyond those
lovely Saturdays of buying precious little things after leisurely brunches together. We did not see that *other* precious little things would be coming along
to destroy the first batch.

UNDERSTANDING DETAILS

1. According to Cosby, exactly what is "the baffling question"? Why is this question "baffling"?
2. If everyone felt as Cosby does about raising children, what kinds of people
   would have children?
3. List three important issues that Cosby believes couples should consider before
   they have children.
4. From Cosby's point of view, in what important ways do children change a couple's life?

THINKING CRITICALLY

5. Why do you think Cosby focuses on the problems children create in a couple's
   life? What effect does this approach have on his main point?
6. What does Cosby mean when he says, "You've decided . . . to abandon the
   joys of leisurely contemplating reproductions of great art for the joys of frantically coping with reproductions of yourselves" (paragraph 1)? Whom is he
   addressing?

Reading Critically

❸ Do you think it's better for couples to have children in their 20s or 30s? Why?

7. Following Cosby's logic, why did he and his wife have children? What examples lead you to this conclusion?

8. In what way is the last sentence in this essay a good summary statement? What specific thoughts does it summarize?

DISCOVERING RHETORICAL STRATEGIES

9. How does the first paragraph set the tone for the rest of the essay?

10. Cosby's primary strategy in this essay is irony. That is, he suggests reasons for having children by listing reasons *not* to have children. What effect is this approach likely to have on his readers?

11. How does Cosby use specific examples to create humor? Is his humor effective? Explain your answer.

12. Cosby is a master of choosing vivid examples to make his point. What other rhetorical strategies does Cosby use to develop his essay? Give examples of each.

MAKING CONNECTIONS

13. Compare Bill Cosby's comments about raising children with those made about our addiction to films by Stephen King in "Why We Crave Horror Movies." To what extent do these authors see our need for children and horror flicks as a kind of self-affirming masochism?

14. How seriously does Cosby intend his readers to take his "advice" about not having children? Do you see any connection between his point of view and that expressed by Jessica Mitford in "Behind the Formaldehyde Curtain"? How do both of these essays work through the rhetorical device of irony (saying the opposite of what they really mean)? Which essay is more effective? Explain your answer.

15. Contrast Cosby's rapport with his children with the parent–child relationships depicted in Lewis Sawaquat's "For My Indian Daughter," Sandra Cisneros's "Only daughter," and/or Michael Dorris's "The Broken Cord." Which parents do you think love their children most? Why do you believe this is true?

IDEAS FOR DISCUSSION/WRITING

Preparing to Write

Write freely about the art of parenthood: From your observations or experience, what are some of the principal problems and joys of parenthood? How is being a parent different from baby-sitting? What pleasant baby-sitting experiences have you had? What unpleasant experiences? What kind of child were you? What specific memories led you to this conclusion?

Choosing a Topic

1. Write an essay for the general public explaining one particular problem or joy of parenthood. In your essay, mimic Cosby's humorous approach to the topic. Use several specific examples to make your point.

2. Write an editorial for your local newspaper on your own foolproof techniques for doing one of the following: (a) baby-sitting, (b) raising children, or (c) becoming a model child. Use specific examples to explain your approach.

3. Interview one or two relatives who are older than you; ask them about the type of child you were. Have them recall some particularly memorable details that characterized your behavior. Then write an essay explaining their predominant impressions of you. Use examples to support these impressions.

4. What is an area in which you are an expert? Select an area in which you feel you have unique expertise. This could be a sport, such as basketball or surfing, or a skill, such as drawing or cooking. Identify your own "baffling question" surrounding the topic, and write an essay that develops this problem. In organizing your essay, consider the types of examples you decide to use. Find facts and/or statistics about your topic online, and determine whether they would serve as effective examples.

Before beginning your essay, you might want to consult the checklists on page 152.

RICHARD RODRIGUEZ   (1944–   )

Public and Private Language

Richard Rodriguez was raised in Sacramento, California, the son of industrious working-class Mexican immigrant parents. He attended parochial schools there and later continued his education at Stanford University, Columbia University, London's Warburg Institute, and, finally, the University of California at Berkeley, where he earned a Ph.D. in English Renaissance literature. A writer and journalist, he is now associate editor of the Pacific News Service in San Francisco. "The Browning of America" is a phrase coined by Rodriguez to describe the cultural, racial, and ethnic blending of the population in the U.S. during the 20th and 21st centuries. In 1982, he received wide critical acclaim for the publication of his autobiography, *Hunger of Memory: The Education of Richard Rodriguez,* which detailed his struggle to succeed in a totally alien culture. A regular contributor to the *Los Angeles Times,* he has also published essays in *New Republic, Time, Harper's, American Scholar, Columbia Forum,* and *College English.* His most recent books are *Days of Obligation: An Argument with My Mexican Father* (1992), an autobiographical study of Mexican immigrants in America, and *Brown: The Last Discovery of America* (2002). Asked to provide advice for students using *The Prose Reader,* Rodriguez explained that "there is no 'secret' to becoming a writer. Writing takes time—and patience, more than anything else. If you are willing to rewrite and rewrite and rewrite, you will become a good writer."

Preparing to Read

This essay was originally published in *Hunger of Memory,* an autobiography that Rodriguez wrote in 1982 about the experience of growing up in a culture alien to his cultural and ethnic heritage.

Exploring Experience: Before you actually read this essay, think about a time you tried to fit in somewhere: What were the circumstances? What did you do to fit in? Was your attempt successful? If you were unsuccessful, what went wrong? How important to you is "fitting in" or "assimilating" into a particular group? Why is assimilation important or unimportant to you? Explain your answer.

Learning Online: Visit the Language Games Web site (http://www .languagegames.org), and select an easy game in a language you don't speak: perhaps Spanish, French, German, or Italian. See how playing even a simple game, such as a word search or hangman, can be difficult when you're using vocabulary you are not familiar with. Consider this challenge as you read about Rodriguez's struggles with learning English in the following excerpt.

Supporters of bilingual education today imply that students like me miss   1
a great deal by not being taught in their family's language. What they
seem not to recognize is that, as a socially disadvantaged child, I considered Spanish to be a private language. What I needed to learn in school
was that I had the right—and the obligation—to speak the public language
of *los gringos.* ● The odd truth is that my first-grade classmates could have
become bilingual, in the conventional sense of that word, more easily than
I. Had they been taught (as upper-middle-class children are often taught
early) a second language like Spanish or French, they could have regarded it
simply as that: another public language. In my case such bilingualism could
not have been so quickly achieved.[What I did not believe was that I could
speak a single public language.]

Without question, it would have pleased me to hear my teachers address   2
me in Spanish when I entered the classroom. I would have felt much less
afraid. I would have trusted them and responded with ease. But I would have
delayed—for how long postponed?—having to learn the language of public society. I would have evaded—and for how long could I have afforded to
delay?—learning the great lesson of school, that I had a public identity. ●

Fortunately, my teachers were unsentimental about their responsibility.   3
What they understood was that I needed to speak a public language. So their
voices would search me out, asking me questions. Each time I'd hear them,
I'd look up in surprise to see a nun's face frowning at me. I'd mumble, not
really meaning to answer. The nun would persist, "Richard, stand up. Don't
look at the floor. Speak up. Speak to the entire class, not just to me!" But I
couldn't believe that the English language was mine to use. (In part, I did not
want to believe it.) I continued to mumble. I resisted the teacher's demands.
(Did I somehow suspect that once I learned public language my pleasing
family life would be changed?) Silent, waiting for the bell to sound, I remained dazed, diffident, afraid.

Because I wrongly imagined that English was intrinsically a public lan-   4
guage and Spanish an intrinsically private one, I easily noticed the difference between classroom language and the language of home. At school,
words were directed to a general audience of listeners. ("Boys and girls.")
Words were meaningfully ordered. And the point was not self-expression
alone but to make oneself understood by many others. The teacher quizzed,
"Boys and girls, why do we use that word in this sentence? Could we think

---

Reading Critically

● To what extent do you feel that immigrants to this country have a "right" and an "obligation" to learn English?

● How is Rodriguez's "public identity" connected with learning the English language?

of a better word to use there? Would the sentence change its meaning if the words were differently arranged? And wasn't there a better way of saying much the same thing?" (I couldn't say. I wouldn't try to say.)

Three months. Five. Half a year passed. Unsmiling, ever watchful, my teachers noted my silence. They began to connect my behavior with the difficult progress my older sister and brother were making. Until one Saturday morning three nuns arrived at the house to talk to our parents. Stiffly, they sat on the blue living room sofa. From the doorway of another room, spying the visitors, I noted the incongruity—the clash of two worlds, the faces and voices of school intruding upon the familiar setting of home. I overheard one voice gently wondering, "Do your children speak only Spanish at home, Mrs. Rodriguez?" While another voice added, "That Richard especially seems so timid and shy." 5

That Rich-heard! 6

With great tact the visitors continued, "Is it possible for you and your husband to encourage your children to practice their English when they are home?" Of course, my parents complied. What would they not do for their children's well-being? And how could they have questioned the Church's authority which those women represented? ❸ In an instant, they agreed to give up the language (the sounds) that had revealed and accentuated our family's closeness. The moment after the visitors left, the change was observed. *"Ahora, speak to us en ingles,"* my father and mother united to tell us. 7

At first, it seemed a kind of game. After dinner each night, the family gathered to practice "our" English. (It was still then *ingles,* a language foreign to us, so we felt drawn as strangers to it.) Laughing, we would try to define words we could not pronounce. We played with strange English sounds, often over-anglicizing our pronunciations. And we filled the smiling gaps of our sentences with familiar Spanish sounds. But that was cheating, somebody shouted. Everyone laughed. In school, meanwhile, like my brother and sister, I was required to attend a daily tutoring session. I needed a full year of special attention. I also needed my teachers to keep my attention from straying in class by calling out, *Rich-heard*—their English voices slowly prying loose my ties to my other name, its three notes. *Ri-car-do.* ❹ Most of all I needed to hear my mother and father speak to me in a moment of seriousness in broken—suddenly heartbreaking—English. The scene was inevitable: One Saturday morning I entered the kitchen where my parents were talking in Spanish. I did not realize that they were talking in Spanish 8

Reading Critically

❸ What is the relationship between the nuns' request and their religious authority?

❹ How do the English and Spanish pronunciations of the author's first name help reinforce his distinction between public and private language?

however until, at the moment they saw me, I heard their voices change to speak English. Those *gringo* sounds they uttered startled me. Pushed me away. In that moment of trivial misunderstanding and profound insight, I felt my throat twisted by unsounded grief. I turned quickly and left the room. But I had no place to escape to with Spanish. (The spell was broken.) My brother and sisters were speaking English in another part of the house.

Again and again in the days following, increasingly angry, I was obliged   9 to hear my mother and father: "Speak to us *en ingles.*" *(Speak)*. Only then did I determine to learn classroom English. Weeks after, it happened: One day in school I raised my hand to volunteer an answer. I spoke out in a loud voice. And I did not think it remarkable when the entire class understood. That day, I moved very far from the disadvantaged child I had been only days earlier. The belief, the calming assurance that I belonged in public, had at last taken hold.

Shortly after, I stopped hearing the high and loud sounds of *los gringos*. A   10 more and more confident speaker of English, I didn't trouble to listen to *how* strangers sounded, speaking to me. And there simply were too many English-speaking people in my day for me to hear American accents anymore. Conversations quickened. Listening to persons who sounded eccentrically pitched voices, I usually noted their sounds for an initial few seconds before I concentrated on *what* they were saying. Conversations became content-full. Transparent. Hearing someone's *tone* of voice—angry or questioning or sarcastic or happy or sad—I didn't distinguish it from the words it expressed. Sound and word were thus tightly wedded. At the end of a day, I was often bemused, always relieved, to realize how "silent," though crowded with words, my day in public had been. (This public silence measured and quickened the change in my life.)

At last, seven years old, I came to believe what had been technically true   11 since my birth: I was an American citizen. ◈ 5

But the special feeling of closeness at home was diminished by then. Gone   12 was the desperate, urgent, intense feeling of being at home: rare was the experience of feeling myself individualized by family intimates. We remained a loving family, but one greatly changed. No longer so close; no longer bound tight by the pleasing and troubling knowledge of our public separateness. Neither my older brother nor sister rushed home after school anymore. Nor did I. When I arrived home there would often be neighborhood kids in the house. Or the house would be empty of sounds.

Following the dramatic Americanization of their children, even my par-   13 ents grew more publicly confident. Especially my mother. She learned the

---

Reading Critically

◈ 5 Why do you think Rodriguez uses a one-sentence paragraph at this particular moment in the essay?

names of all the people on our block. And she decided we needed to have a telephone installed in the house. My father continued to use the word *gringo*. But it was no longer charged with the old bitterness or distrust. (Stripped of any emotional content, the word simply became a name for those Americans not of Hispanic descent.) Hearing him, sometimes, I wasn't sure if he was pronouncing the Spanish word *gringo* or saying gringo in English.

Matching the silence I started hearing in public was a new quiet at home.   14
The family's quiet was partly due to the fact that, as we children learned more and more English, we shared fewer and fewer words with our parents. [6] Sentences needed to be spoken slowly when a child addressed his mother or father. (Often the parent wouldn't understand.) The child would need to repeat himself. (Still the parent misunderstood.) The young voice, frustrated, would end up saying, "Never mind"—the subject was closed. Dinners would be noisy with the clinking of knives and forks against dishes. My mother would smile softly between her remarks; my father at the other end of the table would chew and chew at his food, while he stared over the heads of his children.

My *mother!* My *father!* After English became my primary language, I no   15
longer knew what words to use in addressing my parents. The old Spanish words (those tender accents of sound) I had used earlier—*mama* and *papa*— I couldn't use anymore. They would have been too painful reminders of how much had changed in my life. On the other hand, the words I heard neighborhood kids call *their* parents seemed equally unsatisfactory. *Mother* and *Father; Ma, Papa, Pa, Dad, Pop* (how I hated the all-American sound of that last word especially)—all these terms I felt were unsuitable, not really terms of address for *my* parents. As a result, I never used them at home. Whenever I'd speak to my parents, I would try to get their attention with eye contact alone. In public conversations, I'd refer to "my parents" or "my mother and father."

My mother and father, for their part, responded differently, as their chil-   16
dren spoke to them less. She grew restless, seemed troubled and anxious at the scarcity of words exchanged in the house. It was she who would question me about my day when I came home from school. She smiled at small talk. She pried at the edges of my sentences to get me to say something more. (What?) She'd stopped her children's talking. By contrast, my father seemed reconciled to the new quiet. Though his English improved somewhat, he retired into silence. At dinner he spoke very little. One night his children and even his wife helplessly giggled at his garbled English pronunciation of the Catholic Grace before Meals. Thereafter he made his wife recite the

---

Reading Critically
[6] Why does the author's home life become more quiet?

prayer at the start of each meal, even on formal occasions, when there were guests in the house. Hers became the public voice of the family. ❼On official business, it was she, not my father, one would usually hear on the phone or in stores, talking to strangers. His children grew so accustomed to his silence that, years later, they would speak routinely of his shyness. (My mother would often try to explain: Both his parents died when he was eight. He was raised by an uncle who treated him like little more than a menial servant. He was never encouraged to speak. He grew up alone. A man of few words.) But my father was not shy, I realized, when I'd watch him speaking Spanish with relatives. Using Spanish, he was quickly effusive. Especially when talking with other men, his voice would spark, flicker, flare alive with sounds. In Spanish, he expressed ideas and feelings he rarely revealed in English. With firm Spanish sounds, he conveyed confidence and authority English would never allow him.

The silence at home, however, was finally more than a literal silence. Fewer   17
words passed between parent and child, but more profound was the silence that resulted from my inattention to sounds. At about the time I no longer bothered to listen with care to the sounds of English in public, I grew careless about listening to the sounds family members made when they spoke. Most of the time I heard someone speaking at home and didn't distinguish his sounds from the words people uttered in public. I didn't even pay much attention to my parents' accented and ungrammatical speech. At least not at home. Only when I was with them in public would I grow alert to their accents. Though, even then, their sounds caused me less and less concern. For I was increasingly confident of my own public identity.

I would have been happier about my public success had I not sometimes   18
recalled what it had been like earlier, when my family had conveyed its intimacy through a set of conveniently private sounds. Sometimes in public, hearing a stranger, I'd hark back to my past. A Mexican farmworker approached me downtown to ask directions to somewhere. "Hijito . . . ?" he said. And his voice summoned deep longing. Another time, standing beside my mother in the visiting room of a Carmelite convent, before the dense screen which rendered the nuns' shadowy figures, I heard several Spanish-speaking nuns—their busy, singsong overlapping voices—assure us that yes, yes, we were remembered, all our family was remembered in their prayers. (Their voices echoed faraway family sounds.) Another day, a dark-faced old woman—her hand light on my shoulder—steadied herself against me as she boarded a bus. She murmured something I couldn't quite comprehend. Her Spanish voice came near, like the face of a never-before-seen relative in the instant before I was kissed. Her voice, like so many of the Spanish voices I'd

---

Reading Critically

❼ Why did Rodriguez's mother become the public voice of the family?

hear in public, recalled the golden age of my youth. **8** Hearing Spanish then, I continued to be a careful, if sad, listener to sounds. Hearing a Spanish-speaking family walking behind me, I turned to look. I smiled for an instant, before my glance found the Hispanic-looking faces of strangers in the crowd going by.

UNDERSTANDING DETAILS

1. In what ways was Spanish a private language for Rodriguez?
2. What happened when Rodriguez's two worlds met through the nuns who visited his home?
3. What "spell" is Rodriguez referring to in paragraph 8: "The spell was broken." How was it broken?
4. How did the author finally assert his public self? What language was consistent with this identity?

THINKING CRITICALLY

5. How are language and identity connected for this author?
6. Why do you think Rodriguez didn't feel he had the right to use English as his language?
7. In the author's view, why was concentrating on "content-full" (paragraph 10) conversations good for him?
8. What does Rodriguez mean when he says, "This public silence measured and quickened the change in my life" (paragraph 10)?

DISCOVERING RHETORICAL STRATEGIES

9. Why do you think Rodriguez lets a single sentence stand as a paragraph in paragraph 11? What effect does this choice create in the essay?
10. Why did the family's mastery of English change the interaction of Rodriguez's family?
11. When in the essay does Rodriguez refer to the public confidence he and his family experience? What does he mean by this phrase? What is the context of each of the references to this notion?
12. Do you think the brief reference to the Spanish-speaking family is an effective conclusion to this essay? Why or why not?

MAKING CONNECTIONS

13. Compare and contrast Rodriguez's devotion to his own cultural heritage to that expressed by Lewis Sawaquat ("For My Indian Daughter"), Amy Tan ("Mother Tongue"), Brent Staples ("A Brother's Murder"), and/or Sucheng

---

Reading Critically
8 How do the nuns' Spanish prayers remind the author of the "golden age" of his youth?

Chan ("You're Short, Besides!"). Which author is most intimately connected to his/her heritage? Why do you think this is so?

14. Which author is the best storyteller: Rodriguez, Russell Baker ("The Saturday Evening Post"), Garrison Keillor ("How the Crab Apple Grew"), or Malcolm X ("Learning to Read")? Why?

15. How would Mary Pipher ("Beliefs About Families"), Amy Tan ("Mother Tongue"), and/or Erma Bombeck ("Grandma") feel about Rodriguez's growing estrangement from his parents due to their difficulties with English?

IDEAS FOR DISCUSSION/WRITING

Preparing to Write

Write freely about the importance of "fitting in" or "assimilating" in your life. To what degree is assimilation important to you? Why is it important? What does assimilation into a particular group mean to you? What is more important than assimilation in your life today? What is less important? What does assimilation signify to you? Why do you think it carries this level of priority?

Choosing a Topic

1. The Board of Education for your high school district is thinking of offering classes in several different languages that are spoken in your area. This would allow students who speak a second language at home to do their school work in that language as well. What would be the advantages of this approach? The disadvantages? Prepare a statement for a community meeting with the Board arguing for or against this decision.

2. What specific actions create an intimacy in your family that matches the intimacy Rodriguez lost? Explain this intimacy to someone from another country and discuss its value in your life.

3. You have been asked by a group of friends to attend a concert with them. You really want to go because you like the group of friends and the performers. So you decide to ask your parents to give you the money for the trip. Use your best reasoning on one or both of your parents or guardians to get them to fund this request.

4. Go to the Center for Digital Storytelling Web site (http://storycenter.org/whatis.html), and read this short information page. Then view the two-minute digital story example by Thenmozhi Soundarajan called *Momnotmom*. Using that video as inspiration, choose one of your own family members, and consider what kind of digital story you could create as a tribute to that person. What memories would you include that would be good examples of his or her importance to you? In essay form, describe the video you would create, including as many specific details as possible. List the memories you would mention, the pictures you would use, and the background music you would select.

Before beginning your essay, you might want to consult the checklists on page 152.

HAROLD KRENTS   (1944–1987)

Darkness at Noon

Raised in New York City, Harold Krents earned a B.A. and a law degree at Harvard, studied at Oxford University, worked as a partner in a Washington, D.C., law firm, was the subject of a long-running Broadway play, and wrote a popular television movie—all despite the fact that he was born blind. His "1-A" classification by a local draft board, which doubted the severity of his handicap, brought about the 1969 Broadway hit play *Butterflies Are Free* by Leonard Gershe. Krents once explained that he was merely the "prototype" for the central character: "I gave the story its inspiration—the play's plot is not my story; its spirit is." In 1972, Krents wrote *To Race the Wind,* which was made into a CBS-TV movie in 1980. During his career as a lawyer, Krents worked hard to expand legal protection for the handicapped and fought to secure their right to equal opportunity in the business world. He died in 1987 of a brain tumor.

Preparing to Read

In the following article, originally published in *The New York Times* in 1976, the author gives examples of different kinds of discrimination he has suffered because of his blindness.

Exploring Experience: As you prepare to read this essay, take a few minutes to think about disabilities or handicaps in general: Do you have a disability? If so, how are you treated by others? How do you feel others respond to your handicap? Do you know someone else who has a disability? How do you respond to that person? How do you think he or she wants to be treated? To what extent do you think disabilities should affect a person's job opportunities? What can be done to improve society's prejudices against the disabled?

Learning Online: In this essay, Harold Krents describes his frustrations with people's misconceptions about his disability. To gain a better understanding of his experience, go to http://www. nfb.org/futref.htm, the National Federation of the Blind's Web site for parents and teachers of blind children. The bottom of the page contains links to its magazine, *Future Reflections.* Select the most current issue, and pick a topic that sounds interesting. Consider the experiences mentioned on the Web site as you read Krents's account.

Blind from birth, I have never had the opportunity to see myself and 1
have been completely dependent on the image I create in the eye of
the observer. ◆ To date it has not been narcissistic.

There are those who assume that since I can't see, I obviously also can- 2
not hear. Very often people will converse with me at the top of their lungs,
enunciating each word very carefully. Conversely, people will also often whisper, assuming that since my eyes don't work, my ears don't either.

For example, when I go to the airport and ask the ticket agent for assis- 3
tance to the plane, he or she will invariably pick up the phone, call a ground
hostess and whisper: "Hi, Jane, we've got a 76 here." I have concluded that
the word "blind" is not used for one of two reasons: Either they fear that if
the dread word is spoken, the ticket agent's retina will immediately detach,
or they are reluctant to inform me of my condition of which I may not have
been previously aware.

On the other hand, others know that of course I can hear, but believe 4
that I can't talk. Often, therefore, when my wife and I go out to dinner, a
waiter or waitress will ask Kit if "*he* would like a drink" to which I respond
that "indeed *he* would."

This point was graphically driven home to me while we were in England. 5
I had been given a year's leave of absence from my Washington law firm to
study for a diploma in law degree at Oxford University. During the year I
became ill and was hospitalized. Immediately after admission, I was wheeled
down to the X-ray room. Just at the door sat an elderly woman—elderly I
would judge from the sound of her voice. "What is his name?" the woman
asked the orderly who had been wheeling me.

"What's your name?" the orderly repeated to me.   6
"Harold Krents," I replied.   7
"Harold Krents," he repeated.   8
"When was he born?"   9
"When were you born?"   10
"November 5, 1944," I responded.   11
"November 5, 1944," the orderly intoned. ❷   12

This procedure continued for approximately five minutes at which point 13
even my saint-like disposition deserted me. "Look," I finally blurted out,
"this is absolutely ridiculous. Okay, granted I can't see, but it's got to have become pretty clear to both of you that I don't need an interpreter."

"He says he doesn't need an interpreter," the orderly reported to the 14
woman.

Reading Critically

❶ What "image" do you create in the eye of your observer? To what extent is this image dependent on visual stimuli?

❷ Why is the exchange between Krents and the hospital orderly funny?

The toughest misconception of all is the view that because I can't see, I   15
can't work. I was turned down by over forty law firms because of my blindness, even though my qualifications included a cum laude degree from Harvard College and a good ranking in my Harvard Law School class.

The attempt to find employment, the continuous frustration of being told   16
that it was impossible for a blind person to practice law, the rejection letters,
not based on my lack of ability but rather on my disability, will always remain one of the most disillusioning experiences of my life.

I therefore look forward to the day, with the expectation that it is certain   17
to come, when employers will view their handicapped workers as a little
child did me years ago when my family still lived in Scarsdale.

I was playing basketball with my father in our backyard according to pro-   18
cedures we had developed. My father would stand beneath the hoop, shout,
and I would shoot over his head at the basket attached to our garage. Our
next-door neighbor, aged five, wandered over into our yard with a playmate.
"He's blind," our neighbor whispered to her friend in a voice that could be
heard distinctly by Dad and me. Dad shot and missed; I did the same. Dad
hit the rim; I missed entirely; Dad shot and missed the garage entirely. "Which
one is blind?" ❸ whispered back the little friend.

I would hope that in the near future when a plant manager is touring the   19
factory with the foreman and comes upon a handicapped and nonhandi-
capped person working together, his comment after watching them work will
be, "Which one is disabled?"

UNDERSTANDING DETAILS

1. According to Krents, what are three common misconceptions about blind people?
2. What important details did you learn about Krents's life from this essay? How
does he introduce this information?
3. In what ways was Krents frustrated in his search for employment? Was he qualified for the jobs he sought? Why or why not?
4. What attitude toward the handicapped does Krents look forward to in the future?

THINKING CRITICALLY

5. What does Krents mean when he says that his self-image gained through the
eyes of others "has not been narcissistic" (paragraph 1)? Why do you think this
is the case?

Reading Critically

❸ How does the author use humor in this essay to humanize the situation and put his readers at ease?

6. What is Krents's attitude toward his handicap? What parts of his essay reveal that attitude?
7. How do you account for the reactions to his blindness that Krents tells about in this essay? Are you aware of such behavior in yourself? In others?
8. Do you think we will ever arrive at the point in the working world that Krents describes in the last paragraph? How can we get there? What advantages or disadvantages might accompany such a change?

DISCOVERING RHETORICAL STRATEGIES

9. How does Krents organize the three main points in his essay? Why does he put them in this order? What is the benefit of discussing employment last?
10. Krents often offers specific examples in the form of dialogue or spoken statements. Are these effective ways to develop his main points? Explain your answer.
11. Krents establishes a fairly fast pace in this essay as he discusses several related ideas in a small amount of space. How does he create this sense of speed? What effect does this pace have on his essay as a whole?
12. Although the author's dominant rhetorical mode is example in this essay, what other strategies does he use to develop his ideas? Give examples of each of these strategies.

MAKING CONNECTIONS

13. Compare the employment discrimination faced by Krents because of his blindness with the racial and social discrimination suffered by Lewis Sawaquat ("For My Indian Daughter") and/or Franklin Zimring ("Confessions of an Ex-Smoker"). Which person has been treated most unfairly by society? Explain your answer.
14. How similar is Krents's use of humor to that of Russell Baker ("The Saturday Evening Post") and/or Bill Cosby ("The Baffling Question")? Which author do you find most amusing? Why? Is humor used in a different way in Krents's essay than it is in the Cosby essay? If so, how?
15. How many examples does Krents use in his essay? Does Krents use more or fewer examples per page than Bill Cosby ("The Baffling Question") and/or Brent Staples ("A Brother's Murder")? How does the number of examples affect the believability of each author's argument?

IDEAS FOR DISCUSSION/WRITING

Preparing to Write

Write freely about disabilities: If you are disabled, what is your response to the world? Why do you respond the way you do? How does society respond to you? Are you pleased or not with your relationship to society in general? If you are not disabled, what do you think your attitude would be if you were disabled? How do you respond to disabled people? To what extent does your response depend upon the disability? Are you satisfied with your reaction to other people's disabilities? Are you prejudiced in any way against people with disabilities? Do you think our society as a whole demonstrates any prejudices toward the disabled? If so, how can we correct these biases?

Choosing a Topic

1. As a reporter for your campus newspaper, you have been assigned to study and write about the status of services for the disabled on your campus. Is your school equipped with parking for the handicapped? A sufficient number of ramps for wheelchairs? Transportation for the handicapped? Other special services for the handicapped? Interview some disabled students to get their views on these services. Write an example essay for the newspaper, explaining the situation.

2. With your eyes closed, take a walk through a place that you know well. How does it feel to be nearly sightless? What senses begin to compensate for your loss of vision? Write an essay for your classmates detailing your reactions. Use specific examples to communicate your feelings.

3. Do you have any phobias or irrational fears that handicap you in any way? Write a letter to a friend explaining one of these "handicaps" and your method of coping with it.

4. Select three of your favorite Web sites, and spend a few minutes visiting each one. Now return to them and consider how you would use the site if you were either blind or deaf. What accommodations, if any, have the Web sites made to accommodate differently abled users? Using Krents's article and your experiences with these Web sites as examples, write an essay evaluating the accessibility of the Internet for those who are disabled. Following Krents's writing style, consider the effect of different ways of organizing your examples.

Before beginning your essay, you might want to consult the checklists on page 152.

AMY TAN   (1952–   )

Mother Tongue

In a very short time, Amy Tan has established herself as one of the foremost Chinese-American writers. Her first novel, *The Joy Luck Club* (1989), which was praised as "brilliant . . . a jewel of a book" by *The New York Times Book Review,* focuses on the lives of four Chinese women in pre-1949 China and their American-born daughters in modern-day California. Through a series of vignettes, Tan weaves together the dreams and sorrows of these mothers and daughters as they confront oppression in China and equally difficult cultural challenges in the new world of the United States. Like the protagonists in *The Joy Luck Club,* Tan's parents, a Baptist minister and a licensed vocational nurse, emigrated to America shortly before Tan's birth. She showed an early talent for writing when, at age eight, she won an essay contest (and a transistor radio) with a paper entitled "Why I Love the Library." Following the tremendous success of her first novel, Tan apparently had great difficulty writing her second book, *The Kitchen God's Wife* (1991). As she was working on it, she began grinding her teeth, which resulted in two broken molars and a sizable dental bill. "I am glad that I shall never again have to write a second book," the author has confessed. "Actually, I cannot recall any writer—with or without a splashy debut—who said the second book came easily." Successful film and stage adaptations of *The Joy Luck Club* in 1993 were followed by *The Chinese Siamese Cat* (1994), *The Hundred Secret Senses* (1995), *The Year of No Flood* (1996), *The Bonesetter's Daughter* (2001), *The Opposite of Fate: A Book of Musings* (2003), and *Saving Fish From Drowning* (2005).

Preparing to Read

In the following essay, originally published in *The Threepenny Review,* Amy Tan explains the different "Englishes" she learned to use in her youth. These had a significant effect on her as she grew up to be a successful writer.

Exploring Experience: As you prepare to read this essay, take a few minutes to think about the different varieties of English that you use: How do you change your use of English when you relay the same message to different people? Why do you make these changes? Do you feel as if you do well in English class? On English tests? How could you become an even better writer and speaker of English than you already are?

Learning Online: To better understand Tan's cultural context, conduct an Internet search on the experience of Chinese immigrants in the United States. To start your search, you may want to visit "Becoming an American: The Chinese Experience" located at http://www.pbs.org/becomingamerican. Pay special attention to the Chinese/American women's experience.

I am not a scholar of English or literature. I cannot give you much more   1
than personal opinions on the English language and its variations in this
country or others.

I am a writer. And by that definition, I am someone who has always loved   2
language. I am fascinated by language in daily life. I spend a great deal of my
time thinking about the power of language—the way it can evoke an emotion, a visual image, a complex idea, or a simple truth. Language is the tool
of my trade. And I use them all—all the Englishes I grew up with. 1

Recently, I was made keenly aware of the different Englishes I do use. I   3
was giving a talk to a large group of people, the same talk I had already given
to half a dozen other groups. The nature of the talk was about my writing,
my life, and my book, *The Joy Luck Club*. The talk was going along well
enough, until I remembered one major difference that made the whole talk
sound wrong. My mother was in the room. And it was perhaps the first time
she had heard me give a lengthy speech, using the kind of English I have never
used with her. I was saying things like, "The intersection of memory upon
imagination" and "There is an aspect of my fiction that relates to thus-and-
thus"—a speech filled with carefully wrought grammatical phrases, bur-
dened, it suddenly seemed to me, with nominalized forms, past perfect tenses,
conditional phrases, all the forms of standard English that I had learned in
school and through books, the forms of English I did not use at home with
my mother.

Just last week, I was walking down the street with my mother, and I again   4
found myself conscious of the English I was using, the English I do use with
her. We were talking about the price of new and used furniture and I heard
myself saying this: "Not waste money that way." My husband was with us as
well, and he didn't notice any switch in my English. And then I realized why.
It's because over the twenty years we've been together I've often used the
same kind of English with him, and sometimes he even uses it with me. It
has become our language of intimacy, 2 a different sort of English that relates to family talk, the language I grew up with.

So you'll have some idea of what this family talk I heard sounds like, I'll   5
quote what my mother said during a recent conversation which I videotaped and then transcribed. During this conversation, my mother was talking about a political gangster in Shanghai who had the same last name as her
family's, Du, and how the gangster in his early years wanted to be adopted
by her family, which was rich by comparison. Later, the gangster became

---

Reading Critically
1 Why does Tan use the word "Englishes" to describe her love of language?
2 What does the author mean by the phrase "our language of intimacy"?

more powerful, far richer than my mother's family, and one day showed up at my mother's wedding to pay his respects. Here's what she said in part:

"Du Yusong having business like fruit stand. Like of the street kind. He is 6 Du like Du Zong—but not Tsung-ming Island people. The local people call *putong,* the river east side, he belong to that side local people. That man want to ask Du Zong father take him in like become own family. Du Zong father wasn't look down on him, but didn't take seriously, until that man big like become a mafia. Now important person, very hard to inviting him. Chinese way, came only to show respect, don't stay for dinner. Respect for making big celebration, he shows up. Mean gives lots of respect. Chinese custom. Chinese social life that way. If too important won't have to stay too long. He come to my wedding. I didn't see, I heard it. I gone to boy's side, they have YMCA dinner, Chinese age I was nineteen." ❸

You should know that my mother's expressive command of English be- 7 lies how much she actually understands. She reads the *Forbes* report, listens to *Wall Street Week,* converses daily with her stockbroker, reads all of Shirley MacLaine's books with ease—all kinds of things I can't begin to understand. Yet some of my friends tell me they understand 50 percent of what my mother says. Some say they understand 80 to 90 percent. Some say they understand none of it, as if she were speaking pure Chinese. But to me, my mother's English is perfectly clear, perfectly natural. It's my mother tongue. Her language, as I hear it, is vivid, direct full of observation and imagery. That was the language that helped shape the way I saw things, expressed things, made sense of the world.

Lately, I've been giving more thought to the kind of English my mother 8 speaks. Like others, I have described it to people as "broken" or "fractured" English. But I wince when I say that. It has always bothered me that I can think of no way to describe it other than "broken," as if it were damaged and needed to be fixed, as if it lacked a certain wholeness and soundness. I've heard other terms used, "limited English," for example. But they seem just as bad, as if everything is limited, including people's perceptions of the limited English speaker.

I know this for a fact, because when I was growing up, my mother's "lim- 9 ited" English limited *my* perception of her. ❹ I was ashamed of her English. I believed that her English reflected the quality of what she had to say. That is, because she expressed them imperfectly, her thoughts were imperfect. And I had plenty of empirical evidence to support me: the fact that people in

---

Reading Critically

❸ What is the author's main point here? Why does the gangster come to Tan's mother's wedding?

❹ How true is this in your life? To what extent do you judge others by their use of English?

department stores, at banks, and at restaurants did not take her seriously, did not give her good advice, pretended not to understand her, or even acted as if they did not hear her.

My mother has long realized the limitations of her English as well. When   10 I was fifteen, she used to have me call people on the phone and pretend I was she. In this guise, I was forced to ask for information or even to complain and yell at people who had been rude to her. One time it was a call to her stockbroker in New York. She had cashed out her small portfolio, and it just so happened we were going to go to New York the next week, our very first trip outside California. I had to get on the phone and say in an adolescent voice that was not very convincing, "This is Mrs. Tan."

And my mother was standing in the back whispering loudly, "Why he don't   11 send me check, already two weeks late. So mad he lie to me, losing my money."

And then I said in perfect English, "Yes, I'm getting rather concerned.   12 You had agreed to send the check two weeks ago, but it hasn't arrived."

Then she began to talk more loudly. "What he want, I come to New York   13 tell him front of his boss, you cheating me?" And I was trying to calm her down, make her be quiet, while telling the stockbroker, "I can't tolerate any more excuses. If I don't receive the check immediately, I am going to have to speak to your manager when I'm in New York next week." And sure enough, the following week there we were in front of this astonished stockbroker, and I was sitting there red-faced and quiet, and my mother, the real Mrs. Tan, was shouting at his boss in her impeccable broken English. 🔶5

We used a similar routine just five days ago, for a situation that was far less   14 humorous. My mother had gone to the hospital for an appointment, to find out about a benign brain tumor a CAT scan had revealed a month ago. She said she had spoken very good English, her best English, no mistakes. Still, she said, the hospital did not apologize when they said they had lost the CAT scan and she had come for nothing. She said they did not seem to have any sympathy when she told them she was anxious to know the exact diagnosis, since her husband and son had both died of brain tumors. She said they would not give her any more information until the next time and she would have to make another appointment for that. So she said she would not leave until the doctor called her daughter. She wouldn't budge. And when the doctor finally called her daughter, me, who spoke in perfect English— lo and behold—we had assurances the CAT scan would be found, promises

---

Reading Critically

🔶5 Why does Tan use the oxymoron "impeccable broken English" here? What does the phrase mean?

that a conference call on Monday would be held, and apologies for any suffering my mother had gone through for a most regrettable mistake.

I think my mother's English almost had an effect on limiting my possibilities in life as well. Sociologists and linguists probably will tell you that a person's developing language skills are more influenced by peers. But I do think that the language spoken in the family, especially in immigrant families which are more insular, plays a large role in shaping the language of the child. ⑥ And I believe that it affected my results on achievement tests, IQ tests, and the SAT. While my English skills were never judged as poor, compared to math, English could not be considered my strong suit. In grade school I did moderately well, getting perhaps B's, sometimes B-pluses, in English and scoring perhaps in the sixtieth or seventieth percentile on achievement tests. But those scores were not good enough to override the opinion that my true abilities lay in math and science, because in those areas I achieved A's and scored in the ninetieth percentile or higher.

This was understandable. Math is precise; there is only one correct answer. ⑦ Whereas, for me at least, the answers on English tests were always a judgment call, a matter of opinion and personal experience. Those tests were constructed aråound items like fill-in-the-blank sentence completion, such as "Even though Tom was _____, Mary thought he was _____." And the correct answer always seemed to be the most bland combinations of thoughts, for example, "Even though Tom was shy, Mary thought he was charming," with the grammatical structure "even though" limiting the correct answer to some sort of semantic opposites, so you wouldn't get answers like, "Even though Tom was foolish, Mary thought he was ridiculous." Well, according to my mother, there were very few limitations as to what Tom could have been and what Mary might have thought of him. So I never did well on tests like that.

The same was true with word analogies, pairs of words in which you were supposed to find some sort of logical, semantic relationship—for example, "Sunset is to nightfall as _____ is to _____." And here you would be presented with a list of four possible pairs, one of which showed the same kind of relationship: *red* is to *stoplight, bus* is to *arrival, chills* is to *fever, yawn* is to *boring.* Well, I could never think that way. I knew what the tests were asking, but I could not block out of my mind the images already created by the first pair, *"sunset is to nightfall"*—and I would see a burst

15

16

17

Reading Critically

⑥ Do you think this is true? How has the English you heard as a child influenced your use of language today?

⑦ Which subject do you like better—math or English? Why?

of colors against a darkening sky, the moon rising, the lowering of a curtain of stars. And all the other pairs of words—red, bus, stoplight, boring—just threw up a mass of confusing images, making it impossible for me to sort out something as logical as saying: "A sunset precedes nightfall" is the same as "a chill precedes a fever." The only way I would have gotten that answer right would have been to imagine an associative situation, for example, my being disobedient and staying out past sunset, catching a chill at night, which turns into feverish pneumonia as punishment, which indeed did happen to me.

I have been thinking about all this lately, about my mother's English, about   18 achievement tests. Because lately I've been asked, as a writer, why there are not more Asian Americans represented in American literature. Why are there few Asian Americans enrolled in creative writing programs? Why do so many Chinese students go into engineering? Well, these are broad sociological questions I can't begin to answer. But I have noticed in surveys—in fact, just last week—that Asian students, as a whole, always do significantly better on math achievement tests than in English. And this makes me think that there are other Asian-American students whose English spoken in the home might also be described as "broken" or "limited." And perhaps they also have teach- ers who are steering them away from writing and into math and science, which is what happened to me. ⑧

Fortunately, I happen to be rebellious in nature and enjoy the challenge   19 of disproving assumptions made about me. I became an English major my first year in college, after being enrolled as pre-med. I started writing non- fiction as a freelancer the week after I was told by my former boss that writ- ing was my worst skill and I should hone my talents toward account management.

But it wasn't until 1985 that I finally began to write fiction. And at first I   20 wrote using what I thought to be wittily crafted sentences, sentences that would prove I had mastery over the English language. Here's an example from the first draft of a story that later made its way into *The Joy Luck Club,* but without this line: "That was my mental quandary in its nascent state." A terrible line, which I can barely pronounce.

Fortunately, for reasons I won't get into today, I later decided I should   21 envision a reader for the stories I would write. And the reader I decided upon was my mother, because these were stories about mothers. So with this reader in mind—and in fact she did read my early drafts—I began to write stories using all the Englishes I grew up with: the English I spoke to

---

Reading Critically

⑧ Do you think ethnic bias exists in the career advice students receive in high school and college?

my mother, which for lack of a better term might be described as "simple"; the English she used with me, which for lack of a better term might be described as "broken"; my translation of her Chinese, which could certainly be described as "watered down"; and what I imagined to be her translation of her Chinese if she could speak in perfect English, her internal language, [9] and for that I sought to preserve the essence, but neither an English nor a Chinese structure. I wanted to capture what language ability tests can never reveal: her intent, her passion, her imagery, the rhythms of her speech, and the nature of her thoughts.

Apart from what any critic had to say about my writing, I knew I had succeeded where it counted when my mother finished reading my book and gave me her verdict: "So easy to read."   22

UNDERSTANDING DETAILS

1. What do you think is Tan's main reason for writing this essay?
2. What are the four "Englishes" that Tan grew up with? Explain each in your own words.
3. What is Tan referring to when she uses the term "mother tongue"?
4. How did Tan feel about her mother's "limited English" in the past?

THINKING CRITICALLY

5. How did Amy Tan become a writer? In what way did her rebellious nature help her make this decision?
6. How do all the Englishes Tan grew up with help her as a writer? Explain your answer.
7. What relationship does Tan see between achievement test scores and actual abilities?
8. Why did Tan choose her mother as the audience she envisions when she writes?

DISCOVERING RHETORICAL STRATEGIES

9. Why does Tan actually quote some of her mother's language early in her essay? What effect does this example have on you as a reader?
10. List Tan's main points in this essay. Why do you think she deals with these topics in this particular order?
11. Describe Tan's intended audience in as much detail as possible. Why do you think she aims her essay at this particular group?
12. What other rhetorical strategies does Tan use to help make her point? Give examples of each of these strategies.

Reading Critically

[9] What does Tan mean when she refers to her mother's "internal language"?

MAKING CONNECTIONS

13. Compare and contrast Amy Tan's relationship with her mother and the parent–child relationships examined in any or all of the following essays: Lewis Sawaquat's "For My Indian Daughter," Russell Baker's "The Saturday Evening Post," Bill Cosby's "The Baffling Question," and Wallerstein and Blakeslee's "Second Chances for Children of Divorce."

14. In her essay, Tan describes her love of English and her avocation as a writer despite her relatively weak performance on English achievement tests as a child. Examine the manner in which other people exceeded the expectations placed on them as expressed in Maya Angelou's "New Directions," Russell Baker's "The Saturday Evening Post," Harold Krents's "Darkness at Noon," and/or Alice Walker's "Beauty: When the Other Dancer Is the Self."

15. Discuss the theme of "the limitations of language" as it appears in the following essays: Amy Tan's "Mother Tongue," Stephanie Ericsson's "The Ways We Lie," Mary Roach's "Meet the Bickersons," and/or Sherman Alexie's "The Joy of Reading and Writing: Superman and Me."

IDEAS FOR DISCUSSION/WRITING

Preparing to Write

Write freely about your own abilities in English: Do you feel you use more than one version of English? How does your oral English differ from your written English? Is English your first language? What do you think of yourself as a writer? As a reader? How well do you perform on English achievement tests?

Choosing a Topic

1. As a college student, you see different people approaching their writing assignments in different ways every day. Some students get right down to work. Others procrastinate until the last minute. Some write in spurts until they have finished the task. Write an essay for your school newspaper explaining your observations about the different ways people write. Use carefully chosen examples to illustrate your observations. You might even want to interview some of your peers about their writing rituals.

2. You have been asked to respond to a national survey on the role of education in our lives. The organization conducting the survey wants to know the extent to which education has helped or hindered you in achieving your goals. In a well-developed essay written for a general audience, explain the benefits and liabilities of education in your life at present. Use specific examples to develop your essay.

3. In her essay, Tan refers to the fact that her teachers steered her "away from writing and into math and science" (paragraph 18) primarily because of her test scores. But she believes her test scores were not an accurate measurement of her ability in English because of her background in the language. Do you think test scores are ever used inappropriately to advise students? Or do you think these scores are the best way we currently have to measure ability and aptitude?

Direct your comments to the general public, and use several specific examples to support your opinion.

4. Tan refers to the ways in which family, culture, and education affect how she speaks and writes. Using recent e-mails you have written, examine the "different Englishes" and other languages you use when communicating with diverse audiences. For example, what words do you use when writing to your friends, your family, or your teachers? How do your language choices differ in each instance? What social pressures affect your use of "different Englishes"? Write an essay that examines your different uses of English and/or other languages. Consider your reasons for using various words when communicating with different people. Use specific examples from your e-mails to support and develop your essay.

Before beginning your essay, you might want to consult the checklists on page 152.

BRENT STAPLES   (1951–   )

A Brother's Murder

Brent Staples was the first of nine children born to a truck driver and a housewife in Chester, Pennsylvania, a factory town fifteen miles south of Philadelphia. He was educated at the Philadelphia Military College and Penn Moton College, eventually graduating from Widener College with honors. A prestigious Danforth Fellowship took him to the University of Chicago, where he earned a Ph.D. in Psychology. His brilliant memoir, *Parallel Time: Growing Up in Black and White* (published by Pantheon Books in 1994), was a finalist for the *Los Angeles Times* Book Award and a winner of the Annisfield Wolff Award, which had previously been won by such luminaries as James Baldwin, Ralph Ellison, and Zora Neale Hurston. A past editor of the *New York Times* Book Review section and an assistant metropolitan editor, Staples currently writes on politics and culture for the *Times* editorial page. He is an avid gardener and is especially fond of roses. When asked to give some advice to college writers, he explained that "ninety percent of writing is rewriting. The simple declarative sentence is your best friend in the world."

Preparing to Read

"A Brother's Murder" was first published in an anthology of African-American writing entitled *Bearing Witness*. In this emotional account of his brother's death, Staples realizes many important truths about the role of violence among African-American men.

Exploring Experience: Before reading this essay, think for a few moments about violence in general: From your observations, which kinds of people are most violent? Why do these people use violence? What do you think is the cause of most violent acts? In your opinion, why is the crime rate so high in American society today? Can we do anything to reduce this crime rate? What are some of your constructive suggestions for controlling violence today? Which are most realistic?

Learning Online: Brent Staples uses personal examples to explore the causes and effects of youth violence in his hometown. Visit the "Building Blocks for Youth" Web site located at http://www.buildingblocksforyouth .org/. Click on the "Research" button, and read one of their online articles about violence in African-American communities. Consider the use of examples, such as statistics and dates, in the article as you read Brent Staples's essay.

I t has been more than two years since my telephone rang with the news 1
that my younger brother Blake—just 22 years old—had been murdered.
The young man who killed him was only 24. Wearing a ski mask, he
emerged from a car, fired six times at close range with a massive .44 Magnum, then fled. The two had once been inseparable friends. A senseless rivalry—beginning, I think, with an argument over a girlfriend—escalated from posturing, to threats, to violence, to murder. The way the two were living, death could have come to either of them from anywhere. In fact, the assailant had already survived multiple gunshot wounds from an incident much like the one in which my brother lost his life.

As I wept for Blake, I felt wrenched backward into events and circum- 2
stances that had seemed light-years gone. Though a decade apart, we both
were raised in Chester, Pennsylvania, an angry, heavily black, heavily poor,
industrial city southwest of Philadelphia. There, in the 1960s, I was introduced
to mortality, not by the old and failing, but by beautiful young men who lay
wrecked after sudden explosions of violence. The first, I remember from my
14th year—Johnny, brash lover of fast cars, stabbed to death two doors from
my house in a fight over a pool game. The next year, my teen-age cousin,
Wesley, whom I loved very much, was shot dead. The summers blur. Milton,
an angry young neighbor, shot a crosstown rival, wounding him badly.
William, another teen-age neighbor, took a shotgun blast to the shoulder in
some urban drama and displayed his bandages proudly. His brother, Leonard,
severely beaten, lost an eye and donned a black patch. It went on.

I recall not long before I left for college, two local Vietnam veterans— 3
one from the Marines, one from the Army—arguing fiercely, nearly at
blows about which outfit had done the most in the war. The most killing,
they meant. Not much later, I read in a magazine article that set that dispute in a context. In the story, a noncommissioned officer—a sergeant, I
believe—said he would pass up any number of affluent, suburban-born recruits to get hard-core soldiers from the inner city. They jumped into the
rice paddies with "their manhood on their sleeves," I believe he said. These
two items—the veterans arguing and the sergeant's words—still characterize for me the circumstances under which black men in their teens and 20's
kill one another with such frequency. With a touchy paranoia born of living battered lives, they are desperate to be *real* men. ◆ Killing is only
machismo taken to the extreme. Incursions to be punished by death were
many and minor, and they remain so: they include stepping on the wrong

---

Reading Critically

◆ What did wearing "their manhood on their sleeves" have to do with being "real" men for
Blake's group? What other actions or rituals might be more civilized and productive in
helping young people define themselves as "real"?

toe, literally; cheating in a drug deal; simply saying "I dare you" to someone holding a gun; crossing territorial lines in a gang dispute. My brother
grew up to wear his manhood on his sleeve. And when he died, he was in
that group—black, male, and in its teens and early 20's—that is far and
away the most likely to murder or be murdered.

I left the East Coast after college, spent the mid- and late-1970's in Chicago   4
as a graduate student, taught for a time, then became a journalist. Within 10
years of leaving my hometown, I was overeducated and "upwardly mobile,"
ensconced on a quiet, tree-lined street where voices raised in anger were
scarcely ever heard. ❷ The telephone, like some grim umbilical, ❸ kept me
connected to the old world with news of deaths, imprisonings, and misfor-
tune. I felt emotionally beaten up. Perhaps to protect myself, I added a psychological dimension to the physical distance I had already achieved. I rarely
visited my hometown. I shut it out.

As I fled the past, so Blake embraced it. On Christmas of 1983, I traveled   5
from Chicago to a black section of Roanoke, Virginia, where he then lived. ·
The desolate public housing projects, the hopeless, idle young men crashing
against one another—these reminded me of the embittered town we'd grown
up in. It was a place where once I would have been comfortable, or at least
sure of myself. Now, hearing of my brother's forays into crime, his scrapes with
police and street thugs, I was scared, unsteady on foreign terrain.

I saw Blake's romance with the street life, and the hustler image had flow-   6
ered dangerously. One evening that late December, standing in some
Roanoke dive among drug dealers and grim, hair-trigger losers, I told him
I feared for his life. He had affected the image of the tough he wanted to be.
But behind the dark glasses and the swagger, I glimpsed the baby-faced tod-
dler I'd once watched over. I nearly wept. I wanted desperately for him to
live. The young think themselves immortal, and a dangerous light shone in
his eyes as he spoke laughingly of making fools of the policemen who had
raided his apartment looking for drugs. He cried out as I took his right hand.
A line of stitches lay between the thumb and index finger. Kickback from a
shotgun, he explained, nothing serious. Gunplay had become part of his life.

I lacked the language simply to say: Thousands have lived this for you and   7
died. ❹ I fought the urge to lift him bodily and shake him. This place and the
way you are living smells of death to me, I said. Take some time away, I said.
Let's go downtown tomorrow and buy a plane ticket anywhere, take a bus

---

Reading Critically

❷ How did Brent escape the claustrophobic environment of the ghetto, while his brother
did not?

❸ How does the concept of mortality (para. 2) relate to the "grim umbilical" in para. 4?

❹ What does the author mean when he writes "Thousands have lived this for you and died"?

trip, anything to get away and cool things off. He took my alarm casually. We arranged to meet the following night—an appointment he would not keep. We embraced as though through glass. I drove away.

As I stood in my apartment in Chicago holding the receiver that evening 8 in February 1984, I felt as though part of my soul had been cut away. I questioned myself then, and I still do. Did I not reach back soon or earnestly enough for him? For weeks I awoke crying from a recurrent dream in which I chased him, urgently trying to get him to read a document I had, as though reading it would protect him from what had happened in waking life. His eyes shining like black diamonds, he smiled and danced just out of my grasp. When I reached for him, I caught only the space where he had been. ◈

UNDERSTANDING DETAILS

1. What does Staples mean when he refers to his brother's death by saying, "The way the two were living, death could have come to either of them from anywhere" (paragraph 1)?
2. What stages did Staples's brother and his murderer go through before Blake was killed?
3. Why do you think Staples wrote this essay? What is his main point?
4. What did Staples learn about African-American males by examining his brother's life?

THINKING CRITICALLY

5. In what ways does Brent Staples's brother represent an important segment of the African-American male population?
6. Why did Staples create a distance between his present life and his past?
7. What examples does Staples use to prove his theory that "killing is only *machismo* taken to the extreme" (paragraph 3)? Do you agree with this conclusion? Can you think of any examples that demonstrate the opposite position?
8. What was "Blake's romance with the street life" (paragraph 6)?

DISCOVERING RHETORICAL STRATEGIES

9. Describe in as much detail as possible Staples's intended audience. Why do you think he aims his essay at this particular group?

Reading Critically

◈ How did the "spaces" these two men lived in help shape their lives? Which spaces best define your life? To what extent are you a different person when you move from one space to another?

10. In what way does Staples's recurring dream (paragraph 8) symbolize the author's relationship with his brother? How does this final paragraph sum up Staples's feelings about the plight of African-American males in American society today?

11. In paragraph 7, Staples uses a simile (a special comparison between two unlike items, using *like* or *as*): "We embraced as though through glass." This image adds an extra dimension to Staples's description. Find another simile in this essay, and explain its effect on you.

12. This essay progresses most obviously through the use of examples. What other rhetorical strategies support this dominant mode? In what ways do they add to Staples's main point?

MAKING CONNECTIONS

13. Through hard work and a college education, Brent Staples was able to rise above the violent environment that contributed to his brother's death. Consider any of the following essays you have read, and explain how the central characters escaped their own difficult environments: Maya Angelou's "New Directions," Harold Krents's "Darkness at Noon," and Wallerstein and Blakeslee's "Second Chances for Children of Divorce."

14. Compare and contrast Staples's comments about violence with opinions on the topic voiced by Kimberly Wozencraft's "Notes from the Country Club," Bruce Catton's "Grant and Lee: A Study in Contrasts," Stephen King's "Why We Crave Horror Movies," Dave Grossman's "We Are Training Our Kids to Kill," and/or Barbara Ehrenreich's "The Ecstasy of War."

15. How do Brent Staples's insights about the community in which his brother lived differ from the sense of "community" in the following essays: William Ouchi's "Japanese and American Workers: Two Casts of Mind," Robert Ramirez's "The Barrio," and/or Scott Russell Sanders's "Homeplace"?

IDEAS FOR DISCUSSION/WRITING

Preparing to Write

Write freely about your view of violence in American society today: What is the source of most of this violence? How can we control violence in American society? Why do you think violence is increasing? How else might we channel our innate violent reactions? What other suggestions do you have for reducing violent crimes today?

Choosing Your Topic

1. Write an essay for a college-educated audience based on one of the following statements: "Current pressure in contemporary society causes most of the violence today" or "People's natural instincts cause most of the violence in contemporary society."

2. Interview some people about how they manage their anger: What do they do when they get mad? How do they control their reactions? Have they ever be-

come violent? Then write an essay for the students in your English class explaining your findings.

3. According to Staples, the military frame of mind—the urge to kill—is at the heart of "the circumstances under which black men in their teens and 20's kill one another with such frequency" (paragraph 3). Do you agree or disagree with this statement? Write a well-developed essay, using examples from your experience, to support your opinion.

4. Staples relates his painful experience to help explain the pervasiveness of youth violence. He selects personal examples rather than statistics or news stories to present his argument. Choose an issue about which you feel strongly, and write an essay in which you argue your position using carefully selected relevant examples. Try to clarify general concepts by using specific details as Staples does. Use the Internet to find statistics or case studies, if necessary, to support your argument.

Before beginning your essay, you might want to consult the checklists on page 152.

Chapter Writing Assignments

Practicing Example

1. Think about some qualities that irritate you in other people's behavior (such as how someone drives, how someone talks on the phone, or how someone laughs). In an essay, use examples to explain a behavior that irritates you and the reason it bothers you so much.

2. Think about all the different roles people play, such as father, teacher, big brother, or sister. Who in your experience provides the best example of how this "role" should be performed? Write an essay that explains why this person is the best example of this role.

3. What do you do best as a writer? Which parts of the writing process do you seem to deal with most successfully? Taking examples from your own writing, compose an essay that discusses your strengths as a writer.

Exploring Ideas

4. Should America as a country promote the use of a single national language, or should we instead acknowledge and encourage the use of multiple languages? Write an essay that explores the advantages and/or disadvantages of either single or multiple languages in American society. As you write, use specific examples to support your position.

5. In what ways do all forms of the media use stereotypes? Choose a specific "type" (such as liberal, conservative, radical, athlete), and, using as many specific examples as possible, explain how the media help or hinder our understanding of a certain personality or issue.

6. Discuss a time when someone embarrassed you publicly. Describe what happened and how it affected you. What, if anything, did you learn from the experience?

Analyzing Visual Images

AP Wide World Photos.

7. The photo above is entitled "Miracle on Ice" and reflects the moment the United States defeated, against all odds, the Russians in the 1980 Olympic games before going on to win the gold medal in ice hockey. This victory is an example of team members pulling together to accomplish a major goal and an improbable upset. Think of a time when you had to accomplish a difficult feat—against all odds—and needed others to help you overcome these obstacles. Write a narrative essay about this time, using specific examples to support your points.

8. Look at the picture on page 143 at the beginning of this chapter. How does it make you feel? Think about other places in your own city that make you feel the same way, and explain your response in a narrative essay. Remember to use specific examples to help illustrate your point.

Chapter 4

PROCESS ANALYSIS
Explaining Step by Step

Human nature is characterized by the perpetual desire to understand and analyze the process of living well. The best-seller list is always crowded with books on how to know yourself better, how to be assertive, how to become famous, how to survive a natural disaster, or how to be rich and happy—all explained in three easy lessons. Open almost any popular magazine, and you will find numerous articles on how to lose weight, how elections are run in this country, how to dress for success, how a political rally evolved, how to gain power, or how to hit a successful topspin backhand. People naturally gravitate toward material that tells them how something is done, how something happened, or how something works, especially if they think the information will help them improve their lives in a significant way.

DEFINING PROCESS ANALYSIS

A *process* is a procedure that follows a series of steps or stages; *analysis* involves taking a subject apart and explaining its components in order to better understand the whole. Process analysis, then, explains an action, a mechanism, or an event from beginning to end. It concentrates on either a mental or a physical operation: how to solve a chemistry problem, how to tune up your car, how John F. Kennedy was shot, how the telephone system works. In fact, the explanation of the writing process beginning on page 18

188

of this book is a good case in point: It divides writing into three interrelated verbal activities and explains how they each work—separately and together.

A process analysis can take one of two forms: (1) It can give directions, thereby explaining how to do something (directive), or (2) it can give information about how something happened or how something works (informative). The first type of analysis gives directions for a task the reader may wish to attempt in the future. Examples include how to make jelly, how to lose weight, how to drive to Los Angeles, how to assemble stereo equipment, how to make money, how to use a microscope, how to knit, how to resuscitate a dying relationship, how to win friends, how to discipline your child, and how to backpack.

The second type of analysis furnishes information about what actually occurred in specific situations or how something works. Examples include how Hiroshima was bombed, how certain Hollywood stars live, how the tax system works, how the movie *Chicago* was filmed, how Babe Ruth earned a place in the Baseball Hall of Fame, how gold was first discovered in California, how computers work, how a kibbutz functions, and how the Gulf War began. These subjects and others like them respond to a certain fascination we all have with mastering some processes and understanding the intricate details of others. They all provide us with opportunities to raise our own standard of living, either by helping us directly apply certain processes to our own lives or by increasing our understanding of how our complex world functions.

The following student paragraph analyzes the process of constructing a garden compost pit. Written primarily for people who might wish to make such a pit, this piece is directive rather than informative. Notice in particular the amount of detail the student calls upon to explain each stage of the process and the clear transitions she uses to guide us through her analysis.

No garden is complete without a functioning compost pit. Here's a simple, inexpensive way to make your garbage work for you! To begin with, make a pen out of hog wire or chicken wire, four feet long by eight feet wide by four feet high, splitting it down the middle with another piece of wire so that you end up with a structure that looks like a capital "E" on its side. This is a compost duplex. In the first pen, place a layer of soda ash, just sprinkled on the surface of the dirt. Then pile an inch or so of leaves, grass clippings, or sawdust on top of the soda ash. You're now ready for the exciting part. Start throwing in all the organic refuse from your kitchen (no meat, bones, or grease, please). After the food is a foot or so deep, throw in a shovelful of steer manure, and cover the entire mess with a thin layer of dirt. Then water it down. Continue this layering process until the pile is three to three-and-a-half feet high. Allow the pile to sit until it decomposes (from one month in warm climates to six months in colder weather). Next, take your pitchfork and start slinging the contents of pen one into pen two (which will land in reverse order, of course, with the top on the bottom and the bottom on the top). This ensures that everything will decompose evenly. Water this down and begin making a new pile in pen one. That's all there is to it! You now have a ready supply of fertilizer for your garden.

THINKING CRITICALLY THROUGH PROCESS ANALYSIS

Thinking

Reading · Writing

- Slow down.
- Gain a clear perspective on your subject.
- Be aware of the total product or event.

Process analysis embodies clear, careful, step-by-step thinking that takes one of three different forms: chronological, simultaneous, or cyclical. The first follows a time sequence from "first this" to "then that." The second forces you to deal with activities or events that happen or happened at the same time, such as people quietly studying or just getting home from work when the major 1994 earthquake hit Los Angeles. And the third requires you to process information that is continuous, like the rising and setting of the sun. No other thinking pattern will force you to slow down as much as process analysis because the process you are explaining probably won't make any sense if you leave out even the slightest detail.

Good process analysis can truly help your reader see an event in a totally new light. An observer looks at a product already assembled or at a completed event and has no way of knowing without the help of a good process analysis how it got to this final stage. Such an analysis gives the writer or speaker as well as the observer a completely new way of "seeing" the subject in question. Separating process analysis from the other rhetorical modes lets you practice this method of thinking so that you will have a better understanding of the various mental procedures going on in your head. Exercising this possibility in isolation will help you feel its range and its intricacies so that you can become more adept at using it, fully developed, in combination with other modes of thought.

1. In the picture on the next page, the photographer manipulates our view by using a particular lens and by positioning the photo so that the man on the surfboard is almost in the middle of the scene. What are other ways we manipulate or influence people's views? Brainstorm about how you influence the views or ideas of people around you? What are your most effective techniques? Explain to someone else in class how you effectively

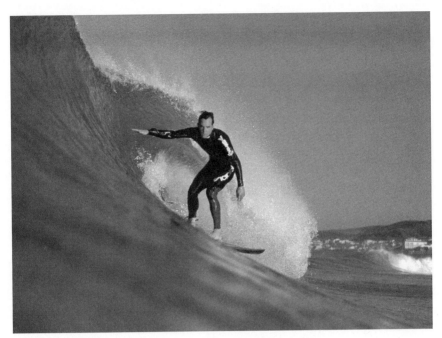

© Rick Doyle/CORBIS.

influence people you know, or explain how to avoid unfairly manipulating or influencing others.

2. List as many examples of each type of process (chronological, simultaneous, and cyclical) that you can think of. Share your list with the class.

3. Write a paragraph telling how *not* to do something. Practice your use of humor as a technique for creating interest in the essay by emphasizing the "wrong" way, for example, to wash a car or feed a dog.

Reading and Writing Process Analysis Essays

Your approach to a process analysis essay should be fairly straightforward. As a reader, you should be sure you understand the author's statement of purpose and then try to visualize each step as you go along. As a writer, you need to adapt the mechanics of the way you normally write to the demands of a process analysis paper, beginning with an interesting topic and a number of clearly explained ideas or stages. As usual, the intended audience determines the choice of words and the degree of detail.

READING PROCESS ANALYSIS ESSAYS

Thinking

Reading   Writing

- Is the essay *directive* or *informative?*
- What is the author's general message?

Preparing to Read.   Preparing to read a process analysis essay is as uncomplicated as the essay itself. The title of Edwin Bliss's essay in this chapter, "Managing Your Time," tells us exactly what we are going to learn about. Julia Bourland's title, "Getting Out of Debt (and Staying Out)," also lets us know what we are going to get. Scanning each selection to assess the author's audience will give you an even better idea of what to expect in these essays, while the synopsis of each in the Rhetorical Table of Contents will help focus your attention on its subject.

Also important as you prepare to read these essays are the qualifications of each author to write on their subject: Has he or she performed the task, worked with the mechanism, or seen the event? Is the writer's experience firsthand? When Edwin Bliss discusses "Managing Your Time," is he writing from his personal experience? What is Jessica Mitford's experience with mortuaries? How does she know what goes on "Behind the Formaldehyde Curtain"? The biography preceding each essay will help you uncover this information and find out other publication details that will encourage you to focus on the material you are about to read.

Finally, before you begin reading, answer the prereading questions, and then do some brainstorming on the subject of the essay: What do you want to know about sports heroes (Jay Weiner)? How well do you read, and what do you think you can learn about the subject from Malcolm X?

Reading.   When you read the essays in this chapter for the first time, record your initial reactions to them. Consider the preliminary information you have been studying in order to create a context for each author's composition: What circumstances prompted Mitford's "Behind the Formaldehyde Curtain"? Why did Jay Weiner write "Sports Centered"? Who do you think is Bourland's target audience in "Getting Out of Debt (and Staying Out)"?

Some questions at the bottom of the pages of these essays are designed to help you understand the essay and make connections that you might not otherwise see. These questions will encourage you to generate ideas that will be essential to completing the exercises and writing assignments that follow the essays. If you respond to them as you read, they will give you new ideas to work with as you continue to read. Recording your answers to these questions would be especially beneficial to your thought processes.

Included in these essays at the bottom of the pages are questions to help you think critically about the content and structure of each essay. These questions will provide ways for you to process the content and understand the structure of each essay so that you will be prepared to answer the questions and do the writing assignments at the end of the reading selections. They essentially help you build a mental bridge from the prereading activities that appear before each essay to those at the end of your reading assignments. Responding to these inquiries in writing will help you get the biggest benefit from this feature of the text because you will already have some thoughts on paper when you get your next writing task.

Also determine at this point whether the essay you are reading is *directive* (explaining how to do something) or *informative* (giving information about how something happened or how something works). This fundamental understanding of the author's intentions, along with a reading of the questions following the essay, will prepare you to approach the contents of each selection critically when you read it a second time.

Rereading.   As you reread these process analysis essays, look for an overview of the process at the beginning of the essay so you know where each writer is headed. The body of each essay, then, is generally a discussion of the stages of the process.

The central portion of the essay is often organized *chronologically* (as in Mitford's essay on current practices in mortuaries and Malcolm X's essay on his self-education), with clear transitions so that readers can easily follow the writer's train of thought. Other methods of organization are *cyclical* (such as the Bourland essay on debt), describing a process that has no clear beginning or end, and *simultaneous* (such as the essays by Bliss on organizing one's time and by Weiner on writing about sports), in which many activities occur at the same time with a clear beginning and end. Most of these essays discuss the process as a whole at some point. During this second reading, you will also benefit from discovering what rhetorical modes each writer uses to support his or her process analysis and why these rhetorical modes work effectively. What does Bliss's cause/effect reasoning add to his essay on time management? And how do the descriptions in Mitford's essay on embalming heighten the horror of the American mortuary business? Do the examples that Malcolm X gives help explain how reading changed his life? How do all the rhetorical modes in each essay help create a coherent whole? After reading each essay for a second time, answer the questions that follow the selection to see if you are understanding your reading material on the literal, interpretive, and analytical levels before you take on the discussion/writing assignments.

For an overview of the entire reading process, you might consult the checklists on page 29 of the Introduction.

WRITING PROCESS ANALYSIS ESSAYS

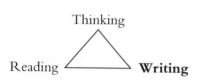

Thinking

Reading ————— **Writing**

- Provide an overview of the process.
- Draft a purpose statement or thesis.
- Make your essay *directive* or *informative*.
- Organize your essay chronologically, simultaneously, or cyclically.
- End with a description of the process as a whole.

Prewriting.   As you begin a process analysis assignment, you first need to become as familiar as you can with the action, mechanism, or event you are going to describe. If possible, try to go through the process yourself at least once or twice. If you can't actually carry out the procedure, going through the process mentally and taking notes is a good alternative. Then, try to read something about the process. After all this preparation (and careful consideration of your audience and purpose), you should be ready to brainstorm, freewrite, cluster, or use your favorite prewriting technique (see pages 19–21 of the Introduction) in response to the prewriting questions before you start composing your paper.

Writing.   The essay should begin with an overview of the process or event to be analyzed. This initial section should introduce the subject, divide it into a number of recognizable steps, and describe the result once the process is complete. Your thesis in a process essay is usually a purpose statement that clearly and briefly explains your approach to the procedure you will discuss: "Building model airplanes can be divided into four basic steps" or "The American courts follow three stages in prosecuting a criminal case."

Next, a directive or informative essay should proceed logically through the various stages of the process, from beginning to end. The parts of a process usually fall nicely into chronological order, supported by such transitions as "at first," "in the beginning," "next," "then," "after that," and "finally." Some processes, however, are either simultaneous, forcing the writer to choose a more complex logical order for the essay (such as classification), or cyclical, requiring the writer to choose a starting point and then explain the cycle stage by stage. Playing the guitar, for example, involves two separate and simultaneous components that must work together: holding the strings against the frets with the fingers of one hand and strumming with the other hand. In analyzing this procedure, you would probably want to describe both parts of the process and then explain how the hands work together to produce music. An example of a cyclical process would be the changing of the seasons. To explain this concept to a reader, you would need to pick a starting point, such as spring, and describe the entire cycle, stage by stage, from that point onward.

In a process paper, you need to be especially sensitive to your intended audience, or they will not be able to follow your explanation. The amount of information, the number of examples and illustrations, and the terms to be defined all depend on the prior knowledge and background of your readers. A writer explaining to a group of amateur cooks how to prepare a soufflé would take an entirely different approach to the subject than he or she would if the audience were a group of bona fide chefs hoping to land jobs in elegant French restaurants. The professional chefs would need more sophisticated and precise explanations than their recreational counterparts, who would probably find such an approach tedious and complicated because of the extraneous details.

The last section of a process analysis paper should consider the process as a whole. If, for example, the writer is giving directions on how to build a model airplane, the essay might end with a good description or drawing of the plane. The informative essay on our legal system might offer a summary of the stages of judging and sentencing a criminal. And the essay on cooking a soufflé might finish with a photograph of the mouth-watering dish.

Rewriting.   In order to revise a process analysis essay, first make sure your main purpose is apparent throughout your paper:

- Is your purpose statement clear?

  Next, you need to determine if your paper is aimed at the proper audience:

- Have you given your readers an overview of the process you are going to discuss?
- Do you go through the process step by step?
- At the end of the essay, do you help your readers see the process as a whole?

The checklists on page 30 will give you further guidelines for writing, revising, and proofreading.

STUDENT ESSAY: PROCESS ANALYSIS AT WORK

The student essay that follows analyzes the process of using a "home permanent" kit. Notice that, once the student gives an overview of the process, she discusses the steps one at a time, being careful to follow a logical order (in this case, chronological) and to use clear transitions. Then, see how the end of the essay shows the process as a whole.

Follow the Simple Directions

Although fickle hairstylists in Paris and Hollywood decide what is currently "in," many romanticists disregard fashion and yearn for a mane of delicate tendrils. <u>Sharing this urge but resenting the cost, I opted for a "home perm" kit.</u> Any literate person with normal dexterity could follow illustrated directions, I reasoned, and the eight easy steps would energize my limp locks in less than two hours. "Before" and "after" photos of flawless models showed the metamorphosis one might achieve. Confidently, I assembled towels, rollers, hair clips, waving lotion, neutralizer, end papers, and a plastic cap. <u>While shampooing,</u> I chortled about my ingenuity and economy.

<u>After towel-drying my hair,</u> I applied the gooey, acidic waving lotion thoroughly. Then I wrapped an end paper around a parted section and rolled the first curl ("securely but not too tightly"). Despite the reassuring click of the fastened rollers, as I sectioned each new curl the previous one developed its own volition and slowly unrolled itself. Resolutely, I reapplied waving lotion and rewound—and rewound— each curl. <u>Since my hair was already saturated, I regarded the next direction skeptically:</u> "Apply waving lotion to each curl." Faithfully, however, I complied with the instructions. <u>Ignoring the fragile state of the fastened rollers,</u> I then feigned assurance and enclosed my entire head in a plastic cap. In forty minutes, chemical magic would occur.

Restless with anticipation, I puttered about the house; while absorbed in small chores, I felt the first few drops of lotion escape from the plastic tent. Stuffing wads of cotton around the cap's edges did not help, and the small drops soon became rivulets that left red streaks on my neck and face and splattered on the floor. (Had I overdone the waving lotion?) Ammonia fumes so permeated each room that I was soon asked to leave. Retreating to the bathroom, I opened the window and dreamed of frivolous new hairstyles.

<u>Finally, the waving time had elapsed; neutralizing was next.</u> I removed my plastic cap, carefully heeding

[margin notes:]

Purpose statement for informative process analysis

Overview

First step, (chronological order)

Transition

Second step

Third step

Transition

Fourth step

Transition

Fifth step

Transition

Sixth step

the caution: "Do not disturb curlers as you rinse waving lotion from hair." With their usual impudence, however, all the curlers soon bobbed in the sink; undaunted, I continued. "This next step is critical," warned the instructions. Thinking half-hearted curls were better than no curls at all, I poured the entire

Transition
Seventh
step

bottle of neutralizer on my hair. After a drippy ten-minute wait, I read the next step: "Carefully remove rollers." As this advice was superfluous, I moved anxiously to the finale: "Rinse all solution from your hair, and enjoy your curls."

Transition

Eighth step

Final
product

Lifting my head from the sink and expecting visions of Aphrodite, I saw instead Medusa's image in the mirror. Limp question-mark spirals fell over my eyes, and each "curl" ended in an explosion of steel-wool frizz. Reflecting on my ineptitude, I knew why the direction page was illustrated only with drawings. After washing a large load of ammonia-scented towels, I took two aspirin and called my hairdresser. Some repair services are cheap at any price.

Concluding
remark

Student Writer's Comments

Any person with normal dexterity can probably do a successful perm, but I sure had trouble! I decided I wanted to communicate that trouble in my process analysis essay. When I was given this writing assignment, I knew immediately that I wanted to explain how to do a perm. But I didn't know how to handle the humor that had resulted from my misguided attempt to administer a perm to myself. Part of my response to this assignment resides deep within my personality (I'm a closet comedian), but part of it simply has to do with the relationship between me and permanents (actually, anything having to do with cosmetics). But as I started out on this project, I had no idea if I could mold the comedy into a step-by-step analysis of a process.

First, I went to the store and bought a brand-new home perm, so I could review the guidelines step by step. On a piece of paper, I listed the procedures for giving myself a perm. On another sheet of paper, I wrote down any stories or associations I had with each stage of the process. Some of the notes on the second sheet of paper took the form of full paragraphs, others a list of words and phrases, and still others a combination of lists and full sentences. I found myself laughing aloud at some of the memories the home perm directions triggered.

I knew I was writing a directive essay for someone who might actually want to try a home perm. After making my preliminary lists of ideas, I just let my natural sense of humor direct my writing. My overview and purpose statement came easily. Next, I went through the directions one by one, laughing at myself and the process along the way. Before I knew it, I found myself writing, "After washing a large load of ammonia-scented towels, I took two aspirin and called my hairdresser"—the perfect end, or so I thought, to my comedy of errors. I had written the whole first draft from start to finish without once surfacing for air.

When I reread my draft, I realized that the approach I had taken to this process analysis assignment was a satirical one. It allowed me to go through the proper procedure of giving myself a home perm while simultaneously poking fun at myself along the way. As I revised my essay, I tried to exaggerate some of the humorous sections that demonstrated my ineptness or my failure to follow the directions correctly, hoping they would communicate the true ridiculousness of this entire situation. After omitting some details and embellishing others, I came up with the current last sentence of the essay: "Some repair services are cheap at any price." This new concluding remark took the edge off the whiny tone of the previous sentence and brought the essay to an even lighter close than before. I ended up liking the way the humor worked in the essay, because besides accurately capturing my most recent process analysis experience, it made a potentially dull essay topic rather entertaining. My only problem now is that I'm still not sure I got all the frizz out of my hair!

SOME FINAL THOUGHTS ON PROCESS ANALYSIS

In this chapter, a single process dictates the development and organization of each of the essays that follow. Both directional and informational methods are represented here. Notice in particular the clear purpose statements that set the focus of the essays in each case, as well as the other rhetorical modes (such as narration, comparison/contrast, and definition) that are used to help support the writers' explanations.

PROCESS ANALYSIS IN REVIEW

Reading Process Analysis Essays

Preparing to Read

✓ What assumptions can you make from the essay's title?

✓ Can you guess what the general mood of the essay is?

✓ What is the essay's purpose and audience?

✓ What does the synopsis tell you about the essay?

✓ What can you learn from the author's biography?

✓ Can you predict the author's point of view toward the subject?

Reading

✓ Is the essay *directive* (explaining how to do something) or *informative* (giving information about how something happened)?

✓ What is the author's general message?

Rereading

✓ Does the author furnish an overview of the process?

✓ How is the essay organized—chronologically, cyclically, or simultaneously?

✓ What other rhetorical modes does the author use?

Writing Process Analysis Essays

Preparing to Write

✓ What is your purpose?

✓ Who is your audience?

Writing

✓ Do you provide an overview of the process at the beginning?

✓ Does your first paragraph introduce your subject, divide it into steps, describe the result of the process, and include a purpose statement as your thesis?

✓ Is your process analysis essay either *directive* or *informative*?

✓ Are the essay's details organized chronologically, simultaneously, or cyclically?

✓ Does the essay end with the process as a whole?

Rewriting

✓ Is your purpose statement clear?

✓ Have you given your readers an overview of the process you are going to discuss?

✓ Do you go through the process step by step?

✓ At the end of the essay, do you help your readers see the process as a whole?

EDWIN BLISS   (1923–   )

Managing Your Time

An internationally known consultant on time-management techniques, Edwin Bliss earned his B.S. and M.S. degrees at the University of Utah, worked as a reporter for the *Columbus Dispatch,* taught journalism at a variety of schools, and was a lobbyist for the National Industrial Council and the U.S. Chamber of Commerce. Not until he became a member of the Washington staff of Senator Wallace F. Bennett, however, did he begin to understand the importance of time management. Since then, Bliss has put his management techniques to work as a consultant for a number of businesses in America and abroad through public seminars sponsored by a company called CareerTrack. "Organizing your time properly is especially important for college students," he claims; "a knowledge of time-management skills can help you avoid writers' block so that you turn your papers in on time." His first book, *Getting Things Done: The ABC's of Time Management,* was published in 1976 (updated and reissued in 1991); his second, *Doing It Now: A Twelve-Step Program for Overcoming Procrastination,* came out in 1983; and his third, *Are Your Employees Stealing You Blind?* (coauthored with Isamu Aoki), appeared in 1993. Bliss currently lives in central California, where he is writing a book on how to operate a small business.

Preparing to Read

In the following essay, which is taken from *Getting Things Done: The ABC's of Time Management,* Bliss offers a number of specific suggestions to help you organize your time more efficiently.

Exploring Experience: Before reading his essay, take a few minutes to think about how you arrange your days: How carefully do you schedule your time? Do you make lists of things you want to do every day? Do you usually accomplish more or less than you wanted to in a typical day? How well do you concentrate on a single activity? Are you able to say *no* to events you don't want to participate in? How much do you procrastinate? Are all aspects of your life in a healthy balance (e.g., work, recreation, school, and family)? If not, what could you do to create a more balanced life for yourself?

Learning Online: Conduct an Internet search on the phrase "time management," and visit two or more Web sites that appear in the results list. Is time management described as a process on these pages? If so, how do you know it is a process? If not, how is it described? Consider different techniques for presenting time management while reading Bliss's article.

I first became interested in the effective use of time when I was an assis-   1
tant to a U.S. Senator. Members of Congress are faced with urgent and
conflicting demands on their time—for committee work, floor votes,
speeches, interviews, briefings, correspondence, investigations, constituents'
problems, and the need to be informed on a wide range of subjects. The
more successful Congressmen develop techniques for getting maximum benefit from minimum investments of time. If they don't, they don't return.

Realizing that I was not one of those who use time effectively, I began to   2
apply in my own life some of the techniques I had observed. Here are ten I
have found most helpful. ⬥[1]

Plan.   You need a game plan for your day. Otherwise, you'll allocate   3
your time according to whatever happens to land on your desk. And you will
find yourself making the fatal mistake of dealing primarily with problems
rather than opportunities. Start each day by making a general schedule, with
particular emphasis on the two or three major things you would like to accomplish—including things that will achieve long-term goals. Remember,
studies prove what common sense tells us: The more time we spend planning
a project, the less total time is required for it. Don't let today's busywork
crowd planning-time out of your schedule.

Concentrate.   Of all the principles of time management, none is more   4
basic than concentration. People who have serious time-management problems invariably are trying to do too many things at once. The amount of
time spent on a project is not what counts: It's the amount of *uninterrupted*
time. Few problems can resist an all-out attack; few can be solved piecemeal.

Take Breaks.   To work for long periods without taking a break is not an   5
effective use of time. Energy decreases, boredom sets in, and physical stress
and tension accumulate. Switching for a few minutes from a mental task to
something physical—isometric exercises, walking around the office, even
changing from a sitting position to a standing position for a while—can provide relief.

Merely resting, however, is often the best course, and you should not think   6
of a "rest" break as poor use of time. Not only will being refreshed increase
your efficiency, but relieving tension will benefit your health. Anything that
contributes to health is good time management.

Avoid Clutter.   Some people have a constant swirl of papers on their   7
desks and assume that somehow the most important matters will float to the

---

Reading Critically

⬥[1] Do you think a list of ten techniques is too large or too small? Can you suggest a more
manageable number?

top. In most cases, however, clutter hinders concentration and can create tension and frustration—a feeling of being "snowed under." [2]

Whenever you find your desk becoming chaotic, take time out to reor-   8 ganize. Go through all your papers (making generous use of the wastebasket) and divide them into categories: (1) Immediate action, (2) Low priority, (3) Pending, (4) Reading material. Put the highest priority item from your first pile in the center of your desk, then put everything else out of sight. Remember, you can think of only one thing at a time, and you can work on only one task at a time, so focus all your attention on the most important one. A final point: Clearing the desk completely, or at least organizing it, each evening should be standard practice. It gets the next day off to a good start.

Don't Be a Perfectionist.   There is a difference between striving for excellence and striving for perfection. [3] The first is attainable, gratifying, and   9 healthy. The second is often unattainable, frustrating, and neurotic. It's also a terrible waste of time. The stenographer who retypes a lengthy letter because of a trivial error, or the boss who demands such retyping, might profit from examining the Declaration of Independence. When the inscriber of that document made two errors of omission, he inserted the missing letters between the lines. If this is acceptable in the document that gave birth to American freedom, surely it would be acceptable in a letter that will be briefly glanced at en route to someone's file cabinet or wastebasket.

Don't Be Afraid to Say No.   Of all the time-saving techniques ever de-   10 veloped, perhaps the most effective is frequent use of the word *no*. Learn to decline, tactfully but firmly, every request that does not contribute to your goals. If you point out that your motivation is not to get out of work but to save your time to do a better job on the really important things, you'll have a good chance of avoiding unproductive tasks. Remember, many people who worry about offending others wind up living according to other people's priorities.

Don't Procrastinate.   Procrastination is usually a deeply rooted habit. [4]   11 But we can change our habits provided we use the right system. William James, the father of American psychology, discussed such a system in his famous *Principles of Psychology,* published in 1890. It works as follows:

1. Decide to start changing as soon as you finish reading this article, while you are motivated. Taking that first step promptly is important.

Reading Critically

[2] What does Bliss mean by his assertion that "clutter hinders concentration"? Do you agree?

[3] What is the difference between "striving for excellence" and "striving for perfection"? Which do you think is better?

[4] What are the drawbacks and rewards of procrastination?

2. Don't try to do too much too quickly. Just force yourself right now to do one thing you have been putting off. Then, beginning tomorrow morning, start each day by doing the most unpleasant thing on your schedule. Often it will be a small matter: an overdue apology; a confrontation with a fellow worker; an annoying chore you know you should tackle. Whatever it is, do it before you begin your usual morning routine. This simple procedure can well set the tone for your day. You will get a feeling of exhilaration from knowing that although the day is only 15 minutes old, you have already accomplished the most unpleasant thing you have to do all day.

There is one caution: Do not permit any exceptions. William James compared it to rolling up a ball of string; a single slip can undo more than many turns can wind up. Be tough with yourself, for the first few minutes of each day, for the next two weeks, and I promise you a new habit of priceless value. 12

Apply Radical Surgery.   Time-wasting activities are like cancers. They drain off vitality and have a tendency to grow. The only cure is radical surgery. If you are wasting your time in activities that bore you, divert you from your real goals, and sap your energy, cut them out, once and for all. 13

The principle applies to personal habits, routines, and activities as much as to ones associated with your work. Check your appointment calendar, your extracurricular activities, your reading list, your television viewing habits, and ax everything that doesn't give you a feeling of accomplishment or satisfaction. 14

Delegate.   An early example of failure to delegate is found in the Bible. ⑤ Moses, having led his people out of Egypt, was so impressed with his own knowledge and authority that he insisted on ruling personally on every controversy that arose in Israel. His wise father-in-law, Jethro, recognizing that this was poor use of a leader's time, recommended a two-phase approach: First, educate the people concerning the laws; second, select capable leaders and give them full authority over routine matters, freeing Moses to concentrate on major decisions. The advice is still sound. 15

You don't have to be a national leader or a corporate executive to delegate, either. Parents who don't delegate household chores are doing a disservice to themselves and their children. Running a Boy Scout troop can be as time-consuming as running General Motors if you try to do everything yourself. One caution: Giving subordinates jobs that neither you nor anyone else wants to do isn't delegating, it's assigning. Learn to delegate the 16

Reading Critically

⑤ Why do you think the author refers to the Bible here? How does this allusion help his argument?

challenging and rewarding tasks, along with sufficient authority to make necessary decisions. It can help to free your time.

Don't Be a "Workaholic."   Most successful executives I know work long   17
hours, but they don't let work interfere with the really important things in life, such as friends, family, and fly fishing. This differentiates them from the workaholic who becomes addicted to work just as people become addicted to alcohol. Symptoms of work addiction include refusal to take a vacation, inability to put the office out of your mind on weekends, a bulging brief-case, and a spouse, son, or daughter who is practically a stranger. [6]

Counseling can help people cope with such problems. But for starters, do   18
a bit of self-counseling. Ask yourself whether the midnight oil you are burn-ing is adversely affecting your health. Ask where your family comes in your list of priorities, whether you are giving enough of yourself to your children and spouse, and whether you are deceiving yourself by pretending that the sacrifices you are making are really for them.

Above all else, good time management involves an awareness that today   19
is all we ever have to work with. The past is irretrievably gone; the future is only a concept. British art critic John Ruskin had the word "TODAY" carved into a small marble block that he kept on his desk as a constant reminder to "Do It Now." But my favorite quotation is by an anonymous philosopher:

> Yesterday is a canceled check.
> Tomorrow is a promissory note.
> Today is ready cash. Use it!

UNDERSTANDING DETAILS

1. What are the ten techniques for managing time that Bliss learned from ob-serving successful members of Congress at work? Explain each in your own words.
2. According to Bliss, what is the difference between "delegating" and "assigning" chores (paragraph 16)?
3. What is a "workaholic" (paragraph 17)? What characteristics identify this type of person?
4. Explain Bliss's favorite quotation:

> Yesterday is a canceled check.
> Tomorrow is a promissory note.
> Today is ready cash. Use It!

What does this saying have to do with time management?

Reading Critically

[6] Do you know any "workaholics"? How does their addiction to work affect the people around them?

THINKING CRITICALLY

5. Why is concentration such an important part of time management? Have you found this to be true in your own experience? Explain your answer.
6. Which of Bliss's guidelines for managing time could you benefit from most? How could it help you? Why do you have trouble in this area?
7. Why does Bliss advise us not to be workaholics? Does this advice conflict with the other guidelines Bliss lists in this essay? Why or why not?
8. In what parts of the essay does Bliss refer to our personal lives? According to the author, how can we balance our personal and professional lives? How realistic are these ideas?

DISCOVERING RHETORICAL STRATEGIES

9. Bliss introduces each new suggestion for managing time as a command and then fully explains each command. How effective is this approach? What effect would headings beginning with present participles have on the essay (e.g., planning, taking breaks, avoiding clutter)?
10. How does Bliss organize his techniques for managing time? Is this order successful? Explain your answer.
11. What is Bliss's general attitude toward time management? In your opinion, is this an efficient attitude toward the subject?
12. What other rhetorical modes does Bliss use to support this process analysis essay? Give examples of each of these modes.

MAKING CONNECTIONS

13. How would William Ouchi ("Japanese and American Workers: Two Casts of Mind") respond to Bliss's essay? Would he agree or disagree with the author's recommendations and conclusions? Do Bliss's suggestions about time management sound more "Japanese" or "American," according to Ouchi's definition of each society's business practices?
14. Bliss's essay analyzing the process of managing our time and Jessica Mitford's essay ("Behind the Formaldehyde Curtain") analyzing funeral customs both try to persuade us to adopt a certain opinion as they describe a process. Which essay is more convincing to you? Explain your answer in detail.
15. Pretend that you are Edwin Bliss giving advice to young Russell Baker ("The Saturday Evening Post"), who wants to become a good salesperson. Which of Bliss's suggestions should Baker follow most earnestly? Why? Which of these suggestions would be most helpful in your own life?

IDEAS FOR DISCUSSION/WRITING

Preparing to Write

Write freely about various aspects of time management: Do you manage time well from day to day? What benefits can you receive from managing your time better? Can you identify any disadvantages that could result from managing your time better? How can you avoid these problems? Are you a workaholic, or do you strike a good balance between the various aspects of your life? What is the relationship between time management and quality of life?

Choosing a Topic

1. You have been asked by the editor of your campus newspaper to adapt Bliss's suggestions to the life of a student. Write a process analysis essay adjusting Bliss's ten guidelines to a college environment.
2. Interview someone in your class about his or her ability to use time wisely. Use Bliss's guidelines to establish whether the person manages time well. Then, direct a process analysis essay to this person, briefly evaluating his or her time-management skills and then offering suggestions for improvement.
3. At times, Bliss's approach to time management (do all you can in a day) seems to conflict with the fundamental tenets for leading a quality life (relax and enjoy yourself). Do you think these two aspects of life are incompatible, or are there ways to reconcile the two? Write an essay for your classmates detailing a solution to this dilemma.
4. Along with two of your classmates, write a process for using a computer program on the Internet. You can describe how to use email, how to attach a file, or how to create a table in Microsoft Word, for example. You could also describe how to conduct Internet research or create a Power Point presentation. Consider whether your essay will be informative or directive and whether you will use the chronological, simultaneous, or cyclical approach.

Before beginning your essay, you might want to consult the checklists on page 199.

Behind the Formaldehyde Curtain

Once called "Queen of the Muckrakers" in a *Time* magazine review, Jessica Mitford has written scathing exposés of the Famous Writers' School, American funeral directors, television executives, prisons, a "fat farm" for wealthy women, and many other venerable social institutions. She was born in England into the gentry, immigrated to the United States, and later became a naturalized American citizen. After working at a series of jobs, she achieved literary fame at age forty-six with the publication of *The American Way of Death* (1963), which relentlessly shatters the image of funeral directors as "compassionate, reverent family-friends-in-need." Her other major works include *Kind and Unusual Punishment: The Prison Business* (1973); *Poison Penmanship: The Gentle Art of Muckraking* (1979), an anthology of Mitford's articles in the *Atlantic, Harper's,* and other periodicals covering a twenty-two-year time span; two volumes of autobiography, *Daughters and Rebels* (1960) and *A Fine Old Madness* (1977); *Faces of Philip: A Memoir of Philip Toynbee* (1984); *Grace Had an English Heart: The Story of Grace Darling, Heroine and Victorian Superstar* (1988); and *The American Way of Birth* (1992). Superbly skilled in the techniques of investigative reporting, satire, and black humor, Mitford was described in a *Washington Post* article as "an older, more even-tempered, better-read Jane Fonda who has maintained her activism long past middle age."

Preparing to Read

The following essay, taken from *The American Way of Death,* clearly illustrates the ruthless manner in which Mitford exposes the greed and hypocrisy of the American mortuary business.

Exploring Experience: As you prepare to read this article, think for a few minutes about funeral customs in our society: Have you attended a funeral service recently? Which rituals seemed particularly vivid to you? What purpose did these symbolic actions serve? What other interesting customs are you aware of in American society? What purpose do these customs serve? What public images do these customs have? Are these images accurate? Do you generally approve or disapprove of these customs?

Learning Online: In this controversial essay, Jessica Mitford graphically describes the embalming process. Before reading her article, familiarize yourself with some technical mortuary terms by visiting HBO's "Six Feet Under" Web site (http://www. hbo.com/sixfeetunder). Select "Video" from the menu options to view farcical commercials that poke fun at the funeral industry.

T he drama begins to unfold with the arrival of the corpse at the   1
mortuary.

Alas, poor Yorick! How surprised he would be to see how his   2
counterpart of today is whisked off to a funeral parlor and is in short order
sprayed, sliced, pierced, pickled, trussed, trimmed, creamed, waxed, painted,
rouged, and neatly dressed—transformed from a common corpse into a
Beautiful Memory Picture. This process is known in the trade as embalming and restorative art and is so universally employed in the United States and
Canada that the funeral director does it routinely, without consulting corpse
or kin. He regards as eccentric those few who are hardy enough to suggest
that it might be dispensed with. Yet no law requires embalming, no religious
doctrine commends it, nor is it dictated by considerations of health, sanitation, or even of personal daintiness. In no part of the world but in Northern America is it widely used. The purpose of embalming is to make the
corpse presentable for viewing in a suitably costly container; and here too
the funeral director routinely, without first consulting the family, prepares
the body for public display.

Is all this legal? The processes to which a dead body may be subjected are   3
after all to some extent circumscribed by law. In most states, for instance, the
signature of next of kin must be obtained before an autopsy may be performed,
before the deceased may be cremated, before the body may be turned over to
a medical school for research purposes; or such provision must be made in the
decedent's will. In the case of embalming, no such permission is required nor
is it ever sought. A textbook, *The Principles and Practices of Embalming,* comments on this: "There is some question regarding the legality of much that is
done within the preparation room." The author points out that it would be
most unusual for a responsible member of a bereaved family to instruct the
mortician, in so many words, to "*embalm*" the body of a deceased relative. The
very term "embalming" is so seldom used that the mortician must rely upon
custom in the matter. The author concludes that unless the family specifies
otherwise, the act of entrusting the body to the care of a funeral establishment
carries with it an implied permission to go ahead and embalm.

Embalming is indeed a most extraordinary procedure, and one must won-   4
der at the docility of Americans who each year pay hundreds of millions of
dollars for its perpetuation, blissfully ignorant of what it is all about, what is
done, how it is done. Not one in ten thousand has any idea of what actually
takes place. Books on the subject are extremely hard to come by. They are
not to be found in most libraries or bookshops.

Reading Critically

How do Mitford's description of the embalming process as a "drama" and her reference
to Shakespeare's *Hamlet* ("Alas, poor Yorick!") help set the tone for this essay?

In an era when huge television audiences watch surgical operations in 5 the comfort of their living rooms, when, thanks to the animated cartoon, the geography of the digestive system [2] has become familiar territory even to the nursery school set, in a land where the satisfaction of curiosity about almost all matters is a national pastime, the secrecy surrounding embalming can, surely, hardly be attributed to the inherent gruesomeness of the subject. Custom in this regard has within this century suffered a complete reversal. In the early days of American embalming, when it was performed in the home of the deceased, it was almost mandatory for some relative to stay by the embalmer's side and witness the procedure. Today, family members who might wish to be in attendance would certainly be dissuaded by the funeral director. All others, except apprentices, are excluded by law from the preparation room.

A close look at what does actually take place may explain in large measure the undertaker's intractable reticence concerning a procedure that has become his major *raison d'être*. Is it possible he fears that public information about embalming might lead patrons to wonder if they really want this service? [3] If the funeral men are loath to discuss the subject outside the trade, the reader may, understandably, be equally loath to go on reading at this point. For those who have the stomach for it, let us part the formaldehyde curtain,

The body is first laid out in the undertaker's morgue—or rather, Mr. Jones 7 is reposing in the preparation room—to be readied to bid the world farewell.

The preparation room in any of the better funeral establishments has the 8 tiled and sterile look of a surgery, [4] and indeed the embalmer–restorative artist who does his chores there is beginning to adopt the term "dermasurgeon" (appropriately corrupted by some mortician-writers as "demisurgeon") to describe his calling. His equipment, consisting of scalpels, scissors, augers, forceps, clamps, needles, pumps, tubes, bowls, and basins, is crudely imitative of the surgeon's, as is his technique, acquired in a nine- or twelve-month post-high-school course in an embalming school. He is supplied by an advanced chemical industry with a bewildering array of fluids, sprays, pastes, oils, powders, creams, to fix or soften tissue, shrink or distend it as needed, dry it here, restore the moisture there. There are cosmetics, waxes and paints to fill and cover features, even plaster of Paris to replace entire limbs. There are ingenious aids to prop and stabilize the cadaver: A Vari-Pose Head

---

Reading Critically

[2] What does the author mean by the phrase "the geography of the digestive system"?

[3] Do you think this assertion is true? Would most of us choose not to have our loved ones embalmed if we understood more about the actual process?

[4] What does Mitford mean by the British term "surgery"?

Rest, the Edwards Arm and Hand Positioner, the Repose Block (to support the shoulders during the embalming), and the Throop Foot Positioner, which resembles an old-fashioned stocks.

Mr. John H. Eckels, president of the Eckels College of Mortuary Science, thus describes the first part of the embalming procedure: "In the hands of a skilled practitioner, this work may be done in a comparatively short time and without mutilating the body other than by slight incision—so slight that it scarcely would cause serious inconvenience if made upon a living person. It is necessary to remove the blood, and doing this not only helps in the disinfecting, but removes the principal cause of disfigurements due to discoloration." 9

Another textbook discusses the all-important time element: "The earlier this is done, the better, for every hour that elapses between death and embalming will add to the problems and complications encountered. . . ." Just how soon should one get going on the embalming? The author tells us, "On the basis of such scanty information made available to this profession through its rudimentary and haphazard system of technical research, we must conclude that the best results are to be obtained if the subject is embalmed before life is completely extinct—that is, before cellular death has occurred. In the average case, this would mean within an hour after somatic death." [5] For those who feel that there is something a little rudimentary, not to say haphazard, about this advice, a comforting thought is offered by another writer. Speaking of fears entertained in early days of premature burial, he points out, "One of the effects of embalming by chemical injection, however, has been to dispel fears of live burial." How true; once the blood is removed, chances of live burial are indeed remote. 10

To return to Mr. Jones, the blood is drained out through the veins and replaced by embalming fluid pumped in through the arteries. As noted in *The Principles and Practices of Embalming,* "every operator has a favorite injection and drainage point—a fact which becomes a handicap only if he fails or refuses to forsake his favorites when conditions demand it." Typical favorites are the carotid artery, femoral artery, jugular vein, subclavian vein. There are various choices of embalming fluid. If Flextone is used, it will produce a "mild, flexible rigidity. [6] The skin retains a velvety softness, the tissues are rubbery and pliable. Ideal for women and children." It may be blended with B. and G. Products Company's Lyf-Lyk tint, which is guaranteed to reproduce "nature's own skin texture . . . the velvety appearance of living tissue." 11

Reading Critically

[5] What is the difference between "somatic death" and "cellular death"? Why is this distinction important to the funeral profession?

[6] Why is the oxymoron "mild, flexible rigidity" humorous?

Suntone comes in three separate tints: Suntan; Special Cosmetic Tint, a pink shade "especially indicated for young female subjects"; and Regular Cosmetic Tint, moderately pink.

About three to six gallons of a dyed and perfumed solution of formaldehyde, glycerin, borax, phenol, alcohol, and water is soon circulating through Mr. Jones, whose mouth has been sewn together with a "needle directed upward between the upper lip and gum and brought out through the left nostril," with the corners raised slightly "for a more pleasant expression." If he should be bucktoothed, his teeth are cleaned with Bon Ami and coated with colorless nail polish. His eyes, meanwhile, are closed with flesh-tinted eye caps and eye cement. 12

The next step is to have at Mr. Jones with a thing called a trocar. This is a long, hollow needle attached to a tube. It is jabbed into the abdomen, poked around the entrails and chest cavity, the contents of which are pumped out and replaced with "cavity fluid." This done, and the hole in the abdomen sewn up, Mr. Jones's face is heavily creamed (to protect the skin from burns which may be caused by leakage of the chemicals), and he is covered with a sheet and left unmolested for a while. ⑦ But not for long—there is more, much more, in store for him. He has been embalmed, but not yet restored, and the best time to start the restorative work is eight to ten hours after embalming, when the tissues have become firm and dry. 13

The object of all this attention to the corpse, it must be remembered, is to make it presentable for viewing in an attitude of healthy repose. ⑧ "Our customs require the presentation of our dead in the semblance of normality . . . unmarred by the ravages of illness, disease, or mutilation," says Mr. J. Sheridan Mayer in his *Restorative Art*. This is rather a large order since few people die in the full bloom of health, unravaged by illness and unmarked by some disfigurement. The funeral industry is equal to the challenge: "In some cases the gruesome appearance of a mutilated or disease-ridden subject may be quite discouraging. The task of restoration may seem impossible and shake the confidence of the embalmer. This is the time for intestinal fortitude and determination. Once the formative work is begun and affected tissues are cleaned or removed, all doubts of success vanish. It is surprising and gratifying to discover the results which may be obtained." 14

The embalmer, having allowed an appropriate interval to elapse, returns to the attack, but now he brings into play the skill and equipment of sculptor and cosmetician. Is a hand missing? Casting one in plaster of Paris is a simple 15

Reading Critically

⑦ How do such phrases as "have at Mr. Jones with a thing called a trocar" and "left unmolested for a while" help Mitford satirize the embalming process?

⑧ What is ironic about the phrase "in an attitude of healthy repose"?

matter. "For replacement purposes, only a cast of the back of the hand is necessary; this is within the ability of the average operator and is quite adequate." If a lip or two, a nose or an ear should be missing, the embalmer has at hand a variety of restorative waxes with which to model replacements. Pores and skin texture are simulated by stippling with a little brush, and over this cosmetics are laid on. Head off? Decapitation cases are rather routinely handled. [9] Ragged edges are trimmed, and head joined to torso with a series of splints, wires, and sutures. It is a good idea to have a little something at the neck—a scarf or a high collar—when time for viewing comes. Swollen mouth: Cut out tissue as needed from inside the lips. If too much is removed, the surface contour can easily be restored by padding with cotton. Swollen necks and cheeks are reduced by removing tissue through vertical incisions made down each side of the neck. "When the deceased is casketed, the pillow will hide the suture incisions. . . . As an extra precaution against leakage, the suture may be painted with liquid sealer."

16   The opposite condition is more likely to present itself—that of emaciation. His hypodermic syringe now loaded with massage cream, the embalmer seeks out and fills the hollowed and sunken areas by injection. In this procedure the backs of the hands and fingers and the under-chin area should not be neglected.

17   Positioning the lips is a problem that recurrently challenges the ingenuity of the embalmer. Closed too tightly, they tend to give a stern, even disapproving expression. Ideally, embalmers feel, the lips should give the impression of being ever so slightly parted, the upper lip protruding slightly for a more youthful appearance. This takes some engineering, however, as the lips tend to drift apart. Lip drift [10] can sometimes be remedied by pushing one or two straight pins through the inner margin of the lower lip and then inserting them between the two front upper teeth. If Mr. Jones happens to have no teeth, the pins can just as easily be anchored in his Armstrong Face Former and Denture Replacer. Another method to maintain lip closure is to dislocate the lower jaw, which is then held in its new position by a wire run through holes which have been drilled through the upper and lower jaws at the midline. As the French are fond of saying, *il faut souffrir pour être belle.*

18   If Mr. Jones had died of jaundice, the embalming fluid will very likely turn him green. Does this deter the embalmer? Not if he has intestinal fortitude. Masking pastes and cosmetics are heavily laid on, burial garments and casket interiors are color-correlated with particular care, and Jones is displayed

---

Reading Critically

[9] What does Mitford mean when she says that "Decapitation cases are rather routinely handled"?

[10] What is "Lip drift"? How can funeral directors solve this problem?

beneath rose-colored lights. Friends will say "How *well* he looks." Death by carbon monoxide, on the other hand, can be rather a good thing from the embalmer's viewpoint: "One advantage is the fact that this type of discoloration is an exaggerated form of a natural pink coloration." This is nice because the healthy glow is already present and needs but little attention. [11]

The patching and filling completed, Mr. Jones is now shaved, washed, and dressed. Cream-based cosmetic, available in pink, flesh, suntan, brunette, and blond, is applied to his hands and face, his hair is shampooed and combed (and, in the case of Mrs. Jones, set), his hands manicured. For the horny-handed son of toil special care must be taken; cream should be applied to remove ingrained grime, and the nails cleaned. "If he were not in the habit of having them manicured in life, trimming and shaping is advised for appearance—never questioned by kin."   19

Jones is now ready for casketing (this is the present participle of the verb "to casket"). In this operation his right shoulder should be depressed slightly "to turn the body a bit to the right and soften the appearance of lying flat on the back." Positioning the hands is a matter of importance, and special rubber positioning blocks may be used. The hands should be cupped slightly for a more lifelike, relaxed appearance. [12] Proper placement of the body requires a delicate sense of balance. It should lie as high as possible in the casket, yet not so high that the lid, when lowered, will hit the nose. On the other hand, we are cautioned, placing the body too low "creates the impression that the body is in a box."   20

Jones is next wheeled into the appointed slumber room where a few last touches may be added—his favorite pipe placed in his hand or, if he was a great reader, a book propped into position. (In the case of little Master Jones a Teddy bear may be clutched.) Here he will hold open house for a few days, visiting hours 10 A.M. to 9 P.M.   21

All now being in readiness, the funeral director calls a staff conference to make sure that each assistant knows his precise duties. Mr. Wilber Kriege writes, "This makes your staff feel that they are a part of the team, with a definite assignment that must be properly carried out if the whole plan is to succeed. You never heard of a football coach who failed to talk to his entire team before they go on the field. They have drilled on the plays they are to execute for hours and days, and yet the successful coach knows the importance of making even the bench-warming third-string substitute feel that he is important if the game is to be won." The winning of *this* game is   22

Reading Critically

[11] Why is death by carbon monoxide poisoning "a good thing from the embalmer's viewpoint"?

[12] Why would a mortician wish to create "a more lifelike, relaxed appearance" in the corpses?

predicated upon glass-smooth handling of the logistics. The funeral director has notified the pallbearers whose names were furnished by the family, has arranged for the presence of clergyman, organist, and soloist, has provided transportation for everybody, has organized and listed the flowers sent by friends. In *Psychology of Funeral Service,* Mr. Edward A. Martin points out: "He may not always do as much as the family thinks he is doing, but it is his helpful guidance that they appreciate in knowing they are proceeding as they should....The important thing is how well his services can be used to make the family believe they are giving unlimited expression to their own sentiment." [13]

The religious service may be held in a church or in the chapel of the fu-   23
neral home; the funeral director vastly prefers the latter arrangement, for not only is it more convenient for him but it affords him the opportunity to show off his beautiful facilities to the gathered mourners. After the clergyman has had his say, the mourners queue up to file past the casket for a last look at the deceased. The family is *never* asked whether they want an open-casket ceremony; in the absence of their instruction to the contrary, this is taken for granted. Consequently, well over 90 percent of all American funerals feature the open casket—a custom unknown in other parts of the world. [14] Foreigners are astonished by it. An English woman living in San Francisco described her reaction in a letter to the writer:

> I myself have attended only one funeral here—that of an elderly fellow worker of mine. After the service I could not understand why everyone was walking towards the coffin (sorry, I mean casket), but thought I had better follow the crowd. It shook me rigid to get there and find the casket open and poor old Oscar lying there in his brown tweed suit, wearing a suntan makeup and just the wrong shade of lipstick. If I had not been extremely fond of the old boy, I have a horrible feeling that I might have giggled. Then and there I decided that I could never face another American funeral—even dead.

The casket (which has been resting throughout the service on a Classic   24
Beauty Ultra Metal Casket Bier) is now transferred by a hydraulically operated device called Porto-Lift to a balloon-tired, Glide Easy casket carriage which will wheel it to yet another conveyance, the Cadillac Funeral Coach. This may be lavender, cream, light green—anything but black. Interiors, of course, are color-correlated, "for the man who cannot stop short of perfection."

At graveside, the casket is lowered into the earth. This office, once the   25
prerogative of friends of the deceased, is now performed by a patented me-

---

Reading Critically

[13] What does the author mean by the phrase "giving unlimited expression to their own sentiment" when discussing the involvement of the deceased's family.

[14] How do you feel about "open casket" funeral ceremonies? Why?

chanical lowering device. A "Life-time Green" artificial grass mat is at the ready to conceal the sere earth, and overhead, to conceal the sky, is a portable Steril Chapel Tent ("resists the intense heat and humidity of summer and the terrific storms of winter . . . available in Silver Grey, Rose, or Evergreen"). Now is the time for the ritual scattering of earth over the coffin, as the solemn words "earth to earth, ashes to ashes, dust to dust" are pronounced by the officiating cleric. This can today be accomplished "with a mere flick of the wrist with the Gordon Leak-Proof Earth Dispenser. No grasping of a handful of dirt, no soiled fingers. Simple, dignified, beautiful, reverent! The modern way!" The Golden Earth Dispenser (at $5) is of nickel-plated brass construction. It is not only "attractive to the eye and long wearing"; it is also "one of the 'tools' for building better public relations" if presented as "an appropriate non-commercial gift" to the clergyman. It is shaped something like a saltshaker.

Untouched by human hand, the coffin and the earth are now united.[15]   26

It is in the function of directing the participants through the maze of gad-   27 getry that the funeral director has assigned to himself his relatively new role of "grief therapist." He has relieved the family of every detail, he has re-vamped the corpse to look like a living doll, he has arranged for it to nap for a few days in a slumber room, he has put on a well-oiled performance in which the concept of *death* has played no part whatsoever—unless it was inconsiderately mentioned by the clergyman who conducted the religious service. He has done everything in his power to make the funeral a real plea-sure for everybody concerned. He and his team have given their all to score an upset victory over death.

UNDERSTANDING DETAILS

1. List the major steps of the embalming process that the author reveals in this essay.
2. Why, according to Mitford, do funeral directors not want to make public the details of embalming? To what extent do you think their desire for secrecy is warranted?
3. Why isn't the permission of a family member needed for embalming? From Mitford's perspective, what does this custom reveal about Americans?
4. In what ways has embalming become the undertaker's *raison d'être*? How do American funeral customs encourage this procedure?

Reading Critically

[15] Why do you think it's important for the coffin and the earth to be united "Untouched by human hand"? In what way is this comment ironic?

THINKING CRITICALLY

5. What is Mitford's primary purpose in this essay? Why do you think she has analyzed this particular process in such detail?
6. Explain the title of this essay.
7. Do you think the author knows how gruesome her essay is? How can you tell? What makes the essay so horrifying? How does such close attention to macabre detail help Mitford accomplish her purpose?
8. What does Mitford mean when she argues that the funeral director and his team "have given their all to score an upset victory over death" (paragraph 27)? Who or what is "the team"? Why does Mitford believe death plays no part in American burial customs?

DISCOVERING RHETORICAL STRATEGIES

9. Why does Mitford begin her essay with a one-sentence paragraph? Is it effective? Why or why not?
10. A euphemism is a deceptively pleasant term used in place of a straightforward, less pleasant one. In what way is "Beautiful Memory Picture" (paragraph 2) a euphemism? How are we reminded of this phrase throughout the essay? What other euphemisms can you find in this selection?
11. What tone does Mitford establish in the essay? What is her reason for creating this particular tone? What is your reaction to it?
12. What other rhetorical strategies does Mitford use besides gruesome examples and illustrations to make her point? Give examples of each of these different strategies.

MAKING CONNECTIONS

13. Imagine that Stephen King ("Why We Crave Horror Movies") has just read Mitford's essay on funeral customs. According to King, what would be the source of our fascination with these macabre practices? Why do essays like Mitford's both intrigue and repulse us at the same time?
14. Compare and contrast Mitford's use of examples with those used by Harold Krents ("Darkness at Noon") and/or Amy Tan ("Mother Tongue"). How often does each author use examples? What is the relationship between the frequency of examples in each essay and the extent to which you are convinced by the author's argument?
15. In this essay, Mitford lifts the curtain on certain bizarre funeral practices in much the same way that Judith Wallerstein and Sandra Blakeslee expose the trauma of divorce ("Second Chances for Children of Divorce"), Jay Weiner uncovers corporate greed in athletics ("Sports Centered"), and Barbara Ehrenreich discloses the pleasures of combat ("The Ecstasy of War"). Which of these "exposés" that you have read seems most complete and devastating to you? Explain your answer.

IDEAS FOR DISCUSSION/WRITING

Preparing to Write

Write freely about a particularly interesting custom in America or in another country: Why does this custom exist? What role does it play in the society? What value does it have? What are the details of this custom? In what way is this custom a part of your life? Your family's life? What purpose does it serve for you? Is it worth continuing? Why or why not?

Choosing a Topic

1. In a process analysis essay directed to your classmates, explain a custom you do not approve of. Decide on your tone and purpose before you begin to write.
2. In a process analysis essay directed to your classmates, explain a custom you approve of. Select a specific tone and purpose before you begin to write.
3. You have been asked to address a group of students at a college of mortuary science. In this role, you have an opportunity to influence the opinion of these students concerning the practice of embalming. Write a well-reasoned lecture to this group arguing either for or against the process of embalming.
4. Not all process descriptions are as explicit as Mitford's article. Why do you think she felt it was necessary to provide such disturbing descriptions in her process analysis? Consider a task you find unpleasant. How can you connect this unpleasant task with an important issue? For example, perhaps you dislike writing papers. Perhaps you could connect the unpleasant task of writing papers with the actual volume of paper you use and/or throw away. This could lead to a paper about either tree conservation or the need to recycle in order to avoid negatively affecting landfills. Write a process analysis with a purpose. Using Mitford's style as a guideline, incorporate relevant issues into your process analysis and offer specific solutions.

Before beginning your essay, you might want to consult the checklists on page 199.

JAY WEINER   (1954–   )

Sports Centered

A sports writer for the *Minneapolis Star Tribune,* Jay Weiner was born in
Philadelphia and educated at Temple University, where he earned an
interdisciplinary degree in Sports Studies. He has been a sports journalist
for the past twenty-five years, specializing in off-the-field articles that relate
to business and social issues. His most recent book, *Stadium Games: Fifty Years
of Big League Greed and Bush League Boondoggles* (2006), is an analysis of
professional sports facilities in Minnesota. He has, in addition, published
articles on sports in the *New York Times, Business Week, TV Guide,
Newsweek.com,* the *Utne Reader,* and many other newspapers and periodicals,
and he is a frequent contributor to Minnesota Public Radio on the topic
of athletics. In his spare time, he runs, rides a bicycle, and admits to watching
"a lot of ESPN." His advice to students using *The Prose Reader* is to "read
and write a great deal." Although "the very best writers seem to have God-
given talents, the rest of us can steadily improve the way we write through
constant practice." He counsels students who want to go into journalism
to "read as many newspapers each day as you can, which will help you learn
your craft."

Preparing to Read

The following essay from the *Utne Reader* discusses ways to bridge the gap
that the author believes has developed between sports and the public. He
reminisces about sports heroes and suggests some new approaches to
professional sports in the future.

Exploring Experience: As you prepare to read this article, pause for a
moment to consider your own interest in sports: Do you participate in any
sports? If so, which ones? Do you like athletics? Why or why not? What role
do sports play in American society? Why do you think they have become
such a big business in this country? Have you gotten more or less involved in
spectator sports over the past few years? What is the primary reason for this
change?

Learning Online: Choose the name of a famous athlete who still actively
competes in his or her sport. Conduct an Internet search on the athlete's
name. What types of links appear? Do the Web sites bearing the name of your
chosen athlete focus on athletic ability and recent performance, or do the sites
concentrate more on physical appearance, advertising, or social gossip?
Consider your findings while reading Weiner's article.

How far back must we go to remember that sports matter? How deeply into our personal and national pasts must we travel to recall that we once cared? ❶

Do we have to return to 1936? Adolf Hitler tried to make the Olympics into a propaganda machine for anti-Semitism and racism. In that case, American track star Jesse Owens, demonstrating that the master race could be mastered at racing, stole Hitler's ideological show. Were not sports a vehicle of significant political substance then?

Or should we return to 1947 and Jackie Robinson? A baseball player integrated our "national pastime" a year before the U.S. Army considered African Americans equal. Robinson's barrier-break may have been largely based on ticket-selling economics for the Brooklyn Dodgers' owners, but didn't sports do something good?

Their fists raised, their dignity palpable, track stars Tommie Smith and John Carlos spread the American black power and student protest movements to the world when they stood on the victory stand at the 1968 Olympics in Mexico City. Politics and sports mixed beautifully then.

Remember when tennis feminist Billie Jean King took on an old fart named Bobby Riggs in 1973, boldly bringing the women's movement to the playing fields? That moment of sports theater stirred up sexual politics as much as any Betty Friedan essay or Miss America bra burning could ever do.

Sports had meaning. And sports were accessible.

Remember when your grandfather or your uncle—maybe your mother—took you to a game when you were a little kid? The hot dog was the best. The crowd was mesmerizing. The colors were bright. The crack of the bat under the summer sun or the autumn chill wrapped around that touchdown run was unforgettable. Back then, some nobody became your favorite player, somebody named Johnny Callison or Hal Greer or Clarence Peaks or Vic Hadfield, someone who sold cars in the off-season and once signed autographs for your father's men's club for a $50 appearance fee. Those "heroes" were working-class stiffs, just like us.

Now you read the sports pages—or, more exactly, the business and crime pages—and you realize you've disconnected from the institution and it from you. Sports is distant. It reeks of greed. Its politics glorify not the majestic drama of pure competition, but a drunken, gambling masculinity epitomized by sports-talk radio, a venue for obnoxious boys on car phones. ❷

Reading Critically

❶ How much do you care about sports? How important are they to our entire nation?

❷ Can you think of a modern sports star who is greedy or ill-mannered?

How can we reconcile our detachment from corporatized pro sports, pro- 9
fessionalized college sports—even out-of-control kids' sports—with our appreciation for athleticism, with our memories? And how, after we sort it all
out, can we take sports back?

Part of the problem is that we want sports to be mythological when, in 10
our hearts, we know they aren't. So reclaiming sports requires that we come
to grips with our own role in the myth-making. Owens, Robinson, Smith,
Carlos, and King played to our highest ideals and so have been enshrined in
our sports pantheon. But we've also made heroes of some whose legacies are
much less clear-cut. Take Joe Namath, the 1960s quarterback who represented sexual freedom, or Bill Walton, the 1970s basketball hippie who symbolized the alienated white suburban Grateful Dead sports antihero. Neither
deserves the reverence accorded Owens or Robinson or even King, but both
captured the essence of their era. Or how about relief pitcher Steve Howe,
who symbolized the evils of drug addiction in the '80s, or Mike Tyson, who
currently plays the archetypal angry black male? No less than Tommie Smith
and John Carlos, these anti-icons were emblematic of their age.

It may be discomfiting, but it's true: The power of sports and sports he- 11
roes to mirror our own aspirations have also contributed to the sorry state
of the institution today. The women's sports movement Billie Jean King
helped create proved a great leap forward for female athletes, but it also created a generation of fitness *consumers,* whose appetite for Nikes and Reeboks
created a new generation of Asian sweatshops.

Fans applauded the courage of renegade Curt Flood, the St. Louis Car- 12
dinals outfielder who in 1969 refused to be traded, arguing that baseball
players should be free to play where they want to play. We cheered—all the
way to the Supreme Court—his challenge to the cigar-smoking owners'
hold on their pinstripe-knickered chattel. Now players can sell their services
to the highest bidder, but their astronomical salaries—deserved or not—
alienate us from the games as much as the owners' greed.

The greed isn't new, of course. ❸ The corporate betrayal of the fan is as 13
traditional as the seventh-inning stretch. The Boston Braves moved to Mil-
waukee in 1953, and the Dodgers and New York Giants fled to California
in 1958, for money, subsidized facilities, and better TV contracts. But what
has always been a regrettable by-product of sports has suddenly become its
dominant ethos. Our worship of sports and our worship of the buck have
now become one and the same. So it shouldn't surprise us that we get the
heroes we expect—and maybe deserve.

Reading Critically

❸ What other careers seem to attract greedy individuals?

So how do we as a society reclaim sports from the corporate entertain- 14
ment behemoth that now controls it? Some modest proposals:

- **Deprofessionalize college and high school sports.**   15

Let's ban college athletic scholarships in favor of financial aid based on
need, as for any other student. And let's keep high school athletics in perspective. Why should local news coverage of high school sports exceed coverage given to the band, debating society, or science fair? Sports stars are
introduced to the culture of athletic privilege at a very young age. ◆4

- **Allow some form of public ownership of professional**   16
  sports teams.

Leagues and owners ask us to pay for the depreciating asset of a stadium
but give us no share of the appreciating asset of a franchise. Lease agreements
between teams and publicly financed stadiums should also include enforce-
able community-involvement clauses.

- **Make sports affordable again.**   17

Sports owners call their games "family entertainment." For whose family? Bill Gates'? Owners whose teams get corporate subsidies should set aside
20 percent of their tickets at prices no higher than a movie admission. And,
like any other business feeding at the public trough, they should be required
to pay livable wages even to the average schmoes who sell hot dogs.

- **Be conscious of the messages sport is sending.**   18

Alcohol-related advertising should be banned from sports broadcasting.
Any male athlete convicted of assaulting a woman should be banned from college and pro sports. Fighting in a sports event should be at least a misde-
meanor and maybe a felony, rather than a five-minute stay in the penalty box.
Let's take the sports establishment by its lapels and shake it back toward us.   19
Because even with all the maddening messages of male dominance, black ser-
vility, homophobia, corporate power, commercialism, and brawn over brains,
sports still play an important role in many lives. When we watch a game, we
are surrounded by friends and family. There are snacks and beverages. We sit in
awe of the players' remarkable skills. We can't do what they do. They extend
our youth. ◆5 The tension of the competition is legitimate. The drama is high.

Reading Critically

◆4 How do you feel about these suggestions? How well do you think they would work?
◆5 To what extent do athletic superstars "extend our youth"?

And therein lies the essence of modern American sport. It's a good show,   20
albeit bread and circuses. And we just can't give it up. So why not take it back
for ourselves as best we can, looking for ways to humanize an institution
that mirrors our culture, understanding that those who own sport won't give
it up without a fight, knowing that we like it too much to ever just walk away.

UNDERSTANDING DETAILS

1. In what ways do sports reflect our culture? Explain your answer in detail.
2. Why does Weiner think sports have drifted away from the American public?
3. According to Weiner, how can we "take sports back"? Summarize the author's
   suggestions.
4. What does the author believe is the main purpose of modern American sports?

THINKING CRITICALLY

5. What is the principal purpose of this essay? To what extent do you think it ac-
   complishes its goals? Explain your answer.
6. Why do you think Weiner says we want to mythologize our love of sports?
7. How have "our worship of sports and our worship of the buck . . . become one
   and the same" (paragraph 13)? Explain your answer.
8. What does Weiner mean when he says, "The corporate betrayal of the fan is as
   traditional as the seventh inning stretch" (paragraph 13)?

DISCOVERING RHETORICAL STRATEGIES

9. How does Weiner organize the ideas in his essay? Why does he choose this particular order? Is it effective in achieving his purpose? Why or why not?
10. Describe in detail Weiner's intended audience. How did you come to this con-
    clusion?
11. Analyze Weiner's use of examples throughout this essay. How does he raise our
    awareness regarding the relationship between sports and culture?
12. Weiner uses examples to set up his essay. What other rhetorical strategies does
    he use to make his point about sports? Give an example of each of these
    strategies.

MAKING CONNECTIONS

13. Imagine that Jay Weiner, Gloria Steinem ("The Politics of Muscle"), and/or
    Barrett Seaman ("How Bingeing Became the New College Sport") are hav-
    ing a discussion about the role of sports in America. To what extent would each
    say that stereotypes help contribute to the moral and ethical decay of our coun-
    try?
14. What advice would Julia Bourland ("Getting Out of Debt (and Staying Out)")
    give to Weiner about coping with the corporate takeover of American profes-
    sional sports?

15. Compare and contrast the growing inaccessibility of professional sports decried in Weiner's article with the loss of our wilderness areas in John McPhee's "The Pines," the loss of cultural heritage in Richard Rodriguez's "Public and Private Language," and/or the loss of control over our country's borders debated by Michael Scott's and Richard Rayner's articles on immigration controls. Which "loss" will be most detrimental to the United States in the long run? Why do you think this is so?

IDEAS FOR DISCUSSION/WRITING

Preparing to Write

Write freely about your impressions of sports today: Do you enjoy participating in sports? Do you like watching sports? What specific pleasures do you derive from watching or participating in sports? What role do sports play in American society? How did they get so much influence over our lives? Are sports mostly a positive or negative influence on our younger generation?

Choosing a Topic

1. One of your friends who is still in high school has asked you for information about social activities in college. Write to this friend, using process analysis to explain how to survive college while having a life full of outside activities. Decide on a purpose and a point of view before you begin to write.
2. Greed is evident throughout American society. Where else, in addition to sports, do you see examples of greed? How does greed become the motivating force behind an organization? Write an essay suggesting how a company or organization can avoid greed and still remain focused and successful.
3. Take one of Weiner's suggestions and develop it into an essay explaining how to accomplish this particular recommendation. Flesh out the essay with as many details as possible.
4. Weiner uses process analysis to suggest a method through which society can "reclaim sports from the corporate entertainment behemoth that now controls it" (paragraph 14). Using the information you gained from an Internet search on a famous athlete, write a process analysis outlining the athlete's rise to fame. How did your chosen athlete rise from the ranks of amateur to professional? Use your process analysis to either support or refute Weiner's claims. Did your athlete benefit from athletic scholarships, competitive salaries, and/or prize money? Do you feel that similar athletes will excel in the future if Weiner's recommendations are adopted?

Before beginning your essay, you might want to consult the checklists on page 199.

Learning to Read

Born Malcolm Little in Omaha, Nebraska, the author later changed his name to Malcolm X when he joined the Nation of Islam in 1953. He explained his new name by saying that the "X" stood for what he had been and what he had become: "Ex-smoker, Ex-drinker, Ex-Christian, Ex-slave." The "X" also represented the unknown original names of the slaves from whom he descended, as opposed to the fictitious names which would have been given by the slaves' "owners." A Boston street hustler in his youth, he was arrested in 1946 at the age of twenty on charges of breaking and entering, carrying firearms, and larceny and sentenced to eight years in prison, where he learned to read and became fascinated with the Nation of Islam's leader, Elijah Muhammad. Upon his release, he was a changed man, giving fervent, inspirational speeches and rising to the number two person in Muhammad's organization, with which he later became disenchanted. He was also responsible for inspiring the famous heavyweight champion Cassius Clay to join the Nation of Islam and change his name to Muhammad Ali. In 1963, he began collaboration with Alex Haley (author of *Roots*) on *The Autobiography of Malcolm X,* which was published soon after his assassination two years later. Malcolm X will be remembered as a controversial, charismatic leader who advocated black pride, economic self-reliance, and political involvement.

Preparing to Read

This excerpt was first published in 1964 in *The Autobiography of Malcolm X,* written by Malcolm X and Alex Haley. It illustrates Malcolm X's view of the world that was fostered by his insatiable appetite for reading.

Exploring Experience: As you prepare to read this essay, think about one activity that defines you and your current life: What is that activity: How does it define you? How has this activity enriched your life? What have you gained from this activity that would otherwise not have enriched your life?

Learning Online: While he was in prison, Malcolm X was exposed to more books than ever before in his life. Today, we have free public libraries overflowing with reading material, but with the increasing popularity of the Internet, many books in their full-text forms are also available online. Visit the Bibliomania website at http://www.bibliomania.com, and examine the immense selection of fiction, drama, poetry, and short stories. Click on "Fiction" and scroll through the list of available novels. How many of them have you read? Consider the benefits of reading a book online compared to holding the book in your hands.

It was because of my letters that I happened to stumble upon starting to acquire some kind of a homemade education.

I became increasingly frustrated at not being able to express what I wanted to convey in letters that I wrote, especially those to Mr. Elijah Muhammad. In the street, I had been the most articulate hustler out there— I had commanded attention when I said something. But now, trying to write simple English, I not only wasn't articulate, I wasn't even functional. How would I sound writing in slang, the way I would *say* it, something such as "Look, daddy, let me pull your coat about a cat, Elijah Muhammad—" ◆

Many who today hear me somewhere in person, or on television, or those who read something I've said, will think I went to school far beyond the eighth grade. This impression is due entirely to my prison studies.

It had really begun back in the Charlestown Prison, when Bimbi first made me feel envy of his stock of knowledge. Bimbi had always taken charge of any conversation he was in, and I had tried to emulate him. But every book I picked up had few sentences which didn't contain anywhere from one to nearly all of the words that might as well have been in Chinese. When I just skipped those words, of course, I really ended up with little idea of what the book said. So I had come to the Norfolk Prison Colony still going through only book-reading motions. Pretty soon, I would have quit even these motions, unless I had received the motivation that I did.

I saw that the best thing I could do was get hold of a dictionary—to study, to learn some words. I was lucky enough to reason also that I should try to improve my penmanship. It was sad. I couldn't even write in a straight line. It was both ideas together that moved me to request a dictionary along with some tablets and pencils from the Norfolk Prison Colony school.

I spent two days just riffling uncertainly through the dictionary's pages. I'd never realized so many words existed! I didn't know which words I needed to learn. Finally, just to start some kind of action, I began copying.

In my slow, painstaking, ragged handwriting, I copied into my tablet everything printed on that first page, down to the punctuation marks.

I believe it took me a day. Then, aloud, I read back, to myself, everything I'd written on the tablet. Over and over, aloud, to myself, I read my own handwriting.

I woke up the next morning, thinking about those words—immensely proud to realize that not only had I written so much at one time, but I'd written words that I never knew were in the world. Moreover, with a little effort, I also could remember what many of these words meant. I reviewed the

---

Reading Critically

◆ How often do you communicate in slang? How powerful is this form of written communication?

words whose meanings I didn't remember. Funny thing, from the dictionary first page right now, that "aardvark" springs to my mind. The dictionary had a picture of it, a long-tailed, long-eared, burrowing African mammal, which lives off termites caught by sticking out its tongue as an anteater does for ants. ❷

I was so fascinated that I went on—I copied the dictionary's next page. 10 And the same experience came when I studied that. With every succeeding page, I also learned of people and places and events from history. Actually the dictionary is like a miniature encyclopedia. Finally the dictionary's A section had filled a whole tablet—and I went on into the B's. That was the way I started copying what eventually became the entire dictionary. It went a lot faster after so much practice helped me to pick up handwriting speed. Between what I wrote in my tablet, and writing letters, during the rest of my time in prison I would guess I wrote a million words.

I suppose it was inevitable that as my word-base broadened, I could for 11 the first time pick up a book and read and now begin to understand what the book was saying. ❸ Anyone who has read a great deal can imagine the new world that opened. Let me tell you something: from then until I left that prison, in every free moment I had, if I was not reading in the library, I was reading on my bunk. You couldn't have gotten me out of books with a wedge. Between Mr. Muhammad's teachings, my correspondence, my visitors—usually Ella and Reginald—and my reading of books, months passed without my even thinking about being imprisoned. In fact, up to then, I never had been so truly free in my life. ❹

The Norfolk Prison Colony's library was in the school building. A variety of classes was taught there by instructors who came from such places as Harvard and Boston universities. The weekly debates between inmate teams were also held in the school building. You would be astonished to know how worked up convict debaters and audiences would get over subjects like "Should Babies Be Fed Milk?"

Available on the prison library's shelves were books on just about every 13 general subject. Much of the big private collection that Parkhurst had willed to the prison was still in crates and boxes in the back of the library—thousands of old books. Some of them looked ancient: covers faded, old-time parchment-looking binding. Parkhurst, I've mentioned, seemed to have been

---

Reading Critically

❷ Have you ever browsed through the dictionary? Do you think this would be an effective way of increasing your vocabulary? Why or why not?

❸ What was the relationship between the author's new-found interest in words and his appetite for reading?

❹ Why does reading make Malcolm X feel "truly free" even though he is still in prison?

principally interested in history and religion. He had the money and the special interest to have a lot of books that you wouldn't have in general circulation. Any college library would have been lucky to get that collection.

As you can imagine, especially in a prison where there was heavy emphasis   14
on rehabilitation, [5] an inmate was smiled upon if he demonstrated an unusually intense interest in books. There was a sizable number of well-read inmates, especially the popular debaters. Some were said by many to be practically walking encyclopedias. They were almost celebrities. No university would ask any student to devour literature as I did when this new world opened to me, of being able to read and *understand*.

I read more in my room than in the library itself. An inmate who was   15
known to read a lot could check out more than the permitted maximum number of books. I preferred reading in the total isolation of my own room.

When I had progressed to really serious reading, every night at about ten   16
P.M. I would be outraged with the "lights out." It always seemed to catch me right in the middle of something engrossing.

Fortunately, right outside my door was a corridor light that cast a glow   17
into my room. The glow was enough to read by, once my eyes adjusted to it. So when "lights out" came, I would sit on the floor where I could continue reading in that glow.

At one-hour intervals the night guards paced past every room. Each time   18
I heard the approaching footsteps, I jumped into bed and feigned sleep. And as soon as the guard passed, I got back out of bed onto the floor area of that light-glow, where I would read for another fifty-eight minutes—until the guard approached again. That went on until three or four every morning. Three or four hours of sleep a night was enough for me. Often in the years in the streets I had slept less than that.

The teachings of Mr. Muhammad stressed how history had been   19
"whitened"—when white men had written history books, the black man simply had been left out. Mr. Muhammad couldn't have said anything that would have struck me much harder. I had never forgotten how when my class, me and all of those whites, had studied seventh-grade United States history back in Mason, the history of the Negro had been covered in one paragraph, and the teacher had gotten a big laugh with his joke, "Negroes' feet are so big that when they walk they leave a hole in the ground."

This is one reason why Mr. Muhammad's teachings spread so swiftly *all*   20
over the United States, among *all* Negroes, whether or not they became followers of Mr. Muhammad. The teachings ring true—to every Negro. You can

---

Reading Critically

[5] Do you think prisons actually rehabilitate their inmates? Why or why not?

hardly show me a black adult in America—or a white one, for that matter—who knows from the history books anything like the truth about the black man's role. [6] In my own case, once I heard of the "glorious history of the black man," I took special pains to hunt in the library for books that would inform me on details about black history.

I can remember accurately the very first set of books that really impressed me. I have since bought that set of books and have it at home for my children to read as they grow up. It's called *Wonders of the World*. It's full of pictures of archeological finds, statues that depict, usually, non-European people. [21]

I found books like Will Durant's *Story of Civilization*. I read H. G. Wells' *Outline of History. Souls of Black Folk* by W. E. B. DuBois gave me a glimpse into the black people's history before they came to this country. Carter G. Woodson's *Negro History* opened my eyes about black empires before the black slave was brought to the United States, and the early Negro struggles for freedom. [22]

J. A. Rogers' three volumes of *Sex and Race* told about race mixing before Christ's time; about Aesop being a black man who told fables; about Egypt's Pharaohs; about the great Coptic Christian Empires; about Ethiopia, the earth's oldest continuous black civilization, as China is the oldest continuous civilization. [23]

Mr. Muhammad's teaching about how the white man had been created led me to *Findings in Genetics* by Gregor Mendel. (The dictionary's G section was where I had learned what "genetics" meant.) I really studied this book by the Austrian monk. Reading it over and over, especially certain sections, helped me to understand that if you started with a black man, a white man could be produced; but starting with a white man, you never could produce a black man—because the white gene is recessive. And since no one disputes that there was but one Original Man, the conclusion is clear. [7] [24]

During the last year or so, in the *New York Times,* Arnold Toynbee used the word "bleached" in describing the white man. (His words were "White (i.e., bleached) human beings of North European origin. . . .") Toynbee also referred to the European geographic area as only a peninsula of Asia. He said there is no such thing as Europe. And if you look at the globe, you will see for yourself that America is only an extension of Asia. (But at the same time Toynbee is among those who have helped to bleach history. He has written that Africa was the only continent that produced no history. He won't write that again. Every day now, the truth is coming to light.) [25]

Reading Critically

[6] This essay was written in 1965. Do you think the author's conclusions about the lack of black history in textbooks is still true today?

[7] What is the author's argument concerning the relationship between the recessive nature of the white gene and the origins of life?

I never will forget how shocked I was when I began reading about slav- 26
ery's total horror. It made such an impact upon me that it later became one
of my favorite subjects when I became a minister of Mr. Muhammad's. The
world's most monstrous crime, the sin and the blood on the white man's
hands, are almost impossible to believe. Books like the one by Frederick
Olmstead opened my eyes to the horrors suffered when the slave was landed
in the United States. The European woman, Fannie Kimball, who had married a Southern white slaveowner, described how human beings were de-
graded. Of course I read *Uncle Tom's Cabin*. In fact, I believe that's the only
novel I have ever read since I started serious reading. [8]

Parkhurst's collection also contained some bound pamphlets of the Abo- 27
litionist Anti-Slavery Society of New England. I read descriptions of atrocities, saw those illustrations of black slave women tied up and flogged with
whips; of black mothers watching their babies being dragged off, never to be
seen by their mothers again; of dogs after slaves, and of the fugitive slave
catchers, evil white men with whips and clubs and chains and guns. I read
about the slave preacher Nat Turner, who put the fear of God into the white
slavemaster. Nat Turner wasn't going around preaching pie-in-the-sky and
"non-violent" freedom for the black man. There in Virginia one night in
1831, Nat and seven other slaves started out at his master's home and through
the night they went from one plantation "big house" to the next, killing,
until by the next morning 57 white people were dead and Nat had about
70 slaves following him. White people, terrified for their lives, fled from their
homes, locked themselves up in public buildings, hid in the woods, and some
even left the state. A small army of soldiers took two months to catch and
hang Nat Turner. Somewhere I have read where Nat Turner's example is
said to have inspired John Brown to invade Virginia and attack Harper's Ferry
nearly thirty years later, with thirteen white men and five Negroes.

I read Herodotus, "the father of History," or, rather, I read about him. And 28
I read the histories of various nations, which opened my eyes gradually, then
wider and wider, to how the whole world's white men had indeed acted
like devils, pillaging and raping and bleeding and draining the whole world's
nonwhite people. I remember, for instance, books such as Will Durant's story
of Oriental civilization, and Mahatma Gandhi's accounts of the struggle to
drive the British out of India.

Book after book showed me how the white man had brought upon the 29
world's black, brown, red, and yellow peoples every variety of the sufferings
of exploitation. I saw how since the sixteenth century, the so-called "Christian
trader" white man began to ply the seas in his lust for Asian and African

---

Reading Critically

[8] Have you ever read *Uncle Tom's Cabin*? Why was this novel so interesting to Malcolm X?

empires, and plunder, and power. I read, I saw, how the white man never has
gone among the non-white peoples bearing the Cross in the true manner
and spirit of Christ's teachings—meek, humble, and Christ-like.

I perceived, as I read, how the collective white man had been actually   30
nothing but a piratical opportunist who used Faustian machinations to make
his own Christianity his initial wedge in criminal conquests. [9] First, always
"religiously," he branded "heathen" and "pagan" labels upon ancient non-
white cultures and civilizations. The stage thus set, he then turned upon his
non-white victims his weapons of war.

I read how, entering India—half a *billion* deeply religious brown people—   31
the British white man, by 1759, through promises, trickery and manipula-
tions, controlled much of India through Great Britain's East India Company.
The parasitical British administration kept tentacling out to half of the sub-
continent. In 1857, some of the desperate people of India finally mutinied—
and, excepting the African slave trade, nowhere has history recorded any
more unnecessary bestial and ruthless human carnage than the British sup-
pression of the non-white Indian people.

Over 115 million African blacks—close to the 1930s population of the   32
United States—were murdered or enslaved during the slave trade. And I read
how when the slave market was glutted, the cannibalistic [10] white powers of
Europe next carved up, as their colonies, the richest areas of the black continent. And Europe's chancelleries for the next century played a chess game
of naked exploitation and power from Cape Horn to Cairo.

Ten guards and the warden couldn't have torn me out of those books. Not   33
even Elijah Muhammad could have been more eloquent than those books
were in providing indisputable proof that the collective white man had acted
like a devil in virtually every contact he had with the world's collective non-
white man. I listen today to the radio, and watch television, and read the headlines about the collective white man's fear and tension concerning China.
When the white man professes ignorance about why the Chinese hate him
so, my mind can't help flashing back to what I read, there in prison, about how
the blood forebears of this same white man raped China at a time when
China was trusting and helpless. Those original white "Christian traders" sent
into China millions of pounds of opium. By 1839, so many of the Chinese
were addicts that China's desperate government destroyed twenty thousand
chests of opium. The first Opium War was promptly declared by the white
man. Imagine! Declaring war upon someone who objects to being narcotized!
The Chinese were severely beaten, with Chinese-invented gunpowder.

Reading Critically

[9] With what "criminal conquests" does the author charge white men?
[10] How were the white powers of Europe "cannibalistic"?

The Treaty of Nanking made China pay the British white man for the de-   34
stroyed opium; forced open China's major ports to British trade; forced China
to abandon Hong Kong; fixed China's import tariffs so low that cheap British
articles soon flooded in, maiming China's industrial development.

After a second Opium War, the Tientsin Treaties legalized the ravaging   35
opium trade, legalized a British-French-American control of China's customs. China tried delaying that Treaty's ratification; Peking was looted and
burned.

"Kill the foreign white devils!" was the 1901 Chinese war cry in the   36
Boxer Rebellion. Losing again, this time the Chinese were driven from
Peking's choicest areas. The vicious, arrogant white man put up the famous
signs, "Chinese and dogs not allowed."

Red China after World War II closed its doors to the Western white world.   37
Massive Chinese agricultural, scientific, and industrial efforts are described
in a book that *Life* magazine recently published. Some observers inside Red
China have reported that the world never has known such a hate-white
campaign as is now going on in this non-white country where, present birth-
rates continuing, in fifty more years Chinese will be half the earth's population. And it seems that some Chinese chickens will soon come home to
roost, with China's recent successful nuclear tests.

Let us face reality. We can see in the United Nations a new world order   38
being shaped, along color lines—an alliance among the non-white nations. **11**
America's U.N. Ambassador Adlai Stevenson complained not long ago that in
the United Nations "a skin game" was being played. He was right. He was facing reality. A "skin game" is being played. But Ambassador Stevenson sounded
like Jesse James accusing the marshal of carrying a gun. Because who in the
world's history ever has played a worse "skin game" than the white man?

Mr. Muhammad, to whom I was writing daily, had no idea of what a new   39
world had opened up to me through my efforts to document his teachings
in books.

When I discovered philosophy, I tried to touch all the landmarks of philo-   40
sophical development. Gradually, I read most of the old philosophers, Occidental and Oriental. The Oriental philosophers were the ones I came to
prefer; finally, my impression was that most Occidental philosophy had largely
been borrowed from the Oriental thinkers. Socrates, for instance, traveled in
Egypt. Some sources even say that Socrates was initiated into some of the
Egyptian mysteries. Obviously Socrates got some of his wisdom among the
East's wise men.

Reading Critically

11 Do you think this assertion is still true? Is a new world order "being shaped along color
lines"? Is this true in the middle East and elsewhere?

I have often reflected upon the new vistas that reading opened to me. [12]   41
I knew right there in prison that reading had changed forever the course of
my life. As I see it today, the ability to read awoke inside me some long dor-
mant craving to be mentally alive. I certainly wasn't seeking any degree, the
way a college confers a status symbol upon its students. My homemade education gave me, with every additional book that I read, a little bit more
sensitivity to the deafness, dumbness, and blindness that was afflicting the
black race in America. Not long ago, an English writer telephoned me from
London, asking questions. One was, "What's your alma mater?" I told him,
"Books." You will never catch me with a free fifteen minutes in which I'm
not studying something I feel might be able to help the black man.

Yesterday I spoke in London, and both ways on the plane across the At-   42
lantic I was studying a document about how the United Nations proposes
to insure the human rights of the oppressed minorities of the world. The
American black man is the world's most shameful case of minority oppression. What makes the black man think of himself as only an internal United
States issue is just a catch-phrase, two words, "civil rights." How is the black
man going to get "civil rights" before first he wins his human rights? If
American black man will start thinking about his *human* rights, and then
start thinking of himself as part of one of the world's greatest peoples, he
will see he has a case for the United Nations.

I can't think of a better case! Four hundred years of black blood and sweat   43
invested here in America, and the white man still has the black man begging
for what every immigrant fresh off the ship can take for granted the minute
he walks down the gangplank.

But I'm digressing. I told the Englishman that my alma mater was books,   44
a good library. Every time I catch a plane, I have with me a book that I want
to read—and that's a lot of books these days. If I weren't out here every day
battling the white man, I could spend the rest of my life reading, just satisfying my curiosity—because you can hardly mention anything I'm not curious about. I don't think anybody ever got more out of going to prison
than I did. In fact, prison enabled me to study far more intensively than I
would have if my life had gone differently and I had attended some college.
I imagine that one of the biggest troubles with colleges is there are too many
distractions, too much panty-raiding, fraternities, and boola-boola and all of
that. Where else but prison could I have attacked my ignorance by being
able to study intensely sometimes as much as fifteen hours a day? [13]

Reading Critically

[12] What "new vistas" did reading open for Malcolm X? What vistas has reading opened for
you?

[13] Why does Malcolm X think he got a lot out of going to prison? How did the prison experience change his life?

UNDERSTANDING DETAILS

1. Why did Malcolm X start to educate himself?
2. What does Malcolm X mean by the phrase "homemade education" (paragraph 1)?
3. In what ways is the dictionary like an encyclopedia? What did Malcolm X learn from copying the dictionary pages?
4. Name three details that Malcolm X learned about "slavery's total horror" (paragraph 26)?

THINKING CRITICALLY

5. What does Malcolm X mean when he says "Four hundred years of black blood and sweat invested here in America, and the white man still has the black man begging for what every immigrant fresh off the ship takes for granted the minute he walks down the gangplank" (paragraph 43)?
6. Why did reading make Malcolm X feel "truly free" (paragraph 11)?
7. Why do you think debating was so popular in prison?
8. How does Malcolm X characterize the relationship between whites and nonwhites in his reading? What is the main conflict according to the author?

DISCOVERING RHETORICAL STRATEGIES

9. Malcolm X starts this essay with a one-sentence paragraph. What effect does this beginning have on you?
10. In what way does Malcolm X feel white people misused Christianity in their treatment of the nonwhite population? How does the author use examples to make this case?
11. Malcolm X names actual books that he read and explains what impression they made on him. Is this an effective way to document his understanding of history? What do all these examples demonstrate? What other way could the author have explained his experience? Would this way have been more or less effective than giving examples from his reading?
12. In what way does Malcolm X make a comparison between African Americans and the Chinese?

MAKING CONNECTIONS

13. Compare and contrast Malcolm X's awakening about his ethnic and racial identity with similar experiences by Lewis Sawaquat ("For My Indian Daughter"), Sandra Cisneros ("Only daughter"), and/or Sucheng Chan ("You're Short, Besides!"). Which author seems most devoted to his personal identity? Why do you think this is so?
14. How does the act of reading bring enlightenment to Malcolm X, Sherman Alexie ("The Joy of Reading and Writing: Superman and Me"), and/or Richard Wright ("The Library Card")?

15. How is the time spent in prison different for Malcolm X and Kimberly Wozen-craft ("Notes from the Country Club")? Which author has used his/her time more effectively? Why do you think this is so?

IDEAS FOR DISCUSSION/WRITING

Preparing to Write

Write freely about the topics that stimulate your curiosity? What fuels this curiosity? How does this desire to learn and understand affect your development as a person? What would you be like without this basic curiosity?

Choosing a Topic

1. What one activity captures you as a person? How does this activity represent you? Write an essay explaining to your classmates how this activity defines your personality.
2. Malcolm X is quite clear about how his view of the world took shape through a combination of prison and reading. Write an essay explaining what has contributed most dramatically to your perspective on life? What is that perspective? In what way does it make you a unique human being?
3. List five books, articles, essays, or comic books that you have read recently, and in a coherent essay, explain their effect on you and your view of the world.
4. Imagine that a paper shortage exists, and publishers are no longer printing books in hard copy. Hereafter, all reading material is being made available online only. Write an essay about the process you would go through to read a novel online. What computer would you use? Would you be able to take notes on what you read? Revisit the Bibliomania Web site (http://www.bibliomania.com) to get an idea of this experience.

Before beginning your essay, you might want to consult the checklists on page 199.

JULIA BOURLAND   (1970-   )

Getting Out of Debt (and Staying Out)

Born and raised in Dallas, Texas, Julia Bourland moved to California in 1989, where she graduated from Mills College with a B.A. in Political Science. A full-time writer, she is the author of two extremely popular books—*The Go-Girl Guide: Surviving Your 20's with Savvy, Soul, and Style* (2000) and *Hitched: The Go-Girl Guide to the First Year of Marriage* (2003)—along with numerous articles in such periodicals as *Bride's Magazine, Shape, 7 × 7, Parenting,* and many others. Her past positions include senior producer of the Relationships Channel at *Women.com* and associate editor of *Parenting* magazine. Recently married, she enjoys hiking, cycling, running, and practicing yoga. Her advice to students using *The Prose Reader* is to "allow yourself time every day just for unedited, free-flowing writing. Twenty minutes in the morning or evening can really open up any blockage you may be experiencing, especially knowing that this writing doesn't 'count.' By that, I mean that no one ever has to see it. Don't get out of the habit. It's like going to the gym—you've got to do it every day, or else you start mentally resisting it. Also, read other good writers for inspiration." Bourland currently lives near San Francisco, where she is working on her third book.

Preparing to Read

The following essay, from a book called *The Go-Girl Guide: Surviving Your 20s with Savvy, Soul, and Style,* offers extremely helpful advice for getting and staying out of debt. With national credit card interest payments in the trillions of dollars each year and with students getting multiple credit card offers even before they graduate, everyone can use a little help in this area.

Exploring Experience: As you prepare to read this essay, take a few minutes to think about money in general: Which do you enjoy more: making or spending money? Do you work? If so, do you feel you are paid fairly? Are you comfortable spending money? Do you ever buy on credit? Do you have trouble limiting your spending to the money you earn? How much difficulty do you have controlling your spending?

Learning Online: Visit the Motley Fool Web site (http://www.fool.com/ccc/debt/debt01.htm), or go to your campus financial aid Web site. Read a few paragraphs describing ways to get out of debt or methods for paying student loans. How do the techniques suggested in these Web sites differ from Bourland's advice?

I'm going to make the bold assumption that you have incurred a little debt   1
during your great entrance into adulthood, from either student loans,
devilish credit cards, or that car loan you recently signed with its 36 easy
installment payments. If you haven't tasted debt, you are abnormally perfect
and un-American and can just skip on down to the next section on retirement planning and chill out until the rest of us catch up with you. ◆

Some debt, such as student loans, is money well borrowed and an invest-   2
ment in your future. Because of their relatively low interest rates, manageable
(though seemingly eternal) repayment plans, and reasonable deferment options, student loans should not be the source of midnight panic attacks during your second semester of senior year, even if you've incurred thousands and
thousands of dollars to fund your education and still don't have a job that
suggests that all the debt was worth it. If you haven't graduated yet, toward
the end of your final semester, your college student loan officer will give you
all the dirty details of your repayment schedule (hopefully armed with ample
tissue for the tears that are certain to flood your contacts), as well as tell you
how to defer paying back your loans if you aren't employed by the time your
repayment grace period is up, as was my case. The cheery thing I discovered
about deferring repayment is that the groovy government actually paid the
interest I owed during my six-month deferment. That's not the case with all
student loans, but you'll find that out when you start reading the fine print.

If you're like me, you may have several loans to repay. Again, you probably   3
got (or will get) the skinny from your financial aid administrator at college, but
in case he or she is on drugs, I'll summarize. There are a few consolidation
plans that can make the whole process of paying back your loans less horrifying. Consolidating means that you will be able to merge all of your loans into
one giant superloan that offers a low interest rate, as well as various options for
shortening or lengthening your repayment schedule (which will increase or decrease the amount you owe each month, thereby increasing or decreasing the
amount of interest you ultimately end up paying). But the best reason to consolidate your loans is that you will receive only one bill every month, which
means you have to think and stress about all the student loan money you owe
only once every 30 days! I highly recommend consolidation, if only for that.

If you have several loans from one financial institution, contact your lender   4
directly about its consolidation options, or try these two programs: Federal
Direct Consolidation Loan Program (800-557-7392; www.ed.gov/
directloan) and Student Loan Marketing Association (a.k.a. Sallie Mae) Smart
Loan Account (800-524-9100; www.salliemae.com).

Reading Critically

◆ What does Bourland mean by the terms "devilish credit cards" and "un-American"? How
do they help set the tone and direction of her essay?

Student loans are much less threatening and guilt-provoking than credit 5
card debt, to which we 20-somethings are painfully vulnerable. ❷ There are
so many things we want and need. Credit card companies seize upon our vulnerability, especially during college, sending us application after application
with such enticing incentives as a *free water bottle, a two-pound bag of M & Ms,
a 10% discount* on first purchases, *free checks* to spend anywhere we please, our
very own *head shot* on the card, a *4.9% introductory interest rate,* and *bonus airline miles.* My first advice on the whole matter of credit card debt is to avoid
it like the devil! I know many honest, smart girls who've become submerged
in debt through the seductive power of plastic.

Our society once thrived without credit, so it *is* possible to stay out of debt 6
as we begin our adult lives. But since you will probably experiment with
credit despite the danger, memorize these eight guidelines compliments of
those who've battled the plastic demons:

#1: No Department Store Credit Cards

In-store credit usually carries a much higher interest rate than credit cards 7
issued by banks. If you don't pay your debt back right away, what you buy
is going to cost you much more than you bargained for. The only exception
is if you have money to pay off your debt as soon as the bill arrives, and sign-
ing up for a card gives you a substantial discount on your first purchase. In
these cases, get the card (and discount), pay your bill in full, and immediately
cancel the card and shred it into a million pieces, lest you be tempted to use
it again without the discount and money to pay for it. Note: If the discount
isn't more than $10 or 20, don't even bother, because when you sign on,
you'll probably get put on some annoying direct-mail list that will be sold
to a bunch of trashy companies who will send you junk mail every single day.

#2: One Card Only

The fewer little plastic rectangles you have, the less you'll be tempted to 8
live beyond your meager means (and the fewer hysteria-provoking bills ❸
you'll receive). Ideally, you should use your card only for items that you know
you can pay off with your next paycheck or for unavoidable emergencies, like
getting new brakes for your clunker or fillings for your insatiable sweet tooth.
The ideal cards have fixed annual percentage rates ranging from 9 to 12 percent, or less if you can find them, no annual fee, and a grace period that
doesn't start charging interest on what you buy until the bill's due date. If

---

Reading Critically

❷ Why do you think "20-somethings" are so "painfully vulnerable" to credit card debt?

❸ Do you own a credit card? Have you ever received a "hysteria-provoking" bill? Why were
you so deeply in debt?

you are a conscientious customer, you will be inundated with appealing offers for new cards boasting Platinum status and $25,000 credit lines. When you receive these, gingerly toss them into the recycling bin. Opening them will only lead you into trouble. There is one exception to this rule, but I'll get to that when we talk about transferring balances. First, a few more basic tips.

#3: Use Your ATM Credit/Debit Card Instead

If you're diligent about balancing your checkbook, there's no reason to fear   9
the credit card capabilities of your ATM card, which most banks are offering these days. Keep the receipt for whatever you purchase with your card as you would had you withdrawn money from the bank, and record the amount in your checkbook ledger as you would a check. Your debit card is just as convenient as a credit card, but your purchase won't accrue interest, which will save you money. Definitely use your debit card instead of a real credit card when grocery shopping or buying little things at the pharmacy, unless you like the idea of paying 18 percent interest on cereal and tampons. Trust your elders: the interest on all the little things makes them as costly as a raging girls' night out.

#4: Pay Back as Much as You Can, as Soon as You Can

If we take the *minimum* payment request on our monthly statements to   10
heart, we may not pay off our account in full until we qualify for social security. That's because interest continues to accrue on our balance each month. If we don't pay off everything we owe, the remainder plus the interest we've amassed will be charged interest the following month and the month after that, which means our balance continues to grow at the speed of our card's annual percentage rate (APR) despite the fact that we pay our minimum due every month and have hidden our credit card in the closet under five shoe boxes. That's how credit card companies make so much money and why we should avoid getting into debt in every humanly possible (but legal) way.

If you have debt from several sources, pay back whatever has higher in-   11
terest rates first—usually your credit cards—then tackle the typically lower-rated student loan and car loan debts. [4] If your credit card debt is spiraling out of control, you could refinance your student or car loans so that you will owe less on them each month, using the extra money to pay off your credit cards. Then, when your costlier debts have been paid off (and cards dumped in the nearest incinerator), you can designate all your funds to

---

Reading Critically

[4] Do you know the interest rates you are paying on all your debts? Which is highest? Which is lowest?

paying back your temporarily neglected student and car loans as quickly as you can.

#5: Trash Those Credit Card Checks That Come with Your Statement, and Shun Cash Advances from the ATM

Both checks and cash advances will cost you dearly, since many card com- 12
panies tack on an additional finance charge to your bill when you use them, plus impose an interest rate for the amount you borrow that's much higher than the rate you have for normal purchases. That means that if you withdraw $100 from your card at a bank or ATM or use one of those checks for your rent, you'll be paying back your credit card company a lot more than the amount you borrowed.

6: Switch to a Card with a Lower Interest Rate

I said earlier that you should throw away offers for additional credit cards, 13
and that is a good rule unless you are carrying a balance on a card (or cards) with an outrageous interest rate, say more than 12 percent. In that case, it's a good financial move to transfer your balance(s) to one card with the lowest rate you can find. Some offer temporary introductory interest rates as low as 2.9 percent on all transferred balances; when you apply, make sure you note the expiration date for those low rates on your calendar, and have another card offer lined up and ready to take on the load when the time comes. I know this sounds tedious, but careful organization and diligence will save you money as you attempt to pay the whole balance off.

If you play credit card musical chairs, keep three things in mind. **⑤** First, 14
some balance transfer offers have associated fees or finance charges that aren't exactly highlighted in their promotions. Always inquire about transfer fees, and try to talk them out of it; many issuers are willing to waive the fees upon request. Second, even after you transfer your balance in full, the account remains open. To close it, you must officially cancel. The issuing bank won't automatically cancel a zero-balance account, so if you don't, your access to that credit line will remain on your credit report. That could be problematic later on when you're applying for a mortgage and have thousands of dollars worth of potential debt in your financial profile—something that makes lenders skittish. The other reason to cancel is to avoid the temptation to start using that clean slate of credit that your old card suddenly presents. And the third caveat: when you transfer your balance, do not use this new card to purchase new things. Declare it a debt repayment card only, and stick that shiny piece of plastic in the file where you keep your monthly statements. Here's why:

Reading Critically
⑤ What does the author mean by the term "credit card musical chairs"?

When you charge new items on a card that has adopted old debt, many   15
card issuers apply a different (and uber-exorbitant) interest rate to those new
purchases. The higher interest rate will remain on the amount of your new
purchases until your entire debt has been repaid. Therefore, when you are trying to pay off a large debt, you should try to have two credit cards—one
with a very low balance-transfer interest rate for your main debt and another with a reasonable interest rate on new purchases that you will use for
emergencies only, since you are, after all, trying to get out of the hole, not
rack up new debt. A good resource for finding low-rate, no-fee cards is a
company called CardWeb.com, Inc., which publishes a newsletter called
CardTrak that lists these desirable cards. You can access the newsletter and
other credit card consumer information on its website (www.cardweb.com)
or by calling (800) 344-7714.

#7: Apply for a Secured Credit Card if Your Credit Is Screwed

If you have damaged your credit rating by defaulting on a loan or debt,   16
your main priority (besides coming up with a repayment plan that suits all
your creditors) is to rebuild your credit. Secured credit cards can help. You
give the issuer a certain sum of money up front, which is kept in an account
for you as a security deposit. Depending on the terms of your agreement,
you can then charge a specified amount on that card. Once you've proved
that you can repay your debts in this secured way, you may be offered a new
card with real credit that doesn't require you to put up money ahead of time.
CardWeb.com, Inc. (cited in the previous entry) can provide a list of secured
credit cards as well as low-rate, no-fee cards.

If you are in a bad situation and creditors are calling you about monster   17
debt that you can't currently pay off, don't pack up and move to North
Dakota, thinking creditors won't be able to find you—they will. A couple of
nonprofit credit counseling organizations can help with debt-repayment
planning assistance: Consumer Credit Counseling Services, associated with
the National Foundation for Consumer Credit (800-388-2227; www.nfcc
.org), and Debt Counselors of America (800-698-3782 www.dca.org).

#8: Check Your Credit Report

I've already expounded on why a clean credit report is so important, so I   18
won't beat that dead horse, [6] but I will add that it's wise to check up on your
report every now and then to make sure there are no surprises (or mistakes)
that need mending. There are three agencies that compile credit reports, and

---

Reading Critically

[6] What is the meaning of the metaphor "to beat a dead horse"?

they all get their information separately, so what one company says is part of your credit history may differ from what another company includes. You can get copies of your credit report from each company for $8 or less, depending on your state of residence. If you have had bad credit in the past but believe you've been exonerated (usually after seven years), you should make sure all three companies are showing you in the proper light.

The three agencies keeping tabs are Experian (formerly TRW) (888-397- 19
3742; www.experian.com/ecommerce/consumercredit.html); Equifax (800-685-1111. www.econsumer.equifax.com), and Trans Union (800-888-4213; www.transunion.com/Personal/PersonalSolutions.jsp).

UNDERSTANDING DETAILS

1. According to Bourland, what types of debts are worthwhile?
2. What does "consolidating loans" (paragraph 3) mean? What are the benefits of consolidating loans?
3. What are Bourland's eight guidelines for avoiding credit card debt? Summarize each guideline.
4. How can you check your credit rating?

THINKING CRITICALLY

5. Have you incurred any debts in your life so far? Explain your answer by giving specifics.
6. Why does Bourland think debts are a normal part of life?
7. Why are young adults especially vulnerable to credit card debt?
8. Which of Bourland's guidelines are most likely to help you now and in the future? Explain your answer.

DISCOVERING RHETORICAL STRATEGIES

9. How would you characterize the tone of this essay? What specific details bring you to this conclusion?
10. Who do you think is Bourland's primary audience in this essay? On what do you base your answer?
11. What method does Bourland use to organize her advice in this essay?
12. What other rhetorical strategies, besides process analysis, does Bourland use to strengthen her argument about handling debt? Give an example of each of these strategies.

MAKING CONNECTIONS

13. Compare and contrast the advice Julia Bourland provides about managing your money with similar suggestions by Edwin Bliss about managing your time. Which type of advice will be most useful to you in the future? Why do you think so?

14. How is Bourland's description of the process of staying out of debt similar to the process of embalming dead bodies described by Jessica Mitford in "Behind the Formaldehyde Curtain"? Which process seems most difficult to you? Explain your answer.

15. What advice would K. C. Cole ("Calculated Risks") give to Julia Bourland about the risks and rewards of money management? Which of these two authors would be more likely to make a big financial gamble in her life? Explain your answer.

IDEAS FOR DISCUSSION/WRITING

Preparing to Write

Write freely about your spending habits: Do you spend money wisely? Do you usually spend more than you make? How do you establish limits for your spending? Do you follow these limits? Have you built up a lot of debt? How do you plan to pay off this debt?

Choosing a Topic

1. Debt is widespread in contemporary American society, especially among college students. As a result, your college newspaper is running a special series of articles focusing on debt in college. Find out as much as you can about this problem, its causes, and its solutions, and write an article for your campus newspaper on the various causes of student debt and some ways to avoid it.

2. Most people hope to find a job that fulfills and interests them as their lives progress. But they generally don't start out with the job of their dreams. Write a letter to a high school student offering realistic advice on securing a good job during college.

3. Using Hansen's advice, explain what characterizes successful money management in your opinion. Direct your essay to college students.

4. Using Bourland's essay as a model, write an article entitled "How I Got into Debt," "How I Stay Out of Debt," or "How I Plan to Stay Out of Debt." Where applicable, cite Web sites that either provide additional resources or support your claims.

Before beginning your essay, you might want to consult the checklists on page 199.

Chapter Writing Assignments

Practicing Process Analysis

1. Make a list of some of the activities you do well. Choose one activity, and think about exactly what you must do to perform this skill. Write an essay that describes to another person the process of doing this activity well. Be as specific and clear in your directions as you can.

2. Identify a task or responsibility that seems impossible for you to do well. What keeps you from performing this task with skill or efficiency? Write an essay that describes how to fail at this activity. Describe this method for failure in a humorous or sarcastic manner.

3. What is your best method for solving major life problems? Think of times in your life when you have had to solve a problem or make an important decision. Write an essay that explains to a person looking for problem-solving ideas the method you rely on when faced with important problems that need to be solved.

Exploring Ideas

4. How do you think your ability to manage money affects your daily life? Do you think this ability has mostly positive or negative effects on your lifestyle? Use specific examples to support your opinion.

5. Find a recent advertisement on television, in the newspaper, on a billboard, or on the radio that you think is especially successful. Examine this ad, and write an essay explaining its success. What makes it good? Whom does it reach? How effectively does it address its target population?

6. Should we "force" students to stay in school until the age of sixteen, or should we allow students who do not choose to go to school the right to drop out before they finish high school? Respond to these questions in an organized essay.

Analyzing Visual Images

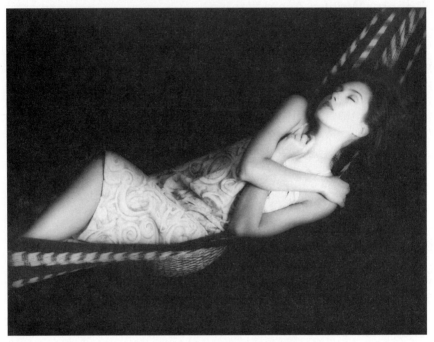

Image the copyright property of Michael Greco, www.visionlightgallery.com.

7. How do you achieve complete relaxation? Provide a step-by-step guide to accomplishing the kind of tranquility you see in the photograph above.

8. Look at the picture on page 191 at the beginning of this chapter. Imagine having to explain the steps of surfing to someone who knew nothing about the sport. Think of a sport you know well, and try to explain the basic rules of that activity to someone who knows little or nothing about it.

Chapter 5

DIVISION/CLASSIFICATION
Finding Categories

Both division and classification play important roles in our everyday lives: Bureau drawers separate one type of clothing from another; kitchen cabinets and drawers organize food, dishes, and utensils into groups; grocery stores shelve similar items together so shoppers can easily locate what they want to buy; school notebooks with tabs help students divide up their academic lives; newspapers classify local and national events in order to organize a great deal of daily information for the general public; and our own personal classification systems assist us in separating what we like from what we don't so that we can have access to our favorite foods, our favorite cars, our favorite entertainment, our favorite people. The two processes of division and classification are so natural to us, in fact, that we sometimes aren't even aware that we are using them.

DEFINING DIVISION/CLASSIFICATION

Division and classification are actually mirror images of each other. Division is the basic feature of process analysis, which we studied in the last chapter; it moves from a general concept to subdivisions of that concept or from a single category to multiple subcategories. Classification works in the opposite direction, moving from specifics to a group with common traits or from multiple subgroups to a single, larger, and more inclusive category.

245

These techniques work together in many ways: A college, for example, is *divided* into departments (single to multiple), whereas courses are *classified* by department (multiple to single); the medical field is *divided* into specialties, whereas doctors are *classified* by a single specialty; a cookbook is *divided* into chapters, whereas recipes are *classified* according to type; and athletics is *divided* into specific sports, whereas athletes are *classified* by the sport in which they participate. Division is the separation of an idea or an item into its basic parts, such as a home into rooms, a course into assignments, or a job into various duties or responsibilities; classification is the organization of items with similar features into a group or groups, such as finding all green-eyed people in a large group, omitting all carbohydrates from your diet, or watching only the track and field events during the Olympics.

Classification is an organizational system for presenting a large amount of material to a reader or listener. This process helps us make sense of the complex world we live in by letting us work with smaller, more understandable units of that world. Classification must be governed by some clear, logical purpose (such as focusing on all lower-division course requirements), which will then dictate the system of categories to be used. The plan of organization that results should be as flexible as possible, and it should illustrate the specific relationship to each other of items in a group and of the groups themselves to one another.

As you already know, many different ways of classifying the same elements are possible. If you consider the examples at the outset of this chapter, you will realize that bureau drawers vary from house to house and even from person to person; that no one's kitchen is set up exactly the same way as someone else's; and that grocery stores have similar but not identical systems of classification. (Think, for instance, of the many different schemes for organizing dairy products, meats, foreign foods, etc.) In addition, your friends probably use a method different from yours to organize their school notebooks; different newspapers vary their presentation of the news; and two professors will probably teach the same course material in separate ways. We all have distinct and uniquely logical methods of classifying the elements in our own lives.

The following student paragraph about friends illustrates both division and classification. As you read it, notice how the student writer moves back and forth smoothly from general to specific and from multiple to single:

> *The word* friend *can refer to many different types of relationships. Close friends are "friends" at their very best: people for whom we feel respect, esteem, and, quite possibly, even love. We regard these people and their well being with kindness, interest, and goodwill; we trust them and will go out of our way to help them. Needless to say, we could all use at least one close friend. Next come*

"casual friends," people with whom we share a particular interest or activity. The investment of a great amount of time and energy in developing this type of friendship is usually not required, though casual friends often become close friends with the passage of time. The last division of "friend" is most general and is composed of all those individuals whose acquaintance we have made and who feel no hostility toward us. When one is counting friends, this group should certainly be included, since such friendships often develop into "casual" or "close" relationships. Knowing people in all three groups is necessary, however, because all types of friends undoubtedly help us live healthier, happier lives.

THINKING CRITICALLY THROUGH DIVISION/CLASSIFICATION

- Focus on similarities and differences.
- Move freely between dividing and classifying.
- Let meaning emerge from your categories.

The thinking strategies of division and classification are the flip sides of each other: Your textbook is *divided* into chapters (one item divided into many), but chapters are *classified* (grouped) into sections or units. Your brain performs these mental acrobatics constantly, but to be as proficient at this method of thinking as possible, you need to be aware of the cognitive activities you go through. Focusing on these two companion patterns of thought will develop your skill in dealing with these complex schemes as it simultaneously increases your overall mental capabilities.

You might think of division/classification as a driving pattern that goes forward and then doubles back on itself in reverse. Division is a movement from a single concept to multiple categories, while classification involves gathering multiple concepts into a single group. Dividing and/or classifying helps us make sense of our subject by using categories to highlight similarities and differences. In the case of division, you are trying to find what differences break the items into separate groups, while, with classification, you let the similarities among the items help you put the material into meaningful categories. Processing your material in this way helps your readers see your particular subject in a new way and often brings renewed insights to both reader and writer.

Experimenting with division and classification is important to your growth as a critical thinker. It will help you process complex information so you can understand more fully your options for dealing with material in all subject areas. Practicing division and classification separate from other rhetorical modes makes you concentrate on improving this particular pattern of thinking before adding it to your expanding arsenal of critical thinking skills.

Bill Carden.

1. Describe the people, windows, and doors in this photograph by Bill Carden. How could they be divided and classified into groups? What do you learn by looking at the photograph in this way?

2. Study the table of contents of a magazine that interests you. Into what sections is the magazine divided? What distinguishing features does each section have? Now study the various advertisements in the same magazine. What different categories would you use to classify these ads? List the ads in each category.

3. Make a chart classifying the English instructors at your school. Explain your classification system to the class.

Reading and Writing Division/Classification Essays

Though writers of division/classification essays will probably use both division and classification in their essays, they should decide if they are primarily going to break down a topic into many separate parts or group together similar items into one coherent category; a writer's purpose will, of course, guide him or her in this decision. Readers must likewise recognize and understand which of these two parallel operations an author is using to structure an essay. Another important identifying feature of division/classification essays is an explanation (explicit or implicit) of the significance of a particular system of organization.

READING DIVISION/CLASSIFICATION ESSAYS

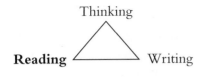

- What is the essay's context?
- Does the essay divide and/or classify?

Preparing to Read.   As you approach the selections in this chapter, you should study all the material that precedes each essay so you can prepare yourself for your reading. First of all, what hints does the title give you about what you are going to read? To what extent does K. C. Cole reveal his attitude toward risks? Who do you think Judith Wallerstein and Sandra Blakeslee's audience is in "Second Chances for Children of Divorce"? Does Stephanie Ericsson's title give us any indication about her point of view in "The Ways We Lie"? Then see what you can learn from scanning each essay and reading its synopsis in the Rhetorical Table of Contents.

Also important as you prepare to read the essays in this chapter is your knowledge about each author and the conditions under which each essay was written: What does the biographical material tell you about Phyllis Schneider's "Memory: Tips You'll Never Forget"? About Franklin Zimring's "Confessions of an Ex-Smoker"? Knowing where these essays were first published will give you even more information about each author's purpose and audience.

Finally, before you begin to read, answer the Preparing to Read questions, and then think freely for a few minutes about the general topic: What do you want to know about children of divorce from Wallerstein and Blakeslee? What are some different types of lies you have told (Viorst)?

Reading.   As you read each essay for the first time, write down your initial reactions to the topic itself, to the preliminary material, to the mood the writer sets, or to a specific incident in the essay. Make associations between the essay and your own experiences.

In addition, create a context for each essay by drawing on the preliminary material you just read about the essay: What is Schneider implying about the relationship between remembering and forgetting, and why does she care about this relationship? What is significant about Zimring's point of view in "Confessions of an Ex-Smoker"? According to Ericsson, why are some lies necessary? Also in this first reading, notice when the writers divided (split up) or classified (gathered together) their material to make their point.

At the bottom of the pages of these essays are several questions that will help you think critically about the topics in this chapter. They prompt you to understand the writers' reasoning and the structure of each essay. Your responses to these questions will give you ideas to use in response to the exercises and writing assignments after each essay, providing a "bridge" from the activities before to the tasks after each essay. Writing out your responses is always the way to get the most benefit out of these questions so that you have ideas to work with when you compose your own essays.

Finally, read the questions after each essay, and let them guide your second reading of the selection.

Rereading.   When you read these division/classification essays a second time, notice how the authors carefully match their dominant rhetorical approach (in this case, division or classification) to their purpose in a clear thesis. What, for example, is Cole's dominant rhetorical approach to his subject? How does this approach further his purpose? What other rhetorical strategies support his thesis? Then see how these writers logically present their division or classification systems to their readers, defining new categories as their essays progress. Finally, notice how each writer either implicitly or explicitly explains the significance or value of his or her division/classification system. How do Wallerstein and Blakeslee explain their system of organization? And how does Ericsson give her organizing principle significance? Now answer the questions after each essay to check your understanding and to help you analyze your reading in preparation for the discussion/writing topics that follow.

For a more complete survey of reading guidelines, you may want to consult the checklists on page 29 of the Introduction.

WRITING DIVISION/CLASSIFICATION ESSAYS

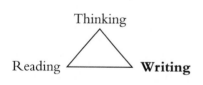

- Decide on a purpose/thesis.
- Divide the subject into categories.
- Arrange the categories logically.
- Define each category.
- Explain the significance of your approach.

Preparing to Write.   You should approach a division/classification essay in the same way you have begun all your other writing assignments— with some kind of prewriting activity that will help you generate ideas, such as the Preparing to Write questions featured in this chapter. The prewriting techniques outlined in the Introduction on pages 19–21 can help you approach these questions imaginatively. Before you even consider the selection and arrangement of details, you need to explore your subject, choose a topic, and decide on a specific purpose and audience. The best way to explore your subject is to think about it, read about it, and then write about it. Look at it from all possible angles, and see what patterns and relationships emerge. To choose a specific topic, you might begin by listing any groups, patterns, or combinations you discover within your subject matter. Your purpose should take shape as you form your thesis, and your audience is probably dictated by the assignment. Making these decisions before you write will make the rest of your task much easier.

Writing.   As you begin to write, certain guidelines will help you structure your ideas for a division/classification essay:

1. First, declare an overall purpose for your division/classification.
2. Then divide the item or concept you are dealing with into categories.
3. Arrange these categories into a logical sequence.
4. Define each category, explaining the difference between your categories and demonstrating that difference through examples.
5. Explain the significance of your classification system (Why is it worth reading? What will your audience learn from it?).

All discussion in such an essay should reinforce the purpose stated at the beginning of your paper. Other rhetorical modes—such as narration, example, and comparison/contrast—will naturally be used to supplement your classification.

To make your division/classification as workable as possible, take special care that your categories do not overlap and that all topics fall into their proper places. If, for example, you were dividing/classifying all the jobs performed by students in your writing class, the categories of (1) indoor work and (2) outdoor work would probably be inadequate because some jobs fit into both categories. At a pizza parlor, a florist, or a gift shop, for example, a delivery person's time would be split between indoor and outdoor work. So you would need to alter the classification system to avoid this problem. The categories of (1) indoor work, (2) outdoor work, and (3) a combination of indoor and outdoor work would be much more useful for this task. Making sure your categories don't overlap will help make your classification essays more readable and more accurate.

Rewriting.   As you rewrite your division/classification essays, consider carefully the probable reactions of your readers to the form and content of your paper:

- Does your thesis communicate your purpose clearly?
- Have you divided your topic into separate categories?
- Are these categories arranged logically?
- Do you explain the significance of your classification system?

More guidelines for writing and rewriting are available on page 30 of the Introduction.

STUDENT ESSAY: DIVISION/CLASSIFICATION AT WORK

The following student essay divides skiers into interesting categories based on their physical abilities. As you read it, notice how the student writer weaves the significance of his study into his opening statement of purpose. Also, pay particular attention to his logical method of organization and clear explanation of categories as he moves with ease from multiple to single and back to multiple again throughout the essay.

People on the Slopes

When I first learned to ski, I was amazed by the shapes who whizzed by me and slipped down trails marked only by a black diamond signifying "most difficult," while others careened awkwardly down the "bunny slopes." These skiers, I discovered, could be divided into distinct categories—for my own entertainment and for the purpose of finding appropriate skiing partners.

First are the "poetic skiers." They glide down the mountainside silently with what seems like no effort at all. They float from side to side on the intermediate slopes, their knees bent perfectly above parallel skis, while their sharp skills allow them to bypass slower skiers with safely executed turns at remarkable speeds.

The "crazy skiers" also get down the mountain quickly, but with a lot more noise attending their descent. At every hill, they yell a loud "Yahoo!" and slam their skis into the snow. These go-for-broke athletes always whiz by faster than everyone else, and they especially seem to love the crowded runs where they can slide over the backs of other people's skis. I often find crazy skiers in mangled messes at the bottoms of steep hills, where they are yelling loudly, but not the famous "Yahoo!"

Margin annotations: Subject · Thesis statement · Overall purpose · First category · Definition · Supporting details · Second category · Definition · Supporting details (with humor)

Third category — Transition — After being overwhelmed by the crazy skiers, I am always glad to find other skiers like myself: "the average ones." We are polite on the slopes, concentrate on improving our technique with every run, and ski the beginner slopes only at the beginning of the day to warm up. We go over the moguls (small hills) much more cautiously than the crazy or poetic skiers, but we still seek adventure with a little jump or two each day. We remain a silent majority on the mountain.

Definition — Supporting details (comparative)

Fourth category — Transition — Below us in talent, but much more evident on the mountainside, are what I call the "eternal beginners." These skiers stick to the same beginner slope almost every run of every day during their vacation. Should they venture onto an intermediate slope, they quickly assume the snowplow position (a pigeon-toed stance) and never leave it. Eternal beginners weave from one side of the run to the other and hardly ever fall, because they proceed so slowly; however, they do yell quite a bit at the crazies who like to run over the backs of their skis.

Definition — Supporting details

Transition — Having always enjoyed people-watching, I have fun each time I am on the slopes observing the myriad of skiers around me. I use these observations to pick out possible ski partners for myself and others. Since my mother is an eternal beginner, she has more fun skiing with someone who shares her interests than with my dad, who is a poetic skier with solitude on his mind. After taking care of Mom, I am free to find a partner I'll enjoy. My sister, the crazy skier of the family, just heads for the rowdiest group she can find! As the years go by and my talents grow, I am trusting my perceptions of skier types to help me find the right partner for life on and off the slopes. No doubt watching my fellow skiers will always remain an enjoyable pastime.

Significance of classification system

Concluding remarks

Student Writer's Comments

To begin this paper—the topic of which occurred to me as I flew over snow-capped mountains on a trip—I brainstormed. I jotted down the general groups of skiers I believed existed on the slopes and recorded characteristics of each group as they came to me. The ideas flowed quite freely at this point, and I enjoyed imagining the people I was describing. This prewriting stage brought back some great memories from the slopes that cluttered my thinking at times, but in most cases one useless memory triggered two or three other details or skiing stories that helped me make sense of my division/classification system.

I then felt ready to write a first draft but was having a lot of trouble coming up with a sensible order for my categories. So I just began to write. My categories were now clear to me, even though I wanted to work a little more on their labels. And the definitions of each category came quite naturally as I wrote. In fact, the ease with which they surfaced made me believe that I really had discovered some ultimate truth about types of skiers. I also had tons of details and anecdotes to work with from my brainstorming session. When I finished the body of my first draft (it had no introduction or conclusion yet), I realized that every paragraph worked nicely by itself—four separate category paragraphs. But these paragraphs didn't work together yet at all.

As I reworked the essay, I knew my major job was to reorganize my categories in some logical way and then smooth out the prose with transitions that would make the essay work as a unified whole. To accomplish this, I wrote more drafts of this single paper than I can remember writing for any other assignment. But I feel that the order and the transitions finally work now. The essay moves logically from type to type, and I think my transitions justify my arrangement along the way. My overall purpose came to me as I was reorganizing my categories, at which point I was able to write my introduction and conclusion. After I had put my purpose into words, the significance of my division/classification system became clear. I saved it, however, for the conclusion.

The most exciting part of this paper was realizing how often I had used these mental groupings in pairing my family and friends with other skiers. I had just never labeled, defined, or organized the categories I had created. Writing this paper helped me verbalize these categories and ended up being a lot of fun (especially when it was finished).

SOME FINAL THOUGHTS ON DIVISION/CLASSIFICATION

The essays collected in this chapter use division and/or classification as their primary organizing principle. All of these essays show both techniques at work to varying degrees. As you read these essays, you might also want to be aware of the other rhetorical modes that support these division/classification essays, such as description and definition. Finally, pay special attention to how these authors bring significance to their systems of classification and, as a result, to their essays themselves.

DIVISION/CLASSIFICATION IN REVIEW

Reading Division/Classification Essays

Preparing to Read

✓ What assumptions can you make from the essay's title?

✓ Can you guess what the general mood of the essay is?
✓ What is the essay's purpose and audience?
✓ What does the synopsis tell you about the essay?
✓ What can you learn from the author's biography?
✓ Can you predict the author's point of view toward the subject?

Reading

✓ What is the context of the essay?
✓ Did the author divide or classify?

Rereading

✓ How does division or classification help the author accomplish his/her purpose?
✓ What other rhetorical strategies does the author use?
✓ How does the writer explain the significance of his/her approach?

Writing Division/Classification Essays

Preparing to Write

✓ What is your purpose?
✓ Who is your audience?

Writing

✓ Do you declare an overall purpose in your thesis?
✓ Do you divide your subject into distinct categories?
✓ Do you arrange the categories into a logical sequence?
✓ Do you define each category?
✓ Do you explain the significance of your approach?

Rewriting

✓ Does your thesis communicate your purpose clearly?
✓ Have you divided your topic into separate categories?
✓ Are these categories arranged logically?
✓ Do you explain the significance of your classification system?

Memory: Tips You'll Never Forget

Born in Seattle, Washington, Phyllis Schneider received her B.A. in English at Pacific Lutheran University and her M.A. in Advanced Writing at the University of Washington. She has been articles editor at *Seventeen* magazine, founding editor of *YM* magazine, and managing editor of *Weight Watchers* magazine. She currently works for Consumers Union, the publisher of *Consumer Reports,* for whom she has written a fundraising newsletter and various promotional materials. She has also published articles in *Working Woman, Redbook, Woman's Day, New Choices, Parents* magazine, and many other periodicals, and she writes health-care career supplements for the Greater New York Hospital Association and *The New York Times.* One recent article, entitled, "Oh, My Aching Back," evaluates the many different causes of lower back pain and argues that rest, physical therapy, and other conservative treatments are often better than surgery, which is riskier and more costly. Another, titled "A Buyer's Guide for Herbs," urges caution in purchasing products from health food stores, which can be like walking into a "jungle" for unwary consumers. A lover of animals (she has a mixed-breed dog named "Jenny"), she also enjoys making jewelry in her spare time and serving as an associate at an Episcopal convent. Her advice to students using *The Prose Reader* is to "learn grammar." "Many young people have the enthusiasm to write well," she explains, "but not the proper skills."

Preparing to Read

The following essay, originally published in *New Choices,* offers us some important insights into the strengths and weaknesses of our memories in an attempt to classify some of the typical memory lapses we all experience on a daily basis.

Exploring Experience: Prior to reading this essay, consider the strengths and weaknesses of your own memory. What information do you remember best? What do you have trouble remembering? Do you have any minor problems with your memory on a daily basis? Do your memory lapses fall into any particular categories? What are these categories? How do you deal with these memory lapses?

Learning Online: How do you organize your life? Look at files on your computer hard drive or e-mail "Inbox," and consider the techniques you use for remembering where you store important information. What are some of your categories? What method do you use to create these classifications?

When my husband, Ted, started "losing" our car, I began to worry. In his 30s and 40s, he'd leave a store or a theater and head straight for our vehicle—no problem. But shortly after his 50th birthday, Ted walked into a mall parking garage and stopped short. Scratching his head, he asked, "Where did we park?"

In the ensuing months, there were times when Ted would forget where he put his glasses, his keys, his wallet. And walking by a restaurant one day, he remarked, "Remember what a great dinner we had there"? I'd never been in that restaurant and said so. But he insisted: he'd ordered the sole, and I'd had the salmon; we had both agreed it was one of the best restaurants we'd ever been to. ◆

Though I found Ted's memory lapses troublesome, most experts would say that such forgetfulness doesn't necessarily signal trouble. "You needn't worry about these lapses unless you experience a noticeable and consistent decline in memory or you aren't able to function at work," says psychologist Daniel L. Schacter of Harvard University. At that point, of course, you should see a doctor.

For most people, such lapses are just a normal—if annoying—part of life. Mild deficits in memory do begin in the 40s and 50s and increase in later years, but stress, fatigue, and a mere lack of attention all can trigger temporary memory glitches in people of all ages.

Here are some common types and strategies for minimizing difficulties.

"It's on the Tip of My Tongue."   You start to introduce an old friend to someone, and suddenly you can't remember that someone's name—even though you sense it just beyond the grasp of your memory. Or you can't quite retrieve the name of a movie you just saw. Such tip-of-the-tongue—or TOT—incidents happen to most everyone, notes Deborah Burke, a psychologist at Pomona College in Claremont, Calif.

These lapses have nothing to do with remembering the meaning of a word, but rather with its sound, "Often, the sound of a word is arbitrary and senseless," says Burke. This sheer arbitrariness sometimes can make word retrieval challenging.

The best way to prevent the problem is to use the name of a person or object as frequently as possible. "I tell clients to do what salespeople often do—repeat people's names several times just before you plan to see them," says psychologist Liz Zelinski of the University of Southern California in Los Angeles.

Reading Critically

◆ Have you ever had a similar experience? Why do you think Schneider begins her essay with these personal examples of memory loss?

A TOT experience can seem worse when a similar-sounding, but incor-   9
rect, word pops into your head and stays there. Burke tells the story of a student who was trying to remember the name of a particular recreational
vehicle. The student wanted the word *Winnebago,* but she could only come
up with *rutabaga.* When this happens shift your focus to something else, suggests Burke. ❷ "If you stop fretting about it, the correct word eventually will
come to you."

"Where Did I Put My Keys?"   Most episodes of absent-mindedness—   10
forgetting where you left something or wondering why you just entered a
room—are caused by a simple lack of attention, says Harvard's Schacter.
"You're supposed to remember something, but you haven't encoded it
deeply." ❸

Encoding, Schacter explains, is a special way of paying attention to an event   11
that has a major impact on recalling it later. Failure to encode properly can
create annoying situations. If you put your cell phone in a pocket, for example, and don't pay attention to what you did because you're involved in a
conversation, you'll probably forget that the phone is in the jacket now hanging in your closet. "Your memory per se isn't failing you," says Schacter.
"Rather, you didn't give your memory system the information it needed."

Lack of interest can also lead to absent-mindedness. "A man who can re-   12
cite baseball scores from 30 years ago," says Zelinski, "may not remember to
drop a letter in the mailbox." Women have slightly better memories than
men, possibly because they pay more attention to their environment, and
memory relies on just that.

Visual cues can help prevent absent-mindedness, says Schacter. "But be sure   13
the cue is clear and available," he cautions. If you want to remember to take a
medication with lunch, put the pill bottle on the kitchen table—don't leave it
in the medicine chest and write yourself a note that you tuck in a pocket.

Another common episode of absent-mindedness: walking into a room   14
and wondering why you're there. Most likely, you were thinking about something else. "Everyone does this from time to time," says Zelinski. The best
thing to do is to return to where you were before entering the room, and
you'll likely remember.

"That's Not the Way I Remember It."   Most of us occasionally experience   15
a memory error called "misattribution." You correctly remember something
that happened but attribute it to the wrong source. For example, you share

---

Reading Critically

❷ How could shifting "your focus to something else" help restore someone's memory?
❸ What memories have you "encoded" recently? Why were they especially important
to you?

a story with a friend and credit it to your mutual acquaintance Jim. Although the incident actually happened to John—from whom you heard of it in the first place—you remain convinced that it originated with Jim.

In a similar way, people often come up with ideas that were someone   16 else's to begin with—a phenomenon known as unintentional plagiarism. ◆4 At dinner one night, a friend related "her" recent experience at a store: Seeing a mother carrying her baby in a backpack, she remarked on the cute toy clutched in the infant's fist. "Oh, no—that's not hers!" the mother exclaimed. "She must have grabbed it from a shelf."

Then my friend's daughter piped up: "Mom, that happened to me. I told   17 you about it last month."

False memory, another trick the mind can play, is closely related to mis-   18 attribution. You may "remember" that you fell off the pier when your father took you fishing, though in reality you only witnessed such a scene in a movie many years ago.

As annoying as these kinds of memory lapses can be, there's a positive   19 side, says Schacter. If our brains did store all that we saw, heard, or read, we'd be overwhelmed. Our ability to splice together bits of necessary information and throw out the rest is essential for sound thinking. ◆5

I find this theory reassuring. Now when my husband forgets where the   20 car is, I tell myself that he's busy selecting and storing information that is really important to him—like ordering tickets to a sporting event—instead of concentrating on trivial stuff. And when we pass the restaurant that he insists we dined at years ago, I just smile and let him savor his memory of a delectable—and obviously unforgettable—dinner.

UNDERSTANDING DETAILS

1. What exactly is Schneider classifying in this essay? Explain her three categories.
2. What is the positive side of memory lapses, according to Schneider?
3. Which of these memory problems have you experienced? How did you solve the problem?
4. What are some of the main causes of memory lapses?

THINKING CRITICALLY

5. Are you surprised to know that experts agree that lapses in memory don't "necessarily signal trouble" (paragraph 3)? Explain your answer.

Reading Critically

◆4 What is "unintentional plagiarism"? Have you ever been guilty of this?
◆5 When Schneider talks about "our ability to splice together bits of necessary information," where does the metaphor come from? What else do we "splice" together?

6. Which of Schneider's categories do you suppose is most common among students?
7. Why do you think Schneider cited so many experts in this essay? What do these authoritative voices add to her essay?
8. What do all the solutions Schneider proposes for each type of memory lapse have in common?

DISCOVERING RHETORICAL STRATEGIES

9. In what ways does Schneider use division and classification in this essay? How does she give significance or value to her system of organization? What other rhetorical techniques does she use to accomplish her purpose?
10. What types of memory lapses do you experience in a typical day? How would you classify these lapses?
11. What is Schneider's point of view toward forgetfulness in general?
12. Why do you think Schneider opened and closed her essay with references to her husband? Are her beginning and ending effective? Explain your answer.

MAKING CONNECTIONS

13. Examine the tricks memory plays on us by contrasting Schneider's essay with Malcolm Cowley's "The View from 80," Russell Baker's "The Saturday Evening Post," Robert Ramirez's "The Barrio," and/or Michael Dorris's "The Broken Cord."
14. Compare and contrast the way Schneider categorizes her advice with the organizational techniques of Edwin Bliss's "Managing Your Time," K. C. Cole's "Calculated Risks," and/or Stephanie Ericsson's "The Ways We Lie."
15. Schneider defines *encoding* as "a special way of paying attention to an event that has a major impact on recalling it later." What advice do you think any of the following authors would give us about "encoding" important events in life: Ray Bradbury ("Summer Rituals"), Russell Baker ("The Saturday Evening Post"), and Roger Rosenblatt ("I Am Writing Blindly")?

IDEAS FOR DISCUSSION/WRITING

Preparing to Write

Write freely about various memory lapses you have experienced. What activities do they involve? Are they easily classified? Do they occur frequently in your life? When do they happen?

Choosing a Topic

1. Your English teacher has asked about the accuracy of your memory. Respond to this question by classifying for this teacher all the different types of memory work you do in a typical day. Remember that each memory task you do should fit into a specific category. Decide on a point of view before you begin to write.

2. Speculate about the memory of a close friend or relative by analyzing that person's behavior and preferences. Remember that analysis is based on the process of division. Divide this person's behavior and preferences into logical parts; then study those parts so that you can better understand the person's reasoning techniques. Decide on a purpose and audience before you begin to write.

3. If the mental activities we perform say something important about us, analyze yourself by writing an essay that classifies the different mental activities you have carried out in the last week. Discuss your choices as you proceed.

4. Pretend you are writing a "how-to" Web site. Select a topic such as time management, exercise, or organization, and divide your topic into clear and separate categories. Write an article for online publication that provides an overview of your topic, describes the challenges associated with it, and classifies your method into clear categories.

Before beginning your essay, you might want to consult the checklists on page 255.

K.C. COLE   (1946–   )

Calculated Risks

K. C. Cole spent her early childhood in Rio de Janeiro, then grew up in Port Washington, New York, and Shaker Heights, Ohio. After graduating from Barnard College with a B.A. in political science, she worked for Radio Free Europe as an editor and subsequently lived in Czechoslovakia, the Soviet Union, and Hungary. While working as a writer and editor at the *Saturday Review* in San Francisco, she developed a love for physics and started writing about science. In the 1970s, she became an editor at *Newsday*, for which she wrote personal essays on politics, humor, and women's issues. Her first book, *What Only a Mother Can Tell You*, was published in 1982; a collection of essays titled *Between the Lines* came out two years later. She has also written *Sympathetic Vibrations: Reflections on Physics as a Way of Life* (1985, with an introduction by Frank Oppenheimer), *The Universe and the Teacup* (1998), and *The Hole in the Universe* (2001). Since 1994, she has covered physical science for *The Los Angeles Times,* where she also writes the column "Mind Over Matter." Her recreational activities include rollerblading, hiking, listening to Bach, and watching *Six Feet Under* and *Sex in the City.* Her advice to students using *The Prose Reader* is "to be passionate. There's no point in writing if you don't really care about what you say. And don't be afraid to make mistakes. If you don't make mistakes, you aren't taking enough risks."

Preparing to Read

The following essay first appeared in K. C. Cole's book entitled *The Universe and the Teacup: The Mathematics of Truth and Beauty* (1998). It suggests that the way we calculate risks in our lives doesn't make much sense.

Exploring Experience: As you prepare to read this article, take a few moments to think about how you analyze potential risks in your life: What constitutes a "risk" for you? What risks do you take every day? Do you take these risks readily and willingly? Give some examples. When do you avoid risks? Is taking risks a positive or negative force in your life? In what ways does taking risks influence your life? How does taking risks energize or diminish your actions?

Learning Online: K. C. Cole claims, "Risk assessment is rarely based on purely rational considerations." Before reading her essay, read a humorous approach to fear and evaluating risk. Go to Michael Moore's "Bowling for Columbine" Web site (http://www.bowlingforcolumbine.com), and select "Film Clips and Soundtracks." In the "Film Clips" category, choose "A Brief History of America." Consider how this presentation of risk assessment relates to Cole's theories.

Newsweek magazine plunged American women into a state of near   1
panic some years ago when it announced that the chances of a
college-educated thirty-five-year-old woman finding a husband was
less than her chance of being killed by a terrorist. Although Susan Faludi
made mincemeat of this so-called statistic in her book *Backlash,* the notion that we can precisely quantify risk has a strong hold on the Western
psyche. ◆ Scientists, statisticians, and policy makers attach numbers to the risk
of getting breast cancer or AIDS, to flying and food additives, to getting hit
by lightning or falling in the bathtub.

Yet despite (or perhaps because of) all the numbers floating around, most   2
people are quite properly confused about risk. I know people who live happily on the San Andreas Fault and yet are afraid to ride the New York sub-
ways (and vice versa). I've known smokers who can't stand to be in the same
room with a fatty steak and women afraid of the side effects of birth control pills who have unprotected sex with strangers. Risk assessment is rarely
based on purely rational considerations—even if people could agree on what
those considerations were. We worry about negligible quantities of Alar in
apples, yet shrug off the much higher probability of dying from smoking. We
worry about flying, but not driving. We worry about getting brain cancer
from cellular phones, although the link is quite tenuous. ◆ In fact, it's easy
to make a statistical argument—albeit a fallacious one—that cellular phones
prevent cancer, because the proportion of people with brain tumors is smaller
among cell phone users than among the general population.

Even simple pleasures such as eating and breathing have become suspect.   3
Love has always been risky, and AIDS has made intimacy more perilous than
ever. On the other hand, not having relationships may be riskier still. According to at least one study, the average male faces three times the threat of
early death associated with not being married as he does from cancer.

Of course, risk isn't all bad. Without knowingly taking risks, no one would   4
ever walk out the door, much less go to school, drive a car, have a baby, submit a proposal for a research grant, fall in love, or swim in the ocean. It's hard
to have any fun, accomplish anything productive, or experience life without
taking on risks—sometimes substantial ones. Life, after all, is a fatal disease,
and the mortality rate for humans, at the end of the day, is 100 percent.

Yet, people are notoriously bad at risk assessment. I couldn't get over this   5
feeling watching the aftermath of the crash of TWA Flight 800 and the
horror it spread about flying, with the long lines at airports, the increased

---

Reading Critically

◆ How much do you think about the element of risk in your life? Do you think Cole is right
in her assertion that most Americans try to "quantify risk" as much as possible?

◆ What specific risks do you worry about most?

security measures, the stories about grieving families day after day in the newspaper, the ongoing attempt to figure out why and who and what could be done to prevent such a tragedy from happening again.

Meanwhile, tens of thousands of children die every day around the world   6
from common causes such as malnutrition and disease. That's roughly the same as a hundred exploding jumbo jets full of children every single day. ❸ People who care more about the victims of Flight 800 aren't callous or ignorant. It's just the way our minds work. Certain kinds of tragedies make an impact; others don't. Our perceptual apparatus is geared toward threats that are exotic, personal, erratic, and dramatic. This doesn't mean we're ignorant, just human.

This skewed perception of risk has serious social consequences, however.   7
We aim our resources at phantoms, while real hazards are ignored. Parents, for example, tend to rate drug abuse and abduction by strangers as the greatest threats to their children. Yet hundreds of times more children die each year from choking, burns, falls, drowning, and other accidents that public safety efforts generally ignore. . . .

Even in terms of simple dollars, our policies don't make any sense. It's   8
well known, for example, that prenatal care for pregnant women saves enormous amounts of money—in terms of care infants need in the first year of life—and costs a pittance. Yet millions of low-income women don't get it.

Numbers are clearly not enough to make sense of risk assessment. Con-   9
text counts, too. Take cancer statistics. It's always frightening to hear that cancer is on the rise. However, at least one reason for the increase is simply that people are living longer—long enough to get the disease.

What you consider risky, after all, depends somewhat on the circumstances   10
of your life and lifestyle. People who don't have enough to eat don't worry about apples contaminated with Alar. People who face daily violence at their front door don't worry about hijackings on flights to the Bahamas. Attitudes toward risk evolve in cultural contexts and are influenced by everything from psychology to ethics to beliefs about personal responsibility.

In addition to context, another factor needed to see through the maze of   11
conflicting messages about risk is human psychology. For example, imminent risks strike much more fear in our hearts than distant ones; it's much harder to get a teenager than an older person to take long-term dangers like smoking seriously.

Smoking is also a habit people believe they can control, which makes the   12
risk far more acceptable. ❹ (People seem to get more upset about the effects

---

Reading Critically

❸ How effective is the author's "jumbo jet" analogy?

❹ What is the relationship between control and risk?

of passive smoking than smoking itself—at least in part because smokers get to choose, and breathers don't.)

As a general principle, people tend to grossly exaggerate the risk of any   13
danger perceived to be beyond their control, while shrugging off risks they think they can manage. Thus, we go skiing and skydiving, but fear asbestos. We resent and fear the idea that anonymous chemical companies are putting additives into our food; yet the additives we load onto our own food—salt, sugar, butter—are millions of times more dangerous.

This is one reason that airline accidents seem so unacceptable—because   14
strapped into our seats in the cabin, what happens is completely beyond our control. In a poll taken soon after the TWA Flight 800 crash, an overwhelming majority of people said they'd be willing to pay up to fifty dollars more for a round-trip ticket if it increased airline safety. Yet the same people resist moves to improve automobile safety, for example, especially if it costs money.

The idea that we can control what happens also influences who we blame   15
when things go wrong. Most people don't like to pay the costs for treating people injured by cigarettes or riding motorcycles because we think they brought these things on themselves. Some people also hold these attitudes toward victims of AIDS or mental illness, because they think the illness results from lack of character or personal morals. ⑤

In another curious perceptual twist, risks associated with losing some-   16
thing and gaining something appear to be calculated in our minds according to quite different scales. In a now-classic series of studies, Stanford psychologist Amos Tversky and colleague Daniel Kahneman concluded that most people will bend over backward to avoid small risks, even if that means sacrificing great potential rewards. "The threat of a loss has a greater impact on a decision than the possibility of an equivalent gain," they concluded.

In one of their tests, Tversky and Kahneman asked physicians to choose   17
between two strategies for combating a rare disease, expected to kill 600 people. Strategy A promised to save 200 people (the rest would die), while Strategy B offered a one-third probability that everyone would be saved, and a two-thirds probability that no one would be saved. Betting on a sure thing, the physicians choose A. But presented with the identical choice, stated differently, they choose B. The difference in language was simply this: Instead of stating that Strategy A would guarantee 200 out of 600 saved lives, it stated that Strategy A would mean 400 sure deaths.

People will risk a lot to prevent a loss, in other words, but risk very little   18
for possible gain. Running into a burning house to save a pet or fighting

---

Reading Critically

⑤ Is the concept of risk somehow less meaningful if people are perceived to have brought tragedy upon themselves?

back when a mugger asks for your wallet are both high-risk gambles that people take repeatedly in order to hang on to something they care about. [6] The same people might not risk the hassle of, say, fastening a seat belt in a car even though the potential gain might be much higher.

The bird in the hand always seems more attractive than the two in the   19
bush. Even if holding on to the one in your hand comes at a higher risk and the two in the bush are gold-plated.

The reverse situation comes into play when we judge risks of commis-   20
sion versus risks of omission. A risk that you assume by actually doing something seems far more risky than a risk you take by not doing something, even though the risk of doing nothing may be greater.

Deaths from natural causes, like cancer, are more readily acceptable than   21
deaths from accidents or murder. That's probably one reason it's so much easier to accept thousands of starving children than the death of one in a drive-by shooting. The former is an act of omission—a failure to step in and help, send food or medicine. The latter is the commission of a crime—somebody pulled the trigger.

In the same way, the Food and Drug Administration is far more likely to   22
withhold a drug that might help a great number of people if it threatens to harm a few; better to hurt a lot of people by failing to do something than act with the deliberate knowledge that some people will be hurt. Or as the doctors' credo puts it: First do no harm.

For obvious reasons, dramatic or exotic risks [7] seem far more dangerous   23
than more familiar ones. Plane crashes and AIDS are risks associated with ambulances and flashing lights, sex and drugs. While red dye #2 strikes terror in our hearts, that great glob of butter melting into our baked potato is accepted as an old friend. "A woman drives down the street with her child romping around in the front seat," says John Allen Paulos. "Then they arrive at the shopping mall, and she grabs the child's hand so hard it hurts, because she's afraid he'll be kidnapped."

Children who are kidnapped are far more likely to be whisked away by   24
relatives than strangers, just as most people are murdered by people they know.

Familiar risks creep up on us like age and are often difficult to see until   25
it's too late to take action. Mathematician Sam C. Saunders of Washington State University reminds us that a frog placed in hot water will struggle to escape, but the same frog placed in cool water that's slowly warmed up will sit peacefully until it's cooked. "One cannot anticipate what one does not

---

Reading Critically

[6] What do you care most about in life? Who or what would you risk your life to save?

[7] What is an "exotic risk"?

perceive," he says, which is why gradual accumulations of risk due to lifestyle choices (like smoking or eating) are so often ignored. We're in hot water, but it's gotten hot so slowly that no one notices. **8**

To bring home his point, Saunders asks us to imagine that cigarettes are not harmful—with the exception of an occasional one that has been packed with explosives instead of tobacco. These dynamite-stuffed cigarettes look just like normal ones. There's only one hidden away in every 18,250 packs—not a grave risk, you might say. The only catch is, if you smoke one of those explosive cigarettes, it might blow your head off.   26

The mathematician speculates, I think correctly, that given such a situation, cigarettes would surely be banned outright. After all, if 30 million packs of cigarettes are sold each day, an average of 1,600 people a day would die in gruesome explosions. Yet the number of deaths is the same to be expected from normal smoking. "The total expected loss of life or health to smokers using dynamite-loaded (but otherwise harmless) cigarettes over forty years would not be as great as with ordinary filtered cigarettes," says Saunders.   27

We can accept getting cooked like a frog, in other words, but not getting blown up like a firecracker.   28

It won't come as a great surprise to anyone that ego also plays a role in the way we assess risks. Psychological self-protection leads us to draw consistently wrong conclusions. In general, we overestimate the risks of bad things happening to others, while vastly underrating the possibility that they will happen to ourselves. **9** Indeed, the lengths people go to minimize their own perceived risks can be downright "ingenious," according to Rutgers psychologist Neil Weinstein. For example, people asked about the risk of finding radon in their houses always rate their risk as "low" or "average," never "high." "If you ask them why," says Weinstein, "they take anything and twist it around in a way that reassures them. Some say their risk is low because the house is new; others, because the house is old. Some will say their risk is low because their house is at the top of a hill; others, because it's at the bottom of a hill."   29

Whatever the evidence to the contrary, we think, "It won't happen to me." Weinstein and others speculate that this has something to do with preservation of self-esteem. We don't like to see ourselves as vulnerable. We like to think we've got some magical edge over the others. Ego gets involved especially in cases where being vulnerable to risk implies personal failure—for   30

Reading Critically

8 How does the author's analogy about a frog placed in hot water help us understand the concept of "familiar risks"?

9 Do you think Cole is right in her assertion that "we over-estimate the risks of bad things happening to others, while vastly underrating the possibility that they will happen to ourselves"? Why do you think this is so?

example, the risk of depression, suicide, alcoholism, drug addiction. "If you admit you're at risk," says Weinstein, "you're admitting that you can't handle stress. You're not as strong as the next person."

Average people, studies have shown, believe that they will enjoy longer   31
lives, healthier lives, and longer marriages than the "average" person. Despite the obvious fact that they themselves are, well, average people too. According to a recent poll, 3 out of 4 baby boomers (those born between 1946 and 1964) think they look younger than their peers, and 4 out of 5 say they have fewer wrinkles than other people their age—a statistical impossibility.

Kahneman and Tversky studied this phenomenon as well and found that   32
people think they'll beat the odds because they're special. This is no doubt a necessary psychological defense mechanism, or no one would ever get married again without thinking seriously about the potential for divorce. A clear view of personal vulnerability, however, could go a long way toward preventing activities like drunken driving. But then again, most people think they are better than average drivers—even when intoxicated.

We also seem to believe it won't happen to us if it hasn't happened yet.   33
That is, we extrapolate from the past to the future. "I've been taking that highway at eighty miles per hour for ten years and I haven't crashed yet," we tell ourselves. This is rather like reasoning that flipping a coin ten times that comes up heads guarantees that heads will continue to come up indefinitely.

Curiously, one advertising campaign against drunken driving that was   34
quite successful featured the faces of children killed by drunken drivers.[10] These children looked real to us. We could identify with them in the same way as we could identify with the people on TWA Flight 800. It's much easier to empathize with someone who has a name and a face than a statistic.

That explains in part why we go to great expense to rescue children who   35
fall down mine shafts, but not children dying from preventable diseases. Economists call this the "rule of rescue."[11] If you know that someone is in danger and you know that you can help, you have a moral obligation to do so. If you don't know about it, however, you have no obligation. Columnist Roger Simon speculates that's one reason the National Rifle Association lobbied successfully to eliminate the program at the Centers for Disease Control that keeps track of gun deaths. If we don't have to face what's happening, we won't feel obligated to do anything about it.

Even without the complication of all these psychological factors, however,   36
calculating risks can be tricky because not everything is known about every

---

Reading Critically

[10] Why did the advertising campaign featuring the faces of children killed by drunk drivers work so well?

[11] What is the "rule of rescue"?

situation. "We have to concede that a single neglected or unrecognized risk can invalidate all the reliability calculations, which are based on known risk," writes Ivar Ekeland. There is always a risk, in other words, that the risk assessment itself is wrong.

Genetic screening, like tests for HIV infection, has a certain probability of being wrong. If your results come back positive, how much should you worry? If they come back negative, how safe should you feel?   37

The more factors involved, the more complicated the risk assessment becomes. When you get to truly complex systems like nationwide telephone networks and power grids, worldwide computer networks and hugely complex machines like space shuttles, the risk of disaster becomes infinitely harder to pin down. [12] No one knows when a minor glitch will set off a chain reaction of events that will culminate in disaster. Potential risks in complex systems, in other words, are subject to exponential amplification.   38

Needless to say, the way a society assesses risk is very different from the way an individual views the same choices. Whether or not you wish to ride a motorcycle is your own business. Whether society pays the bills for the thousands of people maimed by cycle accidents, however, is everybody's business. Any one of us might view our own survival on a transatlantic flight as more important than the needs of the nation's children. Governments, one presumes, ought to have a somewhat different agenda.   39

But how far does society want to go in strictly numerical accounting? It certainly hasn't helped much in the all-important issue of health care, where an ounce of prevention has been proven again and again to be worth many pounds of cures. Most experts agree that we should be spending much more money preventing common diseases and accidents, especially in children. But no one wants to take health dollars away from precarious newborns or the elderly—where most of it goes. These are decisions that ultimately will not be made by numbers alone. Calculating risks only helps us to see more clearly what exactly is going on.   40

According to anthropologist Melvin Konner, author of *Why the Reckless Survive,* our poor judgment about potential risks may well be the legacy of evolution. [13] Early peoples lived at constant risk from predators, disease, accidents. They died young. And in evolutionary terms, "winning" means not longevity, but merely sticking around long enough to pass on your genes to the next generation. Taking risks was therefore a "winning" strategy, especially if it meant a chance to mate before dying. Besides, decisions had to be made quickly. If going for a meal of ripe berries meant risking an attack from a   41

Reading Critically

[12] What is the relationship between complexity and risk?
[13] Why is our poor judgment about potential risks "the legacy of evolution"?

saber-toothed tiger, you dove for the berries. For a half-starved cave dweller, this was a relatively simple choice. Perhaps our brains are simply not wired, speculates Konner, for the careful calculations presented by the risks of modern life.

UNDERSTANDING DETAILS

1. Why does Cole claim that people are basically confused about risk assessment (paragraph 2)?
2. What role does "context" play in our assessment of risks?
3. What three psychological factors affect people's perceptions of risk? Explain each in your own words.
4. In what ways does an individual calculate risk differently from the way society calculates risk?

THINKING CRITICALLY

5. What is the overall purpose of Cole's essay? How do you know? What clues make this purpose clear?
6. Why are faces and names more persuasive to us than statistics when considering risks in our own lives?
7. According to Cole, how do we form our own personal attitudes about risks? What does our lifestyle have to do with these attitudes?
8. Why does Cole think risk assessment is such a complex and difficult process?

DISCOVERING RHETORICAL STRATEGIES

9. Where in this essay does the author use division? Where does she use classification? Give specific examples. What other rhetorical modes does Cole use in her essay?
10. List the topics of each section of the body of this essay (paragraphs 9–40) (i.e., list one topic for each section). What advantages does this order have over other possible arrangements of the same ideas? How would the effect have been altered if Cole had changed the order of these ideas?
11. Why does Cole quote Melvin Kooner at the end of the essay: "Perhaps our brains are simply not wired, speculates Kooner, for the careful calculations presented by the risks of modern life" (paragraph 41). What does this quote mean in the context of Cole's essay?
12. What point of view does Cole take in her article? What tone results from this point of view?

MAKING CONNECTIONS

13. If K. C. Cole were having a round-table discussion with Brent Staples ("A Brother's Murder"), Julia Bourland ("Getting Out of Debt (and Staying Out)"), and/or Michael Dorris ("The Broken Cord"), which of the four would speak

most forcefully for the value and necessity of taking risks in life? Explain your answer.

14. What would Stephanie Ericsson ("The Ways We Lie") say about the kinds of lies we tell ourselves every day concerning the many risks we take? To what extent do you think K. C. Cole would agree with her?

15. Compare and contrast the way K. C. Cole divides and classifies types of risks with similar techniques of division and classification used by Franklin Zimring ("Confessions of an Ex-Smoker") and/or Phyllis Schneider ("Memory: Tips You'll Never Forget").

IDEAS FOR DISCUSSION/WRITING

Preparing to Write

Write freely about the risks you take: What criteria do you use to decide whether or not to take a particular risk? What risks do you confront on a daily basis? What risks have you taken beyond your daily routine? Why do you take these risks? How often do you seek out risks? Which risks do you avoid most aggressively? Why? What do risks add or detract from your life?

Choosing a Topic

1. Use division/classification to explain the types of risks you deal with in your life. Divide the risks you face into categories, and then discuss those categories in an essay written for your English class. Make sure you decide on a purpose and a point of view before you begin to write.

2. How do you make decisions? Use division/classification to explain how you approach a decision and make up your mind. Decide on a purpose and point of view before you begin to write.

3. Write an essay for your classmates in which you convince them to take a specific risk that you have taken. This might be anything from riding a roller coaster to filling out a job application. Be creative in your essay.

4. Visit your favorite online news source. What are today's most important headlines? How do they fit into K. C. Cole's categories of risk taking? Select a current event, and write an essay in which you analyze its actual risk using K. C. Cole's method of classification.

Before beginning your essay, you might want to consult the checklists on page 255.

JUDITH WALLERSTEIN   (1921–   )

SANDRA BLAKESLEE   (1943–   )

Second Chances for Children of Divorce

Judith Wallerstein grew up in New York City, earned her Ph.D. at Lund University in Sweden, and now lives and works in Marin County, California, where she serves as director of the Center for the Family in Transition. Since 1965, she has taught psychology at the University of California at Berkeley, where she specializes in divorce and its effect on family members. Her first book, *Surviving the Breakup* (coauthored by Joan Kelly, 1980), analyzes the impact of divorce on young children in the family. Her next, *Second Chances: Men, Women, and Children a Decade After Divorce* (1989), is a study of the long-term effects of divorce on teenagers and young adults. Her most recent book, *The Unexpected Legacy of Divorce* (2000), is a study of the effects of divorce on children twenty-five years after their parents' breakup. She is currently hard at work on a study of happy marriages. An avid reader, she collects ideas the way "other people collect recipes." She advises college students to read as much as possible: "The first prerequisite a writer must have is a love of reading." Her coauthor on *Second Chances*, Sandra Blakeslee, was born in Flushing, New York, and earned her B.S. degree at Berkeley, where her specialty was neurobiology. She is currently the West Coast science and medicine correspondent for the *New York Times*. A former Peace Corps volunteer in Borneo, she advises students using *The Prose Reader* to travel as much as possible: "You need a wide range of experiences to be a good writer." Blakeslee goes mountain biking and running in her spare time. She and Wallerstein recently collaborated on a new book entitled *What About the Kids? Raising Your Children Before, During, and After Divorce* (2003).

Preparing to Read

In the following essay from *Second Chances*, Wallerstein and Blakeslee classify the psychological tasks children who have suffered through the divorce of their parents must complete to free themselves from the past.

Exploring Experience: As you prepare to read this article, take a few minutes to think about the effects of divorce on yourself or someone you know: How close have you been to a divorce experience? What differences did you notice in the way adults and children responded to the same situation? Why do you think the divorce rate has been so high during the last fifty years?

Learning Online: Conduct an Internet search using the term *divorce statistics*. Keep in mind your findings when reading Wallerstein and Blakeslee's description of the different ways in which children are affected by divorce.

A t each stage in the life cycle, children and adults face predictable and particular issues that represent the coming together of the demands of society and a biological and psychological timetable. Just as we physically learn to sit, crawl, walk, and run, we follow an equivalent progression in our psychological and social development. Each stage presents us with a sequence of tasks we must confront. We can succeed or fail in mastering them, to varying degrees, but everyone encounters the tasks. They begin at birth and end at death. 1

Children move upward along a common developmental ladder, although each goes it alone at his or her own pace. Gradually, as they pass through the various stages, children consolidate a sense of self. They develop coping skills, conscience, and the capacity to give and receive love. 2

Children take one step at a time, negotiating the rung they are on before they can move up to the next. They may—and often do—falter in this effort. The climb is not steady under the best of circumstances, and most children briefly stand still in their ascent. They may even at times move backward. [1] Such regressions are not a cause for alarm; rather, they may represent an appropriate response to life's stresses. Children who fail one task are not stalled forever; they will go on to the next stage, although they may be weakened in their climb. Earlier failures will not necessarily imperil their capacity as adults to trust a relationship, make a commitment, hold an appropriate job, or be a parent—to make use of their second chances at each stage of development. 3

I propose that children who experience divorce face an additional set of tasks specific to divorce in addition to the normal developmental tasks of growing up. Growing up is inevitably harder for children of divorce [2] because they must deal with psychological issues that children from well-functioning intact families do not have to face. 4

The psychological tasks of children begin as difficulties, escalate between the parents during the marriage, and continue through the separation and divorce and throughout the postdivorce years. 5

Task: Understanding the Divorce

The first and most basic task at the time of separation is for the children to understand realistically what the divorce means in their family and what its concrete consequences will be. Children, especially very young children, are thrown back on frightening and vivid fantasies of being abandoned, being 6

Reading Critically

[1] Try to remember a time when you "moved backward" in your social development? What was the long-term result of this change in your life?

[2] Why do you think growing up is more difficult for children of divorce?

placed in foster care, or never seeing a departed parent again, or macabre fantasies such as a mother being destroyed in an earthquake or a father being destroyed by a vengeful mother. All of these fantasies and the feelings that accompany them can be undone only as the children, with the parents' continuing help, begin to understand the reality and begin to adjust to the actual changes that the divorce brings.

The more mature task of understanding what led to the marital failure   7 awaits the perspective of the adolescent and young adult. Early on, most children regard divorce as a serious error, but by adolescence most feel that their parents never should have married. The task of understanding occurs in two stages. The first involves accurately perceiving the immediate changes that divorce brings and differentiating fantasy fears from reality. The second occurs later, when children are able at greater distance and with more mature understanding to evaluate their parents' actions and can draw useful lessons for their own lives. [3]

Task: Strategic Withdrawal

Children and adolescents need to get on with their own lives as soon as   8 possible after the divorce, to resume their normal activities at school and at play, to get back physically and emotionally to the normal tasks of growing up. Especially for adolescents who may have been beginning to spread their wings, the divorce pulls them back into the family orbit, where they may become consumed with care for siblings or a troubled parent. It also intrudes on their academic and social life, causing them to spend class time preoccupied with worry and to pass up social activities because of demands at home. This is not to say that children should ignore the divorce. Their task is to acknowledge their concern and to provide appropriate help to their parents and siblings, but they should strive to remove the divorce from the center of their own thoughts so that they can get back to their own interests, pleasures, problems, and peer relationships. To achieve this task, children need encouragement from their parents to *remain* children.

Task: Dealing with Loss

In the years following divorce, children experience two profound losses.   9 One is the loss of the intact family together with the symbolic and real protection it has provided. [4] The second is the loss of the presence of one parent, usually the father, from their daily lives.

Reading Critically

[3] Analyze one insight about your parents' relationship that you became aware of recently.

[4] What do you think is the difference between the "symbolic" and the "real" protection our family structure offers?

In dealing with these losses, children fall back on many fantasies to mask   10
their unhappiness. As we have seen, they may idealize the father as representative of all that is lacking in their current lives, thinking that if only he
were present, everything would be better.

The task of absorbing loss is perhaps the single most difficult task im-   11
posed by divorce. At its core, the task requires children to overcome the profound sense of rejection, humiliation, unlovability, and powerlessness they
feel with the departure of one parent. When the parent leaves, children of all
ages blame themselves. They say, "He left me because I was not lovable. I was
not worthy." They conclude that had they been more lovable, worthy, or different, the parent would have stayed. In this way, the loss of the parent and
lowered self-esteem become intertwined.

To stave off these intensely painful feelings of rejection, children contin-   12
ually try to undo the divorce scenario, to bring their parents back together,
or to somehow win back the affection of the absent parent.[5] The explanation "Had he loved me, he would not have left the family" turns into a new
concern. "If he loved me, he would visit more often. He would spend more
time with me." With this in mind, the children not only are pained at the outset but remain vulnerable, sometimes increasingly, over the years. Many reach
out during adolescence to increase contact with the parent who left, again
to undo the sad scenario and to rebuild their self-esteem as well.

This task is easier if parents and children have a good relationship, within   13
the framework of a good visiting or joint custody arrangement.

Some children are able to use a good, close relationship with the visiting   14
parent to promote their growth within the divorced family. Others are able
to acknowledge and accept that the visiting parent could never become
the kind of parent they need, and they are able to turn away from blaming
themselves. Still others are able to reject, on their own, a rejecting parent or
to reject a role model that they see as flawed. In so doing, these youngsters
are able to effectively master the loss and get on with their lives.[6]

Task: Dealing with Anger

Divorce, unlike death, is always a voluntary decision for at least one of the   15
partners in a marriage. Everyone involved knows this. The child understands
that divorce is not a natural disaster like an earthquake or tornado; it is caused
by the decision of one or both of the parents to separate. Its true cause lies in
the parents' failure to maintain the marriage, and someone is culpable.

Reading Critically

[5] How and why do children "continually try to undo the divorce scenario"?

[6] To what extent do you believe divorce is seen as a "loss" by the children of the
relationship?

Given this knowledge, children face a terrible dilemma. They know that   16
their unhappiness has been caused by the very people charged with their
protection and care—their parents are the agents of their distress. Furthermore, the parents undertook this role voluntarily. This realization puts children in a dreadful bind because they know something that they dare not
express—out of fear, out of anxiety, out of a wish to protect their parents.

Children get angry at their parents, experiencing divorce as indifference   17
to their needs and perceiving parents sometimes realistically as self-centered
and uncaring, as preaching a corrupt morality, and as weak and unable to deal
with problems except by running away.

At the same time, children are aware of their parents' neediness, weak-   18
nesses, and anxiety about life's difficulties. Although children have little understanding of divorce, except when the fighting has been open and violent,
they fully recognize how unhappy and disorganized their parents become,
and this frightens them very much. Caught in a combination of anger and
love, the children are frightened and guilty about their anger because they
love their parents and perceive them as unhappy people who are trying to
improve their lives in the face of severe obstacles. Their concern makes it difficult even to acknowledge their anger.

A major task, then, for children is to work through this anger, to recog-   19
nize their parents as human beings capable of making mistakes, and to respect
them for their real efforts and their real courage. [7]

Cooling of anger and the task of forgiveness go hand in hand with chil-   20
dren's growing emotional maturity and capacity to appreciate the various
needs of the different family members. As anger diminishes, young people are
better able to put the divorce behind them and experience relief. As children
forgive their parents, they forgive themselves for feeling anger and guilt and
for failing to restore the marriage. In this way, children can free themselves
from identification with the angry or violent parent or with the victim.

TASK: Working Out Guilt

Young children often feel responsible for divorce, thinking that their mis-   21
behavior may have caused one parent to leave. Or, in a more complicated way,
they may feel that their fantasy wish to drive a wedge between their mother
and father has been magically granted. Many guilty feelings arise at the time
of divorce but dissipate naturally as children mature. Others persist, usually
with roots in a profound continuing sense of having caused the unthink-
able—getting rid of one parent so as to be closer to the other.

Reading Critically

[7] Have you ever tried to "work through" anger about something? How successful were you
in doing so?

Other feelings of guilt are rooted in children's realization that they were   22
indeed a cause of marital difficulty. Many divorces occur after the birth of a
child, and the child correctly comprehends that he or she really did drive a
wedge between the adults.

We see another kind of guilt in girls who, in identifying with their troubled   23
mothers, become afraid to surpass their mothers. These young women have
trouble separating from their mothers, whom they love and feel sorry for, and
establishing their own successful relationships with suitable young men. The
children of divorce need to separate from guilty ties that bind them too closely
to a troubled parent and to go on with their lives with compassion and love.

TASK: Accepting the Permanence of the Divorce

At first, children feel a strong and understandable need to deny the divorce.   24
Such early denial may be a first step in the coping process. Like a screen that
is alternately lowered and raised, the denial helps children confront the full
reality of the divorce, bit by bit. They cannot take it in all at once.

Nevertheless, we have learned that five and even ten years after divorce,   25
some children and adolescents refuse to accept the divorce as a permanent
state of affairs. They continue to hope, consciously or unconsciously, that the
marriage will be restored, finding omens of reconciliation even in a harmless handshake or a simple friendly nod.

In accepting permanence, the children of divorce face a more difficult   26
task than children of bereavement. Death cannot be undone, but divorce
happens between living people who can change their minds. A reconciliation fantasy [8] taps deep into children's psyches. Children need to feel that
their parents will still be happy together. They may not overcome this fantasy of reconciliation until they themselves finally separate from their parents
and leave home.

TASK: Taking a Chance on Love

This is perhaps the most important task for growing children and for so-   27
ciety. Despite what life has dealt them, despite lingering fears and anxieties,
the children of divorce must grow, become open to the possibility of success
or failure, and take a chance on love. They must hold on to a realistic vision
that they can both love and be loved.

This is the central task for youngsters during adolescence and at entry   28
into young adulthood. And as we have seen, it is the task on which so many
children tragically flounder. Children who lose a parent through death must

---

Reading Critically

[8] What is a "reconciliation fantasy"?

take a chance on loving with the knowledge that all people eventually die and that death can take away our loved ones at any time. Children who lose the intact family through divorce must also take a chance on love, knowing realistically that divorce is always possible but being willing nevertheless to remain open to love, commitment, marriage, and fidelity.

More than the ideology of hoping to fall in love and find commitment, 29 this task involves being able to turn away from the model of parents who could not stay committed to each other. While all the young people in our study were in search of romantic love, a large number of them lived with such a high degree of anxiety over fears of betrayal or of not finding love that they were entirely unable to take the kind of chances necessary for them to move emotionally into successful young adulthood.

This last task, taking a chance on love, [9] involves being able to venture, 30 not just thinking about it, and not thinking one way and behaving another. It involves accepting a morality that truly guides behavior. This is the task that occupies children of divorce throughout their adolescence. It is what makes adolescence such a critical and difficult time for them. The resolution of life's tasks is a relative process that never ends, but this last task, which is built on successfully negotiating all the others, leads to psychological freedom from the past. This is the essence of second chances for children of divorce.

UNDERSTANDING DETAILS

1. Name the seven categories into which Wallerstein and Blakeslee divide the psychological growth of the children of divorce. How long will it take most children to go through these stages?
2. Choose one of these tasks and explain it in your own words.
3. According to Wallerstein and Blakeslee, what is probably the most difficult task that results from divorce? Why do the authors believe this stage is so painful?
4. What did Wallerstein and Blakeslee find out about their subjects' ability to deal with love in their lives?

THINKING CRITICALLY

5. In your opinion, which of the emotional tasks that Wallerstein and Blakeslee describe is likely to be most traumatic in a child's life after a divorce? On what do you base your conclusion?
6. What is the relationship suggested in this essay between the parents' divorce and a child's sense of rejection?

Reading Critically

[9] According to the authors, why is "taking a chance on love" tougher for children of divorce?

7. In what ways does dealing with all facets of their anger create a problem for children of divorce? Do you know anyone who has worked through such a problem? Explain your answer in detail.
8. How might an understanding of the seven tasks discussed in this essay help people deal more effectively with children affected by divorce?

DISCOVERING RHETORICAL STRATEGIES

9. How do Wallerstein and Blakeslee organize their categories in this essay? Why do they place these tasks in this particular order?
10. What is the authors' general attitude toward divorce? What references in the essay reveal this point of view?
11. Describe the authors' intended audience. What makes you think they are directing their comments to this group?
12. What other rhetorical modes do Wallerstein and Blakeslee use in this essay besides division and classification? How do these other modes support the authors' division/classification system?

MAKING CONNECTIONS

13. Compare and contrast the love and support needed by children of divorce with the love and support provided naturally by the different types of families described in Mary Pipher's "Beliefs About Families."
14. What are the principal differences between Wallerstein and Blakeslee's prescriptions for how a child can best cope with the death of his or her parents' relationship and the way in which funeral directors in Jessica Mitford's "Behind the Formaldehyde Curtain" try to help us endure the death of a friend or relative? Which coping mechanisms are the same? Which are different?
15. Wallerstein and Blakeslee divide their essay into seven "tasks" that must be accomplished by children of divorce. Find a division/classification essay in this section of *The Prose Reader* that has more subdivisions. Then, find one that has fewer. How does the number of subdivisions in a division/classification essay affect your ability to understand the author's entire argument? Which of these essays is the easiest to follow? Which is the most difficult? Why?

IDEAS FOR DISCUSSION/WRITING

Preparing to Write

Write freely about your thoughts on divorce and the effects of divorce on others: Do you know anyone who has gone through a divorce? How did the experience affect the couple getting divorced? How did it affect their friends, their relatives, and their children? How do you think the high divorce rate is affecting Americans in general? Why is America's national divorce rate so high? What changes could we make to lower the divorce rate?

Choosing a Topic

1. Assume that you are an expert on the variety and scope of college relationships. In an essay written for your classmates, divide your observations on different types of relationships into categories that will show students the full range of these associations in a college setting.

2. Because you have been involved with divorce in some way, you have been asked to submit to your college newspaper an editorial classifying the various ways in which different types of people react to divorce (husbands, wives, children, friends, and so on). You have been told to pay particular attention to the reactions of college students whose parents are going through or have gone through a divorce.

3. In an essay written for the general public, speculate about the reasons for the high national divorce rate. Use your own experience, interview others, or consult sources in the library to investigate the reasons for this trend. Suggest how we could solve this problem in America.

4. What other important issues affect children? Visit the United Nations Children's Fund Web site (http://www.unicef.org), and explore issues affecting children internationally. Write an essay in which you either select a single issue and divide it into subsections or you classify several different topics into a thematic order.

Before beginning your essay, you might want to consult the checklists on page 255.

Confessions of an Ex-Smoker

Born in Los Angeles, Franklin Zimring earned his B.A. at Wayne State University and his law degree at the University of Chicago and then served for ten years as the director of the Center for Studies in Criminal Justice at the University of Chicago before moving to his present post as director of the Earl Warren Legal Institute at the University of California at Berkeley. A specialist in legal policy, he has published a number of books on a wide variety of topics, many of which were coauthored with colleague Gordon Hawkins, including *The Citizen's Guide to Gun Control* (1987), *The Scale of Imprisonment* (1991), *The Search for Rational Drug Control* (1992), *Incapacitation: Penal Confinement and the Restraint of Crime* (1995), *Crime Is Not the Problem: Lethal Violence in America* (1997), *American Youth Violence* (1998), *Punishment and Democracy: Three Strikes and You're Out* (2000), and *The Contradictions of Capital Punishment* (2003). He has also written articles on similar topics, including "The Executioner's Dissonant Song: On Capital Punishment and American Legal Values," which was published in *Killing State: Capital Punishment in Law, Politics, and Culture* (1999). His advice to students using *The Prose Reader* is to "listen to your own internal prompter as you write." A great believer in E. M. Forster's famous question "How do I know what I think till I see what I say?," Zimring counsels students to "relax and decide what you really think about a topic, and then express it as clearly and concisely as possible." The author's own relaxation comes from the sport of swimming, to which he confesses a "religious devotion."

Preparing to Read

Originally published in *Newsweek* magazine (April 20, 1987), the following article is one in a series of "Mid-Life Memoranda" that Zimring has been writing since 1985. It offers a witty classification of ex-smokers into four distinct groups: zealots, evangelists, the elect, and the serene.

Exploring Experience: As you prepare to read this essay, think for a few moments about your own addictions: Have you ever had any addictions? Were they good addictions or bad? Are any of these addictions still with you? Why are these addictions part of your life? Do you want to change the status of these addictions? Why or why not? What do you think causes people to be addicted to certain substances or behavior? How can we break away from addictions successfully?

Learning Online: Using Google's search engine (http://www.google .com), click on the "Images" tab to conduct a picture search for the term *cigarette ads*. What differences do you find in how smokers are portrayed in the past and present?

Americans can be divided into three groups—smokers, nonsmokers, and that expanding pack of us who have quit. Those who have never smoked don't know what they're missing, but former smokers, ex-smokers, reformed smokers can never forget. We are veterans of a personal war, linked by that watershed experience of ceasing to smoke and by the temptation to have just one more cigarette. For almost all of us ex-smokers, smoking continues to play an important part in our lives. And now that it is being restricted in restaurants around the country and will be banned in almost all indoor public places in New York State, it is vital that everyone understand the different emotional states cessation of smoking can cause. I have observed four of them; and in the interest of science I have classified them as those of the zealot, the evangelist, the elect, and the serene. Each day, each category gains new recruits.

Not all antitobacco zealots are former smokers, but a substantial number of fire-and-brimstone opponents do come from the ranks of the reformed. ◆ Zealots believe that those who continue to smoke are degenerates who deserve scorn not pity and the penalties that will deter offensive behavior in public as well. Relations between these people and those who continue to smoke are strained.

One explanation for the zealot's fervor in seeking to outlaw tobacco consumption is his own tenuous hold on abstaining from smoking. But I think part of the emotional force arises from sheer envy as he watches and identifies with each lung-filling puff. By making smoking in public a crime, the zealot seeks reassurance that he will not revert to bad habits; give him strong social penalties, and he won't become a recidivist.

No systematic survey has been done yet, but anecdotal evidence suggests that a disproportionate number of doctors who have quit smoking can be found among the fanatics. ◆ Just as the most enthusiastic revolutionary tends to make the most enthusiastic counterrevolutionary, many of today's vitriolic zealots include those who had been deeply committed to tobacco habits.

By contrast, the antismoking evangelist does not condemn smokers. Unlike the zealot, he regards smoking as an easily curable condition, as a social disease, and not a sin. The evangelist spends an enormous amount of time seeking and preaching to the unconverted. He argues that kicking the habit is not *that* difficult. After all, *he* did it; moreover, as he describes it, the benefits of quitting are beyond measure and the disadvantages are nil.

The hallmark of the evangelist is his insistence that he never misses tobacco. Though he is less hostile to smokers than the zealot, he is resented more. Friends and loved ones who have been the targets of his preachments

---

Reading Critically

◆ What is a "zealot"? What are you zealous about?

◆ According to Zimring, why are physicians who have quit smoking often the most fanatic about their conversion from cigarettes?

frequently greet the resumption of smoking by the evangelist as an occasion for unmitigated glee.

Among former smokers, the distinctions between the evangelist and the elect are much the same as the differences between proselytizing and non-proselytizing religious sects. While the evangelists preach the ease and desirability of abstinence, the elect do not attempt to convert their friends. They think that virtue is its own reward and subscribe to the Puritan theory of pre-destination. Since they have proved themselves capable of abstaining from tobacco, they are therefore different from friends and relatives who continue to smoke. They feel superior, secure that their salvation was foreordained. These ex-smokers rarely give personal testimony on their conversion. ❸ They rarely speak about their tobacco habits, while evangelists talk about little else. Of course, active smokers find such blue-nosed behavior far less offensive than that of the evangelist or the zealot, yet they resent the elect simply because they are smug. Their air of self-satisfaction rarely escapes the notice of those lighting up. For active smokers, life with a member of the ex-smoking elect is less stormy than with a zealot or evangelist, but it is subtly oppressive nonetheless.

I have labeled my final category of former smokers the serene. This classification is meant to encourage those who find the other psychic styles of ex-smokers disagreeable. Serenity is quieter than zealotry and evangelism, and those who qualify are not as self-righteous as the elect. The serene ex-smoker accepts himself and also accepts those around him who continue to smoke. This kind of serenity does not come easily nor does it seem to be an immediate option for those who have stopped. Rather it is a goal, an end stage in a process of development during which some former smokers progress through one or more of the less-than-positive psychological points en route. For former smokers, serenity is thus a positive possibility that exists at the end of the rainbow. But all former smokers cannot reach that promised land.

What is it that permits some former smokers to become serene? I think the key is self-acceptance and gratitude. The fully mature former smoker knows he has the soul of an addict and is grateful for the knowledge. He doesn't regret that he quit smoking, nor any of his previous adventures with tobacco. As a former smoker, he is grateful for the experience and memory of craving a cigarette.

Serenity comes from accepting the lessons of one's life. ❹ And ex-smokers who have reached this point in their world view have much to be grateful for. They have learned about the potential and limits of change. In

---

Reading Critically

❸ Why does the author shift into religious imagery here?

❹ Which of life's lessons have you accepted with the most serenity? How did you learn these lessons?

becoming the right kind of former smoker, they developed a healthy sense of self. This former smoker, for one, believes that it is better to crave (one hopes only occasionally) and not to smoke than never to have craved at all. And by accepting that fact, the reformed smoker does not need to excoriate, envy, or disassociate himself from those who continue to smoke.

UNDERSTANDING DETAILS

1. What are the four categories of reformed smokers that Zimring has observed? What characterizes each type?
2. What is the difference between the "elect" and the "serene" ex-smokers according to the author?
3. What is the general purpose of this division/classification essay?
4. How are becoming "the right kind of former smoker" and "a healthy sense of self" (paragraph 10) related? How do they affect one another?

THINKING CRITICALLY

5. How does Zimring portray smokers in this essay? What effect does this attitude have on the rest of the essay?
6. What type of ex-smoker do you think would be most difficult to live with and why?
7. Why do you think many doctors who stop smoking become zealots?
8. Do you agree with Zimring that the key to being a "serene" ex-smoker is "self-acceptance and gratitude" (paragraph 9)? Are these positive qualities in an ex-smoker? Explain your answer in detail.

DISCOVERING RHETORICAL STRATEGIES

9. Who do you think is Zimring's specific audience for this essay? Explain your answer.
10. What do you think is Zimring's purpose in writing this essay? How did you come to this conclusion?
11. Zimring discusses these types of reformed smokers in a specific order. Explain this progression and discuss whether it is effective in achieving Zimring's overall purpose.
12. What rhetorical modes support the author's division/classification? Give examples of each.

MAKING CONNECTIONS

13. Compare Zimring's description of the addictive nature of tobacco with Michael Dorris's account of alcohol addiction in "The Broken Cord." Which substance do you think is most addictive? Explain your answer.

14. Use Zimring's definition of a "zealot" to help analyze essays by Gloria Steinem ("The Politics of Muscle"), Dave Grossman ("We Are Training Our Kids to Kill"), and/or Barbara Ehrenreich ("The Ecstasy of War"). To what extent are these authors zealots in support of their cause? Which author is most passionate in his or her opinion? Which is the least? Are you zealous about any particular issue? If so, which one?

15. Examine Jessica Mitford's "Behind the Formaldehyde Curtain," Scott Russell Sanders' "Homeplace," and/or Sucheng Cahn's "You're Short, Besides!" in order to determine whether any of these authors have reached Zimring's level of "serenity" in life. Which of these writers would you characterize as "zealots"? Which as "evangelists"? Which as "the elect"? What are the principal differences in the approaches of these three authors?

IDEAS FOR DISCUSSION/WRITING

Preparing to Write

Write freely about the role addiction plays in our lives in America: What do you know about addiction in general? What different substances and activities can people be addicted to? How can they break an addiction? What addictions are most dominant in American society? In what ways have you avoided addiction? In what ways are you addicted? What are your worst addictions? What are some of your friends' addictions? What do your addictions say about your personality? What do your friends' addictions say about them? What are some of America's major addictions? How could we alleviate these problems?

Choosing a Topic

1. Your high school graduating class has decided to put together a brochure about substance abuse and addiction for students starting high school. You have been asked to explain addiction and its consequences to this audience. Make your essay as vivid as possible.

2. Pretend that your college newspaper is running a special issue distinguishing between different generations of students. In a coherent essay written for the readers of this newspaper, classify the students of your generation in some logical, interesting fashion. Remember that classification is a rhetorical movement from "many" to "one." Group the members of your generation by some meaningful guidelines or general characteristics that you establish. Be sure to decide on a purpose and a point of view before you begin to write.

3. You have had many different types of friends over the years. Discuss one type of friend by dividing into logical categories the actual behavior of that type of person. Discuss each part of your division, giving examples as frequently as possible. Decide on a purpose and a point of view before you begin to write.

4. Zimring uses humor to classify former smokers that he observes. Spend some time watching the way people use one of the following: computers, the Internet, or e-mail. You may do this by reading through your e-mails or spending time in a campus computer lab, library, or coffee shop. How do people differ in their

use of this technological equipment? Write a humorous essay in which you divide the users you observe into specific groups. Use concrete details to support your categories.

Before beginning your essay, you might want to consult the checklists on page 255.

STEPHANIE ERICSSON (1953–   )

The Ways We Lie

Born in Dallas, Stephanie Ericsson grew up in San Francisco and lived in London, Spain, New York, and Los Angeles before settling in Minneapolis, Minnesota, where she currently lives with her two children. Following a filmmaking degree in college, she worked in advertising and then became a screenwriter's assistant and later a writer of situation comedies. After overcoming substance abuse problems, she published *Shamefaced: The Road to Recovery* (1985) and *Women of AA: Recovering Together* (1985). When she was 32 years old, her husband died suddenly of a heart attack while she was two and a half months pregnant, thereby inspiring a number of journal entries and two frank and wrenching books on grief: *Companion Through the Darkness: Inner Dialogues on Grief* (1993) and *Companion Into the Dawn: Inner Dialogues on Loving* (1994). Defining grief as "the constant reawakening that things are now different," she argues that it "shears away the masks of normal life and forces brutal honesty out of your mouth before propriety can stop you. It shoves away friends and scares away so-called friends and rewrites your address book for you." Her unique prose style is a very effective combination of her own diary entries mixed with brief essays that vividly chronicle wrenching emotions of grief. A frequent speaker on the subject of loss, Ericsson has written extensively on human psychology and the mental and physical repercussions of addiction and deceit.

Preparing to Read

In this essay, first published in the *Utne Reader,* Stephanie Ericsson categorizes the different types of lies we all tell in an attempt to portray the reality we all live in.

Exploring Experience: As you prepare to read this selection, consider how often you lie or stretch the truth in a typical day: Do you find that you don't tell the truth in every situation? When do you stretch the truth? Why do you do it? What are the consequences of these lies? Do you feel guilty when you don't tell the whole truth? Why do you think you feel this way?

Learning Online: Visit the Blifaloo Web site selection "How to Detect Lies" (http://www.blifaloo.com/info/lies.php), and read this short article on the common signs of deception. According to the essay, what are some of the physical gestures, facial expressions, and verbal indicators that people display when they are lying? Have you ever been aware of these indicators in yourself or someone else? You also might read the companion article "Eye Direction and Lying" (http://www.blifaloo.com/info/lies_eyes.php).

The bank called today and I told them my deposit was in the mail, even   1
though I hadn't written a check yet. It'd been a rough day. The baby
I'm pregnant with decided to do aerobics on my lungs for two hours,
our three-year-old daughter painted the living-room couch with lipstick,
the IRS put me on hold for an hour, and I was late to a business meeting
because I was tired.

I told my client that traffic had been bad. When my partner came home,   2
his haggard face told me his day hadn't gone any better than mine, so when
he asked, "How was your day?" I said, "Oh, fine," knowing that one more
straw might break his back. A friend called and wanted to take me to lunch.
I said I was busy. Four lies in the course of a day, none of which I felt the
least bit guilty about.

We lie. We all do. We exaggerate, we minimize, we avoid confrontation,   3
we spare people's feelings, we conveniently forget, we keep secrets, we justify lying to the big-guy institutions. Like most people, I indulge in small
falsehoods and still think of myself as an honest person. Sure I lie, but it
doesn't hurt anything. Or does it? [1]

I once tried going a whole week without telling a lie, and it was paralyz-   4
ing. I discovered that telling the truth all the time is nearly impossible. It means
living with some serious consequences: The bank charges me $60 in overdraft
fees, my partner keels over when I tell him about my travails, my client fires
me for telling her I didn't feel like being on time, and my friend takes it personally when I say I'm not hungry. There must be some merit to lying.

But if I justify lying, what makes me any different from slick politicians   5
or the corporate robbers who raided the S&L industry? Saying it's okay to
lie one way and not another is hedging. I cannot seem to escape the voice
deep inside me that tells me: When someone lies, someone loses.

What far-reaching consequences will I, or others, pay as a result of my   6
lie? [2] Will someone's trust be destroyed? Will someone else pay my penance
because I ducked out? We must consider the *meaning of our actions*. Deception, lies, capital crimes, and misdemeanors all carry meanings. *Webster's*
definition of *lie* is specific:

1. a false statement or action especially made with the intent to deceive;
2. anything that gives or is meant to give a false impression.

A definition like this implies that there are many, many ways to tell a lie.   7
Here are just a few.

Reading Critically

[1] Do you think lying "doesn't hurt anything"? Have you ever been harmed by a lie?
[2] Have your lies ever hurt another person? How did the situation make you feel?

The White Lie

A man who won't lie to a woman has very little consideration for her feelings.
                                                                —*Bergen Evans*

The white lie assumes that the truth will cause more damage than a sim-   8
ple, harmless untruth. Telling a friend he looks great when he looks like hell
can be based on a decision that the friend needs a compliment more than a
frank opinion. But, in effect, it is the liar deciding what is best for the lied
to. Ultimately, it is a vote of no confidence. It is an act of subtle arrogance
for anyone to decide what is best for someone else.

Yet not all circumstances are quite so cut and dried. Take, for instance, the   9
sergeant in Vietnam who knew one of his men was killed in action but listed
him as missing so that the man's family would receive indefinite compensation instead of the lump sum pittance the millitary gives widows and children. His intent was honorable. Yet for twenty years this family kept their
hopes alive, unable to move on to a new life. ❸

Façades

Et tu, Brute?

                                                                —*Caesar*

We all put up façades to one degree or another. When I put on a suit to   10
go to see a client, I feel as though I am putting on another face, obeying the
expectation that serious businesspeople wear suits rather than sweatpants. But
I'm a writer: Normally, I get up, get the kid off to school, and sit at my computer in my pajamas until four in the afternoon. When I answer the phone,
the caller thinks I'm wearing a suit (though the UPS man knows better).

But façades can be destructive because they are used to seduce others into   11
an illusion. For instance, I recently realized that a former friend was a liar.
He presented himself with all the right looks and the right words and offered
lots of new consciousness theories, fabulous books to read, and fascinating
insights. Then I did some business with him, and the time came for him to
pay me. He turned out to be all talk and no walk. I heard a plethora of reasonable excuses, including in-depth descriptions of the big break around the
corner. In six months of work, I saw less than a hundred bucks. When I confronted him, he raised both eyebrows and tried to convince me that I'd heard
him wrong, that he'd made no commitment to me. A simple investigation into
his past revealed a crowded graveyard of disenchanted former friends. ❹

Reading Critically

❸ Do you approve of the sergeant's lie? Why or why not?

❹ What does the metaphor "a crowded graveyard of disenchanted former friends" mean to
you?

Ignoring The Plain Facts

Well, you must understand that Father Porter is only human.

—*A Massachusetts Priest*

In the '60s, the Catholic Church in Massachusetts began hearing complaints that Father James Porter was sexually molesting children. Rather than relieving him of his duties, the ecclesiastical authorities moved him from one parish to another between 1960 and 1967, actually providing him with a fresh supply of unsuspecting families and innocent children to abuse. After treatment in 1967 for pedophilia, he went back to work, this time in Minnesota. The new diocese was aware of Father Porter's obsession with children, but they needed priests and recklessly believed treatment had cured him. More children were abused until he was relieved of his duties a year later. By his own admission, Porter may have abused as many as a hundred children.   12

Ignoring the facts may not in and of itself be a form of lying, but consider the context of this situation. If a lie is a false action done with the intent to deceive, then the Catholic Church's conscious covering for Porter created irreparable consequences. The church became a co-perpetrator with Porter.   13

Deflecting

When you have no basis for an argument, abuse the plaintiff

—*Cicero*

I've discovered that I can keep anyone from seeing the true me by being selectively blatant. I set a precedent of being up-front about intimate issues, but I never bring up the things I truly want to hide; I just let people assume I'm revealing everything. It's an effective way of hiding. ⑤   14

Any good liar knows that the way to perpetuate an untruth is to deflect attention from it. When Clarence Thomas exploded with accusations that the Senate hearings were a "high-tech lynching," he simply switched the focus from a highly charged subject to a radioactive subject. Rather than defending himself, he took the offensive and accused the country of racism. It was a brilliant maneuver. Racism is now politically incorrect in official circles— unlike sexual harassment, which still rewards those who can get away with it.   15

Some of the most skilled deflectors are passive-aggressive people who, when accused of inappropriate behavior, refuse to respond to the accusations. This you-don't-exist stance infuriates the accuser, who, understandably, screams something obscene out of frustration. The trap is sprung and the act of deflection successful, because now the passive aggressive person can indignantly say, "Who can talk to someone as unreasonable as you?" The real   16

Reading Critically

⑤ What does the term "deflecting" mean? Have you ever been guilty of this type of lying?

issue is forgotten and the sins of the original victim become the focus. Feeling guilty of name-calling, the victim is fully tamed and crawls into a hole, ashamed. I have watched this fighting technique work thousands of times in disputes between men and women, and what I've learned is that the real culprit is not necessarily the one who swears the loudest.

Omission

The cruelest lies are often told in silence.

—*R. L. Stevenson*

Omission involves telling most of the truth minus one or two key facts   17
whose absence changes the story completely. You break a pair of glasses that are guaranteed under normal use and get a new pair, without mentioning that the first pair broke during a rowdy game of basketball. Who hasn't tried something like that? But what about omission of information that could make a difference in how a person lives his or her life?

For instance, one day I found out that rabbinical legends tell of another   18
woman in the Garden of Eden before Eve. I was stunned. The omission of the Sumerian goddess Lilith from Genesis—as well as her demonization by ancient misogynists as an embodiment of female evil—felt like spiritual robbery. I felt like I'd just found out my mother was really my stepmother. To take seriously the tradition that Adam was created out of the same mud as his equal counterpart, Lilith, redefines all of Judeo-Christian history.

Some renegade Catholic feminists introduced me to a view of Lilith that   19
had been suppressed during the many centuries when this strong goddess was seen only as a spirit of evil. Lilith was a proud goddess who defied Adam's need to control her, attempted negotiations, and when this failed, said adios and left the Garden of Eden.

This omission of Lilith from the Bible was a patriarchal strategy to keep   20
women weak. Omitting the strong-woman archetype of Lilith from Western religions and starting the story with Eve the Rib has helped keep Christian and Jewish women believing they were the lesser sex for thousands of years.

Stereotypes and Clichés

Where opinion does not exist, the status quo becomes stereotyped and all originality is discouraged.

—*Bertrand Russell*

Stereotype and cliché serve a purpose as a form of shorthand. [6] Our need   21
for vast amounts of information in nanoseconds has made the stereotype

---

Reading Critically

[6] In what way are stereotype and cliché a "form of shorthand"?

vital to modern communication. Unfortunately, it often shuts down original thinking, giving those hungry for the truth a candy bar of misinformation instead of a balanced meal. The stereotype explains a situation with just enough truth to seem unquestionable.

All the "isms"—racism, sexism, ageism, et al.—are founded on and fueled by the stereotype and the cliché, which are lies of exaggeration, omission, and ignorance. They are always dangerous. They take a single tree and make it a landscape. They destroy curiosity. They close minds and separate people. The single mother on welfare is assumed to be cheating. Any black male could tell you how much of his identity is obliterated daily by stereotypes. Fat people, ugly people; beautiful people, old people, large-breasted women, short men, the mentally ill, and the homeless man could tell you how much more they are like us than we want to think. I once admitted to a group of people that I had a mouth like a truck driver. Much to my surprise, a man stood up and said, "I'm a truck driver, and I never cuss." Needless to say, I was humbled.

Groupthink

Who is more foolish, the child afraid of the dark, or the man afraid of the light?
—*Maurice Freehill*

Irving Janis, in *Victims of Group Think,* defines this sort of lie as a psychological phenomenon within decision-making groups in which loyalty to the group has become more important than any other value, with the result that dissent and the appraisal of alternatives are suppressed. If you've ever worked on a committee or in a corporation, you've encountered groupthink. ⑦ It requires a combination of other forms or lying—ignoring facts, selective memory, omission, and denial, to name a few.

The textbook example of groupthink came on December 7, 1941. From as early as the fall of 1941, the warnings came in, one after another, that Japan was preparing for a massive military operation. The navy command in Hawaii assumed Pearl Harbor was invulnerable—the Japanese weren't stupid enough to attack the United States' most important base. On the other hand, racist stereotypes said the Japanese weren't smart enough to invent a torpedo effective in less than 60 feet of water (the fleet was docked in 30 feet); after all, US technology hadn't been able to do it.

On Friday, December 5, normal weekend leave was granted to all the commanders at Pearl Harbor even though the Japanese consulate in Hawaii was busy burning papers. Within the tight, good-ole-boy cohesiveness of the

---

Reading Critically

⑦ What is "groupthink"? Have you ever been involved in it?

US command in Hawaii, the myth of invulnerability stayed well entrenched. No one in the group considered the alternatives. The rest is history. [8]

Out-And-Out Lies

The only form of lying that is beyond reproach is lying for its own sake.
                                                                —Oscar Wilde

Of all the ways to lie, I like this one the best, probably because I get tired   26
of trying to figure out the real meanings behind things. At least I can trust the bald-faced lie. I once asked my five-year-old nephew, "Who broke the fence?" (I had seen him do it.) He answered, "The murderers." Who could argue?

At least when this sort of lie is told it can be easily confronted. As the   27
person who is lied to, I know where I stand. The bald-faced lie doesn't toy with my perceptions—it argues with them. It doesn't try to refashion reality, it tries to refute it. *Read my lips.* . . . No sleight of hand. No guessing. If this were the only form of lying, there would be no such things as floating anxiety or the adult-children-of-alcoholics movement.

Dismissal

Pay no attention to that man behind the curtain! I am the Great Oz!
                                                                —The Wizard of Oz

Dismissal is perhaps the slipperiest of all lies. Dismissing feelings, percep-   28
tions, or even the raw facts of a situation ranks as a kind of lie that can do as much damage to a person as any other kind of lie.

The roots of many mental disorders can be linked back to the dismissal   29
of reality. Imagine that a person is told from the time she is a tot that her perceptions are inaccurate. *"Mommy, I'm scared."* "No you're not, darling." *"I don't like that man next door, he makes me feel icky."* "Johnny, that's a terrible thing to say, of course you like him. You go over there right now and be nice to him."

I've often mused over the idea that madness is actually a sane reaction to   30
an insane world. [9] Psychologist R. D. Laing supports this hypothesis in *Sanity, Madness and The Family,* an account of his investigation into the families of schizophrenics. The common thread that ran through all of the families he studied was a deliberate, staunch dismissal of the patient's perceptions from a very early age. Each of the patients started out with an accurate grasp

---

Reading Critically

[8] What specific "history" is the author referring to?

[9] Do you agree that "madness is actually a sane reaction to an insane world"? Why or why not?

of reality, which, through meticulous and methodical dismissal, was demolished until the only reality the patient could trust was catatonia.

Dismissal runs the gamut. Mild dismissal can be quite handy for forgiving the foibles of others in our day-to-day lives. Toddlers who have just learned to manipulate their parents' attention sometimes are dismissed out of necessity. Absolute attention from the parents would require so much energy that no one would get to eat dinner. But we must be careful and attentive about how far we take our "necessary" dismissals. Dismissal is a dangerous tool, because it's nothing less than a lie. 31

Delusion

We lie loudest when we lie to ourselves.

—*Eric Hoffer*

I could write the book on this one. Delusion, a cousin of dismissal, is the tendency to see excuses as facts. It's a powerful lying tool because it filters out information that contradicts what we want to believe. Alcoholics who believe that the problems in their lives are legitimate reasons for drinking rather than results of the drinking offer the classic example of deluded thinking. Delusion uses the mind's ability to see things in myriad ways to support what it wants to be the truth. 32

But delusion is also a survival mechanism we all use. If we were to fully contemplate the consequences of our stockpiles of nuclear weapons or global warming, we could hardly function on a day-to-day level. We don't want to incorporate that much reality into our lives because to do so would be paralyzing. 33

Delusion acts as an adhesive to keep the status quo intact. It shamelessly employs dismissal, omission, and amnesia, among other sorts of lies. Its most cunning defense is that it cannot see itself. 34

The liar's punishment [. . .] is that he cannot believe anyone else.

—*George Bernard Shaw*

These are only a few of the ways we lie. Or are lied to. As I said earlier, it's not easy to entirely eliminate lies from our lives. No matter how pious we may try to be, we will still embellish, hedge, and omit to lubricate the daily machinery of living. ⑩ But there is a world of difference between telling functional lies and living a lie. Martin Buber once said, "The lie is the spirit committing treason against itself." Our acceptance of lies becomes a cultural cancer that eventually shrouds and reorders reality until moral garbage becomes as invisible to us as water is to a fish. 35

Reading Critically

⑩ In what way do lies "lubricate the daily machinery of living"?

How much do we tolerate before we become sick and tired of being sick   36
and tired? When will we stand up and declare our *right* to trust? When do
we stop accepting that the real truth is in the fine print? Whose lips do we
read this year when we vote for president? When will we stop being so ret-
icent about making judgments? When do we stop turning over our personal
power and responsibility to liars?

Maybe if I don't tell the bank the check's in the mail I'll be less tolerant   37
of the lies told me every day. A country song I once heard said it all for me:
"You've got to stand for something or you'll fall for anything."

UNDERSTANDING DETAILS

1. According to Ericsson, why do we all lie?
2. What are the ten types of lies the author delineates?
3. How do we justify lying in our lives?
4. Why does Ericsson claim that telling the truth all the time is "almost impossible" (paragraph 4)?

THINKING CRITICALLY

5. What are some of the consequences Ericsson is referring to at the beginning
   of this essay?
6. Which of these types of lies do you tell most often? Why do you resort to them?
7. Which of these types of lies would you say is most damaging? Why is this so?
8. What is the difference between "telling functional lies and living a lie" (paragraph 35)?

DISCOVERING RHETORICAL STRATEGIES

9. What do the quotes that the author uses to introduce each type of lie add to
   the explanations of each category?
10. Why does Ericsson end her essay with lyrics from a song? What do they mean?
    What significance do they have in this essay?
11. What does the definition from Webster's dictionary add to Ericsson's essay?
12. What other rhetorical strategies does the author use besides division/classifica-
    tion?

MAKING CONNECTIONS

13. To what extent would Ericsson and/or Jessica Mitford ("Behind the Formalde-
    hyde Curtain") agree on the need for "façades" in life?
14. Read Ericsson's section on "Stereotypes and Clichés," and then analyze Mal-
    colm Cowley's "The View from 80," Sandra Cisneros' "Only daughter," Gloria
    Steinem's "The Politics of Muscle," and/or Sucheng Chan's "You're Short,

Besides!" in terms of how much each of these authors has suffered from being a member of a group that society sometimes stereotypes.

15. Contrast the ways in which Ericsson, K. C. Cole ("Calculated Risks"), and/or Franklin Zimring ("Confessions of an Ex-Smoker") divide their various topics.

IDEAS FOR DISCUSSION/WRITING

Preparing to Write

Write freely about the role of lies in your life: What types of lies do you tell most often? Why do you tell these lies? How are these lies necessary to your life? How do you justify these lies? Would telling the truth all the time have any negative consequences for you? If so, what would these consequences be?

Choosing a Topic

1. A friend found out you lied to him or her and demands an explanation. Instead of talking to your friend, you decide to write an explanation of the history of the lie, your justification for this lie, and an apology (if appropriate).

2. Write an essay explaining and analyzing our behavior when we lie. Use information you learned from Ericsson and your own experience when appropriate.

3. John Webster once said, "There is nothing so powerful as truth—and often nothing so strange." What does this statement mean to you? Write an essay to Ericsson explaining this concept.

4. At the bottom of the Blifaloo article "How to Detect Lies" (http://www.blifaloo.com/info/lies.php) is a section inviting readers to post comments. Read the comments that others have posted, and then write a response that you would like to post in response to the article.

Before beginning your essay, you might want to consult the checklists on page 255.

Chapter Writing Assignments

Practicing Division/Classification

1. Do you think public schools should teach students ethics and personal values? If so, which values should schools teach in order to produce "good citizens"? Classify these values in an essay, and explain how these categories would have fit into your high school curriculum.

2. What problems are most destructive to a healthy relationship? Choose a specific type of relationship (friend, spouse, parent–child), and write an essay discussing various categories of problems that can cause the most trouble in this type of relationship. Explain why the qualities you identify would be destructive in the kind of relationship you describe.

3. Think about the ideal _____ (fill in the blank with one of the many roles we play every day [for example, wife, husband, teacher, student, friend, or cousin]). List the qualities that person needs. What categories do these qualities fall into? Why are these characteristics ideal? Write an essay explaining the categories you have developed for the role you chose to discuss.

Exploring Ideas

4. We all have bad habits, but few people know how to break them. What advice do you have for people who want to change their behavior in some important way or break a bad habit? How do you know your method works?

5. Explain a cultural tradition we are in danger of losing in society today. Discuss the value of the tradition itself and the ways this tradition is changing, along with the value and effects of this change. Make sure you discuss this topic in an unbiased way.

6. How do a person's cultural views and beliefs affect the educational process? In what ways does our current system of education acknowledge, hinder, or ignore our diverse cultural backgrounds? In a well-developed essay, discuss how our educational system successfully or unsuccessfully deals with our various cultural differences. Are the categories in your essay distinct from one another? What rhetorical strategies support your essay?

Analyzing Visual Images

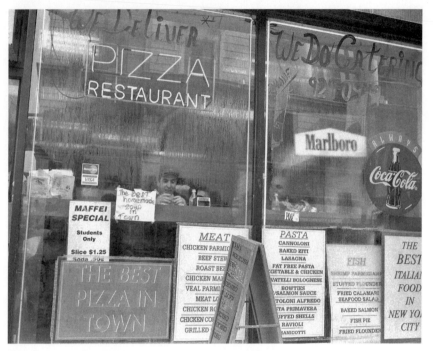

Dave Beckerman Photography.

7. The photo above classifies the food available at this restaurant. Choose a common topic like food, houses, or clothing (or another subject that interests you), and discuss in essay form how we could classify the items in that category. For example, we could discuss types of cars according to the characteristics of the people who are likely to buy them.

8. Look at the picture on page 248 at the beginning of this chapter. What do you think these people are doing? Why are they here? Consider the various reasons people might be in this particular place, and write an essay classifying them according to your assumptions.

Chapter 6

COMPARISON/CONTRAST
Discovering Similarities and Differences

Making comparisons is such a natural and necessary part of our everyday lives that we often do so without conscious effort. When we were children, we compared our toys with those of our friends, we contrasted our height and physical development to other children's, and we constantly evaluated our happiness in comparison with that evidenced by our parents and childhood companions. As we grew older, we habitually compared our dates, teachers, parents, friends, cars, and physical attributes. In college, we learn about anthropology by writing essays on the similarities and differences between two African tribes, about political science by contrasting the Republican and Democratic platforms, about business by comparing annual production rates, and about literature by comparing Shakespeare with Marlowe or Browning with Tennyson. Comparing and contrasting various elements in our lives helps us make decisions, such as which course to take or which house to buy, and it justifies preferences that we already hold, such as liking one city more than another or loving one person more than the next. In these ways and in many others, the skillful use of comparison and contrast is clearly essential to our social and professional lives.

DEFINING COMPARISON/CONTRAST

Comparison and contrast allow us to understand one subject by putting it next to another. Comparing involves discovering likenesses or similarities, whereas contrasting is based on finding differences. Like division and classification, comparison and contrast are generally considered part of the same process, because we usually have no reason for comparing unless some contrast is also involved. Each technique implies the existence of the other. For this reason, the word *compare* is often used to mean both techniques.

Comparison and contrast are most profitably applied to two items that have something in common, such as cats and dogs or cars and motorcycles. A discussion of cats and motorcycles, for example, would probably not be very rewarding or stimulating, because they do not have much in common. If more than two items are compared in an essay, they are still most profitably discussed in pairs: for instance, motorcycles and cars, cars and bicycles, or bicycles and motorcycles.

An analogy is an extended, sustained comparison. Often used to explain unfamiliar, abstract, or complicated thoughts, this rhetorical technique adds energy and vividness to a wide variety of college-level writing. The process of analogy differs slightly from comparison/contrast in three important ways: Comparison/contrast begins with subjects from the same class and places equal weight on both of them. In addition, it addresses both the similarities and the differences of these subjects. Analogy, conversely, seldom explores subjects from the same class and focuses principally on one familiar subject in an attempt to explain another, more complex one. Furthermore, it deals only with similarities, not with contrasts. A comparison/contrast essay, for example, might study two veterans' ways of coping with the trauma of the War in Iraq by pointing out the differences in their methods as well as the similarities. An analogy essay might use the familiar notion of a fireworks display to reveal the chilling horror of the lonely hours after dark during this war: "Nights in Bagdad were similar to a loud, unending fireworks display. We had no idea when the next blast was coming, how loud it would be, or how close. We cringed in terror after dark, hoping the next surprise would not be our own death." In this example, rather than simply hearing about an event, we participate in it through this highly refined form of comparison.

The following student paragraph compares and contrasts married and single life. As you read it, notice how the author compares similar social states and, in the process, justifies her current lifestyle:

Recently I saw a bumper sticker that read, "It used to be wine, women, and song, and now it's beer, the old lady, and TV." Much truth may be found in this comparison of single and married lifestyles. When my husband and I used to date, for example, we'd go out for dinner and drinks and then maybe see a play or concert. Our discussions were intelligent, often ranging over global politics, science, literature, and other lofty topics. He would open doors for me, buy me flowers, and make sure I was comfortable and happy. Now, three years later, after marriage and a child, the baby bottle has replaced the wine bottle, the smell of diapers wipes out the scent of roses, and our nights on the town are infrequent, cherished events. But that's all right. A little bit of the excitement and mystery may be gone, but these intangible qualities have given way to a sturdy, dependable trust in each other and a quiet confidence about our future together.

THINKING CRITICALLY THROUGH COMPARISON/CONTRAST

Thinking

Reading   Writing

- Find similarities and differences.
- Classify your ideas by similarities.
- Look for clusters of thoughts.

Comparison and contrast are basic to a number of different thought processes. We compare and contrast quite naturally on a daily basis, but all of us would benefit greatly from being more aware of these companion strategies in our own writing. They help us not only in perceiving our environment but also in understanding and organizing large amounts of information.

The basic skill of finding similarities and differences will enhance your ability to create accurate descriptions, to cite appropriate examples, to present a

© Zach Gold/CORBIS.

full process analysis, and, of course, to classify and label subjects. It is a pattern of thought that is essential to more complex thinking strategies, so perfecting the ability to use it is an important step in your efforts to improve your critical thinking.

Once again, we are going to practice this strategy in isolation to get a strong sense of its mechanics before we combine it with other rhetorical modes. Isolating this mode will make your reading and writing even stronger than they are now, because the individual parts of the thinking process will be more vigorous and effective, thus making your academic performance more powerful than ever.

1. Make a list of similarities and differences for the photograph on page 301. What messages or ideas do you think the photographer is able to communicate through this photograph?
2. Find magazine ads that use comparison/contrast to make a point or sell a product. What is the basis of each comparison? How effective or ineffective is each comparison?
3. Have you ever been to the same place twice? Think for a moment about how the first and second visits to this place differed. How were they similar? What were the primary reasons for the similarities and differences in your perceptions of these visits?

Reading and Writing Comparison/Contrast Essays

Many established guidelines regulate the development of a comparison/contrast essay and should be taken into account from both the reading and the writing perspectives. All good comparative studies serve a specific purpose. They attempt either to examine their subjects separately or to demonstrate the superiority of one over the other. In evaluating two different types of cars, for example, a writer might point out the amazing gas mileage of one model and the smooth handling qualities of the other or the superiority of one car's gas mileage over that of another. Whatever the intent, comparison/contrast essays need to be clear and logical and have a precise purpose.

READING COMPARISON/CONTRAST ESSAYS

- What is the writer comparing?
- What is the essay's thesis?
- How is the essay organized?

Preparing to Read.   As you begin reading this chapter, pull together as much preliminary material as possible for each essay so you can focus your attention and have the benefit of prior knowledge before you start to read. In particular, you should try to discover what is being compared or contrasted and why. From the title of his essay, can you tell what Bruce Catton is comparing in "Grant and Lee: A Study in Contrasts"? What does William Ouchi's title ("Japanese and American Workers: Two Casts of Mind") suggest to you? From glancing at the essay itself and reading the synopsis in the Rhetorical Table of Contents, what do you think Sucheng Chan's essay will try to accomplish?

Also, before you begin to read these essays, try to discover information about the author and about the conditions under which each essay was written. What is Gloria Steinem's stand on women's bodybuilding? To what extent do you expect her opinions on this topic to color her comparison of women's past and present physical strength? Why is Ouchi qualified to write about Japanese and American workers? How does he reveal his background in his essay?

Finally, just before you begin to read, answer the Preparing to Read questions, and then make some free associations with the general topic of each essay: For example, what do you think are some of the comparisons and contrasts in "Homeplace" (Scott Russell Sanders)? What is your general view on women's bodybuilding (Gloria Steinem)?

Reading.   As you read each comparison/contrast essay for the first time, be sure to record your own feelings and opinions. Some of the issues presented in this chapter are highly controversial. You will often have strong reactions to them, which you should try to write down as soon as possible.

In addition, you may want to comment on the relationship between the preliminary essay material, the author's stance in the essay, and the content of the essay itself. For example, what motivated Sanders to write "Homeplace"? Who is his primary audience? What is Chan's tone in "You're Short, Besides!," and how does it advance her purpose? Answers to questions such as these will provide you with a context for your first reading of these essays and will assist you in preparing to analyze the essays in more depth on your second reading.

Critical thinking questions are provided with each essay at the bottom of the pages in this chapter. If you dig in and try to answer each one, they will lead you to higher levels of thinking on these particular issues. They are designed to bridge the gap in understanding between the prereading and postreading activities surrounding each essay. Writing your responses to these questions will provide you with the best opportunity to learn how to think analytically about these topics.

At this point in the chapter, you should make certain you understand each author's thesis and then take a close look at his or her principal method of organization: Is the essay arranged (1) point by point, (2) subject by subject, (3) as a combination of these two, or (4) as separate discussions of similarities and differences between two subjects? (See the chart on page 306 for an illustration of these options.) Last, preview the questions that follow the essay before you read it again.

Rereading.   When you read these essays a second time, you should look at the comparison or contrast much more closely than you have up to now. First, look in detail at the writer's method of organization (see the chart on page 306). How effective is it in advancing the writer's thesis?

Next, you should consider whether each essay is fully developed and balanced: Does Catton compare similar items? Does Baca discuss the same elements of his subjects? Does Ouchi deal with all aspects of the comparison between Japanese and American workers? Is Steinem's treatment of her subjects well balanced? And does Chan give her audience enough specific details to clarify the extent of her comparison? Do all the writers in this chapter use well-chosen transitions so you can move smoothly from one point to the next? Also, what other rhetorical modes support each comparison/contrast in this chapter?

Finally, the answers to the questions after each selection will let you evaluate your understanding of the essay and help you analyze its contents in preparation for the discussion/writing topics that follow.

For a more thorough inventory of the reading process, you should turn to page 29 in the Introduction.

WRITING COMPARISON/CONTRAST ESSAYS

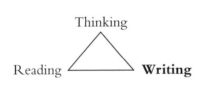

- Draft a thesis.
- Choose items in the same category.
- Introduce your subjects and your reason for comparing them.
- Include the limits of your discussion.
- Organize your essay.
- Balance the treatment of your subjects.

Preparing to Write. As you consider various topics for a comparison/contrast essay, you should answer the Preparing to Write questions that precede the assignments and then use the prewriting techniques explained in the Introduction (pp. 19–21) to generate even more ideas on these topics.

As you focus your attention on a particular topic, keep the following suggestions in mind:

1. Always compare/contrast items in the same category (e.g., compare two professors, but not a professor and a swimming pool).
2. Have a specific purpose or reason for writing your essay.
3. Discuss the same qualities of each subject (if you evaluate the teaching techniques of one professor, do so for the other professor as well).
4. Use as many pertinent details as possible to expand your comparison/contrast and to accomplish your stated purpose.
5. Deal with all aspects of the comparison that are relevant to the purpose.
6. Balance the treatment of the different subjects of your comparison (i.e., don't spend more time on one than on another).
7. Determine your audience's background and knowledge so that you will know how much of your comparison should be explained in detail and how much can be skimmed over.

Next, in preparation for a comparison/contrast project, you might list all the elements of both subjects that you want to compare. This list can then help you give your essay structure as well as substance. At this stage in the writing process, the task may seem similar to pure description, but a discussion of two subjects in relation to one another rapidly changes the assignment from description to comparison.

Writing.   The introduction of your comparison/contrast essay should (1) clearly identify your subjects, (2) explain the basis of your comparison/contrast, and (3) state your purpose and the overall limits of your particular study. Identifying your subject is, of course, a necessary and important task in any essay. Similarly, justifying the elements you will be comparing and contrasting creates interest and gives your audience some specifics to look for in the essay. Finally, your statement of purpose or thesis (for example, to prove that one professor is superior to another) should include the boundaries of your discussion. You cannot cover all the reasons for your preference in one short essay, so you must limit your consideration to three or four basic categories (perhaps teaching techniques, the clarity of the assignments given, classroom attitude, and grading standards). The introduction is the place to make all these limits known.

You can organize the body of your paper in one of four ways: (1) a point-by-point, or alternating, comparison; (2) a subject-by-subject, or divided, comparison; (3) a combination of these two methods; or (4) a division between the similarities and differences (see chart on page 306).

The point-by-point comparison evaluates both subjects in terms of each category. If the issue, for example, is which of two cars to buy, you might discuss both models' gasoline mileage first; then, their horsepower; next, their ease in handling; and, finally, their standard equipment. Following the second method of organization, subject by subject, you would discuss the gasoline mileage, horsepower, ease in handling, and standard equipment of car A first and then

Point by Point	**Subject by Subject**
MPG, car A MPG, car B Horsepower, car A Horsepower, car B Handling, car A Handling, car B Equipment, car A Equipment, car B	MPG, car A Horsepower, car A Handling, car A Equipment, car A MPG, car B Horsepower, car B Handling, car B Equipment, car B

Combination	**Similarities/Differences**

Equipment, car A
Equipment, car B
 	
———
 	
MPG, car A
Horsepower, car A
Handling, car A
 	
MPG, car B
Horsepower, car B
Handling, car B
	Similarities:
	  MPG, cars A & B
	
	Differences:
	  Horsepower, cars A & B
	  Handling, cars A & B
	  Equipment, cars A & B

follow the same format for car B. The third option would allow you to introduce, say, the standard equipment of each car point by point (or car by car) and then explain the other features in your comparison (miles per gallon, horsepower, and ease in handling) subject by subject. To use the last method of organization, you might discuss the similarities between the two models first and the differences second (or vice versa). If the cars you are comparing have similar miles-per-gallon (MPG) ratings but completely different horsepower, steering systems, and optional equipment, you could discuss the gasoline mileage and then emphasize the differences by mentioning them later in the essay. If, instead, you are trying to emphasize the fact that the MPG ratings of these models remain consistent despite their differences, then reverse the order of your essay.

When confronted with the task of choosing a method of organization for a comparison/contrast essay, you need to find the pattern that best suits your purpose. If you want single items to stand out in a discussion, for instance, the best choice will be the point-by-point system; it is especially appropriate for long essays but has a tendency to turn into an exercise in listing if you don't pay careful attention to your transitions. If, however, the subjects themselves (rather than the itemized points) are the most interesting feature of your essay, you should use the subject-by-subject comparison; this system is particularly good for short essays in which the readers can retain what was said about one subject while they read about a second subject. Through this second method of organization, each subject becomes a unified whole, an approach to an essay that is generally effective unless the theme becomes awkwardly divided into two separate parts. You must also remember, if you choose this second method of organization, that the second (or last) subject is in the most emphatic position because that is what your readers will have seen most recently. The final two options for organizing a comparison/contrast essay give you some built-in flexibility so that you can create emphasis and attempt to manipulate reader opinion simply by the structure of your essay.

Using logical transitions in your comparison/contrast essays will establish clear relationships between the items in your comparisons and will also move your readers smoothly from one topic to the next. If you wish to indicate comparisons, use such words as *like, as, also, in like manner, similarly,* and *in addition;* to signal contrasts, try *but, in contrast to, unlike, whereas,* and *on the one hand/on the other hand.*

The conclusion of a comparison/contrast essay summarizes the main points and states the deductions drawn from those points. As you choose your method of organization, remember not to get locked into a formulaic approach to your subjects, which will adversely affect the readability of your essay. To avoid making your reader feel like a spectator at a verbal table tennis match, be straightforward, honest, and patient as you discover and recount the details of your comparison.

Rewriting.   When you review the draft of your comparison/contrast essay, you need once again to make sure that you communicate your purpose as effectively as possible to your intended audience. Two guidelines previously mentioned should help you accomplish this goal:

- Does your thesis state the purpose and limits of your study?

You will also need to pay close attention to the following in the development of your essay:

- Do you compare/contrast items from the same general category?
- Do you discuss the same qualities of each subject?
- Do you balance the treatment of your topics?
- Do you organize your essay as effectively as possible?
- Does your conclusion summarize and analyze your main points?

For further information on writing and revising your comparison/contrast essays, consult the checklists on page 30 of the Introduction.

STUDENT ESSAY: COMPARISON/CONTRAST AT WORK

The following student essay compares the advantages and disadvantages of macaroni and cheese versus tacos in the life of a harried college freshman. As you read it, notice that the writer states his intention in the first paragraph and then expands his discussion with appropriate details to produce a balanced essay. Also, try to determine what effect he creates by using two methods of organization: first subject by subject, then point by point.

Dormitory Chef

To this day, I will not eat either macaroni and cheese or tacos. No, it's not because of any allergy; it's because during my freshman year at college, I prepared one or the other of these scrumptious dishes more times than I care to remember. However, my choice of which culinary delight to cook on any given night was not as simple a decision as one might imagine.

Topics

Basis of comparison

Thesis statement: Purpose and limits of comparison

Macaroni and cheese has numerous advantages for the dormitory chef. First of all, it is inexpensive. No matter how poor one may be, there's probably enough change under the couch cushion to buy a box at the market. All that starch for only $5.29. What a bargain! Second, it can be prepared in just one pan. This is especially important given the meager resources of the average dorm kitchen. Third, and perhaps most important, macaroni and cheese is odorless. By odorless, I mean that no one else can smell it. It is a well-known fact that dorm residents hate to cook and that they love nothing better than to wander dejectedly around the kitchen with big, sad eyes after someone else has been cooking. But with macaroni and cheese, no enticing aromas are going to find their way into the nose of any would-be mooch.

Paragraph on Subject A: Macaroni and cheese

Point 1 (Price)

Point 2 (Preparation)

Point 3 (Odor)

Tacos, on the other hand, are a different matter altogether. For the dorm cook, the most significant difference is obviously the price. To enjoy tacos for dinner, the adventurous dorm gourmet must purchase no fewer than five ingredients from the market: corn tortillas, beef, lettuce, tomatoes, and cheese. Needless to say, this is a major expenditure. Second, the chef must adroitly shuffle these ingredients back and forth among his or her very limited supply of pans and bowls. And finally, tacos smell great. That wouldn't be a problem if the tacos didn't also smell great to about

Paragraph on Subject B: Tacos

Transition

Point 1 (Price)

Point 2 (Preparation)

Point 3 (Odor)

twenty of the cook's newest—if not closest—friends, who appear with those same pathetic, starving eyes mentioned earlier. When this happens, the cook will be lucky to get more than two of his own creations.

Subject B | Paragraph on Point 4: Taste

Tacos, then, wouldn't stand much of a chance if they didn't outdo macaroni and cheese in one area: taste. Taste is almost—but not quite—an optional requirement in the opinion of a frugal dormitory hash-slinger. Taste is just important enough so that tacos are occasionally prepared, despite their disadvantages.   *Transition · Subject A*

Transition | Paragraph on Point 5: Color

But tacos have other advantages besides their taste. With their enticing, colorful ingredients, they even look good. The only thing that can be said about the color of macaroni and cheese is that it's a color not found in nature.   *Subject B · Subject A*

Transition | Paragraph on Point 6: Time

On the other hand, macaroni and cheese is quick. It can be prepared in about ten minutes, while tacos take more than twice as long. And there are occasions—such as final exam week—when time is a scarce and precious resource.   *Subject A · Subject B*

Transition | Analysis

As you can see, quite a bit of thinking went into my choice of food in my younger years. These two dishes essentially got me through my freshman year and indirectly taught me how to make important decisions (like what to eat). But I still feel a certain revulsion when I hear their names today.   *Summary · Concluding statement*

Student Writer's Comments

I compare and contrast so many times during a typical day that I took this rhetorical technique for granted. In fact, I had overlooked it completely. The most difficult part of writing this essay was finding two appropriate subjects to compare. Ideally, I knew they should be united by a similarity. So I brainstormed to come up with some possible topics. Then, working from this list of potential subjects, I began to freewrite to see if I could come up with two topics in the same category on which I could write a balanced comparison. Out of my freewriting came this reasoning: Macaroni and cheese and tacos, in reality, are two very different kinds of food from the same category. Proving this fact is easy and might even result in an interesting essay. Their similar property of being popular dorm foods unites the two despite their differences and also gives me two important reasons for writing the comparison: to discover why they are both popular dorm delicacies and to determine which one has more advantages for my particular purposes. In proportion to writing and revising, I spent most of my time choosing my topic, brainstorming, freewriting, and rebrainstorming to make sure I could develop every aspect of my comparison adequately. Most of my prewriting work took the form of two columns, in which I recorded my opinions on the choice between macaroni and cheese versus tacos.

Sitting down to mold my lists into an essay posed an entirely new set of problems. From the copious notes I had taken, I easily wrote the introductory paragraph, identifying my topics, explaining the basis of my comparison/contrast, and stating the purpose and limits of my study (my thesis statement). But now that I faced the body of the essay, I needed to find the best way to organize my opinions on these two dorm foods: point by point, subject by subject, a combination of these two, or a discussion of similarities and differences?

I wrote my first draft discussing my topics point by point. Even with an occasional joke and a few snide comments interjected, the essay reminded me of a boring game of ping pong with only a few attempts at changing the pace. I started over completely with my second draft and worked through my topics subject by subject. I felt this approach was better, but not quite right for my particular purpose and audience. I set out to do some heavy-handed revising.

Discussing my first three points (price, preparation, and odor) subject by subject seemed to work quite well. I was actually satisfied with the first half of my discussion of these two subjects. But the essay really started to get sluggish when I brought up the fourth point: taste. So I broke off my discussion there and rewrote the second half of my essay point by point, dealing with taste, color, and time each in its own paragraph. This change gave my essay the new direction it needed to keep the readers' attention and also offered me some new insights into my comparison. Then I returned to the beginning of my essay and revised it for readability, adding transitions and making sure the paper now moved smoothly from one point or subject to the next. Finally, I added my final paragraph including a brief summary of my main points and an explanation of the deductions I had made. My concluding remark ("But I still feel a certain revulsion when I hear their names today.") came to me as I was putting the final touches on this draft.

What I learned from writing this particular essay is that comparison/contrast thinking, more than thinking in other rhetorical modes, is much like a puzzle. I really had to spend an enormous amount of time thinking through, mapping out, and rethinking my comparison before I could start to put my thoughts in essay form. The results are rewarding, but I sure wore out a piece of linoleum on the den floor on the way to my final draft.

SOME FINAL THOUGHTS ON COMPARISON/CONTRAST

The essays in this section demonstrate various methods of organization as well as a number of distinct stylistic approaches to writing a comparison/contrast essay. As you read these selections, pay particular attention to the clear, well-focused introductions; the different logical methods of organization; and the smooth transitions between sentences and paragraphs.

COMPARISON/CONTRAST IN REVIEW

Reading Comparison/Contrast Essays

Preparing to Read

✓ What assumptions can you make from the essay's title?

✓ Can you guess what the general mood of the essay is?

✓ What is the essay's purpose and audience?

✓ What does the synopsis tell you about the essay?

✓ What can you learn from the author's biography?

✓ Can you predict the author's point of view toward the subject?

Reading

✓ What is the writer comparing?

✓ What is the essay's thesis?

✓ How is the essay organized?

Rereading

✓ Is the writer's method of organization effective?

✓ Is the essay fully developed?

✓ What other rhetorical strategies does the author use?

Writing Comparison/Contrast Essays

Preparing to Write

✓ What is your purpose?

✓ Who is your audience?

Writing

✓ Did you draft a thesis?

✓ Are you comparing items in the same general category?

✓ Does your introduction (1) identify your subjects, (2) explain the basis of your comparison, and (3) state the purpose and limits of your study?

✓ Does your thesis include the boundaries of your discussion?

✓ Is your paper organized point by point, subject by subject, as a combination of the two, or as a discussion of similarities and differences?

✓ Do you balance the treatment of your subjects?

Rewriting

✓ Does your thesis state the purpose and limits of your study?

✓ Do you compare/contrast items from the same general category?

✓ Do you discuss the same qualities of each subject?

✓ Do you balance the treatment of your topics?

✓ Do you organize your essay as effectively as possible?

✓ Does your conclusion summarize and analyze your main points?

BRUCE CATTON   (1899–1978)

Grant and Lee: A Study in Contrasts

Bruce Catton was a much-loved and respected historian of the U.S. Civil War, whose many books and articles have brought an "eyewitness" vividness to this crucial period in American development. Believing that history "ought to be a good yarn," Catton saw himself as more of a reporter than a historian, stripping away the romantic glamour of war to reveal with vigor and clarity the reality of this important historical era. A native of Benzonia, Michigan, the author was fascinated during his childhood by stories told by the many Civil War veterans who had returned to his small town. Catton attended Oberlin College, worked for a time as a newspaper reporter, and then turned his attention principally to researching and writing about the Civil War. His most popular and influential book was *A Stillness at Appomattox* (the third part of his *Army of the Potomac* trilogy), which won both the Pulitzer Prize and the National Book Award for history in 1954. Among his many other books are *This Hallowed Ground* (1956), *The Coming Fury* (1961), *Terrible Swift Sword* (1963), *Grant Takes Command* (1969), and *Michigan: A Bicentennial History* (1976). As historian Oliver Jensen has explained, "There is a near-magic power of imagination in Catton's work that seemed to project him physically into the battlefields, along the dusty roads and to the campfires of another age." For the last twenty-four years of his life, Catton was also editor of *American Heritage* magazine.

Preparing to Read

The following essay is taken from *The American Story* (1956), a collection of essays by distinguished historians; it examines the similarities and differences between Generals Grant and Lee at the conclusion of the Civil War.

Exploring Experience: As you prepare to read this article, take a few moments to consider heroes in your life: What special qualities turn people into heroic figures? Why do you think some heroes are admired more than others? What historical events bring forth heroes? How does American society act in general toward these people? Why do most of us seem to need heroic figures in our lives? What roles do heroes play in society today?

Learning Online: In this essay, Catton describes the historic meeting between Grant and Lee at the Appomattox Courthouse. To view a photo and brief history of the courthouse, go to the National Park Service Web site (http://www.nps.gov/apco).

When Ulysses S. Grant and Robert E. Lee met in the parlor of a   1
modest house at Appomattox Court House, Virginia, on April 9,
1865, to work out the terms for the surrender of Lee's Army of
Northern Virginia, a great chapter in American life came to a close, and a
great new chapter began. [1]

These men were bringing the Civil War to its virtual finish. To be sure,   2
other armies had yet to surrender, and for a few days the fugitive Confederate government would struggle desperately and vainly, trying to find some
way to go on living now that its chief support was gone. But in effect it was
all over when Grant and Lee signed the papers. And the little room where
they wrote out the terms was the scene of one of the poignant, dramatic
contrasts in American history.

They were two strong men, these oddly different generals, and they rep-   3
resented the strengths of two conflicting currents that, through them, had
come into final collision.

Back of Robert E. Lee was the notion that the old aristocratic concept   4
might somehow survive and be dominant in American life.

Lee was tidewater Virginia, and in his background were family, culture, and   5
tradition . . . the age of chivalry transplanted to a New World which was
making its own legends and its own myths. He embodied a way of life that
had come down through the age of knighthood and the English country
squire. America was a land that was beginning all over again, dedicated to
nothing much more complicated than the rather hazy belief that all men
had equal rights and should have an equal chance in the world. In such a land
Lee stood for the feeling that it was somehow of advantage to human society to have a pronounced inequality in the social structure. [2] There should
be a leisure class, backed by ownership of land; in turn, society itself should
be keyed to the land as the chief source of wealth and influence. It would
bring forth (according to this ideal) a class of men with a strong sense of
obligation to the community; men who lived not to gain advantage for themselves, but to meet the solemn obligations which had been laid on them by
the very fact that they were privileged. From them the country would get
its leadership; to them it could look for the higher values—of thought, of
conduct, of personal deportment—to give it strength and virtue.

Lee embodied the noblest elements of this aristocratic ideal. Through him, the   6
landed nobility justified itself. For four years, the Southern states had fought a desperate war to uphold the ideals for which Lee stood. In the end, it almost seemed

---

Reading Critically

[1] Why does Catton's essay start by depicting the Civil War metaphorically as a book, with
one "chapter" closing and another beginning?

[2] Why do you believe Lee thought that "a pronounced inequality in the social structure"
was an "advantage to human society"?

as if the Confederacy fought for Lee; as if he himself was the Confederacy . . . the best thing that the way of life for which the Confederacy stood could ever have to offer. He had passed into legend before Appomattox. Thousands of tired, underfed, poorly clothed Confederate soldiers, long since past the simple enthusiasm of the early days of the struggle, somehow considered Lee the symbol of everything for which they had been willing to die. But they could not quite put this feeling into words. If the Lost Cause, sanctified by so much heroism and so many deaths, had a living justification, its justification was General Lee.

Grant, the son of a tanner on the Western frontier, was everything Lee was   7 not. He had come up the hard way and embodied nothing in particular except the eternal toughness and sinewy fiber of the men who grew up beyond the mountains. He was one of a body of men who owed reverence and obeisance to no one, who were self-reliant to a fault, ❸ who cared hardly anything for the past but who had a sharp eye for the future.

These frontier men were the precise opposites of the tidewater aristo-   8 crats. Back of them, in the great surge that had taken people over the Alleghenies and into the opening Western country, there was a deep, implicit dissatisfaction with a past that had settled into grooves. They stood for democracy, not from any reasoned conclusion about the proper ordering of human society, but simply because they had grown up in the middle of democracy and knew how it worked. Their society might have privileges, but they would be privileges each man had won for himself. Forms and patterns meant nothing. No man was born to anything, except perhaps to a chance to show how far he could rise. Life was competition.

Yet along with this feeling had come a deep sense of belonging to a na-   9 tional community. The Westerner who developed a farm, opened a shop, or set up in business as a trader could hope to prosper only as his own community prospered—and his community ran from the Atlantic to the Pacific and from Canada down to Mexico. If the land was settled, with towns and highways and accessible markets, he could better himself. He saw his fate in terms of the nation's own destiny. As its horizons expanded, so did his. He had, in other words, an acute dollars-and-cents stake in the continued growth and development of his country.

And that, perhaps, is where the contrast between Grant and Lee becomes   10 most striking. The Virginia aristocrat, inevitably, saw himself in relation to his own region. He lived in a static society which could endure almost anything except change. Instinctively, his first loyalty would go to the locality in which that society existed. He would fight to the limit of endurance to defend it, because in defending it he was defending everything that gave his own life its deepest meaning.

Reading Critically

❸ What does the phrase "self-reliant to a fault" mean to you?

The Westerner, on the other hand, would fight with an equal tenacity for the broader concept of society. ❹ He fought so because everything he lived by was tied to growth, expansion, and a constantly widening horizon. What he lived by would survive or fall with the nation itself. He could not possibly stand by unmoved in the face of an attempt to destroy the Union. He would combat it with everything he had, because he could only see it as an effort to cut the ground out from under his feet.   11

So Grant and Lee were in complete contrast, representing two diametrically opposed elements in American life. Grant was the modern man emerging; beyond him, ready to come on the stage, was the great age of steel and machinery, of crowded cities and a restless burgeoning vitality. Lee might have ridden down from the old age of chivalry, lance in hand, silken banner fluttering over his head. Each man was the perfect champion of his cause, drawing both his strengths and his weaknesses from the people he led.   12

Yet it was not all contrast, after all. Different as they were—in background, in personality, in underlying aspiration—these two great soldiers had much in common. Under everything else, they were marvelous fighters. Furthermore, their fighting qualities were really very much alike.   13

Each man had, to begin with, the great virtue of utter tenacity and fidelity. Grant fought his way down the Mississippi Valley in spite of acute personal discouragement and profound military handicaps. Lee hung on in the trenches at Petersburg after hope itself had died. ❺ In each man there was an indomitable quality. . . . the born fighter's refusal to give up as long as he can still remain on his feet and lift his two fists.   14

Daring and resourcefulness they had, too; the ability to think faster and move faster than the enemy. These were the qualities which gave Lee the dazzling campaigns of Second Manassas and Chancellorsville and won Vicksburg for Grant.   15

Lastly, and perhaps greatest of all, there was the ability, at the end, to turn quickly from war to peace once the fighting was over. ❻ Out of the way these two men behaved at Appomattox came the possibility of a peace of reconciliation. It was a possibility not wholly realized, in the years to come, but which did, in the end, help the two sections to become one nation again . . . after a war whose bitterness might have seemed to make such a reunion wholly impossible. No part of either man's life became him more than the part he played in this brief meeting in the McLean house at Appomattox. Their behavior there put all succeeding generations of Americans in their debt. Two great Americans, Grant and Lee—very different, yet under every-   16

Reading Critically

❹ How was Grant's concept of society "broader" than Lee's?

❺ Rephrase the metaphor "after hope itself had died" in more literal terms.

❻ How did the ability to turn quickly from war to peace help America?

thing very much alike. Their encounter at Appomattox was one of the great moments of American history.

UNDERSTANDING DETAILS

1. What two conflicting views of American life does the author believe these two generals represented?
2. What special qualities of Grant and Lee does Catton contrast to achieve his purpose? What qualities does he compare?
3. How did both Grant and Lee respond to progress and change in general? Explain your answer in detail.
4. What does Catton imply about the behavior of these two generals at Appomattox Court House? According to this essay, why was the encounter of Grant and Lee at Appomattox "one of the great moments of American history" (paragraph 16)?

THINKING CRITICALLY

5. What is Catton's purpose in this essay? What truths, according to the author, needed to be made clear about these two great Civil War generals? Why did Catton study similarities as well as differences in these two men?
6. What does Catton mean when he says, "Life was competition" (paragraph 8) in Grant's philosophy? What aspects of this philosophy do you see in today's society?
7. In what ways were Lee and Grant emblems of the past and the future, respectively?
8. About the actions of these men at Appomattox, Catton says, "Their behavior there put all succeeding generations of Americans in their debt" (paragraph 16). What does he mean by this statement? What influences of these two men can we still see in our culture today?

DISCOVERING RHETORICAL STRATEGIES

9. Which of the four main methods of organizing a comparison/contrast essay does Catton use? How many paragraphs does the author spend on each part of his comparison? Why do you think he spends this amount of time on each?
10. What transitional words or phrases does the author use to move from one part of this essay to the next? Give at least three specific examples. Do these devices hold the essay together effectively? Explain your answer.
11. In what ways does the last paragraph of this essay echo the first paragraph? Why is this echoing technique an effective way to end the essay?
12. What other rhetorical strategies besides comparison and contrast does Catton use to achieve his purpose in this essay? Give examples of each strategy.

MAKING CONNECTIONS

13. Like Bruce Catton, Alice Walker ("Beauty: When the Other Dancer Is the Self") describes one particular moment in time when life was changed forever. What similarities can you find between the two important events described by each of these authors?

14. First, Catton contrasts Grant and Lee, and then he compares them. How is this structural approach different from the comparison/contrast essays written by Sucheng Chan ("You're Short, Besides!") and/or William Ouchi ("Japanese and American Workers: Two Casts of Mind")? Which organizational technique do you find most effective? Explain your answer.

15. According to Catton, Grant and Lee each represented "the strengths of two conflicting currents that, through them, had come into final collision" (paragraph 3). Along the same lines, how does strength signify power for Gloria Steinem in "The Politics of Muscle," and/or how does an "unfamiliar country" symbolize old age for Malcolm Cowley in "The View from 80"? In other words, how do these three authors use symbols to give significance to everyday events?

IDEAS FOR DISCUSSION/WRITING

Preparing to Write

Write freely about heroes and heroines in American society: Name some public figures you respect. Why do you admire them? What qualifies someone as a heroic figure in your opinion? What do most of the heroes and heroines you admire have in common? How are they different? How are history and heroic figures related in your mind?

Choosing a Topic

1. In an essay written for your classmates, compare and/or contrast two famous people in history. As Catton did, try to explain what forces in society these figures represent. Decide on a clear focus and point of view before you begin.

2. Choose two people who have had a significant influence on your life. Then, compare and/or contrast how they have affected you.

3. America has had many new beginnings throughout its history. The time at the end of the Civil War, discussed in this essay, was one of them. Explain to your classmates another new beginning for America. What were the details of this new start? Who were the heroes? Where, when, how, and why did it take place?

4. Visit your favorite online news source. Who is in the headlines? Select a person in today's news. Following Catton's example, compare this person with someone who may share some character traits but seems diametrically opposed in every other way. Write an essay in which you use Catton's method of presenting each person, while comparing and contrasting their backgrounds and actions.

Before beginning your essay, you might want to consult the checklists on page 311.

SCOTT RUSSELL SANDERS   (1945–)

Homeplace

Scott Sanders has been connected to many places in his life. Born in Memphis, he descended from a father related to cotton farmers in Mississippi and a mother from an immigrant doctor's family in Chicago. He studied physics and English at Brown University, then earned his Ph.D. in English at Cambridge University in England. Since 1971, he has been a professor of English at Indiana University, where he has won a number of teaching awards. His fiction and essays have been published in a wide variety of journals, including *Audubon, Harper's, North American Review, Georgia Review,* and *Resurgence.* He has also been literary editor of *The Cambridge Review,* fiction editor for *The Minnesota Review,* a columnist for the *Chicago Sun-Times,* and a contributing editor for *Audubon.* Among his nineteen books are *Wilderness Plots* (1983), *Blow* (1985), *Bad Man Ballad* (1986), *The Paradise of Bombs* (1987), *In Limestone Country* (1991), *Staying Put* (1993), and *The Force of Spirit* (2000). His most recent book is *A Private History of Awe* (2006), which is simultaneously a coming of age memoir, a love story, and a spiritual testament. Like most of his other written work, it celebrates the triumph of social justice, the search for divine truth, and the sense of community so lacking in our busy modern lives. He and his wife, Ruth, a biochemist, live in Bloomington in the White River Valley.

Preparing to Read

This essay was first published in 1992 in a journal called *Orion.* In it, Sanders addresses the innate desire in our culture to keep moving, exploring, and growing.

Exploring Experience: As you prepare to read this essay, consider your natural inclination to move or to stay in the same place: Do you feel genuinely connected to the place you call "home," or are you always looking for a chance to move? What value do you derive from settling down? From staying on the move? Do you feel you are working with or against our culture? In what ways? Do you think this culture varies by geographic region? Explain your answer.

Learning Online: In his essay, Sanders points out that Americans have created more transportation systems than any other nation in the world. Visit the *America on the Move* project sponsored by the Smithsonian National Museum of American History (http://americanhistory.si.edu/onthemove). Take some time to view the pictures and read the history of American transportation.

s a boy in Ohio, I knew a farm family, the Millers, who suffered from   1
three tornadoes. The father, mother, and two sons were pulling into
their driveway after church when the first tornado hoisted up their
mobile home, spun it around, and carried it off. With the insurance money,
they built a small frame house on the same spot.

Several years later, a second tornado peeled off the roof, splintered the   2
garage, and rustled two cows. The Millers rebuilt again, raising a new garage
on the old foundation and adding another story to the house. That upper
floor was reduced to kindling by a third tornado, which also pulled out half
the apple trees and slurped water from the stock pond. Soon after that I left
Ohio, snatched away by college as forcefully as by any cyclone. Last thing I
heard, the family was preparing to rebuild yet again. ❶

Why did the Millers refuse to move? I knew them all enough to say they were   3
neither stupid nor crazy. Plain stubbornness was a factor. These were people
who, once settled, might have remained at the volcano or on the bank of a
flood-prone river or beside an earthquake fault. They had relatives nearby, helpful neighbors, jobs and stores and schools within a short drive, and those were
all good reasons to stay. But the main reason, I believe, was that the Millers had
invested so much of their lives in the land, ❷ planting orchards and gardens,
spreading manure on the fields, digging ponds, building sheds, seeding pastures.
Out back of the house were groves of walnuts, hickories, and oaks, all started
by hand from acorns and nuts. April through October, perennial flowers in the
yard pumped out a fountain of blossoms. This farm was not just so many acres
of dirt, easily exchanged for an equal amount elsewhere; it was a particular
place, intimately known, worked on, dreamed over, cherished.

Psychologists tell us that we answer trouble with one of two impulses, ei-   4
ther fight or flight. I believe that the Millers exhibited a third instinct, that
of staying put. They knew better than to fight a tornado, and they chose not
to flee. Their commitment to the place may have been foolhardy, but it was
also grand. I suspect that most human achievements worth admiring are the
result of such devotion.

The Millers dramatize a choice we are faced with constantly: whether to   5
go or stay, whether to move to a situation that is safer, richer, easier, more attractive, or to stick where we are and make what we can of it. If the shine
goes off our marriage, our house, our car, do we trade it for a new one? If
the fertility leaches out of our soil, the creativity out of our job, the money

---

Reading Critically

❶ Why do you think the family kept rebuilding their home? Would you have done the same
thing? Why or why not?

❷ Have you or your family "invested" your lives in any particular place? What does the
metaphor "invested" mean to you?

out of our pocket, do we start over somewhere else? [3] There are voices enough, both inner and outer, urging us to deal with difficulties by pulling up stakes and heading for new territory. I know them well, for they have been calling to me all my days. I wish to raise here a contrary voice, to say a few words on behalf of staying put, learning the ground, going deeper.

Claims for the virtues of moving on are familiar and seductive to Amer- 6 icans, this nation founded by immigrants and shaped by restless seekers. From the beginning, our heroes have been sailors, explorers, cowboys, prospectors, speculators, backwoods ramblers, rainbow chasers, vagabonds of every stripe. Our Promised Land has always been over the next ridge or at the end of the trail, never under our feet. In our national mythology, the worst fate is to be trapped on a farm, in a village, in the sticks, in some dead-end job or unglamorous marriage or played-out game.

Stand still, we are warned, and you die. Americans have dug the most 7 canals, laid the most rails, built the most roads and airports of any nation. In a newspaper I read that, even though our sprawling system of interstate highways is crumbling, politicians think we should triple its size. Only a populace drunk on driving, [4] a populace infatuated with the myth of the open road, could hear such a proposal without hooting.

Novelist Salman Rushdie chose to leave his native India for England, where 8 he has written a series of brilliant books from the perspective of a cultural immigrant. In his book of essays *Imaginary Homelands* he celebrates the migrant sensibility: "The effect of mass migrations has been the creation of radically new types of human being: people who root themselves in ideas rather than places, [5] in memories as much as in material things." He goes on to say that "to be a migrant is, perhaps, to be the only species of human being free of the shackles of nationalism (to say nothing of its ugly sister, patriotism)." Lord knows we could do with less nationalism (to say nothing of its ugly siblings, racism, religious sectarianism, and class snobbery). But who would pretend that a history of migration has immunized the United States against bigotry? And even if, by uprooting ourselves, we shed our chauvinism, is that all we lose?

In this hemisphere, many of the worst abuses—of land, forests, animals, and 9 communities—have been carried out by "people who root themselves in ideas rather than places." Migrants often pack up their visions and values with the rest of their baggage and carry them along. The Spaniards devastated Central and South America by imposing on this New World the religion,

---

Reading Critically

[3] How does creativity "leach" out of a job?
[4] Do you agree that our society is "drunk on driving"? In what ways is this metaphor especially true?
[5] Do you root yourself in ideas or in places? What is the difference?

economics, and politics of the old. Colonists brought slavery with them to North America, along with smallpox and Norway rats. The Dust Bowl of the 1930s was caused not by drought but by the transfer onto the Great Plains of farming methods that were suitable to wetter regions. The habit of our industry and commerce has been to force identical schemes onto differing locales, as though the mind were a cookie cutter and the land were dough.

I quarrel with Rushdie because he articulates as eloquently as anyone the   10
orthodoxy that I wish to counter: the belief that movement is inherently good, staying put is bad; that uprooting brings tolerance, while rootedness breeds intolerance; that to be modern, enlightened, fully of our time is to be displaced. Wholesale displacement may be inevitable in today's world; but we should not suppose that it occurs without disastrous consequences for the earth and for ourselves. People who root themselves in places are likelier to know and care for those places than are people who root themselves in ideas. When we cease to be migrants and become inhabitants, ⑥ we might begin to pay enough heed and respect to where we are. By settling in, we have a chance of making a durable home for ourselves, our fellow creatures, and our descendants.

The poet Gary Snyder writes frequently about our need to "inhabit" a   11
place. One of the key problems in American society now, he points out, is people's lack of commitment to any given place:

> Neighborhoods are allowed to deteriorate, landscapes are allowed to be strip-mined, because there is nobody who will live there and take responsibility; they'll just move on. The reconstruction of a people and a life in the United States depends on people, neighborhood by neighborhood, county by county, deciding to stick it out and make it work where they are rather than flee.

But if you stick in one place, won't you become a stick-in-the-mud? If you stay put, won't you be narrow, backward, dull? You might. I have met ignorant people who never moved; and I have also met ignorant people who never stood still. Committing yourself to a place does not guarantee that you will become wise, but neither does it guarantee that you will become parochial.

To become intimate with your home region, to know the territory as well   12
as you can, to understand your life as woven into the local life does not prevent you from recognizing and honoring the diversity other places, cultures, ways. On the contrary, how can you value other places if you do not have one of your own? If you are not yourself placed, then you wander the world like a sightseer, a collector of sensations, with no gauge for measuring what you see. Local knowledge is the grounding for global knowledge. Those who care about nothing beyond the confines of their parish are in truth parochial, and

---

Reading Critically

⑥ Do you agree with the author's assertion that when we "cease to be migrants" we "become inhabitants"?

are at least mildly dangerous to their parish; on the other hand, those who *have* no parish, those who navigate ceaselessly among postal zones and area codes, those for whom the world is only a smear of highways and bank accounts and stores, [7] are a danger not just to their parish but to the planet.

Since birth, my children have regularly seen images of the earth as viewed   13 from space, images that I first encountered when I was in my 20s. Those photographs show vividly what in our sanest moments we have always known—that the earth is a closed circle, lovely and rare. On the wall beside me as I write is a poster of the big blue marble encased in its white swirl of clouds. That is one pole of my awareness; but the other pole is what I see through my window. I try to keep both in sight at once.

For all my convictions, I still have to wrestle with the fear—in myself, in   14 my children, and even in some of my neighbors—that our place is too re- mote from the action. This fear drives many people to pack their bags and move to some resort or burg they have seen on television, leaving behind what they learn to think of as the boondocks. I deal with my own unease by asking just what action I am remote from—a stock market? a debating chamber? a drive-in mortuary? The action that matters, the work of nature and community, goes on everywhere.

Since Copernicus, we have known better than to see the earth as the cen-   15 ter of the universe. Since Einstein, we have learned that there is no center; or alternatively, that any point is as good as any other for observing the world. I find a kindred lesson in the words of the Zen master Thich Nhat Hanh: "This spot where you sit is your own spot. It is on this very spot and in this very moment that you can become enlightened. You don't have to sit beneath a special tree in a distant land." If you stay put, your place may become a holy center, [8] not because it gives you special access to the divine, but because in your stillness you hear what might be heard anywhere.

I think of my home ground as a series of nested rings, with house and fam-   16 ily and marriage at the center, surrounded by the wider and wider hoops of neighborhood and community, the bioregion within walking distance of my door, the wooded and rocky hills of southern Indiana, the watershed of the Ohio Valley, and so on outward—and inward—to the ultimate source.

The longing to become an inhabitant rather than a drifter sets me against   17 the current of my culture, which nudges everyone into motion. [9] Newton

---

Reading Critically

[7] What does Sanders mean when he refers to the world as a "smear of highways and bank accounts and stores"?

[8] How can your place "become a holy center" if you "stay put"? Paraphrase this concept in your own words.

[9] According to the author, how does our culture "nudge" everyone into motion?

taught us that a body at rest tends to stay at rest, unless it is acted on by an outside force. We are acted on ceaselessly by outside forces—advertising, movies, magazines, speeches—and also by the inner force of biology. I am not immune to their pressure. Before settling in my present home, I lived in seven states and two countries, tugged from place to place in childhood by my father's work and in early adulthood by my own. This itinerant life is so common among the people I know that I have been slow to conceive of an alternative. Only by knocking against the golden calf of mobility, which looms so large and shines so brightly, have I come to realize that it is hollow. Like all idols, it distracts us from what is truly divine.

I am encouraged by the words of a Crow elder, quoted by Gary Snyder   18 in The Practice of the Wild: "You know, I think if people stay somewhere long enough—even white people—the spirits will begin to speak to them. It's the power of the spirits coming up from the land. The spirits and the old powers aren't lost, they just need people to be around long enough and the spirits will begin to influence them."

As I write this, I hear the snarl of earth movers and chain saws a mile   19 away destroying a farm to make way for another shopping strip. I would rather hear a tornado, whose damage can be undone. The elderly woman who owned the farm had it listed in the National Register, then willed it to her daughters on condition they preserve it. After her death, the daughters, who live out of state, had the will broken, so the land could be turned over to the chain saws and earth movers. The machines work around the clock. Their noise wakes me at midnight, at three in the morning, at dawn. The roaring abrades my dreams. The sound is a reminder that we are living in the midst of a holocaust. I do not use the word lightly. The earth is being pillaged, and every one of us, willingly or grudgingly, is taking part. We ask how sensible, educated, supposedly moral people could have tolerated slavery or the slaughter of Jews. Similar questions will be asked about us by our descendants, to whom we bequeath an impoverished planet. They will demand to know how we could have been party to such waste and ruin. [10]

What does it mean to be alive in an era when earth is being devoured,   20 and in a country that has set the pattern for that devouring? What are we called to do? I think we are called to the work of healing, both inner and outer: healing of the mind through a change in consciousness, healing of the earth through a change in our lives. We can begin that work by learning how to inhabit a place.

Reading Critically

[10] Do you agree with Sanders that the mistreatment of our planet is similar to the horrors of slavery and the holocaust? Why or why not?

"The man who is often thinking that it is better to be somewhere else than   21
where he is excommunicates himself," we are cautioned by Thoreau, that
notorious stay-at-home. The metaphor is religious: To withhold yourself
from where you are is to be cut off from communion with the source. It has
taken me half a lifetime of searching to realize that the likeliest path to the
ultimate ground leads through my local ground. I mean the land itself, with
its creeks and rivers, its weather, seasons, stone outcroppings, and all the plants
and animals that share it. I cannot have a spiritual center without having a
geographical one; I cannot live a grounded life without being grounded in
a place.

   In belonging to a landscape, one feels a rightness, an at-homeness, a knit-   22
ting of self and world. ⟐ This condition of clarity and focus, this being fully
present, is akin to what the Buddhists call mindfulness, what Christian con-
templatives refer to as recollection, what Quakers call centering down. I am
suspicious of any philosophy that would separate this-worldly from other-
worldly commitment. There is only one world, and we participate in it here
and now, in our flesh and our place.

UNDERSTANDING DETAILS

1. Why does Sanders believe the Millers didn't move—even after three tornadoes
    devastated their house?
2. What is associated with a commitment to place for the author?
3. According to Sanders, how does being committed to a place help us appreci-
    ate other places and cultures?
4. What does Sanders mean when he says, "By settling in, we have a chance of
    making a durable home for ourselves, our fellow creatures, and our descen-
    dants" (paragraph 10)?

THINKING CRITICALLY

5. How does being committed to a place work against our heritage in the United
    States?
6. What does Sanders imply about the difference between a commitment to place
    and a commitment to ideas?
7. What is the significance of the move from migrants to inhabitants in the Amer-
    ican culture?
8. In paragraph 12, Sanders says, "Local knowledge is the grounding for global
    knowledge." Do you agree or disagree with this statement? Explain your answer.

Reading Critically

⟐ What does the author mean by "a knitting of self and world"?

DISCOVERING RHETORICAL STRATEGIES

9. Explain the title of this selection?
10. Is the story about the Millers an effective beginning for this essay?
11. Sanders divides his essay into four sections. What is the main idea of each section?
12. What rhetorical strategies besides comparison/contrast does Sanders use to make his point?

MAKING CONNECTIONS

13. How is Sanders's devotion to the sense of place echoed in the following essays: Ray Bradbury's "Summer Rituals," John McPhee's "The Pines," and/or Bruce Catton's "Grant and Lee: A Study in Contrasts"?
14. In what important ways does Sanders's comparison/contrast technique differ from those used by William Ouchi ("Japanese and American Workers: Two Casts of Mind"), Gloria Steinem ("The Politics of Muscle"), and/or Sucheng Chan ("You're Short, Besides!")?
15. Compare and contrast the resilience of the Millers (paragraphs 1–3) in Sanders's essay with similar stories of persistence in Maya Angelou's "New Directions," Harold Krentz's "Darkness at Noon," and/or Malcolm X's "Learning to Read."

IDEAS FOR DISCUSSION/WRITING

Preparing to Write

Write freely about your desire or lack of desire for change: How many times have you moved to a new residence during your life so far? Have you moved by choice or by necessity? Do you welcome major changes in your life? Do you make commitments easily? Do these commitments last? What is your strongest current commitment? Will this commitment ever change? What leads you to this conclusion?

Choosing a Topic

1. Someone is considering moving into your neighborhood. In preparation for talking to this neighbor, record your thoughts in essay form about whether or not this would be a good idea.
2. Compare and contrast your level of commitment with that of someone else whom you know very well.
3. Are you more committed to places or ideas? Defend your choice in a well-developed essay modeled on Sanders's selection.
4. Take the brief online travel quiz sponsored by Travel-Journal (http://www .travel-journal.org/quiz), and find out your "travel personality." After receiving the results of the quiz, write an essay describing the type of traveler you are. Compare the quiz results with your own self-evaluation to determine the accuracy of the quiz.

Before beginning your essay, you might want to consult the checklists on page 311.

WILLIAM OUCHI   (1943–)

Japanese and American Workers: Two Casts of Mind

Born in Honolulu, Hawaii, William Ouchi is an internationally known expert
on business management—particularly on the relationship between American
and Japanese corporations. Ouchi was educated at Williams College, Stanford
University, and the University of Chicago; since then, he has taught in business
programs at several major American universities, most recently at the Anderson
Graduate School of Management at UCLA, where he is vice dean and faculty
director of the Executive Education Program. The author has also served as
associate study director for the National Opinion Research Center and as a
business consultant for many of America's most successful companies. He has
written three books on organization and management: *Theory Z: How American
Business Can Meet the Japanese Challenge* (1981) is a thorough analysis of the
differences between American and Japanese industrial productivity; *The
M-Form Society: How American Teamwork Can Recapture the Competitive Edge*
(1984) is the result of a three-year study by a team of sixteen researchers led
by Ouchi; and *Organizational Economics* (1986) is a textbook coedited with
Jay Barney. His latest book is titled *Making Schools Work: A Revolutionary Plan
to Get Your Children the Education They Need* (2003). He advises students using
The Prose Reader to spend plenty of time revising their material. "No one
writes a good first draft," he explains. "You must continue to revise your work
till you understand exactly what you want to say and you have constructed a
group of sentences that say it clearly." Ouchi lives with his wife and three
children in Santa Monica, California, where he enjoys playing golf as frequently
as his busy schedule allows.

Preparing to Read

The following essay, excerpted from *Theory Z,* compares and contrasts
Japan's collective work ethic with the American spirit of individualism.

Exploring Experience: As you prepare to read this essay, think about your
own work ethic: When you study, for example, do you prefer working alone
or with a group of people? What kinds of jobs have you held during your
life? Did they stress individual or collective behavior? Were you often rewarded
for individual achievement, or did you work mostly within a group? In what
sort of work environment are you most productive? Most satisfied?

Learning Online: Select an industry such as cars or electronics. Find Web
sites for an American company and a Japanese company in your chosen
industry. Try to access the companies' mission statements, and think about
ways in which their company philosophies are both similar and different.

Perhaps the most difficult aspect of the Japanese for Westerners to com- 1 prehend is the strong orientation to collective values, ◆ particularly a collective sense of responsibility. Let me illustrate with an anecdote about a visit to a new factory in Japan owned and operated by an American electronics company. The American company, a particularly creative firm, frequently attracts attention within the business community for its novel approaches to planning, organizational design, and management systems. As a consequence of this corporate style, the parent company determined to make a thorough study of Japanese workers and to design a plant that would combine the best of East and West. In their study they discovered that Japanese firms almost never make use of individual work incentives, such as piecework or even individual performance appraisal tied to salary increases. They concluded that rewarding individual achievement and individual ability is always a good thing.

In the final assembly area of their new plant long lines of young Japanese 2 women wired together electronic products on a piece-rate system: The more you wired, the more you got paid. About two months after opening, the head foreladies approached the plant manager. "Honorable plant manager," they said humbly as they bowed, "we are embarrassed to be so forward, but we must speak to you because all of the girls have threatened to quit work this Friday." (To have this happen, of course, would be a great disaster for all concerned.) "Why," they wanted to know, "can't our plant have the same compensation system as other Japanese companies? When you hire a new girl, her starting wage should be fixed by her age. An eighteen-year-old should be paid more than a sixteen-year-old. Every year on her birthday, she should receive an automatic increase in pay. The idea that any one of us can be more productive than another must be wrong, because none of us in final assembly could make a thing unless all of the other people in the plant had done their jobs right first. To single one person out as being more productive is wrong and is also personally humiliating to us." ◆ The company changed its compensation system to the Japanese model.

Another American company in Japan had installed a suggestion system 3 much as we have in the United States. Individual workers were encouraged to place suggestions to improve productivity into special boxes. For an accepted idea the individual received a bonus amounting to some fraction of the productivity savings realized from his or her suggestion. After a period of six months, not a single suggestion had been submitted. The American managers were puzzled. They had heard many stories of the inventiveness,

---

Reading Critically

◆ What does the term "collective values" mean to you?

◆ Why were the workers humiliated? How did the plant solve the problem?

the commitment, and the loyalty of Japanese workers, yet not one suggestion to improve productivity had appeared.

The managers approached some of the workers and asked why the suggestion system had not been used. The answer: "No one can come up with a work improvement idea alone. We work together, and any ideas that one of us may have are actually developed by watching others and talking to others. If one of us was singled out for being responsible for such an idea, it would embarrass all of us." The company changed to a group suggestion system, in which workers collectively submitted suggestions. Bonuses were paid to groups which would save bonus money until the end of the year for a party at a restaurant or, if there was enough money, for family vacations together. The suggestions and productivity improvements rained down on the plant. ❸

One can interpret these examples in two quite different ways. Perhaps the Japanese commitment to collective values is an anachronism that does not fit with modern industrialism but brings economic success despite that collectivism. Collectivism seems to be inimical to the kind of maverick creativity exemplified in Benjamin Franklin, Thomas Edison, and John D. Rockefeller. Collectivism does not seem to provide the individual incentive to excel which has made a great success of American enterprise. Entirely apart from its economic effects, collectivism implies a loss of individuality, a loss of the freedom to be different, to hold fundamentally different values from others.

The second interpretation of the examples is that the Japanese collectivism is economically efficient. It causes people to work well together and to encourage one another to better efforts. Industrial life requires interdependence of one person on another. ❹ But a less obvious but far-reaching implication of the Japanese collectivism for economic performance has to do with accountability.

In the Japanese mind, collectivism is neither a corporate or individual goal to strive for nor a slogan to pursue. Rather, the nature of things operates so that nothing of consequence occurs as a result of individual effort. Everything important in life happens as a result of teamwork or collective effort. Therefore, to attempt to assign individual credit or blame to results is unfounded. A Japanese professor of accounting, a brilliant scholar trained at Carnegie-Mellon University who teaches now in Tokyo, remarked that the status of accounting systems in Japanese industry is primitive compared to those in the United States. Profit centers, transfer prices, and computerized

---

Reading Critically

❸ How did the shift to a "group suggestion system" affect morale and productivity at the plant? Why was this simple change so successful?

❹ How is this concept of "interdependence" developed at your college? At your job?

information systems are barely known even in the largest Japanese companies, whereas they are commonplace in even small United States organizations. Though not at all surprised at the difference in accounting systems, I was not at all sure that the Japanese were primitive. In fact, I thought their system a good deal more efficient than ours.

Most American companies have basically two accounting systems. One 8
system summarizes the overall financial state to inform stockholders, bankers, and other outsiders. That system is not of interest here. The other system, called the managerial or cost accounting system, exists for an entirely different reason. ⑤ It measures in detail all of the particulars of transactions between departments, divisions, and key individuals in the organization, for the purpose of untangling the interdependencies between people. When, for example, two departments share one truck for deliveries, the cost accounting system charges each department for part of the cost of maintaining the truck and driver, so that at the end of the year, the performance of each department can be individually assessed, and the better department's manager can receive a larger raise. Of course, all of this information processing costs money, and furthermore may lead to arguments between the departments over whether the costs charged to each are fair.

In a Japanese company a short-run assessment of individual perfor- 9
mance is not wanted, so the company can save the considerable expense of collecting and processing all of that information. Companies still keep track of which department uses a truck how often and for what purposes, but like-minded people can interpret some simple numbers for themselves and adjust their behavior accordingly. Those insisting upon clear and precise measurement for the purpose of advancing individual interests must have an elaborate information system. Industrial life, however, is essentially integrated and interdependent. No one builds an automobile alone, no one carries through a banking transaction alone. In a sense the Japanese value of collectivism fits naturally into an industrial setting, whereas the Western individualism provides constant conflicts. The image that comes to mind is of Chaplin's silent film Modern Times in which the apparently insignificant hero played by Chaplin successfully fights against the unfeeling machinery of industry. Modern industrial life can be aggravating, even hostile, or natural: All depends on the fit between our culture and our technology. ⑥

Reading Critically

⑤ Why are there two systems of accounting?

⑥ What do you think the author means by "the fit between our culture and our technology."

The *shinkansen* or "bullet train" speeds across the rural areas of Japan giv-   10
ing a quick view of cluster after cluster of farmhouses surrounded by rice
paddies. This particular pattern did not develop purely by chance, but as a
consequence of the technology peculiar to the growing of rice, the staple of
the Japanese diet. The growing of rice requires construction and maintenance of an irrigation system, something that takes many hands to build.
More importantly, the planting and the harvesting of rice can only be done
efficiently with the cooperation of twenty or more people. The "bottom
line" is that a single family working alone cannot produce enough rice to survive, but a dozen families working together can produce a surplus. Thus the
Japanese have had to develop the capacity to work together in harmony, no
matter what the forces of disagreement or social disintegration, in order to
survive.

Japan is a nation built entirely on the tips of giant, suboceanic volcanoes. [7]   11
Little of the land is flat and suitable for agriculture. Terraced hillsides make
use of every available square foot of arable land. Small homes built very close
together further conserve the land. Japan also suffers from natural disasters
such as earthquakes and hurricanes. Traditionally homes are made of light
construction materials, so a house falling down during a disaster will not
crush its occupants and also could be quickly and inexpensively rebuilt. During the feudal period until the Meiji restoration of 1868, each feudal lord
sought to restrain his subjects from moving from one village to the next for
fear that a neighboring lord might amass enough peasants with which to
produce a large agricultural surplus, hire an army, and pose a threat. Apparently bridges were not commonly built across rivers and streams until the late
nineteenth century, since bridges increased mobility between villages.

Taken all together, this characteristic style of living paints the picture of   12
a nation of people who are homogeneous with respect to race, history, language, religion, and culture. [8] For centuries and generations these people have
lived in the same village next door to the same neighbors. Living in close
proximity and in dwellings which gave very little privacy, the Japanese survived through their capacity to work together in harmony. In this situation,
it was inevitable that the one most central social value which emerged, the
one value without which the society could not continue, was that an individual does not matter.

To the Western soul this is a chilling picture of society. Subordinating in-   13
dividual tastes to the harmony of the group and knowing that individual

---

Reading Critically

[7] What is the relationship between Japan's geography and its business practices?

[8] What is the effect of homogeneity on business?

needs can never take precedence over the interests of all is repellent to the Western citizen. But a frequent theme of Western philosophers and sociologists is that individual freedom exists only when people willingly subordinate their self-interests to the social interest. A society composed entirely of self-interested individuals is a society in which each person is at war with the other, a society which has no freedom. This issue, constantly at the heart of understanding society, comes up in every century, and in every society, whether the writer be Plato, Hobbes, or B. F. Skinner. The question of understanding which contemporary institutions lie at the heart of the conflict between automatism and totalitarianism remains. In some ages, the kinship group, the central social institution, mediated between these opposing forces to preserve the balance in which freedom was realized; in other times the church or the government was most critical. Perhaps our present age puts the work organization as the central institution.

In order to complete the comparison of Japanese and American living   14 situations, consider a flight over the United States. Looking out of the window high over the state of Kansas, we see a pattern of a single farmhouse surrounded by fields, followed by another single homestead surrounded by fields. In the early 1800s in the state of Kansas there were no automobiles. Your nearest neighbor was perhaps two miles distant; the winters were long, and the snow was deep. Inevitably, the central social values were self-reliance and independence. Those were the realities of that place and age that children had to learn to value.

The key to the industrial revolution was discovering that non–human   15 forms of energy substituted for human forms could increase the wealth of a nation beyond anyone's wildest dreams. But there was a catch. To realize this great wealth, non–human energy needed huge complexes called factories with hundreds, even thousands of workers collected into one factory. Moreover, several factories in one central place made the generation of energy more efficient. Almost overnight, the Western world was transformed from a rural and agricultural country to an urban and industrial state. ⑨ Our technological advance seems to no longer fit our social structure: In a sense, the Japanese can better cope with modern industrialism. While Americans still busily protect our rather extreme form of individualism, the Japanese hold their individualism in check and emphasize cooperation.

Reading Critically
⑨ How was the Western world transformed overnight "from a rural and agricultural country to an urban and industrialized state"?

UNDERSTANDING DETAILS

1. Describe in your own words the two different philosophies Ouchi is comparing in this essay.
2. What is Ouchi's main point in this essay? Where does he introduce his purpose?
3. According to the author, what is the most difficult aspect of the Japanese business ethic for Westerners to understand?
4. Why does "collectivism" work better for the Japanese than for the Americans? What is its history in Japan? How is it different from Western "individualism"?

THINKING CRITICALLY

5. What is Ouchi's personal opinion of the two value systems he is comparing? At what points does he reveal his preference?
6. Why does the author introduce the origins of American and Japanese living conditions?
7. Which set of business values do you prefer after reading Ouchi's comparison? Explain the reasons for your preference.
8. In what ways is the "work organization" the middle ground between automatism and totalitarianism today? Give examples of this observation from your own experience.

DISCOVERING RHETORICAL STRATEGIES

9. How does Ouchi organize this essay? Outline the main points he covers for each subject.
10. Why do you think the author introduces the two anecdotes at the outset of this essay? How do these stories help Ouchi achieve his purpose?
11. Who do you think is the author's intended audience? How much knowledge about these two subjects does he assume they have? What evidence can you give to support your answer?
12. What other rhetorical strategies besides comparison and contrast does Ouchi use to achieve his purpose in this essay? Give examples of each strategy.

MAKING CONNECTIONS

13. Ouchi argues persuasively that geography has played a major role in Japan's orientation toward "collective" values. Scarcity of land and crowded conditions have forced Japanese citizens to work together harmoniously in ways that seem alien to our concept of self-reliance and independence born on the wide-open American frontier. In what similar ways does geography play a part in the essays by John McPhee ("The Pines"), Bruce Catton ("Grant and Lee: A Study in Contrasts"), and/or Scott Russell Sanders ("Homeplace")?
14. Imagine that Ouchi, Robert Ramirez ("The Barrio"), and Mary Pipher ("Beliefs About Families") are having a conversation about the importance of cooperation among people who live close together. What would these authors

say are the principal difficulties of achieving such necessary cooperation? What would they say are the main rewards? How "cooperative" is the neighborhood in which you live? Do you wish it were more so? Why or why not?

15. Compare the suggestions made by Ouchi and Edwin Bliss ("Managing Your Time") concerning how American businesses could work more effectively and efficiently. What ideas would you like to share with our business leaders to help make American industry more productive?

IDEAS FOR DISCUSSION/WRITING

Preparing to Write

Write freely about the work ethic that characterizes your immediate environment—at school, at home, or on the job: How do the people in each of these environments feel about one another? How do you feel about them? When are you most productive in these environments? What are the circumstances? Do you work better individually or collectively? Why?

Choosing a Topic

1. Would you prefer to live your social life individually or collectively (as Ouchi defines the two methods)? Explain your preference to a friend, comparing the advantages and disadvantages of both situations. What implications does your preference have? Be sure to make your purpose as clear as possible.

2. Would you rather work in a factory that follows the Japanese or the American method of organization outlined by Ouchi? Explain your preference to your best friend or your immediate supervisor at work. Compare the advantages and disadvantages of both situations. What implications does your preference have? Be sure to make your purpose as clear as possible.

3. *Leisure* magazine has asked you to compare work and leisure from a college student's point of view. Consider the advantages and disadvantages of each. Be sure to decide on a purpose before you begin to write your comparison.

4. Ouchi explores "Two Casts of Mind" in the business world. Have you observed differences in perspective based on age, gender, or culture outside the business arena? How do these differences in perspective affect individual or collective behavior? Select an online magazine whose audience would be interested in your observations. Using Ouchi's technique of alternating comparisons, prepare an article that compares and contrasts these differences in perspective and analyzes their effect on individual and/or collective behavior.

Before beginning your essay, you might want to consult the checklists on page 311.

The Politics of Muscle

Once described as a writer with "unpretentious clarity and forceful expression," Gloria Steinem is one of the foremost organizers and champions of the modern women's movement. She was born in Toledo, Ohio, earned a B.A. at Smith College, and pursued graduate work in political science at the universities of Delhi and Calcutta in India before returning to America to begin a freelance career in journalism. One of her earliest and best-known articles, "I Was a Playboy Bunny," was a witty exposé of the entire Playboy operation written in 1963 after she had worked undercover for two weeks in the New York City Playboy Club. In 1968 she and Clay Felker founded *New York* magazine; then, in 1972, they started *Ms.* magazine, which sold out its entire 300,000–copy run in eight days. Steinem's subsequent publications have included *Outrageous Acts and Everyday Rebellions* (1983), *Marilyn: Norma Jean* (1986), *Bedside Book of Self-Esteem* (1989), and *Moving Beyond Words* (1994). An articulate and passionate spokesperson for feminist causes, Steinem has been honored nine times by the *World Almanac* as one of the twenty-five most influential women in America.

Preparing to Read

Taken from the author's newest book, *Moving Beyond Words,* "The Politics of Muscle" is actually an introduction to a longer essay entitled "The Strongest Woman in the World," which celebrates the virtues of women's bodybuilding champion Bev Francis.

Exploring Experience: As you prepare to read this essay, examine for a few minutes your own thoughts about the associations Americans make with weakness and strength in both men and women: Which sex do you think of as stronger? In America, what does strength have to do with accomplishment? With failure? Do these associations vary for men and women? What does weakness suggest in American culture? Do these suggestions vary for men and women? What are the positive values Americans associate with muscles and strength? With helplessness and weakness? What are the negative values Americans associate with muscles and strength? With helplessness and weakness? What connections have you made from your experience between physical strength and gender roles?

Learning Online: Read expert opinions about Gloria Steinem by conducting an Internet search using the terms "Perspectives of Gloria Steinem." As you read these perspectives, consider the ways Steinem uses her writing for social and political activism.

I come from a generation of women who didn't do sports. Being a cheer-   1
leader or a drum majorette was as far as our imaginations or role models could take us. Oh yes, there was also being a strutter—one of a group
of girls (and we were girls then) who marched and danced and turned cart-
wheels in front of the high school band at football games. Did you know that
big football universities actually gave strutting scholarships? That shouldn't
sound any more bizarre than football scholarships, yet somehow it does.
Gender politics strikes again.

But even winning one of those rare positions, the stuff that dreams were   2
made of, was more about body display than about the considerable skill they
required. ◆ You could forget about trying out for them if you didn't have
the right face and figure, and my high school was full of girls who had learned
to do back flips and twirl flaming batons, all to no avail. Winning wasn't
about being the best in an objective competition or achieving a personal
best, or even about becoming healthy or fit. It was about *being chosen.*

That's one of many reasons why I and other women of my generation   3
grew up believing—as many girls still do—that the most important thing
about a female body is not what it does but how it looks. The power lies not
within us but in the gaze of the observer. In retrospect, I feel sorry for the
protofeminist gym teachers who tried so hard to interest us in half-court
basketball and other team sports thought suitable for girls in my high school,
while we worried about the hairdo we'd slept on rollers all night to achieve.
Gym was just a stupid requirement you tried to get out of, with ugly gym
suits whose very freedom felt odd on bodies accustomed to being constricted
for viewing. ◆ My blue-collar neighborhood didn't help much either, for it
convinced me that sports like tennis or golf were as remote as the country
clubs where they were played—mostly by men anyway. That left tap dancing and ballet as my only exercise, and though my dancing school farmed us
out to supermarket openings and local nightclubs, where we danced our
hearts out in homemade costumes, those events were about display too, about
smiling and pleasing and, even during the rigors of ballet, about looking
ethereal and hiding any muscles or strength.

My sports avoidance continued into college, where I went through shock   4
about class and wrongly assumed athletics were only for well-to-do prep
school girls like those who brought their own lacrosse sticks and riding
horses to school. With no sports training to carry over from childhood—and
no place to become childlike, as we must when we belatedly learn basic

---

Reading Critically

◆ What does Steinem mean by the term "body display"?
◆ To what extent are women's bodies still "constricted for viewing" today?

skills—I clung to my familiar limits. Even at the casual softball games where *Ms.* played the staffs of other magazines, I confined myself to cheering. As the *Ms.* No Stars, we prided ourselves on keeping the same lineup, win or lose, and otherwise disobeying the rules of the jockocracy, so I contented myself with upsetting the men on the opposing team by cheering for their female team members. [3] It's amazing how upset those accustomed to conventional divisions can become when others refuse to be divided by them.

In my case, an interest in the politics of strength had come not from my own experience but from observing the mysterious changes in many women around me. Several of my unathletic friends had deserted me by joining gyms, becoming joggers, or discovering the pleasure of learning to yell and kick in self-defense class. Others who had young daughters described the unexpected thrill of seeing them learn to throw a ball or run with a freedom that hadn't been part of our lives in conscious memory. On campuses, I listened to formerly anorexic young women who said their obsession with dieting had diminished when they discovered strength as a third alternative to the usual fat-versus-thin dichotomy. [4] Suddenly, a skinny, androgynous, "boyish" body was no longer the only way to escape the soft, female, "victim" bodies they associated with their mothers' fates. Added together, these examples of before-and-after-strength changes were so dramatic that the only male analogues I could find were Vietnam amputees whose confidence was bolstered when they entered marathons in wheelchairs or on artificial legs, or paralyzed accident survivors whose sense of themselves was changed when they learned to play wheelchair basketball. Compared to their handicapped female counterparts, however, even those men seemed to be less transformed. Within each category, women had been less encouraged to develop whatever muscle and skills we had.

Since my old habits of ignoring my body and living inside my head weren't that easy to break, it was difficult to change my nonathletic ways. Instead, I continued to learn secondhand from watching my friends, from reading about female strength in other cultures, and from asking questions wherever I traveled.

Though cultural differences were many, there were political similarities in the way women's bodies were treated that went as deep as patriarchy itself. Whether achieved through law and social policy, as in this and other industrialized countries, or by way of tribal practice and religious ritual, as in older cultures, an individual woman's body was far more subject to other people's

---

Reading Critically

[3] What do you think the author means by a "jockocracy"? What are some of its "rules"?

[4] In what way is "strength" a "third alternative to the usual fat-versus-thin-dichotomy"?

rules than was that of her male counterpart. Women always seemed to be owned to some degree as the means of reproduction. [5] And as possessions, women's bodies then became symbols of men's status, with a value that was often determined by what was rare. Thus, rich cultures valued thin women, and poor cultures valued fat women. Yet all patriarchal cultures valued weakness in women. How else could male dominance survive? In my own country, for example, women who "belong" to rich white men are often thinner (as in "You can never be too rich or too thin") than those who "belong" to poor men of color; yet those very different groups of males tend to come together in their belief that women are supposed to be weaker than men; that muscles and strength aren't "feminine."

If I had any doubts about the psychological importance of cultural emphasis on male/female strength difference, listening to arguments about equality put them to rest. Sooner or later, even the most intellectual discussion came down to men's supposedly superior strength as a justification for inequality, whether the person arguing regretted or celebrated it. What no one seemed to explore, however, was the inadequacy of physical strength as a way of explaining oppression in other cases. Men of European origin hadn't ruled in South Africa because they were stronger than African men, and blacks hadn't been kept in slavery or bad jobs in the United States because whites had more muscles. On the contrary, males of the "wrong" class or color were often confined to laboring positions precisely because of their supposedly greater strength, just as the lower pay females received was often rationalized by their supposedly lesser strength. [6] Oppression has no logic—just a self-fulfilling prophecy, justified by a self-perpetuating system. 8

The more I learned, the more I realized that belief in great strength differences between women and men was itself part of the gender mind-game. In fact, we can't really know what those differences might be, because they are so enshrined, perpetuated, and exaggerated by culture. They seem to be greatest during the childbearing years (when men as a group have more speed and upper-body strength, and women have better balance, endurance, and flexibility) but only marginal during early childhood and old age (when females and males seem to have about the same degree of physical strength). Even during those middle years, the range of difference *among* men and *among* women is far greater than the generalized difference *between* males and females as groups. In multiracial societies like ours, where males of some races are smaller than females of others, judgments based on sex make even 9

Reading Critically

[5] How are women "owned"? How are their bodies "status symbols"?

[6] According to the author, what is the relationship between muscles and social class?

less sense. Yet we go right on assuming and praising female weakness and male strength.

But there is a problem about keeping women weak, even in a patriarchy. 10 Women are workers, as well as the means of reproduction. Lower-class women are especially likely to do hard physical labor. So the problem becomes: How to make sure female strength is used for work but not for rebellion? The answer is: Make women ashamed of it. Though hard work requires lower-class women to be stronger than their upper-class sisters, for example, those strong women are made to envy and imitate the weakness of women who "belong" to, and are the means of reproduction for, upper-class men—and so must be kept even *more* physically restricted if the lines of race and inheritance are to be kept "pure." That's why restrictive dress, from the chadors, or full-body veils, of the Middle East to metal ankle and neck rings in Africa, from nineteenth-century hoop skirts in Europe to corsets and high heels here, started among upper-class women and then sifted downward as poor women were encouraged to envy or imitate them. So did such bodily restrictions as bound feet in China, or clitoridectomies and infibulations in much of the Middle East and Africa, both of which practices began with women whose bodies were the means of reproduction for the powerful, and gradually became generalized symbols of femininity. ⓻ In this country, the self-starvation known as anorexia nervosa is mostly a white, upper-middle-class, young-female phenomenon, but all women are encouraged to envy a white and impossibly thin ideal.

Sexual politics are also reflected through differing emphases on the re- 11 productive parts of women's bodies. Whenever a patriarchy wants females to populate a new territory or replenish an old one, big breasts and hips become admirable. Think of the bosomy ideal of this country's frontier days, or the *zaftig,* Marilyn Monroe-type figure that became popular after the population losses of World War II. As soon as increased population wasn't desirable or necessary, hips and breasts were deemphasized. Think of the Twiggy look that arrived in the 1960s.

But whether bosomy or flat, *zaftig* or thin, the female ideal remains weak, 12 and it stays that way unless women ourselves organize to change it. Suffragists shed the unhealthy corsets that produced such a tiny-waisted, big-breasted look that fainting and smelling salts became routine. Instead, they brought in bloomers and bicycling. Feminists of today are struggling against social pressures that exalt siliconed breasts but otherwise stick-thin silhouettes. Introducing health and fitness has already led to a fashion industry effort to

---

Reading Critically

⓻ How are "bound feet" and "clitoridectomies" in other cultures symbols of femininity? Name some symbols of femininity in American culture today?

reintroduce weakness with the waif look, but at least it's being protested. The point is: Only when women rebel against patriarchal standards does female muscle become more accepted. [8]

For these very political reasons, I've gradually come to believe that society's acceptance of muscular women may be one of the most intimate, visceral measures of change. Yes, we need progress everywhere, but an increase in our physical strength could have more impact on the everyday lives of most women than the occasional role model in the boardroom or in the White House.   13

UNDERSTANDING DETAILS

1. According to Steinem, what is "gender politics" (paragraph 1)?
2. In what ways does Steinem equate "winning" with "being chosen" (paragraph 2)? Why is this an important premise for her essay?
3. What does Steinem mean when she says, "Oppression has no logic" (paragraph 8)? Explain your answer in detail.
4. In what ways does "power" lie with the observer rather than within the female?

THINKING CRITICALLY

5. Why does Steinem call the female body a "victim" body (paragraph 5)? What did girls' mothers have to do with this association?
6. Do you agree with the author that a woman's body is "far more subject to other people's rules than that of her male counterpart" (paragraph 7)? Explain your answer, giving examples from your own experience.
7. What is Steinem implying about the political overtones connected with female weakness and male strength? According to Steinem, why are these judgments so ingrained in American social and cultural mores?
8. What are Steinem's reasons for saying that "society's acceptance of muscular women may be one of the most intimate, visceral measures of change" (paragraph 13)? Do you agree with this statement or not? Explain your reaction in detail.

DISCOVERING RHETORICAL STRATEGIES

9. Who do you think is Steinem's intended audience for this essay? On what do you base your answer?
10. In your opinion, what is Steinem's primary purpose in this essay? Explain your answer in detail.

Reading Critically
[8] Why will female muscle become more accepted when women rebel against patriarchal standards? Do you agree with this assertion? Why or why not?

11. How appropriate is the title of this essay? What would be some possible alternate titles?

12. What rhetorical modes support the author's comparison/contrast? Give examples of each.

MAKING CONNECTIONS

13. To what extent would Erma Bombeck ("Grandma"), Mary Pipher ("Beliefs About Families"), and/or Barbara Ehrenreich ("The Ecstasy of War") agree with Gloria Steinem's assertion that "the most important thing about a female body is not what it does but how it looks" (paragraph 3)? Do you agree or disagree with this assertion? Give at least three reasons for your opinion.

14. If Steinem is correct that American women have not traditionally found power in their muscles, where have they found it? If you were able to ask Sandra Cisneros ("Only daughter") this same question, what do you think her response would be? With whom would you agree more? Explain your answer.

15. How would Lyn Mikel Brown and Meda Chesney-Lind ("Bad Girls, Bad Girls, Whatcha Gonna Do?") feel about the revolution Steinem describes in women's bodybuilding that is bringing renewed power and strength to women of all ages. To what extent might they see this trend as an antidote to the growing epidemic of "girlfighting"?

IDEAS FOR DISCUSSION/WRITING

Preparing to Write

Write freely about the definition and role of strength and weakness in American society: What does strength generally mean in American society? What does weakness mean? What associations do you have with both modes of behavior? Where do these associations come from? What are the political implications of these associations? The social implications? In what ways are strength and weakness basic to the value system in American culture?

Choosing a Topic

1. Compare two different approaches to the process of succeeding in a specific job or activity. Develop your own guidelines for making the comparison; then, write an essay for your fellow students about the similarities and differences you have observed between these two different approaches. Be sure to decide on a purpose and a point of view before you begin to write.

2. Interview your mother and your father about their views on physical strength in their separate family backgrounds. If you have grandparents or stepparents, interview them as well. Then compare and contrast these various influences in your life. Which of them are alike? Which are different? How have you personally dealt with these similarities and differences? Be sure to decide on a purpose and a point of view before you begin to write.

3. In her essay, Steinem argues that "an increase in our [women's] physical strength could have more impact on the everyday lives of most women than the occasional role model in the boardroom or in the White House" (paragraph 13). Do you agree with the author? Write an essay to be published in your hometown newspaper explaining your views on this issue.

4. Gloria Steinem organizes her comparison of males and females around the issue of "muscle." What other comparisons can be made between men and women? Visit both an online men's magazine and an online women's magazine, and examine the headings. Find an issue that is explored in both magazines, and write an essay that analyzes their similarities and differences. Following Steinem's example, organize your analysis around a single issue, and include your own perspective where appropriate.

Before beginning your essay, you might want to consult the checklists on page 311.

SUCHENG CHAN   (1941–   )

You're Short, Besides!

Sucheng Chan was born in the Peoples' Republic of China and emigrated to the United States in 1957 at the age of sixteen. Following a B.A. at Swarthmore College, an M.A. from the University of Hawaii, and a Ph.D. at the University of California, Berkeley, she held a number of prestigious academic positions, including Assistant Professor of History at Sonoma State University; Professor of History and Provost of Oakes College at the University of California, Santa Cruz; and Professor of Global Studies and Chair of Asian Studies at the University of California, Santa Barbara, where she is now a distinguished professor emeritus. Among her many influential books are *This Bittersweet Soil* (1986), *Asian Americans: An Interpretive History* (1990), *Entry Denied: Exclusion and the Chinese Community in America* (1991), *Peoples of Color in the American West* (1994), *Not Just Victims: Conversations With Cambodian Community Leaders in the United States* (2003), and *In Defense of Asian American Studies* (2005). Her advice to students using *The Prose Reader* is to "read as much good writing as you can, and be sure to read different genres of writing. That will help you pick up (often subconsciously) the sounds and rhythms of felicitous prose. Of course, writing classes also help." Chan currently lives in Santa Barbara, where she continues to publish books and articles in the field of Asian Studies.

Preparing to Read

The following essay, from *Making Space, Making Soul: Creative Perspectives by Women of Color,* edited by Gloria Anzalvúa (1990), gives us many valuable insights into the life of a handicapped person. In it, the author presents a resilient self-concept that had to be adjusted several times to cope with new circumstances.

Exploring Experience: As you prepare to read this essay, examine for a few minutes your own ideas about the handicapped: If you are handicapped, how would your life be different as an able-bodied person? If you are able-bodied, how would your life be different as a handicapped person? How physically independent could you be in either situation? Is physical independence important to you? In what ways? How dependent are you on others in your daily life? Does this dependence bother you in any way? To what extent are your goals in life influenced by your dependence on other people?

Learning Online: Visit the "Americans with Disabilities" Web site (http://www.ada.gov), and spend a few moments exploring some of the frequent issues people with disabilities face. When reading Sucheng Chan's article, consider the way she presents her experience and how she compares the differences in Asian and American perspectives.

W hen asked to write about being a physically handicapped Asian-   1
American woman, I considered it an insult. [1] After all, my accomplishments are many, yet I was not asked to write about any
of them. Is being handicapped the most salient feature about me? The fact
that it might be in the eyes of others made me decide to write the essay as
requested. I realized that the way I think about myself may differ considerably from the way others perceive me. And maybe that's what being physically handicapped is all about.

I was stricken simultaneously with pneumonia and polio at the age of   2
four. Uncertain whether I had polio of the lungs, seven of the eight doctors
who attended me—all practitioners of Western medicine—told my parents
they should not feel optimistic about my survival. A Chinese fortune teller
my mother consulted also gave a grim prognosis, but for an entirely different reason: I had been stricken because my name was offensive to the gods. [2]
My grandmother had named me "grandchild of wisdom," a name that the
fortune teller said was too presumptuous for a girl. So he advised my parents to change my name to "chaste virgin." All these pessimistic predictions
notwithstanding, I hung onto life, if only by a thread. For three years, my body
was periodically pierced with electric shocks as the muscles of my legs at-
rophied. Before my illness, I had been an active, rambunctious, precocious,
and very curious child. Being confined to bed was thus a mental agony as
great as my physical pain. Living in war-torn China, I received little medical attention; physical therapy was unheard of. But I was determined to
walk. So one day, when I was six or seven, I instructed my mother to set up
two rows of chairs to face each other so that I could use them as I would parallel bars. I attempted to walk by holding my body up and moving it forward
with my arms while dragging my legs along behind. Each time I fell, my
mother gasped, but I badgered her until she let me try again. After four non-
ambulatory years, I finally walked once more by pressing my hands against
my thighs so my knees wouldn't buckle.

My father had been away from home during most of those years because   3
of the war. When he returned, I had to confront the guilt he felt about my
condition. In many East Asian cultures, there is a strong folk belief that a
person's physical state in this life is a reflection of how morally or sinfully he
or she lived in previous lives. Furthermore, because of the tendency to view
the family as a single unit, it is believed that the fate of one member can be
caused by the behavior of another. Some of my father's relatives told him that

---

Reading Critically

[1] Why was Chan insulted when she was asked to write about being a "physically handicapped Asian-American woman"?

[2] How was Chan's name "offensive to the gods"?

my illness had doubtless been caused by the wild carousing he did in his youth. A well-meaning but somewhat simple man, my father believed them.

Throughout my childhood, he sometimes apologized to me for having to suffer retribution for his former bad behavior. This upset me; it was bad enough that I had to deal with the anguish of not being able to walk, but to have to assuage his guilt as well was a real burden! In other ways, my father was very good to me. He took me out often, carrying me on his shoulders or back, to give me fresh air and sunshine. He did this until I was too large and heavy for him to carry. And ever since I can remember, he has told me that I am pretty. ❸ 4

After getting over her anxieties about my constant falls, my mother decided to send me to school. I had already learned to read some words of Chinese at the age of three by asking my parents to teach me the sounds and meaning of various characters in the daily newspaper. But between the ages of four and eight, I received no education since just staying alive was a full-time job. Much to her chagrin, my mother found no school in Shanghai, where we lived at the time, which would accept me as a student. Finally, as a last resort, she approached the American School, which agreed to enroll me only if my family kept an *amah* (a servant who takes care of children) by my side at all times. The tuition at the school was twenty U.S. dollars per month—a huge sum of money during those years of runaway inflation in China—and payable only in U.S. dollars. My family afforded the high cost of tuition and the expense of employing a full-time *amah* for less than a year. 5

We left China as the Communist forces swept across the country in victory. We found an apartment in Hong Kong across the street from a school run by Seventh-Day Adventists. By that time I could walk a little, so the principal was persuaded to accept me. An *amah* now had to take care of me only during recess when my classmates might easily knock me over as they ran about the playground. 6

After a year and a half in Hong Kong, we moved to Malaysia, where my father's family had lived for four generations. There I learned to swim in the lovely warm waters of the tropics and fell in love with the sea. On land I was a cripple; in the ocean I could move with the grace of a fish. ❹ I liked the freedom of being in the water so much that many years later, when I was a graduate student in Hawaii, I became greatly enamored with a man just because he called me a "Polynesian water nymph." 7

As my overall health improved, my mother became less anxious about all aspects of my life. She did everything possible to enable me to lead as normal a life as possible. I remember how once some of her colleagues in the 8

Reading Critically

❸ Why was Chan pleased that her father told her often that she was pretty?

❹ Why did the author fall in love with the sea? Do you enjoy being around the sea? Why or why not?

high school where she taught criticized her for letting me wear short skirts. They felt my legs should not be exposed to public view. My mother's response was, "All girls her age wear short skirts, so why shouldn't she?"

The years in Malaysia were the happiest of my childhood, even though I 9 was constantly fending off children who ran after me calling, "*Baikah! Baikah!*" ("Cripple! Cripple!" in the Hokkien dialect commonly spoken in Malaysia). The taunts of children mattered little because I was a star pupil. I won one award after another for general scholarship as well as for art and public speaking. Whenever the school had important visitors, my teacher always called on me to recite in front of the class.

A significant event that marked me indelibly occurred when I was twelve. 10 That year my school held a music recital, and I was one of the students chosen to play the piano. I managed to get up the steps to the stage without any problem, but as I walked across the stage, I fell. Out of the audience, a voice said loudly and clearly, "Ayah! A *baikah* shouldn't be allowed to perform in public." I got up before anyone could get on stage to help me and, with tears streaming uncontrollably down my face, I rushed to the piano and began to play. Beethoven's "Für Elise" had never been played so fiendishly fast before or since, but I managed to finish the whole piece. That I managed to do so made me feel really strong. I never again feared ridicule. 5

In later years I was reminded of this experience from time to time. During 11 my fourth year as an assistant professor at the University of California at Berkeley, I won a distinguished teaching award. Some weeks later I ran into a former professor who congratulated me enthusiastically. But I said to him, "You know what? I became a distinguished teacher by *limping* across the stage of Dwinelle 155!" (Dwinelle 155 is a large, cold classroom that most colleagues of mine hate to teach in.) I was rude not because I lacked graciousness but because this man, who had told me that my dissertation was the finest piece of work he had read in fifteen years, had nevertheless advised me to eschew a teaching career.

"Why?" I asked. 12

"Your leg . . ." he responded. 13

"What about my leg?" I said, puzzled. 14

"Well, how would you feel standing in front of a large lecture class?" 15

"If it makes any difference, I want you to know I've won a number of 16 speech contests in my life, and I am not the least bit self-conscious about speaking in front of large audiences. . . . Look, why don't you write me a letter of recommendation to tell people how brilliant I am and let *me* worry about my leg!"

Reading Critically

5 How does finishing her piano solo give the author strength?

This incident is worth recounting only because it illustrates a dilemma that   17
handicapped persons face frequently: those who care about us sometimes
get so protective that they unwittingly limit our growth.[6] This former professor of mine had been one of my greatest supporters for two decades. Time
after time, he had written glowing letters of recommendation on my behalf. He had spoken as he did because he thought he had my best interests
at heart; he thought that if I got a desk job rather than one that required
me to be a visible, public person, I would be spared the misery of being
stared at.

Americans, for the most part, do not believe as Asians do that physically   18
handicapped persons are morally flawed. But they are equally inept at interacting with those of us who are not able-bodied. Cultural differences in the
perception and treatment of handicapped people are most clearly expressed
by adults.[7] Children, regardless of where they are, tend to be openly curious about people who do not look "normal." Adults in Asia have no hesita-
tion in asking visibly handicapped people what is wrong with them, often
expressing their sympathy with looks of pity, whereas adults in the United
States try desperately to be polite by pretending not to notice.

One interesting response I often elicited from people in Asia but have   19
never encountered in America is the attempt to link my physical condition
to the state of my soul. Many a time while living and traveling in Asia people would ask me what religion I belonged to. I would tell them that my
mother is a devout Buddhist, that my father was baptized a Catholic but has
never practiced Catholicism, and that I am an agnostic. Upon hearing this,
people would try strenuously to convert me to their religion so that
whichever God they believed in could bless me. If I would only attend this
church or that temple regularly, they urged, I would surely get cured.[8]
Catholics and Buddhists alike have pressed religious medallions into my
palm, telling me if I would wear these, the relevant deity or saint would make
me well. Once while visiting the tomb of Muhammad Ali Jinnah in Karachi,
Pakistan, an old Muslim, after finishing his evening prayers, spotted me, ges-
tured toward my legs, raised his arms heavenward, and began a new round
of prayers, apparently on my behalf.

In the United States adults who try to act "civilized" toward handicapped   20
people by pretending they don't notice anything unusual sometimes end up

---

Reading Critically

[6] In what way did Chan's professor "unwittingly limit" her growth?

[7] How do adults in Asia and America differ in their treatment of handicapped people?
Which approach is better in your opinion? Why?

[8] What is the relationship between religion and cure in these examples? Do you agree with
this relationship? Why or why not?

ignoring handicapped people completely. In the first few months I lived in this country, I was struck by the fact that whenever children asked me what was the matter with my leg, their adult companions would hurriedly shush them up, furtively look at me, mumble apologies, and rush their children away. After a few months of such encounters, I decided it was my responsibility to educate these people. So I would say to the flustered adults, "It's okay, let the kid ask." Turning to the child, I would say, "When I was a little girl, no bigger than you are, I became sick with something called polio. The muscles of my leg shrank up and I couldn't walk very well. You're much luckier than I am because now you can get a vaccine to make sure you never get my disease. So don't cry when your mommy takes you to get a polio vaccine, okay?" Some adults and their little companions I talked to this way were glad to be rescued from embarrassment; others thought I was strange.

Americans have another way of covering up their uneasiness: they become jovially patronizing. Sometimes when people spot my crutch, they ask if I've had a skiing accident. When I answer that unfortunately it is something less glamorous than that they say, "I bet you *could* ski if you put your mind to it!" Alternately, at parties where people dance, men who ask me to dance with them get almost belligerent when I decline their invitation. They say, "Of course you can dance if you *want* to!" Some have given me pep talks about how if I would only develop the right mental attitude, I would have more fun in life. [9]   21

Different cultural attitudes toward handicapped persons came out clearly during my wedding. My father-in-law, as solid a representative of middle America as could be found, had no qualms about objecting to the marriage on racial grounds, but he could bring himself to comment on my handicap only indirectly. He wondered why his son, who had dated numerous high school and college beauty queens, couldn't marry one of them instead of me. My mother-in-law, a devout Christian, did not share her husband's prejudices, but she worried aloud about whether I could have children. [10] Some Chinese friends of my parents, on the other hand, said that I was lucky to have found such a noble man, one who would marry me despite my handicap. I, for my part, appeared in church in a white lace wedding dress I had designed and made myself—a miniskirt!   22

How Asian Americans treat me with respect to my handicap tells me a great deal about their degree of acculturation. Recent immigrants behave just like Asians in Asia; those who have been here longer or who grew up in the   23

Reading Critically

[9] Why do some people say that the "right mental attitude" could help Chan have more fun in life?

[10] What is the difference in reactions to Chan by her mother-in-law and father-in-law?

United States behave more like their white counterparts. I have not encountered any distinctly Asian American pattern of response. What makes the experience of Asian American handicapped people unique is the duality of responses we elicit.

Regardless of racial or cultural background, most handicapped people have to learn to find a balance between the desire to attain physical independence and the need to take care of ourselves by not overtaxing our bodies. In my case. I've had to learn to accept the fact that leading an active life has its price. Between the ages of eight and eighteen. I walked without using crutches or braces, but the effort caused my right leg to become badly misaligned. Soon after I came to the United States, I had a series of operations to straighten out the bones of my right leg; afterwards, though my leg looked straighter and presumably better, I could no longer walk on my own. Initially my doctors fitted me with a brace, but I found wearing one cumbersome and soon gave it up. I could move around much more easily—and more important, faster—by using one crutch. One orthopedist after another warned me that using a single crutch was a bad practice. ⚓ They were right. Over the years my spine developed a double-S curve, and for the last twenty years I have suffered from severe, chronic back pains, which neither conventional physical therapy nor a lighter work load can eliminate.   24

The only thing that helps my backaches is a good massage, but the soothing effect lasts no more than a day or two. Massages are expensive, especially when one needs them three times a week. So I found a job that pays better, but at which I have to work longer hours, consequently increasing the physical strain on my body—a sort of vicious circle. When I was in my thirties, my doctors told me that if I kept leading the strenuous life I did, I would be in a wheelchair by the time I was forty. They were right on target: I bought myself a wheelchair when I was forty-one. But being the incorrigible character that I am, I use it only when I am *not* in a hurry!   25

It is a good thing, however, that I am too busy to think much about my handicap or my backaches because pain can physically debilitate as well as cause depression. And there are days when my spirits get rather low. What has helped me is realizing that being handicapped is akin to growing old at an accelerated rate. The contradiction I experience is that often my mind races along as though I'm only twenty while my body feels about sixty. But fifteen or twenty years hence, unlike my peers who will have to cope with aging for the first time, I shall be full of cheer because I will have already fought, and I hope won, that battle long ago.   26

Reading Critically

⚓ Why was using a single crutch a bad practice?

Beyond learning how to be physically independent and, for some of us, 27 living with chronic pain or other kinds of discomfort, the most difficult thing a handicapped person has to deal with, especially during puberty and early adulthood, is relating to potential sexual partners. Because American culture places so much emphasis on physical attractiveness, a person with a shriveled limb, or a tilt to the head, or the inability to speak clearly, experiences great uncertainty—indeed trauma—when interacting with someone to whom he or she is attracted. My problem was that I was not only physically handicapped, small, and short, but worse, I also wore glasses and was smarter than all the boys I knew! Alas, an insurmountable combination. 12 Yet somehow I have managed to have intimate relationships, all of them with extraordinary men. Not surprisingly, there have also been countless men who broke my heart—men who enjoyed my company "as a friend," but who never found the courage to date or make love with me, although I am sure my experience in this regard is no different from that of many able-bodied persons.

The day came when my backaches got in the way of having an active sex 28 life. Surprisingly, that development was liberating because I stopped worrying about being attractive to men. No matter how headstrong I had been, I, like most women of my generation, had had the desire to be alluring to men ingrained into me. And that longing had always worked like a brake on my behavior. When what men think of me ceased to be compelling, I gained greater freedom to be myself. 13

I've often wondered if I would have been a different person had I not 29 been physically handicapped. I really don't know, though there is no question that being handicapped has marked me. But at the same time I usually do not *feel* handicapped—and consequently, I do not *act* handicapped. People are therefore less likely to treat me as a handicapped person. There is no doubt, however, that the lives of my parents, sister, husband, other family members, and some close friends have been affected by my physical condition. They have had to learn not to hide me away at home, not to feel embarrassed by how I look or react to people who say silly things to me, and not to resent me for the extra demands my condition makes on them. Perhaps the hardest thing for those who live with handicapped people is to know when and how to offer help. There are no guidelines applicable to all situations. My advice is, when in doubt, ask, but ask in a way that does not

---

Reading Critically

12 How many "handicaps" does Chan have? Which do you think was the most difficult for her to cope with? Why?

13 How did Chan begin to gain greater freedom to be herself when she stopped worrying about what men thought of her?

smack of pity or embarrassment. Most important, please don't talk to us as though we are children.

So, has being physically handicapped been a handicap? It all depends on   30
one's attitude. Some years ago, I told a friend that I had once said to an affirmative action compliance officer (somewhat sardonically, since I do not believe in the head count approach to affirmative action) that the institution which employs me is triply lucky because it can count me as non-white, female and handicapped. He responded, "Why don't you tell them to count you four times? . . . Remember, you're short, besides!"

UNDERSTANDING DETAILS

1. What "folk belief" (paragraph 3) did Chan's family think might be the cause of her condition?
2. How was Chan finally able to walk after four years of not walking?
3. What specific event enabled the author to tolerate ridicule without fear?
4. In what ways have Chan's friends and family had to adjust to her condition?

THINKING CRITICALLY

5. What is Chan comparing in this essay? Explain three topics that she discusses in her comparison.
6. According to Chan, why do most handicapped people need to "find a balance between the desire to attain physical independence and the need to take care of ourselves by not overtaxing our bodies" (paragraph 24)? Explain your answer.
7. How does Chan plan to win the battle against aging before her peers take it on?
8. Why was giving up on sex a liberating experience for Chan? Explain your answer.

DISCOVERING RHETORICAL STRATEGIES

9. In what way does the background information Chan gives us in the first paragraph set up the entire essay? Explain your answer.
10. Who do you think is Chan's intended audience? On what evidence do you base your answer?
11. What is the author's attitude toward her subject in this essay? What details in the essay reveal this point of view?
12. Which rhetorical modes does Chan use to support her comparison? How effective are these choices in fulfilling her purpose?

MAKING CONNECTIONS

13. Imagine that Chan, Harold Krents ("Darkness at Noon"), and Alice Walker ("Beauty: When the Other Dancer Is the Self") are having a discussion about whether their physical disability has been a "handicap" to them. Which of these

authors do you think would feel least handicapped by his or her disability? Why?

14. Chan, Amy Tan ("Mother Tongue"), and William Ouchi ("Japanese and American Workers: Two Casts of Mind") all exhibit distinctive Eastern views of life. In what ways do these authors share similar philosophies? How are they different?

15. How do Chan's comparison/contrast techniques differ from those used by Gloria Steinem ("The Politics of Muscle")?

IDEAS FOR DISCUSSION/WRITING

Preparing to Write

Write freely about your own physical independence: If you are handicapped, how "independent" do you feel? If you are able bodied, are you aware of your physical independence? How much do you value your independence? In what ways is it a part of your identity? What would happen if your independence were threatened or taken away? How is physical independence related to your identity?

Choosing a Topic

1. In a magazine popular with your peers, explain some specific elements in your ideal life by comparing and contrasting them to those aspects in other people's lives. Is your ideal based on anyone's life in particular? In what way is he or she a role model for you? Does this person play an active role in helping you achieve your ideal existence?

2. Write a comparison essay explaining your attraction to the types of people you date or have married. Why do you like these people? What do your feelings about this type of person tell other people about you?

3. Discuss the concepts of independence and dependence by comparing these ideas to one another. Give examples to support your main points.

4. Select two Web sites that address either a specific disability or disabilities in general. First, identify their commonalities, and then compare the ways in which they are different. Write an essay comparing the two Web sites' approaches and perspectives toward disability. Following Chan's example, integrate your perspective into your examples.

Before beginning your essay, you might want to consult the checklists on page 311.

Chapter Writing Assignments

Practicing Comparison/Contrast

1. Compare one feature of your culture to the same aspect of someone else's culture. Make sure you are not making random or biased judgments, but are exploring similarities, differences, and their significance.

2. Compare the styles of two different writers in *The Prose Reader*. First, identify the major features of each writer's style. Then narrow your ideas to a few points of comparison. For example, perhaps one writer is serious and another funny; one writer may write long, complex sentences, while another writes mostly simple sentences. Discuss the effects each essay has on its readers based on these specific differences in style.

3. Discuss the major differences between two views of a political issue or between two political candidates. Identify the main sources of the differences, and then defend the point of view you believe is most reasonable.

Exploring a Theme

4. What does being "an individual" mean? How important is individualism to you personally? When might being an individual clash with the needs of society? Identify and discuss a situation in which individualism and the needs of society might conflict. If such a conflict occurs, which needs should prevail and why?

5. Identify a disturbing trend that you see in American society. Describe this trend in an essay, providing examples from your observations and experiences.

6. Think about a business or organization that is not what it appears to be. Then write an essay explaining the differences between the image this business or organization projects and the way it actually functions. Include specific examples to illustrate the differences between its image and the reality experienced by its customers or clients.

Analyzing Visual Images

Dave Beckerman Photography.

7. Based on the photo above, we can see that couples behave very differently. Compare a relationship you have had with a relationship you've
   seen, such as your parents' relationship or marriage, a previous relationship in which you were involved, or the relationship of someone else you
   know that seems very different from your own.

8. Look at the picture on page 301 at the beginning of the chapter. Do you
   think the woman in the photograph is holding up a picture of herself
   or someone else, possibly a daughter or sister? Explain your answer by
   discussing the different comparisons/contrasts you considered in order
   to reach your conclusion.?

Chapter 7

DEFINITION
Limiting the Frame of Reference

Definitions help us function smoothly in a complex world. All effective communication, in fact, is continuously dependent on our unique human ability to understand and employ accurate definitions of a wide range of words, phrases, and abstract ideas. If we did not work from a set of shared definitions, we would not be able to carry on coherent conversations, write comprehensible letters, or respond to even the simplest radio and television programs. Definitions help us understand basic concrete terms (such as automobiles, laser beams, and the gross national product), discuss various events in our lives (such as snowboarding, legal proceedings, and a Cinco de Mayo celebration), and grasp difficult abstract ideas (such as democracy, ambition, and resentment). The ability to comprehend definitions and use them effectively helps us keep our oral and written level of communication accurate and accessible to a wide variety of people.

DEFINING DEFINITION

Definition is the process of explaining a word, object, or idea in such a way that the reader (or listener) knows as precisely as possible what we mean. A good definition sets up intellectual boundaries by focusing on the special qualities of a word or phrase that set it apart from other similar words or phrases. Clear definitions always give the writer and the reader a mutual starting point on the sometimes bumpy road to successful communication.

Definitions vary from short, dictionary-length summaries to longer, "extended" accounts that determine the form of an entire essay. Words or ideas that require expanded definitions are usually abstract, complex, or unavoidably controversial; they generally bear many related meanings or many shades of meaning. Definitions can be *objective* (technically precise and generally dry) or *subjective* (colored with personal opinion), and they can be used to instruct, to entertain, or to accomplish a combination of these two fundamental rhetorical goals.

In the following paragraph, a student defines "childhood" by putting it into perspective with other important stages of life. Though mostly entertaining, the paragraph is also instructive as the student objectively captures the essence of this phase of human development:

> *Childhood is a stage of growth somewhere between infancy and adolescence. Just as each developmental period in our lives brings new changes and concerns, childhood serves as the threshold to puberty—the time we learn to discriminate between good and bad, right and wrong, love and lust. Childhood is neither a time of irresponsible infancy nor responsible adulthood. Rather, it is marked by duties that we don't really want, challenges that excite us, feelings that puzzle and frighten us, and limitless opportunities that help us explore the world around us. Childhood is a time when we solidify our personalities in spite of pressures to be someone else.*

THINKING CRITICALLY THROUGH DEFINITION

- Focus on single words and word associations.
- Explain abstract concepts.
- Find meaning in your definitions.

Definitions are building blocks in communication that help us make certain we are functioning from the same understanding of terms and ideas. They give us a foundation to work from in both reading and writing. Definitions force us to think about meanings and word associations that make other logical strategies stronger and easier to work with.

The process of thinking through our definitions forces us to come to some understanding about a particular term or concept we are mentally wrestling with. Articulating that definition helps us move to other modes of thought and higher levels of understanding. Practicing definitions in isolation to get a feel for them is much like separating the skill of pedaling from the process of riding a bike. The better you get at pedaling, the more natural the rest of the cycling process becomes. The following exercises ask you to practice definitions in a number of different ways. Being more conscious of what definition entails will make it more useful to you in both your reading and your writing.

Mel Curtis/Getty Images—Photodisc.

1. What does the ring in this photograph mean? Identify at least three ways in which people could define this ring. Write your definitions as precisely as possible, and share one with your class.
2. Define in one or two sentences one of the concrete words and one of the abstract words listed here.
    Concrete: *cattle, book, ranch, water, gum*
    Abstract: *freedom, progress, equality, fairness, boredom*
    What were some of the differences between the process you went through to explain the concrete word and the abstract word? What can you conclude from this brief exercise about the differences in defining abstract and concrete words?
3. Define the word *grammar*. Consult a dictionary, several handbooks, and maybe even some friends to get their views on the word's meaning. Then write a humorous definition of *grammar* that consolidates all these views into a single definition.

Reading and Writing Definition Essays

Extended definitions, which may range from two or three paragraphs to an entire essay, seldom follow a set pattern of development or organization. Instead, as you will see from the examples in this chapter, they draw on a number of different techniques to help explain a word, object, term, concept, or phenomenon.

READING DEFINITION ESSAYS

Thinking

Reading   Writing

- What is the essay's context?
- How is the definition introduced?
- Is the essay objective or subjective?
- What other rhetorical modes support the definition?

Preparing to Read.   As you begin to read each of the definition essays in this chapter, take some time to consider the author's title and the synopsis of the essay in the Rhetorical Table of Contents: What do you sense is the general mood of Mary Pipher's "Beliefs About Families"? What do you think Stephen Jay Gould's attitude is in "Dorothy, It's Really Oz"? How much can you learn about Lyn Mikel Brown and Meda Chesney-Lind's topic from their title, "Bad Girls, Bad Girls, Watcha Gonna Do?"

Equally important as you prepare to read is scanning an essay and finding information from its prefatory material about the author and the circumstances surrounding the composition of the essay. What can you learn about Erma Bombeck and the role of grandmothers in our lives? And what do you think is Robert Ramirez's purpose in his definition of the barrio?

Last, as you prepare to read these essays, answer the prereading questions before each essay, and then spend a few minutes thinking freely about the general subject of the essay at hand: What do you want to know from Pipher about families? What role does religion or science play in your life (Gould)? What interests you about aggressive behavior in others (Brown and Chesney-Lind)?

Reading.   As you read a definition essay, as with all essays, be sure to record your initial reactions to your reading material. What are some of your thoughts or associations in relation to each essay?

As you get more involved in the essay, reconsider the preliminary material so you can create a context within which to analyze what the writer is saying: What is Bombeck's purpose in writing "Grandma"? Does her tone effectively support that purpose? Who do you think is Ramirez's primary audience? Do you think his essay will effectively reach that group of people? In what ways is Gould qualified to write about science and religion?

Throughout each essay in this chapter are provocative questions at the bottom of the pages meant to guide you to analysis and critical thinking. These questions ask you to consider the authors' ideas as they relate to one another and to your own experience. Your responses to these questions will then give you thoughtful material to work with on the tasks after each essay. So these questions essentially bridge the gap between the prereading questions and the activities after each essay. Writing down your thoughts will be especially beneficial to you as you gather your own ideas together in response to a writing assignment.

Finally, determine at this point whether the author's treatment of his or her subject is predominantly objective or subjective. Then, make sure you understand the main points of the essay on the literal, interpretive, and analytical levels by reading the questions that follow.

Rereading.   When you read these definition essays for a second time, check to see how each writer actually sets forth his or her definition: Does the writer put each item in a specific category with clear boundaries? Do you understand how the item being defined is different from other items in the same category? Did the author name the various components of the item, explain its etymology (linguistic origin and history), discuss what it is not, or perform a combination of these tasks?

To evaluate the effectiveness of a definition essay, you need to reconsider the essay's primary purpose and audience. If Bombeck is trying to get the general reader to understand the vital role of a grandmother in a typical family, how effective is she? In like manner, is Pipher successful in communicating to the same audience the value of the family unit?

Especially applicable is the question of what other rhetorical strategies help the author communicate this purpose. What other modes does Ramirez use to help him define the barrio? Through what other modes do Brown and Chesney-Lind define "bad girls"?

For an inventory of the reading process, you can review the guidelines on page 29 of the Introduction.

WRITING DEFINITION ESSAYS

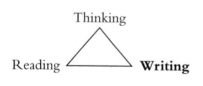

Thinking

Reading — Writing

- Compose a thesis statement.
- Approach the definition creatively.
- Define the word or concept.
- Use other rhetorical strategies to support your definition.

Preparing to Write.   As with other essays, you should begin the task of writing a definition essay by answering the prewriting questions featured in this text and then by exploring your subject and generating other ideas. (See the explanation of various prewriting techniques on pages 19–21 of the Introduction.) Be sure you know what you are going to define and how you will approach your definition. You should then focus on a specific audience and purpose as you approach your writing assignment.

Writing.   The next step toward developing a definition essay is usually to describe the general category to which the word belongs and then to contrast the word with all other words in that group. To define *exposition,* for example, you might say that it is a type of writing. Then, to differentiate it from other types of writing, you could go on to say that its main purpose is to "expose," or present information, as opposed to rhetorical modes such as description and narration, which describe and tell stories. In addition, you might want to cite some expository methods, such as example, process analysis, division/classification, and comparison/contrast.

Yet another way to begin a definition essay is to provide a term's etymology. Tracing a word's origin often illuminates its current meaning and usage as well. *Exposition,* for example, comes from the Latin *exponere,* meaning "to put forth, set forth, display, declare, or publish" (*ex* = out; *ponere* = to put or place). This information can generally be found in any good dictionary or encyclopedia.

Another approach to defining a term is to explain what it does *not* mean. For example, *exposition* is not creative writing. By limiting the readers' frame of reference in these various ways, you are helping to establish a working definition for the term under consideration.

Finally, rhetorical methods that we have already studied, such as description, narration, example, process analysis, division/classification, and comparison/contrast, are particularly useful to writers in expanding their definitions. To clarify the term *exposition,* you might **describe** the details of an expository theme, **narrate** a story about the wide use of the term in today's classroom, or **give examples** of assignments that would produce good expository writing. In other situations, you could **analyze** various writing assignments and discuss the **process** of producing an expository essay, **classify** exposition apart from creative writing and then **divide** it into categories similar to the headings of this book, or **compare** and **contrast** it with creative writing. Writers also use definition quite often to support other rhetorical modes.

Rewriting.   Reviewing and revising a definition essay is a relatively straightforward task:

- Have you chosen an effective beginning for your paper?
- Did you create a reasonable context for your definition?
- Have you used appropriate rhetorical strategies to develop your ideas?
- Have you achieved your overall purpose as effectively as possible?

Other guidelines to direct your writing and revising appear on page 30 of the Introduction.

STUDENT ESSAY: DEFINITION AT WORK

In the following essay, a student defines "the perfect yuppie." Notice how the writer puts this term in a category and then explains the limits of that category and the uniqueness of this term within the category. To further inform her audience about the features of "yuppiedom," the student calls on the word's etymology, its dictionary definition, an itemization of the term's basic characteristics, a number of examples that explain those characteristics, and, finally, a general discussion of causes and effects that regulate a yuppie's behavior.

The Perfect Yuppie

Many people already know that the letters YUP stand for "young urban professional." *Young* in this context is understood to mean fortyish; *urban* often means suburban; and *professional* means most definitely college-educated. Double the *P* and add an *I* and an *E* at the end, and you get *yuppie*—that 1980s' bourgeois, the marketers' darling, and the 1960s' inheritance. But let's not generalize. Not every forty-year-old suburban college graduate qualifies as a yuppie. Nor is every yuppie in his or her forties. True yuppiness involves much more than the words that make up the acronym. Being the little sister of a couple of yups, I am in an especially good position to define the perfect yuppie. I watched two develop.

The essence of yuppiness is generally new money. In the yuppie's defense, I will admit that most yuppies have worked hard for their money and social status. Moreover, the baby boom of which they are a part has caused a glut of job seekers in their age bracket, forcing them to be competitive if they want all the nice things retailers have designed for them. But with

Margin annotations:
- Etymology/ dictionary definition
- General category of word being defined
- Subject
- Limitations set
- Why the dictionary definition is inadequate
- Writer's credibility
- General characteristic
- Cause/ Effect

General charac-teristic new money comes <u>an interesting combination of wealth, naiveté, and pretentiousness</u>.

Specific example For example, most yuppies worthy of the title have long ago <u>traded in their fringed suede jackets for fancy fur coats</u>. Although they were animal rights activists in the 1960s, they will not notice the irony of this change. In fact, they may be shameless enough to <u>parade in their fur coats—fashion-show style—for friends and family</u>. Because of their "innocence," yuppies generally will not see the vulgarity of their actions.   Cause/ Effect   Specific example

General charac-teristic Because they are often quite wealthy, yuppies <u>tend to have a lot of "things."</u> They are simply overwhelmed by the responsibility of spending all that money. For example, <u>one yup I know has fourteen pairs of sunglasses and seven watches</u>. She, her husband, and their three children own at least <u>twenty collections of everything from comic books to Civil War memorabilia</u>. Most yuppies have so much money that I often wonder why the word "yuppie" does not have a dollar sign in it somewhere.   Specific example   Specific example

General charac-teristic Perhaps in an effort to rid themselves of this financial burden, <u>all good yuppies go to Europe</u> as soon as possible. Not Germany or France or Portugal, mind you, but Europe. They do not know what they are doing there and thus generally spend much more money than they need to—but, after all, no yuppie ever claimed to be frugal. Most important, they <u>bring home slides of Europe and show them</u> to everyone they know. A really good yuppie will forget and show you his or her slides more than once. Incidentally, when everyone has seen the slides of Europe twice, the yuppie's next stop is Australia.   Cause/ Effect   Cause/ Effect

General charac-teristic A favorite pastime of yuppies is having <u>wine-tasting parties</u> for their yuppie friends. At these parties, they must <u>make a great to-do about tasting the wine</u>, cupping their faces over the glass with their palms (as if they were having a facial), and even sniffing the cork, for goodness sake. I once knew a yuppie who <u>did not understand that a bottle of wine could not be rejected simply because he found he "did not like that kind."</u> <u>Another enjoyed making a show of having his wife</u>   Specific example   Specific example

Specific example

What it is not — choose and taste the wine occasionally, which they both thought was adorable.

Some yuppie wanna-bes drive red or black BMWs, but don't let them fool you. A genuine, hard-core yuppie will usually own a gold or silver Volvo station wagon. *[General characteristic]* In this yuppie-mobile, the yuppie wife will chauffeur her young yupettes to and from their mod-

Specific examples — eling classes, track meets, ballet, the manicurist, and boy scouts, for the young yuppie is generally as com- *[Cause/Effect]* petitive and socially active as his or her parents. On the same topic, one particularly annoying trait of yuppie parents is bragging about their yupettes. You will

General characteristic — know yuppies by the fact that they have the smartest, most talented children in the world. They will show you their kids' report cards, making sure you notice *[Specific example]* any improvements from last quarter.

Perhaps I have been harsh in my portrayal of the perfect yuppie, and, certainly, I will be accused by some

Division/ Classification — of stereotyping. But consider this: I never classify peo- *[General characteristic and concluding statement]* ple as yuppies who do not so classify themselves. The ultimate criterion for being yuppies is that they will always proudly label themselves as such.

Student Writer's Comments

The most difficult part about writing this definition essay was choosing a topic. I knew it had to be a word or phrase with different shades of meaning, but it also had to be either something I knew more about than the average person or something I had an unusual perspective on. I figured *yuppie* was a good word, not only because it has different meanings for different people, but also because it is an acronym, and acronyms tend to be greater than the sum of their parts.

I started by looking the word up in the dictionary and writing down its etymology (which I later referred to in my opening sentence). I then used freewriting to record the various meanings and natural associations I have with the word *yuppie,* which helped me discover relationships between these meanings and associations. I felt my mind wandering freely over all aspects of this word as I filled up pages and pages of freewriting. I then felt as if I had enough material to work with, so I began to write a draft of my essay.

I started writing the essay from the beginning, a process that was a real novelty for me. After citing the etymology of my word and placing it in a general category, I explained why the dictionary definition was inadequate. Then,

I let the general characteristics I associate with the word take me step by step through the essay. As I wrote, I found myself mentally reorganizing my prewriting notes so that I could stay slightly ahead of my actual writing. I kept looping back and forth into my notes, looking for the next best characters to introduce, then writing, then going back to my notes again. I generated my entire first draft this way and revised the order only slightly in my final draft.

As I reworked my essay before handing it in, I added some humor from my own experience with my older sisters and looked closely at other rhetorical modes I had used to support my definition. Naturally, I had scattered examples throughout my essay and had discussed causes and effects quite openly. I revised my paper to make some of the connections I had in mind clearer by either adding transitions or explaining the relationships in other words. I found that this process lengthened my essay quite a bit as I revised. I also worked on the essay at this point to bring out a secondary point I had in mind, which is that some yuppies have lost the 1960s values they once had but often don't even realize it.

I spent the remainder of my time on my conclusion, which I rewrote from scratch four times. I finally ended up directly addressing the classification of yuppies, at which point I stumbled on the ultimate criterion for being a yuppy: "They will always proudly label themselves as such." When I reached this insight, I knew my paper was finished, and I was content with the results. I also realized that rewriting the conclusion so many times had given me a headache, but the pain was worth it.

SOME FINAL THOUGHTS ON DEFINITION

The following selections feature extended definitions whose main purpose is to explain a specific term or idea to their readers. Each essay in its own way helps its audience identify with various parts of the definitions, and each successfully communicates the unique qualities of the term or idea in question. Notice what approaches to definition each writer takes and how these approaches limit the readers' frame of reference in the process of effective communication.

DEFINITION IN REVIEW

Reading Definition Essays

Preparing to Read

✓ What assumptions can you make from the essay's title?

✓ Can you guess what the general mood of the essay is?

✓ What is the essay's purpose and audience?

✓ What does the synopsis tell you about the essay?

✓ What can you learn from the author's biography?

✓ Can you predict the author's point of view toward the subject is?

Reading

✓ What is the essay's context?

✓ How is the definition introduced?

✓ Is the essay objective or subjective?

✓ What other rhetorical modes support the thesis?

Rereading

✓ How does the author lay out the definition?

✓ What is the essay's main purpose and audience?

✓ What other rhetorical strategies does the author use?

Writing Definition Essays

Preparing to Write

✓ Do you know what you are going to define and how you will approach your topic?

✓ Who is your audience?

Writing

✓ Did you compose a thesis statement?

✓ Does the beginning of your essay suit your purpose?

✓ Do you use effective strategies to define your word or concept effectively?

✓ What rhetorical strategies do you use to expand your definition essay?

Rewriting

✓ Have you chosen an effective beginning for your paper?

✓ Did you create a reasonable context for your definition?

✓ Have you used appropriate rhetorical strategies to develop your ideas?

✓ Have you achieved your overall purpose as effectively as possible?

ERMA BOMBECK   (1927–1996)

Grandma

One of our country's best-loved humorists, Erma Bombeck made a brilliant career out of satirizing the trials of the American housewife. Born in Dayton, Ohio, she was intrigued by journalism at an early age, working part-time for the *Dayton Journal Herald* while she was in high school and college. After graduating from the University of Dayton with a degree in English, she became a full-time staff writer for the newspaper. Bombeck then took off twelve years to raise her three children, returning to journalism in 1965 to write a humorous column for homemakers, for which she was originally paid three dollars per column. Later syndicated under the title "At Wit's End," it was carried by over seven-hundred newspapers prior to her death in 1996 from kidney disease. Most of her books are extensions of her column, including such classics as *Just Wait Till You Have Children of Your Own* (1971), *I Lost Everything in the Post-Nasal Depression* (1973), *The Grass Is Always Greener Over the Septic Tank* (1976), *If Life Is a Bowl of Cherries, What Am I Doing in the Pits* (1978), *Motherhood: The Second Oldest Profession* (1983), and *Family: The Ties That Bind . . . and Gag!* (1987). For over three decades, she did all her columns on an old IBM Selectric. "I tried to write on a computer for a while," she explained, "but it didn't write funny. Maybe you have to pay more." *Forever, Erma* (1996), released eight months after the author's death, is a collection of two hundred of her most loved columns.

Preparing to Read

The following nostalgic essay, originally published in *At Wit's End,* attempts to define grandmothers. Bombeck supports her definition with stories, examples, comparisons, and a discussion of causes and effects that helps us understand the valuable role of grandmothers in our lives.

Exploring Experience: As you prepare to read this essay, pause a few moments to think about any associations you make with the word *grandmother:* Do you have a good relationship with your grandmothers? What special qualities characterize those relationships? How close are you to your grandparents? How did you develop your relationship with them? What have you learned about your parents from them? What do you think your kids will learn about you from your parents? If you have children, what have they already learned about you from your parents?

Learning Online: Visit the Erma Bombeck Museum online to become acquainted with the life of Erma Bombeck (http://www. ermamuseum.org).

grandma (grand/ma), n.   The mother of one's father or mother.

The role of a grandmother has never been really defined. Some sit in 1
rockers, some sky dive, some have careers. Others clean ovens. Some
have white hair. Others wear wigs. Some see their grandchildren once
a day (and it's not enough). Others, once a year (and that's too much). ❶

Once I conducted an interesting survey among a group of eight-year- 2
olds on grandmas. I asked them three questions. One, what is a grandmother?
Two, what does she do? And three, what is the difference between a grandmother and a mother?

To the first question, the answers were rather predictable. "She's old (about 3
eighty), helps around the house, is nice and kind, and is Mother's mother or
Father's mother, depending on the one who is around the most."

To the second question, the answers again were rather obvious. Most of 4
them noted grandmothers knit, do dishes, clean the bathroom, make good
pies; and a goodly number reveled in the fact that Grandma polished their
shoes for them.

It was the third question that stimulated the most reaction from them. Here 5
is their composite of the differences between a mother and a grandmother.
"Grandma has gray hair, lives alone, takes me places, and lets me go into her
attic. She can't swim. Grandma doesn't spank you and stops Mother when
she does. Mothers scold better and more. Mothers are married. Grandmas
aren't.

"Grandma goes to work and my mother doesn't do anything. Mom gives 6
me shots, but Grandma gives me frogs. Grandma lives far away. A mother
you're born from. A grandmother gets married to a grandfather first, a mother
to a father last.

"Grandma always says, 'Stay in, it's cold outside,' and my mother says, 'Go 7
out, it's good for you.'" ❷

And here's the clincher. Out of thirty-nine children queried, a total of 8
thirty-three associated the word "love" with Grandma. One summed up the
total very well with, "Grandma loves me all the time."

Actually this doesn't surprise me one small bit. On rare occasions when 9
I have had my mother baby-sit for me, it often takes a snake whip and a
chair to restore discipline when I get them home.

"Grandma sure is a neat sitter," they yawn openly at the breakfast table. 10
"We had pizza and cola and caramel popcorn. Then we watched Lola Brook-
lynbridgida on the late show. After that we played Monopoly till you came

---

Reading Critically

❶ Which of the types of grandmothers described by Bombeck is most like yours?
❷ According to the author, what is the difference between the ways in which mothers and
grandmothers deal with children?

home. She said when you were a kid you never went to bed. One night you even heard them play 'The Star-Spangled Banner' before the station went off."

"Did Grandma tell you I was twenty-eight at the time?" I snapped. 11

"Grandma said twenty-five cents a week isn't very much money for an al- 12 lowance. She said we could make more by running away and joining the Peace Corps. She said you used to blow that much a week on jawbreakers."

"Well, actually," I said grimacing, "Grandma's memory isn't as good as it 13 used to be. She was quite strict, and as I recall my income was more like ten cents a week, and I bought all my own school clothes with it."

"Grandma sure is neat all right. She told us you hid our skateboard be- 14 hind the hats in your closet. She said that was dirty pool. What's dirty pool, Mama?"

"It's Grandma telling her grandchildren where their mother hid the skate- 15 board."

"Mama, did you really give a live chicken to one of your teachers on class 16 day? And did you really play barbershop once and cut off Aunt Thelma's hair for real? Boy, you're neat!" They looked at me in a way I had never seen before.

Naturally I brought Mother to task for her indiscretion. "Grandma," I 17 said, "you have a forked tongue and a rotten memory. You've got my kids believing I'm 'neat.' Now I ask you, what kind of an image is that for a mother?"

"The same image your grandmother gave me," she said. ❸ 18

Then I remembered Grandma. What a character. 19

In fact, I never see a Japanese war picture depicting kamikaze pilots stand- 20 ing erect in their helmets and goggles, their white scarfs flying behind them, toasting their last hour on earth with a glass of sake, that I don't think of riding to town with my grandma on Saturdays.

We would climb into her red and yellow Chevy coupe and jerk in first 21 gear over to the streetcar loop, where Grandma would take her place in line between the trolley cars. Due to the rigorous concentration it took to stay on the tracks and the innumerable stops we had to make, conversation was kept to a minimum. A few times a rattled shopper would tap on the window for entrance, to which Grandma would shout angrily, "If I wanted passengers, I'd dingle a bell!"

Once, when I dared to ask why we didn't travel in the same flow of traf- 22 fic as the other cars, Grandma shot back, "Laws, child, you could get killed out there." Our first stop in town was always a tire center. I could never figure this out. We'd park in the "For Customers Only" lot, and Grandma would walk through the cool building. She'd kick a few tires, but she never

---

Reading Critically

❸ Why shouldn't kids think their parents are "neat"?

purchased one. One day she explained, "The day I gain a new tire is the day I lose the best free parking spot a woman ever had."

I don't have Grandma's guts in the traffic or her cunning. But I thought 23 about her the other day as I sat bumper to bumper in the hot downtown traffic. "Hey, lady," yelled a voice from the next car, "wanta get in our pool? Only cost a quarter. We're putting odds on the exact minute your radiator is going to blow. You can have your choice of two minutes or fifteen seconds." Boy, Grandma would have shut his sassy mouth in a hurry.

We had an understanding, Grandma and I. She didn't treat me like a child, 24 and I didn't treat her like a mother. We played the game by rules. If I didn't slam her doors and sass, then she didn't spank and lecture me. Grandma treated me like a person already grown up.

She let me bake cookies with dirty hands . . . pound on the piano just be- 25 cause I wanted to . . . pick the tomatoes when they were green . . . use her clothespins to dig in the yard . . . pick her flowers to make a necklace chain. Grandma lived in a "fun" house. 4 The rooms were so big you could skate in them. There were a hundred thousand steps to play upon, a big eave that invited cool summer breezes and where you could remain "lost" for hours. And around it all was a black, iron fence.

I liked Grandma the best, though, when she told me about my mama, be- 26 cause it was a part of Mama I had never seen or been close to. I didn't know that when Mama was a little girl a photographer came one day to take a picture of her and her sister in a pony cart. I couldn't imagine they had to bribe them into good behavior by giving them each a coin. In the picture Mama is crying and biting her coin in half. It was a dime, and she wanted the bigger coin—the nickel—given to her sister. Somehow, I thought Mama was born knowing the difference between a nickel and a dime.

Grandma told me Mama was once caught by the principal for writing in 27 the front of her book, "In Case of Fire, Throw This in First." I had never had so much respect for Mama as the day I heard this.

From Grandma I learned that Mama had been a child and had traveled 28 the same route I was traveling now. I thought Mom was "neat." (And what kind of an image is that for a mother?) 5

If I had it to do all over again, I would never return to Grandma's house 29 after she had left it. No one should. For that grand, spacious house tended to shrink with the years. 6 Those wonderful steps that I played upon for

---

Reading Critically

4 Why is each of these activities enjoyable? What did you like to do for fun when you were a child?

5 What important insight does Bombeck learn from her mother?

6 To what extent do all our memories "shrink with the years"? Why do you think this happens?

hours were broken down and rather pathetic. There was a sadness to the tangled vines, the peeling paint, and the iron fence that listed under the burden of time. The big eave was an architectural "elephant" and would mercifully crumble under the ax of urban renewal.

Grandmas defy description. They really do. They occupy such a unique   30
place in the life of a child. They can shed the yoke of responsibility, relax, and enjoy their grandchildren in a way that was not possible when they were raising their own children. And they can glow in the realization that here is their seed of life that will harvest generations to come.

UNDERSTANDING DETAILS

1. What three questions did Bombeck ask on her survey about grandmothers?
2. Summarize the answers she received to the first two questions on the survey.
3. Analyze the answers to question 3 in Bombeck's survey, and explain the main difference in the answers between mothers and grandmothers.
4. How does each generation in Bombeck's family learn that their mothers were actually normal kids when growing up?

THINKING CRITICALLY

5. Why do you think one child from the survey said, "Grandma loves me all the time" (paragraph 8)?
6. How did the stories Bombeck's mother told her children make the kids believe their mom was really "neat"? How did they develop a new appreciation for her?
7. Why was returning to Grandma's house not a good idea for Bombeck?
8. What does Bombeck mean when she says, "Grandmas defy description" (paragraph 30)?

DISCOVERING RHETORICAL STRATEGIES

9. Several details in this essay give us clues about when it was written. What specific information helps you guess the approximate date of this essay? What do you think that date is?
10. How does Bombeck organize her essay? How does she introduce each new generation?
11. What is the tone of this essay? What details bring you to this decision?
12. What rhetorical strategies, besides definition, does Bombeck use in this essay? Give examples of each strategy.

MAKING CONNECTIONS

13. Compare and contrast the view of older people offered by Bombeck, Malcolm Cowley ("The View from 80"), Sandra Cisneros ("Only daughter"), and/or Amy Tan ("Mother Tongue"). Which of these authors seems to depict seniors

in the most favorable way? Which the least? How do you account for this difference in perspectives?

14. How do Bombeck, Mary Pipher ("Beliefs About Families"), and/or Robert Ramirez ("The Barrio") differ in the ways they define the subject of their essays. Which definition seems most clear to you? Why?

15. Imagine that Bombeck, Gloria Steinem ("The Politics of Muscle"), Mary Roach ("Meet the Bickersons"), and/or Lyn Mikel Brown and Meda Chesney-Lind ("Bad Girls, Bad Girls, Whatcha Gonna Do?") were having a discussion about the role of women in today's society. Which author would probably adopt the most traditional view? Which the most *avant-garde?* With which of these writers would you most likely agree? Explain your answer.

IDEAS FOR DISCUSSION/WRITING

Preparing to Write

Write freely about the different relationships in your family: What special qualities characterize each of these family members? Whom do you like the best? How many different roles do you play in your family (i.e., father/mother, son/daughter, brother/sister, husband/wife)? Which of these roles do you like best? Why? What makes some of your relationships with family members better than others? To what extent are you able to control these relationships?

Choosing a Topic

1. In a humorous and coherent essay written for your classmates, define a relative other than a grandmother. What special qualities characterize this relative in most families? Why are these qualities prominent in this particular relative?

2. You play many roles in relation to the members of your family. You are a son or daughter, and also perhaps an aunt, uncle, cousin, parent, or nephew. What is your favorite role in your family? Why is it your favorite? Do you think your opinion about this role will change over time? Why or why not?

3. Choose one of the definitional techniques explained in the introduction to this chapter, and define the word *family* in a well-developed, logically organized essay written for the general public. Introduce your main topic at the beginning of your essay; then explain and illustrate it clearly as your essay progresses. You may use other definition techniques in addition to your main choice.

4. Write an e-mail to a family member, mentor, or close friend. Define the role the person plays or has played in your life. Using Bombeck's style, start with a general definition/description of the role and then shift to a more personal definition of the person's importance in your life. Strengthen your definition by using descriptive examples.

Before beginning your essay, you might want to consult the checklists on page 364.

ROBERT RAMIREZ   (1949–   )

The Barrio

Robert Ramirez was born and raised in Edinburg, a southern Texas town near the Mexican border in an area that has been home to his family for almost two hundred years. After graduating from the University of Texas–Pan American, he taught freshman composition and worked for a while as a photographer. For the next several years, he was a salesman, reporter, and announcer/anchor for the CBS affiliate station KGBT-TV in Harlingen, Texas. His current job has brought him full circle, back to the University of Texas–Pan American, where he serves as a development officer responsible for alumni fundraising. He loves baseball and once considered a professional career, but he now contents himself with bike riding, swimming, and playing tennis. A conversion to the Baha'i faith in the 1970s has brought him much spiritual happiness. When asked to give advice to students using *The Prose Reader,* Ramirez responded, "The best writing, like anything else of value, requires a great deal of effort. Rewriting is 90 percent of the process. Sometimes, if you are fortunate, your work can take on a life of its own, and you end up writing something important that astounds and humbles you. This is what happened with 'The Barrio,' which is much better than the essay I originally intended. There's an element of the divine in it, as there is in all good writing."

Preparing to Read

First titled "The Woolen Sarape," Ramirez's essay was written while he was a student at the University of Texas-Pan American. His professor, Edward Simmens, published it in an anthology entitled *Pain and Promise: The Chicano Today* (1972). In it, the author defines the exciting, colorful, and close-knit atmosphere typical of many Hispanic barrios or communities.

Exploring Experience: As you prepare to read this essay, take a few moments to think about a place that is very special to you: What are its physical characteristics? What memories are connected to this place for you? What kinds of people live there? What is the relationship of these people to each other? To people in other places? Why is this place so special to you? Is it special to anyone else?

Learning Online: Gain a stronger perspective on Robert Ramirez's definition of home by visiting the Web site for the PBS series "American Family" (http://www.pbs.org/americanfamily/). Click on the link for "Cisco's Journal" to see an artistic interpretation of life in the *barrio.*

The train, its metal wheels squealing as they spin along the silvery   1
tracks, rolls slower now. Through the gaps between the cars blinks a
streetlamp, and this pulsing light on a barrio street corner beats slower,
like a weary heartbeat, until the train shudders to a halt, the light goes out,
and the barrio is deep asleep.

Throughout Aztlán (the Nahuatl term meaning "land to the north"),   2
trains grumble along the edges of a sleeping people. From Lower California,
through the blistering Southwest, down the Rio Grande to the muddy Gulf,
the darkness and mystery of dreams ◆ engulf communities fenced off by
railroads, canals, and expressways. Paradoxical communities, isolated from the
rest of the town by concrete columned monuments of progress, and yet
stranded in the past. They are surrounded by change. It eludes their reach,
in their own backyards, and the people, unable and unwilling to see the future, or even touch the present, perpetuate the past.

Leaning from the expressway or jolting across the tracks, one enters a dif-   3
ferent physical world permeated by a different attitude. The physical dimensions are impressive. It is a large section of town which extends for fifteen
blocks north and south along the tracks, and then advances eastward, thin-
ning into nothingness beyond the city limits. Within the invisible (yet sensible) walls of the barrio are many, many people living in too few houses. The
homes, however, are much more numerous than on the outside.

Members of the barrio describe the entire area as their home. It is a home,   4
but it is more than this. The barrio is a refuge from the harshness and the
coldness of the Anglo world. ◆ It is a forced refuge. The leprous people are
isolated from the rest of the community and contained in their section of
town. The stoical pariahs of the barrio accept their fate, and from the angry
seeds of rejection grow the flowers of closeness between outcasts, not the
thorns of bitterness and the mad desire to flee. There is no want to escape,
for the feeling of the barrio is known only to its inhabitants, and the material needs of life can also be found here.

The *tortillería* fires up its machinery three times a day, producing steam-   5
ing, round, flat slices of barrio bread. In the winter, the warmth of the tortilla factory is a wool sarape in the chilly morning hours, but in the summer,
it unbearably toasts every noontime customer.

The *panadería* sends its sweet messenger aroma down the dimly lit street,   6
announcing the arrival of fresh, hot, sugary *pan dulce*.

Reading Critically

◆ Why do you think Ramirez describes dreams as mysterious?

◆ Do you think the "Anglo world" is harsh and cold? Why or why not?

The small corner grocery serves the meal-to-meal needs of customers, and   7
the owner, a part of the neighborhood, willingly gives credit to people unable to pay cash for foodstuffs.

The barbershop is a living room with hydraulic chairs, radio, and televi-   8
sion, where old friends meet and speak of life as their salted hair falls aim-
lessly about them.

The pool hall is a junior level country club where 'chucos, strangers in   9
their own land, get together to shoot pool and rap, while veterans, unaware
of the cracking, popping balls on the green felt, complacently play dominoes
beneath rudely hung *Playboy* foldouts.

The *cantina* is the night spot of the barrio. It is the country club and the   10
den where the rites of puberty are enacted. Here the young become men. ❸
It is in the taverns that a young dude shows his *machismo* through the quantity of beer he can hold, the stories of *rucas* he has had, and his willingness
and ability to defend his image against hardened and scarred old lions.

No, there is no frantic wish to flee. It would be absurd to leave the familiar   11
and nervously step into the strange and cold Anglo community when the
needs of the Chicano can be met in the barrio.

The barrio is closeness. From the family living unit, familial relationships   12
stretch out to immediate neighbors, down the block, around the corner, and
to all parts of the barrio. The feeling of family, a rare and treasurable sentiment, pervades and accounts for the inability of the people to leave. The
barrio is this attitude manifested on the countenances of the people, on the
faces of their homes, and in the gaiety of their gardens.

The color-splashed homes arrest your eyes, arouse your curiosity, and   13
make you wonder what life scenes are being played out in them. The flimsy,
brightly colored, wood-frame houses ignore no neon-brilliant color. Houses
trimmed in orange, chartreuse, lime green, yellow, and mixtures of these and
other hues beckon the beholder to reflect on the peculiarity of each home.
Passing through this land is refreshing like Brubeck, not narcoticizing like re-
volting rows of similar houses, which neither offend nor please.

In the evenings, the porches and front yards are occupied with men calmly   14
talking over the noise of children playing baseball in the unpaved extension
of the living room, while the women cook supper or gossip with female
neighbors as they water the *jardines.* The gardens mutely echo the expressive
verses of the colorful houses. The denseness of multicolored plants and trees
gives the house the appearance of an oasis or a tropical isand hideaway, shel-
tered from the rest of the world.

Reading Critically
❸ What relationship does the author imply between drinking and maturity?

Fences are common in the barrio, but they are fences and not the walls   15
of the Anglo community. [4] On the western side of town, the high wooden
fences between houses are thick, impenetrable walls, built to keep the neighbors at bay. In the barrio, the fences may be rusty, wire contraptions or thick
green shrubs. In either case you can see through them and feel no sense of
intrusion when you cross them.

Many lower-income families of the barrio manage to maintain a com-   16
fortable standard of living through the communal action of family members
who contribute their wages to the head of the family. Economic need creates interdependence and closeness. Small barefooted boys sell papers on
cool, dark Sunday mornings, deny themselves pleasantries, and give their
earnings to *mamá*. The older the child, the greater the responsibility to help
the head of the household provide for the rest of the family.

There are those, too, who for a number of reasons have not achieved a rel-   17
ative sense of financial security. Perhaps it results from too many children
too soon, but it is the homes of these people and their situation that numbs
rather than charms. Their houses, aged and bent, oozing children, are fissures
in the horn of plenty. Their wooden homes may have brick-pattern asbestos
tile on the outer walls, but the tile is not convincing.

Unable to pay city taxes or incapable of influencing the city to live up to   18
its duty to serve all the citizens, the poorer barrio families remain trapped in
the nineteenth century and survive as best they can. The backyards have
well-worn paths to the outhouses, which sit near the alley. Running water
is considered a luxury in some parts of the barrio. Decent drainage is usually unknown, and when it rains, the water stands for days, an incubator of
health hazards and an avoidable nuisance. Streets, costly to pave, remain rough,
rocky trails. Tires do not last long, and the constant rattling and shaking grind
away a car's life and spread dust through screen windows.

The houses and their *jardines,* the jollity of the people in an adverse world,   19
the brightly feathered alarm clock pecking away at supper and cautiously
eyeing the children playing nearby, produce a mystifying sensation at finding
the noble savage alive in the twentieth century. [5] It is easy to look at the
positive qualities of life in the barrio and look at them with a distantly envious feeling. One wishes to experience the feelings of the barrio and not the
hardships. Remembering the illness, the hunger, the feeling of time running

---

Reading Critically

[4] According to Ramirez, how are "fences" different from "walls"? Which do you have around
your house?

[5] What is a "noble savage"? How does the author use the term in this context?

out on you, the walls, both real and imagined, reflecting on living in the past, one finds his envy becoming more elusive, until it has vanished altogether.

Back now beyond the tracks, the train creaks and groans, the cars jostle   20
each other down the track, and as the light begins its pulsing, the barrio, with all its meanings, greets a new dawn with yawns and restless stretchings.

UNDERSTANDING DETAILS

1. Define the barrio in your own words.
2. What is the difference between fences in the barrio and in the Anglo community?
3. In Ramirez's view, what creates "interdependence and closeness" (paragraph 16)? How does this phenomenon work in the barrio?
4. According to Ramirez, why are the houses in the barrio so colorful? What do you think is the relationship between color and happiness in the barrio?

THINKING CRITICALLY

5. Why does Ramirez call the people in the barrio "leprous" (paragraph 4)?
6. What does the author mean when he says, "The barrio is closeness" (paragraph 12)? How does this statement compare with the way you feel about your neighborhood? Why can't people leave the barrio?
7. Why might people look at the barrio with "a distantly envious feeling" (paragraph 19)? What other feelings may alter or even erase this sense of envy?
8. In what ways does the barrio resemble the communal living of various social groups in the 1960s?

DISCOVERING RHETORICAL STRATEGIES

9. How does Ramirez use the train to help him define the barrio? In what ways would the essay be different without the references to the train?
10. Ramirez uses metaphors masterfully throughout this essay to help us understand the internal workings of the barrio. He relies on this technique especially in paragraphs 4 through 10. For example, a metaphor that explains how relationships develop in the barrio is "The stoical pariahs of the barrio accept their fate, and from the angry seeds of rejection grow the flowers of closeness between outcasts, not the thorns of bitterness and the mad desire to flee" (paragraph 4). In this garden metaphor, "rejection" is likened to "angry seeds," "closeness between outcasts" to "flowers," and "bitterness" to "thorns." Find four other metaphors in these paragraphs, and explain how the comparisons work. What are the familiar and less familiar items in each comparison?
11. What tone does Ramirez establish in this essay? How does he create this tone?
12. The dominant method the author uses to organize his essay is definition. What other rhetorical strategies does Ramirez use to support his definition?

MAKING CONNECTIONS

13. Compare and contrast the "feeling of family" described by Ramirez with that depicted by Sandra Cisneros ("Only daughter") and/or Mary Pipher ("Beliefs About Families").

14. Ramirez does a wonderful job of creating a sensual experience in his essay as he chronicles the vivid sights, sounds, smells, tastes, and textures of life in the barrio. In the same way, Ray Bradbury ("Summer Rituals") and John McPhee ("The Pines") appeal to our senses in their descriptive essays. Which author's prose style (of the essays you have read) do you find most sensual? Explain your answer.

15. While Ramirez defines the "barrio" through description, Stephen Jay Gould ("Dorothy, It's Really Oz") defines his principal topic in a different fashion. How do the two authors differ in constructing their definitions? Which technique do you find most persuasive? Explain your answer.

IDEAS FOR DISCUSSION/WRITING

Preparing to Write

Write freely about a place that is special to you: Describe this place from your perspective. Is this place special to anyone else? Describe this place from someone else's perspective. How do these descriptions differ? What characteristics differentiate this place from other places? What makes this place special to you?

Use some metaphors to relay your feelings to your readers about certain features of this place. Do you think this place will always be special to you? Why or why not?

Choosing a Topic

1. Ramirez's definition of the barrio demonstrates a difference between an insider's view and an outsider's view of the same location. In an essay for your classmates, define your special place from both the inside and the outside. Then discuss the similarities and differences between these two points of view.

2. In essay form, define the relationships among the people who are your extended family. These could be people from your neighborhood, your school, your job, or a combination of places. How did these relationships come about? Why are you close to these people? Why are these people close to you? To each other?

3. What primary cultural or social traditions have made you what you are today? In an essay written to a close friend, define the two or three most important traditions you practiced as a child, and explain what effects they had on you.

4. Ramirez defines *barrio* by using rich description. What does the term *home* mean to you? Create a virtual tour of a place you have lived. Describe each room, the neighborhood, or the region. Develop your definition of *home* so that the reader can walk with you through each detail.

Before beginning your essay, you might want to consult the checklists on page 364.

MARY PIPHER   (1947–   )

Beliefs About Families

The oldest of seven children, Mary Pipher was born in Springfield, Missouri. She earned her B.A. in cultural anthropology at the University of California, Berkeley, and her Ph.D. in clinical psychology at the University of Nebraska. Currently a professor in the graduate clinical training program at the University of Nebraska, she became a writer only after her children had been raised, declaring that "Writing has been the great gift of my middle years. It is my reason to wake up in the morning." Her first book, *Hunger Pains: The Modern Woman's Tragic Quest for Thinness* (1987), was followed by *Reviving Ophelia: Saving the Selves of Adolescent Girls* (1994), an enormously influential study of the world of teenage girls. Her most recent books are *The Shelter of Each Other: Rebuilding Our Families* (1996), which examines family relationships in America today; *Another Country: Navigating the Emotional Terrain of Our Elders* (1999), an analysis of how the United States isolates and misunderstands its senior citizens; *The Middle of Everywhere: The World's Refugees Come to Our Town* (2002); *Letters to a Young Therapist: The Art of Mentoring* (2003), and *Writing to Change the World* (2006). An avid outdoorswoman who loves hiking, backpacking, and watching sunsets, Pipher has the following advice for students using *The Prose Reader:* "What all writers have in common is a yearning to communicate."

Preparing to Read

The following essay from *The Shelter of Each Other: Rebuilding Our Families* attempts to define the notion of "family" in contemporary society.

Exploring Experience: As you prepare to read this essay, take a few moments to think about the role family plays in your life: Are you close to your biological family? Are you a part of any other groups that function like a family? How do they work? Are you aware of your roles in these various groups? What is the relationship betwen your role in your immediate family and your personal goals?

Learning Online: To gain a perspective on the varied media representations of "family," go to the TV Land Web site (http://www.tvland.com). Choose "shows" from the menu, and then select the "Leave it to Beaver" link from the alphabetized list. Peruse the episode descriptions, sound bytes, and photos from the sitcom. Contrast this family with the one portrayed in "American Beauty." Visit the Internet Movie Database Web site (http://www.imdb.com), enter "American Beauty" into the search field, and view the movie trailer. Consider how these "families" relate to Pipher's definition as you read her essay.

When I speak of families, I usually mean biological families. There
is a power in blood ties that cannot be denied. ◆ But in our frag-
mented, chaotic culture, many people don't have biological families nearby. For many people, friends become family. Family is a collection
of people who pool resources and help each other over the long haul. Families love one another even when that requires sacrifice. Family means that
if you disagree, you still stay together.

Families are the people for whom it matters if you have a cold, are feud-
ing with your mate or training a new puppy. Family members use magnets
to fasten the newspaper clippings about your bowling team on the refrigerator door. They save your drawings and homemade pottery. They like to hear
stories about when you were young. They'll help you can tomatoes or change
the oil in your car. They're the people who will come visit you in the hospital, will talk to you when you call with "a dark night of the soul" and will
loan you money to pay the rent if you lose your job. Whether or not they
are biologically related to each other, the people who do these things are
family. ❷

If you are very lucky, family is the group you were born into. But some
are not that lucky. When Janet was in college, her parents were killed in a car
wreck. In her early twenties she married, but three years later she lost her husband to leukemia. She has one sister, who calls mainly when she's suicidal or
needs money. Janet is a congresswoman in a western state, a hard worker and
an idealist. Her family consists of the men, women, and children she's grown
to depend on in the twenty-five years she's lived in her community. Except
for her beloved dog, nobody lives with her. But she brings the cinnamon rolls
to one family's Thanksgiving dinner and has a Mexican fiesta for families at
her house on New Year's Eve. She attends Bar Mitzvahs, weddings, school
concerts, and soccer matches. She told me with great pride, "When I sprained
my ankle skiing last year, three families brought me meals."

I think of Morgan, a jazz musician who long ago left his small town and
rigid, judgmental family. He had many memories of his father whipping him
with a belt or making him sleep in the cold. Once he said to me, "I was
eighteen years old before anyone ever told me I had something to offer." Indeed he does. He plays the violin beautifully. He teaches improvisation and
jazz violin and organizes jazz events for his town. His family is the family of
musicians and music lovers that he has built around him over the years.

Reading Critically

◆ What does Pipher mean when she says "There is a power in blood ties that cannot be
denied"?

❷ What is your definition of "family"? How is it different from Pipher's?

If you are very unlucky, you come from a nuclear family[3] that didn't
care for you. Curtis, who as a boy was regularly beaten by his father, lied
about his age so that he could join the Navy at sixteen. Years later he wrote
his parents and asked if he could return home for Christmas. They didn't
answer his letter. When I saw him in therapy, I encouraged him to look for
a new family, among his cousins and friends from the Navy. Sometimes cut-
offs, tragic as they are, are unavoidable.

I think of Anita, who never knew her father and whose mother abandoned
her when she was seven. Anita was raised by an aunt and uncle, whom she loved
very much. As an adult she tracked down her mother and tried to establish a
relationship, but her mother wasn't interested. At least Anita was able to find other
family members to love her. She had a family in her aunt and uncle.

Family need not be traditional or biological. But what family offers is not
easily replicated. Let me share a Sioux word, *tiospaye,* which means the people with whom one lives. The *tiospaye* is probably closer to a kibbutz than to
any other Western institution. The *tiospaye* gives children multiple parents,
aunts, uncles and grandparents. It offers children a corrective factor for problems in their nuclear families. If parents are difficult, there are other adults
around to soften and diffuse the situation. Until the 1930s, when the *tiospaye*
began to fall apart with sale of land, migration and alcoholism, there was not
much mental illness among the Sioux. When all adults were responsible for
all children, people grew up healthy.

What *tiospaye* offers and what biological family offers is a place that all
members can belong to regardless of merit. Everyone is included regardless
of health, likability or prestige. What's most valuable about such institutions
is that people are in by virtue of being born into the group. People are in
even if they've committed a crime, been a difficult person, become physically
or mentally disabled or are unemployed and broke. That ascribed status was
what Robert Frost valued when he wrote that home "was something you
somehow hadn't to deserve."[4]

Many people do not have access to either a supportive biological family
or a *tiospaye.* They make do with a "formed family." Others simply prefer a
community of friends to their biological families. The problem with formed
families is they often have less staying power. They might not take you in,
give you money if you lose a job or visit you in a rest home if you are

---

Reading Critically

[3] Why does the author think that people who come from families that don't care for them
are "unlucky"?

[4] Why does the author quote from the poet Robert Frost? What special insight does this
quotation bring to Pipher's essay?

paralyzed in a car crash. My father had a stroke and lost most of his sight and speech. Family members were the people who invited him to visit and helped him through the long tough years after his stroke. Of course, there are formed families who do this. With the AIDS crisis, many gays have supported their friends through terrible times. Often immigrants will help each other in this new country. And there are families who don't stick together in crisis. But generally blood is thicker than water. Families come through when they must.

Another problem with formed families is that not everyone has the skills   10
to be included in that kind of family. Friendship isn't a product that can be obtained for cash. People need friends today more than ever, but friends are harder to make in a world where people are busy, moving, and isolated. Some people don't have the skills. They are shy, abrasive, or dull. Crack babies have a hard time making friends, as do people with Alzheimer's. Formed families can leave many people out.

From my point of view the issue isn't biology. Rather the issues are com-   11
mitment and inclusiveness. I don't think for most of us it has to be either/or. A person can have both a strong network of friends and a strong family. ⑤   It is important to define family broadly so that all kinds of families, such as single-parent families, multigenerational families, foster families and the families of gays are included. But I agree with David Blankenberg's conclusion in his book *Rebuilding the Nest:* "Even with all the problems of nuclear families, I will support it as an institution until something better comes along."

Americans hold two parallel versions of the family—the idealized ver-   12
sion and the dysfunctional version. The idealized version portrays families as wellsprings of love and happiness, loyal, wholesome, and true. This is the version we see in *Leave It to Beaver* or *Father Knows Best*. The dysfunctional version depicts families as disturbed and disturbing, and suggests that salvation lies in extricating oneself from all the ties that bind. Both versions have had their eras. In the 1950s the idealized version was at its zenith. Extolling family was in response to the Depression and war, which separated families. People who had been wrenched away from home missed their families and thought of them with great longing. They idealized how close and warm they had been.

In the 1990s the dysfunctional version of family seems the most influen-   13
tial. This belief system goes along with the culture of narcissism, which sells

---

Reading Critically

⑤ Do you have a strong network of friends and family? Which group is most important to you now? Which group do you think will be more important to you twenty years from now?

people the idea that families get in the way of individual fulfillment. Currently, many Americans are deeply mistrustful of their own and other people's families. Pop psychology presents families as pathology-producing. Talk shows make families look like hotbeds of sin and sickness. Day after day people testify about the diverse forms of emotional abuse that they suffered in their families. Movies and television often portray families as useless impediments.

In our culture, after a certain age, children no longer have permission to love their parents. We define adulthood as breaking away, disagreeing and making up new rules. [6] Just when teenagers most need their parents, they are encouraged to distance themselves from them. A friend told me of walking with her son in a shopping mall. They passed some of his friends, and she noticed that suddenly he was ten feet behind, trying hard not to be seen with her. She said, "I felt like I was drooling and wearing purple plaid polyester." Later her son told her that he enjoyed being with her, but that his friends all hated their parents and he would be teased if anyone knew he loved her. He said, "I'm confused about this. Am I supposed to hate you?"   14

This socialized antipathy toward families is unusual. Most cultures revere and respect family. In Vietnam, for example, the tender word for lover is "sibling." In the Kuma tribe of Papua New Guinea, family members are valued above all others. Siblings are seen as alter egos [7] essential parts of the self. The Kuma believe that mates can be replaced, but not family members. Many Native American tribes regard family members as connected to the self. To be without family is to be dead.   15

From the Greeks, to Descartes, to Freud and Ayn Rand, Westerners have valued the independent ego. But Americans are the most extreme. Our founders were rebels who couldn't tolerate oppression. When they formed a new government they emphasized rights and freedoms.   16

American values concerning independence may have worked better when we lived in small communities surrounded by endless space. But we have run out of space and our outlaws live among us. At one time the outlaw mentality was mitigated by a strong sense of community. Now the values of community have been superseded by other values.   17

We have pushed the concept of individual rights to the limits. Our laws let adults sell children harmful products. But laws are not our main problem.   18

Reading Critically

[6] Do you agree with Pipher that adulthood means "breaking away, disagreeing and making up new rules"? Why or why not?

[7] Do you have a sibling? In what sense is he or she an "alter ego"?

People have always been governed more by community values than by laws. [8] Ethics, rather than laws, determine most of our behavior. Unwritten rules of civility—for taking turns, not cutting in lines, holding doors open for others and lowering our voices in theaters—organize civic life. Unfortunately, those rules of civility seem to be crumbling in America. We are becoming a nation of people who get angry when anyone gets in our way.

Rudeness is everywhere in our culture. Howard Stern, G. Gordon Liddy, and Newt Gingrich are rude. It's not surprising our children copy them. Phil Donahue and Jay Leno interrupt, and children learn to interrupt. A young man I know was recently injured on a volleyball court. The player who hurt him didn't apologize or offer to help him get to an emergency room. An official told him to get off the floor because he was messing it up with his blood and holding up the game. I recently saw an old man hesitate at a busy intersection. Behind him drivers swore and honked. He looked scared and confused as he turned into traffic and almost wrecked his car. At a festival a man stood in front of the stage, refusing to sit down when people yelled out that they couldn't see. Finally another man wrestled him to the ground. All around were the omnipresent calls of "Fuck You." Over coffee a local politician told me she would no longer attend town meetings. She said, "People get out of control and insult me and each other. There's no dialogue, it's all insults and accusations." 19

We have a crisis in meaning in our culture. The crisis comes from our isolation from each other, from the values we learn in a culture of consumption and from the fuzzy, self-help message that the only commitment is to the self and the only important question is—Am I happy? We learn that we are number one and that our own immediate needs are the most important ones. The crisis comes from the message that products satisfy and that happiness can be purchased. 20

We live in a money-driven culture. [9] But the bottom line is not the only line, or even the best line for us to hold. A culture organized around profits instead of people is not user friendly to families. We all suffer from existential flu, as we search for meaning in a culture that values money, not meaning. Everyone I know wants to do good work. But right now we have an enormous gap between doing what's meaningful and doing what is reimbursed. 21

Reading Critically

[8] What is the difference between "community values" and "laws"? Can you give an example of each?

[9] Do you agree that we live in a "money-driven" culture? Explain your answer.

UNDERSTANDING DETAILS

1. How does Pipher define *families?* What particular activities characterize a "family" member?
2. What do "commitment and inclusiveness" (paragraph 11) have to do with being in a family?
3. According to Pipher, what are the two parallel versions of the family and when were they dominant?
4. According to Pipher, what poses the biggest problem to the integrity of the family as a unit?

THINKING CRITICALLY

5. In what way does the Sioux word *tiospaye* (paragraph 7) describe the traits of a family?
6. According to Pipher, why do "people need friends today more than ever" (paragraph 10)?
7. What is difficult about "formed families" (paragraph 10)?
8. Do you agree with Pipher that we have "a crisis of meaning in our culture" (paragraph 20)? Explain your answer in detail.

DISCOVERING RHETORICAL STRATEGIES

9. Why does the author introduce the stories of Janet, Morgan, Curtis, and Anita?
10. What do you think Pipher's purpose is in this essay?
11. Pipher approaches her definition from many different angles before suggesting that the American culture is facing a crisis in understanding and agreeing upon what a family is. How do her various definitions support her statement about a crisis? Explain your answer.
12. What rhetorical modes support the author's definition? Give examples of each.

MAKING CONNECTIONS

13. Which parts of Mary Pipher's definition of "family" would Judith Wallerstein and Sandra Blakeslee ("Second Chances for Children of Divorce"), Robert Ramirez ("The Barrio"), and/or Ray Bradbury ("Summer Rituals") most agree with? Why?
14. Imagine that Russell Baker ("The Saturday Evening Post"), Mary Roach ("Meet the Bickersons"), and/or Mary Pipher are discussing the extent to which people in a family have to compromise. Which author would you probably agree with and why?
15. Compare and contrast the ways in which Erma Bombeck ("Grandma"), Robert Ramirez ("The Barrio"), and/or Lyn Mikel Brown and Meda Chesney-Lind ("Bad Girls, Bad Girls, Whatcha Gonna Do?") begin their definition essays.

IDEAS FOR DISCUSSION/WRITING

Preparing to Write

Write freely about the qualities that constitute a good family member: How do you recognize a good family member? What characterizes him or her? Do you personally appreciate your biological family? Are you a part of other families? If so, what are the characteristics of these families? Why is some type of family important to our well-being? What role does the notion of family play in your self-definition?

Choosing a Topic

1. Write an essay for your classmates defining "a family" that you belong to.
2. In a well-organized essay, use examples to define the dysfunctional family as it exists today. Be as specific as possible.
3. The relationship between family and individual has changed since your parents were in school. Explain to them the current relationship between you and your family. What are the connections between your personal goals and your role in your immediate family?
4. Conduct Internet research on international representations of "family." Start with the United Nations Children's Fund (UNICEF) Web site (http://www.unicef.org). Use terms such as *family practices* to begin your search. Write an essay in which you expand Pipher's definition of *family* to include at least three detailed examples of globalfamily practices. Use Pipher's developed example of Sioux customs as a model for your expanded descriptions.

Before beginning your essay, you might want to consult the checklists on page 364.

STEPHEN JAY GOULD   (1941–   )

Dorothy, It's Really Oz

Paleontologist and biologist Stephen Jay Gould was raised in New York and earned his B.A. at Antioch College and his Ph.D. at Columbia University. Currently a professor of zoology and Curator of the Museum of Comparative Zoology at Harvard, he has achieved international fame through his many books and articles that translate obscure scientific topics into language the average reader can easily understand. His earliest book was *Ever Since Darwin: Reflections in Natural History* (1977), which was soon followed by *Ontogeny and Phylogeny* (1977) and *The Panda's Thumb: More Reflections in Natural History* (1980). Subsequent books have included *A View of Life* (1981), *Hen's Teeth and Horses' Toes* (1983), *The Flamingo's Smile* (1985), *Time's Arrow, Time's Cycle* (1987), *An Urchin in the Storm* (1987), *Dinosaur in a Haystack* (1995), *Crossing Over: Where Art and Science Meet* (2000), *The Structure of Evolutionary Theory* (2002), and *The Hedgehog, the Fox, and the Magister's Pox* (2003). Several of these books are collections of essays first published in a column entitled "This View of Life," which he has written for many years in *Natural History* magazine. Gould lives near Harvard, where he enjoys playing an occasional game of baseball—a sport which he celebrates in one of his recent books titled *Triumph and Tragedy in Mudville: A Lifelong Passion for Baseball* (2003).

Preparing to Read

This essay first appeared in *Time* magazine in 1999. In it, Gould claims that religion and science, often considered rivals, can peacefully coexist in our society.

Exploring Experience: As you prepare to read this essay, think about your own position in relation to religion and science: Do you subscribe to any specific religious beliefs? Do these beliefs conflict with any facts you've learned in science classes? Explain your answer. What do you know about evolution? Do any of the details associated with evolution threaten your religious beliefs? Do you know any science majors or scientists who are also religious?

Learning Online: Go to the Web site http://www.becominghuman.org, sponsored by the Institute of Human Origins. Click on the "Becoming Human" documentary, and take some time to watch this video about the anthropological discoveries researchers have made over the years. The documentary is divided into sections, so you might have to click on "Play the Documentary" at the beginning of each section.

The Kansas Board of Education voted 6 to 4 to remove evolution,   1
and the Big Bang theory as well, from the state's science curriculum. In so doing, the board transported its jurisdiction to a never-
never land where a Dorothy of the new millennium might exclaim, "They
still call it Kansas, but I don't think we're in the real world anymore." ❶ The
new standards do not forbid the teaching of evolution, but the subject will
no longer be included in statewide tests for evaluating student—a virtual
guarantee, given the realities of education, that this central concept of biology will be diluted or eliminated, thus reducing courses to something like
chemistry without the periodic table, or American history without Lincoln.

The Kansas skirmish marks the latest episode of a long struggle by reli-   2
gious Fundamentalists and their allies to restrict or eliminate the teaching of
evolution in public schools—a misguided effort that our courts have quashed
at each stage, and that saddens both scientists and most theologians. No scientific theory, including evolution, can pose any threat to religion—for these
two great tools of human understanding operate in complementary (not
contrary) fashion in their totally separate realms: science as an inquiry about
the factual state of the natural world, religion as a search for spiritual meaning and ethical values. ❷

In the early 1920s, several states simply forbade the teaching of evolution   3
outright, opening an epoch that inspired the infamous 1925 Scopes trial
(leading to the conviction of a Tennessee high school teacher) and that ended
only in 1968, when the Supreme Court declared such laws unconstitutional
on First Amendment grounds. In a second round in the late 1970s, Arkansas
and Louisiana required that if evolution be taught, equal time must be given
to Genesis literalism, masquerading as oxymoronic "creation science." ❸ The
Supreme Court likewise rejected those laws in 1987.

The Kansas decision represents creationism's first—and surely tempo-   4
rary—success with a third strategy for subverting a constitutional imperative:
that by simply deleting, but not formally banning, evolution, and by not demanding instruction in a biblically literalist "alternative," their narrowly partisan religious motivations might not derail their goals.

Given this protracted struggle, Americans of goodwill might be excused   5
for supposing that some genuine scientific or philosophical dispute motivates this issue: Is evolution speculative and ill founded? Does evolution

---

Reading Critically

❶ How does Gould's allusion to *The Wizard of Oz* at the beginning and ending of his essay
help strengthen his attack on the Kansas Board of Education decision about the teaching
of evolution?

❷ How does the author distinguish between the inquiries of science and religion?

❸ Why does Gould think the term "creation science" is an oxymoron?

threaten our ethical values or our sense of life's meaning? As a paleontologist by training, and with abiding respect for religious traditions, I would raise three points to alleviate these worries:

First, no other Western nation has endured any similar movement, with any   6
political clout, against evolution—a subject taught as fundamental, and without dispute, in all other countries that share our major socio-cultural traditions.

Second, evolution is as well documented as any phenomenon in science,   7
as strongly as the earth's revolution around the sun rather than vice versa. In this sense, we can call evolution a "fact." (Science does not deal in certainty, so "fact" can only mean a proposition affirmed to such a high degree that it would be perverse to withhold one's provisional assent.)

The major argument advanced by the school board—that large-scale evo-   8
lution must be dubious because the process has not been directly observed—smacks of absurdity and only reveals ignorance about the nature of science. Good science integrates observation with inference. No process that unfolds over such long stretches of time (mostly, in this case, before humans appeared), or at an infinitude beneath our powers of direct visualization (subatomic particles, for example), can be seen directly. If justification required eyewitness testimony, we would have no sciences of deep time—no geology, no ancient human history either. [4] (Should I believe Julius Caesar ever existed? The hard bony evidence for human evolution surely exceeds our reliable documentation of Caesar's life.)

Third, no factual discovery of science (statements about how nature "is") can,   9
in principle, lead us to ethical conclusions (how we "ought" to behave) or to convictions about intrinsic meaning (the "purpose" of our lives). These last two questions—and what more important inquiries could we make?—lie firmly in the domains of religion, philosophy and humanistic study. Science and religion should be equal, mutually respecting partners, each the master of its own domain, and with each domain vital to human life in a different way.

Why get excited over this latest episode in the long, sad history of Amer-   10
ican anti-intellectualism? Let me suggest that, as patriotic Americans, we should cringe in embarrassment that, at the dawn of a new, technological millennium, a jurisdiction in our heartland has opted to suppress one of the greatest triumphs of human discovery. Evolution is not a peripheral subject but the central organizing principle of all biological science. No one who has not read the Bible or the Bard can be considered educated in Western traditions; so no one ignorant of evolution can understand science. [5]

Reading Critically

[4] How does the lack of "eyewitness testimony" help those who wish to ban the teaching of evolution in the schools?

[5] Do you agree with the author that the theory of evolution is just as central to our education as are the Bible and the works of Shakespeare in today's world? Why or why not?

Dorothy followed her yellow brick road as it spiraled outward toward re-   11
demption and homecoming (to the true Kansas of our dreams and possibilities). The road of the newly adopted Kansas curriculum can only spiral
inward toward restriction and ignorance.

UNDERSTANDING DETAILS

1. What did the Kansas Board of Education establish by a vote of 6 to 4?
2. What laws preceded the "Kansas decision" (paragraph 4)? On what grounds
    were these laws considered unconstitutional?
3. What group is behind the Kansas decision? How does this political move sup-
    port the group's goals?
4. In what ways do people think the study of evolution threatens certain religious
    beliefs or traditions?

THINKING CRITICALLY

5. How do science and religion function in "separate realms" (paragraph 2)? Give
    examples that support your reasoning.
6. Do you agree with Gould that science and religion are each "vital to human
    life in a different way" (paragraph 9)? Explain your reasoning.
7. What do Dorothy and "her yellow brick road" (paragraph 11) have to do with
    this essay? How is the title related to these references?
8. What does Gould mean when he says, "No one ignorant of evolution can un-
    derstand science" (paragraph 10)?

DISCOVERING RHETORICAL STRATEGIES

9. What are Gould's three main arguments? Are they in an effective order?
10. Gould opens and closes this essay with references to Dorothy. Is this approach
    effective or not? Explain your answer.
11. How would you characterize the tone or mood of this essay? Is it appropriate
    for this original audience?
12. Explain the title of this essay.

MAKING CONNECTIONS

13. Imagine that Gould is having a discussion about "American anti-intellectualism"
    (paragraph 10) with K. C. Cole ("Calculated Risks"), Seaman Barrett ("How
    Bingeing Became the New College Sport"), and/or Rita Mae Brown ("Writ-
    ing as a Moral Act"). In your opinion, which of these authors would argue most
    convincingly that our country needs to put more emphasis on the education
    of its youth?
14. Compare and contrast the ways in which Gould, Ramirez ("The Barrio"),
    and/or Erma Bombeck ("Grandma") use the technique of definition in their
    essays. Which definition is most clear to you? Why?

15. Examine the use of scientific details and examples in essays by Gould, Jessica Mitford ("Behind the Formaldehyde Curtain"), and/or the articles on DNA testing by O'Brien, Dao, and Roff. Which of these essays is most convincing to you? Why?

IDEAS FOR DISCUSSION/WRITING

Preparing to Write

Write freely about the importance of religion and science in America today: What roles do these two fields play in our society? In what ways are they both important? Is either one unimportant? Why do you think these two fields are often in conflict? How can this conflict be resolved?

Choosing a Topic

1. You are a principal in a Kansas high school who has just learned about this new mandate. Write a letter to the Kansas Board of Education either supporting or refuting their decision.

2. Why are schools always at the center of the debate between science and religion? What is the purpose of education? Should it confirm or challenge our beliefs? Write an editorial for your local newspaper that outlines the role of education in the debate over evolution and creationism?

3. Why would religious fundamentalists want to eliminate the topic of evolution from the curriculum in public schools? What are the advantages of this strategy? The disadvantages? Write an essay analyzing this ongoing battle in social and historical terms. What does this debate reveal about our society?

4. Go online to the Smithsonian Institution Archives Web site dedicated to the 1925 Scopes Trial (http://siarchives.si.edu/research/scopes.html). Read the background and view the pictures concerning this landmark court decision prohibiting the teaching of evolution in high school biology classses. Using information from the "Becoming Human" video noted earlier (http://www.becominghuman.org) along with your personal knowledge, write an essay in which you define both "evolution" and "religion," then discuss the similarities and differences between the two terms.

Before beginning your essay, you might want to consult the checklists on page 364.

LYN MIKEL BROWN   (1956–   )
AND MEDA CHESNEY–LIND   (1947–   )

Bad Girls, Bad Girls, Whatcha Gonna Do?

Lyn Mikel Brown is a Professor of Women's Studies, Education, and Human Development at Colby College in Waterville, Maine. She earned her Ed.D. from Harvard University's Graduate School of Education. Her first book (written with Carol Gilligan), *Meeting at the Crossroads* (1992), was a *New York Times* Notable Book of the Year, while her second, *Raising Their Voices: The Politics of Girls' Anger* (1998), offered a study of how girls express anger. She is currently finishing a book on girls' friendships tentatively titled *Girlfighting: Betrayal, Teasing, and Rejection Among Girls.* Her hobbies include "raising a preteen daughter," creating perennial gardens, and talking with close friends. When asked to provide advice for students using *The Prose Reader,* Brown said to "take time each day to breathe, reflect, and sit with your feelings. Write a little every day, be brave, and dare to move out of your comfort zone." Meda Chesney-Lind earned her B.A. at Whitman College and her M.A. and Ph.D. at the University of Hawaii. She is currently a professor of Women's Studies at the University of Hawaii at Manoa, where she has published three books on women and crime—*Girls, Delinquency, and Juvenile Justice* (1992, with Randall Shelden), *The Female Offender* (1997), and *Female Gangs in America* (1999, with John Hagedorn)—plus over fifty articles on related topics. Her recreational activities include walking and haunting thrift shops. She advises student writers to "trust your instincts in order to become better writers, which also requires patience, discipline, and a healthy sense of humor."

Preparing to Read

This essay was first published on a web site called "Critical Criminology" ("Criticrim" for short). In it, the authors analyze the causes and effects of female aggression in society today.

Exploring Experience: As you prepare to read this essay, consider how our society deals with anger in girls: What do you think are the general causes of this anger? Should we make girls control this anger or allow them to vent their frustration? What are some acceptable ways of expressing anger? What are some of the social consequences of expressing one's anger?

Learning Online: StopHazing.org is a popular online site that deals with many types of hazing—in schools, in fraternity and sorority groups, in the military, and in athletics. Read the article titled "Myths and Facts about Hazing" at http://www.stophazing.org/mythsandfacts.html. Six common myths are outlined in the article. Do you think any of these "myths" are true?

S uddenly the world is filled with nasty girls. ❶ "Girls just want to be   1
mean," the *New York Times Magazine* announced last year as a slew of
new books on girls' relational aggression told us how "to tame them,"
to use the *Times'* own words.

Girls will be (backstabbing, catty) girls—the latest flavor de jour of the   2
American media's love affair with "bad" girls. Hardly a new idea in a country that grew up reading Longfellow's poem about his daughter: "When she
was good, she was very very good, but when she was bad she was horrid."

Now comes the ultimate girl fight in living color. Full-scale "savagery in   3
the Chicago suburbs," *Newsweek* called it. Junior girls from the privileged
Glenbrook North High School paid for the right to be hazed by seniors at
the annual powder puff football game. After the beatings and humiliations
ended, five girls were sent to the hospital, one with a broken ankle, another
with a concussion so serious it caused memory loss, another to receive 10
stitches in her scalp.

As authors who write about girls' anger, aggression and violence, we are   4
troubled, for reasons that are obvious and some that are less so. Violence that
girls perpetrate on other girls, whether it's emotional or physical, is cause
for concern. But the media frenzy that greeted the lurid and voyeuristic
video of girls fighting other girls is also problematic. In fact, it signals another
major issue for those concerned about girls' development. Girls grow up in
a world that has long encouraged them to turn their rage against one another—and then likes to be in the audience for the fight. Like the Glenbrook
parents, they might even supply the beer.

Girls' anger has a long history of being dismissed ("she's just a bitch," "it   5
must be PMS") and trivialized ("you're beautiful when you're angry"). ❷
Girls violence is generally either ignored entirely or sensationalized and sex-
ualized. Girlfighting, in particular, is often presented as a spectacle (consider
mud or Jello wrestling) enjoyed for its eroticism as much as its entertainment value (think Jerry Springer).

The hazing we watched up-close and personal, over and over again, was   6
horrifying, but questions about how and why the episode gripped the nation are at least as troubling. Who was it watching the events unfold on the
field? Why was it caught on videotape to begin with? How was it passed on
to cable and network television? Who made the decision to run it repeatedly? Why was it international news?

Girlfighting as spectator sport. Again.   7

Reading Critically

❶ Does the essay's first sentence catch your attention? Why or why not?

❷ Do you agree with the authors that anger among girls is often dismissed or trivialized?

Why, when boys perpetrate 80 percent of serious violence in the U.S., is   8
this the story that captivates us—and helps define a generation of girls?

In the shock and awe, we've missed the point. The school principal sug-   9
gests this is just kids with "old scores to settle." That doesn't tell us enough
and, worse, it fudges the real issues.

This was girls fighting over boyfriends and popularity. The seniors used   10
words like "bitches," "wimps," and "sluts" to shame the juniors into staying
on the field. In what many think of as post-feminist America, ❸ it's not popular to raise issues of power and subordination, but the fact that girls are
fighting other girls in front of videotaping boys, is hardly insignificant. That
girls used sexist and misogynistic language to control other girls during and
after the event and that their fights were primarily for boys' attention and
favor is a symptom of deeper cultural problems. As with many girl fights, boys
are both the "cause" of girl's violence and the real audience.

We need to ask harder, more critical questions about why girls are fight-   11
ing. Why embrace insults that ratify the sexual double standard? Why is
strength in women always devalued as "bitchiness?" Why the endless competition among girls for male approval? And why fight each other instead of
against a culture still rife with sexism and violence toward women?

Girlfighting gets acted out horizontally on other girls because this is the   12
safest and easiest outlet for their outrage and frustration. Girls are essentially
accessing and mimicking the male violence they sometimes know all too
well; and they are choosing victims that are societally approved—other
girls. ❹ This pattern of horizontal aggression has long characterized subordinate groups since it manages the inevitable anger in the group being controlled without jeopardizing the over all structure of male privilege.

Girls' violence also served one additional purpose. It's not uncommon for   14
the targets of that violence to, themselves, be the group members that are
challenging the rigid norms of girlhood. Why, for example, wouldn't the
girlfighters go after those "girly girls" that the media continuously tells them
are weak, vapid, and stupid? From the evil head cheerleaders in the Disney
Channel's *Kim Possible* and *Lizzie McGuire,* to *The Man Show's* Juggy Squad
on Comedy Central, to *Thong Song* wannabes, these girls make easy targets.

Girls who take out other girls for being "dykes," "hos," and "bitches" can   15
prove they are different, worth taking seriously, a force to contend with. No
wimps, wusses, or victims here. But this posturing is short-lived protection
at best, because selling out other girls this way only continues a climate of

---

Reading Critically
❸ What do the authors mean by the phrase "post-feminist America"?
❹ Why, according to the authors, are girls victims that society approves of?

misogyny, and any wrong move can quickly turn the perpetrator into a victim.

The problem is not girls; the problem is a culture that denigrates, com- 16 modifies and demoralizes women⁵ and then gets a kick out of watching the divide and conquer consequences.

There's an old saying, "men kill their weak, women kill their strong." If 17 we would give girls legitimate avenues to power, value their minds as much as their bodies, they'd be less likely to go down those nasty, underhanded or openly hostile roads, less likely to take their legitimate rage out on other girls. Let's face it, "meanness" and other covert aggressions are, in the final analysis, weapons of the weak; horizontal violence ultimately ratifies boy not girl power. When we join with girls to create real pathways to power and possibility, we'll have a lot less to video tape and we'd have a lot more to be proud of both in ourselves and in our daughters.

UNDERSTANDING DETAILS

1. Explain the basic problem that Brown and Chesney-Lind are addressing?
2. In what way is "girlfighting" a spectator sport in American society?
3. How can boys be both the cause and the audience for girls' violence?
4. What do the authors suggest to solve the problem of female anger and aggression?

THINKING CRITICALLY

5. Why did the media's reaction to the "girlfighting" bother the authors? What are the implications of these fights? Their social consequences?
6. From your own experience, in what ways is girls' anger "dismissed"?
7. Why is American society fascinated by girls' fighting?
8. Why do the authors believe that girls choose other girls to vent their rage on?

DISCOVERING RHETORICAL STRATEGIES

9. List the main points the authors make. Why do the authors address these points in this particular order?
10. Who do you think is the intended audience of this essay?
11. What rhetorical modes do the authors draw on to produce this essay? Give an example of each strategy.
12. How would you characterize the tone of this essay?

Reading Critically

⑤ Do you believe our culture "denigrates, commodifies, and demoralizes" women? What does each of these terms mean?

MAKING CONNECTIONS

13. To what extent do you think that Brown and Chesney-Lind would agree with Sandra Cisneros ("Only daughter"), Gloria Steinem ("The Politics of Muscle"), and/or Kim Severson ("I'm Not Willing to Settle for Crumbs") about the need for traditional roles for women in today's society? With which author would you most likely agree? Why?

14. Compare and contrast the opinions of Brown and Chesney-Lind with Stephen King ("Why We Crave Horror Movies") and/or Dave Grossman ("We Are Training Our Kids to Kill") about the level of violence in America today, its causes, and its effects on our society.

15. Write an essay on "Bad Boys" using examples taken from essays by Brent Staples ("A Brother's Murder"), Bruce Catton ("Grant and Lee: A Study in Contrasts"), and/or Barbara Ehrenreich ("The Ecstasy of War").

IDEAS FOR DISCUSSION/WRITING

Preparing to Write

Write freely about the anger in American society today: What events or actions are likely to bring anger to the surface? What are some acceptable ways of expressing anger? Why is girls' anger more sensational than boys' anger? How does society react to anger and aggression from these two groups? What are the consequences of any type of anger? Why is anger so difficult to control?

Choosing a Topic

1. Imagine that you are the head counselor at your high school, and you have noticed a serious increase in aggression from both male and female students at your school. You call an assembly to discuss this issue and make students realize the seriousness of their behavior. Because you have very little time with them, you write your speech out in the form of an essay on the day before you deliver it. What could you say to make the students look closely at their anger and change their behavior?

2. *Psychology Today* has asked you, as an adolescent psychologist, to write an essay analyzing the differences and similarities between girls' anger and boys' anger in high school. They need you to write two to three typed pages for their journal.

3. Having survived high school, you are in a position of being able to advise younger students. In a well-developed essay, give a younger girl whom you know some advice about managing anger during her high school years.

4. Most schools have anti-hazing policies, many of which are available online. Using Google's search engine (http://www.google.com), type in the name of your school and then "hazing policy" to find the guidelines enforced on your campus. If you cannot find your own school's policy, you can broaden your search and read one from another school (such as Fort Hays State University's at http://www.fhsu.edu/staffairs/hazing.shtml). Using the online policy state-

ment for information, write a one- to two-paragraph definition of what you consider unacceptable student behavior. Then write a one-paragraph statement explaining the appropriate penalty for students who display such behavior. Be as specific as possible.

Before beginning your essay, you might want to consult the checklists on page 364.

Chapter Writing Assignments

Practicing Definition

1. Identify a term people use to describe you (for example, *trustworthy*, *sloppy*, or *athletic*). In a well-developed essay, define this term as clearly as you can, and discuss whether or not it accurately represents you. Support your claim with carefully chosen details.
2. In what ways do our families define us? How do our families shape who we are and who we have become? In an essay, define the concept of family by explaining how your family members relate to each other.
3. Think of an object you value greatly. For example, a ring might represent a special relationship. Then, in essay form, explain what this object says about you. Why is it your favorite? What does it mean to you?

Exploring Ideas

4. Have you ever felt jealous? What do you think are the most common sources of jealousy? Do you think that jealousy is mostly a productive or unproductive emotion? Write an essay discussing the main qualities of jealousy. What do most people need to know about this feeling?
5. Think of all the "communities" to which you belong (for example, school, church, neighborhood, friends). Choose one that is really important to you, and, in an essay, identify the major features of this community. What makes this community so important in your life?
6. In essay form, describe an ugly part of your campus or city, and explore some important ways this place could be improved or changed. What effects do you think these changes might have on your community or campus? How did you come to this conclusion?

Analyzing Visual Images

Reuters/Anthony Correla/Landov LLC.

7. The photo above was taken shortly after 9/11. Looking at this picture carefully, how would you characterize the scene in words—confusion, rescue efforts, heroes, terrorism? Explore the associations you have with this photograph, and then write an essay in which you clearly define one of these terms. Use examples to clarify your definition.

8. Look at the picture on page 356 at the beginning of this chapter. Why do you think the man is holding this ring? Based on your answer, what do you think this ring signifies—love, honor, deceit, betrayal, etc.? Write an essay that explains how this picture captures the word you associate with it.

Chapter 8

CAUSE/EFFECT
Tracing Reasons and Results

Wanting to know why things happen is one of our earliest, most basic instincts: Why can't I go out, Mommy? Why are you laughing? Why won't the dog stop barking? Why can't I swim faster than my big brother? These questions, and many more like them, reflect the innately inquisitive nature that dwells within each of us. Closely related to this desire to understand *why* is our corresponding interest in *what* will happen in the future as a result of some particular action: What will I feel like tomorrow if I stay up late tonight? How will I perform in the track meet Saturday if I practice all week? What will be the result if I mix together these two potent chemicals? What will happen if I turn in my next English assignment two days early?

A daily awareness of this intimate relationship between causes and effects allows us to begin to understand the complex and interrelated series of events that make up our lives and the lives of others. For example, trying to understand the various causes of the conflict between Palestine and Israel teaches us about international relations; knowing our biological reactions to certain foods helps us make decisions about what to eat; understanding the interrelated reasons for the outbreak of World War II offers us insight into historical trends and human nature; knowing the effects of sunshine on various parts of our bodies helps us make decisions about how much ultraviolet exposure we can tolerate and what suntan lotion to use; and understanding the causes of America's most recent recession will help us respond appropriately to the next economic crisis we encounter. More than anything else, tracing causes and effects teaches us how to think clearly and react intelligently to our multifaceted environment.

In college, you will often be asked to use this natural interest in causes and effects to analyze particular situations and to discern general principles. For example, you might be asked some of the following questions on essay exams in different courses:

Anthropology: Why did the Mayan culture disintegrate?

Psychology: Why do humans respond to fear in different ways?

Biology: How do lab rats react to caffeine?

History: What were the positive effects of the Spanish-American War?

Business: Why did so many computer manufacturing companies go bankrupt in the early 1980s?

Your ability to answer such questions will depend in large part on your skill at understanding cause/effect relationships.

DEFINING CAUSE/EFFECT

Cause/effect analysis requires the ability to look for connections between different elements and to analyze the reasons for those connections. As the name implies, this rhetorical mode has two separate components: cause and effect. A particular essay might concentrate on cause (Why do you live in a dorm?), on effect (What are the resulting advantages and disadvantages of living in a dorm?), or on some combination of the two. In working with causes, we are searching for any circumstances from the past that may have caused a single event; in looking for effects, we seek occurrences that took place after a particular event and resulted from that event. Like process analysis, cause/effect makes use of our intellectual ability to analyze. Process analysis addresses *how* something happens, whereas causal analysis discusses *why* it happened and *what* the result was. A process analysis paper, for example, might explain how to advertise more effectively to increase sales, whereas a cause/effect study would discover that three specific elements contributed to an increase in sales: effective advertising, personal service, and selective discounts. The study of causes and effects, therefore, provides many different and helpful ways for humans to make sense of and clarify their views of the world.

Looking for causes and effects requires an advanced form of thinking. It is more complex than most rhetorical strategies we have studied because it can exist on a number of different and progressively more difficult levels. The most accurate and effective causal analysis accrues from digging for the real or ultimate causes or effects, as opposed to those that are merely superficial or immediate. Actress Angela Lansbury would have been out of work on an episode of the television show *Murder, She Wrote,* for example, if her character had stopped her investigation at the immediate cause of death (slipping in the bathtub) rather than searching diligently for the *real* cause (an overdose of cocaine administered by an angry companion, which resulted in the slip in the tub). Similarly, voters would be easy to manipulate if they considered only the immediate effects of a tax increase (a slightly higher tax bill) rather than the ultimate benefits that would result (the many years of improved education that our children would receive because of the specialized programs created by such an increase). Only the discovery of the actual reasons for an event or an idea will lead to the logical and accurate analysis of causes and effects important to a basic understanding of various aspects of our lives.

Faulty reasoning assigns causes to a sequence of actions without adequate justification. One such logical fallacy is called *post hoc, ergo propter hoc* ("after this, therefore because of this"): The fact that someone lost a job after walking under a ladder does not mean that the two events are causally related; by the same token, if we get up every morning at 5:30 A.M., just before the sun rises, we cannot therefore conclude that the sun rises *because* we get up (no matter how self-centered we are!). Faulty reasoning also occurs when we oversimplify a particular situation. Most events are connected to a multitude of causes and effects. Sometimes one effect has many causes: A student may fail a history exam because she's been working two part-time jobs, she was sick, she didn't study hard enough, and she found the instructor very boring. One cause may also have many effects. If a house burns down, the people who lived in it will be out of a home. If we look at such a tragic scene more closely, however, we may also note that the fire traumatized a child who lived there, helped the family learn what good friends they had, encouraged the family to double their future fire insurance, and provided the happy stimulus that they needed to make a long-dreamed-of move to another city. One event has thus resulted in many interrelated effects. Building an argument on insecure foundations or oversimplifying the causes or effects connected with an event will seriously hinder the construction of a rational essay. No matter what the nature of the cause/effect analysis, it must always be based on clear observation, accurate facts, and rigorous logic.

In the following paragraph, a student writer analyzes some of the causes and effects connected with the controversial issue of euthanasia. Notice how he makes connections and then analyzes those connections as he consistently explores the immediate and ultimate effects of being able to stretch life beyond its normal limits through new medical technology:

Along with the many recent startling advancements in medical technology have come a number of complex moral, ethical, and spiritual questions that beg to be answered. We now have the ability to prolong the life of the human body for a very long time. But what rights do patients and their families have to curtail cruel and unusual medical treatment that stretches life beyond its normal limits? This dilemma has produced a ripple effect in society. Is the extension of life an unquestionable goal in itself, regardless of the quality of that life? Modern scientific technology has forced doctors to reevaluate the exact meaning and purpose of their profession. For example, many medical schools and undergraduate university programs now routinely offer classes on medical ethics—an esoteric and infrequently taught subject only a few years ago. Doctors and scholars alike are realizing that medical personnel alone cannot be expected to decide on the exact parameters of life. In like manner, the judicial process must now evaluate the legal complexities of mercy killings and the rights of patients to die with dignity and without unnecessary medical intervention. The insurance business, too, wrestles with the catastrophic effects of new technology on the costs of today's hospital care. In short, medical progress entails more than microscopes, chemicals, and high-tech instruments. If we are to develop as a thoughtful, just, and merciful society, we must consider not only the physical well-being of our nation's patients, but their emotional, spiritual, and financial status as well.

THINKING CRITICALLY THROUGH CAUSE/EFFECT

- Search for relationships between ideas.
- Make sense of these relationships.
- Analyze causes and effects.

Thinking about causes and effects is one of the most advanced mental activities that we perform. It involves complex operations that we must think through carefully, making sure all connections are reasonable and accurate. Unlike other rhetorical patterns, cause/effect thinking requires us to see specific relationships between two or more items. To practice this strategy, we need to look for items or events that are causally related—that is, one that has caused the other. Then, we can focus on either the causes (the initial stimulus), the effects (the results), or a combination of the two.

Searching for causes and effects requires a great deal of digging that is not necessary for most of the other modes. Cause/effect necessitates the ultimate in investigative work. The mental exertion associated with this thinking strategy is sometimes exhausting, but it is always worth going through when you discover relationships that you never saw before or when you uncover links in your reasoning that were previously unknown or obscure to you.

If you've ever had the secret desire to be a private eye or an investigator of any sort, practicing cause/effect reasoning can be lots of fun. It forces you to see relationships among multiple items and then to make sense of those connections. Completing exercises in this skill by itself will once again help you perfect the logistics of cause/effect thinking before you mix and match it with other thinking strategies.

Sam Shere/UPI/Corbis Bettmann.

1. In Sam Shere's famous 1937 photo of the Hindenburg bursting into flames, we can see that this voyage of the zeppelin from Germany to the United States ended in disaster. Ninety-seven people were aboard when the Hindenberg went down, and none of them expected to die. Think of other examples of technological inventions or changes where the outcome was different from what people expected. Identify the expectations, the actual results, and what can be learned from these results.

2. Choose a major problem you see in our society, and list what you think are the main causes of this problem on one side of a piece of paper and the effects on the other side. Compare the two lists to see how they differ. Then, compare and contrast your list with those written by other students.

3. What "caused" you to become a student? What influences led you to this choice at this point in your life? How has being a student affected your life? List several overall effects.

Reading and Writing Cause/Effect Essays

Causal analysis is usually employed for one of three main purposes: (1) to prove a specific point (such as the necessity for stricter gun control), in which case the writer generally deals totally with facts and with conclusions drawn from those facts; (2) to argue against a widely accepted belief (for example, the assertion that cocaine is addictive), in which case the writer relies principally on facts, with perhaps some pertinent opinions; or (3) to speculate on a theory (for instance, why the crime rate is higher in most major cities than it is in rural areas), in which case the writer probably presents hypotheses and opinions along with facts. This section will explore these purposes in cause/effect essays from the standpoint of both reading and writing.

READING CAUSE/EFFECT ESSAYS

- What is the essay's thesis?
- What are the real causes and effects?
- What are the author's assertions?

Preparing to Read.   As you set out to read the essays in this chapter, begin by focusing your attention on the title and the synopsis of the essay you are about to read and by scanning the essay itself: What do you think Stephen King is going to talk about in "Why We Crave Horror Movies"? What does the synopsis in the Rhetorical Table of Contents tell you about Michael Dorris's "The Broken Cord" or about Sherman Alexie's "The Joy of Reading and Writing: Superman and Me"?

Also, at this stage in the reading process, you should try to learn as much as you can about the author of the essay and the reasons he or she wrote it. Ask yourself questions like the following: What is King's intention in "Why We Crave Horror Movies"? Who is Mary Roach's intended audience in "Meet the Bickersons"? And what is Alice Walker's point of view in "Beauty: When the Other Dancer Is the Self"?

Finally, before you begin to read, answer the prereading questions for each essay and then consider the proposed essay topic from a variety of perspectives: For example, concerning Alexie's topic, how important to you is reading and/or writing? Which segments of American society are most aware of the value of these skills? Which the least? What do you want to know from Roach about people and arguing? Do you have a desire to understand relationships better?

Reading.   As you read each essay in this chapter for the first time, record your spontaneous reactions to it, drawing as often as possible on the preliminary material you already know: What do you think of horror movies (King)? What is Dorris suggesting about fetal alcohol babies? Have you experienced an addiction of any kind? Why did Roach choose the title she did?

Whenever you can, try to create a context for your reading: What is the tone of Alexie's comments about reading and writing? How does this tone help him communicate with his audience? What do you think Walker's purpose is in her essay concerning her childhood accident? How clearly does she get this purpose across to you?

Also, during this reading, note the essay's thesis and check to see if the writer thoroughly explores all possibilities before settling on the primary causes and/or effects of a particular situation; in addition, determine whether the writer clearly states the assertions that naturally evolve from a discussion of the topic.

At the base of the essay's pages in this chapter are some questions that will help you process this reading material critically or analytically. These questions are designed to provide a bridge that will connect your thoughts before you read the essay with your tasks at the end of your reading by helping you see relationships among ideas that will lead you to higher levels of thinking. Recording your answers in writing is the best way to approach these questions although your instructor might have some other guidelines for you.

Finally, read the questions following each essay to get a sense of the main issues and strategies in the selection.

Rereading.   When you reread these essays, you should focus mainly on the writer's craft. Notice how the authors narrow and focus their material, how they make clear and logical connections between ideas in their essays, how they support their conclusions with concrete examples, how they use other rhetorical modes to accomplish their cause/effect analysis, and how they employ logical transitions to move us smoothly from one point to another. Most important, however, ask yourself if the writer actually discusses the real causes and/or effects of a particular circumstance: What does King say are the primary reasons people crave horror movies? According to Roach, why do many couples have trouble in their marriages? What are the primary causes and effects of Walker's childhood injury?

For a thorough outline of the reading process, consult the checklist on page 29 of the Introduction.

WRITING CAUSE/EFFECT ESSAYS

Thinking

Reading   Writing

• State your purpose in your thesis.
• Explore all causes and effects.
• Use concrete evidence.
• Summarize and draw conclusions.

Preparing to Write.   Beginning a cause/effect essay requires—as does any other essay—exploring and limiting your subject, specifying a purpose, and identifying an audience. The Preparing to Write questions before the essay assignments, coupled with the prewriting techniques outlined in the Introduction (pp. 19–21), encourage you to consider specific issues related to your reading. The assignments themselves will then help you limit your topic and determine a particular purpose and audience for your message. For cause/effect essays, determining a purpose is even more important than usual, because your readers can get hopelessly lost unless your analysis is clearly focused.

Writing.   For all its conceptual complexity, a cause/effect essay can be organized quite simply. The introduction generally presents the subject(s) and states the purpose of the analysis in a clear thesis. The body of the paper then explores all relevant causes and/or effects, typically progressing either from least to most influential or from most to least influential. Finally, the concluding section summarizes the various cause/effect relationships established in the body of the paper and clearly states the conclusions that can be drawn from those relationships.

The following additional guidelines should assist you in producing an effective cause/effect essay in all academic disciplines:

1. Narrow and focus your material as much as possible.
2. Consider all possibilities before assigning real or ultimate causes or effects.
3. Show connections between ideas by using transitions and key words—such as *because, reasons, results, effects,* and *consequences*—to guide your readers smoothly through your essay.
4. Support all inferences with concrete evidence.
5. Be as objective as possible in your analysis so that you don't distort logic with personal biases.
6. Understand your audience's opinions and convictions so that you know what to emphasize in your essay.
7. Qualify your assertions to avoid overstatement and oversimplification.

These suggestions apply to both cause/effect essay assignments and exam questions.

Rewriting.   As you revise your cause/effect essays, ask yourself the following important questions:

- Is your thesis stated clearly at the outset of your paper?
- Does it include your subject and your purpose?
- Do you explore all relevant causes and/or effects?
- Do you accomplish your purpose as effectively as possible?
- Do you use logical reasoning throughout the essay?
- Do you state clearly the conclusions that can be drawn from your paper?

More specific guidelines for writing and revising your essays appear on page 30 of the Introduction.

STUDENT ESSAY: CAUSE/EFFECT AT WORK

In the following essay, the student writer analyzes the effects of contemporary TV soap operas on young people: Notice that she states her subject and purpose at the beginning of the essay and then presents a combination of facts and opinions in her exploration of the topic. Notice also that, in her analysis, the writer is careful to draw clear connections between her perceptions of the issue and various objective details in an attempt to trace the effects of this medium in our society today. At the end of her essay, look at her summary of the logical relationships she establishes in the body of the essay and her statements about the conclusions she draws from these relationships.

Distortions of Reality

Background   Television's contributions to society, positive and negative, have been debated continually since this piece of technology invaded the average American household in the 1950s. Television has brought an unlimited influx of new information, ideas, and cultures into our homes. However, based on my observations of my thirteen-year-old cousin, Katie, and her friends, I think we need to take a closer look at the effects of soap operas on adolescents today. <u>The distortions of reality portrayed on these programs are frighteningly misleading and, in my opinion, can be very confusing to young people.</u>   Thesis statement

Transition   <u>During the early 1990s, the lifestyle of the typical soap opera "family" has been radically transformed from comfortable pretentiousness to blatant and unrealistic decadence. The characters neither live nor dress</u>   First distortion of reality like the majority of their viewers, who are generally middle-class Americans. These television families live in large, majestic homes that are flawlessly decorated. The

Concrete examples actors are often adorned in beautiful designer clothing, fur coats, and expensive jewelry, and this opulent lifestyle is sustained by people with no visible means of income. Very few of the characters seem to "work" for a living. When they do, upward mobility—without the benefit of the proper education or suitable training—and a well-planned marriage come quickly.

Transition   From this constant barrage of conspicuous consumption, my cousin and her friends seem to have a *First effect* distorted view of everyday economic realities. I see Katie and her group becoming obsessed with the ap-

Concrete examples pearance of their clothes and possessions. I frequently hear them criticize their parents' jobs and modest homes. With noticeable arrogance, these young adolescents seem to view their parents' lives as "failures" when compared to the effortless, luxurious lifestyles portrayed in the soaps.

Transition   One of the most alluring features of this genre is its masterful use of deception. Conflicts between characters in soap operas are based on secrecy and misin-

Concrete examples formation. Failure to tell the truth and to perform honorable deeds further complicates the entangled lives and love affairs of the participants. But when the *Second distortion of reality* truth finally comes out and all mistakes and misdeeds become public, the culprits and offenders hardly ever suffer for their actions. In fact, they appear to leave the scene of the crime guilt-free.

Transition   Regrettably, Katie and her friends consistently express alarming indifference to this lack of moral in-

Concrete examples tegrity. In their daily viewing, they shrug off underhanded scenes of scheming and conniving, and they marvel at how the characters manipulate each other into positions of powerlessness or grapple in distasteful love scenes. I can only conclude that contin- *Second effect* ued exposure to this amoral behavior is eroding the fundamental values of truth and fidelity in these kids.

Transition   Also in the soaps, the powers-that-be conveniently *Third distortion of reality* disregard any sense of responsibility for wrongdoing. Characters serve jail terms quickly and in relative

Concrete examples comfort. Drug or alcohol abuse does not mar any-one's physical appearance or behavior, and poverty is virtually nonexistent. Usually, the wrongdoer's position, wealth, and prestige are quickly restored—with little pain and suffering.

Third effect <u>Adolescents are clearly learning that people can act without regard for the harmful effects of their actions on themselves and others when they see this type of behavior go unpunished.</u> Again, I notice the result of this delusion in my cousin. Recently, when a businessman in our community was convicted of embezzling large sums of money from his clients, Katie was Concrete examples outraged because he was sentenced to five years in prison, unlike her daytime TV "heartthrob," who had been given a suspended sentence for a similar crime. With righteous indignation, Katie claimed that the victims, many of whom had lost their entire savings, should have realized that any business investment involves risk and the threat of loss. Logic and common sense evaded Katie's reasoning as she insisted on comparing television justice with real-life jurisprudence.

The writers and producers of soap operas argue that the shows are designed to entertain viewers and are not meant to be reflections of reality. Theoretically, this may be true, but I can actually see how these soap operas are affecting my cousin and her crowd. Although my personal observations are limited, I cannot believe they are unique or unusual. <u>Too many</u> Ultimate effect <u>young people think that they can amass wealth and material possessions without an education, hard work, or careful financial planning; that material goods are the sole measure of a person's success in life; and that honesty and integrity are not necessarily admirable qualities.</u>

Proposed solution <u>Soap operas should demonstrate a realistic lifestyle and a responsible sense of behavior.</u> The many hours adolescents spend in front of the television can obviously influence their view of the world. As a society, we cannot afford the consequences resulting from the distortions of reality portrayed every day in these shows.

Student Writer's Comments

In general, writing this essay was not as easy as I had anticipated during my prewriting phase. Although I was interested in and familiar with my topic, I had trouble fitting all the pieces together: matching causes with effects, examples with main points, and problems with solutions.

My prewriting activities were a combination of lists and journal entries that gave me loads of ideas and phrasing to work with in my drafts. From this initial thinking exercise, I created an informal outline of the points I wanted to make. I played with the order of these topics for a while and then began to write.

Because I had spent so much time thinking through various causal relationships before I began to write, I generated the first draft with minimal pain. But I was not happy with it. The examples that I had chosen to support various points I wanted to make did not fit as well as they could, and the whole essay was scattered and incoherent. Although all writing requires support and focus, I realized that a cause/effect essay demands special attention to the relationship between specific examples and their ultimate causes and/or effects. As a result, I had to begin again to revise my sprawling first draft.

I spent my first revising session on the very sloppy introduction and conclusion. I felt that if I could tighten up these parts of the essay, I would have a clearer notion of my purpose and focus. I am convinced now that the time I spent on the beginning and ending of my essay really paid off. I rewrote my thesis several times until I finally arrived at the statement in the draft printed here. This final thesis statement gave me a clear sense of direction for revising the rest of my paper.

I then worked through my essay paragraph by paragraph, verifying that the examples and illustrations I cited supported as effectively as possible each of my points. I made sure that the causes and effects were accurately paired, and I reorganized sections of the essay that didn't yet read smoothly. I put the final touches on my conclusion and handed in my paper—with visions of causes, effects, and soap opera characters still dancing around in my head.

SOME FINAL THOUGHTS ON CAUSE/EFFECT

The essays in this chapter deal with both causes and effects in a variety of ways. As you read each essay, try to discover its primary purpose and the ultimate causes and/or effects of the issue under discussion. Note also the clear causal relationships that each author sets forth on solid foundations supported by logical reasoning. Although the subjects of these essays vary dramatically, each essay exhibits the basic elements of effective causal analysis.

CAUSE/EFFECT IN REVIEW

Reading Cause/Effect Essays

Preparing to Read

✓ What assumptions can you make from the essay's title?

✓ Can you guess what the general mood of the essay is?

✓ What is the essay's purpose and audience?

✓ What does the synopsis tell you about the essay?

✓ What can you learn from the author's biography?

✓ Can you predict the author's point of view toward the subject?

Reading

✓ What is the essay's thesis?

✓ What are the real causes and/or effects?

✓ What are the author's assertions?

Rereading

✓ How does the writer narrow and focus the essay?

✓ Does the writer make clear and logical connections between the ideas?

✓ What concrete examples support the author's conclusions?

✓ Does the writer discuss the real causes and effects?

Writing Cause/Effect Essays

Preparing to Write

✓ What is your purpose?

✓ Who is your audience?

Writing

✓ Do you state your purpose in your thesis?

✓ Do you explore all causes and effects?

✓ Do you use concrete evidence?

✓ Do you summarize and draw conclusions?

Rewriting

✓ Is your thesis stated clearly at the outset of your paper?

✓ Does it include your subject and your purpose?

✓ Do you explore all relevant causes and/or effects?

✓ Do you accomplish your purpose as effectively as possible?

✓ Do you use logical reasoning throughout the essay?

✓ Do you state clearly the conclusions that can be drawn from your paper?

STEPHEN KING   (1947–   )

Why We Crave Horror Movies

"People's appetites for terror seem insatiable," Stephen King once remarked, an insight that may help justify his phenomenal success as a writer of horror fiction since the mid-1970s. His books have sold over one hundred million copies, and the movies made from them have generated more income than the gross domestic product of several small countries. After early jobs as a janitor, a laundry worker, and a high school English teacher in Portland, Maine, King turned to writing full time following the spectacular sales of his first novel, *Carrie* (1974), which focuses on a shy, socially ostracized young girl who takes revenge on her cruel classmates through newly developed telekinetic powers. King's subsequent books have included *The Shining* (1976), *Firestarter* (1980), *Cujo* (1981), *Christine* (1983), *Pet Sematary* (1983), *Misery* (1987), *The Stand* (1990), *The Waste Lands* (1992), *Delores Claiborne* (1993), *Desperation* (1996), *Bag of Bones* (1999), *Dreamcatcher* (2001), and *The Dark Tower V: Wolves of the Calla* (2003). Asked to explain why readers and moviegoers are so attracted to his tales of horror, King explained that most people's lives "are full of fears—that their marriage isn't working, that they aren't going to make it on the job, that society is crumbling all around them. But we're really not supposed to talk about things like that, and so they don't have any outlets for all those scary feelings. But the horror writer can give them a place to put their fears." A cheerful though somewhat superstitious person, King, who now lives in Bangor, Maine, admits to doing most of his best writing during the morning hours. "You think I want to write this stuff at night?" he once asked a reviewer.

Preparing to Read

This essay, originally published in *Playboy* magazine, attempts to explain why horror movies satisfy our most basic instincts.

Exploring Experience: As you prepare to read this article, consider your thoughts on America's emotional condition: How emotionally healthy are Americans? Were they more emotionally healthy twenty years ago? A century ago? What makes a society emotionally healthy? Emotionally unhealthy? How can a society maintain good health? What is the relationship between emotional health and a civilized society?

Learning Online: Conduct an Internet search on two recently released horror movies. Use the title of the film as well as the phrase "movie trailer" as your search terms. Find links that allow you to watch each film's preview trailer. How do you feel after watching the trailer? Do you like or dislike this type of film genre?

I think that we're all mentally ill; those of us outside the asylums only hide 1
it a little better—and maybe not all that much better, after all. We've all
known people who talk to themselves, people who sometimes squinch
their faces into horrible grimaces when they believe no one is watching,
people who have some hysterical fear—of snakes, the dark, the tight place,
the long drop . . . and, of course, those final worms and grubs that are waiting so patiently underground. ❶

When we pay our four or five bucks and seat ourselves at tenth-row cen- 2
ter in a theater showing a horror movie, we are daring the nightmare.

Why? Some of the reasons are simple and obvious. To show that we can, 3
that we are not afraid, that we can ride this roller coaster. ❷ Which is not to
say that a really good horror movie may not surprise a scream out of us at
some point, the way we may scream when the roller coaster twists through
a complete 360 or plows through a lake at the bottom of the drop. And horror movies, like roller coasters, have always been the special province of the
young; by the time one turns 40 or 50, one's appetite for double twists or
360-degree loops may be considerably depleted.

We also go to reestablish our feelings of essential normality; the horror 4
movie is innately conservative, even reactionary. Freda Jackson as the horrible melting woman in *Die, Monster, Die!* confirms for us that no matter how
far we may be removed from the beauty of a Robert Redford or a Diana
Ross, we are still light-years from true ugliness.

And we go to have fun. 5

Ah, but this is where the ground starts to slope away, isn't it? Because this 6
is a very peculiar sort of fun, indeed. The fun comes from seeing others men-
aced—sometimes killed. One critic has suggested that if pro football has become the voyeur's version of combat, then the horror film has become the
modern version of the public lynching.

It is true that the mythic, "fairy-tale" horror film intends to take away the 7
shades of gray. . . . It urges us to put away our more civilized and adult pen-
chant for analysis and to become children again, seeing things in pure blacks
and whites. It may be that horror movies provide psychic relief on this level
because this invitation to lapse into simplicity, irrationality, and even outright madness is extended so rarely. We are told we may allow our emotions
a free rein . . . or no rein at all.

Reading Critically

❶ What are the worms and grubs waiting for?
❷ How does King use the image of a roller coaster as a metaphor? What is it that we really
"ride"?

If we are all insane, then sanity becomes a matter of degree. If your insanity   8
leads you to carve up women, like Jack the Ripper or the Cleveland Torso
Murderer, we clap you away in the funny farm (but neither of those two
amateur-night surgeons was ever caught, heh-heh-heh); if, on the other
hand, your insanity leads you only to talk to yourself when you're under
stress or to pick your nose on your morning bus, then you are left alone to
go about your business . . . though it is doubtful that you will ever be invited
to the best parties.

The potential lyncher is in almost all of us [3] (excluding saints, past and   9
present; but then, most saints have been crazy in their own ways), and every
now and then, he has to be let loose to scream and roll around in the grass.
Our emotions and our fears form their own body, and we recognize that it
demands its own exercise to maintain proper muscle tone. Certain of these
emotional muscles are accepted—even exalted—in civilized society; they
are, of course, the emotions that tend to maintain the status quo of civilization itself. Love, friendship, loyalty, kindness—these are all the emotions that
we applaud, emotions that have been immortalized in the couplets of Hallmark cards and in the verses (I don't dare call it poetry) of Leonard Nimoy.

When we exhibit these emotions, society showers us with positive rein-   10
forcement; we learn this even before we get out of diapers. When, as children, we hug our rotten little puke of a sister and give her a kiss, all the aunts
and uncles smile and twit and cry, "Isn't he the sweetest little thing?" Such
coveted treats as chocolate-covered graham crackers often follow. But if we
deliberately slam the rotten little puke of a sister's fingers in the door, sanc-
tions follow—angry remonstrance from parents, aunts, and uncles; instead
of a chocolate-covered graham cracker, a spanking.

But anticivilization emotions [4] don't go away, and they demand periodic   11
exercise. We have such "sick" jokes as, "What's the difference between a truckload of bowling balls and a truckload of dead babies?" (You can't unload a
truckload of bowling balls with a pitchfork . . . a joke, by the way, that I heard
originally from a ten-year-old.) Such a joke may surprise a laugh or a grin
out of us even as we recoil, a possibility that confirms the thesis: If we share
a brotherhood of man, then we also share an insanity of man. None of which
is intended as a defense of either the sick joke or insanity but merely as an
explanation of why the best horror films, like the best fairy tales, manage to
be reactionary, anarchistic, and revolutionary all at the same time.

Reading Critically

[3] Do you agree with the author that a "potential lyncher" lurks inside all of us? Why or why
not?

[4] What are "anticivilization emotions"? Do you have any?

The mythic horror movie, like the sick joke, has a dirty job to do. It de- 12
liberately appeals to all that is worst in us. It is morbidity unchained, our
most base instincts let free, our nastiest fantasies realized . . . , and it all happens, fittingly enough, in the dark. For those reasons, good liberals often shy
away from horror films. For myself, I like to see the most aggressive of them—
Dawn of the Dead, for instance—as lifting a trap door in the civilized forebrain and throwing a basket of raw meat to the hungry alligators swimming
around in that subterranean river beneath.

Why bother? Because it keeps them from getting out, man. It keeps them 13
down there and me up here. It was Lennon and McCartney who said that
all you need is love, and I would agree with that.

As long as you keep the gators fed. 14

UNDERSTANDING DETAILS

1. Why, in King's opinion, do civilized people enjoy horror movies?
2. According to King, in what ways are horror movies like roller coasters?
3. According to King, how are horror films like public lynchings?
4. What is the difference between "emotions that tend to maintain the status quo
   of civilization" (paragraph 9) and "anticivilization emotions" (paragraph 11)?

THINKING CRITICALLY

5. How can horror movies "reestablish our feelings of essential normality" (paragraph 4)?
6. What is "reactionary, anarchistic, and revolutionary" (paragraph 11) about fairy
   tales? About horror films?
7. Why does the author think we need to exercise our anticivilization emotions?
   What are some other ways we might confront these emotions?
8. Explain the last line of King's essay: "As long as you keep the gators fed" (paragraph 14).

DISCOVERING RHETORICAL STRATEGIES

9. What is the cause/effect relationship King notes in society between horror
   movies and sanity?
10. Why does King begin his essay with such a dramatic statement as "I think that
    we're all mentally ill" (paragraph 1)?
11. Who do you think is the author's intended audience for this essay? Describe
    them in detail. How did you come to this conclusion?
12. What different rhetorical strategies does King use to support his cause/effect
    analysis? Give examples of each.

MAKING CONNECTIONS

13. Apply Stephen King's definition of *horror* to such frightening experiences as the preparation of a dead body for its funeral (Jessica Mitford, "Behind the Formaldehyde Curtain") and/or caring for a fetal alcohol syndrome child (Michael Dorris, "The Broken Cord"). In what way is each of these events "horrible"? What are the principal differences between watching a horror movie and living through a real-life horror?

14. In this essay, King gives us important insights into his own writing process, especially into how horror novels and movies affect their audiences. Compare and contrast his revelation of the techniques of his trade with those advanced by Amy Tan ("Mother Tongue"), Roger Rosenblatt ("I am Writing Blindly"), and/or Rita Mae Brown ("Writing as a Moral Act"), all of whom discuss the writing process. Whose comments are most helpful to you? Explain your answer.

15. Compare King's remarks about "fear" with similar insights into the topic by such other authors as Barbara Ehrenreich ("The Ecstasy of War") and/or Alice Walker ("Beauty: When the Other Dancer Is the Self"). How would each of these writers define the term differently? With which author's definition would you most likely agree? Explain your answer.

IDEAS FOR DISCUSSION/WRITING

Preparing to Write

Write freely about how most people maintain a healthy emotional attitude: How would you define emotional well-being? When are people most emotionally healthy? Most emotionally unhealthy? What do your friends and relatives do to maintain a healthy emotional life? What do you do to maintain emotional health? What is the connection between our individual emotional health and the extent to which our society is civilized?

Choosing a Topic

1. Think of a release other than horror films for our most violent emotions. Is it an acceptable release? Write an essay for the general public explaining the relationship between this particular release and our "civilized" society.

2. If you accept King's analysis of horror movies, what role in society do you think other types of movies play (e.g., love stories, science-fiction movies, and comedies)? Choose one type, and explain its role to your college composition class.

3. Your psychology instructor has asked you to explain your opinions on the degree of sanity or insanity in America at present. In what ways are we sane? In what ways are we insane? Write an essay for your psychology instructor explaining in detail your observations along these lines.

4. King's essay focuses on the benefits of watching horror films. What are other practices we have that on the surface may seem silly or trivial, but actually serve

an important purpose? Select one such practice, and write an essay in which you identify its causes and effects. Conduct an Internet search on your topic, and use credible references to support your theories. Try to use relevant, vivid imagery, as King does, to engage your audience.

Before beginning your essay, you might want to consult the checklists on page 410.

MICHAEL DORRIS   (1945–1997)

The Broken Cord

Michael Dorris, a descendant of Modoc American Indians and Irish and French settlers, grew up in Kentucky and Montana. He earned his B.A. at Georgetown University and his Master of Arts degree at Yale and was for many years a professor of anthropology and Native-American Studies at Dartmouth, where he was also head of the Native-American Studies program. His training was quite eclectic. "I came to cultural anthropology," he has explained, "by way of an undergraduate program in English and classics and a Master's Degree in history of the theater." He was also a Guggenheim Fellow (1978), a Rockefeller Fellow (1985), a member of the Smithsonian Institution Council, a National Endowment for the Humanities consultant, a National Public Radio commentator, and a member of the editorial board of the *American Indian Culture and Research Journal* during his distinguished academic career. His many publications included *Native Americans: Five Hundred Years After* (1975); a bestselling novel, *A Yellow Raft in Blue Water* (1987); *The Broken Cord* (1989), a work of nonfiction that won the Heartland Prize, the Christopher Medal, and the National Book Critics Circle Award; *Morning Girl* (1992), a book of short stories; and two more novels, *Working Men* (1993) and *Rooms in the House of Stone* (1993). Dorris also coauthored several books with his wife, Louise Erdrich, including *Route Two and Back* (1991), a collection of travel essays. Prior to his death, he advised students using *The Prose Reader* to "work at as many kinds of jobs as possible while they are young and keep daily journals of their experiences and impressions."

Preparing to Read

The following excerpt from *The Broken Cord* details some of Dorris's frustrations in raising his adopted son, Adam, who suffered from fetal alcohol syndrome until his death in 1991.

Exploring Experience: As you prepare to read this article, take a few moments to think about your own physical and mental growth: What do you know about your birth? How did you develop as a child? Are you reaching your physical and mental potential? How do you know? Are there any barriers between you and this potential? What are they? How can you surmount them? How will you maintain your potential?

Learning Online: Conduct an Internet search on the term *Fetal Alcohol Syndrome* to find facts and photos about the condition described so vividly in Dorris's essay.

A dam's birthdays are, I think, the hardest anniversaries, even though as   1
an adoptive father I was not present to hear Adam's first cry, to feel
the aspirated warmth of his body meeting air for the first time. I was
not present to count his fingers, to exclaim at the surprise of gender, to be
comforted by the hope at the heart of his new existence.

From what I've learned, from the sum of gathered profiles divided by the   2
tragedy of each case, the delivery of my premature son was unlikely to have
been a joyous occasion. Most fetal alcohol babies emerge not in a tide, the
facsimile of saline, primordial, life-granting sea, but instead enter this world
tainted with stale wine. Their amniotic fluid literally reeks of Thunderbird
or Ripple, and the whole operating theater stinks like the scene of a three-
day party. Delivery room staff who have been witness time and again tell of
undernourished babies thrown into delirium tremens when the cord that
brought sustenance and poison is severed. 🔹 Nurses close their eyes at the
memory. An infant with the shakes, as cold turkey as a raving derelict deprived
of the next fix, is hard to forget.

Compared to the ideal, Adam started far in the hole, differently from the   3
child who began a march through the years without the scars of fetters on
his ankles, with eyes and ears that worked, with nothing to carry except
what he or she collected along the path.

Adam's birthdays are reminders for me. For each celebration commem-   4
orating that he was born, there is the pang, the rage, that he was not born
whole. I grieve for what he might have, what he should have been. I magnify and sustain those looks of understanding or compassion or curiosity
that fleet across his face, fast as a breeze, unexpected as the voice of God—
the time he said to me in the car, the words arising from no context I could
see, "Kansas is between Oklahoma and Texas." But when I turned in amazement, agreeing loudly, still ready after all these years to discover a buried talent or passion for geography, for anything, that possible person had
disappeared.

"What made you say that?" I asked.   5

"Say what?" he answered. "I didn't say anything."   6

The sixteenth birthday, the eighteenth. The milestones. The driver's li-   7
cense, voting, the adult boundary-marker birthdays. The days I envisioned
while watching the mail for the response to my first adoption application,
the days that set forth like distant skyscrapers as I projected ahead through
my years of fatherhood. I had given little specific consideration to what
might come between, but of those outstanding days I had been sure. They
were the pillars I followed, the oases of certainty. Alone in the cabin in Alaska

---

Reading Critically

🔹 Why is it ironic that the umbilical cord brings both "sustenance and poison"?

or in the basement apartment near Franconia while I waited for the defin- ition of the rest of my life to commence, I planned the elaborate cake deco- rations for those big birthdays, the significant presents I would save to buy. Odd as it may seem, the anticipation of the acts of letting Adam go began before I even knew his name. ❷ I looked forward to the proud days on which the world would recognize my son as progressively more his own man. Those were among the strongest hooks that bonded me to him in my imagination.

As each of these anniversaries finally came and went, nothing like I ex- pected them to be, I doubly mourned. First, selfishly, for me, and second for Adam, because he didn't know what he was missing, what he had already missed, what he would miss. I wanted to burst through those birthdays like a speeding train blasts a weak gate, to get past them and back into the anony- mous years for which I had made no models, where there were no obvious measurements, no cakes with candles that would never be lit. 8

It was a coincidence that Adam turned twenty-one as this book neared completion, but it seemed appropriate. On the morning of his birthday, I rose early and baked him a lemon cake, his favorite, and left the layers to cool while I drove to Hanover to pick him up. His gifts were wrapped and on the kitchen table—an electric shaver, clothes, a Garfield calendar. ❸ For his special dinner he had requested tacos, and as always I had reserved a magic candle—the kind that keeps reigniting no matter how often it is blown out—for the center of his cake. 9

I was greeted at Adam's house by the news that he had just had a seizure, a small one this time, but it had left him groggy. I helped him on with his coat, bent to tie his shoelace, all the while talking about the fun we would have dur- ing the day. He looked out the window. Only the week before he had been laid off from his dishwashing job. December had been a bad month for seizures, some due to his body's adjustment to a change in dosage and some occurring because Adam had skipped taking medicine altogether. The bowl- ing alley's insurance carrier was concerned and that, combined with an after- Christmas slump in business, decided the issue. Now he was back at Hartford for a few weeks while Ken Krambert and his associates sought a new work placement. I thought perhaps Adam was depressed about this turn of events, so I tried to cheer him up as we drove south on the familiar road to Cornish. 10

"So, Adam," I said, making conversation, summoning the conventional words, "do you feel any older? What's good about being twenty-one?" 11

He turned to me and grinned. There *was* something good. 12

Reading Critically

❷ Why does Dorris anticipate "letting Adam go" before he even knows his name?

❸ How does the odd combination of an electric shaver and a Garfield calendar help us un- derstand Adam's predicament?

"Well," he answered, "now the guys at work say I'm old enough to drink."   13

His unexpected words kicked me in the stomach. They crowded every   14
thought from my brain.

"Adam, you can't," I protested. "I've told you about your birth-mother,   15
about your other father. Do you remember what happened to them?" I knew
he did. I had told him the story several times, and we had gone over it together as he read, or I read to him, parts of this book.

Adam thought for a moment. "They were sick?" he offered finally. "That's   16
why I have seizures?"

"No, they weren't sick. They died, Adam. They died from drinking. If you   17
drank, it could happen to you." My memory played back all the statistics
about sons of alcoholic fathers and their particular susceptibility to substance
abuse. "It would not mix well with your medicine."

Adam sniffed, turned away, but not before I recognized the amused dis-   18
belief in his expression. He did not take death seriously, never had. It was an
abstract concept out of his reach and therefore of no interest to him. Death
was less real than Santa Claus—after all, Adam had in his album a photograph
of himself seated on Santa Claus's lap. Death was no threat, no good reason
to refuse his first drink.

My son will forever travel through a moonless night with only the roar   19
of wind for company. ◆ Don't talk to him of mountains, of tropical beaches.
Don't ask him to swoon at sunrises or marvel at the filter of light through
leaves. He's never had time for such things, and he does not believe in them.
He may pass by them close enough to touch on either side, but his hands are
stretched forward, grasping for balance instead of pleasure. He doesn't wonder where he came from, where he's going. He doesn't ask who he is, or
why. Questions are a luxury, the province of those at a distance from the periodic shock of rain. Gravity presses Adam so hard against reality that he
doesn't feel the points at which he touches it. A drowning man is not separated from the lust for air by a bridge of thought—he is one with it—and
my son, conceived and grown in an ethanol bath, lives each day in the act
of drowning. For him there is no shore.

© Michael Dorris 1989.

UNDERSTANDING DETAILS

1. Why are Adam's birthdays difficult for Dorris?
2. What are some of the problems Adam was born with?

Reading Critically

◆ Explain the following metaphor in your own words: "My son will forever travel through
a moonless night with only the roar of wind for company."

3. Why will Adam never reach his full potential?

4. In what ways did Dorris feel Adam's birthdays would be "oases of certainty" (paragraph 7)? How did the actual celebrations differ from these expectations?

THINKING CRITICALLY

5. Why does Dorris "doubly" mourn (paragraph 8) his son's birthdays? Explain your answer.

6. In what way was "the definition of the rest of [Dorris's] life" (paragraph 7) connected with his son's birthdays?

7. In what way is death like Santa Claus for Adam? Explain your answer.

8. What does Dorris mean when he says "Questions are a luxury" for his son (paragraph 19)?

DISCOVERING RHETORICAL STRATEGIES

9. At what points in this essay does Dorris either directly or indirectly analyze the causes of Adam's behavior? When does he study its effects (on either himself or his son)? Divide a piece of paper in half. List the causes of Adam's behavior on one side and the effects on the other. Record the paragraph references in each case. Then, discuss the pattern that emerges from your two lists. Does Dorris give more attention to the causes or the effects of Adam's behavior? Why do you think the author develops his essay around this particular emphasis?

10. Dorris uses several comparisons to help his readers understand what raising a fetal alcohol child is like. Look, for example, at paragraph 19, in which he compares Adam's life to "a moonless night" and to "the act of drowning." Find two other vivid comparisons in this essay. What do all these comparisons add to the essay? What effect do they have on the essay as a whole?

11. What tone does Dorris establish in his essay? Describe it in three or four well-chosen words. How does he create this tone? What effect does this particular tone have on you as a reader?

12. What rhetorical strategies does Dorris use to support his cause/effect analysis? Give examples of each.

MAKING CONNECTIONS

13. Contrast Dorris's definition of "addiction" with the definitions in the following essays that discuss other addictive topics: Kimberly Wozencraft's "Notes from the Country Club," Franklin Zimring's "Confessions of an Ex-Smoker," and/or Stephen King's "Why We Crave Horror Movies." What specific substance is addictive in these essays? Which addiction do you think would be most difficult to recover from? Explain your answer.

14. Love and concern for a child is the principal topic of Dorris's essay, as it is in Lewis Sawaquat's "For My Indian Daughter," Russell Baker's "The Saturday Evening Post," Bill Cosby's "The Baffling Question," and Judith Wallerstein and Sandra Blakeslee's "Second Chances for Children of Divorce." If we were able to get all these authors together in a roundtable discussion about parent–child

relationships, do you think they would agree on any of the issues? If so, what would these areas of agreement be?

15. Birthdays are milestones in Dorris's essay, just as they are for Malcolm Cowley in "The View from 80." What are the principal differences in the ways each author celebrates these birthdays? Why do these differences exist?

IDEAS FOR DISCUSSION/WRITING

Preparing to Write

Write freely about the process of growing up and reaching your potential: What special problems did you experience while growing up? How did you deal with these problems? How did your parents deal with these problems? Do you feel you are heading toward your full potential, or have you already reached it? How do you plan to reach or maintain your potential? What experiences or people have disappointed you mainly because they were not what you expected? What were their shortcomings? Can these shortcomings be remedied? What effects do such shortcomings have on society as a whole?

Choosing a Topic

1. In a conversation with your mother, father, or another close relative, explain what problems you found most difficult as you were growing up, and speculate about the causes of those problems. In dialogue form, record the conversation as accurately as possible. Add an introduction, a conclusion, and an explanation of your discussion in order to mold the conversation into an essay.

2. In the last paragraph of his essay, Dorris implies that his son is slowly drowning in his birth-mother's alcohol abuse. This essay is Dorris's process of grieving about "what [his son] was missing, what he had already missed, what he would miss" (paragraph 8). In an essay of your own, explain something (a process, a person, an event, a relationship, or an activity) that disappointed you mainly because your expectations weren't met. What were the principal reasons for your disappointment? What were the effects of your disappointment? What could have changed the situation?

3. Many forms of addiction and abuse plague our society at present. In an essay written for your composition class, choose one of these problems and speculate on its primary causes and effects in society today. As often as possible, give specific examples to support your observations.

4. In his article, Dorris personalizes the effects of alcoholism on unborn children. Conduct an Internet search on other threats to infant and child health. To begin your search, you may want to visit the Centers for Disease Control and Prevention's Web site (http://www.cdc.gov). Choose a topic that interests you, and write an article for your campus's student health Web site. Describe the causes and effects of your chosen topic. Find a way to personalize your essay so that it will strike a nerve with your intended audience.

Before beginning your essay, you might want to consult the checklists on page 410.

SHERMAN ALEXIE   (1966–   )

The Joy of Reading and Writing: Superman and Me

A Spokane/Coeur d'Alene Indian, Sherman Alexie grew up on a reservation in Wellpinit, Washington, where he read voraciously as a child. Despite suffering seizures due to his hydrocephalic birth, he excelled in school, eventually attending Gonzaga University on a scholarship. Later, while a student at Washington State University, he stumbled into a poetry workshop and fell in love with writing, which became his life's work. His first two poetry collections, *The Business of Fancydancing* (1991) and *I Would Steal Horses* (1993), led to a collection of short stories, *The Lone Ranger and Tonto Fistfight in Heaven* (1993), which won several prestigious awards. After dabbling in stand-up comedy, Alexie wrote his first novel, *Reservation Blues* (1995), which was soon followed by *Indian Killer* (1996), described by the author as "a feel-good novel about interracial murder." His first movie, *Smoke Signals* (1999), won the Filmmaker's Trophy at the Sundance Film Festival. Additional publications include *Old Shirts and New Skins* (1993), *First Indian on the Moon* (1993), *Water Flowing Home* (1995), *The Summer of Black Widows* (1996), and *Ten Little Indians* (2003). Proud of his Native American heritage, Alexie has admitted that he isn't trying to speak for everybody: "I'm one individual heavily influenced by my tribe. And good art doesn't come out of assimilation—it comes out of tribalism."

Preparing to Read

This essay was first published in a collection of essays on reading called *Most Wonderful Books*. In it, the author, Sherman Alexie, describes his love affair with books and explains their role in his success.

Exploring Experience: As you prepare to read this essay, think about how important reading is in your life: What types of books do you read? What percentage of your reading is for school? For pleasure? Do you enjoy reading? What does leisure reading do for you? How are reading and writing related for you? Are you a good writer? How do you account for your writing ability?

Learning Online: Sherman Alexie's enthusiasm about learning and writing has led him to become a very passionate spokesman for education. Using Google's search engine (http://www.google.com), click on the "Images" tab to conduct a picture search. Use the author's name, "Sherman Alexie," and view several pictures of Alexie addressing various audiences. He humorously describes himself as a "Banana Republic kind of Indian." Consider these pictures as you read his essay and listen to the voice in his writing.

I learned to read with a *Superman* comic book. Simple enough, I suppose. 1
I cannot recall which particular Superman comic book I read, nor can
I remember which villain he fought in that issue. I cannot remember
the plot, nor the means by which I obtained the comic book. What I can remember is this: I was three years old, a Spokane Indian boy living with his
family on the Spokane Indian Reservation in eastern Washington state. We
were poor by most standards, but one of my parents usually managed to find
some minimum-wage job or another, which made us middle-class by reservation standards. I had a brother and three sisters. We lived on a combination
of irregular paychecks, hope, fear, and government surplus food. ❶

My father, who is one of the few Indians who went to Catholic school 2
on purpose, was an avid reader of westerns, spy thrillers, murder mysteries,
gangster epics, basketball player biographies, and anything else he could find.
He bought his books by the pound at Dutch's Pawn Shop, Goodwill, Salvation Army, and Value Village. When he had extra money, he bought new novels at supermarkets, convenience stores and hospital gift shops. Our house was
filled with books. They were stacked in crazy piles in the bathroom, bedrooms, and living room. In a fit of unemployment-inspired creative energy,
my father built a set of bookshelves and soon filled them with a random assortment of books about the Kennedy assassination, Watergate, the Vietnam
War, and the entire twenty-three-book series of the Apache westerns. My father loved books, and since I loved my father with an aching devotion, I decided to love books as well. ❷

I can remember picking up my father's books before I could read. The 3
words themselves were mostly foreign, but I still remember the exact moment when I first understood, with a sudden clarity, the purpose of a paragraph. I didn't have the vocabulary to say "paragraph," but I realized that a
paragraph was a fence that held words. ❸ The words inside a paragraph
worked together for a common purpose. They had some specific reason for
being inside the same fence. This knowledge delighted me. I began to think
of everything in terms of paragraphs. Our reservation was a small paragraph
within the United States. My family's house was a paragraph, distinct from
the other paragraphs of the LeBrets to the north, the Fords to our south, and
the Tribal School to the west. Inside our house, each family member existed
as a separate paragraph but still had genetics and common experiences to link

---

Reading Critically

❶ What does the series of "paychecks, hope, fear, and government surplus food" tell us
about Alexie's childhood?

❷ Do you love anything that your father or mother loves? What is it?

❸ Do you believe this is a good definition of a "paragraph"? Can you define a "sentence"
in the same metaphoric way?

us. Now, using this logic, I can see my changed family as an essay of seven paragraphs: mother, father, older brother, the deceased sister, my younger twin sisters, and our adopted little brother.

At the same time I was seeing the world in paragraphs, I also picked up   4
the *Superman* comic book. Each panel, complete with picture, dialogue, and narrative, was a three-dimensional paragraph. In one panel, Superman breaks through a door. His suit is red, blue, and yellow. The brown door shatters into many pieces. I look at the narrative above the picture. I cannot read the words, but I assume it tells me that "Superman is breaking down the door." Aloud, I pretend to read the words and say, "Superman is breaking down the door." Words, dialogue, also float out of Superman's mouth. Because he is breaking down the door, I assume he says, "I am breaking down the door." Once again, I pretend to read the words and say aloud, "I am breaking down the door." In this way, I learned to read.

This might be an interesting story all by itself. A little Indian boy teaches   5
himself to read at an early age and advances quickly. He reads *Grapes of Wrath* in kindergarten when other children are struggling through Dick and Jane. If he'd been anything but an Indian boy living on the reservation, he might have been called a prodigy. But he is an Indian boy living on the reservation and is simply an oddity. ❹ He grows into a man who often speaks of his childhood in the third-person, as if it will somehow dull the pain and make him sound more modest about his talents.

A smart Indian is a dangerous person, widely feared and ridiculed by In-   6
dians and non-Indians alike. I fought with my classmates on a daily basis. They wanted me to stay quiet when the non-Indian teacher asked for answers, for volunteers, for help. We were Indian children who were expected to be stupid. Most lived up to those expectations inside the classroom but sub-verted them on the outside. They struggled with basic reading in school but could remember how to sing a few dozen powwow songs. They were mono-syllabic in front of their non-Indian teachers but could tell complicated sto-ries and jokes at the dinner table. They submissively ducked their heads when confronted by a non-Indian adult but would slug it out with the Indian bully who was ten years older. As Indian children, we were expected to fail in the non-Indian world. Those who failed were ceremonially accepted by other Indians and appropriately pitied by non-Indians.

I refused to fail. I was smart. I was arrogant. I was lucky. I read books late   7
into the night, until I could barely keep my eyes open. I read books at re-cess, then during lunch, and in the few minutes left after I had finished my

---

Reading Critically

❹ What is the difference between a "prodigy" and an "oddity" in the context of the reservation?

classroom assignments. I read books in the car when my family traveled to powwows or basketball games. In shopping malls, I ran to the bookstores and read bits and pieces of as many books as I could. I read the books my father brought home from the pawnshops and secondhand. I read the books I borrowed from the library. I read the backs of cereal boxes. I read the newspaper. I read the bulletins posted on the walls of the school, the clinic, the tribal offices, the post office. I read junk mail. I read auto-repair manuals. I read magazines. I read anything that had words and paragraphs. I read with equal parts joy and desperation. I loved those books, but I also knew that love had only one purpose. I was trying to save my life. ⑤

Despite all the books I read, I am still surprised I became a writer. I was   8
going to be a pediatrician. These days, I write novels, short stories, and poems. I visit schools and teach creative writing to Indian kids. In all my years in the reservation school system, I was never taught how to write poetry, short stories, or novels. I was certainly never taught that Indians wrote poetry, short stories, and novels. Writing was something beyond Indians. I cannot recall a single time that a guest teacher visited the reservation. There must have been visiting teachers. Who were they? Where are they now? Do they exist? I visit the schools as often as possible. The Indian kids crowd the classroom. Many are writing their own poems, short stories, and novels. They have read my books. They have read many other books. They look at me with bright eyes and arrogant wonder. They are trying to save their lives. Then there are the sullen and already defeated Indian kids who sit in the back rows and ignore me with theatrical precision. The pages of their notebooks are empty. They carry neither pencil nor pen. They stare out the window. They refuse and resist. "Books," I say to them. "Books," I say. I throw my weight against their locked doors. ⑥ The door holds. I am smart. I am arrogant. I am lucky. I am trying to save our lives.

UNDERSTANDING DETAILS

1. How did Alexie learn to read? Why was it important to him?
2. How were life and paragraphs related for Alexie?
3. In what ways is the author unique in his own cultural environment?
4. How are reading and writing related for the author?

Reading Critically
⑤ Why does the author think that books will save his life?
⑥ In what sense does Alexie throw his weight against the students' "locked doors"?

THINKING CRITICALLY

5. Why is a smart Indian "a dangerous person" (paragraph 6)? Explain your answer in detail.
6. What did reading have to do with the author's success in life?
7. Why did many Indian children fail in the classroom but succeed on the streets?
8. In what ways can books save lives?

DISCOVERING RHETORICAL STRATEGIES

9. Explain the title of this essay.
10. Alexie starts this essay with background information about his family. Is this an effective beginning? Why or why not?
11. What rhetorical modes does Alexie use to tell his story?
12. What is the main message Alexie is trying to communicate? Does he get his message across effectively? Explain your answer.

MAKING CONNECTIONS

13. Compare and contrast Alexie's love of books with that expressed by Malcolm X in "Learning to Read." Which author's life has been most changed by the act of reading? Why do you think this is so?
14. Which of the following authors overcame the most discrimination and hardship in his or her life: Alexie, Sandra Cisneros ("Only daughter"), Harold Krentz ("Darkness at Noon"), Sucheng Chan ("You're Short, Besides!"), and/or Alice Walker ("Beauty: When the Other Dancer Is the Self")?
15. How do Alexie, Stephen King ("Why We Crave Horror Movies"), Michael Dorris ("The Broken Cord"), and/or Mary Roach ("Meet the Bickersons") use the cause and effect rhetorical mode differently?

IDEAS FOR DISCUSSION/WRITING

Preparing to Write

Write freely about the role of reading and writing in your life: How do they help you? Do they hinder you in any way? How are they related for you? Which one do you enjoy more? Which one is your stronger suit? Why do you think this is the case? In your opinion, can someone be a good writer, but not a good reader? Can someone be a good reader, but not a good writer? Explain your reasoning.

Choosing a Topic

1. Compose an autobiography of your memories about reading, starting with your earliest recollections. Retrace your experiences with reading up to the present, including the kinds of books you have read, the circumstances surrounding your reading experiences, the people who read to you, the places where you read, your feelings about reading, and your current reading habits.

2. Compose a writing autobiography of your memories about writing, starting with your earliest recollections about writing. Retrace your experiences with writing up to the present, including the types of writing you do, the circumstances surrounding your writing experiences, the people or companies you write to, the places where you write, your feelings about writing, and your current writing habits.

3. Analyze the relationship between reading and writing, using your experience and the stories of others to support your main points.

4. In his essay, Alexie explains that Indian children were not expected to be smart or good readers. No matter what other people said, however, he continued to pursue learning because he truly loved it. Think of an important quality about yourself that would surprise other people. It may be a passion you care deeply about, a secret talent you are especially proud of, or even a goal you have for the future. Write a short essay about this "unexpected characteristic" that you could post on your personal home page.

Before beginning your essay, you might want to consult the checklists on page 410.

MARY ROACH   (1959–   )

Meet the Bickersons

A native of Hanover, New Hampshire, Mary Roach received her B.A. in psychology from Wesleyan University, then worked as a copy editor and a public relations consultant for the San Francisco Zoo. Following five years in the business world, she began her career as a freelance writer after deciding that "it was a lot easier to write the stuff in the first place than to clean it up after someone else had written it." She has been a contributor for many years to the "Diversions" section of the *San Francisco Examiner Sunday Magazine,* focusing on such quirky, interesting topics as drive-in movies and old black-and-white photo booths. She is currently a contributing editor for such well-known periodicals as *Health, Discover, Wired, Muse* (the Smithsonian Museum's children's magazine), and *SALON.com* (an online journal). Her most recent book is *Stiff: The Curious Lives of Human Cadavers* (2003). Asked to give advice to students using *The Prose Reader,* she confides that "people think writing is harder than it is. They tie themselves up in knots over it. Good writing is really just talking on paper. If it were difficult to do, I would not be that successful at it." Roach now lives in San Francisco, where her hobbies include bird watching, reading, and traveling.

Preparing to Read

The following humorous essay, originally published in *Health* magazine, explains different strategies for arguing among couples. The title "Meet the Bickersons" is drawn from an extremely popular American radio comedy (1946–1951) starring Don Ameche and Frances Langford, which was later made into a TV series of the same name.

Exploring Experience: Before you read this essay, think for a moment about how important arguing fairly is to you: Do you argue fairly? Do you expect your partner to argue fairly? What are the qualities of a fair argument? Do you argue with other people? Are you able to control your temper? Do you feel better after you argue? Why or why not? When is arguing most worthwhile? When is it never worthwhile? Do you have any special ground rules for arguing with the people you love?

Learning Online: Visit "About.com" (http://about.com), and type "Why do couples fight?" into the search field. Read a short article about why couples fight. Consider the format and content of this article as you read Mary Roach's essay. Why is Roach's presentation more effective?

Psychologists have long said it's possible to predict whether a couple will   1
stay happily married simply by looking at how they fight. This did
not bode well for yours truly, who got married not too long ago.
Pretty much all I'd learned about spousal arguing came from *The Newlywed
Game,* which taught us 1) that the proper form of conflict resolution is to
hit your partner over the head with a large piece of poster board and 2) that
most problems can be resolved with the acquisition of a brand-new washer
and dryer or a gift pack of Turtle Wax.

I've been told I'm defensive—"like a cornered mongoose" were the exact   2
words. I've also been criticized for being sarcastic, overreacting, and crying
too easily. I don't deny these things (though if you were to accuse me of
them in the heat of battle, you can be sure I would—vehemently, and with
pointy little teeth bared).

I had a boyfriend who tried to change me. He asked me to use a therapy   3
technique called "active listening," a mainstay of many modern marriage
counselors. ◆ It's supposed to make you a more fair, less combative arguer.
I (and here's something you couldn't see coming) objected to this, stating that
I was already an active listener. My ex countered that deep sighs, nostril
flares, pacing, and storming from the room did not qualify. Active listening
means focusing carefully on what your partner is saying, as though there
were going to be a test, because, in fact, there is. You are required to paraphrase your beloved's misguided rantings—sorry, feelings—beginning with
the phrase "What I hear you saying is . . ."

I agreed to try it. He went first. Minutes passed. Fortunately, we were on   4
the phone at the time, which allowed me to scribble notes. He finished and
fell silent.

"What I hear you saying," I began, "is that you think I'm defensive, and I   5
don't allow you to feel what you're feeling and that makes you incredibly
. . . truncated, wait, flat-footed?"

"Frustrated."   6

"Of course."   7

"You're cheating," he said. "You're writing things down."   8

"Am not."   9

Nothing—not counseling, not even Turtle Wax—was going to save that   10
relationship.

With Ed, I was determined to do things right and asked a friend with a   11
degree in counseling for advice. She encouraged me to use "I" statements because "you" statements put people on the defensive. For instance, one does

---

Reading Critically

◆ What do you think the term "active listening" means?

not say to one's beloved, "You never do the dishes, you self-centered pea brain." One says, "I feel angry and taken advantage of when the people I love leave their dishes for me, especially when it was those people who dirtied them in the first place and ate the leftovers they knew darn well I was planning to have for lunch." ❷

Another suggested technique was validation, in which each partner makes 12
an effort to endorse the other's feelings: "I can see why you'd be upset with my failing to wash one small dish and eating an eighth of a taco. I would be, too, if I were an oversensitive, petty person who only focuses on the negative."

A while back I put all these techniques to work. We were driving, and I 13
had failed to notice a stop sign, which even the most vigilant driver will do from time to time, am I right? Ed did not fail to notice the stop sign, as was evinced by his slamming of the imaginary brakes on his side of the car. "When you constantly remark upon my driving irregularities," I began, "I feel scrutinized and inadequate, and by the way, who was it that nearly got us killed by turning into traffic outside Costco?"

Ed was unperturbed by the Costco barb. What got him was the I-feel-blah- 14
dee-blah business. "Why don't you just get mad and call me a back-seat driver, and that'd be that?"

Later that evening I tried to explain what I'd learned about "you" state- 15
ments and active listening and validating feelings. Ed listened carefully. Then he took my hand in his. "When you talk about things like this, I feel, let me see, like throwing up. How was that?"

Shortly after, Ed left a newspaper clipping on my desk. It described a uni- 16
versity study in which 130 newlywed pairs were videotaped arguing and then tracked for six years. It turns out the couples who stayed married had seldom used techniques like active listening and validation. The researcher was "shocked" to find that the happy couples fought like normal people—getting angry, clearing the air, and making up. (Their spats, however, were tinged with soothing and humor.)

This was one instance in which I was glad to be proved wrong. So thrilled 17
was I at the prospect of never again having to begin a sentence with "What I hear you saying is" that I made a vow on the spot that the next time Ed got mad at me, I would not get defensive.

It happened on a Saturday afternoon. I had thrown away a set of circa-1970 18
stereo speakers that Ed had wanted to keep because they might come in

---

Reading Critically

❷ What is the difference between an "I" statement and a "You" statement? Which do you use most frequently when you're arguing with a loved one?

handy for taking up space in the basement for the next ten years. It didn't go quite the way I'd envisioned. I heard myself lambasting Ed for having gone through the garbage, checking up on what I'd junked. "You're scrutinizing me!"

Ed looked flabbergasted. "You toss things without even asking!"   19

The bell rang, and we withdrew to our corners. ❸ Around dinnertime I   20 appeared in the kitchen with the speakers, dusted and polished. Ed, in turn, promised not to supervise my spring cleaning. He asked me to let him know when I caught him checking over something I'd done. "I'm not even aware of it. So please tell me." He smiled sweetly. "And then I'll deny it."

UNDERSTANDING DETAILS

1. What is "active listening" (paragraph 3)? What verbal technique did Roach learn as an active listener?
2. Explain the technique of "validation" in your own words.
3. Does Roach think she is too defensive? What animal did someone compare her defensiveness to?
4. What did a university study learn about the argumentative habits of 130 newlywed couples? How did Roach feel about the findings of this study?

THINKING CRITICALLY

5. According to psychologists, how does the way couples fight affect the survival of their marriages?
6. Why was Roach trying different strategies for getting along with her partner?
7. Who is Ed? Why was Roach trying so hard to make her relationship with Ed work?
8. What does Roach mean when she says about the first boyfriend, "Nothing—not counseling, not even Turtle Wax—was going to save that relationship" (paragraph 10)?

DISCOVERING RHETORICAL STRATEGIES

9. List the causes and effects that this essay studies.
10. What is the general mood of Roach's essay?
11. Roach begins her essay with some references to the *Newlywed Game*. What do the poster board, a washer and dryer, and Turtle Wax have to do with that game? Do you think this is an effective way to start her essay? Explain your answer.
12. What other rhetorical strategies support this cause/effect essay? Give examples of each.

Reading Critically

❸ What metaphor for fighting is the author using here? How effective is this comparison?

MAKING CONNECTIONS

13. Compare and contrast Roach's conclusions about successful communications within a relationship with similar advice provided in Wallerstein and Blakeslee's "Second Chances for Children of Divorce" and/or Mary Pipher's "Beliefs About Families."
14. Analyze Roach's prescription for dealing with anger in light of the following essays: Lewis Sawaquat's "For My Indian Daughter," Brent Staples's "A Brother's Murder," and/or Michael Dorris's "The Broken Cord."
15. Compare Roach's use of humor in her essay to similar anecdotes in Russell Baker's "The Saturday Evening Post," Garrison Keillor's "How the Crab Apple Grew," and/or Bill Cosby's "The Baffling Question."

IDEAS FOR DISCUSSION/WRITING

Preparing to Write

Write freely about your views on arguing: Do you know how to argue? Have you ever been sorry for anything you said while you were arguing? Do you argue with your parents differently than you argue with your friends? With your boyfriends/girlfriends/spouses? Why do you argue? What do you try to accomplish when you argue? Does arguing usually make you feel better or worse? Is it difficult to make up after you argue? How do you make up?

Choosing a Topic

1. Your college newspaper is accepting essays on your interests in life. Write an essay for the newspaper explaining in detail your most passionate interest. Cover both the causes and effects of this interest. (This interest does not have to be related to school matters.)
2. Your college counselor/adviser wants to know if you consider yourself emotionally healthy. In a detailed essay written for this counselor, who is writing a letter of recommendation for you, explain why you are or are not in good emotional health. What events, attitudes, or activities have played a part in developing your mental health?
3. Americans seem to be obsessed with their health these days. Why do you think this is so? How did this obsession start?
4. What are some other techniques necessary for maintaining healthy relationships? Choose an issue such as compromise, honesty, or communication, and reflect on your experience with this topic. Then write an essay in which you explore the cause and effect of positive—and negative—uses of this technique. Roach supports her personal observations with case studies. Strengthen your essay by using case studies and statistics that you have found online.

Before beginning your essay, you might want to consult the checklists on page 410.

ALICE WALKER   (1944–   )

Beauty: When the Other Dancer Is the Self

Born in Eatonton, Georgia, and educated at Spelman College and Sarah Lawrence College, Alice Walker is best known for her Pulitzer Prize-winning novel *The Color Purple* (1983), which was later made into an immensely popular movie of the same title. The book details a young African-American woman's search for self-identity within a world contaminated by racial prejudice and family crisis. The author has explained that "the Black woman is one of America's greatest heroes," though she has been denied credit for her accomplishments and "oppressed beyond recognition." Most of Walker's other novels and collections of short stories echo the same theme, and most share the "sense of affirmation" featured in *The Color Purple* that overcomes the anger and social indignity suffered by so many of her characters. The author's many other publications include *In Love and Trouble: Stories of Black Women* (1973), *Meridian* (1976), *You Can't Keep a Good Woman Down* (1981), *In Search of Our Mothers' Gardens* (1983), *Living by the Word* (1988), *To Hell with Dying* (1988), *The Temple of My Familiar* (1989), *Possessing the Secret of Joy* (1992), *Everyday Use* (1994), *Alice Walker Banned* (1996), *By the Light of My Father's Smile* (1998), *The Way Forward Is With a Broken Heart* (2000), *Absolute Trust in the Goodness of the Earth: New Poems* (2003), and *Now Is the Time to Open Your Heart* (2004). Walker, who has been a professor and writer-in-residence at Wellesley College, the University of Massachusetts, the University of California at Berkeley, and Brandeis University, currently lives in Mendocino, California.

Preparing to Read

The following essay, from *In Search of Our Mothers' Gardens,* focuses on young Alice Walker's reaction to being blinded in one eye as a result of an accident with a BB gun.

Exploring Experience: As you begin to read this essay, take a few minutes to consider the role of physical appearance in our lives: Do you find that you often judge people based on their physical appearance? Do you feel that people judge you based on your appearance? What other characteristics play a part in your judgment of others? How important are good looks to you? Why do they carry this importance for you? What specific people affect the way you feel about yourself?

Learning Online: In her essay, Alice Walker describes concerns about her own appearance. Look for pictures of Walker online; use *Alice Walker* as your search term. Consider your opinions of her appearance as you read her essay.

I t is a bright summer day in 1947. My father, a fat, funny man with beau- 1
tiful eyes and a subversive wit, is trying to decide which of his eight children he will take with him to the county fair. My mother, of course,
will not go. She is knocked out from getting most of us ready: I hold my neck
stiff against the pressure of her knuckles as she hastily completes the braid-
ing and then beribboning of my hair.

My father is the driver for the rich old white lady up the road. Her name 2
is Miss Mey. She owns all the land for miles around, as well as the house in
which we live. All I remember about her is that she once offered to pay my
mother thirty-five cents for cleaning her house, raking up piles of her mag-
nolia leaves, and washing her family's clothes, and that my mother—she of
no money, eight children, and a chronic earache—refused it. But I do not
think of this in 1947. I am two and a half years old. I want to go everywhere
my daddy goes. I am excited at the prospect of riding in a car. Someone has
told me fairs are fun. That there is room in the car for only three of us doesn't
faze me at all. Whirling happily in my starchy frock, showing off my biscuit-
polished patent-leather shoes and lavender socks, tossing my head in a way
that makes my ribbons bounce, I stand, hands on hips, before my father.
"Take me, Daddy," I say with assurance; "I'm the prettiest!" ❶

Later, it does not surprise me to find myself in Miss Mey's shiny black car, 3
sharing the back seat with the other lucky ones. Does not surprise me that
I thoroughly enjoy the fair. At home that night I tell the unlucky ones all I
can remember about the merry-go-round, the man who eats live chickens,
and the teddy bears, until they say: that's enough, baby Alice. Shut up now,
and go to sleep.

It is Easter Sunday, 1950. I am dressed in a green, flocked, scalloped-hem 4
dress (handmade by my adoring sister, Ruth) that has its own smooth satin
petticoat and tiny hot-pink roses tucked into each scallop. My shoes, new
T-strap patent leather, again highly biscuit-polished. I am six years old and
have learned one of the longest Easter speeches to be heard that day, totally
unlike the speech I said when I was two: "Easter lilies/pure and white/
blossom in/the morning light." When I rise to give my speech I do so on a
great wave of love and pride and expectation. People in the church stop
rustling their new crinolines. They seem to hold their breath. I can tell they
admire my dress, but it is my spirit, bordering on sassiness (womanishness),
they secretly applaud. ❷

Reading Critically

❶ What does the emphasis on clothing here and elsewhere in the essay tell us about the author's childhood memories?

❷ What is the relationship between "sassiness" and "womanishness"?

"That girl's a little *mess*," they whisper to each other, pleased.   5

Naturally I say my speech without stammer or pause, unlike those who   6
stutter, stammer, or, worst of all, forget. This is before the word "beautiful"
exists in people's vocabulary, but "Oh, isn't she the *cutest* thing!" frequently
floats my way. "And got so much sense!" they gratefully add . . . for which
thoughtful addition I thank them to this day.

It was great fun being cute. But then, one day, it ended. ❸   7

I am eight years old and a tomboy. I have a cowboy hat, cowboy boots,   8
checkered shirt and pants, all red. My playmates are my brothers, two and four
years older than I. Their colors are black and green, the only difference in the
way we are dressed. On Saturday nights we all go to the picture show, even
my mother; Westerns are her favorite kind of movie. Back home, "on the
ranch," we pretend we are Tom Mix, Hopalong Cassidy, Lash LaRue (we've
even named one of our dogs Lash LaRue); we chase each other for hours
rustling cattle, being outlaws, delivering damsels from distress. Then my parents decide to buy my brothers guns. These are not "real" guns. They shoot
"BBs," copper pellets my brothers say will kill birds. Because I am a girl, I do
not get a gun. Instantly I am relegated to the position of Indian. Now there
appears a great distance between us. They shoot and shoot at everything with
their new guns. I try to keep up with my bow and arrows.

One day while I am standing on top of our makeshift "garage"—pieces   9
of tin nailed across some poles—holding my bow and arrow and looking out
toward the fields, I feel an incredible blow in my right eye. I look down just
in time to see my brother lower his gun.

Both brothers rush to my side. My eye stings, and I cover it with my hand.   10
"If you tell," they say, "we will get a whipping. You don't want that to happen, do you?" I do not. "Here is a piece of wire," says the older brother, picking it up from the roof; "say you stepped on one end of it and the other flew
up and hit you." The pain is beginning to start. "Yes," I say. "Yes, I will say that
is what happened." If I do not say this is what happened, I know my brothers will find ways to make me wish I had. But now I will say anything that
gets me to my mother.

Confronted by our parents we stick to the lie agreed upon. They place me   11
on a bench on the porch, and I close my left eye while they examine the
right. There is a tree growing from underneath the porch that climbs past the

---

Reading Critically

❸ Why does Walker use italics here and elsewhere? At which moments in the essay does she
use them?

railing to the roof. It is the last thing my right eye sees. ◆ I watch as its trunk, its branches, and then its leaves are blotted out by the rising blood.

I am in shock. First there is intense fever, which my father tries to break   12
using lily leaves bound around my head. Then there are chills: my mother tries to get me to eat soup. Eventually, I do not know how, my parents learn what has happened. A week after the "accident" they take me to see a doctor. "Why did you wait so long to come?" he asks, looking into my eye and shaking his head. "Eyes are sympathetic," he says. "If one is blind, the other will likely become blind too."

This comment of the doctor's terrifies me. But it is really how I look that   13
bothers me most. Where the BB pellet struck there is a glob of whitish scar tissue, a hideous cataract, on my eye. Now when I stare at people—a favorite pastime, up to now—they will stare back. Not at the "cute" little girl, but at her scar. For six years I do not stare at anyone, because I do not raise my head.

Years later, in the throes of a mid-life crisis, I ask my mother and sister   14
whether I changed after the "accident." "No," they say, puzzled. "What do you mean?"

What do I mean?   15

I am eight, and, for the first time, doing poorly in school, where I have   16
been something of a whiz since I was four. ◆ We have just moved to the place where the "accident" occurred. We do not know any of the people around us because this is a different county. The only time I see the friends I knew is when we go back to our old church. The new school is the former state penitentiary. It is a large stone building, cold and drafty, crammed to over-flowing with boisterous, ill-disciplined children. On the third floor there is a huge circular imprint of some partition that has been torn out.

"What used to be here?" I ask a sullen girl next to me on our way past it   17
to lunch.

"The electric chair," says she. ◆   18

At night I have nightmares about the electric chair and about all the peo-   19
ple reputedly "fried" in it. I am afraid of the school, where all the students seem to be budding criminals.

"What's the matter with your eye?" they ask, critically.   20

When I don't answer (I cannot decide whether it was an "accident" or   21
not), they shove me, insist on a fight.

Reading Critically

◆ Why is it significant that a tree is the last thing the author sees with her injured right eye?

◆ How does time pass in the essay? Why does the author choose these particular moments to help tell her story?

◆ How did the former presence of an electric chair help characterize Walker's new school?

My brother, the one who created the story about the wire, comes to my   22
rescue. But then brags so much about "protecting" me, I become sick.

After months of torture at the school, my parents decide to send me back   23
to our old community, to my old school. I live with my grandparents and the
teacher they board. But there is no room for Phoebe, my cat. By the time
my grandparents decide there *is* room, and I ask for my cat, she cannot be
found. Miss Yarborough, the boarding teacher, takes me under her wing and
begins to teach me to play the piano. But soon she marries an African—a
"prince," she says—and is whisked away to his continent.

At my old school there is at least one teacher who loves me. She is the   24
teacher who "knew me before I was born" and bought my first baby clothes.
It is she who makes life bearable. It is her presence that finally helps me turn
on the one child at the school who continually calls me "one-eyed bitch."
One day I simply grab him by his coat and beat him until I am satisfied. It
is my teacher who tells me my mother is ill.

My mother is lying in bed in the middle of the day, something I have   25
never seen. She is in too much pain to speak. She has an abscess in her ear.
I stand looking down on her, knowing that if she dies, I cannot live. She is
being treated with warm oils and hot bricks held against her cheek. Finally
a doctor comes. But I must go back to my grandparents' house. The weeks
pass but I am hardly aware of it. All I know is that my mother might die, my
father is not so jolly, my brothers still have their guns, and I am the one sent
away from home.

"You did not change," they say.   26

Did I imagine the anguish of never looking up?   27

I am twelve. When relatives come to visit I hide in my room. My cousin   28
Brenda, just my age, whose father works in the post office and whose mother
is a nurse, comes to find me. "Hello," she says. And then she asks, looking at
my recent school picture, which I did not want taken, and on which the
"glob," as I think of it, is clearly visible, "You still can't see out of that eye?"

"No," I say, and flop back on the bed over my book.   29

That night, as I do almost every night, I abuse my eye. I rant and rave at   30
it, in front of the mirror. I plead with it to clear up before morning. I tell it
I hate and despise it. I do not pray for sight. I pray for beauty. ⬩

"You did not change," they say.   31

Reading Critically

⬩ Why does the author pray every night for beauty rather than sight? Which is more important to her? Why?

I am fourteen and baby-sitting for my brother Bill, who lives in Boston. He   32
is my favorite brother, and there is a strong bond between us. Understanding my
feelings of shame and ugliness he and his wife take me to a local hospital, where
the "glob" is removed by a doctor named O. Henry. There is still a small bluish
crater where the scar tissue was, but the ugly white stuff is gone. Almost immediately I become a different person from the girl who does not raise her head. ⑧
Or so I think. Now that I've raised my head I win the boyfriend of my dreams.
Now that I've raised my head I have plenty of friends. Now that I've raised my
head classwork comes from my lips as faultlessly as Easter speeches did, and I
leave high school as valedictorian, most popular student, and *queen,* hardly believing my luck. Ironically, the girl who was voted most beautiful in our class (and
was) was later shot twice through the chest by a male companion, using a "real"
gun, while she was pregnant. But that's another story in itself. Or is it?

"You did not change," they say.   33

It is now thirty years since the "accident." A beautiful journalist comes to   34
visit and to interview me. She is going to write a cover story for her magazine that focuses on my latest book. "Decide how you want to look on the
cover," she says. "Glamorous, or whatever."

Never mind "glamorous," it is the "whatever" that I hear. Suddenly all I   35
can think of is whether I will get enough sleep the night before the photography session: if I don't, my eye will be tired and wander, as blind eyes will.

At night in bed with my lover I think up reasons why I should not ap-   36
pear on the cover of a magazine. "My meanest critics will say I've sold out,"
I say. "My family will now realize I write scandalous books."

"But what's the real reason you don't want to do this?" ⑨ he asks.   37

"Because in all probability," I say in a rush, "my eye won't be straight."   38

"It will be straight enough," he says. Then, "Besides, I thought you'd made   39
your peace with that."

And I suddenly remember that I have.   40

I remember: 41

I am talking to my brother Jimmy, asking if he remembers anything un-   42
usual about the day I was shot. He does not know I consider that day the last
time my father, with his sweet home remedy of cool lily leaves, chose me,
and that I suffered and raged inside because of this. "Well," he says, "all I remember is standing by the side of the highway with Daddy, trying to flag
down a car. A white man stopped, but when Daddy said he needed somebody to take his little girl to the doctor, he drove off."

Reading Critically

⑧ How does Walker change when the scar tissue is removed from her eye?
⑨ Why doesn't the author like to be photographed?

I remember: 43

I am in the desert for the first time. I fall totally in love with it. I am so   44
overwhelmed by its beauty, I confront for the first time, consciously, the
meaning of the doctor's words years ago: "Eyes are sympathetic. If one is
blind, the other will likely become blind too." I realize I have dashed about
the world madly, looking at this, looking at that, storing up images against
the fading of the light. *But I might have missed seeing the desert!* The shock of
that possibility—and gratitude for over twenty-five years of sight—sends me
literally to my knees. Poem after poem comes—which is perhaps how poets
pray. [10]

ON SIGHT

I am so thankful I have seen
The Desert
And the creatures in the desert
And the desert Itself.
The desert has its own moon
Which I have seen
With my own eye.
There is no flag on it.

Trees of the desert have arms
All of which are always up
That is because the moon is up
The sun is up
Also the sky
The stars
Clouds
None with flags.

If there were flags, I doubt
the trees would point.
Would you?

But mostly, I remember this: 45

I am twenty-seven, and my baby daughter is almost three. Since her birth   46
I have worried about her discovery that her mother's eyes are different from
other people's. Will she be embarrassed? I think. What will she say? Every day
she watches a television program called *Big Blue Marble*. It begins with a picture of the earth as it appears from the moon. It is bluish, a little battered-
looking, but full of light, with whitish clouds swirling around it. Every time
I see it I weep with love, as if it is a picture of Grandma's house. One day
when I am putting Rebecca down for her nap, she suddenly focuses on my

---

Reading Critically

[10] What do you think Walker means when she says that writing poems is "how poets pray"?

eye. Something inside me cringes, gets ready to try to protect myself. All children are cruel about physical differences, I know from experience, and that they don't always mean to be is another matter. I assume Rebecca will be the same.

But no-o-o-o. She studies my face intently as we stand, her inside and me   47 outside her crib. She even holds my face maternally between her dimpled little hands. Then, looking every bit as serious and lawyerlike as her father, she says, as if it may just possibly have slipped my attention: "Mommy, there's a *world* in your eye." (As in, "Don't be alarmed, or do anything crazy.") And then, gently, but with great interest: "Mommy, where did you *get* that world in your eye?"

For the most part, the pain left then. (So what, if my brothers grew up to   48 buy even more powerful pellet guns for their sons and to carry real guns themselves. So what, if a young "Morehouse man" once nearly fell off the steps of Trevor Arnett Library because he thought my eyes were blue.) Crying and laughing I ran to the bathroom, while Rebecca mumbled and sang herself off to sleep. Yes indeed, I realized, looking into the mirror. There *was* a world in my eye. And I saw that it was possible to love it: that in fact, for all it had taught me of shame and anger and inner vision, I *did* love it. [11] Even to see it drifting out of orbit in boredom, or rolling up out of fatigue, not to mention floating back at attention in excitement (bearing witness, a friend has called it), deeply suitable to my personality, and even characteristic of me.

That night I dream I am dancing to Stevie Wonder's song "Always" (the   49 name of the song is really "As," but I hear it as "Always"). As I dance, whirling and joyous, happier than I've ever been in my life, another bright-faced dancer joins me. We dance and kiss each other and hold each other through the night. The other dancer has obviously come through all right, as I have done. [12] She is beautiful, whole and free. And she is also me.

UNDERSTANDING DETAILS

1. What time frame in the author's life does this essay cover?
2. What is the focal point of the essay? What activities lead up to this "accident"? What are the long-term effects of this "accident"?
3. In what ways does Walker think her life changed after she was shot in the eye?
4. Describe the author's relationship with her brothers, before and after the accident.

Reading Critically

[11] What event enables Walker to begin loving her eye?
[12] Who is "the other dancer"? How is she related to the author?

THINKING CRITICALLY

5. Why is Walker devastated by the scar tissue in her eye? Which bothers her more, the scar tissue or the blindness? Explain your answer.

6. Which of the people introduced in the essay (other than her family members) mean the most to her? List them in order of importance. Then explain why each is important in this cause/effect essay.

7. List the changes that Walker mentions in her actions and personality. Then analyze these changes by discussing their causes and effects.

8. Why is Rebecca's declaration "Mommy, there's a *world* in your eye" (paragraph 47) so important to the author? What changes in Walker result from this particular encounter with her daughter?

DISCOVERING RHETORICAL STRATEGIES

9. Why do you think Walker wrote this essay? What was she trying to accomplish by writing it?

10. How does Walker use blank spaces between her paragraphs? In what ways does this spacing contribute to her essay?

11. Why does Walker put the sentences "It was great fun being cute. But then, one day, it ended" (paragraph 7) by themselves in italics?

12. Explain the emotional ups and downs in the essay. How does Walker's language change in each case?

MAKING CONNECTIONS

13. Walker's essay centers on a single momentous event, the blinding of her right eye, that affected her life from the instant it happened. Similarly significant events shape the lives of the principal characters in Ray Bradbury's "Summer Rituals," Sandra Cisneros's "Only daughter," and Michael Dorris's "The Broken Cord." Compare and contrast the extent to which each of these events influences the characters involved.

14. One of Walker's primary themes involves the eventual acceptance of who we are in life. Find the same theme in Malcolm Cowley's "The View from 80," Lewis Sawaquat's "For My Indian Daughter," or Richard Rodriguez's "Hunger of Memory"; then decide which of these authors seems most content with his or her own self-image. How did you come to this conclusion?

15. The relationship between Walker's original injury and the shyness and insecurity that resulted from it imply a negative cause/effect connection. Find an essay in this chapter of the book that implies a positive connection between a cause and its effect. How are the two essays different? How are they the same?

IDEAS FOR DISCUSSION/WRITING

Preparing to Write

Write freely about your self-esteem and the role of self-esteem in the life of college students: How important is self-esteem to you personally? To your academic performance? What affects your self-esteem most? Why do these events affect you? Do they help or hinder your self-esteem? What elements affect the self-esteem of other students you know? Of friends of yours? Of relatives? What effects have you observed in college students that result from low self-esteem? In friends? In relatives? How do you control your self-esteem? Do you recommend this method to others?

Choosing a Topic

1. Low self-esteem can cause a number of serious problems in different aspects of college students' lives. Conduct a study of the causes and effects of low self-esteem in the lives of several students at your school. Write an essay for the college community explaining these causes and effects.

2. Your campus newspaper is printing a special issue highlighting the psychological health of different generations of college students. Interview some people who represent a generation other than your own. Then characterize the students in this generation for the newspaper. In essay form, introduce the features you have discovered, and then discuss their causes and effects.

3. Some people believe self-esteem is a result of peer groups; others say that it is a result of one's family environment. What do you think? *Time* magazine is soliciting student reactions on this issue and has asked for your opinion. Where do you stand on this question? Give specific examples that support your opinion. Respond in essay form.

4. Despite her concerns about the wound in her eye, photographs of Alice Walker are published in several places on the Internet. How do you feel about having your picture published on the Internet? Do you have any insecurities about your appearance? Write an essay in which you explore these feelings. With Walker's essay as a model, use vivid description in your analysis of the causes of these insecurities and their effects on other aspects of your life.

Before beginning your essay, you might want to consult the checklists on page 410.

Chapter Writing Assignments

Practicing Cause/Effect

1. Think about a time in your life when you had definite, clear expectations of an event or experience. Where did these expectations come from? Were they high or low? Were they fulfilled or not? If not, what went wrong? Explain the situation surrounding this experience in a coherent essay.

2. Brainstorm about some challenges or difficult times you have faced. Then describe the most important challenge you have overcome. Explain why this experience was so difficult and what helped you face and conquer it.

3. What do you believe are the major causes of violence in American society? Write an essay that explains why the causes you cite are real or valid. Can you propose any possible solutions to the predicament you describe?

Exploring Ideas

4. How does our reading help us perceive the world? Do you think short stories, plays, and poems help us understand people's behavior and feelings? Write an essay responding to these questions.

5. Compare your memory of a particular childhood experience with that of another family member. How accurately do you both seem to remember this same event? What do you think accounts for the differences in what we remember about various events? What do these differences say about us? Write an essay exploring these questions, using the event from your childhood to support your discussion.

6. Television has been blamed for causing violent behavior, shortening attention spans, and exposing young people to sexually explicit images. Should we as a society monitor what appears on television more closely, or should parents be responsible for censoring what their children watch? Write an essay that takes a stand on this issue.

Analyzing Visual Images

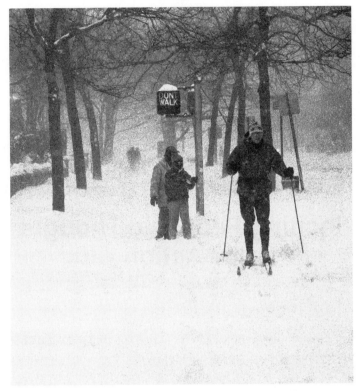

Dave Beckerman Photography.

7. Examine the photo above and think about the roads that we travel in our lives. Discuss a time when you decided to take a different road, and explain the effect this change had on your life.

8. Look at the picture on page 402 at the beginning of this chapter, which depicts the famous Zeppelin Hindenburg (one of the largest airships ever) bursting into flames in 1937. You might be interested in researching the causes and effects of this disaster at http://en.wikipedia.org/wiki/ Hindenburg_disaster#The_Hindenburg. Consider other similar disasters that changed the way people think about traveling, and write an essay explaining all the causes and effects that were connected with this change.

Chapter 9

ARGUMENT AND PERSUASION
Inciting People to Thought or Action

Almost everything we do or say is an attempt to persuade. Whether we dress up to impress a potential employer or argue openly with a friend about an upcoming election, we are trying to convince various people to see the world our way. However, some aspects of life are particularly dependent upon persuasion. Think, for example, of all the television, magazine, and billboard ads we see urging us to buy certain products or of the many impassioned appeals we read and hear on such controversial issues as school prayer, abortion, gun control, and nuclear energy. Religious leaders devote their professional lives to convincing people to live a certain way and believe in certain religious truths, whereas scientists and mathematicians use rigorous logic and natural law to convince us of various hypotheses. Politicians make their living persuading voters to elect them and then support them throughout their terms of office. In fact, anyone who wants something from another person or agency, ranging from federal money for a research project to a new bicycle for Christmas, must use some form of persuasion to get what he or she desires. The success or failure of this type of communication is easily determined: If the people being addressed change their actions or attitudes in favor of the writer or speaker, the attempt at persuasion has been successful.

446

DEFINING ARGUMENT AND PERSUASION

The terms *argument* and *persuasion* are often used interchangeably, but one is actually a subdivision of the other. Persuasion names a purpose for writing. To persuade your readers is to convince them to think, act, or feel a certain way. Much of the writing you have been doing in this book has persuasion as one of its goals: A description of an African tribe might have a "dominant impression" you want your readers to accept; in an essay comparing various ways of celebrating Thanksgiving, you might try to convince your readers to believe that these similarities and differences actually exist; and in writing an essay exam on the causes of the Vietnam War, you are trying to convince your instructor that your reasoning is clear and your conclusions sound. In a sense, some degree of persuasion propels all writing.

More specifically, however, the process of persuasion involves appealing to one or more of the following: to reason, to emotion, or to a sense of ethics. An *argument* is an appeal predominantly to your readers' reason and intellect. You are working in the realm of argument when you deal with complex issues that are debatable; opposing views (either explicit or implicit) are a basic requirement of argumentation. But argument and persuasion are taught together because good writers are constantly blending these three appeals and adjusting them to the purpose and audience of a particular writing task. Although reason and logic are the focus of this chapter, you need to learn to use all three methods of persuasion as skillfully as possible to write effective essays.

An appeal to reason relies on logic and intellect and is usually most effective when you are expecting your readers to disagree with you in some way. This type of appeal can help you change your readers' opinions or influence their future actions through the sheer strength of logical validity. If you want to argue, for example, that pregnant women should refrain from smoking cigarettes, you could cite abundant statistical evidence that babies born to mothers who smoke have lower birth weights, more respiratory problems, and a higher incidence of sudden infant death syndrome than the children of nonsmoking mothers. Because smoking clearly endangers the health of the unborn child, reason dictates that mothers who wish to give birth to the healthiest possible babies should avoid smoking during pregnancy.

Emotional appeals, however, attempt to arouse your readers' feelings, instincts, senses, and biases. Used most profitably when your readers already agree with you, this type of essay generally validates, reinforces, and/or incites in an effort to get your readers to share your feelings or ideas. In order to urge our lawmakers to impose stricter jail sentences for alcohol abuse, you might describe a recent tragic accident involving a local twelve-year-old girl who was killed by a drunk driver as she rode her bicycle to school one morning. By focusing on such poignant visual details as the condition of her mangled bike, the bright red blood stains on her white dress, and the anguish on the faces of parents and friends, you could build a powerfully persuasive essay that would be much more effective than a dull recitation of impersonal facts and nationwide statistics.

An appeal to ethics, the third technique writers often use to encourage readers to agree with them, involves cultivating a sincere, honest tone that will establish your reputation as a reliable, qualified, experienced, well-informed, and knowledgeable person whose opinions on the topic under discussion are believable because they are ethically sound. Such an approach is often used in conjunction with logical or emotional appeals to foster a verbal environment that will result in minimal resistance from its readers. Premier golfer Tiger Woods is a master at creating this ethical, trustworthy persona as he tries to persuade television viewers to buy Nike products. In fact, the old gag question "Would you buy a used car from this man?" is our instinctive response to all forms of attempted persuasion, whether the salesperson is trying to sell us Puppy Chow or gun control, hair spray or school prayer. The more believable we are as human beings, the better chance we will have of convincing our audience.

The following student paragraph is directed primarily toward the audience's logical reasoning ability. Notice that the writer states her assertion and then gives reasons to convince her readers to change their ways. The student writer also brings both emotion and ethics into the argument by choosing her words and examples with great precision.

Have you ever watched a pair of chunky thighs, a jiggling posterior, and an extra-large sweatshirt straining to cover a beer belly and thought, "Thank God I don't look like that! I'm in pretty good shape . . . for someone my age." Well, before you become too smug and self-righteous, consider what kind of shape you're really in. Just because you don't look like Shamu the whale doesn't mean you're in good condition. What's missing, you ask? Exercise. You can diet all day, wear the latest slim-cut designer jeans, and still be in worse shape than someone twice your age if you don't get a strong physical workout at least three times a week. Exercise is not only good for you, but it can also be fun—especially if you find a sport that makes you happy while you sweat. Your activity need not be expensive: Jogging, walking, basketball, tennis, and handball are not costly, unless you're seduced by the glossy sheen of the latest sporting fashions and accessories. Most of all, however, regular exercise is important for your health. You can just as easily drop dead from a sudden heart attack in the middle of a restaurant when you're slim and trim as when you're a slob. Your heart and lungs need regular workouts to stay healthy. So do yourself a favor, and add some form of exercise to your schedule. You'll feel better and live longer, and your looks will improve, too!

THINKING CRITICALLY THROUGH ARGUMENT AND PERSUASION

Thinking

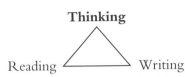

Reading ——————— Writing

- Think logically.
- Draw clear conclusions.
- Find evidence to support your conclusions.

Argument and persuasion require you to present your views on an issue through logic, emotion, and good character in such a way that you convince an audience of your point of view. This rhetorical mode comes at the end of this book because it is an extremely complex and sophisticated method of reasoning. The more proficient you become in this strategy of thinking and presenting your views, the more you will get what you want out of life (and out of school). Winning arguments means getting the pay raises you need, the refund you deserve, and the grades you've worked so hard for.

In a successful argument, your logic must be flawless. Your conclusions should be based on clear evidence, which must be organized in such a way that it builds to an effective, convincing conclusion. You should constantly have your purpose and audience in mind as you build your case; at the same time, issues of emotion and good character should support the flow of your logic.

Exercising your best logical skills is extremely important to all phases of your daily survival—in and out of the classroom. Following a logical argument in your reading and presenting a logical response to your course work are the hallmarks

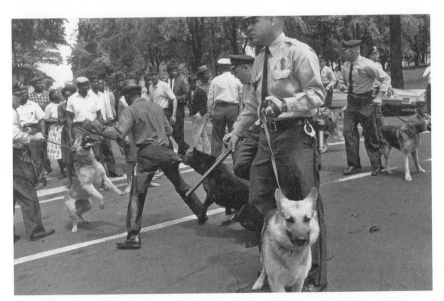

Charles Moore/Black Star.

of a good student. Right now, put your best logic forward and work on your reasoning and persuasive abilities in the following series of exercises. Isolate argument/persuasion from the other rhetorical strategies so that you can practice it and strengthen your ability to argue before you combine it with other methods.

1. Charles Moore uses this photograph to document how the police in Birmingham, Alabama, used a dog to harass a peaceful protester in a 1963 civil rights struggle. Identify another social struggle or protest that you believe is important. Brainstorm about the many views people might hold about this issue. Choose one and identify the types of evidence you would need to support this view, the resolutions you might offer, and the concessions you would be willing to make to resolve the issue. Present a five to ten minute presentation arguing your point to your class or to a small group in your class.

2. Bring to class two magazine ads—one that tries to sell a product and another that tries to convince the reader that a particular action or product is wrong or bad (unhealthy, misinterpreted, politically incorrect, etc.). How does each ad appeal to the reader's logic? How does the advertiser use emotion and character in his or her appeal?

3. Fill in the following blanks: The best way to _____ is to _____. (For example, "The best way to lose weight is to exercise.") Then list ways you might use to persuade a reader to see your point of view in this statement.

Reading and Writing Argument/Persuasion Essays

Although persuasive writing can be approached essentially in three different ways—logically, emotionally, and/or ethically—our stress in this chapter is on logic and reason, because they are at the heart of most college writing. As a reader, you will see how various forms of reasoning and different methods of organization affect your reaction to an essay. Your stand on a particular issue will control the way you process information in argument and persuasion essays. As you read the essays in this chapter, you will also learn to recognize emotional and ethical appeals and the different effects they create. In your role as a writer, you need to be fully aware of the options available to you as you compose. Although the basis of your writing will be logical argument, you will see that you can learn to control your readers' responses to your essays by choosing your evidence carefully, organizing it wisely, and seasoning it with the right amount of emotion and ethics—depending on your purpose and audience.

READING ARGUMENT/PERSUASION ESSAYS

- What is the author's main assertion or thesis?
- What ideas do you agree with?
- What ideas do you disagree with?
- What appeals does the author use?

Preparing to Read.   As you prepare to read the essays in this chapter, spend a few minutes browsing through the preliminary material for each selection: What does bell hooks's title, "Justice: Childhood Love Lessons," prepare you for? What can you learn from scanning Barrett Seaman's essay, "How Bingeing Became the New College Sport," and reading the synopsis of Barbara Kingsolver's essay ("Life Is Precious, Or It's Not") in the Rhetorical Table of Contents?

Also, you should bring to your reading as much information as you can from the authors' biographies: What is the source of Kim Severson's interest in gay marriage ("I'm Not Willing to Settle for Crumbs")? Why do you think Dave Grossman writes about violence and the media? Does he have the proper qualifications to teach us about how "We Are Training Our Kids to Kill"? What perspective does the photo essay ("Tag, You're It!") take? For the essays in this chapter that present several viewpoints on an argument (on immigration, DNA testing, and the Patriot Act), what biographical details prepare us for each writer's stand on the issue? Who were the original audiences for these opposing viewpoints?

Last, before you read these essays, try to generate some ideas on each topic so that you can take the role of an active reader. In this text, the Preparing to Read questions will help you get ready for this task. Then, you should speculate further on the general subject of the essay: What are the main arguments related to disciplining children? What side do you think hooks is on? Where do you stand on the subject? How do you think binge drinking is affecting American society? What would you change about America's approach to this controversial topic? What would you continue?

Reading.   Be sure to record your spontaneous reactions to the persuasive essays in this chapter as you read them for the first time: What are your opinions on each subject? Why do you hold these opinions? Be especially aware of your responses to the essays representing opposing viewpoints at the end of the chapter; know where you stand in relation to each side of the issues here.

Use the preliminary material before an essay to help you create a framework for your responses to it: Who was hooks' primary audience when her essay was first published? In what ways is the tone of her essay appropriate for that audience? What motivated Kingsolver to publish her arguments on violence? What makes Grossman so knowledgeable about children and TV violence? Which argument on immigration do you find most convincing? On postconviction DNA testing? On the Patriot Act?

Throughout each essay in the chapter are questions at the bottom of the pages that further critical thinking. They essentially bridge the gap between the inquiries before each essay and the exercises after the essays. If you answer these questions as they appear in the text, you will be building a framework of understanding that you can draw on when you finally get to the writing assignments at the end of each reading. Putting your responses in writing is the most beneficial way to make the material your own in a way that just thinking about the questions can't accomplish.

Your main job at this stage of reading is to determine each author's primary assertion or proposition (thesis statement) and to create an inquisitive environment for thinking critically about the essay's ideas. In addition, take a look at the questions after each selection to make sure you are picking up the major points of the essay.

Rereading.   As you reread these persuasive essays, notice how the writers integrate their appeals to logic, to emotion, and to ethics. Also, pay attention to the emphasis the writers place on one or more appeals at certain strategic points in the essays: How does hooks integrate these three appeals in "Justice: Childhood Love Lessons"? Which of these appeals does she rely on to help bring her essay to a close? How persuasive is her final appeal? What combination of appeals does Dave Grossman use in "We Are Training Our Kids to Kill"? In what way does the tone of his writing support what he is saying? How does he establish this tone? Which appeal is most prominent in the photo essay?

Also, determine what other rhetorical strategies help these writers make their primary points. How do these strategies enable each writer to establish a unified essay with a beginning, a middle, and an end?

Then answer the questions after each reading selection to make certain you understand the essay on the literal, interpretive, and analytical levels in preparation for the discussion/writing assignments that follow.

For a list of guidelines for the entire reading process, see the checklists on page 29 of the Introduction.

WRITING ARGUMENT/PERSUASION ESSAYS

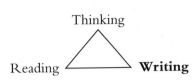

Thinking

Reading   Writing

- Write a debatable thesis.
- Justify the significance of the issue.
- Choose evidence for your thesis.
- Organize your essay effectively.
- Use logical, ethical, and pathetic appeals.
- Conclude with a summary and recommendations.

Preparing to Write.   The first stage of writing an essay of this sort involves, as usual, exploring and then limiting your topic. As you prepare to write your persuasive paper, first try to generate as many ideas as possible—regardless of whether they appeal to logic, emotion, or ethics. To do this, review the prewriting techniques in the Introduction and answer the Preparing to Write questions. Then choose a topic. Next, focus on a purpose and a specific audience before you begin to write.

Writing.   Most persuasive essays should begin with an assertion or a proposition stating what you believe about a certain issue. This thesis should generally be phrased as a debatable statement, such as, "If individual states reinstituted the death penalty, Americans would notice an immediate drop in violent crimes." At this point in your essay, you should also justify the significance of the issue you will be discussing: "Such a decline in the crime rate would affect all our lives and make this country a safer place in which to live."

The essay should then support your thesis in a variety of ways. This support may take the form of facts, figures, examples, opinions by recognized authorities, case histories, narratives/anecdotes, comparisons, contrasts, or cause/effect studies. This evidence is most effectively organized from least to most important when you are confronted with a hostile audience (so that you can lead your readers through your reasoning step by step) and from most to least important when you are facing a supportive audience (so that you can build on their loyalty and enthusiasm as you advance your thesis). In fact, you will be able to engineer your best support if you know your audience's opinions, feelings, and background before you write your essay, so that your intended "target" is as clear as possible. The body of your essay will undoubtedly consist of a combination of logical, emotional, and ethical appeals—all leading to some final summation or recommendation.

The concluding paragraph of a persuasive essay should restate your main assertion (in terms slightly different from your original statement) and should offer some constructive recommendations about the problem you have been discussing (if you haven't already done so). This section of your paper should clearly bring your argument to a close in one final attempt to move your audience to accept or act on the viewpoint you present. Let's look more closely now at each of the three types of appeals used in such essays: logical, emotional, and ethical.

To construct a *logical* argument, you have two principal patterns available to you: inductive reasoning or deductive reasoning. The first encourages an audience to make what is called an "inductive leap" from several particular examples to a single, useful generalization. In the case of the death penalty, for instance, you might cite a number of examples, figures, facts, and case studies illustrating the effectiveness of capital punishment in various states, thereby leading up to your firm belief that the death penalty should be reinstituted. Used most often by detectives, scientists, and lawyers, the process of inductive reasoning addresses the audience's ability to think logically by moving them systematically from an assortment of selected evidence to a rational and ordered conclusion.

In contrast, deductive reasoning moves its audience from a broad, general statement to particular examples supporting that statement. In writing such an essay, you would present your thesis statement about capital punishment first and then offer clear, orderly evidence to support that belief. Although the mental process we go through in creating a deductive argument is quite sophisticated, it is based on a three-step form of reasoning called the *syllogism,* which most logicians believe is the foundation of logical thinking. The traditional syllogism has

A major premise: All humans fear death.

A minor premise: Criminals are humans.

A conclusion: Therefore, criminals fear death.

As you might suspect, this type of reasoning is only as accurate as its original premises, so you need to be sure your premises are true so your argument is valid.

In constructing a logical argument, you should take great care to avoid several types of fallacies in reasoning found most frequently in lower-division college papers. Fallacies occur when you use faulty evidence, when you misrepresent your evidence, or when you use evidence that is irrelevant to your argument. Avoiding fallacies is important because readers who discover a fallacy or problem in logic are likely to question the writer's credibility and perhaps even the writer's interpretation of other evidence. While the following is not an exhaustive list, these fallacies illustrate why most writers would purposely try to avoid using fallacious or faulty reasoning:

Hasty Generalization: When we present a claim that is based on too few examples, we are making a hasty generalization. For example, if we state that students never get enough sleep, we are committing this fallacy. To avoid these kinds of blanket statements, writers need to qualify their claims so they are accurate: Many students don't get enough sleep.

Non Sequitur: A non sequitur occurs when we make a statement that does not logically follow the previous statement. Some people say, for example, "That car she just bought is very expensive. She must be rich." This second sentence is not a conclusion we can draw from the first sentence.

Either/Or Fallacy: Writers commit the either/or fallacy when they present an argument as if only two possible views exist, but actually other views are possible as well. For example, someone might argue that a person could not protest the war in Iraq and still be a patriotic American. A citizen can express a negative view about one policy and still be patriotic, so the explanation of two sides only (supporting the war or being unpatriotic) is an example of the either/or fallacy.

False Cause and Effect: This logical flaw involves making a causal argument based solely on chronology. To avoid this fallacy, the cause must be proved: "First, the group of politicians criticized the war; then the terrorists bombed a building in Baghdad. See what happens when we criticize the war!"

False Authority: An appeal to a false authority occurs when a writer cites an example or opinion of someone who is not an expert in the field. Having an actor advertise a product unrelated to his or her career is an example of this fallacy. When writers choose an expert, they must make sure the person can actually offer a relevant and meaningful testimonial or perspective.

Begging the Question: This is circular logic. For example, skydiving is dangerous because it is not safe. To avoid this fallacy, bring new information into the explanation: Skydiving is dangerous because a lot can go wrong on the way down to the ground.

Bandwagon: This fallacy is based on the false logic that some action is preferable because it is supported by many people. Examples often occur in advertising when companies claim that their product is best because so many people are using it.

If you build your argument on true statements and abundant, accurate evidence, your essay will be effective, and your argument is likely to be persuasive. Avoiding fallacies is also easier when you thoroughly examine your evidence and carefully present supporting ideas and information to your reader. As a writer, you have the ultimate responsibility to find credible evidence and to present it in a well-reasoned and clear essay.

Persuading through *emotion* necessitates controlling your readers' instinctive reactions to what you are saying. You can accomplish this goal in two different ways: (1) by choosing your words with even greater care than usual and (2) by using figurative language whenever appropriate. In the first case, you must be especially conscious of using words that have the same general denotative (or dictionary) meaning but bear decidedly favorable or unfavorable connotative (or implicit) meanings. For example, notice the difference between *slender* and *scrawny, patriotic* and *chauvinistic*, or *compliment* and *flattery*. Your careful attention to the choice of such words can help readers form visual images with certain positive or negative associations that subtly encourage them to follow your argument and adopt your opinions. Second, the effective use of figurative language—especially similes and metaphors—makes your writing more vivid, thus triggering your readers' senses and encouraging them to accept your views. Both of these techniques will help you manipulate your readers into the position of agreeing with your ideas.

Ethical appeals, which establish you as a reliable, well-informed person, are accomplished through (1) the tone of your essay and (2) the number and type of examples you cite. Tone is created through deliberate word choice: Careful attention to the mood implied in the words you use can convince your readers that you are serious, friendly, authoritative, jovial, or methodical—depending on your intended purpose. In like manner, the examples you supply to support your assertions can encourage readers to see you as experienced, insightful, relaxed, or intense. In both of these cases, winning favor for yourself will usually also gain approval for your opinions.

Rewriting.   To rework your persuasive essays, you should play the role of your readers and impartially evaluate the different appeals you have used to accomplish your purpose:

- Is your thesis statement clear?
- Is the main thrust of your essay an appeal to reason?
- Have you chosen examples carefully to support your thesis statement?
- Does your conclusion restate your argument, make a recommendation, and bring your essay to a close?

You should also look closely at the way your appeals work together in your essay:

- When you use logic, is that section of your paper arranged through either inductive or deductive reasoning?
- Is that the most effective order to achieve your purpose?
- In appealing to the emotions, have you chosen your words with proper attention to their denotative and connotative effects?

Any additional guidance you may need as you write and revise your persuasive essays is furnished on page 30 of the Introduction.

STUDENT ESSAY: ARGUMENT AND PERSUASION AT WORK

The following student essay uses all three appeals to make its point about the power of language in shaping our view of the world. First, the writer sets forth her character references (ethical appeal) in the first paragraph, after which she presents her thesis and its significance in paragraph 2. The support for her thesis is a combination of logical and emotional appeals, heavy on the logical, as the writer moves her paragraphs from general to particular in an effort to convince her readers to adopt her point of view and adjust their language use accordingly.

The Language of Equal Rights

Ethical appeal

Up front, I admit it. I've been a card-carrying feminist since junior high school. I want to see an Equal Rights Amendment to the U.S. Constitution, equal pay for equal—and comparable—work, and I go dutch on dates. Furthermore, I am quite prickly on the subject of language. I'm one of those people who bristles at terms like *lady doctor* (you know they don't mean a gynecologist), *female policeman* (a paradox), and *mankind* instead of *humanity* (are they really talking about me?).

Emotional appeal

Many people ask "How important are mere words, anyway? You know what we really mean." A question like this ignores the symbolic and psychological importance of language. What words "mean" can go beyond what a speaker or writer consciously intends, reflecting personal and cultural biases that run so deep that most of the time we aren't even aware they exist. "Mere words" are incredibly important: They are our framework for seeing and understanding the world.

Assertion or thesis statement

Significance of assertion

Man, we are told, means woman as well as man, just as *mankind* supposedly stands for all of humanity.

Logical appeal

Examples organized deductively In the introduction of a sociology textbook I recently read, the author was anxious to demonstrate his awareness of the controversy over sexist language and to assure his female readers that, despite his use of noninclusive terms, he was not forgetting the existence or importance of women in society. He was making a conscious decision to continue to use *man* and *mankind* instead of *people, humanity,* etc., for ease of expression and aesthetic reasons. "Man" simply sounds better, he explained. I flipped through the table of contents and found "Man and Society," "Man and Nature," "Man and Technology," and, near the end, "Man and Woman." Emotional appeal At what point did *Man* quit meaning *people* and start meaning men again? The writer was obviously unaware of the answer to this question, because it is one he would never think to ask. Having consciously addressed the issue only to dismiss it, he reverted to form.

Logical appeal The very ambiguity of *man* as the generic word for our species ought to be enough to combat any arguments that we keep it because we all "know what it means" or because it is both traditional and sounds better. And does it really sound all that much better, or are we just more used to it, more comfortable? Examples organized deductively Our own national history proves that we can be comfortable with a host of words and attitudes that strike us as unjust and ugly today. A lot of white folks probably thought that Negroes were getting pretty stuffy and picky when they began to insist on being called *blacks*. Emotional appeal After all, weren't there more important things to worry about, like civil rights? But black activists recognized the emotional and symbolic significance of having a name that was parallel to the name that the dominant race used for itself—a name equal in dignity, lacking that vaguely alien, anthropological sound. After all, whites were called *Caucasians* only in police reports, textbooks, and autopsies. *Negro* may have sounded better to people in the bad old days of blatant racial bigotry, but we adjusted to the word *black* and have now moved on to *African American,* and more and more people of each race are adjusting to the wider implications and demands of practical, as well as verbal, labels.

Logical appeal

<u>In a world where *man* and *human* are offered as synonymous terms, I don't think it is a coincidence that women are still vastly underrepresented in positions of money, power, and respect</u>. Children grow up learning a language that makes maleness the norm for anything that isn't explicitly designated as female, giving little girls a very limited corner of the universe to picture themselves in. Indeed, the language that non-feminists today claim to be inclusive was never intended to cover women in the first place. "One man, one vote" and "All men are created equal" meant just that. Women had to fight for decades to be included even as an afterthought; it took constitutional amendments to convince the government and the courts that women are human too.

Examples organized deductively

Conclusion/ restatement

The message is clear. <u>We have to start speaking about people, not men, if we are going to start thinking in terms of both women and men. A "female man" will never be the equal of her brother.</u>

Student Writer's Comments

The hardest task for me in writing this essay was coming up with a topic! The second hardest job was trying to be effective without getting preachy, strident, or wordy. I wanted to persuade an audience that would no doubt include the bored, the hostile, and the indifferent, and I was worried about losing their attention.

I chose my topic after several prewriting sessions that generated numerous options for me to write about. I stumbled on the idea of sexist language in one of these sessions and then went on to generate new material on this particular topic. Eventually satisfied that I had enough ideas to stay with this topic, I doubled back and labeled them according to each type of appeal.

Even before I had written my thesis, I had a good idea of what I wanted to say in this essay. I began working from an assertion that essentially remained the same as I wrote and revised my essay. It's more polished now, but its basic intention never changed.

To create my first draft, I worked from my notes, labeled by type of appeal. I let the logical arguments guide my writing, strategically introducing emotional and ethical appeals as I sensed they would be effective. I appealed to ethics in the beginning of the essay to establish my credibility, and I appealed to the readers' emotions occasionally to vary my pace and help my argument gain momentum. I was fully aware of what I was doing when I moved from one appeal to another. I wrote from a passionate desire to change people's thinking about language and its ability to control our perceptions of the world.

Next, I revised my entire essay several times, playing the role of different readers with dissimilar biases in each case. Every time I worked through the essay, I made major changes in the introduction and the conclusion as well. At this point, I paid special attention to the denotation, connotation, and tone of my words (especially highly charged language) and to the examples I had chosen to support each point I decided to keep in my argument. Though I moved a lot of examples around and thought of better ones in some cases, I was eventually happy with the final product. I am especially pleased with the balance of appeals in the final draft.

SOME FINAL THOUGHTS ON ARGUMENT AND PERSUASION

As you can tell from the selections that follow, the three different types of persuasive appeals usually complement one another in practice. Most good persuasive essays use a combination of these methods to achieve their purposes. Good persuasive essays also rely on various rhetorical modes we have already studied—such as example, process analysis, division/classification, comparison/contrast, definition, and cause/effect—to advance their arguments. In the following essays, you will see a combination of appeals and a number of different rhetorical modes at work.

Reading Argument/Persuasion Essays

Preparing to Read

✓ What assumptions can you make from the essay's title?

✓ Can you guess what the general mood of the essay is?

✓ What is the essay's purpose and audience?

✓ What does the synopsis tell you about the essay?

✓ What can you learn from the author's biography?

✓ Can you predict the author's point of view toward the subject?

Reading

✓ What is the author's main assertion or thesis?

✓ What ides do you agree with?

✓ What ideas do you disagree with?

✓ What appeals does the author use?

Rereading

✓ How does the writer integrate the appeals in the essay?

✓ What is the tone of the essay? How does the author establish this tone?

✓ What other rhetorical strategies does the author use?

Writing Argument/Persuasion Essays

Preparing to Write

✓ Do you narrow and focus your material as much as possible?

✓ What is your purpose?

✓ Do you understand your audience's background?

Writing

✓ Did you write a debatable thesis?

✓ Do you justify the significance of the issue?

✓ Did you choose evidence that supports your thesis?

✓ Is your essay organized effectively for what you are trying to accomplish?

✓ Do you use a combination of logical, ethical, and pathetic appeals?

✓ Do you conclude with a summary and recommendations?

Rewriting

✓ Is your thesis statement clear?

✓ Is the main thrust of your essay an appeal to reason?

✓ Have you chosen examples carefully to support your thesis statement?

✓ Does your conclusion restate your argument, make a recommendation, and bring your essay to a close?

Justice: Childhood Love Lessons

Writer, professor, and social critic bell hooks was born Gloria Jean Watkins in Hopkinsville, Kentucky, but has written for many years under the pseudonym "bell hooks" (all lowercase letters) in tribute to her great-grandmother, a woman "who spoke her mind, a woman who was not afraid to talk back." Following a B.A. at Stanford University, an M.A. at the University of Wisconsin, and a Ph.D. at the University of California, Santa Cruz, she embarked on an enviable academic career, first as an assistant professor of African-American Studies and English Literature at Yale University, followed by positions in American Literature and Women's Studies at Oberlin College and in Black Studies at the City College of New York, where she currently teaches. Her prolific and controversial publications have included *Ain't I a Woman: Black Women and Feminism* (1981), *Feminist Theory: From Margin to Center* (1984), *Talking Back: Thinking Feminist, Thinking Black* (1989), *Yearning: Race, Gender, and Cultural Politics* (1990), *Black Looks: Race and Representation* (1992), *Killing Rage: Ending Racism* (1995), *Rock My Soul: Black People and Self-Esteem* (2003), and *We Real Cool: Black Men and Masculinity* (2004). Her works always raise important cultural issues, particularly with regard to the goals of feminism and the place of black women within the movement.

Preparing to Read

In the following essay, originally published in 2000, bell hooks logically and persuasively presents her opinions on the relationship between love and punishment for children.

Exploring Experience: As you prepare to read her essay, take a few moments to focus your own thoughts on the connection between discipline and expressions of love: In what ways do you think children should be disciplined? How should parents express love to their children? Do you believe in hitting children? Why or why not? How else should children be disciplined? Do you believe that discipline and love can coexist?

Learning Online: Conduct an Internet search using the phrase "advice for disciplining children." Explore at least two Web sites. What types of advice do the Web sites offer? How does each site argue its case? Consider these varying opinions while reading bell hooks's essay.

Severe separations in early life leave emotional scars on the brain because they assault the essential human connection: The [parent–child] bond which teaches us that we are lovable. The [parent–child] bond which teaches us how to love. We cannot be whole human beings—indeed, we may find it hard to be human—without the sustenance of this first attachment.

—Judith Viorst

We learn about love in childhood. Whether our homes are happy or 1 troubled, our families functional or dysfunctional, it's the original school of love. ◆ I cannot remember ever wanting to ask my parents to define love. To my child's mind, love was the good feeling you got when family treated you like you mattered and you treated them like they mattered. Love was always and only about good feeling. In early adolescence when we were whipped and told that these punishments were "for your own good" or "I'm doing this because I love you," my siblings and I were confused. Why was harsh punishment a gesture of love? As children do, we pretended to accept this grown-up logic; but we knew in our hearts it was not right. We knew it was a lie. Just like the lie grown-ups told when they explained after harsh punishment, "It hurts me more than it hurts you." There is nothing that creates more confusion about love in the minds and hearts of children than unkind and/or cruel punishment meted out by the grown-ups they have been taught they should love and respect. Such children learn early on to question the meaning of love, to yearn for love even as they doubt it exists.

On the flip side, there are masses of children who grow up confident love 2 is a good feeling who are never punished, who are allowed to believe that love is only about getting your needs met, your desires satisfied. In their child's minds, love is not about what they have to give, love is mostly something given to them. ◆ When children like these are overindulged either materially or by being allowed to act out, this is a form of neglect. These children, though not in any way abused or uncared for, are usually as unclear about love's meaning as their neglected and emotionally abandoned counterparts. Both groups have learned to think about love primarily in relation to good feelings, in the context of reward and punishment. From early childhood on, most of us remember being told we were loved when we did things pleasing to our parents. And we learned to give them affirmations of love when they pleased us. As children grow they associate love more with acts

---

Reading Critically

◆ Why does the author call childhood "the original school of love"? Do you think this is true?

◆ Do you agree with this assertion? Is love "mostly something given" to people?

of attention, affection, and caring. They still see parents who attempt to satisfy their desires as giving love.

Children from all classes tell me that they love their parents and are loved 3 by them, even those who are being hurt or abused. When asked to define love, small children pretty much agree that it's a good feeling, "like when you have something to eat that you really like" especially if it's your f-a-v-o-r-i-t-e. They will say, "My mommy loves me 'cause she takes care of me and helps me do everything right." When asked how to love someone, they talk about giving hugs and kisses, being sweet and cuddly. The notion that love is about getting what one wants, whether it's a hug or a new sweater or a trip to Disneyland, is a way of thinking about love that makes it difficult for children to acquire a deeper emotional understanding.

We like to imagine that most children will be born into homes where 4 they will be loved. But love will not be present if the grown-ups who parent do not know how to love. Although lots of children are raised in homes where they are given some degree of care, love may not be sustained or even present. Adults across lines of class, race, and gender indict the family. Their testimony conveys worlds of childhood where love was lacking—where chaos, neglect, abuse, and coercion reigned supreme. In her recent book *Raised in Captivity: Why Does America Fail Its Children?*, Lucia Hodgson documents the reality of lovelessness in the lives of a huge majority of children in the United States. Every day thousands of children in our culture are verbally and physically abused, starved, tortured, and murdered. They are the true victims of intimate terrorism [3] in that they have no collective voice and no rights. They remain the property of parenting adults to do with as they will.

There can be no love without justice. Until we live in a culture that not only 5 respects but also upholds basic civil rights for children, most children will not know love. In our culture the private family dwelling is the one institutionalized sphere of power that can easily be autocratic and fascistic. As absolute rulers, parents can usually decide without any intervention what is best for their children. If children's rights are taken away in any domestic household, they have no legal recourse. Unlike women who can organize to protest sexist domination, demanding both equal rights and justice, children can only rely on well-meaning adults to assist them if they are being exploited and oppressed in the home.

We all know that, irrespective of class or race, other adults rarely intervene 6 to question or challenge what their peers are doing with "their" children.

Reading Critically

[3] How are children the victims of "intimate terrorism"? What does the word "terrorism" imply in this context?

At a fun party, mostly of educated, well-paid professionals, a multiracial, 7 multi-generational evening, the subject of disciplining kids by hitting was raised. Almost all the guests over thirty spoke about the necessity of using physical punishment. Many of us in the room had been smacked, whipped, or beaten as children. Men spoke the loudest in defense of physical punishment. Women, mostly mothers, talked about hitting as a last resort, but one that they deployed when necessary. ◆4

As one man bragged about the aggressive beatings he had received from 8 his mother, sharing that "they had been good for him," I interrupted and suggested that he might not be the misogynist woman-hater he is today if he had not been brutally beaten by a woman as a child. Although it is too simplistic to assume that just because we are hit as kids we will grow up to be people who hit, I wanted the group to acknowledge that being physically hurt or abused by grown-ups when we are children has harmful consequences in our adult life.

A young professional, the mother of a small boy, bragged about the fact 9 that she did not hit, that when her son misbehaved she clamped down on his flesh, pinching him until he got the message. But this, too, is a form of coercive abuse. The other guests supported this young mother and her husband in their methods. I was astounded. I was a lone voice speaking out for the rights of children.

Later, with other people, I suggested that had we all been listening to a 10 man tell us that every time his wife or girlfriend does something he does not like he just clamps down on her flesh, pinching her as hard as he can, everyone would have been appalled. They would have seen the action as both coercive and abusive. Yet they could not acknowledge that it was wrong for an adult to hurt a child in this way. All the parents in that room claim that they are loving. All the people in that room were college educated. Most call themselves good liberals, supportive of civil rights and feminism. But when it came to the rights of children, they had a different standard.

One of the most important social myths we must debunk if we are to be- 11 come a more loving culture is the one that teaches parents that abuse and neglect can coexist with love. Abuse and neglect negate love. ◆5 Care and affirmation, the opposite of abuse and humiliation, are the foundation of love. No one can rightfully claim to be loving when behaving abusively. Yet parents do this all the time in our culture. Children are told they are loved even though they are being abused.

Reading Critically

◆4 How do you feel about the issue of corporal punishment for children?

◆5 How do abuse and neglect "negate love"?

It is a testimony to the failure of loving practice that abuse is happening   12
in the first place. [6]

Many of the men who offer their personal testimony in *Boyhood, Grow-*   13
ing Up Male tell stories of random violent abuse by parents that inflicted
trauma. In his essay "When My Father Hit Me," Bob Shelby describes the
pain of repeated beatings by his dad, stating, "From these experiences with
my father, I learned about the abuse of power. By physically hitting my
mother and me, he effectively stopped us from reacting to his humiliation
of us. We ceased to protest his violations of our boundaries and his ignoring our sense of being individuals with needs, demands, and rights of our
own." Throughout his essay, Shelby expresses contradictory understand-
ings about the meaning of love. On the one hand, he says, "I have no doubt
that my father loved me, but his love became misdirected. He said he
wanted to give me what he didn't have as a child." On the other hand,
Shelby confesses, "What he most showed me, however, was his difficulty in
being loved. All his life he had struggled with feelings of being unloved."
When Shelby describes his childhood, it is clear that his dad had affection
for him and also gave him care some of the time. However, his dad did
not know how to give and receive love. The affection he gave was under-
mined by the abuse.

Writing from the space of adult recollection, Shelby talks about the im-   14
pact of physical abuse on his boyhood psyche: "As the intensity of the pain
of his hits increased, I felt the hurt in my heart. I realized what hurt me the
most were my feelings of love for this man who was hitting me. I covered
my love with a dark cloth of hate." A similar story is told by other men in
autobiographical narrative—men of all classes and races. One of the myths
about lovelessness is that it exists only among the poor and deprived. Yet
lovelessness is not a function of poverty or material lack. In homes where material privileges abound, children suffer emotional neglect and abuse. In order
to cope with the pain of wounds inflicted in childhood, most of the men in
Boyhood sought some form of therapeutic care. To find their way back to
love they had to heal. [7]

Many men in our culture never recover from childhood unkindnesses.   15
Studies show that males and females who are violently humiliated and abused
repeatedly, with no caring intervention, are likely to be dysfunctional and will
be predisposed to abuse others violently. In Jarvis Jay Masters's book *Finding*

Reading Critically

[6] Why do you think the author uses a one-sentence paragraph here?
[7] Have you ever had to heal an old wound before you could love someone?

Freedom:Writings from Death Row, a chapter called "Scars" recounts his recognition that a vast majority of the scars covering the bodies of fellow inmates (not all of whom were on death row) were not, as one might think, the result of violent adult interactions. These men were covered with scars from childhood beatings inflicted by parenting adults. Yet, he reports, none of them saw themselves as the victims of abuse: "Throughout my many years of institutionalization, I, like so many of these men, unconsciously took refuge behind prison walls. Not until I read a series of books for adults who had been abused as children did I become committed to the process of examining my own childhood." Organizing the men for group discussion, Masters writes, "I spoke to them of the pain I had carried through more than a dozen institutions. And I explained how all these events ultimately trapped me in a pattern of lashing out against everything. Like many abused children, male and female, these men were beaten by mothers, fathers, and other parental caregivers."

When Masters's mother dies, he feels grief that he cannot be with her. The   16
other inmates do not understand this longing, since she neglected and abused him. He responds, "She had neglected me, but am I to neglect myself as well by denying that I wished I'd been with her when she died, that I still love her?" Even on death row, Masters's heart remains open. And he can honestly confess to longing to give and receive love. Being hurt by parenting adults rarely alters a child's desire to love and be loved by them. Among grown-ups who were wounded in childhood, the desire to be loved by uncaring parents persists, even when there is a clear acceptance of the reality that this love will never be forthcoming.

Often, children will want to remain with parental caregivers who have hurt   17
them because of their cathected feelings for those adults. They will cling to the misguided assumption that their parents love them even in the face of remembered abuse, usually by denying the abuse and focusing on random acts of care.

In the prologue to *Creating Love,* John Bradshaw calls this confusion about   18
love "mystification." He shares, "I was brought up to believe that love is rooted in blood relationships. You naturally loved anyone in your family. ⁸ Love was not a choice. The love I learned about was bound by duty and obligation. . . . My family taught me our culture's rules and beliefs above love . . . even with the best intentions our parents often confused love with what we would now

---

Reading Critically

◆ 8 Do you agree that love is always "rooted in blood relationships"? Is there anyone in your family that you don't love? Why?

call abuse." To demystify the meaning of love, the art and practice of loving, we need to use sound definitions of love when talking with children, and we also need to ensure that loving action is never tainted with abuse.

In a society like ours, where children are denied full civil rights, [9] it is ab- 19 solutely crucial that parenting adults learn how to offer loving discipline. Setting boundaries and teaching children how to set boundaries for themselves prior to misbehavior is an essential part of loving parenting. When parents start out disciplining children by using punishment, this becomes the pattern children respond to. Loving parents work hard to discipline without punishment. This does not mean that they never punish, only that when they do punish, they choose punishments like time-outs or the taking away of privileges. They focus on teaching children how to be self-disciplining and how to take responsibility for their actions. Since the vast majority of us were raised in households where punishment was deemed the primary, if not the only, way to teach discipline, the fact that discipline can be taught without punishment surprises many people. One of the simplest ways children learn discipline is by learning how to be orderly in daily life, to clean up any messes they make. Just teaching a child to take responsibility for placing toys in the appropriate place after playtime is one way to teach responsibility and self-discipline. Learning to clean up the mess made during playtime helps a child learn to be responsible. And they can learn from this practical act how to cope with emotional mess. [10]

Were there current television shows that actually modeled loving parent- 20 ing, parents could learn these skills. Television shows oriented toward families often favorably represent children when they are overindulged, are disrespectful, or are acting out. Often they behave in a more adult manner than the parents. What we see on television today actually, at best, models for us inappropriate behavior and in worst-case scenarios, unloving behaviors. A great example of this is a movie like *Home Alone,* which celebrates disobedience and violence. But television can portray caring, loving family interaction. There are whole generations of adults who talk nostalgically about how they wanted their families to be like the fictive portraits of family life portrayed on *Leave It to Beaver* or *My Three Sons.* We desired our families to be like those we saw on the screen [11] because we were witnessing loving parenting, loving house-

---

Reading Critically

[9] Do you agree that children in our society are denied civil rights?

[10] The author argues here that children who clean up the physical mess of playtime learn to clean up their emotional mess later in life. To what extent do you agree with this statement?

[11] Do you think the author is right that shows like *Leave It to Beaver* or *My Three Sons* presented a more positive image of families than current television sitcoms?

holds. Expressing to parents our desire to have families like the ones we saw on the screen, we were often told that the families were not realistic. The reality was, however, that parents who come from unloving homes have never learned how to love and cannot create loving home environments or see them as realistic when watching them on television. The reality they are most familiar with and trust is the one they knew intimately.

There was nothing utopian about the way problems were resolved on   21
these shows. Parent and child discussion, critical reflection, and finding a way to make amends was usually the process by which misbehavior was addressed. On both shows, there was never just one parenting figure. Even though the mother was absent on *My Three Sons,* the lovable Uncle Charlie was a second parent. In a loving household where there are several parental caregivers, when a child feels one parent is being unjust, that child can appeal to another adult for mediation, understanding, or support. We live in a society where there are a growing number of single parents, female and male. But the individual parent can always choose a friend to be another parenting figure, however limited their interaction. This is why the categories of godmother and godfather are so crucial. When my best girlhood friend chose to have a child without a father in the household, I became the godmother, a second parenting figure.

My friend's daughter turns to me to intervene if there is a misunder-   22
standing or miscommunication between her and her mom. Here's one small example. My adult friend had never received an allowance as a child and did not feel she had the available extra money to offer an allowance to her daughter. She also believed her daughter would use all the money to buy sweets. Telling me that her daughter was angry with her over this issue, she opened up the space for us to have a dialogue. I shared my belief that allowances are important ways to teach children discipline, boundaries, and working through desires versus needs. **12** I knew enough about my friend's finances to challenge her insistence that she could not afford to pay a small allowance, while simultaneously encouraging her not to project the wrongs of her childhood onto the present. As to whether the daughter would buy candy, I suggested she give the allowance with a statement of hope that it would not be used for overindulgence and see what happened.

It all worked out just fine. Happy to have an allowance, the daughter   23
chose to save her money to buy things she thought were really important. And candy was not on this list. Had there not been another adult parenting figure involved, it might have taken these two a longer time to resolve

---

Reading Critically
12 Did you have an allowance when you were growing up? What did you learn from the experience?

their conflict, and unnecessary estrangement and wounding might have occurred. Significantly, love and respectful interaction between two adults exemplified for the daughter (who was told about the discussion) ways of problem solving. By revealing her willingness to accept criticism and her capacity to reflect on her behavior and change, the mother modeled for her daughter, without losing dignity and authority, the recognition that parents are not always right.

Until we begin to see loving parenting in all walks of life in our culture, many people will continue to believe we can only teach discipline through punishment and that harsh punishment is an acceptable way to relate to children. Because children can innately offer affection or respond to affectionate care by returning it, it is often assumed that they know how to love and therefore do not need to learn the art of loving. While the will to love is present in very young children, they still need guidance in the ways of love. Grownups provide that guidance.   24

Love is as love does, and it is our responsibility to give children love. When we love children we acknowledge by our every action that they are not property, that they have rights—that we respect and uphold their rights.   25

Without justice there can be no love.   26

UNDERSTANDING DETAILS

1. According to hooks, how do we first learn about love?
2. What two types of activities cause confusion about love in the hearts and minds of children?
3. What age group of parents usually insists on physical punishment for their children?
4. How do abused children generally feel about their parents? Why is this true?

THINKING CRITICALLY

5. Why are children's civil rights so delicate, according to hooks?
6. Why does hooks think we must challenge the idea that "abuse and neglect can coexist with love" (paragraph 11)?
7. Why do we use different standards for the treatment of children and adults?
8. Explain what hooks means in the last sentence of her essay: "Without justice there can be no love"?

DISCOVERING RHETORICAL STRATEGIES

9. Who do you think is hooks' primary audience? How did you come to this conclusion?
10. Why do you think hooks refers to Bob Shelby's story in her essay? Is this reference effective where she has placed it?

11. Are you convinced by this essay that physical punishment and love cannot co-exist in the same household? What details or examples are most persuasive to you?

12. What additional rhetorical strategies does hooks use to develop her argument? Give examples of each.

MAKING CONNECTIONS

13. Imagine that bell hooks, Lewis Sawaquat ("For My Indian Daughter"), Bill Cosby ("The Baffling Question"), Judith Wallerstein and Sandra Blakeslee ("Second Chances for Children of Divorce"), Mary Pipher ("Beliefs About Families"), and/or Michael Dorris ("The Broken Cord") were having a discussion about the best ways to discipline children. Which author would you probably agree with most? Explain your answer.

14. To what extent do you think that bell hooks and Brent Staples ("A Brother's Murder") would agree about the need for physical discipline in inner-city neighborhoods? Do you think the discussion would change dramatically if it were expanded to include the treatment of children from all neighborhoods? Why or why not?

15. According to hooks, what is the proper relationship between love and punishment? What kinds of discipline does she favor? Which of the following authors would most likely agree with her: Kimberly Wozencraft ("Notes from the Country Club"), Bill Cosby ("The Baffling Question"), and/or Lyn Mikel Brown and Meda Chesney-Lind ("Bad Girls, Bad Girls, Whatcha Gonna Do?")?

IDEAS FOR DISCUSSION/WRITING

Preparing to Write

Write freely about your views on disciplining children: Do you think hitting children is ever justified? In what other ways could children be punished? Do children have rights? How do they differ from the rights that adults have? What is the difference between children and adults in terms of humane treatment? Who should receive more respect—adults or children?

Choosing a Topic

1. Your old high school has asked you to talk to its senior psychology class about the topic of child abuse. What constitutes "abuse" in your opinion? Write a well-developed essay on this issue that will start a spirited discussion in class.

2. hooks claims that "No one can rightfully claim to be loving when behaving abusively" (paragraph 11)? Write a well-developed essay arguing for or against this assertion.

3. In your opinion, what is the relationship between civil rights and mutual respect? To what extent are they companion privileges? Take a stand on this question, and use carefully chosen evidence from bell hooks' essay (whenever appropriate) to support your principal points.

4. Do you have an issue about which you feel strongly? Find a credible Web site (ending in ".org," ".gov," or ".edu") that supports your cause. Write an argument that could be published on this Web site. Following bell hooks's example, employ the three types of appeals, and use persuasive evidence to support your claims. Feel free to integrate data and quotes from your chosen Web site.

Before beginning your essay, you might want to consult the checklists on page 461.

Tag, You're It!

The following selection is a pictorial essay compiled from "tagging" or graffiti in various cities throughout the United States.

Preparing to Read

Tagging is an illegal practice that marks a building or structure with the identity of a person or group through graphics of some sort. Most of the graphics make statements—some in aesthetically appealing ways, others with very unappealing results.

Exploring Experience: Before you read this essay, think about your views on graffiti: Do you have any direct experience with graffiti as either a perpetrator or observer? What is that experience? Why do you think graffiti is illegal? Where have you seen graffiti? What messages does graffiti send? Is the graffiti you have seen artistic or not? Do you think people should be allowed to express themselves through graphics in public places? Explain your answer.

Learning Online: Go to http://www.graffiti.org, and look for graffiti from your city or from a city near you. What is your general opinion of the graffiti pictured on this site?

Dallas

Miami

Los Angeles

New Jersey

Chicago

Atlanta

New York

UNDERSTANDING DETAILS

1. Define graffiti from the examples presented here.
2. What two characteristics does this graffiti have in common?
3. Choose a picture from the photo essay, and explain it to the class. Do the colors help convey any part of the message?
4. Which of these examples of graffiti do you like best? Explain your choice.

THINKING CRITICALLY

5. Why do you think graffiti is so popular in urban settings?
6. Why is graffiti illegal?
7. Do you think graffiti defiles its location?
8. Are these examples typical of graffiti in places near you?

DISCOVERING RHETORICAL STRATEGIES

9. Can pictures be read like words? Explain your answer.
10. Who pays attention to graffiti?
11. Do you think we should furnish legal outlets in America for these modes of expression? Explain your answer.
12. What rhetorical strategies are at work in these pictures? Give examples of each.

MAKING CONNECTIONS

13. Compare and contrast the examples of graffiti in this essay. Which looks most like something you might have produced? Explain your answer.
14. Imagine that Brent Staples ("A Brother's Murder"), Robert Ramirez ("The Barrio") and/or the people who created the pictures in this photo essay were discussing the importance of graffiti. Who would argue most strongly that graffiti is a reputable art form. Explain your answer.
15. How is developing the ability to read pictures in this photo essay different from discovering how to read books in Malcolm X's "Learning to Read" and/or Richard Wright's "The Library Card"?

IDEAS FOR DISCUSSION/WRITING

Preparing to Write

Write freely about your views on graffiti: What is your experience with graffiti? What do you think of graffiti in general? Why do people create graffiti? Why do you think graffiti is illegal? Should any form of it be legal? Are there any benefits to graffiti?

Choosing a Topic

1. Your old high school has asked you to talk to its senior class about the topic of graffiti. What constitutes "graffiti" in your opinion? What should we do to control the production of graffiti? Write a well-developed essay on this issue.
2. Can graffiti ever be art? If so, when is this possible? If not, why not?
3. Do you think this type of self-expression should be allowed in public places. If so, explain why, and provide a solution for finding legal avenues for it. If you believe it should not be allowed, explain why, and provide effective ideas for preventing the production of graffiti.
4. Go to the Web site you consulted earlier (www.graffiti.org), and create your own photo essay that deals with graffiti in your area. Choose your pictures carefully with an eye toward your thesis or controlling idea: What do you want to say with your essay? Following your graphic essay, write three discussion questions to focus the readers' attention on your primary message.

Before beginning your essay, you might want to consult the checklists on page 461.

BARBARA KINGSOLVER   (1955–   )

Life Is Precious, or It's Not

A native of Eastern Kentucky, Kingsolver claims she grew up "in the middle of an alfalfa field," where she learned to love the rhythms of rural speech. Following a degree in biology at DePauw University and travel throughout Europe, she earned a masters in biology and ecology at the University of Arizona in Tucson. After graduation, she supported herself with a variety of jobs, including work as a archaeologist, copy editor, X-ray technician, and housecleaner, till a position as a science writer at the University of Arizona led her to feature writing for several different journals and newspapers. Her many books include *The Bean Trees* (1988), *Holding the Line: Women in the Great Arizona Mine Strike of 1983* (1989), *Homeland and Other Stories* (1989), *Animal Dreams* (1990), *Pigs in Heaven* (1993), *High Tide in Tucson* (1995), *Prodigal Summer* (2000), and *Small Wonder* (2002). She and her husband and their two daughters divide their time between Tucson and a farm in Southern Appalachia. Her advice to college writers is useful and succinct: "If you want a slice of life, look out the window. An artist has to isolate one or two suggestive things and embroider them together with poetry and fabrication to create a revelation. If we can't, as artists, improve on real life, we should put down our pencils and go bake bread."

Preparing to Read

This selection, written by Barbara Kingsolver, was first published in a book of essays called *Small Wonder.* In it, Kingsolver tries to explain the violent actions that characterize many U.S. citizens today.

Exploring Experience: Before you read this essay, think about any violent acts that have taken place recently in the United States: What are these acts? Who committed them? Why did these people turn to violence? Do you think that U.S. citizens condone violence in certain situations? If so, what would be the circumstances? Do you think violence is ever warranted? Explain your answer.

Learning Online: The Columbine High School shooting that took place on April 20, 1999, was one of the most devastating incidents of teen violence in America. Using Google's search engine (http://www.google.com), click on the "Images" tab to conduct a picture search. Type in "Columbine High School shooting," and view several pictures of the students and campus during and after the ordeal. If you don't remember the incident, refresh your memory by reading some of the articles attached to the image links.

" "Columbine used to be one of my favorite flowers," my friend   1
told me, and we both fell silent. We'd been talking about
what she might plant on the steep bank at the foot of the
woods above her house, but a single word cut us suddenly adrift from our
focus on the uncomplicated life in which flowers could matter. I understood why she no longer had the heart to plant columbines. I feel that
way, too, and at the same time I feel we ought to plant them everywhere,
to make sure we remember. In our backyards, on the graves of the children lost, even on the graves of the children who murdered, whose
parents must surely live with the deepest emotional pain it is possible
to bear. ❶

In the aftermath of the Columbine High School shootings in Colorado,   2
the whole country experienced grief and shock and very noticeably—the
spectacle of a nation acting bewildered. Even the op-ed commentators who
usually tell us just what to think were asking, instead, what we should think.
How could this happen in an ordinary school, an ordinary neighborhood?
Why would any student, however frustrated with mean spirited tormentors,
believe that guns and bombs were the answer?

I'm inclined to think all of us who are really interested in these questions   3
might have started asking them a long while ago. Why does any person or
nation, including ours, persist in celebrating violence as an honorable expression of disapproval? In, let's say, Iraq, the Sudan, Waco—anywhere we
get fed up with meanspirited tormentors—why are we so quick to assume
that guns and bombs are the answer? ❷

Some accidents and tragedies and bizarre twists of fate are truly senseless,   4
as random as lightning bolts out of the blue. But this one at Columbine
High was not, and to say it was is irresponsible. "Senseless" sounds like "without cause," and it requires no action, so that after an appropriate interval of
dismayed hand-wringing, we can go back to business as usual. What takes guts
is to own up: This event made sense. Children model the behavior of adults,
on whatever scale is available to them. Ours are growing up in a nation
whose most important, influential men—from presidents to the coolest film
characters—solve problems by killing people. Killing is quick and sure and
altogether manly. ❸

Reading Critically

❶ Why does Kingsolver want to plant columbine? What historical event would it remind
her of?

❷ Do you agree with the author that our society is too quick to "assume that guns and
bombs are the answer"?

❸ Why do we feel that killing is "quick and sure and altogether manly"?

It is utterly predictable that some boys who are desperate for admiration 5
and influence will reach for guns and bombs. And it's not surprising that this
happened in a middle-class neighborhood; institutional violence is right at
home in the suburbs. Don't let's point too hard at the gangsta rap in our
brother's house until we've examined the video games, movies, and political choices we support in our own. The tragedy in Littleton grew out of a
culture that is loudly and proudly rooting for the global shootout. That culture is us.

Conventional wisdom tells us that Nazis, the U.S. Marines, the Termina- 6
tor, and the NYPD all kill for different reasons. But as every parent knows,
children are good at ignoring or seeing straight through the subtleties we spin.
Here's what they must surely see: Killing is an exalted tool for punishment
and control. Americans who won't support it are ridiculed, shamed, or even
threatened. The Vietnam War was a morally equivocal conflict by any historical measure, and yet to this day, candidates for public office who avoided
being drafted into that war are widely held to be unfit for leadership.

Most Americans believe bloodshed is necessary for preserving our way of 7
life, even though it means risking the occasional misfire—the civilians strafed
because they happened to live too close to the terrorist, maybe, or the factory that actually made medicines but *might* have been making weapons.
We're willing to sacrifice the innocent man condemned to death row because
every crime must be paid for, and no jury is perfect. The majority position
in our country seems to be that violence is an appropriate means to power, [4]
and that the loss of certain innocents along the way is the sad but inevitable
cost.

I'd like to ask those who favor this position if they would be willing to 8
go to Littleton and explain to some mothers what constitutes an acceptable
risk. Really. Because in a society that embraces violence, this is what "our way
of life" has come to mean. The question can't be *why* but only "Why yours
and not mine?" We have taught our children in a thousand ways, sometimes
with flag-waving and sometimes with a laugh track, that the bad guy deserves
to die. But we easily forget a crucial component of this formula: "Bad" is defined by the aggressor. Any of our children may someday be, in someone's
mind, the bad guy.

For all of us who are clamoring for meaning, aching for the loss of these 9
precious young lives in Littleton to mean something, my strongest instinct
is to use the event to nail a permanent benchmark into our hearts: Life is that

---

Reading Critically

[4] Do you agree that "violence is an appropriate means to power"? Why or why not?

precious, period. It is possible to establish zero tolerance for murder as a solution to anything. Those of us who agree to this contract can start by removing from our households and lives every television program, video game,
film, book, toy, and CD that presents the killing of humans (however symbolic) as an entertainment option, rather than the appalling loss it really is. ⑤
Then we can move on to harder choices, such as discussing the moral lessons
of capital punishment. Demanding from our elected officials the subtleties
and intelligence of diplomacy instead of an endless war budget. Looking
into what we did (and are still doing) to the living souls of Iraq, if we can
bear it. And—this is important—telling our kids we aren't necessarily proud
of the parts of our history that involved bombing people in countries whose
policies we didn't agree with.

Sounds extreme? Let's be honest. *Death* is extreme, and the children are   10
paying attention.

UNDERSTANDING DETAILS

1. What shootings is the author referring to at Columbine High School in Colorado? (Look this information up on the Internet if you need to.)
2. What is one of the main reasons the boys at Columbine High School resorted
   to killing?
3. What is "the tragedy in Littleton" (paragraph 5)?
4. According to Kingsolver, who is "rooting for a global shootout" (paragraph 5)?

THINKING CRITICALLY

5. In your opinion, why do some people think that "guns and bombs are the answer" (paragraph 3)?
6. What prominent people have solved problems by killing? In what ways do these
   people influence the youth in America?
7. What "video games, movies, and political choices" (paragraph 5) characterize
   "your town"?
8. Do you agree with Kingsolver that "most Americans believe bloodshed is necessary for preserving our way of life" (paragraph 7)? Explain your answer.

DISCOVERING RHETORICAL STRATEGIES

9. Explain the title Kingsolver gives this essay.
10. Who do you think was Kingsolver's original audience? Explain your answer.

Reading Critically

⑤ How would your life be different if you removed from it every "entertainment option"
that glorifies killing?

11. What rhetorical strategies does the author use to make her point? Give an example of each one you find.

12. What is the tone of this essay?

MAKING CONNECTIONS

13. Imagine that Kingsolver, Brent Staples ("A Brother's Murder"), Jay Weiner ("Sports Centered"), and/or Dave Grossman ("We Are Training Our Kids to Kill") are having a discussion about the amount of violence in America today. Which author would argue most passionately that we should limit violence in the media? Why do you think this is so?

14. Compare and contrast the use of cause/effect in essays by the following authors: Kingsolver, Stephen King ("Why We Crave Horror Movies"), and/or Michael Dorris ("The Broken Cord"). Who uses this rhetorical technique most skillfully? Why?

15. Do you think that Kingsolver and Lyn Mikel Brown and Meda Chesney-Lind ("Bad Girls, Bad Girls, Whatcha Gonna Do?") would agree that violence is "manly"? Why or why not?

IDEAS FOR DISCUSSION/WRITING

Preparing to Write

Write freely about our exposure to violence in the U.S.: How are we exposed to violence on a daily basis? List as many ways as you can think of. Do you believe these activities affect the crime rate in the U.S.? Explain your answer. How might we decrease the crime rate in the U.S.? How does this crime rate affect the way we live our lives?

Choosing a Topic

1. You have been asked to speak to a group of middle school students about the dangers of violent video games, TV shows, and movies. What do you want to tell them? Write out a draft of your speech.

2. Write an essay from the point of view of a juvenile delinquent called "Life Is Not Precious, or It Is." What would be the focus of such an essay? Develop each paragraph with this person's reasoning.

3. Common, everyday anger has become a dangerous part of our daily lives. In your opinion, where does this problem originate? What can we do as a society to help people curb their rage?

4. Visit these memorial Web sites for Columbine High School victims:

Rachel Scott:	http://www.rachelscott.com or
	http://www.racheljoyscott.com
Daniel Mauser:	http://www.danielmauser.com
Cassie Bernall:	http://www.cassierenebernall.org

Compare these personal sites with the site for an organization called Healing Of People Everywhere (HOPE) Columbine: http://www.hopecolumbine.org. Which Web site appeals to you the most? Which is the most emotionally charged? What characteristics about the Web site attract you? Write a persuasive essay in which you evaluate the Web site and argue that its presentation is most effective. Be sure to use specific details to support your claims.

Before beginning your essay, you might want to consult the checklists on page 461.

BARRETT SEAMAN   (1946–   )

How Bingeing Became the New College Sport

Almost forty years after he graduated from Hamilton College as an undergraduate, former White House correspondent and editor at *Time* magazine Barrett Seaman recently returned to his alma mater and visited twelve other colleges and universities to investigate the culture of America's residential college campuses. The result was *Binge: What Your College Student Won't Tell You* (2005), an unvarnished look at undergraduate life in the early twenty-first century. After two and a half years of living with students in dormitories at Harvard, Middlebury, Duke, Stanford, the University of Virginia, and other prominent schools, Seaman turned his journalist's eye on such controversial topics as binge drinking, casual sex, date rape, "pregaming," and other collegiate rites of passage that, in his opinion, have grown more reckless and impersonal since his graduation from Hamilton in 1967. Now a trustee at the college and the father of three daughters who recently earned their B.A. degrees, Seaman became fascinated with the topic after he accepted an early retirement package from *Time* following the 2001 merger between America Online and Time Warner. Today's college students, he argues, are plagued by anxieties and live in a culture drenched with alcohol and disconnected from the adult world around them. He also decries the decline in academic rigor and the lack of meaningful contact between today's students and their professors, particularly at large research institutions. The author lives in Irvington, New York.

Preparing to Read

This essay was first published in *Time* magazine in August 2005. In it, Barrett Seaman argues that the 21-year-old drinking age in our country is the cause of many serious problems.

Exploring Experience: Before you read this essay, consider what you know about the drinking habits of college students: Does under-age drinking occur at your college? Why does it occur? Do students drink excessively? If so, what do they gain from excessive drinking? Are there other rules that are broken in college? What are they? What are their risks? Where do you stand on the enforcement of these rules?

Learning Online: Take a few minutes to visit the College Drinking Prevention website (http://www.collegedrinkingprevention.gov), and browse the articles, charts, and video clips addressing alcohol abuse in colleges across the United States. Familiarize yourself with the extent of the problem and the consequences faced by the students and their campuses.

In the coming weeks, millions of students will begin their fall semester   1
of college, with all the attendant rituals of campus life: freshman orientation, registering for classes, rushing by fraternities and sororities, and,
in a more recent nocturnal college tradition, "pregaming" in their rooms.

Pregaming is probably unfamiliar to people who went to college before   2
the 1990s. But it is now a common practice among 18-, 19- and 20-year-
old students who cannot legally buy or consume alcohol. It usually involves
sitting in a dorm room or an off-campus apartment and drinking as much
hard liquor as possible before heading out for the evening's parties. ◆ While
reporting for my book *Binge,* I witnessed the hospitalization of several students for acute alcohol poisoning. Among them was a Hamilton College
freshman who had consumed 22 shots of vodka while sitting in a dorm
room with her friends. Such hospitalizations are routine on campuses across
the nation. By the Thanksgiving break of the year I visited Harvard, the
university's health center had admitted nearly 70 students for alcohol
poisoning.

When students are hospitalized—or worse yet, die from alcohol poison-   3
ing, which happens about 300 times each year—college presidents tend to
react by declaring their campuses dry or shutting down fraternity houses. But
tighter enforcement of the minimum drinking age of 21 is not the solution.
It's part of the problem.

Over the past 40 years, the U.S. has taken a confusing approach to the   4
age-appropriateness of various rights, privileges and behaviors. It used to be
that 21 was the age that legally defined adulthood. On the heels of the student revolution of the late '60s, however, came sweeping changes: the voting age was reduced to 18; privacy laws were enacted that protected college
students' academic, health and disciplinary records from outsiders. including
parents; and the drinking age, which had varied from state to state, was lowered to 18.

Then, thanks in large measure to intense lobbying by Mothers Against   5
Drunk Driving, Congress in 1984 effectively blackmailed states into hiking
the minimum drinking age to 21 by passing a law that tied compliance to
the distribution of federal-aid highway funds—an amount that will average
$690 million per state this year. ◆ There is no doubt that the law, which
acheved full 50-state compliance in 1988, saved lives, but it had the unintended consequence of creating a covert culture around alcohol as the young
adult's forbidden fruit.

Reading Critically

1 What is "pregaming"? Have you ever done it?

2 What was the relationship between raising the drinking age to 21 and the distribution of
federal highway funds?

Drinking has been an aspect of college life since the first Western uni-   6
versities in the 14th century. My friends and I drank in college in the 1960s—
sometimes a lot but not so much that we had to be hospitalized. Veteran
college administrators cite a sea change in campus culture that began, not
without coincidence, in the 1990s. It was marked by a shift from beer to
hard liquor, consumed not in large social settings, since that is now illegal,
but furtively and dangerously in students' residences.

In my reporting at colleges around the country, I did not meet any pres-   7
idents or deans who felt that the 21 year age minimum helps their efforts to
curb the abuse of alcohol on their campuses. Quite the opposite. They
thought the law impeded their efforts since it takes away the ability to monitor and supervise drinking activity.

What would happen if the drinking age was rolled back to 18 or 19? Ini-   8
tially, there would be a surge in binge drinking as young adults savored their
newfound freedom. But over time, I predict, U.S. college students would
settle into the saner approach to alcohol I saw on the one campus I visited
where the legal drinking age is 18: Montreal's McGill University, which en-
rolls about 2,000 American undergraduates a year. ❸ Many, when they first
arrive, go overboard, exploiting their ability to drink legally. But by midterms,
when McGill's demanding academic standards must be met, the vast majority have put drinking into its practical place among their priorities.

A culture like that is achievable at U.S. colleges if Congress can muster the   9
fortitude to reverse a bad policy. If lawmakers want to reduce drunk driving, they should do what the Norwegians do: throw the book at offenders
no matter what their age. Meanwhile, we should let the pregamers come
out of their dorm rooms so that they can learn to handle alcohol like the
adults we hope and expect them to be.

UNDERSTANDING DETAILS

1. What is "pregaming" according to this essay?
2. What does Seaman believe is the main cause of binge drinking?
3. How does the 21-year drinking age cause problems for colleges?
4. What is the legal drinking age in Montreal, Canada? How do the students respond to this law at McGill University?

THINKING CRITICALLY

5. In what ways has alcohol become "the young adult's forbidden fruit" (paragraph 5)?

Reading Critically

❸ What would be the short-term result of lowering the drinking age to 18? The long-term
result? Would you be in favor of reducing the drinking age? Why or why not?

6. Do you agree with the author that lowering the drinking age would encourage students to put drinking in their lives into perspective? Explain your answer.
7. Why do you think alcohol consumption is so prevalent on U.S. college campuses?
8. In your opinion, what would be the ideal drinking age in the United States? Explain your reasoning.

DISCOVERING RHETORICAL STRATEGIES

9. Seaman starts his essay with a list of real activities that take place on most college campuses. Is this an effective beginning? Why or why not?
10. List Seaman's topics and make an outline of his essay. Does he cover all the important ideas on this subject?
11. How does the specific reference to McGill University in Montreal affect you? What does it do for the essay?
12. What is the thesis of this essay? Where does this thesis statement appear?

MAKING CONNECTIONS

13. Imagine that Seaman, Franklin Zimring ("Confessions of an Ex-Smoker"), Michael Dorris ("The Broken Cord"), and/or Dave Grossman ("We Are Training Our Kids to Kill") are discussing how tough it is to break an addiction. Which of these addictions do you think would be most difficult to stop? Why?
14. Compare and contrast Seaman's use of examples with those employed by Amy Tan ("Mother Tongue"), Brent Staples ("A Brother's Murder"), and/or Jessica Mitford ("Behind the Formalddehyde Curtain"). Who uses examples most skillfully? Why do you think this is so?
15. Do you think that Michael Dorris ("The Broken Cord") would agree with Seaman that the drinking age ought to be lowered? Whose side would you be on? Why?

IDEAS FOR DISCUSSION/WRITING

Preparing to Write

Write freely about the risks students take in college today: What dangers are most common at your college? Which of these is connected with a law? Why do you think students take risks in college? In what ways is the whole college experience ripe for risk-taking? What risks have you taken in college? Were they worth the danger? Why did you take these risks? Would you take them again? Why or why not?

Choosing a Topic

1. Your old high school has noticed an increase in drinking before high school dances and other social events. Since you used to hold a seat in the student government, your high school has asked you to come back to your school and talk to the seniors about drinking. What will you say? Since this is such a sen-

sitive issue, the school officials have asked to see a copy of your speech before you deliver it. Prepare your talk, being aware that you need to win the students' trust as you also give them realistic warnings.

2. From what you have observed in college so far, analyze the behavior of your peers. How do they generally manage themselves on your campus during the week? How does that change on the weekend? How do you fit into this "routine"? Explain your observations in an essay to your English instructor.

3. What risks have you taken in your life? Why did you take them? Are you glad you did? Why or why not? Focusing on your own behavior, analyze your attitude toward taking risks? What are the advantages? The disadvantages? Use your experiences and observations to support your analysis.

4. Imagine that one of your close friends was recently involved in a "pregaming" party at someone's house before a football game. During the party, your friend drank too much alcohol, lost consciousness, and ended up spending the night passed out in a back bedroom. Your friend does not remember several events that happened that evening, and this greatly concerns you. Write an email to your friend explaining your concern and persuading your friend to pay more attention to the dangers of alcohol abuse.

Before beginning your essay, you might want to consult the checklists on page 461.

DAVE GROSSMAN   (1956–   )

We Are Training Our Kids to Kill

Lieutenant Colonel Dave Grossman is a retired professor of psychology and military science and a former Army Ranger who has recently founded a new field of scientific study he calls "killology," which investigates how and why people kill each other during wartime, the psychological costs of battle, the root causes of violent crime, and the process of healing that victims of violence must go through (see www.killology.com). Following a B.S. at Columbus College in Georgia (where he was elected to Phi Beta Kappa) and an M.Ed. at the University of Texas, Grossman joined the Army, where he rose quickly through the ranks to lieutenant colonel and served as a professor at both the United States Military Academy at West Point and as chair of the Department of Military Science at Arkansas State University. The author of three books— *On Killing: The Psychological Cost of Learning to Kill in War and Society* (1995), *Stop Teaching Our Kids to Kill: A Call to Action Against TV, Movie, and Video Game Violence* (with Gloria deGaetano, 1999), and *On Combat* (2004)—he spends nearly three hundred days on the road each year consulting and giving workshops about combat and violence. He also writes military science fiction and will soon publish a new book entitled *The Two-Space War*. His advice to students using *The Prose Reader* is to avoid a steady diet of violent visual images, which "will lobotomize the brain and make thinking and writing more difficult. If you cleanse your mind (particularly the frontal cortex) with periods of contemplation and reading, you will become a much better writer."

Preparing to Read

The following controversial essay, originally published in the *Saturday Evening Post* in July/August 1999, contains a clear, well-reasoned analysis of the dangers connected with violence on TV and in video games. The author, Dave Grossman, is especially concerned with the way in which these media sources actually train our children to kill.

Exploring Experience: Before you read this essay, think about your views on violence in the media: Do you think watching violence on television and in the movies or playing video games can lead to violent acts? How useful are movie ratings for violence and sex? At what age do you think children should be able to see violence without adult supervision or censorship? Who do you think should control the violence children are exposed to? To what extent should we censor violence in the media? What specific types of violent behavior should be regulated in the media? What should not be censored?

Learning Online: Go to your favorite online news source. How many of the headlines describe violent acts? Consider this information while reading Grossman's argument.

I am from Jonesboro, Arkansas. I travel the world training medical, law enforcement, and U.S. military personnel about the realities of warfare. I try to make those who carry deadly force keenly aware of the magnitude of killing. Too many law enforcement and military personnel act like "cowboys," never stopping to think about who they are and what they are called to do. I hope I am able to give them a reality check.

So here I am, a world traveler and an expert in the field of "killology," ◆ when the (then) largest school massacre in American history happens in my hometown of Jonesboro, Arkansas. That was the March 24, 1998, schoolyard shooting deaths of four girls and a teacher. Ten others were injured, and two boys, ages 11 and 13, were jailed, charged with murder.

Virus of Violence

To understand the why behind Littleton, Jonesboro, Springfield, Pearl, and Paducah, and all the other outbreaks of this "virus of violence," ◆ we need to first understand the magnitude of the problem. The per capita murder rate doubled in this country between 1957—when the FBI started keeping track of the data—and 1992. A fuller picture of the problem, however, is indicated by the rate at which people are attempting to kill one another—the aggravated assault rate. That rate in America has gone from around 60 per 100,000 in 1957 to over 440 per 100,000 in 2002. As bad as this is, it would be much worse were it not for two major factors.

The first is the increased imprisonment of violent offenders. The prison population in America nearly quintupled between 1975 and 2002. According to criminologist John A. DiIulio, "dozens of credible empirical analyses . . . leave no doubt that the increased use of prisons averted millions of serious crimes." ◆ If it were not for our tremendous imprisonment rate (the highest of any industrialized nation), the aggravated assault rate and the murder rate would undoubtedly be even higher.

The second factor keeping the murder rate from being even worse is medical technology. According to the U.S. Army Medical Service Corps, a wound that would have killed nine out of ten soldiers in World War II, nine out of ten could have survived in Vietnam. Thus, by a very conservative estimate, if we still had a 1940-level medical technology today, our murder rate would be ten times higher than it is. The murder rate has been held down by the development of sophisticated lifesaving skills and techniques,

---

Reading Critically
◆ What do you think the term "killology" means?
◆ What does Grossman mean by the "virus of violence" in our country? In what ways is this problem like a disease?
◆ Do you agree with the assertion that "the increased use of prisons averted millions of serious crimes"?

such as helicopter medevacs, 911 operators, paramedics, CPR, trauma centers, and medicines.

Today, both our assault rate and murder rate are at phenomenally high levels. Both are increasing worldwide. In Canada, according to their Center for Justice, per capita assaults increased almost fivefold between 1964 and 2002, attempted murder increased nearly sevenfold, and murders doubled. Similar trends can be seen in other countries in the per capita violent crime rates reported to Interpol between 1977 and 2002. In Australia and New Zealand, the assault rate increased approximately fourfold, and the murder rate nearly doubled in both nations. The assault rate tripled in Sweden and approximately doubled in Belgium, Denmark, England and Wales, France, Hungary, the Netherlands, and Scotland. Meanwhile, all these nations had an associated (but smaller) increase in murder.   6

This virus of violence is occurring worldwide. The explanation for it has to be some new factor that is occurring in all of these countries. There are many factors involved, and none should be discounted: for example, the prevalence of guns in our society. But violence is rising in many nations with Draconian gun laws. And though we should never downplay child abuse, poverty, or racism, there is only one new variable present in each of these countries that bears the exact same fruit: media violence presented as entertainment for children. ❹   7

Killing Is Unnatural

Before retiring from the military, I spent almost a quarter of a century as an army infantry officer and a psychologist, learning and studying how to enable people to kill. Believe me, we are very good at it. But it does not come naturally; you have to be taught to kill. And just as the army is conditioning people to kill, we are indiscriminately doing the same thing to our children, but without the safeguards.   8

After the Jonesboro killings, the head of the American Academy of Pediatrics Task Force on Juvenile Violence came to town and said that children don't naturally kill. It is a learned skill. And they learn it from abuse and violence in the home and, most pervasively, from violence as entertainment in television, the movies, and interactive video games.   9

Killing requires training because there is a built-in aversion to killing one's own kind. ❺ I can best illustrate this fact by drawing on my own military research into the act of killing.   10

Reading Critically

❹ How much violence do you think the average six-year-old child sees on television each day? What is the cumulative effect of watching it for many years?

❺ Do you think this is true? Do most people have an innate aversion to killing other human beings?

We all know how hard it is to have a discussion with a frightened or angry   11
human being. Vasoconstriction, the narrowing of the blood vessels, has literally
closed down the forebrain—that great gob of gray matter that makes one a
human being and distinguishes one from a dog. When those neurons close
down, the midbrain takes over and your thought processes and reflexes are in-
distinguishable from your dog's. If you've worked with animals, you have some
understanding of what happens to frightened human beings on the battlefield. The battlefield and violent crime are in the realm of midbrain responses.

Within the midbrain, there is a powerful, God-given resistance to killing   12
your own kind. Every species, with a few exceptions, has a hardwired resistance to killing its own kind [6] in territorial and mating battles. When animals
with antlers and horns fight one another, they head-butt in a nonfatal fashion. But when they fight any other species, they go to the side to gut and gore.
Piranhas will turn their fangs on anything, but they fight one another with
flicks of the tail. Rattlesnakes will bite anything, but they wrestle one another.
Almost every species has this hard-wired resistance to killing its own kind.

When we human beings are overwhelmed with anger and fear, we slam   13
head-on into that midbrain resistance that generally prevents us from killing.
Only sociopaths—who by definition don't have that resistance—lack this
innate violence immune system.

Throughout all human history, when humans have fought each other,   14
there has been a lot of posturing. Adversaries make loud noises and puff
themselves up, trying to daunt the enemy. There is a lot of fleeing and sub-
mission. Ancient battles were nothing more than great shoving matches. It
was not until one side turned and ran that most of the killing happened, and
most of that was stabbing people in the back. All of the ancient military historians report that the vast majority of killing happened in pursuit when
one side was fleeing.

In more modern times, the average firing rate was incredibly low in Civil   15
War battles. British author Paddy Griffith demonstrates in his book *The Battle Tactics of the Civil War* that the killing potential of the average Civil War regiment was anywhere from five hundred to a thousand men per minute. The
actual killing rate was only one or two men per minute per regiment. At
the Battle of Gettysburg, of the 27,000 muskets picked up from the dead
and dying after the battle, 90 percent were loaded. This is an anomaly, because
it took 90 percent of their time to load muskets and only 5 percent to fire.
But even more amazing, of the thousands of loaded muskets, only half had
multiple loads in the barrel—one had 23 loads in the barrel. [7]

Reading Critically

[6] What does the phrase "hardwired resistance" mean to you?

[7] What do all these statistics imply about the willingness of Civil War soldiers to fire their
muskets?

In reality, the average man would load his musket and bring it to his shoul-   16
der, but he could not bring himself to kill. He would be brave, he would stand
shoulder to shoulder, he would do what he was trained to do; but at the
moment of truth, he could not bring himself to pull the trigger. And so he
lowered the weapon and loaded it again. Of those who did fire, only a tiny
percentage fired to hit. The vast majority fired over the enemy's head.

During World War II, U.S. Army Brig. Gen. S. L. A. Marshall had a team   17
of researchers study what soldiers did in battle. For the first time in history,
they asked individual soldiers what they did in battle. They discovered that
only 15 to 20 percent of the individual riflemen could bring themselves to
fire at an exposed enemy soldier.

That is the reality of the battlefield. Only a small percentage of soldiers   18
are able and willing to participate. Men are willing to die. They are willing
to sacrifice themselves for their nation; but they are not willing to kill. It is
a phenomenal insight into human nature; but when the military became
aware of that, they systematically went about the process of trying to fix this
"problem." From the military perspective, a 15 percent firing rate among riflemen is like a 15 percent literacy rate among librarians. And fix it the military did. By the Korean War, around 55 percent of the soldiers were willing
to fire to kill. And by Vietnam, the rate rose to over 90 percent.

The method in this madness: desensitization.   19

How the military increases the killing rate of soldiers in combat is in-   20
structive because our culture today is doing the same thing to our children.
The training methods militaries use are brutalization, classical conditioning,
operant conditioning, and role modeling. I will explain each of these in the
military context and show how these same factors are contributing to the
phenomenal increase of violence in our culture.

Brutalization and desensitization are what happens at boot camp. From the   21
moment you step off the bus, you are physically and verbally abused: countless push-ups, endless hours at attention or running with heavy loads, while
carefully trained professionals take turns screaming at you. [8] Your head is
shaved; you are herded together naked and dressed alike, losing all individuality. This brutalization is designed to break down your existing mores and
norms, and force you to accept a new set of values that embraces destruction, violence, and death as a way of life. In the end, you are desensitized to
violence and accept it as a normal and essential survival skill in your brutal
new world.

Something very similar to this desensitization toward violence is hap-   22
pening to our children through violence in the media—but instead of

---

Reading Critically

[8] What do you think is the relationship between brutalization and desensitization in armed
forces training?

18-year-olds, it begins at the age of 18 months when a child is first able to discern what is happening on television. At that age, a child can watch something happening on television and mimic that action. But it isn't until children are six or seven years old that the part of the brain kicks in that lets them understand where information comes from. Even though young children have some understanding of what it means to pretend, they are developmentally unable to distinguish clearly between fantasy and reality. [9]

When young children see somebody shot, stabbed, raped, brutalized, de-   23
graded, or murdered on TV, to them it is as though it were actually happening. To have a child of three, four, or five watch a "splatter" movie, learning to relate to a character for the first 90 minutes and then in the last 30 minutes watch helplessly as that new friend is hunted and brutally murdered, is the moral and psychological equivalent of introducing your child to a friend, letting her play with that friend, and then butchering that friend in front of your child's eyes. And this happens to our children hundreds upon hundreds of times.

Sure, they are told, "Hey, it's all for fun. Look, this isn't real; it's just TV."   24
And they nod their little heads and say OK. But they can't tell the difference. Can you remember a point in your life or in your children's lives when dreams, reality, and television were all jumbled together? That's what it is like to be at that level of psychological development. That's what the media are doing to them.

The *Journal of the American Medical Association* published the definitive epi-   25
demiological study on the impact of TV violence. The research demonstrated what happened in numerous nations after television made its appearance as compared to nations and regions without TV. The two nations or regions being compared are demographically and ethnically identical; only one variable is different: the presence of television. In every nation, region, or city with television, there is an immediate explosion of violence on the playground, and within 15 years there is a doubling of the murder rate. Why 15 years? That is how long it takes for the brutalization of a three-to five-year-old to reach the "prime crime age." That is how long it takes for you to reap what you have sown when you brutalize and desensitize a three-year-old. [10]

Today the data linking violence in the media to violence in society are su-   26
perior to those linking cancer and tobacco. Hundreds of sound scientific studies demonstrate the social impact of brutalization by the media. The

---

Reading Critically

[9] According to the author, at what age are children able to understand the difference between fantasy and reality? How does this affect their reaction to televised violence?

[10] How is the brutalization and desensitization of soldiers in training different from the indoctrination of a three-year-old through televised violence?

Journal of the American Medical Association concluded that "the introduction of television in the 1950s caused a subsequent doubling of the homicide rate, i.e., long-term childhood exposure to television is a causal factor behind approximately one half of the homicides committed in the United States, or approximately 10,000 homicides annually." The article went on to say that "if, hypothetically, television technology had never been developed, there would today be 10,000 fewer homicides each year in the United States, 70,000 fewer rapes, and 700,000 fewer injurious assaults" (June 10, 1992).

Classical Conditioning

Classical conditioning is like the famous case of Pavlov's dogs they teach   27
in Psychology 101. The dogs learned to associate the ringing of the bell with food, and once conditioned, the dogs could not hear the bell without salivating.

The Japanese were masters at using classical conditioning with their sol-   28
diers. Early in World War II, Chinese prisoners were placed in a ditch on their knees with their hands bound behind them. And one by one, a select few Japanese soldiers would go into the ditch and bayonet "their" prisoner to death. This is a horrific way to kill another human being. Up on the bank, countless other young soldiers would cheer them on in their violence. Comparatively few soldiers actually killed in these situations, but by making the others watch and cheer, the Japanese were able to use these kinds of atrocities to classically condition a very large audience to associate pleasure with human death and suffering. [11] Immediately afterwards, the soldiers who had been spectators were treated to sake, the best meal they had in months, and to so-called comfort girls. The result? They learned to associate committing violent acts with pleasure.

The Japanese found these kinds of techniques to be extraordinarily ef-   29
fective at quickly enabling very large numbers of soldiers to commit atrocities in the years to come. Operant conditioning (which we will look at shortly) teaches you to kill, but classical conditioning is a subtle but powerful mechanism that teaches you to like it. [12]

This technique is so morally reprehensible that there are very few exam-   30
ples of it in modern U.S. military training, but there are some clear-cut examples of it being done by the media to our children. What is happening to our children is the reverse of the aversion therapy portrayed in the movie *A*

Reading Critically

[11] How and why did the World War II Japanese army teach its soldiers to "associate pleasure with human death and suffering"?

[12] What is the difference between "operant conditioning" and "classical conditioning"? Which do you think is more sinister?

Clockwork Orange. In *A Clockwork Orange,* a brutal sociopath, a mass murderer, is strapped to a chair and forced to watch violent movies while he is injected with a drug that nauseates him. So he sits and gags and retches as he watches the movies. After hundreds of repetitions of this, he associates violence with nausea. And it limits his ability to be violent.

We are doing the exact opposite: Our children watch vivid pictures of   31
human suffering and death, and they learn to associate it with their favorite soft drink and candy bar, or their girlfriend's perfume.

After the Jonesboro shootings, one of the high-school teachers told me   32
how her students reacted when she told them about the shootings at the middle school. "They laughed," she told me with dismay. A similar reaction happens all the time in movie theaters when there is bloody violence. The young people laugh and cheer and keep right on eating popcorn and drinking pop. We have raised a generation of barbarians who have learned to associate violence with pleasure, like the Romans cheering and snacking as the Christians were slaughtered in the Colosseum. [13]

The result is a phenomenon that functions much like AIDS, a phenom-   33
enon I call AVIDS—Acquired Violence Immune Deficiency Syndrome. AIDS has never killed anybody. It destroys your immune system, and then other diseases that shouldn't kill you become fatal. Television violence by itself does not kill you. It destroys your violence immune system and conditions you to derive pleasure from violence. And once you are at close range with another human being and it's time for you to pull that trigger, Acquired Violence Immune Deficiency Syndrome can destroy your midbrain resistance.

Operant Conditioning

The third method the military uses is operant conditioning, a very pow-   34
erful repetitive procedure of stimulus-response, stimulus-response. A benign example is the use of flight simulators to train pilots. An airline pilot in training sits in front of a flight simulator for endless hours; when a particular warning light goes on, he is taught to react in a certain way. When another warning light goes on, a different reaction is required. Stimulus-response, stimulus-response, stimulus-response. One day the pilot is actually flying a jumbo jet; the plane is going down, and 300 people are screaming behind him. He is wetting his seat cushion, and he is scared out of his wits; but he does the right thing. Why? Because he has been conditioned to respond reflexively to this particular crisis.

Reading Critically

[13] Do you agree with the author that "we have raised a generation of barbarians who have learned to associate violence with pleasure"? Why or why not?

When people are frightened or angry, they will do what they have been   35
conditioned to do. In fire drills, children learn to file out of the school in orderly fashion. One day there is a real fire, and they are frightened out of their
wits; but they do exactly what they have been conditioned to do, and it saves
their lives. 14

The military and law enforcement community have made killing a con-   36
ditioned response. This has substantially raised the firing rate on the modern
battlefield. Whereas infantry training in World War II used bull's-eye targets,
now soldiers learn to fire at realistic, man-shaped silhouettes that pop into
their field of view. That is the stimulus. The trainees have only a split second
to engage the target. The conditioned response is to shoot the target, and then
it drops. Stimulus-response, stimulus-response, stimulus-response—soldiers
or police officers experience hundreds of repetitions. Later, when soldiers are
on the battlefield or a police officer is walking a beat and somebody pops up
with a gun, they will shoot reflexively and shoot to kill. We know that 75 to
80 percent of the shooting on the modern battlefield is the result of this
kind of stimulus-response training.

Now, if you're a little troubled by that, how much more should we be   37
troubled by the fact that every time a child plays an interactive point-and-
shoot video game, he is learning the exact same conditioned reflex and motor
skills?

I was an expert witness in a murder case in South Carolina offering mit-   38
igation for a kid who was facing the death penalty. I tried to explain to the
jury that interactive video games had conditioned him to shoot a gun to
kill. He had spent hundreds of dollars on video games learning to point and
shoot, point and shoot. One day he and his buddy decided it would be fun
to rob the local convenience store. They walked in, and he pointed a snub-
nosed .38 pistol at the clerk's head. The clerk turned to look at him, and the
defendant shot reflexively from about six feet. The bullet hit the clerk right
between the eyes—which is a pretty remarkable shot with that weapon at that
range—and killed this father of two. Afterward, we asked the boy what happened and why he did it. It clearly was not part of the plan to kill the guy—
it was being videotaped from six different directions. He said, "I don't know.
It was a mistake. It wasn't supposed to happen."

In the military and law-enforcement worlds, the right option is often not   39
to shoot. But you never, ever put your money in that video machine with
the intention of not shooting. There is always some stimulus that sets you off.
And when he was excited, and his heart rate went up, and vasoconstriction
closed his forebrain down, this young man did exactly what he was condi-

Reading Critically
14 What are some positive uses of "operant conditioning"?

tioned to do: he reflexively pulled the trigger, shooting accurately just like all those times he played video games.

This process is extraordinarily powerful and frightening. The result is ever 40 more "homemade" sociopaths who kill reflexively. Our children are learning how to kill and learning to like the idea of killing; and then we have the audacity to say, "Oh my goodness, what's wrong?" 15

One of the boys involved in the Jonesboro shootings (and they are just 41 boys) had a fair amount of experience shooting real guns. The other one, to the best of our knowledge, had almost no experience shooting. Between them, those two boys fired 27 shots from a range of over 100 yards, and they hit 15 people. That's pretty remarkable shooting. We run into these situations often—kids who have never picked up a gun in their lives pick up a real gun and are incredibly accurate. Why? Video games.

UNDERSTANDING DETAILS

1. According to Grossman, what is the "virus of violence" (paragraph 3)?
2. What evidence does the author use to argue that "killing is unnatural"?
3. What three methods does the military use to train its soldiers to kill?
4. How does Grossman claim we are training our children to kill?

THINKING CRITICALLY

5. What two factors does the author believe control the murder rate in the United States? How do these factors affect this rate?
6. How are the techniques used in video games similar to those taught in military training?
7. How did the U.S. military train more soldiers to actually fire their guns?
8. How can we control this epidemic of violence that Grossman outlines?

DISCOVERING RHETORICAL STRATEGIES

9. What do you think Grossman's purpose is in this essay?
10. Who do you think would be most interested in this essay?
11. What effect do you think this essay will have on parents?
12. Describe the writer's point of view in a complete sentence.

MAKING CONNECTIONS

13. To what extent would Grossman, Brent Staples ("A Brother's Murder"), and/or Barbara Ehrenreich ("The Ecstasy of War") agree that violence is encoded in our human DNA? What outside influences, according to these authors, make us a more violent culture? Which of the three authors makes the most convincing case for his or her point of view? Explain your answer.

Reading Critically

15 How does the author indict all of us in the creation of "homemade sociopaths"?

14. Imagine a conversation between Grossman, Kimberly Wozencraft ("Notes from the Country Club"), and/or Malcolm X ("Learning to Read") about the relationship between societal pressures and incarceration. Why do you think our jails are so crowded? What can be done about this massive increase in America's prison population?

15. How do you think Bill Cosby ("The Baffling Question"), Robert Ramirez ("The Barrio"), Mary Pipher ("Beliefs About Families"), and/or bell hooks ("Justice: Childhood Love Lessons") would each respond to Grossman's implication that parents need to be more vigilant in monitoring what their children watch on television? What is your own opinion on this issue?

IDEAS FOR DISCUSSION/WRITING

Preparing to Write

Write freely about your feelings concerning censorship: Should violence on TV be censored in any way? Why or why not? At what age can children safely watch violence in the media? Do you believe a relationship exists between watching violence and acting in a violent manner? Who is most responsible for restricting or editing the violence that children see?

Choosing a Topic

1. *Time* magazine has asked you to respond directly to Grossman's article. Do you think his argument about the relationship between children and video games is reasonable? Give specific examples to support your contention.

2. As an apprentice at a TV station, you have been asked to represent your age group by giving your opinion on the network's inclusion of violence in their programming. What is your opinion concerning TV violence? In what ways do you think your opinion represents the consensus of American society as a whole?

3. Research and describe the censorship practices of another country. Explain specifically how that country's views on censorship are carried out in practice. Give as many examples as possible to support your explanation.

4. What is the most popular current video game? How violent do you think it is? Do you believe that video games, movies, television shows, or popular music influence youth violence? Write an argument in which you take a position regarding this controversial issue. Following Grossman's style, use several different types of examples to support your claims.

Before beginning your essay, you might want to consult the checklists on page 461.

KIM SEVERSON   (1961–   )

I'm Not Willing to Settle for Crumbs

Born in Eau Claire, Wisconsin, Kim Severson earned her B.A. in journalism at Michigan State University before turning to a career in newspaper writing. Currently a staff writer for the Dining Section of the *New York Times,* she previously wrote about cooking and the culture of food for the *San Francisco Chronicle,* following a seven-year stint as an editor and reporter at the *Anchorage Daily News* in Alaska. Before writing about food full-time, she covered crime, education, social services, and government activities for several daily newspapers on the West Coast. The author of two books—*The New Alaska Cookbook* (2001) and *The Trans Fat Solution: Cooking and Shopping to Eliminate the Deadliest Fat from Your Diet* (2003)—Severson has won several regional and national awards for news and feature writing, including the Casey Medal for Meritorious Journalism for her work on childhood obesity in 2002 and four James Beard awards for food writing. Her hobbies include cooking (no surprise there!), reading, and playing softball in Brooklyn, where she lives with her partner, Katia Hetter. Her advice to students using *The Prose Reader* is to "always keep a notebook for moments of inspiration. Keep writing down any important ideas and thoughts that you have. You will inevitably forget that great idea if it's not in the notebook."

Preparing to Read

This article was originally published in *Newsweek* in 2005. In it, Kim Severson uses personal anecdotes to argue for equal rights for gay couples in marriage.

Exploring Experience: As you prepare to read this essay, consider your views on marriage: What does marriage signify in our society? Why do many people consider marriage "sacred"? What does that mean in this context? Who should be allowed to get married? Should anyone be prohibited from getting married? Why is the institution of marriage important to some and unimportant to others? Where do you stand on the issue of gay marriage?

Learning Online: Visit a retail Web site that features products specifically tailored to same-sex wedding ceremonies, such as http://www.gayweddings .com or http://www.pinkproducts.co.uk. Browse through the products available (i.e., invitations, cake toppers, reception favors, and guest books). Compare these products to those used in traditional heterosexual weddings. Can you think of other items that should be offered?

There is such a sweet light in the face of the straight people who want   1
me to get married. It starts with that sparkly, conspiratorial smile.
They squeeze my arm, leaning in like a favorite auntie. "So," they say,
"are you going to Massachusetts?"

I can barely stand the kick to the curb I'm about to deliver.   2

I would love nothing more than to marry my partner. I love this girl. I   3
want the dinner and the dance and the promise of her Social Security check
if, God forbid, she dies young. I want a joint tax return and the family discount at the health club.

I also want some return for the years I've spent giving straight people   4
wedding presents. I want everyone at the office to gasp at my engagement
ring and pitch in for a bad bakery cake to celebrate. I want the magic of the
day I was conditioned to hope for. ❶

That's not going to happen by going to Massachusetts, where same-sex   5
marriage has been legal since 2003. Sure, I might get the cake and a little slice
of symbolism, but any legal or financial advantage would dissolve once we
left the state. For gay couples like us, marriage is about collecting paper. ❷

Our commitment is measured by the size of our legal files, which grow   6
each time we move to a new state or accumulate property or struggle to
ensure that one person's retirement account will go to the other.

Say my girlfriend and I did take what would be an unquestionably roman-   7
tic trip to Massachusetts. We'd have to start our married life off with a lie, since
you have to declare your intention to live there. We'd have to wait three days
for a license, then get a certificate saying we don't have syphilis and listen to a
lecture on AIDS (a nice bit of equality with our straight brothers and sisters).
For the drive, we'd stock the glove compartment with our medical powers of
attorney and hospital authorization forms. That way, if we got in a car accident
and one of us needed to get into the other's hospital room or make some hard
decisions, we wouldn't get shut out while doctors tried to reach our parents.

Then there's the general power of attorney, which is good, all-round   8
backup. We'd also tuck in the New York City domestic-partnership certificate we got at city hall. It cost us $1 more than the license straight people
buy, for reasons I can't suss out. (My girlfriend says it doesn't really give us
much except the right to visit each other in Rikers. Still, it might work in
a pinch.) All this, on top of the regular pressures of finding a hall, someone
to do the ceremony, and a florist.

Even if we did decide that one more piece of paper might actually make   9
us married, the government wouldn't care. Consider, for example, our medical insurance. She is covered by the domestic-partnership benefits of my

---

Reading Critically

❶ When did you first suspect that this essay was written by a gay author?

❷ Why is marriage "about collecting paper" for Severson and her partner?

job. That's great, until you run headfirst into the federal tax law. Because the Feds don't think gay weddings are real, even if we did get married I'd still have to pay taxes on an extra $9,370.20—what her medical coverage is worth.

Don't get me wrong. I applaud the right-thinking folks in Massachusetts,   10 Vermont and Canada. I appreciate the recent battle in Connecticut, where we get something that looks a lot like marriage but isn't called that. This is a civil-rights battle rooted in love, and it's moving quickly.

I'm grateful that in the Blue States and some of the Red it's not cool to   11 fire me from my job based on my sexual orientation. Except for one incident at a weird resort near Kansas City, Mo., my girlfriend and I have never been hassled when we've asked for a double bed. Even high schools have gay–straight alliances now. The only gay–straight alliance at my school was when the straight kids called me a lezzie.

I understand the emotional draw of a legally sanctioned ceremony. We   12 were living in San Francisco when gay marriage started breaking out all over city hall one Friday afternoon in the winter of last year. My girlfriend was covering it for the daily paper, and she called me to come watch what was a historic moment.

I saw people on the steps of the beaux-arts building, weeping and kiss-   13 ing. On that glorious day, it felt as if I could have what all my straight friends had. I hadn't known how heavy the oppression was until it was lifted, even for a moment.

We didn't get married. My girlfriend believed that as a journalist, she   14 couldn't be a part of a story she was writing about. (The old journalistic-objectivity excuse—like I haven't heard that before.) She didn't buy my argument that straight, married people shouldn't be able to cover it then, either.

The truth was, we didn't want to rush it. Isn't the whole point of getting   15 married to have your brothers make stupid toasts and your mother cry and your friends swear to help keep you together when you're falling apart—to craft a public sharing of love? [3] Marriage is not about driving to a place where you don't live or settling for a ceremony that will be recognized only there.

It's my wedding, damn it. I don't want the crumbs. [4] I want the whole cake.   16

UNDERSTANDING DETAILS

1. What reasons does Severson give for wanting to get married?
2. What is the "little slice of symbolism" Severson is referring to in paragraph 5?
3. In what ways is marriage for gay couples about "collecting paper" (paragraph 5)?
4. Why does Severson believe a Massachusetts marriage is not for her?

Reading Critically

[3] Why does the author want "to craft a public sharing of love"? How is this desire different from the feelings of straight couples?

[4] What does Severson mean when she explains that she doesn't want "the crumbs"?

THINKING CRITICALLY

5. In your opinion, who should be allowed to marry?
6. In what ways is gay marriage "a civil-rights battle rooted in love" (paragraph 10)?
7. What do you think is "the emotional draw of a legally sanctioned ceremony" that Severson refers to in paragraph 12?
8. Explain the last paragraph of Severson's essay.

DISCOVERING RHETORICAL STRATEGIES

9. Explain the title of this essay.
10. Severson uses the word "oppression" in paragraph 13. Define this word in the context of gay rights.
11. Is developing her argument with personal examples and anecdotes effective for this topic, or would a more objective essay be more persuasive?
12. How effective is Severson's argument that she wants "the whole cake" (paragraph 16) effective? Explain your answer.

MAKING CONNECTIONS

13. Compare and contrast the quality of love portrayed by Severson, Garrison Keillor ("How the Crab Apple Grew"), and/or Mary Roach ("Meet the Bickersons").
14. Do you think that Mary Pipher ("Beliefs About Families") would agree with Severson that a gay couple would make a good "family"? Why or why not?
15. How do Severson, Richard Rodriguez ("Hunger of Memory"), Amy Tan ("Mother Tongue"), and/or Jessica Mitford ("Behind the Formaldehyde Curtain") use specific details to help advance their arguments? Which author is most skilled at this technique? Why do you think this is so?

IDEAS FOR DISCUSSION/WRITING

Preparing to Write

Write freely about your views on gay marriage: Is marriage an important ritual to you? Why or why not? Should the institution of marriage be denied to anyone? What do you think is the main reason people decide to get married? How important is marriage to society? Explain your answer. Why is marriage important to some people and not to others? Are there any rituals important to you that you were not allowed to participate in? Why were you excluded? Did the decision make sense to you? How did it make you feel?

Choosing a Topic

1. Write an argument either for or against gay marriage. Before you start writing, gather some information on this topic from the Internet. Then support your position with appropriate evidence.
2. How does disappointment make us stronger? Choose an activity or event that you were excluded from even though participating in it was important to you,

and write an essay discussing the activity and explaining how the disappointment made you a stronger person.

3. You have been asked by the local Psychology Club to be on a panel debating the advantages and disadvantages of marriage in society today. You decide to write out your thoughts before the panel presentation. In essay form, argue for or against marriage as an important institution in our society. What are your reasons? What will be the reasons of the opposition? Can you anticipate and counter the opposition? Explore all angles of this issue so you are well prepared for the debate.

4. Revisit the retail Web site for Pink Products (http://www.pinkproducts.co.uk). Imagine that you are running a similar company that sells all types of wedding products. However, you would like to make as much profit as possible by attracting both straight and gay couples. Create a one-page advertisement or marketing brochure featuring your products. Design it in such a way that it would appeal to both audiences.

Before beginning your essay, you might want to consult the checklists on page 461.

Immigration

The following essays take opposite views on the question of immigration controls. The first, by Michael Scott, argues in favor of more stringent restraint on immigration into the United States. Scott is a graduate of the UCLA School of Management currently employed as a national sales manager for a high-tech electronics firm. His interest in immigration began twelve years ago when he stumbled upon nearly one hundred illegal aliens hiding in the scrub brush in Newport Beach, California. His advice to students using *The Prose Reader* is to concentrate on topics they feel passionate about: "The first draft of an essay should come straight from the heart or gut. Don't worry about spelling or punctuation at that early stage. Just let it all hang out. Then go back and smooth everything out to create the finished product."

Richard Raynor, who takes the other side of the immigration question, is a British-born journalist and Cambridge graduate who has published six novels, among them *The Elephant* (1992), *The Blue Suit: Memoir of a Crime* (1995), *Los Angeles Without a Map* (1997), and *The Cloud Sketcher* (2001, soon to be made into a movie starring Brad Pitt). His advice for aspiring authors is to "write about the kinds of things you like to read, something that will make you want to turn the page. As John Cleese says in a Monty Python sketch, 'it's not just getting the right number of words—it's getting them in the right order.' "

Preparing to Read

The following essays were first published in *The Social Contract* (2000) and *New York Times Magazine* (1996) respectively. They take opposing viewpoints on the many complex issues associated with illegal immigration.

Exploring Experience: Before you begin to read these essays, think about immigration and its effect on society: How do you feel about illegal immigration? Whom should we stop from entering our borders? Whom should we let through? Why is immigration such a major issue in the United States? What do immigrants generally bring to America? What do they take from our country? Do you worry about the expense of illegal aliens? What other issues concern you about this topic?

Learning Online: Visit the U.S. government's Bureau of Citizenship and Immigration Services Web site (http://uscis.gov). Click on the "FAQ" link, and select "Statistics" from its alphabetized list. Read the most recently published statistical report. Pay special attention to the number of illegal immigrants, their regional location, and their average monthly wage. Consider how each writer uses statistics to develop his argument.

MICHAEL SCOTT   (1948–   )

America Must Take Stronger Measures to Halt Illegal Immigration

In 1991, I accidentally stumbled upon a botched illegal immigration op- 1
eration on a nearby Southern California beach—in broad daylight. Nearly
one-hundred illegal immigrants were hiding in a few tiny gullies, partially
protected by a cadre of lookouts, presumably waiting for transportation to
get them to their destinations. Neither the local police nor Los Angeles Immigration and Naturalization Service (INS) showed much concern. This resulted in my researching the background and realities of illegal immigration,
and the more I learned, the worse it got. We've got a ticking time bomb on
our hands, [1] made worse by legions of government officials who just slumber on or push their heads deeper into the sand to curry flavor with those
who support this relentless invasion. Just as bad, lots of Americans have been
sucker-punched into inaction by threats of being called "racist," "bigot" and
sundry yada yada.

Then, in 1999, I had a conversation with Arizona rancher Roger Bar- 2
nett, whose property is under year-round siege by hordes of illegal aliens. His
Chochise County border sector is overwhelmed by about 475,000 illegal
aliens annually. Although Barnett has apprehended over 1000 illegal aliens on
his property and turned them over to the Border Patrol, he's anything but a
vigilante. Roger has lived in Douglas, Arizona, all of his 50-some years and
is infuriated by the on-going destruction of his property caused by incessant
swarms of illegal immigrants, as well as by the repeated failures of the INS
to stem this relentless flood. [2] Barnett and his neighbors have had it with
an unmerciful stealth migration that generates mountains of rotting garbage,
piles of discarded diapers, food containers and plastic water bottles, and sundry
filth everywhere—exacerbated by the stench of excrement, poisoned (or
throat-slit) pets and livestock, and lots of stolen property that wasn't tied
down.

Of special ire is Barnett's 80-year-old widowed neighbor who lives be- 3
hind her chain-link fence, with a shotgun and pistol always near by, and
who's afraid to come out at night and challenge the hoards who have ruined

---

Reading Critically

[1] Do you agree that illegal immigration in this country is a "ticking time bomb"?

[2] How do the metaphors "incessant swarms" and "relentless flood" help the author make
his point?

her crops and garden and made her a virtual prisoner in her own home. She's afraid to buy more guard dogs since the last two were poisoned, probably by "coyotes."

Costs of Illegal Immigration

One look at the ravages of illegal immigration in California is enough to   4 make most Americans sick. At least 40 percent of the nation's 6 million illegal immigrants are here. From a base of 2.4 million illegal immigrants already present, they just keep coming—120,000 net new illegals each year into California (300,000 nationally), and the horrendous social costs just keep rising. There are 408,000 illegal immigrant K–12 students to educate at a cost to California taxpayers of approximately $2.2 billion annually, for example. Never mind that these students can't work, drive, or vote once they graduate, unless they obtain fraudulent documents.

Taxpayers subsidize 96,000 illegal immigrant births in statewide county   5 hospitals (200,000 nationally) at a yearly cost of $352 million. Then we have annual [welfare] costs for these new citizen children of nearly $552 million. Add another $557 million to incarcerate 23,000 illegal alien felons in California, plus $60 million health care costs for various services, and we're over $3.7 billion annually—out of our pockets, and against our overwhelming opposition to such outrages. ❸

Eliminating this brutal migratory devastation involves two basic actions—   6 enforcing our own immigration laws and accepting the ugly reality that "we've met the enemy and it is us."

Enforcing the Law

Three fundamental law enforcement steps must be taken to break the   7 back of illegal immigration. First, our borders must be sealed. No more baloney about how difficult this might be. The INS instituted a Border Patrol crackdown in 1994 in the El Paso sector and then took it to San Diego a year later. In 1993, 90 percent of all illegal aliens crossed at border cities. Today [in 2000], two-thirds cross in remote areas. In 1994, in the San Diego sector, 42 percent of all illegals surged through a 14-mile-corridor near Imperial Beach. Another 22.6 percent entered in and around El Paso. Both sectors are now almost impregnable, as these flows have become trickles. So today's illegals are going where it's easier to get across, like Douglas, Arizona. The inescapable conclusion is that the crackdown has succeeded where sufficient resources have been applied. This isn't a matter of insufficient re-

---

Reading Critically

❸ Why do you think the alleged costs of illegal immigration are used so often to argue against it?

sources or wherewithal; it's a matter of insufficient willpower, as well as a writing-off of those individuals and organizations who want illegal immigration to succeed.

The next critical law enforcement step is to prosecute employers who   8
hire illegal aliens. [4] The Justice Department is hardly lifting a finger in this area. If there were no jobs, most illegal aliens would leave, or most wouldn't come in the first place. The fantasy of illegal immigration cheerleaders that the economy would collapse without illegal labor simply doesn't wash. Since when don't we enforce laws (or break them) in accordance with our own standards of right and wrong? I sometimes speed on California interstates, and I'm prepared for the fines if caught. But this doesn't excuse me from punishment nor the California Highway Patrol (CHP) from enforcement.

This baloney about the need for "guest workers" is pure bunk. Both the   9
California Division of Labor and the General Accounting Office (GAO) have confirmed there are currently two farm workers for every agricultural job in California. This glut of farm workers has depressed agricultural wages over the past twenty years, in inflation adjusted terms, by 20 percent and spawned deplorable working conditions.

Job opportunities for low-skilled workers have been declining for three   10
decades. The continued influx of low-skilled, uneducated immigrants has depressed earnings and limited opportunities. Income disparity has widened as a result of too many low-skilled workers pursuing too few jobs.

A University of California (Davis) agricultural economist (and several   11
other noted researchers) published "Poverty Amid Prosperity," a compilation of research findings on "The processes of immigration and its unexamined impacts on cities and towns" (July 1997; The Urban Institute Press). They offered the following analysis of the impact of farm worker wage increases on both grower expenses and the price of food:

> And suppose that the entire cost of higher farm wages is passed on to consumers, so that the annual cost of the farm labor used to produce the fresh fruit consumed by the average American household rises from $8.60 to $13 and the cost of farm labor rises from $10.20 to $15. If these increased farm labor costs were completely passed on to consumers, spending on fresh fruits and vegetables eaten at home for a typical 2.6 person consumer unit would increase by less than $10, from $270 to almost $280.

I'd welcome the opportunity to pay higher consumer prices to rid our land   12
of illegal immigrants. [5] We'd lift an enormous financial albatross from our backs and provide better educational opportunities for thousands of

---

Reading Critically

[4] Why does the author criticize employers who hire illegal aliens?

[5] Would you be willing to pay higher prices for consumer items such as food in order to "rid our land of illegal immigrants"? Why or why not?

American kids to receive the full attention of teachers in schools crowded with the children of illegal immigrants.

Americans Willing to Work

Finally, to address perhaps the biggest lie of all—that Americans won't do 13 the work that illegals perform—the truth is that uneducated and unskilled Americans won't live in garages with multiple families and endure similar hardships to take on backbreaking work at below minimum wages. Get rid of illegal immigrants, and wages would have to rise to attract those native-born and legal residents who lack the skills and education to do much else. [6]

About deportation. With the exception of illegal alien felons incarcerated 14 in various prisons and those illegals caught by the border patrol (at the border), deportations are virtually nonexistent. Yet there are six million illegal aliens in this country. We could make a huge deportation dent in this stealth population if we only had the commitment and determination to do so. Once again, it's a national administration attempting to curry favor with the wrong people.

About "we've met the enemy and they are us," some conservatives and lib- 15 erals support Cardinal Roger Mahony's statement, "the right to immigrate is more fundamental than that of nations to control their borders"—conservatives because they get their jollies from exploiting cheap labor and liberals because it gives them another opportunity to smother someone with compassion. Added to these afflictions are the wishes of politicians to get re-elected by ducking issues and the hidden agendas of opportunists and ideologues to advance their causes.

Proposition 187

Let's look at California's Proposition 187. This was a 1994 ballot initiative 16 that barred illegal immigrant access to public social services, including education and public health care services, except emergency care. In November of 1994, 59 percent of the California electorate voted for Proposition 187. Of California's 58 counties, 49 voted yes.

The day after Proposition 187 passed, a federal court in Los Angeles and 17 a state court in San Francisco barred enforcement of most of its provisions. A federal judge kept this bottled up for nearly 3½ years before voiding it. Immediately thereafter the State of California appealed the decision, but because a conniving governor was soon thereafter elected—a person opposed to

---

Reading Critically

[6] Do you agree with the author that a decrease in the number of illegal immigrants would prompt a rise in wages for unskilled American workers?

Proposition 187—he saw to it that the initiative never reached the Supreme Court through the appellate process.

Just before Governor Gray Davis strangled Proposition 187 in April 1999,   18
he said with the most angelic of faces, "If this (Proposition 187) were a piece of legislation, I would veto it. But it's not. It's an initiative, passed by nearly 60 percent of the voters through a process specifically designed to go over the heads of the legislature and the governor. If officials choose to selectively enforce only the laws they like, our system of justice will not long endure." Davis then walked off the press conference stage and betrayed the people of California by stabbing them in the back.

Our Own Worst Enemies

Then there's the shameful AFL-CIO [labor union] clamor for amnesty for   19
6 million illegal aliens, hoping lots of them will become union members. ⑦
The AFL-CIO is attempting to line their pockets with membership dues over the short run, while rolling the dice with the futures of American workers. All this will do is end control of our borders and unleash terrible wage depression pressures on millions of American workers as hordes of foreigners surge across unprotected borders looking for American jobs.

We've clearly become our own worst enemies and will suffer a terrible   20
fate unless we end this madness. A series of national administrations have buried their collective heads in the sand and ignored the acrid odors of the white hot burning fuse attached to the illegal immigration time bomb. There just aren't enough Roger Barnetts around, and that's what's necessary for us to retake our country. Just remember folks, the only card your opponents hold in their hands is the race-baiting card, the threat of calling you a racist or a bigot. But the collective votes of an ignored and aggrieved articulate voting population are the strongest cards of all, and if you chose to play them, it's a slam-dunk for the good guys.

Illegal immigration is repudiated by our laws, by the facts, and by most   21
Americans. So, one more time folks, let's seal our borders, deport all illegal aliens, prosecute any employer hiring illegals, throw the rascals out who live on the Planet Beltway and kowtow to the illegal immigration lobby, and begin to pay close attention to the calamity that awaits us unless we do all of these things.

Reading Critically
⑦ According to Scott, why are labor unions in favor of amnesty for illegal aliens?

RICHARD RAYNOR   (1955–   )

Illegal Immigration Does Not Threaten America

Maria T. bites her nails. At 31, with five children, she's one of the 1.7 mil-   1
lion immigrants now estimated to be living in California illegally.
She speaks almost no English, even though she has been in America
for more than eight years. In her clean and sparsely furnished living room, her
kids—Gustavo (11), Mario (7), Maribel (6), Cesar (5) and Joan (4)—are in front
of the TV, laughing first at "Home Improvement," then at "The Simpsons."

The refrigerator is almost empty; it contains only a gallon of milk, some   2
Kool-Aid, a few tortillas. Her life is frugal, a devotion to the future of her children. Though there are three bedrooms in the apartment, all five sleep with
her because she hates to let them out of her sight. Since she has no car and
can rarely afford the bus, the family walks everywhere, Maria leading the
way like Mother Goose with the kids behind toting Batman and Pocahon-
tas backpacks. On a typical day she walks six miles, shuttling between her
apartment and the local school in Van Nuys. **❶**

For her, as for so many, the decision to make the journey to El Norte was   3
the beginning of an epic. Gustavo was 3 at the time, Mario was 8 months,
and she was 5 months pregnant with Maribel. Maria crossed the border with
the help of a "coyote," a guide, but when she arrived in San Diego the woman
who'd paid for her brothers' crossings didn't have any money this time. Maria
was kept a slave in the coyote's house. He beat and raped her until, after three
months, her brother raised $300, half the sum agreed for the crossing, and the
coyote let her go.

She stayed with her brother in Los Angeles, the Pico-Union district, and   4
it was here that Maribel was born. "I'd come out of labor and I was staring
at the wall and I said to my sister-in-law, 'Look, she's there.' She said, 'Who?'
I said, 'The Virgin Mary.' She said, 'There's nothing there. You're crazy.' But
it was true all the same. For eight months the Virgin would appear to me.
She made me strong." **❷**

"At first, I had to beg for food. Sometimes I did day work for Latinos, for   5
$10 a day. I'd take off into the city on the bus, not really knowing where I
was going and get off to beg on the streets. I'm ashamed of that."

Slowly, she clawed her way up. It is in so many ways a classic immigrant's   6
tale, although she has been the beneficiary not just of her own drive, but

---

Reading Critically

❶ Instead of beginning his essay with statistics, Raynor starts with a brief case study of a typical illegal immigrant. How powerful and convincing is this tactic?

❷ Why does the author connect religion with the necessity to immigrate to America?

also of something equally important—welfare. She's here illegally, with fake ID, and she doesn't work. She receives $723 in cash and $226 in food stamps, and Section 8 takes care of more than two-thirds of her $1,000 rent (high, because landlords know illegals won't complain).

It's a myth, however, that anyone can come over the border and start milk- 7 ing the system. Only Medicaid and limited food benefits are available to il- legal immigrants, and most don't apply for these because they fear detection by the Immigration and Naturalization Service (I.N.S.). Maria T. gets what she does because of her children who were born here. ③

Local, state, and federal governments spend about $11.8 billion a year ed- 8 ucating legal and illegal immigrant children, according to the Urban Insti- tute, a nonpartisan research organization, compared with the $227 billion spent to educate all children. Generally, this is more than offset by the taxes that legal and illegal immigrant families pay—$70.3 billion a year, the Urban Institute says—while receiving $42.9 billion in total services. Illegal immi- grants pay $7 billion in taxes.

Maria T., however, represents the nightmare scenario—an illegal immigrant 9 who's sucking money from the system and putting nothing back. Even so, it's not clear that she's a villain. She hopes one day to go to work herself. She hopes and believes that her bright children will become outstanding. She believes in America.

Fears of Strangers

My wife, from Finland, has a green card; I'm English, in the process of ap- 10 plying for one myself; our son was born an American. When we moved into our house in Venice, Calif., one of our neighbors, an elderly white woman with whom we're now very friendly, said, "No Americans live on our block anymore."

Maybe she had the jitters about new neighbors, or maybe there was some- 11 thing else at play. I knew that her father had been born in Germany and had journeyed to Detroit, where she was born. I wanted to say that logically, therefore, our son is every bit as American as she is. But in any debate about nationality, I know, logic fades fast.

My own father once traced our family tree back to 1066, when one Baron 12 de Rainier sailed from Normandy to help conquer England. Since then, give or take the occasional Irish excursion, my progenitors were all born within a hundred or so miles of one another in the north of England. So, when I came to America and found that nearly everyone was from somewhere else if they

---

Reading Critically

③ How do you feel about the legality of granting automatic citizenship to American-born children of illegal immigrants?

stepped back a generation or two, I found myself thrilled and oddly at ease. It explained America's drive, its generosity and up-for-anything energy. As (novelist Herman) Melville wrote, "We are not a nation, so much as a world."

Not everyone sees things this way. Many have drawn a line behind which   13
they stand, true Americans, fearful and angry about the erosion of their identity. With unintended irony they talk of themselves as "natives." ◆ On immigration, they argue that enough is enough, that the borders must be secured and a drastic cutback enforced. Those who are allowed in, they say, must be professionals or skilled workers because the others—mobs of unskilled, third-world peasants—drain resources and take jobs. They cost billions and dilute the gene pool. They are mutating the face of America.

California itself, for instance, passed an anti-immigrant measure with scary   14
ease. In 1994's state election nearly 60 percent voted for Proposition 187, the so-called Save-Our-State initiative, which sought to deny public education, nonemergency health care and welfare to illegal immigrants. By linking illegal immigration to joblessness and crime, Pete Wilson revived his flagging gubernatorial campaign and was swept back into office, even though, as an exit poll showed, few who voted for 187 actually thought it was going to work.

Wilson was avid for votes and a reaction and he got both. Many illegal   15
Latinos, fearful of deportation, refused to go near schools and emergency rooms. There was immigrant bashing and hate mail. Since the Republicans took control of the United States House and Senate, moreover, it seems as though all Washington has been grandstanding on the issue. Dozens of immigration-related bills were introduced.

Many of the proposals are mean-spirited and, to a lot of observers, wrong-   16
headed. One would impose a tax on employers who hire legal aliens. Others would deny citizenship to children born in this country to illegals or eliminate some categories of family immigration. The anti-immigration forces have done an excellent job of creating an atmosphere of crisis in which the debate has focused on how to slow the "flood" of immigration, legal and illegal. But illegal immigration should not be folded over to scapegoat legals as well. The real point is that there isn't any immigration crisis.

How Many Immigrants?

"The perception is that immigration is out of control," says Joel Kotkin,   17
author of *Tribes* and a fellow at the Pepperdine University Institute of Public Policy. "It isn't. ◆ If you say to most Americans, 'We have 800,000 legal immigrants a year,' they're going to reply, 'Hey, that's not so bad.' And this is

---

Reading Critically
◆ Who are the true "natives" of America, according to Raynor?
◆ Do you believe that immigration is "out of control"? Why or why not?

the truth of the situation. But it's somehow been demonized so that people think there are millions coming across the border."

The Border Patrol logged 1,094,718 apprehensions in 1994. On page 26   18
of his *Alien Nation,* a leading restrictionist, Peter Brimelow, writes that legal immigration is "overwhelmed by an estimated 2 to 3 million illegal entries into the country in every recent year." He goes on to note, correctly, that many of these illegal entrants go back home and that some trundle to and fro across the border every day. By page 33, however, he's writing "a remarkable 2 to 3 million illegal immigrants may have succeeded in entering the country in 1993."

Within seven pages illegal entrants have mysteriously become illegal im-   19
migrants, attached to that hyperbolic two to three million, a figure vigorously disputed by I.N.S., which regards as preposterous the idea that for every border crosser caught another three get away. Indeed, throughout the 1970's there were some eight million border apprehensions and during that time, according to the best estimates of I.N.S., about one million illegals came to reside—eight apprehensions per illegal immigrant.

So how many illegals are coming in and staying each year now? The Urban   20
Institute says 250,000 to 300,000. The Center for Immigration Studies, a conservative research group, says 400,000, while I.N.S. says 300,000. The Census Bureau until recently guessed 200,000 to 400,000; now it agrees with the I.N.S.

The 300,000 figure is considered firm because it was based on the years   21
following 1988, when the I.N.S. started to process the genuinely reliable data it amassed following the 1986 amnesty for illegals. Too much of this and the eyes glaze over, but the gist is, the further you get from 1988, the flakier the statistics become. And the argument over the number of illegal immigrants is nothing compared with the furor over how much they cost. [6]

The fact is, no one knows for sure; there is simply no up-to-date research.   22
"The issue has caught political fire," Papademetriou says. "But serious academics haven't got out into the field yet. They're reluctant to play into the hands of the politicians."

Immigration is in the spotlight not because of money but because it so   23
impinges on issues like race, the role of government, national identity, and change. Name an issue and you can hook it to immigration. One side looks at crime, failing schools, and soaring welfare spending and sees too many immigrants. The other sees America, the greatest nation on earth, built on the backs of immigrants and still benefiting enormously from the brains, energy,

---

Reading Critically

[6] The author attacks the notion that illegal immigration is costly to Americans, yet provides no statistics to support his point. Does this tactic help or hurt his argument?

and determination (not to speak of low wages) of the next generation of newcomers. Right now the debate is more emotional than informed. It's all temper tantrums and red-hot sound bites.

Fear of Latinos

When people complain about immigration, about the alien "flood," it's Latin   24
Americans they mean, who from their entry points in California and Miami are fanning out through the country. There's concern about the small minority, who are criminals, and the seeming reluctance of these people to learn English. 🕖 Mixed in with this is the prejudice summarized by D. H. Lawrence in *Mornings in Mexico.* They are other, he concluded; they are dirty; I don't trust them and they stink. There's also the suggestion that Latinos are lazy, though everywhere you look in Los Angeles you see evidence to the contrary.

A Demand for Labor

Historically, immigration has been tolerated, even encouraged during   25
labor shortages. Labor migration has been going on for centuries, and it's hard to see how 300,000 or so illegal immigrants per year will make or break the American economy. Indeed, in Los Angeles they're most likely an asset. The number of illegals in California is thought to be growing by 125,000 a year—hardly an economic catastrophe in a state of 31 million. In Los Angeles, where 80,000 jobs were created last year, it's a definite plus. The city has a thirst for people who will work for $5 or even $3 an hour.

The legal Chinese immigrants who have revitalized the San Gabriel Val-   26
ley, the Latinos who are opening businesses in depressed areas of South Los Angeles, and the Russians and Iranians who are opening businesses all over are the principal reasons the city is so different from, say, Detroit. Says Joel Kotkin, "The only place where American society is evolving is where the immigrant influx is strong. Cities would have no future without them. But if you're sitting in Idaho, it looks different."

The Race Issue

Pro-immigration forces have tended to keep their focus tight on the eco-   27
nomic issues because they sense that Americans don't want to be told they're racist. Nobody does. Yet, one of the problems with the immigration issue is that it does impinge on the race issue and thus appeals temptingly and dangerously to the worst side of all of us. 🔞

A central argument of Brimelow's "Alien Nation" is that America has al-   28
ways had an essential nature, an ethnic core, and that it's white. He writes that

---

Reading Critically
🕖 How do you feel about the alleged reluctance of many immigrants to learn English?
🔞 Do you feel that most people who oppose illegal immigration are racists? Why or why not?

"the first naturalization law, in 1790, stipulated that an applicant must be a 'free white person.' Blacks became full citizens only after the Civil War."

He goes on, "Maybe America should not have been like this. But it was." 29 And now, "Americans are being tricked out of their own identity."

Reading this, I'm overcome with a weird looking–glass giddiness. Some-   30 one's trying to change the rules here, to wipe a rag over history. [9] America's identity is precisely that of mutation, its power drawn from an energetic and quite fearless ability to adapt and win. Its national book, after all, is *The Adventures of Huckleberry Finn,* about a beautiful and dangerous river that never stops changing.

An Immigrant Nation

America is an immigrant nation, indeed, a nation of strangers. I like it   31 that way, though the arguments in favor of the idea are not merely sentimental and historical. Corporate interests value immigration for something that troubles us—keeping wages lower, and these days not just at the level of busboys and dayworkers.

The American economy is in relatively good shape and has pretty much   32 the legal immigration it needs. The system isn't broken, doesn't need fixing—and certainly not in the ways that are now being proposed. Illegal immigration is touchier. Listening to academics makes it easy to forget the racially inflamed brush fire that is the debate in California.

Recent polls show a surprising sympathy even for illegal immigrants, pro-   33 vided they otherwise play by the rules: work, get documentation, learn English. Only 20 percent say immigrants take jobs away from citizens, and 69 percent say they do work that citizens don't necessarily want and that needs to be done. Few say that the American-born children of illegals should be deprived of education and welfare, let alone their citizenship. The message here is a sensible one: beef up the Border Patrol; deport criminals; don't break up families; target labor-enforcement at bad-guy sweatshop employers and make an effort to deal with temporary visa overstays, who surprisingly make up as much as 50 percent of all illegals; supply Federal assistance to heavily impacted areas such as Los Angeles; and forget the idea of a national verification system or an identification card.

Ultimately, this is a debate about values, not money. This is about how   34 America feels about itself. [10]

Reading Critically

[9] What is the meaning of the author's metaphor that some people are trying to "wipe a rag over history"?

[10] How powerful is the author's concluding statement? What do you think this last sentence means?

UNDERSTANDING DETAILS

1. What are Scott ("America Must Take Stronger Measures to Halt Illegal Immigration") and Raynor ("Illegal Immigration Does Not Threaten America") each saying about illegal immigration in these two essays?
2. What arguments can you think of to supplement both of their essays?
3. What three basic steps does Scott say must be taken through law enforcement to stop illegal immigration? Explain each in detail.
4. What does Raynor mean when he says, "Ultimately, this is a debate about values, not money. This is about how America feels about itself"?

THINKING CRITICALLY

5. Which stand on this particular argument is most convincing to you? Which examples or statistics seem most persuasive? Explain your reactions to each of these two positions.
6. Would you agree to pay higher prices "to rid our land of illegal immigrants" (Scott, paragraph 12)?
7. What do you think Melville means by the words "We are not a nation, so much as a world" (Raynor, paragragh 12)? Do you agree with this statement?
8. How might the opinions in these two essays be reconciled? Can you make a compromise prediction that combines both these views of the world?

DISCOVERING RHETORICAL STRATEGIES

9. Who do you think is the intended audience for each of these essays? Are there any important differences between these audiences in your opinion?
10. These two authors make their points with slightly different writing voices. Describe the tone or mood of each essay, and explain whether you think that particular voice is most effective for the author's purpose.
11. How does the organization of the two essays differ? What is the general organizing principle in each case?
12. What other rhetorical strategies does each essay use to make its point? Give examples of each strategy.

MAKING CONNECTIONS

13. Compare and contrast the arguments used by Scott and Raynor. Which essay seems most persuasive to you? Which essay comes closest to matching your own personal viewpoint? Could you conceivably find an essay convincing and well-argued even if it conflicts with your own opinion? Why or why not?
14. If Scott and Raynor were having a conversation with Kimberly Wozencraft ("Notes from the Country Club") about the difficulties in enforcing laws against illegal aliens versus those concerning drug abuse, which issue would the authors say receives less attention from our legal system? Would you agree? What does this disparity in justice tell us about laws in the United States? About the power of special interest groups?

15. Imagine that Scott and Raynor were having a round-table discussion about the topic of illegal immigration with Sandra Cisneros ("Only daughter"), Amy Tan ("Mother Tongue"), Sucheng Chan ("You're Short, Besides!"), and/or Richard Rodriguez ("Public and Private Language"). Which of these authors would speak most vigorously in favor of having the United States truly integrated with people from many different countries? What specific skills and abilities do immigrants bring to America? Do you think the alleged strain on our economy and infrastructure is worth the positive values these immigrants bring to our country? Why or why not?

IDEAS FOR DISCUSSION/WRITING

Preparing to Write

Write freely about your views on the role of immigrants in the United States: What do immigrants offer America? In what ways do immigrants weaken our country? What is your general view of immigrants? Who should be allowed to enter our national borders? What guidelines would you put on immigrants? Why would you establish these guidelines? Explain your answer in as much detail as possible.

Choosing a Topic

1. Whether or not we should pay for the education of illegal aliens has been an issue in politics for quite some time. What is your opinion on this issue. Use facts and statistics from these two essays to support your point of view.
2. Many sociologists and politicians who have studied immigration claim that the issue ultimately centers upon race. Do you agree with this contention? Present your own argument on this statement, supporting your opinion with persuasive examples and facts.
3. Your local library is sponsoring a writing contest with a first place prize of $1000. All contestants must write a 500-word essay on the following topic: "How does understanding other cultures help make us better human beings?" Write an essay on this topic that would win the first place award.
4. Which of the two arguments was presented most effectively? Regardless of your personal feelings about the issue, evaluate which argument presented its case most persuasively. Write an editorial essay for your favorite online news source in which you evaluate both articles and argue that one's presentation is more effective. Be sure to use specific details to support your claims.

Before beginning your essay, you might want to consult the checklists on page 461.

Postconviction DNA Testing

The following three essays each offer a different viewpoint on the controversial question of whether DNA testing should consistently be used in legal cases. Tim O'Brien, who argues that the use of DNA should be encouraged, is an attorney and award-winning journalist who covered the Supreme Court for more than twenty-two years. He also served as the principal Washington correspondent for CNN's "Moneyline." James Dao, who suggests in his article that DNA testing is helpful in some cases and not in others, is a reporter for the *New York Times* who has covered a wide variety of political and social events. And Peter Roff, who argues against the widespread use of DNA testing, is a Senior Political Analyst with United Press International. He is also the editor of the Daily Enterprise, a web blog for the Free Enterprise Fund. DNA testing was pioneered by Sir Alec Jeffreys at the University of Leicester in 1985. Also called "genetic fingerprinting," it identifies subtle differences in DNA sequencing that can be used to help determine guilt or innocence in a court of law, confirm paternity, and establish biogeographic and ethnic heritage.

Preparing to Read

Each of the next three essays takes a different stand on DNA: One talks about using DNA to prove someone's innocence; the second tells us how DNA testing cleared one convict and implicated another; and the third argues for limiting DNA testing on previously convicted prisoners.

Exploring Experience: This series of essays deals with the advantages and disadvantages of DNA testing. As you prepare to read these essays, share with the rest of your class what you know about DNA testing: What are its advantages and disadvantages? What is the source of your information? Why is DNA testing such an interesting feature of most investigations? What makes it so interesting?

Learning Online: Visit the "Facts and Figures" page of the Web site for the National Coalition Against the Death Penalty (NCADP) at http://www.ncadp.org/facts_figures.html. Scroll through the charts and tables of statistics regarding the number of death penalty executions that have taken place over the last several years. Note the number of people currently on death row in each state, and pay particular attention to the disparity according to race. Do any of these numbers surprise you? What are your thoughts about this information?

TIM O'BRIEN   (1946–   )

Postconviction DNA Testing Should Be Encouraged

My editors and I thought it was a good story: the black, one-eyed,   1
homosexual rapist who claimed it was a case of mistaken identity.
P.S.: He also walked with a limp. ❶

The U.S. Supreme Court had agreed to review the case in its 1988 term,   2
because it had raised an important constitutional question: Do the police
have any obligation to preserve potentially exculpatory evidence?

The Case of Larry Youngblood

The defendant, Larry Youngblood, had been convicted of abducting a   3
10-year-old boy from a church carnival and repeatedly sodomizing him.
Youngblood had argued that if the police had preserved semen samples taken
from the boy's clothing, DNA tests would have shown they had arrested the
wrong man.

Never mind that the tests in question weren't ordinarily available at the   4
time of the trial (although they are now routine). Never mind that Youngblood fit the description provided by the victim or that the traumatized child
also identified Youngblood in court as the perpetrator. Never mind that the
evidence appeared so overwhelming that it took the jury only 40 minutes
to convict Youngblood and send him on his way to a 10-year prison term.

The legal issue the case raised was significant; it was to resonate years later   5
in the O.J. Simpson case and doubtless many other lesser cases. In my heart,
I questioned the judgment of the public defenders who would bring such
an important issue to the Supreme Court with such an obviously guilty defendant. If, as Oliver Wendell Holmes put it, hard cases make bad law, then
what do bad cases make? ❷

But public defenders Dan Davis and Carol Witteis seemed less concerned   6
with the precedent the court might set than with winning freedom for their
client. Could they possibly believe he was really innocent? Yes, without a
doubt, they both said. Defense lawyers can believe, or appear to believe,
anything.

Supreme Court justices are supposed to decide cases on the basis of the   7
law, but like all humans, they too can be influenced by the facts. And the
facts in this case couldn't have been worse for Youngblood. Moreover, he

---

Reading Critically
❶ Do you think this is a good start to the essay? Why or why not?
❷ What does this Oliver Wendell Holmes maxim mean to you?

lived alone, had a history of mental illness and had had previous run-ins with the law.

As expected, the Supreme Court upheld Youngblood's conviction, deciding his fate with exceptional speed, just as the jury had two years earlier. Only three justices dissented, with the late Harry Blackmun writing that "the Constitution requires a fair trial, not merely a 'good faith' try at a fair trial." 8

Mistaken Identity

A good story? We didn't know the half of it. [In August 2000] Youngblood's conviction was vacated—thrown out by the Pima County Superior Court in Tucson. While the small amount of semen that was preserved was insufficient for reliable testing at the time of the appeal, new testing procedures that only recently became available were conducted by the Tucson police. They showed conclusively what attorneys Witteis and Davis knew all along: The police really did have the wrong man. It was a case of mistaken identity. ❸ 9

Youngblood may have been less a victim of bad facts than of societal biases that can seep into and poison the criminal justice process. Could his race have been a factor? His multiple disabilities, mental and physical? His perceived sexual orientation? The fact that he had been accused of a horrendous crime that cried out for retribution? 10

There is no scientific way to quantify the effects of these illicit considerations in Youngblood's case, nor anyone else's for that matter. And the Supreme Court, in another case, has ruled that even a statistical probability of bias is insufficient to set aside a conviction, even a death sentence. DNA testing, by providing statistical proof of innocence (or guilt), may be the only way to effectively offset invidious biases. 11

Yet at every turn prosecutors are resisting the use of DNA tests whenever it might mean reopening an old case. There are now hundreds of inmates on death row who claim DNA tests would show they were not guilty of the crimes for which they were convicted. Most, perhaps even all, are mistaken. But in light of what happened to Larry Youngblood, the complaints that such tests are too expensive and time-consuming or that a jury's verdict must be accorded finality ring hollow indeed. The Tucson police have graciously conceded that it was "unfortunate" Youngblood spent so much time incarcerated for a crime he didn't commit, but they say they did what they thought 12

Reading Critically

❸ How did the newly analyzed DNA evidence save this particular defendant?

was right at the time. Youngblood is angry to have been robbed of "the best part of my life," and he wants to sue the police. All agree it should not have happened.

To prevent it from happening again, courts must be receptive to any credible claim that new tests might prove the actual innocence of one who has already been convicted. Had Larry Youngblood been charged with first degree murder, he'd probably be dead now. ◆[4]   13

Note

1. In 1995 former football star O.J. Simpson was found not guilty of murdering his ex-wife and her friend. Controversies over evidence had been a significant factor in the murder trial.

Reading Critically

◆[4] How convincing is this single example? Would you vote to require DNA testing for all such offenses based on this one case? Why or why not?

JAMES DAO   (1942–   )

In Same Case, DNA Clears Convict and Finds Suspect

In his final years in prison, Kirk Bloodsworth had a passing acquaintance   1
with a fellow inmate, Kimberly Shay Ruffner. Mr. Bloodsworth, a prison
librarian, delivered books to Mr. Ruffner. Sometimes they lifted weights
together. But Mr. Bloodsworth said Mr. Ruffner seemed to behave "kind of
peculiar" when they were together.

Mr. Bloodsworth may now know the reason why. This morning, the po-   2
lice in Baltimore County charged Mr. Ruffner in the murder and rape of a
9-year-old in 1984, Dawn Hamilton, the very crime that Mr. Bloodsworth
was serving time for when he met Mr. Ruffner.

"I'm so happy," said Mr. Bloodsworth, 43, a fisherman from Cambridge,   3
Md. "This tells the world that I'm innocent."

The charges against Mr. Ruffner open a new chapter in a case that has be-   4
come a prime example of the two-edged nature of DNA testing: not only
as a means of clearing the wrongly accused, but also of identifying new suspects in cold cases. ❶

In 1993, Mr. Bloodsworth became the first person in the nation con-   5
victed in a death penalty case to be exonerated through DNA testing, which
eliminated him as a source of semen stains on the girl's underpants. He had
served nine years in prison, including two on death row, when he was released
by a judge and pardoned by the governor.

Last spring, a Baltimore County forensic biologist who was studying ev-   6
idence from the case found stains on a sheet that had not been analyzed, a
spokesman for the Police Department said. Investigators conducted DNA
tests on the stains and ran the results through a national database last month.
Mr. Ruffner's name popped up.

The police did not have to go far to charge Mr. Ruffner. He was still   7
serving time for attempted rape and attempted murder in the prison in Baltimore where he had met Mr. Bloodsworth.

Defense lawyers say they hope the dual use of DNA evidence in the case   8
will reduce resistance among prosecutors to allow prisoners to challenge
convictions with DNA tests. They say the case demonstrates that DNA can
not only prove innocence, but also pinpoint culprits. ❷

Reading Critically

❶ What is the "two-edged nature" of DNA testing?

❷ In this particular case, how did DNA testing "prove innocence" and "pinpoint" a culprit?

"Maryland, and the nation, would be remiss if we did not learn from   9
today's news," said Peter Loge, director of the Criminal Justice Reform Education Fund, which has championed Mr. Bloodsworth's case.

The new charges were filed at a crucial time in a debate in Florida over   10
a law from 2001 that will soon bar prisoners from seeking DNA testing for
old cases. The law set Oct. 1 as the deadline for such requests. It also allows
the destruction of DNA evidence, except in death penalty cases.

Defense lawyers contend that the Hamilton case clearly shows how DNA   11
can be used to reopen cold cases. If a law like Florida's had been in effect in
Maryland 12 years ago, they say, Mr. Bloodsworth would still be behind bars.

"This should be a cautionary tale to those in Florida who are insisting on   12
this deadline for destroying biological evidence," said Barry Scheck, co-
director of the Innocence Project at the Benjamin L. Cardozo Law School
in Manhattan. "It's a law enforcement calamity."

Many prosecutors contend that DNA testing, though reliable, is not a   13
sure-fire way to prove innocence where there is other evidence of guilt.
DNA testing, they say, should be seen as only one piece of a bigger evidentiary puzzle. ❸

"I don't know of many people in my business who don't see the accuracy   14
of DNA testing," George W. Clarke, deputy district attorney for San Diego
County, said. "It's more the significance of those results. Those questions
aren't about to go away."

For Mr. Bloodsworth, today's developments had a far more personal sig-   15
nificance. Though he was pardoned a decade ago, he said some people had
continued to view him as a child murderer. Worse, he feared that prosecutors remained convinced of his guilt and might try to bring new charges
against him.

So after the assistant state's attorney who had prosecuted him, Ann Brobst,   16
called him on Thursday night to ask for a meeting, Mr. Bloodsworth and his
wife could not sleep.

"We were prepared for anything," Mr. Bloodsworth's lawyer, Deborah   17
Crandall, said.

Instead, in a meeting this morning at a Burger King, Ms. Brobst told Mr.   18
Bloodsworth of the DNA evidence against Mr. Ruffner and apologized for
wrongly prosecuting him. Mr. Bloodsworth, who has become an outspoken
advocate for reforming federal death penalty laws, said he cried and then
hugged Ms. Brobst.

In an interview, the state's attorney for Baltimore County, Sandra A.   19
O'Connor, said that the police and prosecutors had acted responsibly in the

---

Reading Critically

❸ Do you agree that DNA testing should be seen "as only one piece of a bigger evidentiary
puzzle," or should it be the most important evidence in a court case?

case, but that DNA technology did not exist at the time of Mr. Bloodsworth's trial. What did exist were the statements of five witnesses who said they saw him with the girl on the day she was killed.

"Obviously," Ms. O'Connor said, "the system failed in the case of Mr. Bloodsworth." ◆   20

Reading Critically

◆ How often do you think our judicial system fails?

PETER ROFF   (1966–   )

Postconviction DNA Testing Should Not Be Encouraged

To deprive an individual of their liberty—even for a short time—is to limit their most basic freedom. It is a serious matter and should be done with the utmost care. The Anglo-American system of jurisprudence gives every benefit of every doubt to the accused. At trial, the state must prove guilt beyond a reasonable doubt while the accused is presumed to be innocent.

What Justice Oliver Wendell Holmes said in defense of the Fourth Amendment is generally true where the free exercise of liberty is at issue: "It is less evil that some criminals should escape than that the government should play an ignoble part (in gathering evidence)." ❶

This does not, however, require evidence be re-examined years after the fact because the science changes.

Prisons Full of Innocent People?

Technology may have advanced to the point where certain types of evidence may conclusively identify a guilty party. This is just part of the entire equation, admittedly an important part. Yet the idea that many of the inmates on death row or serving long sentences could be freed by new DNA evidence has been ingrained in the American mind by Hollywood. While dramatic, it is hardly true and runs counter to the argument, most often heard from inmates and their lawyers that the prisons are full of innocent people, wrongfully convicted.

While the presence of DNA at a crime scene can be used to establish guilt in a court of law, the converse is not automatically true. The absence of a particular individual's DNA at a crime scene is not alone proof of their innocence. ❷ Prosecutors and legislators arguing against the unlimited opportunity for taxpayer-funded DNA tests in pursuit of the exoneration of convicted felons are correct in their objections.

It is the entire body of evidence that must be considered, not just the results of lab tests performed on old clothing.

Reading Critically
❶ Paraphrase this quotation in your own words.
❷ Can you think of a recent court case where the absence of DNA was an important piece of the evidence?

Doubtful Evidence

The rights of the accused are protected in the courtroom, often at the expense of the victims'. Physical evidence, eyewitness testimony and evidence often circumstantial in nature but attesting to means, motive, and opportunity are considered during trial under accepted rules of evidence. Can that chain of evidence still be as reliable 10, 15 or 20 years after the fact? It is doubtful. [3]   7

Can the state, fairly and years later, represent the interests of the victim and society as a whole if the judicial system lets doubt—which increases over time—adhere to the benefit of the accused, especially when DNA tests often produce more doubt than proof?   8

In the same way repeated death penalty appeals slowed the wheels of justice for many years these DNA requests will tax the already overburdened legal system, depriving the victims and the wrongfully accused of their day in court in a timely manner.   9

The requests for these tests amount more to lawyerly shams rather [than to] efforts to overcome justice denied. The state is right to limit them.   10

UNDERSTANDING DETAILS

1. According to Tim O'Brien, what facts worked against Youngblood in his trial?
2. How did "the system" fail in Bloodsworth's case (Dao, paragraph 20)?
3. What is Roff's main argument in his essay?
4. Explain Oliver Wendell Holmes' comment in paragraph 2 of the Roff essay: "It is less evil that some criminals should escape than that the government should play an ignoble part (in gathering evidence)."

THINKING CRITICALLY

5. Why does Tim O'Brien say that Youngblood would probably be dead if he were charged with first-degree murder?
6. Why was the Hamilton case a landmark in DNA testing?
7. Why would Bloodsworth still be behind bars if the Florida law about DNA testing were applied to Maryland?
8. In what ways are death penalty appeals and DNA requests similar?

DISCOVERING RHETORICAL STRATEGIES

9. In paragraph 4, O'Brien writes a series of sentences starting with "Never mind." What effect does this group of sentences have on the rest of the essay? How does this paragraph stand apart from the other paragraphs?

Reading Critically

[3] What is the author arguing about the length of time from the original crime and the reliability of the evidence?

10. Is the opening paragraph of the Dao essay effective? Why or why not?
11. Roff includes two subheadings in his essay. In what ways do they help you move logically through this essay?
12. Why does Roff refer to Hollywood in his essay?

MAKING CONNECTIONS

13. Briefly summarize the arguments advanced by O'Brien, Dao, and Roff concerning the use of DNA testing? Which point of view comes closest to your own? Why?
14. Compare and contrast the ways in which all three authors use examples in their essays. Who do you think uses examples most skillfully? Why do you think this is so?
15. Imagine that Kimberly Wozencraft ("Notes From the Country Club") and Brent Staples ("A Brother's Murder") were having a discussion with O'Brien, Dao, and Roff about the necessity of presenting physical evidence in a court of law. Which authors would argue most forcefully that such evidence must be displayed before a conviction can be attained? Why?

IDEAS FOR DISCUSSION/WRITING

Preparing to Write

Write freely about your knowledge of DNA testing after reading these essays: What are its advantages? Its disadvantages? Its limitations? Why is the public so interested in its use? Do you think DNA testing will deter criminals in any way?

Choosing a Topic

1. DNA testing is sensationalized on CSI shows to the point that real-life juries often expect such conclusive evidence when they serve on a case. How might these expectations affect our judicial system? To what extent does Hollywood actually influence what goes on in our courtrooms? Argue for or against putting these unrealistic shows on the air.
2. You have been asked to write a response to Roff's essay for publication as a companion piece. Using his format, develop your own argument for or against limiting DNA testing. Research this issue on the Internet a bit before you begin to write.
3. Americans are currently fascinated with investigative TV shows. *CSI, Law and Order,* and *Forensic Files* are at the top of the Neilson ratings. Do you see any connection between the increasing popularity of these shows and the violent crime rate in America today? Take a stand for or against the airing of this type of show as it relates to crime.
4. The National Coalition Against the Death Penalty has a very interesting fact sheet entitled "Innocence" found online at http://www.ncadp.org/fact_sheet4.html. It begins with general statistics regarding the number of people on death row who have been exonerated. Then the fact sheet highlights stories about specific individuals who were wrongly convicted because DNA testing

was not available at the time of their trials. Notice the appeals to logic (logos) in the overall statistics, and the appeals to emotion and character (pathos and ethos) in the individual stories. Choose one of the personal stories to use for information, and write a letter to a defense attorney requesting that he or she reopen the case to consider new DNA evidence. Try to incorporate all three appeals—to logos, pathos, and ethos—in your letter.

Before beginning your essay, you might want to consult the checklists on page 461.

The Patriot Act

The next three essays each take a different point of view concerning the Patriot Act, which Congress passed following the 9/11 attacks to help protect the security of our country. James X. Dempsey is the Executive Director of the Center for Democracy and Technology, which monitors national privacy and electronic surveillance issues. In his essay, Dempsey argues that we need to be vary careful in making any constitutional or legal changes that weaken our civil liberties, which would be counterproductive in the war on terrorism. Ramesh Ponnuru, a senior editor for the *National Review,* has written widely on public policy issues and has appeared frequently on such television programs as CNN's "Inside Politics," CSPAN's "Washington Journal," and NPR's "Morning Edition." His essay suggests that fears about the Patriot Act have been exaggerated and distorted by civil libertarians. David Cole, a professor at Georgetown University's Law Center and legal affairs correspondent for *The Nation,* has published several books on criminology and terrorism, including *No Equal Justice: Race and Class in the American Criminal Justice System* and *Enemy Aliens: Double Standards and Constitutional Freedoms in the War on Terrorism.* In his essay, he maintains that the Patriot Act unfairly sacrifices immigrants' rights to protect national security.

Preparing to Read

Each of the next three essays takes a different stand on the Patriot Act: One claims that the Patriot Act does not threaten our civil liberties; the second argues that it does threaten our freedom; and the third insists that it unfairly targets immigrants.

Exploring Experience: As you prepare to read these essays, share what you know about the Patriot Act with others in class: What problems does the Patriot Act address? When was it created? Why was it developed? What are the details of this act? Do you think it serves a useful purpose in our country's judicial history? What do you know about its strengths? Its weaknesses?

Learning Online: Visit the US Department of Justice website for the Patriot Act at http://www.lifeandliberty.gov. Then visit the American Civil Liberties Union (ACLU) website for the Patriot Act at http://www.aclu.org/safefree/patriot. How are these two websites alike? How are they different? Compare and contrasts their visual construction. Which is more appealing?

JAMES X. DEMPSEY   (1953–   )

Civil Liberties in a Time of Crisis

The terrorist attacks of September 11 represented a quantum leap in   1
the deadlines and audacity of terror. They revealed a vulnerability
that many in the United States had never before appreciated. And
they spurred adoption of many sound initiatives to better prevent terrorism.
Unfortunately, they also triggered a startling surrender of fundamental democratic principles in an attempt to purchase enhanced security—an effort that
is not only constitutionally unsound but also likely to be counterproductive. ◆ Within weeks of the attacks, thousands of individuals were arrested and
held without criminal charges, under a shroud of secrecy. Attorney General
John Ashcroft compromised the Sixth Amendment right to effective legal
counsel by ordering officials to wiretap attorney–client telephone calls without judicial approval. President Bush authorized the creation of military courts
to secretly try terrorism suspects. And Congress fundamentally rewrote the surveillance laws and increased the powers of both the FBI and the CIA to collect information within the U.S. on citizens and noncitizens alike.

Criticizing these measures does not deny the frightening risks our nation   2
faces. There likely will be additional terrorist attacks on our soil and against
U.S. interests abroad. It is even possible that some attacks will involve biological, chemical, or nuclear materials. Yet, it is precisely because the risk is
so high that we need to preserve the fullest range of due process ◆ and accountability in the exercise of government powers.

The False Trade-Off Between Freedom and Security

The debate over terrorism is often framed as a trade-off between liberty   3
and security. This is a flawed calculus, in several respects. First, many civil liberties, far from being at odds with security, actually enhance the ability of the
government to defend the common good. We guarantee the right to confront one's accusers, for example, not only as an element of human dignity
but also because cross-examination exposes lies and forces the government
to continue looking until the truly guilty party is found. Similarly, we subject government decisions to public scrutiny and judicial review not only to
give voice to individuals but also because openness and accountability can

---

Reading Critically

◆ Which do you think is more important—civil liberties or increased security? Explain
your answer?

◆ What do you think Dempsey means by "due process"?

produce a fuller factual record, expose faulty assumptions, and slow the rash decision making of elected officials acting under pressure. We protect freedom of speech not only because it allows room for personal self-expression, but also because it promotes the stability that comes from the availability of channels for dissent and peaceful change. For these and other reasons, surrender of freedom in the name of fighting terror is not only a constitutional tragedy, it is also likely to be ineffective and worse, counterproductive.

The attorney general has said that foreign terrorists "do not deserve the 4 protection of the American Constitution." ❸ What the attorney general does not seem to appreciate, however, is that it is precisely the procedures of the Constitution by which we reliably determine who is a terrorist and who is not.

Second, policymakers too frequently curtail civil liberties without ever 5 actually analyzing whether civil liberties in fact pose an impediment to security. September 11 proved in the worst way that the U.S. anti-terrorism effort was flawed. The governmental reaction to the events of that day is doubly distressing not merely because it curtails civil liberties but also because it has done so with no consideration of what went wrong in the days and months before and little regard to whether the liberty-curtailing changes will be effective. The fact that U.S. authorities failed to detect the September 11 attack in advance should have prompted a comprehensive review of our intelligence capabilities. But Congress enacted many of the provisions of the Bush administration's anti-terrorism law, the USA Patriot Act (Patriot Act), without ever identifying what problems they were intended to cure or how the additional authorities would make a difference.

Third, trading off civil liberties for real or perceived improvements in na- 6 tional security is the wrong place to start when there are so many things to be done to improve security that do not implicate civil liberties at all. ❹ Take airport security, where luggage screeners deserve job stability and a decent wage, and the technology to detect bombs in luggage should be used consistently. Yet, weeks and even months after September 11, breaches of airport security continue to occur. We need to do a better job of improving the safety and security of nuclear plants and chemical plants, instead of sweeping those problems under the rug as some in industry and Congress have proposed, internationally, we should step up efforts to gain control over and destroy chemical, biological, and nuclear toxins left behind by the Soviet

---

Reading Critically

❸ Do you agree with the attorney general that foreign terrorists "do not deserve the protection of the American constitution"? Why or why not?

❹ What do you think our country could do to improve national security? If you were the president, what specific steps would you take?

Union. Tighter domestic regulation of toxins is needed as well. As of September 11, we did not have an adequate system in place to control the manufacture, transport, and possession of dangerous chemicals and biological materials. There are many ways to improve the use of information in the visa and immigration process that have nothing to do with the political or associational criteria that in the past have been used to deny visas to those critical of U.S. foreign policy.

Finally, even in the area of surveillance and privacy, the choice is not between surveillance powers and no surveillance powers. Civil libertarians engaged in the debate over the new terrorism laws do not argue that the government should be denied the tools it needs to monitor terrorists' communications. Instead, privacy advocates urge that those powers be focused and subject to clear standards and judicial review. The tragedy of the response to September 11 is not that the government has been given new powers—it is that those new powers have been granted without standards or checks and balances.   7

To better understand the disconnect between the danger facing America and some of the measures that have been adopted that curtail civil liberties, it is worth examining, in depth, several of the provisions in the USA Patriot Act, the anti-terrorism law adopted in October 2001.   8

"Sneak and Peek" Searches

The popular notion of search and seizure can be described as follows: the police go before a judge and get a search warrant. They rush to the apartment of the suspect, rap loudly on the door and shout, "Police, open up, we have a warrant to search your apartment" If the person inside doesn't open up right away, the police can kick in the door, but in any event, most people would assume, when the FBI or police want to come into your home or apartment, they have to announce themselves, show their warrant and, if they seize anything, leave an inventory of what they have taken. After all, the police do occasionally make mistakes and go to the wrong address. The homeowner can point this out, and observe the search to ensure the police stay within the terms of the warrant. In Wilson v. Arkansas, 514 U.S. 927 (1995), and Richards v. Wisconsin, 520 U.S. 385 (1997), the Supreme Court reaffirmed this vision, holding that contemporaneous notice was normally constitutionally required, and could be dispensed with only under exceptional circumstances. ⑤   9

Reading Critically

⑤ Why do you think the author cites court precedents here and elsewhere? To what extent do these references help his argument?

The Patriot Act threw out this concept of a normal police search of a   10
home, apartment or office. Section 213 amended section 3103a of Title 18,
United States Code, allowing the FBI to secretly enter your apartment or
house while you are asleep or away, take, alter or copy things, and not tell you
they were there for days, weeks, or even months later. Instead of crafting
specific standards for such searches, Congress incorporated by reference a
delayed notice provision governing the reading of stored e-mail.

Instead of limiting the so-called "sneak and peek" authority to aliens sus-   11
pected of terrorism, Congress applied it to the homes of citizens also. Moreover, what is most remarkable about this provision is that it is not limited to
terrorism cases: it applies to drug cases, tax fraud, providing false information
on student loan applications, or any other federal crime. And it is not subject to the sunset provision under which some of the new law's provisions
expire after four years unless renewed by Congress. Thus, the emergency atmosphere generated by the September 11 attacks was used to make a permanent, fundamental change in law enforcement procedures having nothing
to do with terrorism.

Expanding the Domestic Power of the CIA

When the Central Intelligence Agency was created in 1947, Congress ex-   12
plicitly said that the agency was to have no subpoena or domestic police
powers. Instead, the CIA's operations were intended to be directed overseas,
focused on foreign nationals. Since the CIA was not supposed to engage in
law enforcement, and since its agents were never supposed to appear in court,
the CIA was not given the type of power that law enforcement agencies
wield. [6] And those law enforcement powers are awesome.

One of the most powerful is the grand jury. The grand jury can compel   13
anyone to testify under oath. If you refuse, you can be sent to jail. If you testify and the government believes you are lying, you can be prosecuted for per-
jury. The grand jury can compel any business to turn over any records or
databases, again with the threat of jail time for those who refuse. These powers are subject, however, to two important controls: anything from the grand
jury the government uses in a criminal case is subject to the full panoply of
due process protections, while, on the other hand, anything not used in open
court must be kept secret and used for no other purpose.

Section 203 of the 2001 Patriot Act abolished these limitations, giving   14
the CIA the benefit of the grand jury's powers with none of the protections

---

Reading Critically

[6] How have the powers and responsibilities of the CIA changed over the years?

of the criminal justice system. In a provision that is not subject to the four-year sunset, the new law amended Rule 6(e) of the Federal Rules of Criminal Procedure to allow information collected by grand juries to be shared with the CIA and other intelligence agencies, as well as any national defense or national security official, without the prior approval of a judge. In effect, CIA agents working with law enforcement officers can now jointly draw up subpoenas, obtain the fruits of the grand jury's power, and never have to appear in open court or explain how they used the information.

Evading the Stricter Standards of the Criminal Wiretap Laws

One of the other fundamental changes of the Patriot Act was to allow the FBI to carry out wiretaps and secret physical searches ("black bag jobs") to collect evidence of crimes using the lower standards designed for foreign intelligence gathering. The Foreign Intelligence Surveillance Act (FISA) authorizes the FBI to conduct electronic surveillance and clandestine searches without full probable cause to believe that a crime has been or is about to be committed. Instead, the FISA standard merely requires the government to have probable cause to believe that the target of the intrusion is an agent of a foreign power. If the suspected agent of a foreign power is a U.S. citizen, the government needs additional probable cause, but still less than is required for a wiretap under Title III or a normal search and seizure in a criminal case.   15

The wiretaps and searches authorized by FISA are extraordinary in nature: Most notably, the target of the surveillance is never notified of the intrusion (under Title III and even under the "sneak and peek" authority in the Patriot Act, the subject is eventually notified after the investigation closes). This lack of notice is most significant in cases where the surveillance turns up nothing. Under FISA, a person is notified of surveillance only if he or she is later prosecuted using the evidence seized. Even then, defendants have little opportunity to challenge the validity of the search, for they are never provided the affidavit that served as the basis for the surveillance. In the case of individuals who are not prosecuted—those where the likelihood of government overreaching is the greatest—notice is never given. 🔗   16

This extraordinary authority was justified on the basis that it would not be used for the purpose of investigating crime. Congress recognized that evidence of crimes might be collected—espionage, for example, is a crime—so Congress allowed the use of FISA evidence in criminal cases. But the "purpose" of the investigation had to be the collection of foreign intelli-   17

Reading Critically
🔗 How would you feel if you knew you were under government surveillance?

gence. Otherwise, the statute would serve as an end run around the probable cause requirements of the criminal wiretap statute.

In the Patriot Act, Congress eliminated the primary purpose test, amend-   18
ing FISA to allow wiretaps and physical searches without probable cause so
long as "a significant purpose" of the intrusion is to collect foreign intelligence. The express justification for this was to allow the government to ini-
tiate wiretaps under FISA's lower standard where the primary purpose from
the outset was the collection of criminal evidence. This means that, in cases
involving a foreign government—an investigation, for example, of foreign
contributions to a U.S. political campaign—the Department of Justice can
conduct a criminal investigation involving FBI wiretapping and secret
searches without probable cause to believe that a crime was being committed. If no crime turns up, the government need never tell the person whose
phones were tapped; yet the information obtained can be shared with the
CIA, the National Security Council, and the Pentagon.

The Dragnet Approach

Generally, when the government goes to a bank, credit bureau, telephone   19
company, hospital, or library, it can obtain a person's records only if there is
reason to believe that the particular person was engaged in some wrongdoing. In international terrorism cases, for example, the government formerly
needed some reason to believe that the person whose records it was seeking
was a member of a foreign terrorist group. The Patriot Act wiped out this
limitation. The implications of this change are enormous. Previously, the FBI
could get the credit records of anyone suspected of being an international
terrorist. Under the new 2001 legislation, the FBI can get the entire database of the credit card company. It can go into a public library and ask for
the records on everybody who ever used the library, or who used it on a certain day, or who checked out certain kinds of books. [8] It can do the same
at any bank, any telephone company, any hotel or motel, any hospital, and
any university—merely on the claim that the information is "sought for" an
investigation to protect against international terrorism or clandestine intelligence activities.

Conclusion

In the name of fighting terrorism, changes have been adopted that fun-   20
damentally alter the power of the government. They weaken the role of
the judiciary. They relieve the government of the responsibility to focus its

---

Reading Critically
[8] Do you think that monitoring the titles of books checked out of a public library is too
much power for our federal government to have? Why or why not?

investigations on specific suspects. They permit government agencies to cast their nets far wider than ever before.

These changes do not mean merely that the government is collecting a   21
lot more information on a lot more people in the hope that something will turn up, the investigative and intelligence agencies were already choking on more information than they could digest. Sweeping in even more information will not make the picture any clearer. In this way, the expanded surveillance powers are likely to make counterterrorism efforts more inefficient.

The fight against terrorism is an epic struggle, one that is likely to go on   22
for many years. It is precisely because the stakes are so high that we need to adhere to principles of due process, judicial checks and balances, and openness and accountability in government. CIA agents and law enforcement officers can now jointly draw up subpoenas. Expanded surveillance powers are likely to make counterterrorism efforts more inefficient. **9**

Reading Critically

9 How convincing was this author's essay?

RAMESH PONNURU   (1974–   )

1984 in 2003?

Fears about the Patriot Act are misguided

Has the war on terrorism become a war on Americans' civil liber- 1
ties?[1] A coalition of left- and right-wing groups fears so, and has
been working hard to restrain the law-and-order impulses of the
Bush administration. It's a coalition that includes the ACLU and the American Conservative Union, Nat Hentoff and William Safire, John Conyers and
Dick Armey.

The coalition started to form in 1996, when Congress passed an anti- 2
terrorism bill. But it really took off after September 11. Members of the
coalition believe that Washington's legislative response—called, rather ludi-
crously, the "USA Patriot Act," an acronym for "Uniting and Strengthening
America by Providing Appropriate Tools to Intercept and Obstruct Terrorism"—was a too-hastily conceived, excessive reaction to the atrocities.

Since then, the coalition has regularly found new cause for alarm. It has 3
protested the administration's plans for military tribunals, the president's des-
ignation of "enemy combatants," and the Pentagon's attempts to consolidate data under a program called "Total Information Awareness." This spring,
the civil libertarians of left and right worked together again to block Sen.
Orrin Hatch's attempt to make permanent those provisions of the Patriot Act
which are set to expire next year. They have organized, as well, against the
possibility that the Justice Department will propose another dangerous anti-
terror bill ("Patriot II").

The civil libertarians have had some success. They forced modifications in 4
the Patriot Act before its enactment. They have inspired some cities to pass
resolutions banning their employees from cooperating with federal authorities to implement provisions of the act that violate the Constitution. (Officials in other cities are, presumably, free to violate the Constitution at will.)
They imposed legislative restrictions on Total Information Awareness. They
have inhibited the administration from proposing anti-terror measures that
would generate adverse publicity.

They themselves have gotten favorable publicity. It's an irresistible story 5
for the press: the lion and the lamb lying down together.[2] The press has

---

Reading Critically

[1] Does the first sentence of this essay grab your attention? Why or why not?
[2] In Ponnuru's metaphor, who are represented by the lion and the lamb?

tended to marvel at the mere existence of the coalition. They have not been quick to note that there is a larger bipartisan coalition on the other side, which is why the civil libertarians have been losing most of the battles. The Patriot Act passed 357–66 in the House and 98–1 in the Senate. In early May, the Senate voted 90–4 to approve another anti-terror provision—making it easier to investigate "lone wolf" terrorists with no proven connection to larger organizations—that the civil libertarians oppose.

More important, the press has not adequately scrutinized the civil libertarians' claims. This has kept the debate mired in platitudes about liberty and security. It has also reduced the incentive for the civil libertarians to do their homework, which has in turn made their case both weaker and more hysterical than it might otherwise have been.   6

Take the attack on TIPS, the Terrorist Information and Prevention System. This abortive plan would have encouraged truckers, deliverymen, and the like to report suspicious behavior they observed in the course of their work. How effective this idea would have been is open to question. Most of the criticism, however, echoed former Republican congressman Bob Barr, who said that TIPS "smacks of the very type of fascist or communist government we fought so hard to eradicate in other countries in decades past."   7

But of all the measures the administration has adopted, it's the Patriot Act (along with the possible Patriot II) that has inspired the most overheated criticisms. When it was passed, the Electronic Frontier Foundation wrote that "the civil liberties of ordinary Americans have taken a tremendous blow with this law." The ACLU says the law "gives the Executive Branch sweeping new powers that undermine the Bill of Rights." But most of the concerns about Patriot are misguided or based on premises that are just plain wrong.   8

Roving Wiretaps

Thanks to the Patriot Act, terrorism investigations can use roving wiretaps. Instead of having to get new judicial authorization for each phone number tapped, investigators can tap any phone their target uses. This is important when fighting terrorists whose MO includes frequently switching hotel rooms and cell phones. It's a commonsense measure. It's also nothing new: Congress authorized roving wiretaps in ordinary criminal cases back in 1986. It's hard to see Patriot as a blow to civil liberties on this score.   9

Internet Surveillance

Libertarians have been particularly exercised about Patriot's green light for "spying on the Web browsers of people who are not even criminal suspects"—to quote *Reason* editor Nick Gillespie. This is a misunderstanding of Patriot, as George Washington University law professor Orin Kerr has demonstrated in a law-review article. Before Patriot, it wasn't clear that any   10 statute limited the government's, or even a private party's, ability to obtain basic information about electronic communications (e.g., to whom you're sending e-mails). Patriot required a court order to get that information, and made it a federal crime to get it without one. ❸

Kerr believes that the bar for getting a court order should be raised. But he notes that Patriot made the privacy protections for the Internet as strong as those for phone calls and stronger than for mail. Patriot's Internet provisions, he concludes, "updated the surveillance laws without substantially shifting the balance between privacy and security." 11

James Bovard traffics in another Patriot myth in a recent cover story for *The American Conservative:* that it "empowers federal agents to cannibalize Americans' e-mail with Carnivore wiretaps." Carnivore is an Internet surveillance tool designed by the FBI. Don't be scared by the name. The FBI's previous tool was dubbed "Omnivore," and this new one was so named because it would be more selective in acquiring information, getting only what was covered by a court order and leaving other information private. But even if Carnivore is a menace, it's not the fault of Patriot. As Kerr points out, "The only provisions of the Patriot Act that directly address Carnivore are pro-privacy provisions that actually restrict the use of Carnivore." 12

Hacking

Also in *Reason,* Jesse Walker writes that Patriot "expands the definition of *terrorist* to include such non-lethal acts as computer hacking." That's misleading. Pre-Patriot, an al-Qaeda member who hacked the electric company's computers to take out the grid could not be judged guilty of terrorism, even if he would be so judged if he accomplished the same result with a bomb. Hacking per se isn't terrorism, and Patriot doesn't treat it as such. ❹ 13

Sneak and Peek

The ACLU is running ads that say that Patriot lets the government "secretly enter your home while you're away . . . rifle through your personal belongings . . . download your computer files . . . and seize any items at will." Worst of all, "you may never know what the government has done." Reality check: You will be notified if a sneak-and-peek search has been done, just after the fact—usually within a few days. The feds had the authority to conduct these searches before Patriot. A federal judge has to authorize such a search warrant, and the warrant has to specify what's to be seized. 14

Reading Critically

❸ How would you feel about the government spying on your e-mails and Internet searches?

❹ Do you think that computer hacking should be a federal offense? Why or why not?

Library Records

Bovard is appalled that Patriot allows "federal agents to commandeer li-   15
brary records," and the American Library Association shares his sentiment.
Patriot doesn't mention libraries specifically, but does authorize terrorism
investigators to collect tangible records generally. Law enforcement has, however, traditionally been able to obtain library records with a subpoena. Prof.
Kerr suggests that because of Patriot, the privacy of library records may be
better protected in terrorism investigations than it is in ordinary criminal
ones. [5]

The civil libertarians deserve some credit. Their objections helped to rid   16
Patriot of some provisions—such as a crackdown on Internet gambling—that
didn't belong in an anti-terrorism bill. Armey added the Carnivore protections to the bill. The law, as finally enacted, places limits on how much officials may disclose of the information they gain from Internet and phone
surveillance. Moreover, the civil libertarians make a reasonable demand when
they ask that Patriot be subject to periodic re-authorizations, so that Congress can regularly consider making modifications.

The civil libertarians rarely acknowledge the costs of legal laxity: Re-   17
strictions on intelligence gathering may well have impeded the investigation of Zacarias Moussaoui, the "twentieth hijacker," before 9/11. David
Cole, one of the movement's favorite law professors, goes so far as to lament
that U.S. law makes "mere membership in a terrorist group grounds for exclusion and deportation."

And while civil libertarians may scant the value of Patriot, terrorists do not.   18
Jeffrey Battle, an accused member of a terrorist cell in Portland, complained
about Patriot in a recorded phone call that was recently released in court. People were less willing to provide financial support, he said, now that they were
more likely to be punished for it.

Speaking of the administration's civil-liberties record, Al Gore said last   19
year that President Bush has "taken the most fateful step in the direction of
[a] Big Brother nightmare that any president has ever allowed to occur."
Dick Armey worries about "the lust for power that these people in the Department of Justice have." The civil-liberties debate could use a lot less
rhetoric of this sort—and a lot more attention to detail.

A calm look at the Patriot Act shows that it's less of a threat to civil lib-   20
erties than, say, campaign-finance reform. A lot of the controversy is the result of confusion. Opponents of the Patriot Act are fond of complaining that
few people have bothered to read it. No kidding.

Reading Critically
[5] Does the author argue for or against the privacy of library records?

DAVID COLE   (1958–   )

The Patriot Act Unfairly Targets Immigrants to Enhance National Security

It is often said that civil liberties are the first casualties of war. It may be more   1
accurate to say that immigrants' civil liberties are the first to go. In the wake
of the devastating terrorist attacks of September 11 [2001], we all feel vulnerable in ways that we have never felt before, and many have argued that we
may need to sacrifice our liberty in order to purchase security. In fact, however, what we have done is to sacrifice the liberties of some—immigrants, and
especially Arab and Muslim immigrants—for the purported security of the
rest of us. This double standard ◆ is an all too tempting way to strike the balance—it allows citizens to enjoy a sense of security without sacrificing their
own liberty, but it is an illegitimate trade-off. In the end, moreover, it is likely
to be counterproductive, as it will alienate the very communities that we
most need to work with as we fight the war on terrorism.

Guilt by Association

The problems begin with the USA Patriot Act (Patriot Act), enacted in   2
haste under threats from Attorney General John Ashcroft that if another terrorist incident occurred before the law was signed, Congress would be held
responsible. Among other things, it imposes guilt by association on immigrants, a philosophy that the Supreme Court has condemned as "alien to
the traditions of a free society and the First Amendment itself." Before the
advent of the Patriot Act, aliens were deportable for engaging in or supporting terrorist activity. The Patriot Act makes them deportable for virtually any associational activity with a "terrorist organization," irrespective of
whether the alien's support has any connection to an act of violence, much
less terrorism. And because the Act defines "terrorist activity" to include virtually any use or threat to use a weapon against a person or property, and defines a "terrorist organization" as any group of two or more persons that
engages in such an act, the proscription on political association potentially
encompasses every organization that has ever been involved in a civil war or
a crime of violence, from a pro-life group that once threatened workers at
an abortion clinic, to the ANC [African National Congress], the IRA [Irish
Republican Army], or the Northern Alliance in Afghanistan.

Reading Critically
◆ What "double standard" is Cole discussing?

Once a group is designated as a "terrorist group," aliens are deportable   3
for asking people to join it, fundraising for it, or providing any kind of material support to it, including dues. Indeed, the law extends even to those who
support a group in an effort to counter terrorism. Thus, an immigrant who
offered his services in peace negotiating to the IRA in the hope of further-
ing the peace process in Great Britain could be deported as a terrorist.

This is guilt by association, ❷ because it treats aliens as culpable not for their   4
own acts, but for the acts of those with whom their conduct is associated. Guilt
by association, the Supreme Court has ruled, violates the First and Fifth
Amendments. All people in the United States have a First Amendment right
to associate with groups that have lawful and unlawful ends, so long as they
do not further the group's illegal ends. And the Fifth Amendment dictates
that "in our jurisprudence guilt is personal." Without some connection between the alien's support and terrorist activity, the Constitution is violated.

Some argue that the threat from terrorist organizations abroad requires   5
compromise on the principle prohibiting guilt by association. But this constitutional principle was developed in connection with measures directed at
the Communist Party, an organization that Congress found to be a foreign-
dominated organization that used sabotage and terrorism for the purpose of
overthrowing the United States by force and violence, and that was supported by the world's other great superpower.

Others argue that money is fungible, ❸ so support of a group's lawful ac-   6
tivities will simply free up resources that will be spent on terrorism. But that
argument proves too much, for it would authorize guilt by association whenever any organization engages in some illegal activity. Donations to the
Democratic Party, it could be argued, "free up" resources that are used to
violate campaign finance laws, yet surely we could not criminalize all support to the Democratic Party simply because it sometimes violates the campaign finance laws. Moreover, the fungibility argument assumes that every
marginal dollar provided to a designated group will, in fact, be spent on violence. However, no one would seriously contend that every dollar given to
the ANC for its lawful anti-apartheid work freed up a dollar that was spent
on that organization's terrorist activity.

Ideological Exclusion

The Patriot Act also resurrects ideological exclusion, the practice of deny-   7
ing entry to aliens for pure speech. It excludes aliens who "endorse or es-
pouse terrorist activity," or who "persuade others to support terrorist activity

---

Reading Critically
❷ What does the author mean by "guilt by association"? Why does he think this is a bad practice?
❸ What does the phrase "money is fungible" mean?

or a terrorist organization," in ways that the Secretary of State determines undermine U.S. efforts to combat terrorism. It also excludes aliens who are representatives of groups that "endorse acts of terrorist activity" in ways that similarly undermine U.S. efforts to combat terrorism.

Excluding people for their ideas is flatly contrary to the spirit of freedom   8
for which the United States stands. [4] It was for that reason that Congress repealed all such grounds in the Immigration and Nationality Act in 1990, after years of embarrassing politically motivated visa denials. We are a strong enough country, and our resolve against terrorism is powerful enough, to make such censorship wholly unnecessary.

Detention Versus Due Process

The government has detained well over 1,200 persons in connection with   9
the investigation of the attacks of September 11. (The DOJ [Department of Justice] has halted its practice of publicizing the total number detained so we don't know how much higher the actual figure may be.) As of December 2001, over 500 persons were still being held in federal custody, with an untold number of others being held in state and local custody. Yet, as of that same time, only one person had been charged with involvement in the crimes perpetrated that day—Zaccarias Moussaoui. Department of Justice officials claim that about ten or twelve of the detained may be linked to Al Qaeda, but of course that only raises a question about the rest. The DOJ has been unwilling to disclose even the most basic information about the largest group of detainees, those held on immigration charges. It refuses even to identify who is detained. The immigrants are being tried in secret proceedings, closed to the public, the press, or even family members. Immigration judges are instructed not to list the cases on the docket, and to refuse to confirm or deny that cases even exist. Such practices are unprecedented. But what we do know, mostly from enterprising investigative journalists, suggests that the vast majority have all but the most attenuated connections to the events of that terrible day. Most of those detained appear to be Arabs or Muslims.

The administration has dramatically changed the rules governing its au-   10
thority to detain immigrants. Shortly after September 11, the INS unilaterally amended a regulation governing detention without charges. [5] The regulation had required the INS to file charges within twenty-four hours of detaining an alien; under the new regulations, detention without charges is permissible for forty-eight hours and for an unspecified "reasonable" period beyond forty-eight hours in times of emergency.

Reading Critically

[4] Do you think the United States should be able to exclude people because of their ideas?

[5] Do you believe our government should be able to detain immigrants without charge? Why or why not?

Before September 11, the INS could detain any alien placed in removal   11
proceedings for as long as the proceedings lasted—in many cases several
years. However, it could do so only if it had reason to believe that he or she
posed a threat to national security or a risk of flight, and the alien was entitled to seek release from an immigration judge. Under a new regulation,
however, even if the immigration judge rules that the alien should be released,
INS prosecutors can keep him locked up simply by filing an appeal of the
release order. They need not make any showing that their appeal is likely to
succeed. Appeals of immigration custody decisions routinely take months
and often more than a year to decide.

A Broad Definition

The Patriot Act goes still further, giving the attorney general unilateral au-   12
thority to detain aliens on his say-so, without any opportunity for the alien
to respond to the charges. The attorney general may detain any immigrant
whom he certifies as a "suspected terrorist." The Patriot Act defines a "suspected terrorist" so broadly that it includes virtually every immigrant who
has been involved in a barroom brawl or domestic dispute, as well as aliens
who have never committed an act of violence in their life, and whose only
crime is that he or she provided humanitarian aid to an organization disfa-
vored by the government. [6]

This provision raises several basic constitutional concerns. It mandates   13
preventive detention of persons who pose no threat to national security or
risk of flight, and without any hearing. And it allows the INS to detain such
aliens indefinitely, even where they prevail in their removal proceedings. This
is akin to detaining a prisoner even after he has been pardoned.

The provision permits certification and detention on mere "reasonable   14
grounds to believe" that an alien has engaged in terrorist activity, a standard
that the INS has likened to the "reasonable suspicion" required for a brief stop
and frisk under the Fourth Amendment. But under the Fourth Amendment,
"reasonable suspicion" does not even justify a custodial arrest, much less indefinite detention.

The provision also permits detention for up to seven days without filing   15
any charges. Yet, the Supreme Court has ruled in the criminal setting that
charges must be filed within forty-eight hours except in the most extraordinary circumstances. In short, hundreds of immigrants not charged with
any crime, much less involvement in the September 11 attack, are being detained in secret, even where judges rule that there is no basis for detention,
and without going before a judge at all.

Reading Critically
[6] How does our government define a "suspected terrorist"?

There is good reason to doubt whether these measures will in fact make 16
us safer. By penalizing even wholly lawful, nonviolent, and counter-
terrorist associational activity, we are likely to waste valuable resources tracking innocent political activity, drive other activity underground, encourage
extremists, and make the communities that will inevitably be targeted by
such measures far less likely to cooperate with law enforcement. And by
conducting law enforcement in secret, and jettisoning procedures designed
to protect the innocent and afford legitimacy to the outcome of trials, we
will encourage people to fear the worst about our government. As Justice
Louis Brandeis wrote nearly seventy-five years ago, the framers of our Constitution knew "that fear breeds repression; that repression breeds hate; and
that hate menaces stable government." In other words, freedom and security
need not necessarily be traded off against one another; maintaining our freedoms is itself critical to maintaining our security. 7

UNDERSTANDING DETAILS

1. What are Dempsey's main arguments about the Patriot Act?
2. According to Ponnuru, who is part of the coalition that is "working hard to restrain the law-and-order impulses of the Bush administration" (para. 1)?
3. What five issues in the Patriot Act does Ponnuru address? Why do you think
   he chooses these topics?
4. Summarize David Coles' article ("The Patriot Act Unfairly Targets Immigrants
   to Enhance National Security").

THINKING CRITICALLY

5. In what ways do the changes Dempsey cites in our judicial system affect our
   civil liberties?
6. Why does Ponnuru think most of the criticism directed at the Patriot Act is
   "misguided? (paragraph 8)?
7. In what ways is sacrificing the liberties of immigrants "an illegitimate trade-off"
   (Cole, paragraph 1)?
8. Do you think security and freedom can co-exist in the United States? Explain
   your answer.

DISCOVERING RHETORICAL STRATEGIES

9. Do the subheadings that all three authors use help you through each essay? Explain your answer.
10. Explain the title of Ponnuru's essay.

Reading Critically

7 How convincing was this essay?

11. Outline the main ideas and details used as evidence in all three essays. Which ideas and details are used more than once?

12. Look closely at the outline of Cole's essay, and explain how he moves from one point to the next. How does the order of his ideas support his argument?

MAKING CONNECTIONS

13. Imagine a roundtable discussion about civil liberties featuring Franklin Zimring ("Confessions of an Ex-Smoker"), Sucheng Chan ("You're Short, Besides!"), Kim Severson ("I'm Not Willing to Settle for Crumbs"), and Dempsey, Ponnuru, and Cole. Which of these authors would argue most strongly that we need good laws to protect our civil liberties? Why?

14. Give a brief summary of the arguments by Dempsey, Ponnuru, and Cole. Then explain which side you agree with most.

15. How skillfully do Dempsey, Ponnuru, and Cole use examples to help prove their point? Which author arranges his examples most convincingly? Why do you think this is so?

IDEAS FOR DISCUSSION/WRITING

Preparing to Write

Write freely about the relationship of the attack on 9/11, the Patriot Act, and American civil liberties: What do they all have in common? How are they related? Can the Patriot Act and our civil liberties co-exist? Is one threatened by the other? How could they work together in your opinion? Why have the Patriot Act and our civil liberties come under public scrutiny?

Choosing a Topic

1. You have been invited to return to your middle school in the post-9/11 era to explain the relationship among the 2001 terrorist attack, the Patriot Act, and Americans' civil liberties. Choose a controlling idea that relates to all three events, and explain these historical issues to a group of seventh and eighth graders.

2. Research the Patriot Act, and take a position for or against any of its specific issues. Argue your case with clear examples from your research and from the essays you just read.

3. Choose one of these three essays, and write a direct rebuttal to it. Argue with the essay point by point.

4. Visit the ACLU multimedia page at http://www.aclu.org/multimedia. Scroll down to the TV ads, and click on one or more of them to view the video clips. Then visit the Department of Justice website (http://www.lifeandliberty.gov), and click on the "Anti-Terror Record" link on the left side of the page. In essay form, argue whether or not the steps being taken to protect us are worth the sacrifice of our civil liberties.

Before beginning your essay, you might want to consult the checklists on page 461.

Chapter Writing Assignments

Practicing Argument / Persuasion

1. What is the best method for disciplining a child? What kinds of "discipline" constitute child abuse? What rights should parents have in deciding how to discipline their own children? Write an essay explaining what disciplinary actions you believe are acceptable and arguing why others are not.

2. Many people argue that the media actually run the elections in the United States. What is your opinion on this issue? What should be the role of the media in the political arena? How should we force them to limit themselves to this role? In what ways do the media help us understand certain important issues? In what ways do they hinder our understanding? Write an essay in which you argue for a specific relationship between the media and politics, including elections, referendums, and bond issues. Support your position with concrete details.

3. Look up the term *immigration* in the dictionary. Ask a variety of people about their positive and negative responses to immigration. Write an essay in which you explain your position on immigration, using your interviews as background and support.

Exploring Ideas

4. Do you think people are prone to violence because of inborn qualities or because of learned behavior? Why are some people violent while others are not? Where does this difference come from in your opinion—nature or nurture?

5. Do you think any limits should be put on free speech? If so, what should these limits be? If not, why not? What is the reasoning behind your opinion? Write an essay supporting your position with examples.

6. American society often argues about whether or not voting materials and other government documents should be printed in multiple languages. Does this practice work against the principle of speaking only one language in America? Write an essay that explains your opinion on this issue. Be sure to include specific examples to support your argument.

Analyzing Visual Images

AP Wide World Photos.

7. Choose a current issue and design several slogans that would effectively argue your point of view. Discuss in essay form how effectively these slogans would persuade others.

8. Look at the picture on page 449 at the beginning of this chapter, which captures the Civil Rights movement and the struggle for equal rights. Many today would argue that racism is no longer an issue and that equal rights have, in fact, been given to all races, genders, religious sects, etc. Argue for or against this statement, using examples from your own life or those around you to support your claim.

Chapter 10

THE RESEARCH PAPER
Reading and Writing from Sources

We use sources every day in both informal and formal situations. We explain the source of a phone message, for example, or we refer to an instructor's comments in class. We use someone else's opinion in an essay, or we quote an expert to prove a point. We cite sources both in speaking and in writing through summary, paraphrase, and direct quotation. Most of your college instructors will ask you to write papers using sources so they can see how well you understand the course material. The use of sources in academic papers requires you to understand what you have read and to integrate this reading material with your own opinions and observations—a process that requires a high level of skill in thinking, reading, and writing.

DEFINING RESEARCH PAPERS

Research papers provide you with the opportunity to perform sophisticated and exciting exercises in critical thinking; they draw on the thinking, reading, and writing abilities you have built up over the course of your academic career, and they often require you to put all the rhetorical modes to work at their most analytical level. Research papers demonstrate the process of analytical thinking at its best in different disciplines.

In the academic world, research papers are also called *documented essays, library papers,* and *term papers.* They are generally written for one of three reasons: (1) to **report,** (2) to **interpret,** or (3) to **analyze.**

The most straightforward, uncomplicated type of research paper **reports** information, as in a survey of problems that children have in preschool. The second type of research paper both presents and **interprets** its findings. It examines a number of different views on a specific issue and weighs these views as it draws its own conclusions. A topic that falls into this category would be whether children who have attended preschool are more sociable than those who have not. After considering evidence on both sides, the writer would draw his or her own conclusions on this topic. A research paper that **analyzes** a subject presents a hypothesis, tests the hypothesis, and analyzes or evaluates its conclusions. This type of essay calls for the most advanced form of critical thinking. It might look, for example, at the reasons preschool children are more or less socially flexible than nonpreschool children. At its most proficient, this type of writing requires a sophisticated degree of evaluation that forces you to judge your reading, evaluate your sources, and ultimately scrutinize your own reasoning ability as the essay takes shape. Each of these types of research papers calls for a higher level of thinking, and each evolves from the previous category. In other words, interpreting requires some reporting, and analyzing draws on both reporting and interpreting.

In the following paragraph, a student reports, interprets, analyzes, and uses sources to document the problem of solid waste in America. Notice how the student writer draws her readers into the essay with a commonly used phrase about America and then questions the validity of its meaning. The student's opinions give shape to the paragraph, while her use of sources helps identify the problem and support her contentions as she uses several rhetorical modes to prove her point.

"America the Beautiful" is a phrase used to describe the many wonders of nature found throughout our country. America's natural beauty will fade, however, if solutions to our solid waste problems are not discovered soon. America is a rich nation socially, economically, and politically. But these very elements may be the cause of Americans' wastefulness. Americans now generate approximately 160 million tons of solid waste a year—3½ pounds per person per day. We live in a consumer society where "convenience," "ready-to-use," and "throw-away" are words that spark the consumer's attention (Cook 60). However, many of the products associated with these words create a large part of our problem with solid waste (Grossman 39). We are running out of space for our garbage. The people of America are beginning to produce responses to this problem. Are we too late? A joint effort between individuals, businesses, government industries, and local, state, and federal governments is necessary to establish policies and procedures to combat this war on waste. The problem requires not one solution, but a combination of solutions involving technologies and people working together to provide a safe and healthy environment for themselves and future generations.

Reading and Writing Research Papers

Reading and writing research papers involves the skillful integration of two complex operations: research and writing. Reading research papers or documented essays critically means understanding the material and evaluating the sources as you proceed. Writing documented essays includes reading and understanding sources on the topic you have chosen and then combining this reading with your own conclusions. The two skills are essentially mirror images of one another.

READING RESEARCH PAPERS

Preparing to Read.   You should approach a research paper in much the same way that you approach any essay. First, take a few minutes to look at the preliminary material for each selection: What can you learn from scanning Ehrenreich's essay ("The Ecstasy of War") or from reading the synopsis in the Rhetorical Table of Contents? What does Barbara Ehrenreich's title, "The Ecstasy of War," prepare you to read? And what questions do you have about sleep before you read Nancy Nadolski's essay ("Getting a Good Night's Sleep: Diagnosing and Treating Insomnia")?

Also, you should learn as much as you can from the authors' biographies: What is Nadolski's interest in sleep? What biographical details prepare us for her approach to this topic? What is Edward Ayers' background? Does he have the proper qualifications to write about the American Civil War?

Another important part of preparing to read a documented essay or research paper is surveying the sources cited. Turn to the end of the essay and look at the sources. What publications does Ehrenreich draw from? Are these books and magazines well respected? Do you recognize any of the authorities Nadolski quotes?

Last, before you read these essays, try to generate some ideas on each topic so you can participate as fully as possible in your reading. The Preparing to Read questions will get you ready for this task. Then, try to speculate further on the topic of each essay: What is the connection for Ehrenreich between war and ecstasy? What does this relationship tell us about human nature in general? Why has the relationship between sleep and health gained so much momentum in the United States? Where do you think this momentum will take us in the future?

Reading.   As you react to the material in this chapter, you should respond to both the research and the writing. Record your responses as you read the essay for the first time: What are your reactions to the information you are reading? Are the sources appropriate? How well do they support the author's main points?

Use the preliminary material before each essay to help you create a framework for your responses to it: What motivated Ehrenreich to publish her essay on war? Do you find it convincing? Who was Ayers' primary audience when his essay was first published? In what ways is the tone of his essay appropriate for that audience?

Carefully crafted questions at the bottom of the pages of each essay will guide you from prereading predictions and sentiments to high level forms of critical thinking in preparation for your writing assignments at the end of each selection. These questions are especially helpful with more complex reading tasks like the ones in this chapter. The essays in this chapter are similar to the material you will read in your other courses throughout your college experience. The questions at the bottom of these pages will essentially teach you how to approach this type of reading and understand it in all of its complexity. As in previous chapters, writing out your responses to these questions is the best strategy for shaping your own thoughts about these issues.

Your main job at this stage is to determine each essay's primary assertion (thesis statement), note the sources that support this thesis, and begin to ask yourself questions about the essay so you can respond critically to your reading. In addition, take a look at the questions after each selection to make sure you are comprehending the major ideas of the essay.

Rereading.   As you reread these documented essays, take some time to become aware of the difference between fact and opinion, to weigh and evaluate the evidence brought to bear on the arguments, to consider the sources the writers use, to determine what the writers omitted, and to confirm your own views on the issues at hand. During this stage, you will also need to critique your sources to determine whether or not their information is credible. All these skills demand the use of critical thinking strategies at their most sophisticated level.

You need to approach this type of argument with an inquiring mind, asking questions and looking for answers as you read the essays. Be especially conscious of the appeals (logical, emotional, and ethical) at work in each essay (see "Writing Argument Essays" in the Introduction of Chapter 9), and take note of other rhetorical strategies that support each author's main argument.

Also, be aware of your own thought processes as you sort facts from opinions. Know where you stand personally in relation to each side of the issues.

For a list of guidelines for the entire reading process, see the checklists on page 29 of the Introduction.

WRITING RESEARCH PAPERS

Preparing to Write.   Just as with any writing assignment, you should begin the task of writing a research paper by exploring and limiting your topic. In this case, however, you draw on other sources to help you with this process. You should seek out both primary and secondary sources related to your topic. **Primary sources** are works of literature, historical documents, letters, diaries, speeches, eyewitness accounts, and your own experiments, observations, and conclusions; **secondary sources** explain and analyze information from other sources. Any librarian can help you search for both types of sources related to your topic.

After you have found a few sources on your general topic, you should scan and evaluate what you have discovered so you can limit your topic further. Depending on the required length of your essay, you will want to find a topic broad enough to be researched, established enough to let you discover ample sources on it in the library, and significant enough to demonstrate your abilities to grapple with important ideas and draw meaningful conclusions. The Preparing to Write questions can help you generate and focus your ideas.

Once you have established these limitations, you might try writing a tentative thesis. At this point, asking a question and attempting to find an answer are productive. But you should keep in mind that your thesis is likely to be revised several times as the range of your knowledge changes and your paper takes different turns while you research and write. Then decide on a purpose and audience for your essay.

Once your tentative thesis is formed, you should read your sources for ideas and take detailed notes on your reading. These notes will probably fall into one of four categories: (1) *summary*—a condensed statement of someone else's thoughts or observations; (2) *paraphrase*—a restatement in your own words of someone else's ideas or observations; (3) *direct quotations from sources;* or (4) *a combination of these forms.* Be sure to make a distinction in your notes between actual quotes and paraphrases or summaries. Also, record the sources (including page and/or paragraph numbers) of all your notes—especially of quoted, summarized, and paraphrased material—which you may need to cite in your essay.

The World Wide Web is an exciting source of information for your research papers. Electronic sources include online journals and magazines, CD-ROMs, software programs, newsletters, discussion groups, bulletin boards, gopher sites, and email. But not all electronic sources are equally accurate and reliable. Based on your topic, you need to exercise your best judgment and get your instructor's help in assessing the most useful online sites for your purposes. Most instructors agree that students should use scholarly web sources that have been through a rigorous amount of academic screening. These include academic databases, such as WilsonWeb, EBSCOhost, ABI/INFORM, and LexisNexis, that you can access through your library. These sources are considered credible, while others that are not "peer-reviewed" can be biased and incorrect. So they are less reliable. Check with one of your reference librarians for tips on how to distinguish between these two types of Web-based sources.

As you gather information, you should consider keeping a "research journal" where you can record your own opinions, interpretations, and analyses in response to your reading. This journal should be separate from your notes on sources and is the place where you can make your own discoveries in relation to your topic by jotting down thoughts and relationships among ideas you are exposed to, by keeping a record of sources you read and others you want to look at, by tracking and developing your own ideas and theories, and by clarifying your thinking on an issue.

Finally, before you begin your first draft, you might want to write an informal working outline for your own information. Such an exercise can help you check the range of your coverage and the order and development of your ideas. With an outline, you can readily see where you need more information, less information, or more solid sources. Try to be flexible, however. This outline may change dramatically as your essay develops.

Writing.   Writing the first draft of a research paper is your chance to discover new insights and to find important connections between ideas that you may not be aware of yet. This draft is your opportunity to demonstrate that you understand the issue at hand and your sources on three increasingly difficult levels—literal, interpretive, and analytical; that you can organize your material effectively; that you can integrate your sources (in the form of summaries, paraphrases, or quotations) with your opinions; and that you can document (that is, cite) your sources.

To begin this process, look again at your thesis statement and your working outline, and adjust them to represent any new discoveries you have made as you read your sources and wrote in your research journal. Then, organize your research notes and information in some logical fashion.

When you begin to draft your paper, write the sections of the essay that you feel most comfortable about first. Throughout the essay, feature your own point of view and integrate summaries, paraphrases, and quotations from other sources into your own analysis. Each point you make should be a section of your paper consisting of your own conclusion and your support for that conclusion (in the form of facts, examples, summaries, paraphrases, and quotations). Remember that the primary reason for doing such an assignment is to let you demonstrate your ability to synthesize material, draw your own conclusions, and analyze your sources and your own reasoning.

A documented paper usually blends three types of material:

1. *Common knowledge, such as the places and dates of events (even if you have to look them up).*

   Example: Neil Armstrong and Edwin Aldrin first walked on the moon on July 20, 1969.

2. *Your own thoughts and observations.*

   Example: Armstrong and Aldrin's brief walk on the moon's surface was the beginning of a new era in the U.S. space program.

3. *Someone else's thoughts and observations.*

   Example: President Richard Nixon reacted to the moonwalk in a telephone call to the astronauts: "For one priceless moment in the history of man all the people on this earth are truly one—one in their pride in what you have done and one in our prayers that you will return safely to Earth."

Of these three types of information, you must document or cite your exact source only for the third type. Negligence in citing your sources, whether purposeful or accidental, is called *plagiarism,* which comes from a Latin word meaning "kidnapper." Among student writers, plagiarism usually takes one of three forms: (1) using words from another source without quotation marks; (2) using someone else's ideas in the form of a summary or paraphrase without citing your source; and (3) using someone else's term paper as your own.

Avoiding plagiarism is quite simple: You just need to make sure you acknowledge the sources of ideas or wording that you are using to support your own contentions. Acknowledging your sources also gives you credit for the reading you have done and for the ability you have developed to synthesize and use sources to support your observations and conclusions. To give credit to your sources, you must acknowledge them in two ways: (1) in-text citations that provide your reader with the author, page or paragraph numbers, and sometimes dates for each summary, paraphrase, or direct quotation you use and (2) a list of sources at the end of your paper that provides complete publication information on all the sources you have used in your essay. These two types of documentation work together to provide your readers with all the information they need to understand the exact details of the sources you read.

Two specific forms of documentation cause students some unexpected problems. But if you heed the following warnings, you will avoid these stumbling blocks. First, when you paraphrase (or put another writer's ideas in your own words), you cannot use the author's words or sentence structure. You must also cite your source at the end of a paraphrase. Second, when you put an author's words in quotation marks, you must print them exactly as they are in the original source without making any changes.

As you document your sources, you should know that documentation styles vary from discipline to discipline. Ask your instructor about the particular documentation style he or she wants you to follow. The most common styles are the Modern Language Association (MLA) style, used in humanities courses, and the American Psychological Association (APA) style, used in behavioral science and science courses. You should check the MLA or APA Home Pages for their current guidelines for online documentation: The URL for the Modern Language Association is http://www. mla.org and for the American Psychological Association, http://www.apa.org. (See any writing handbook for more details on documentation formats.)

Even though documentation styles vary somewhat from one field to another, the basic concept behind documentation is the same in all disciplines: You must give proper credit to other writers by acknowledging the sources of the summaries, paraphrases, and quotations that you use to support the ideas in your research paper. Remember that you have two goals in any citation: (1) to acknowledge the author and (2) to help the reader locate the material. Once you grasp this basic concept and accept it, you will have no trouble avoiding plagiarism.

Rewriting.   To rewrite your research paper, you should play the role of your readers and impartially evaluate your argument and the sources you have used as evidence in that argument. To begin with, revise your thesis to represent all the discoveries you made as you wrote your first draft. Then, look for problems in logic throughout the essay; you might even develop an outline at this point to help evaluate your reasoning:

- Are the essay's assertions clear? Are they adequately supported?
- Are other points of view recognized and examined?
- Does the organization of your paper further your argument?

Next, check your documentation style:

- Are your summaries, paraphrases, and quotations presented accurately?
- Do you introduce the sources in your paper when appropriate?
- Are your sources in the proper format (MLA, APA, or another)?

Then, proofread carefully. Finally, prepare your paper to be submitted to your instructor:

- Have you followed your instructor's guidelines for your title page, margins, page numbers, tables, and abstracts?

- Do you have an alphabetical list of your sources at the end of your paper?

Any additional guidance you may need as you write and revise your term papers is furnished on page 30 of the Introduction.

STUDENT ESSAY: DOCUMENTATION AT WORK

The following student research paper uses documented sources to support its observations and conclusions about college students' eating habits today. First, the writer discusses the problem of the "freshman 15." She then goes on to consider why students typically gain weight in their first year of college. After recognizing and refuting some opposing views, this student writer ends her paper by asserting college students need to change various behaviors that are harmful to their health. Throughout the essay, the student writer carefully supports her principal points with summaries, paraphrases, and quotations from other sources. Notice that she uses the MLA documentation style and closes the paper with an alphabetical list of "Works Cited." Look also for her uses of different rhetorical modes, which are identified in the margins in brackets ([ ]).

Food for Thought

[Narration] When parents send their children off to college, they are full of last-minute wisdom they hope their kids will hear: "Make sure you study!" "Don't forget to set your alarm in the morning!" "Remember to eat right!" This last bit of advice is important for new college students because many have never had to worry about their eating habits before. But now, out on their own for the first time, they are responsible for the choices they make regarding their health. The "freshman 15" is a widely known concept, coined because many freshmen gain weight (usually about 15 pounds) in their first year away from home. Most attribute this weight gain to a change in lifestyle and poor eating habits, but perhaps a larger reason for this weight gain is fast food. McDonald's, Taco Bell, Wendy's, and other fast food restaurants have cheap food at all hours of the night, and for college students, the appeal may be too great, leading them to learn firsthand about the freshman 15.

Several researchers have studied the phenomenon of the freshman 15. For example, Washington University scientists believe that "weight gain during the

Margin notes: General information — [Cause/Effect] — Common knowledge

Margin notes (left): Common knowledge — [Definition] — Thesis statement first year of college has been described as a problem for many students, but there is little evidence to support or refute these anecdotal reports" (Racette et al. 245), so these (and several other) scientists set out to determine whether the freshman 15 was fact or fiction. Melody Graham and Amy Jones, researchers from Mercy College in Iowa, determined that the average weight gain for freshmen students was 4.6 pounds, thus refuting the myth that freshmen gain an average of 15 pounds in their first year of school. However, Susan Racette et al., researchers from Washington University, found an increase of approximately 9 pounds for over 70% of 764 students they studied, which shows a "potentially significant weight gain" (249). In addition, Katy Kelly, citing research findings of Cornell professor David Levitsky, explains that "the dreaded 'freshman 15' is a reality. The 60 freshmen Levitsky studied gained about a third of a pound a week—an average of 4.2 pounds during the first 12 weeks on campus" (par. 1). If this campus were on a quarter system, these students would have been well on their way to fulfilling the freshman 15 weight gain. So whether freshmen are gaining 15 pounds or 5, the truth of the matter is that they are, in fact, gaining weight.

One fact that all of the above scientists agree on is that this weight gain is due to a more inactive lifestyle and poor food choices. Kelly concludes that "one of the best predictors of weight gain was eating in all-you-can-eat dining halls" (par. 2) or downing junk food late at night, where the "most available snacks are fattening foods from vending machines" (par. 3). Racette et al. show "evidence that many students in our sample are neither consuming adequate fruits and vegetables nor limiting their consumption of fried and fast foods to appropriate levels" (250). Both researchers offer plausible explanations for the weight gain, but the more likely reason is a combination of the two: students are eating fast foods late at night. Finding 24-hour fast-food restaurants near campuses is hardly difficult, especially since fast food restaurants typically locate themselves close to colleges. In a study con-

ducted near the Boston area, scientists discovered that
fast-food restaurants typically "cluster" around K–12
schools because they know they can sell their products
to children and young adults. Austin et al. claim, "Although fast-food restaurants are located throughout
the city, they are clustered in areas within walking distance from schools" (1578). And anyone who has been
near a college knows that these restaurants expand
their reach to college campuses. College students eat
late, like the cheap bargain menus, and don't typically
care about what they are eating. Further, as if this isn't
enough, techy William Powell explains that McDonald's is including free wireless Internet service in exchange for the "purchase of any Extra Value Meal"
(24). Now, college students can go to McDonald's at
midnight for quick, cheap, meals and do their homework at the same time so they're not wasting valuable
study time.

    The real issue, however, is that students can watch
Morgan Spurlock's 2004 *Super Size Me* documentary
(in which he lives on McDonald's food for 30 days
and gains a lot of weight while at the same time becoming increasingly unhealthy) and still walk into a
McDonald's late at night and order a Big Mac; <u>they
just don't care that they are choosing junk food over
healthy food</u>. Perhaps Kenneth Hein says it best:

      I like fast food. I like big burgers that sweat
    through their paper wrappers as they sit in their
    mini-tanning beds under scorching heat lamps.
    I like the super-sized fries with ample salt, es-
    pecially the "extra" ones at the bottom of the
    bag. And yes, I would like an "apple pie with
    that," and occasionally I like a thick, creamy
    milk shake that barely fits through the straw,
    too. (par. 1)

Hein realistically discusses what college students know:
fast food tastes great, is fast and cheap, and is accessible at all hours of the night. And it's not the place
for dieters to go searching for a healthy meal because
consumers who go to fast-food restaurants are probably not looking for light food (Hein, par. 14). Anyone who listens to the news is likely to hear that

Margin notes:

[Cause/ Effect]

Establishing causes for possible accessibility of fast food restaurants

Establishing a second reason for drawing in college students

Concluding second point

Student shows college students know the truth but just don't care

Establishing third point

[Description]

Quote to establish what many feel about fast food—note block format

Continuation of student's point using paraphrase

people who eat fast food are trying to blame their weight gain on what they eat, as though they didn't understand this consequence. But the truth of the matter is that many choose fast food for the same experience that Hein describes above: There's something satisfying in eating fast food. And for college students, the 99-cent menus and late-night hours are irresistible benefits.

Establishing fault in the choices of fast food consumers, not in fast food restaurants

Even though many fast-food restaurants now include lighter fare, with salads and other calorie-reduced menu items, the fact of the matter is that college students don't frequent McDonald's for their salads. Some, like Spurlock, would argue that the salads aren't, in the end, any benefit for the calorie counters anyway. The truth is that fast foods are just that—fast. So those students who consistently choose McDonald's over fruits and vegetables can hardly expect to maintain their weight. As Hein says, "If you're on a diet, don't eat at Taco Bell" (par. 9). Even *Time* magazine pokes fun at McDonald's:

Start of conclusion

Showing difficulty of choices

Establishing that even healthy choices aren't healthy

Academic use of a cartoon

Clearly, fast food restaurants aren't hiding the fact that their food is fattening; it's a truth any fast-food customer knows. So college students need to make better choices when they get hit by the munchies at midnight to avoid gaining what has proven to be the freshman 15.

Student's final point

[Cause/ Effect]

Works Cited

Austin, S. Bryn, et al. "Clustering of Fast-Food Restaurants Around Schools: A Novel Application of Spatial Statistics to the Study of Food Environments." *American Journal of Public Health* 95.9 (2005): 1575–1581.

Graham, Meolody A., and Amy L. Jones. "Freshman 15: Valid Theory or Harmful Myth?" *Journal of American College Health* 50.4 (2002): 171–173. 12 Jan. 2006 <http://voyager.lib.csub.edu:2068>.

Hein, Kenneth. "Fat Mac? Eat Me Spurlock." *Brandweek* 46.22 (2005): 14 pars. 13 Jan. 2006 <http://voyager.lib.csub.edu:2068>.

Kelly, Katy. "The 'Freshman 15.' " *U.S. News & World Report* 135.4 (2003): 3 pars. 11 Jan. 2006 <http://voyager.lib.csub.edu:2105>.

Powell, William. "A Burger and Wi-Fi." T+D, 57.6 (2003): 24. 12 Jan. 2006 <http://voyager.lib.csub.edu:2068>.

Racette, Susan B., et al. "Weight Changes, Exercise, and Dietary Patterns During Freshman and Sophomore Years of College." *Journal of American College Health* 53.6 (2005): 245–251. 12 Jan. 2006 <http://voyager.lib.csub.edu:2068>.

Smith, Mike. "McDonald's." Cartoon. *Time* 7, Nov. 2005. 20.

Super Size Me. Screenplay by Morgan Spurlock. Dir. and prod. Morgan Spurlock. Perf. Morgan Spurlock. 2004. DVD. Roadside Attractions and Samuel Goldwyn Films, 2004.

Beginning of MLA reference page in alphabetical order

Student Writer's Comments

From the moment this term paper was assigned, I knew my topic would be fast food and gaining weight, because I felt the key to a convincing argument was to select a subject I was passionate about. Since I've been in college, gaining weight is a topic I can discuss passionately. I wanted to bring together the ideas about the "freshman 15" and fast food in a way that I thought would be new, and once I found the articles on Wi-Fi and the location of fast-food restaurants, I knew I had an angle to attack: I could talk about how fast-food places target college students because students can't resist the many lures of these quick, cheap meals. I wanted to be honest as I appealed to the emotions, concerns, and ethics of my audience (not to mention their bodies), so that my message would not be taken lightly and so future college students might reconsider those late-night excursions to Taco Bell or McDonald's. Even though I knew students would never stop going to such places, maybe learning that fast food restaurants seek out college students' lifestyles might help students make better choices at midnight.

I began the process of writing this paper by getting on the computer every chance I had (between classes, during lunch, and at night before I went home) and collecting information about the "freshman 15" and fast-food "nutrition." I found plenty of material about all three, but I also uncovered some counterarguments that I really didn't expect to find. I was fascinated by the information—both facts and opinions—that I discovered. But the material wasn't taking any shape at all yet; the only common denominators were the general topic and my interest level.

I was taking notes on notecards, so I had filled quite a stack of cards when I stopped to reread all my material to see if I could put it into any coherent categories. Happily, my notes fell quite naturally into three divisions: (1) the "freshman 15," (2) the practices of fast-food restaurants targeting kids and young adults, and (3) fast food nutrition and choices. I could see right away that I had enough material from reputable sources on the "freshman 15." My notes on fast food would also be sufficient with a few more research sessions. I had some stray notes that didn't fit any of these categories, but I decided to worry about those later. I tried my hand at a thesis statement, which I think had been floating around in my head for days. Then I wrote the paper topic by topic over a period of several days. I didn't attempt the introduction and the conclusion until I began to rewrite. As I composed the essay, I was especially aware of the types of material I had to support each of my topics. I had a good distribution of summaries, paraphrases, and quotations and had remembered to keep careful notes on my sources, so I put my source and page numbers (or paragraph numbers) into my first draft. I also had several examples for each of my topics and a good blend of facts and opinions.

When I rewrote my essay, I kept in mind that I would be successful in arguing my case only if my words caused the readers to make a change, however small, in their own behavior. I reworked my research paper several times as I played different readers with various biases, paying special attention to word choice and sentence structure.

Overall, writing this paper gave me a great deal of pleasure. I feel even stronger in my determination to avoid fast food—at least late at night when I know I should make better choices.

SOME FINAL THOUGHTS ON RESEARCH PAPERS

The three essays that follow offer vigorous exercises in critical thinking. They also use a combination of the three different types of persuasive appeals we studied in Chapter 9 (logical, emotional, and ethical) and draw several different rhetorical modes that we have studied throughout the book. In the first essay, Barbara Ehrenreich illustrates the Modern Language Association documentation style as she uses sources to support her thesis that people do not have a natural instinct to kill. The second essay, by Nancy Nadolski, explains the connection between a good night's sleep and your general health; its use of sources illustrates the American Psychological Association documentation style. Finally, Edward Ayers, in "The American Civil War, Emancipation, and Reconstruction on the World Stage," discusses some of the mysteries of the Civil War, using Chicago Manual documentation style. As you read these essays, be aware of the combination of appeals at work, the various rhetorical modes each author uses to further his or her argument, and the way the authors use sources to support the topics within each essay.

RESEARCH PAPERS IN REVIEW

Reading Research Papers

Preparing to Read

✓ What assumptions can you make from the essay's title?

✓ Can you guess what the general mood of the essay is?

✓ What is the essay's purpose and audience?

✓ What does the synopsis tell you about the essay?

✓ What can you learn from the author's biography?

Reading

✓ What is the author's main assertion or thesis?

✓ What sources does the author cite to support the thesis?

✓ What questions do you have about this topic?

Rereading

✓ How does the author use facts and opinions in the essay?

✓ Are the sources the writer cites valid and reliable?

✓ Does the author interpret facts accurately?

Writing Research Papers

Preparing to **Write**

✓ What is your purpose?

✓ Who is your audience?

Writing

✓ Do you have a thesis statement?

✓ Have you organized your material effectively?

✓ Have you avoided plagiarism and cited your sources correctly?

✓ Do you use the appropriate documentation style?

Rewriting

✓ Are the essay's assertions clear? Are they adequately supported?

✓ Are other points of view recognized and examined?

✓ Does the organization of your paper further your argument?

✓ Are your summaries, paraphrases, or quotations presented accurately?

✓ Do you introduce the sources in your paper when appropriate?

✓ Are your sources in the proper format (MLA, APA, or another)?

✓ Have you followed your instructor's guidelines for your title page, margins, page numbers, tables, and abstracts?

✓ Do you have an alphabetical list of sources for the end of your paper?

BARBARA EHRENREICH   (1941–   )

The Ecstasy of War

Barbara Ehrenreich is a respected author, lecturer, and social commentator with opinions on a wide range of topics. After earning a B.A. from Reed College in chemistry and physics and a Ph.D. from Rockefeller University in cell biology, she turned almost immediately to freelance writing, producing a succession of books and pamphlets on a dazzling array of subjects. Early publications examined student uprisings, health care in America, nurses and midwives, poverty, welfare, economic justice for women, and the sexual politics of disease. Her most recent books include *The Hearts of Men: American Dreams and the Flight from Commitment* (1983), *Fear of Falling: The Inner Life of the Middle Class* (1989), *The Worst Years of Our Lives: Irreverent Notes from a Decade of Greed* (1990), *Blood Rites: Origins and History of the Passions of War* (1997), *Nickel and Dimed* (2001), and *Bait and Switch: The (Futile) Pursuit of the American Dream* (2005). Ehrenreich is also well known as a frequent guest on television and radio programs, including *The Today Show, Good Morning America, Nightline, Crossfire,* and *The Phil Donohue Show.* Her many articles and reviews have appeared in the *New York Times Magazine, Esquire,* the *Atlantic Monthly,* the *New Republic, Vogue, Harper's,* and the *Wall Street Journal.* She has been an essayist for *Time* since 1990. Ehrenreich, whose favorite hobby is "voracious reading," lives in Syosset, New York.

Preparing to Read

Taken from *Blood Rites: Origins and History of the Passions of War* (1997), the following essay analyzes the psychology of war. Its citations and bibliography illustrate proper MLA (Modern Language Association) documentation form.

Exploring Experience: As you prepare to read this article, take a few minutes to think about aggression in society today: Do you think aggression plays a significant role in American society? In other societies? What do you think is the origin of aggression? In your opinion, what role does aggression play in war? In everyday life? How do you react to aggressive behavior? How do people you associate with react to aggressive behavior?

Learning Online: Review the descriptions of current video games with a war theme. You may visit Web sites for Electronic Arts, Activision, or Take 2 Interactive to peruse their current game lists. Consider the techniques and intents of these games while reading Ehrenreich's essay.

"So elemental is the human need to endow the shedding of blood with some great and even sublime significance that it renders the intellect almost entirely helpless"
(Van Creveld 166).

Different wars have led to different theories of why men fight them. ◆ 1
The Napoleonic Wars, which bore along with them the rationalist spirit of the French Revolution, inspired the Prussian officer Carl von Clausewitz to propose that war itself is an entirely rational undertaking, unsullied by human emotion. War, in his famous aphorism, is merely a "continuation of policy . . . by other means," with policy itself supposedly resulting from the same kind of clearheaded deliberation one might apply to a game of chess. Nation-states were the leading actors on the stage of history, and war was simply one of the many ways they advanced their interests against those of other nation-states. If you could accept the existence of this new super-person, the nation, a battle was no more disturbing and irrational than, say, a difficult trade negotiation—except perhaps to those who lay dying on the battlefield.

World War I, coming a century after Napoleon's sweep through Europe   2
and northern Africa, led to an opposite assessment of the human impulse to war. World War I was hard to construe as in any way "rational," especially to that generation of European intellectuals, including Sigmund Freud, who survived to ponder the unprecedented harvest of dead bodies. History textbooks tell us that the "Great War" grew out of the conflict between "competing imperialist states," but this Clausewitzian interpretation has little to do with the actual series of accidents, blunders, and miscommunications that impelled the nations of Europe to war in the summer of 1914.[1] At first swept up in the excitement of the war, unable for weeks to work or think of anything else, Freud was eventually led to conclude that there is some dark flaw in the human psyche, a perverse desire to destroy, countering Eros and the will to live (Stromberg 82).

So these are, in crude summary, the theories of war which modern wars   3
have left us with: That war is a means, however risky, by which men seek to advance their collective interests and improve their lives. Or, alternatively, that war stems from sub-rational drives not unlike those that lead individuals to commit violent crimes. In our own time, most people seem to hold both views at once, avowing that war is a gainful enterprise, intended to meet the material needs of the groups engaged in it, and, at the same time, that it fulfills deep and "irrational" psychological needs. ◆ There is no question about the first part of this proposition—that wars are designed, at least

---

Reading Critically

◆ Why do you think most wars are fought?
◆ How do you think war "fulfills deep and irrational psychological needs"?

ostensibly, to secure necessaries like land or oil or "geopolitical advantage." The mystery lies in the peculiar psychological grip war exerts on us.

In the 1960s and '70s, the debate on the psychology of war centered on   4 the notion of an "aggressive instinct," peculiar to all humans or only to human males. This is not the place to summarize that debate, with its endless examples of animal behavior and clashes over their applicability to human affairs. Here I would simply point out that, whether or not there is an aggressive instinct, there are reasons to reject it as the major wellspring of war.

Although it is true that aggressive impulses, up to and including murder-   5 ous rage, can easily take over in the heat of actual battle, even this statement must be qualified to take account of different weaponry and modes of fighting. Hand-to-hand combat may indeed call forth and even require the emotions of rage and aggression, if only to mobilize the body for bursts of muscular activity. In the case of action-at-a-distance weapons, however, like guns and bows and arrows, emotionality of any sort can be a distinct disadvantage. ❸ Coolness, and the ability to keep aiming and firing steadfastly in the face of enemy fire, prevails. Hence, according to the distinguished American military historian Robert L. O'Connell, the change in the ideal warrior personality wrought by the advent of guns in the fifteenth and sixteenth centuries, from "ferocious aggressiveness" to "passive disdain" (119). So there is no personality type—"hot-tempered," "macho," or whatever—consistently and universally associated with warfare.

Furthermore, fighting itself is only one component of the enterprise we   6 know as war. Wars are not barroom brawls writ large, or domestic violence that has been somehow extended to strangers. In war, fighting takes place within battles—along with much anxious waiting, of course—but wars do not begin with battles and are often not decided by them either. Most of war consists of *preparation* for battle—training, the organization of supplies, marching and other forms of transport—activities which are hard to account for by innate promptings of any kind. There is no plausible instinct, for example, that impels a man to leave his home, cut his hair short, and drill for hours in tight formation. As anthropologists Clifton B. Kroeber and Bernard L. Fontana point out, "It is a large step from what may be biologically innate leanings toward individual aggression to ritualized, socially sanctioned, institutionalized group warfare" (166).

War, in other words, is too complex and collective an activity to be ac-   7 counted for by a single warlike instinct lurking within the individual psyche. Instinct may, or may not, inspire a man to bayonet the first enemy he

---

Reading Critically
❸ Do you agree with Ehrenreich that emotionality can be a disadvantage in war? Why or why not?

encounters in battle. But instinct does not mobilize supply lines, manufacture rifles, issue uniforms, or move an army of thousands from point A on the map to B.[4] These are "complicated, orchestrated, highly organized" activities, as social theorist Robin Fox writes, undertaken not by individuals but by entities on the scale of nations and dynasties (15). "The hypothesis of a killer instinct," according to a commentator summarizing a recent conference on the anthropology of war, is "not so much wrong as irrelevant" (Clark McCauley in Haas 2).

In fact, throughout history, individual men have gone to near-suicidal   8 lengths to avoid participating in wars—a fact that proponents of a warlike instinct tend to slight. Men have fled their homelands, served lengthy prison terms, hacked off limbs, shot off feet or index fingers, feigned illness or insanity, or, if they could afford to, paid surrogates to fight in their stead. "Some draw their teeth, some blind themselves, and others maim themselves, on their way to us" (Mitchell 42), the governor of Egypt complained of his peasant recruits in the early nineteenth century. So unreliable was the rank and file of the eighteenth-century Prussian army that military manuals forbade camping near a woods or forest: The troops would simply melt away into the trees (Delbrück 303).

Proponents of a warlike instinct must also reckon with the fact that even   9 when men have been assembled, willingly or unwillingly, for the purpose of war, fighting is not something that seems to come "naturally" to them. In fact, surprisingly, even in the thick of battle, few men can bring themselves to shoot directly at individual enemies.[2] The difference between an ordinary man or boy and a reliable killer, as any drill sergeant could attest, is profound. A transformation is required: The man or boy leaves his former self behind and becomes something entirely different, perhaps even taking a new name. In small-scale, traditional societies, the change was usually accomplished through ritual drumming, dancing, fasting, and sexual abstinence—all of which serve to lift a man out of his mundane existence and into a new, warriorlike mode of being, denoted by special body paint, masks, and headdresses.

As if to emphasize the discontinuity between the warrior and the ordi-   10 nary human being, many cultures require the would-be fighting man to leave his humanness behind and assume a new form as an animal.[3][5] The young Scandinavian had to become a bear before he could become an elite warrior, going "berserk" (the word means "dressed in a bear hide"), biting and chasing people. The Irish hero Cuchulain transformed himself into a

---

Reading Critically
[4] According to the author, what is the role of instinct in a war effort?
[5] Why do you think so many cultures have encouraged their warriors to become like animals in order to fight well?

monster in preparation for battle: "He became horrible, many-shaped, strange, and unrecognizable," with one eye sucked into his skull and the other popping out of the side of the face (Davidson 84). Apparently this transformation was a familiar and meaningful one, because similarly distorted faces turn up frequently in Celtic art.

Often the transformation is helped along with drugs or social pressure of various kinds. Tahitian warriors were browbeaten into fighting by functionaries called Rauti, or "exhorters," who ran around the battlefield urging their comrades to mimic "the devouring wild dog" (Keeley 146). The ancient Greek hoplites drank enough wine, apparently, to be quite tipsy when they went into battle (Hanson 126); Aztecs drank pulque; Chinese troops at the time of Sun Tzu got into the mood by drinking wine and watching "gyrating sword dancers" perform (Sun Tzu 37). Almost any drug or intoxicant has served, in one setting or another, to facilitate the transformation of man into warrior. [6] Yanomamo Indians of the Amazon ingest a hallucinogen before battle; the ancient Scythians smoked hemp, while a neighboring tribe drank something called "hauma," which is believed to have induced a frenzy of aggression (Rolle 94–95). So if there is a destructive instinct that impels men to war, it is a weak one and often requires a great deal of help. [11]

In seventeenth-century Europe, the transformation of man into soldier took on a new form, more concerted and disciplined, and far less pleasant, than wine. New recruits and even seasoned veterans were endlessly drilled, hour after hour, until each man began to feel himself part of a single, giant fighting machine. The drill was only partially inspired by the technology of firearms. It's easy enough to teach a man to shoot a gun; the problem is to make him willing to get into situations where guns are being shot and to remain there long enough to do some shooting of his own. So modern military training aims at a transformation parallel to that achieved by "primitives" with war drums and paint: In the fanatical routines of boot camp, a man leaves behind his former identity and is reborn as a creature of the military—an automaton and also, ideally, a willing killer of other men. [12]

This is not to suggest that killing is foreign to human nature or, more narrowly, to the male personality. Men (and women) have again and again proved themselves capable of killing impulsively and with gusto. But there is a huge difference between a war and an ordinary fight. War not only departs from the normal; it inverts all that is moral and right: [7] In war one *should* kill, *should* steal, *should* burn cities and farms, *should* perhaps even rape matrons and little girls. Whether or not such activities are "natural" or at some level [13]

Reading Critically

[6] What role have intoxicants played in warfare in past centuries?

[7] How does war invert "all that is moral and right"?

instinctual, most men undertake them only by entering what appears to be an "altered state"—induced by drugs or lengthy drilling, and denoted by face paint or khakis.

The point of such transformative rituals is not only to put men "in the 14 mood." Returning warriors may go through equally challenging rituals before they can celebrate victory or reenter the community—covering their heads in apparent shame, for example; vomiting repeatedly; abstaining from sex (Keeley 144). Among the Maori, returning warriors could not participate in the victory celebration until they had gone through a whaka-hoa ritual, designed to make them "common" again: The hearts of slain enemies were roasted, after which offerings were made to the war god Tu, and the rest was eaten by priests, who shouted spells to remove "the blood curse" and enable warriors to reenter their ordinary lives (Sagan 18). Among the Taulipang Indians of South America, victorious warriors "sat on ants, flogged one another with whips, and passed a cord covered with poisonous ants, through their mouth and nose" (Métraux 397). Such painful and shocking postwar rites impress on the warrior that war is much more than a "continuation of policy . . . by other means." In war men enter an alternative realm of human experience, as far removed from daily life as those things which we call "sacred."

Notes

1. See, for example, Stoessinger, *Why Nations Go to War,* 14–20.
2. See Grossman, *On Killing.*
3. In the mythologies of the Indo-European tradition, Dumézil relates, thanks "either to a gift of metamorphosis, or to a monstrous heredity, the eminent warrior possesses a veritable animal nature" (Dumézil 140).

Works Cited

Davidson, Hilda Ellis. *Myths and Symbols in Pagan Europe: Early Scandinavian and Celtic Religions.* Syracuse: Syracuse UP, 1988.

Delbrück, Hans. *The Dawn of Modern Warfare.* Lincoln: U of Nebraska P, 1985.

Dumézil, Georges. *Destiny of the Warrior.* Chicago: U of Chicago P, 1969.

Fox, Robin. "Fatal Attraction: War and Human Nature." *National Interest Winter* 1992/93: 11–20.

Grossman, Lt. Col. Dave. *On Killing: The Psychological Cost of Learning to Kill in War and Society.* Boston: Little, Brown, 1995.

Haas, Jonathan, ed. *The Anthropology of War.* Cambridge: Cambridge UP, 1990.

Hanson, Victor Davis. *The Western Way of War: Infantry Battle in Classical Greece.* New York: Knopf, 1989.

Keeley, Lawrence H. *War Before Civilization: The Myth of the Peaceful Savage.* New York: Oxford UP, 1996.

Kroeber, Clifton B., and Bernard L. Fontana. *Massacre on the Gila: An Account of the Last Major Battle Between American Indians, with Reflections on the Origin of War.* Tucson: U of Arizona P, 1986.

Métraux, Alfred. "Warfare, Cannibalism, and Human Trophies." *Handbook of South American Indians.* Vol. 5. Ed. Julian H. Steward. New York: Cooper Square, 1963.

Mitchell, Timothy. *Colonizing Egypt.* Berkeley: U of California P, 1991.

O'Connell, Robert L. *Of Arms and Men: A History of War, Weapons, and Aggression.* New York: Oxford UP, 1989.

Rolle, Renate. *The World of the Scythians.* Berkeley: U of California P, 1989.

Sagan, Eli. *Cannibalism: Human Aggression and Cultural Form.* New York: Harper and Row, 1974.

Stoessinger, John G. *Why Nations Go to War.* New York: St. Martin's, 1993.

Stromberg, Roland. *Redemption by War: The Intellectuals and 1914.* Lawrence: U of Kansas P, 1982.

Sun Tzu. *The Art of War.* Translated and with an introduction by Samuel B. Griffith. London: Oxford University Press, 1971.

Van Creveld, Martin. *The Transformation of War.* New York: Free Press, 1991.

UNDERSTANDING DETAILS

1. What do you think Ehrenreich's main purpose is in this essay?
2. According to Ehrenreich, what is the difference between hand-to-hand combat and fighting at a distance?
3. What does Ehrenreich say are the various components of what we call "war"?
4. In what ways do some cultures ritualize the transformation from regular citizen to warrior? Give three examples.

THINKING CRITICALLY

5. Do you believe that war can ever be emotionless and rational, like "a difficult trade negotiation" (paragraph 1)?
6. What do Kroeber and Fontana mean when they say, "It is a large step from what may be biologically innate leanings toward individual aggression to ritualized, socially sanctioned, institutionalized group warfare" (paragraph 6)?
7. Why is "the hypothesis of a killer instinct" "not so much wrong as irrelevant" to the "anthropology of war" (paragraph 7)?
8. Are you convinced by this essay that "in war men enter an alternative realm of human experience, as far removed from daily life as those things which we call 'sacred' " (paragraph 14)?

DISCOVERING RHETORICAL STRATEGIES

9. Who do you think is Ehrenreich's main audience? How did you come to this conclusion?

10. The author begins her discussion of war with different "theories of why men fight" wars (paragraph 1). Is this an effective beginning for what Ehrenreich is trying to accomplish? Explain your answer.

11. What information in this essay is most persuasive to you? What is least persuasive?

12. What tone does the author establish by citing frequent statistics and referring to other sources in her essay?

MAKING CONNECTIONS

13. Compare and contrast Ehrenreich's insights on the psychology of war with Stephen King's theories on "Why We Crave Horror Movies." How do their ideas support one another? How do they contradict each other?

14. Compare Ehrenreich's use of examples with those of Jessica Mitford in "Behind the Formaldehyde Curtain"). Which author uses them more skillfully? Why do you think this is true?

15. In a conversation among Ehrenreich, Brent Staples ("A Brother's Murder"), bell hooks ("Justice: Childhood Love Lessons"), and/or Dave Grossman ("We Are Training Our Kids to Kill") about the "aggressive instinct" in people, on what principal points would they agree and disagree? Give examples.

IDEAS FOR DISCUSSION/WRITING

Preparing to Write

Write freely about aggression in general: Why do people fight? Why do countries go to war? What are some ways in which people take out their aggression? Have you ever noticed people fighting just for the sake of fighting? When is aggression acceptable? When is it unacceptable?

Choosing a Topic

1. Ehrenreich claims that "even when men have been assembled, willingly or unwillingly, for the purpose of war, fighting is not something that seems to come 'naturally' to them" (paragraph 9). Do you agree or disagree with this statement? Explain your reaction in a clearly reasoned argumentative essay. Cite Ehrenreich's selection whenever necessary.

2. In the last paragraph of her essay, Ehrenreich suggests that warriors often have to go through rituals to return to their civilizations. Use Ehrenreich's article as one of your sources; then read further on such transformations. Next write a clear, well-documented argument expressing your opinion on a specific transformation. Organize your paper clearly, and present your suggestions logically, using proper documentation (citations and bibliography) to support your position.

3. Use additional sources to study the circumstances of a war you are familiar with. Then, referring to Ehrenreich's explanation of "the anthropology of war" (paragraph 7), write a well-documented argument explaining the causes and effects of the war by discussing or analyzing in depth the consequences you have discovered.

4. Video games simulate war situations involving strategy, combat, and sometimes killing. Ehrenreich claims that no personality type has a "single warlike instinct" (paragraph 7). How do her theories apply to video game users? Develop a research paper in which you test Ehrenreich's theories by applying them to video game users. Be sure to use credible sources to support your claims.

Before beginning your essay, you might want to consult the checklists on page 560.

NANCY NADOLSKI   (1950–   )

Getting a Good Night's Sleep: Diagnosing and Treating Insomnia

Born in Cleveland, Nancy Nadolski earned her B.S. in Nursing at Washington State University, then worked in the medical profession for several years before returning to school at age 40 for a Masters in Counseling at Albertsons College and a Masters in Nursing at Gonzaga University. She is currently a family nurse practitioner at Foothills Psychiatry in Boise, Idaho, where she spends her time conducting community workshops on health issues within a 9,000 square mile area of the Idaho countryside. She has a special interest in women's health, including depression, anxiety, and menopausal sleep problems. Nadolski, who has given papers and presentations as far away as Groningen, Netherlands, is also a founder and director of the Foothills Foundation, an organization supporting mental health education for professionals and the public. Her hobbies include whitewater rafting, especially on the Middle Fork of the Salmon River in Idaho. Asked for advice for students using *The Prose Reader,* the author encouraged them to "write with confidence. Just get your ideas down on paper, and then edit and refine them later. Be courageous and be open to feedback from your professors and peers."

Preparing to Read

This essay was first published in a journal for nurses. In it, Nancy Nadolski lays out the basic trials, tribulations, and medication options associated with insomnia.

Exploring Experience: As you prepare to read this essay, think about your general health: How well do you take care of yourself? Do you eat well, exercise, and get enough sleep to function at your optimum level? If you are under stress or deadlines, where do you cut corners? Do these short cuts take a toll on your health? What motivates you to make these choices when you are under pressure? How important do you think sleep is to your general health? Do you have any sleep problems?

Learning Online: Visit the Web site http://www.shuteye.com, which is sponsored by a pharmaceutical company called Sanofi-Aventis. Rate the quality of your sleep by clicking on the "Sleep Assessor" link on the left side of the page, and then take the interactive quiz. Do you suffer from any form of insomnia? Keep your answers in mind as you read Nadolski's essay.

My mind clicks on and off . . . I try letting one eyelid close at a time while I prop the other open with my will. My whole body argues dully that nothing, nothing life can attain, is quite so desirable as sleep.
                    —*Charles Lindbergh, as quoted from* The Spirit of St. Louis

Most of us do not spend 33 hours flying an airplane across the   1
Atlantic Ocean as Charles Lindbergh did, but for each 16-hour
period we are awake, we drive cars, work with technical data, and
make critical decisions with people everyday.

What's The Big Deal About Sleep?

Insomnia is a public health problem. [1] In the primary care setting, in-   2
somnia is the second most common complaint, after pain. The prevalence of
excessive daytime sleepiness is reported by up to 31% of the adult population at any one time (Gallop Organization, 1995). The consequences of poor
sleep quality can be significant, including accidents, negative economic and
public health outcomes, reduced performance at work and school, and impaired psychosocial functioning (see Table 1) (Leger, 2000).

Major industrial disasters, such as those at Chernobyl, Three Mile Island,   3
and Bhopal and serious accidents, including the *Exxon Valdez* and the *Chall-
enger,* have been officially attributed to errors in judgment caused by sleepiness in the workplace. The U.S. National Traffic Safety Board reports the
death rate related to drowsy driving may well surpass that of alcohol-related
crashes among young Americans. [2]

Table 1:   Impact of Insomnia

Insomnia can have a very serious impact on quality of life, productivity, and safety.

- People with insomnia are four times as likely to suffer from depression than people who sleep well.
- Lack of sleep due to insomnia may contribute to illness, including heart disease.
- Safety on the job, at home, and on the road may be affected by sleepiness.
- People with insomnia may miss more time from work or receive fewer promotions.
- After a poor night's sleep, many people report accomplishing fewer daily tasks and enjoying activities less.

Reading Critically

[1] Have you ever had difficulty getting a good night's sleep? How did you resolve the situation?

[2] What specific problems are associated with sleep deprivation?

Defining Insomnia

The Greeks were the first to describe insomnia, and it wasn't until the   4
1970s that criteria were established to describe different kinds of sleep disorders. There are over 70 specific sleep disorders, and insomnia is the most
common. Insomnia is defined as difficulty falling asleep, trouble staying asleep,
waking up too early in the morning, and nonrestorative sleep (American
Psychiatric Association, 1994). In fact, next-day consequences are the single
most important factor that supports a diagnosis of insomnia.

Primary Insomnia   A primary insomnia is the main pathological condition.   5
It is treatable and takes time to unravel the patterns that have created this condition.

Psychophysiological insomnia is a learned sleep-preventing association   6
that results in a complaint of poor sleep and daytime fatigue.

Idiopathic or childhood-onset insomnia is a lifelong inability to get ade-   7
quate sleep that is due to problems with the control of the sleep-wake system.

Sleep-state misperception is the reporting of the inability to sleep that is   8
without any objective sleep study findings (Attarian, 2004).

Secondary Insomnia   Secondary insomnias are conditions where the in-   9
somnia is a symptom of another disorder. ③ Forty-two percent of middle-
aged women experience menopause-related insomnia, which is secondary
insomnia (Attarian, 2004). Ninety percent of those diagnosed with depression report insomnia, which would also be considered a secondary insomnia (Ford & Kamerow, 1989). Psychiatric as well as medical and neurological
conditions and the medications used to treat them can disrupt sleep (Simon
& Vonkoff, 1997). Secondary insomnias are more easily identified and most
often respond to treatment of the underlying cause.

A Closer Look At Sleep

Sleep is objectively measured and recorded by electrical activity from the   10
cerebral cortex with an electroencephalography (EEG), eye movements
recorded with electro-oculography (EOG), and electromyelography (EMG)
to record muscle activity. Patterns of the measurements change as one moves
through the sleep stages. Here is a look at a 10-year-old girl's sleep pattern.

It's a school night for Maxine. Around 9:00, she is finishing her homework   11
and knows it is time for bed. She brushes her teeth, puts on her pajamas,
makes sure her stuffed animals are where she can find them, and calls for the

---

Reading Critically
③ What physical disorders can contribute to sleep problems?

family cat or dog to join her. She employs these rituals to get ready for bed. As Maxine puts her head on her pillow, she feels the fabric of her blanket against her skin. She hears the sound of the dishwasher or maybe the buzz of her parents talking in the other room. She thinks about the past day or maybe what lies ahead tomorrow. ◆ [4]

- Sleep stage 1—As Maxine lies still in her bed, she loses awareness of her surroundings. While the blanket is still touching her skin, she moves into the first stage of non-REM sleep called stage 1, and her awareness of the blanket changes. Her eyes roll back and forth and her muscles relax. Maxine's EEG shows alpha waves with a mix of theta waves. If we were to wake her now, she would arouse easily and possibly deny that she was asleep. In this stage she might experience a feeling of falling, something we call hypnic myoclonia, or sudden muscle contractions causing her leg to jerk. While these contractions are benign, sleep specialists do not know the cause of this phenomenon.

- Sleep stage 2—The household noises continue around Maxine, but she moves deeper and deeper into sleep. Stage 2 non-REM sleep is established when her EEG shows theta waves, K-complexes, and sleep spindles. Her eye movement stops and her brain waves become slower.

- Sleep stage 3—Stage 3 sleep is the beginning of deep non-REM sleep. Her EEG shows the extremely slow delta waves. These delta waves are periodically interrupted by the smaller theta waves. She is deeply asleep with her heart and breathing rate regular and slow.

- Sleep stage 4—During this stage of non-REM sleep, delta waves predominate and no eye movement or muscle activity occurs. It would be extremely difficult to arouse Maxine at this time. Stage 4 sleep allows for the body to rebuild and repair itself. During the first deep sleep of the night, Maxine's body secretes growth hormone, which helps cells divide and multiply, building new tissue for growth. Her cells are being repaired and regenerated and until she reaches age 18, this is where she will spend most of her sleep time. This is also the time when children might experience bedwetting, night terrors, and sleep walking.

- REM sleep—Maxine weaves in and out of stages 1 to 4 and then engages in rapid eye movement or REM sleep. On the EEG, REM sleep appears with choppy theta waves with short bursts of alpha and beta waves that look much like the EEC of wakefulness. At this time her breathing becomes more rapid, irregular, and shallow. Her eyes jerk rapidly in various

---

Reading Critically

◆ [4] How does the use of a specific person named "Maxine" help the author make her point?

directions and the peripheral muscles become temporarily paralyzed. REM sleep is dream time. If she woke at this time, she would describe her dream in detail. Significant data explain why we have non-REM sleep; however, REM sleep cannot be easily explained. Robert Stickgold with Harvard Medical School suggests that REM sleep helps lay down memory. One thing for certain is our dreams can be nonsensical. That is because the part of the brain active during REM sleep is not connecting with the part of our brain that provides logical and linear thought. [5]

Maxine moves in and out of these cycles through the night with the complete sleep cycle lasting 90 to 110 minutes. The first REM stage occurs during the last 20 minutes of the first cycle. As the night progresses, REM stages become longer and deep sleep gets shorter. By the end of the night, most sleep is in stages 1 and 2 or REM.   12

Newborns have REM onset with their sleep stages and spend little time in stages 1 and 2. The elderly are just the opposite, spending most of their time in stages 1 and 2, with less percentage of time in stages 3 to 4 and REM (Ancoli-lsreal, 2000). This explains why many elders describe sleep interruptions since they spend more time in the stages of sleep where they can be easily aroused. [6]   13

Overall, the healthy adult spends 50% of sleep in stages 1 and 2, 20% is spent in REM sleep, and the remaining 30% is spent in stages 3 and 4. People dream for about 2 hours each night. Should one have a poor night's sleep, the human body compensates for the loss by increasing the time spent in stages 3 and 4 as well as REM sleep. A sleep-deprived person will move quickly through stages 1 and 2 to get to the stages that allow for physical restoration.   14

You've Got Rhythm (Circadian, That Is)

Body functions are directed by a biological clock or circadian rhythm (Smolensky & Lamberg, 2000). Circadian is Latin for "about a day." The circadian rhythm is the maestro that keeps the body on track for stability and change. William Dement writes in *The Promise of Sleep* (1999) that the rotation of our planet as it spins its way around the sun is represented in miniature within our cells. The requirement for sleep and wakefulness, cognitive function, hormonal secretions, and other physiologic functions cycle regularly across each day. The circadian rhythms are generated by an internal pacemaker located in the suprachiasmic nucleus (SCN) of the hypothalamus. The main role of the SCN is to synchronize bodily functions with the   15

Reading Critically

[5] What is REM sleep? How important is it to our overall health?
[6] How do our sleep habits change as we get older?

environmental light-dark cycle. Light is the most potent stimulus for shifting the phase of our circadian cycle.

Circadian rhythms shift body temperatures and the drive to sleep corre- 16
lates with times when our temperature is at its lowest levels. The strongest drive to sleep coincides approximately at 2 to 4 AM for most individuals and the lesser vulnerable period at approximately 2 to 4 PM. While it is good to surrender to the drive in the early morning hours during our regular sleep time, our culture does not encourage or reward the afternoon siesta.

Many hormones are affected by these rhythms. Growth hormone is se- 17
creted during stages 3 and 4 during the night. Blood pressure increases in the morning, asthma worsens at night, and allergies get worse in the morning. The body's production of gastric acid reaches a pinnacle late at night and coincides with the pain of an ulcer. [7]

Circadian Sleep Disorders   Jet lag is a relatively new human phenomenon. It 18
occurs when we rapidly change time zones as a result of air travel. While your body is in the new time zone, your circadian rhythm is still in your home zone. [8]

Shift Work Sleep Disorder is the result of shifting sleep times to accom- 19
modate work and social activities several times during a week or month. The discomfort occurs as the body functions are trying to synchronize with the different times and duration of sleep (Buysse, 1990). It takes up to a week to resynchronize to working at night because humans are biologically organized for sleeping at night and active during the day. More than 15 million Americans have nontraditional work schedules that may conflict with their biological clocks. According to the 2002 *Sleep in America* poll (National Sleep Foundation, 2005), shift workers get less sleep on week-nights than regular day workers (6.5 versus 6.8 hours/night) and are more likely to sleep less than 6 hours per night (25% versus 13%). Many recovery room nurses have had patients who were slow to wake up after surgery. Some of these patients are midnight workers and may also admit to having worked the midnight shift the night before surgery. Although it would seem that a sleepless night before surgery would have some effect on the process and outcome of the patient receiving anesthesia for surgery, there is no clinical research to support or refute that. According to Dr. Michael McCue (personal communication, September 2, 2005), staff anesthesiologist and William Beaumont Hospital in Royal Oak, Michigan, the patient who has had little sleep the night before surgery does not require more or less anesthesia for surgery, nor is the patient more difficult to wake up postoperatively. Many recovery room nurses

---

Reading Critically

[7] How do you feel when you've had a good night's sleep?
[8] Have you ever had jet lag? How did it affect your sleeping habits?

have observed that such patients would like to sleep all day, and thus present a challenge to timely discharge from the outpatient surgical area.

How Much Sleep Do You Need?

Napoleon advocated six hours of sleep for a man, seven hours for a woman, and eight hours for a fool.

—*Anonymous*

Age is the main determinant of the sleep required each night. Newborns require 16 to 24 hours per day. Taken in 3 to 4 hour intervals throughout the day in the first few months of life, by age 2, the sleep need drops to 9 to 12 hours. Teens need 9 to 10 hours of sleep, and middle-aged adults need 7 to 9 hours. The elderly also require 7 to 8 hours of sleep, despite the myth that we require less sleep as we age.   20

Short sleepers thrive on only 4 to 5 hours of sleep each night. While these short sleepers are a rare breed, they do exist and are puzzled by the need for 7 to 8 hours of sleep by the rest of us. Again, the best way to determine sleep need is to evaluate how you feel the next day. [9]   21

During childhood, bedtime can be established about 9 to 10 PM. Most healthy children get in bed and are asleep within 20 to 30 minutes. This sleep cycle changes with adolescents. While they still need 9 to 10 hours each night, they have a delayed sleep onset, making it difficult for them to get to sleep until after midnight. Most adolescents have a difficult time getting up for school at 5:30 or 6:00 AM because they are only halfway through their sleep cycle. Thank goodness for weekends; that's when most teens make up the sleep they have missed during the week, only to have it disrupted again on Monday morning.   22

The elderly need 7 to 8 hours of sleep each night, but their sleep cycles also shift. Opposite from the adolescent delayed sleep onset, they have an advanced sleep onset. In other words, Grandma heads to bed early and gets up early, whereas the teenager goes to bed late and wants to sleep late. Considering comorbidities, such as benign prostatic hypertrophy or congestive heart failure, an elderly person can wake up 3 to 4 times a night and have difficulty getting back to sleep (Hauri, 1998).   23

Screening and Diagnosis

Any office visit provides an opportunity to discuss the risk or presence of problems with sleep. Since most patients do not offer this information, they need to be asked specific questions (National Institutes of Health, 1998). It   24

Reading Critically

[9] How many hours of sleep do you generally get each night? How many hours do you need?

is important to speak with family members who can provide helpful information about the patient's sleep habits and snoring.

- When did the problem begin?
- Do you or the person you sleep with snore?
- Do you have difficulty falling asleep?
- Do you wake up during the night and have trouble getting back to sleep?
- Do you feel sleepy during the day?
- Do you use any medications?
- What is your intake of alcohol, caffeine, or tobacco? [10]

A sleep diary is an excellent tool to increase awareness of patterns that are 25 barriers to a good night's sleep. Sleep diaries need to record a patient's bedtime, time to sleep onset, number of awakenings, total sleep time, use of sleep medications, time out of bed in the morning, and a subjective rating of sleep quality and daytime functioning. Patients need to document mealtimes, exercise times, and use of medications and alcohol. Sleep diaries can help uncover sleep problems, circadian sleep disorders, and poor sleep hygiene.

Depression, anxiety, menopause medications, or medical problems that 26 cause secondary insomnia need to be ruled out (Owens & Matthews, 1998). Once secondary insomnia has been ruled out and primary insomnia is identified, it is important to refer to a sleep specialist for further evaluation. Sleep specialists may order a sleep study to evaluate the patient's specific sleep architecture and make recommendations based on the findings.

It is common to hear the remark that the hospital is no place to get any 27 rest! There are many environmental factors in the hospital (noise, nursing routines, unfamiliar environment, uncomfortable mattress, no control over the thermostat, roommates, etc.) that interfere with sleep. In addition, the postoperative patient may be in pain or required to sleep in an uncustomary position. [11]

Perioperative insomnia appears to be a long standing phenomenon that 28 persists after discharge. Postoperative, self-rated insomnia is multifactorial and mainly explained by the amount of postoperative pain (Beydon, et al., 1994). According to Yasuma and Okada (1989), the incidence of insomnia (defined by early awakenings, initiating, and maintaining sleep) amounted to 72.9% on the night of two days before surgery, 86% on the night before the surgery, and 86.6% on the first night after surgery.

Reading Critically

[10] How would you answer all these questions?

[11] Have you ever tried to sleep in a hospital? How successful was the attempt?

Treating Insomnia with Behavioral and Pharmacological Interventions

The goals of treatment for patients with insomnia are four-fold: (1) resolve   29
the underlying problem(s), (2) prevent progression from acute to chronic insomnia, (3) restore and improve sleep quality and duration, and (4) improve
the quality of life (Becker, 1993).

Identifying the specific problem(s) is the start to effective treatment (Na-   30
tional Sleep Foundation, 2000). However, all insomniacs benefit from behavioral interventions (see Table 2). Sleep-deprived patients are usually
skeptical about trying behavioral techniques. Most have tried "just about
everything" before they seek medical help for the problem (Richardson,
2000). Educating about sleep stages and the importance of each will enroll
the patient and the family to try new interventions.

Table 2   Sleep Guidelines Used by Washington University Sleep
Medicine Center

1. Standardize sleep time—our bodies love rituals and go to bed only when sleepy.
2. Use the bed for sleep and sex only. Do not read, watch television, or eat in bed.
3. If unable to sleep, get up and move to another room. Stay up until you are definitely sleepy and then return to bed.
4. Set the alarm and get up at the same time every morning, regardless of how much you have slept through the night.
5. Do not nap.
6. Do not exercise just before going to bed.
7. Do not engage in stimulating activity just before bed.
8. Do not drink alcohol close to bedtime.
9. Eliminate clocks in the bedroom.
10. Before bedtime, schedule a period to review stressful events of the day.
11. Promote relaxation and sleep by focusing on quiescent tasks that occupy the mind, such as reading or listening to music.

Sleep Aids/Hypnotics   Mention sleep aids to most of the general public and   31
visions of Marilyn Monroe and Jimi Hendrix dance through their heads.
Sleep aids have gotten a bad rap. Not because of what they do, but what
happens when they are not taken as prescribed. Marilyn and Jimi are examples of "it's not the pill, it's the patient." Self-medication is usually
the first step for treating insomnia (National Institutes of Health Consensus Conference, 1984). Over-the-counter sleep aids and alcohol are the
most commonly used, with alcohol the first line of treatment for most insomniacs. General considerations for prescribing hypnotics are shown in
Table 3.

Table 3   Prescribing Hypnotics: General Considerations

- Use individual prescriptions for each patient.
- Prescribe the lowest effective dosage for the shortest amount of time.
- Consider the onset and duration of the medication.
- Consider prescribing a lower dosage for elderly patients and for patients with hepatic or renal disease.
- Use with caution in patients with compromised respiratory function.

The sleep/wake cycle is controlled by the frontal cortex and is influenced 32 by several neurotransmitters. Those that play a pivotal role in the wake cycle include dopamine, norepinephrine, histamine, acetylcholine, and glutamate (Ashlon, 1994). Neurotransmitters that are associated with sleep include serotonin, adenosine, and gamma-aminobutyric acid (GABA). Pharmaceutical agents aimed at inducing sleep will either antagonize the "wakefulness" neurotransmitters or stimulate the "sleepiness" neurotransmitiers. Barbiturates, benzodiazepines, and imidazopyradines or nonbenzodiazepines all push the GABA pedal to turn on sleep. Barbiturates act nonselectively, sort of a shotgun approach, to the GABA receptor creating multiple side effects. Benzodiazepines are a little bit more selective at the GABA receptor and are specific to muscle relaxation, reducing anxiety, and inducing sleep. The imidazopyradines or nonbenzodiazepines (Ambien, Sonata, Lunesta) are currently the most GABA-specific to induce sleep. 12

The first medications to treat insomnia were brought to market to treat 33 other symptoms and sedation was a side effect that proved beneficial. Until the 19th century, sleep aids contained opium or alcohol. While both worked to induce sleep, they came with the price tag of addiction, long half-life, next-day consequences, and were unsafe at high doses. The 1900s brought the development of the anesthesia compound called barbiturates that were prescribed as sleeping pills. Secobarbital (Seconal), amobarbitol (Amytol), and pentobarbital (Nembutal) had problems with developing tolerance and after several nights of use, the body needed higher doses for the same effect. The space between a therapeutic dose and lethal dose is very narrow with these medications and can induce deep unconsciousness and respiratory depression at high doses.

By the 1970s, benzodiazepines came on the market to be used for the 34 treatment of anxiety. Again, the benzodiazepines, and their side effect of sedation, were used to treat insomnia. They hoped they would avoid the

Reading Critically

12 Have you ever tried a prescription sleeping pill? Did you sleep well after taking it?

problems shown by the barbiturates until Valium caused wide publicity and was found to be addictive. The Food and Drug Administration (FDA) approved flurazepam (Dalmane), with a long half-life, as the first benzodiazepine for sleep. Halcion, with a shorter half-life, was the next FDA-approved sleeping pill. The FDA found the drugs to be entirely safe when taken at the recommended doses. Benzodiazepines act nonselectively at two central receptor sites in the GABA complex.

The relatively new class of medications called imidazopyradines, or non-benzodiazepines, are the most selective in inducing sleep in the GABA complex. Advantages of these non-benzodiazepines include a short sleep onset and short half-life, creating no next-day residual effects as well as little or no interference of sleep architecture (Stimmel, 1999). Zolpidem (Ambien) is the most prescribed hypnotic in the United States. Starting in France, Zolpidem has been available for 12 years and is safe and effective due to its specificity. The FDA has recently approved Ambien CR for insomnia, Ambien CR has a 6-hour half-life and can treat sleep onset, as well as sleep maintenance.   35

A new non-benzodiazepine called eszopiclone (Lunesta) became available in January 2005. It is the S isomer of zopiclone, with a 6-hour half-life, and is FDA approved for long-term treatment. Lunesta's 12-month study was the first of its kind for a prescription non-benzodiazepine for the treatment of insomnia.   36

The latest sleep medication, Rozerem, is a non-scheduled medication. It is a melatonin agonist (M1 and M2 receptors). It works in the melatonin pathway to turn off the alerting mechanism in the brain. The FDA approved this medication in July of 2005 for treating sleep onset insomnia.   37

Over-the-Counter Medications   Histamine is a neurotransmitter that keeps us awake. The over-the-counter (OTC) sleep aids were originally antihistamines used as allergy medications affecting the mast cells in the immune system. Antihistamines induce sleepiness by antagonizing histamine and the alertness function in the brain. It is not receptor specific and has side effects of dry mouth, dehydration, fatigue, difficulty concentrating, and constipation. With regular use (more than several nights in a row), they can quickly lose their effectiveness and may also interfere with normal sleep architecture by suppressing REM sleep.   38

In 1978, the FDA approved a new drug application providing for OTC marketing of doxylamine succinate for nighttime sleep-aid use. In 1982, the agency authorized the initial marketing of diphenhydramine Hcl and diphenhydramine citrate for this use. The only safe and effective nonprescription insomnia ingredients are antihistamines: diphenhydramine Hcl 50 mg (Unisom SleepGels, Sleepinal, Compoz, Simply Sleep) and doxylamine succinate 25 mg (Unisom SleepTabs). Diphenhydramine acts quickly, usu-   39 ally between 15 to 30 minutes and has a half-life of between 3 and 12 hours in adults.

Other prescribed medications work on the histamine receptors. Trazadone, 40 which is FDA approved to treat depression, creates significant sedation. It was not very successful as an antidepressant because of its sedating side effects. While it is not FDA approved for insomnia, it is widely used because of its effectiveness in inducing sleep and it is inexpensive (Mendelson & Aikens, 1999). Next-day consequences can be significant because the half-life of trazadone is 8 to 12 hours.

Melatonin[13] is a natural hormone with a sleep phase-shifting effect on 41 circadian rhythm. A placebo-controlled, cross-over study conducted on older adults with insomnia showed that melatonin at a physiologic dose (0.1), and intermediate dose (0.3), and a pharmacologic dose (3 mg) improved sleep efficiency. However, only the intermediate dose restored sleep to its normal quality. The challenge with over-the-counter products such as melatonin is there are no FDA controls in the manufacturing of these substances.

Summary

Healthcare providers are in a perfect position to help make sleep a prior- 42 ity in patient's lives. At the preoperative visit, the nurse has the opportunity to assess the patients sleep pattern and should encourage good sleep for the weeks prior to surgery. Just as we ask patients to stop smoking and taking specific medications (e.g., aspirin), we can counsel the patient to avoid a sleep deficit prior to surgery.

For a nurse to help patients improve their sleep hygiene, the nurse needs 43 to take care of his or her own sleep needs. Nursing education continues to lack in training to make sleep as important as the food groups and daily exercise. In 2002, The National Commission on Sleep Disorders Research (1993) determined that 63% of nursing schools had less than one hour curriculum on normal sleep, and 56% of programs had less than one hour of curriculum on sleep disorders. Graduate schools did not fare much better, with 86% showing less than five hours on sleep disorders and 17% provided no instruction of any form.[14] Research continues to show how insomnia has adverse effects not only on the individual suffering, but also on families and communities. The economic impact can be huge. (For example, the

---

Reading Critically

[13] Have you ever tried an over-the-counter sleep aid like melatonin? How useful was it in helping you get a good night's sleep?

[14] How much education on sleep disorders do medical students and nurses typically receive? Given the magnitude of sleep problems in our country, do you think this education is enough? Why or why not?

ambulatory surgery patients who are slow to wake up are slower to discharge from the hospital. This influences how many patients can be accommodated in the surgical areas.) The most effective treatment for most patients with insomnia is a multidisciplined approach consisting of appropriate use of hypnotics, improved sleep hygiene, and behavioral changes.

References

American Psychiatric Association (APA). (1994). *Diagnostic and Statistical Manual of Mental Disorders* [DSM-IV] (4th ed.). Washington, DC: APA.

Ancoli-lsreal, S. (2000). Insomnia in the elderly: A review for the primary care practitioner. *Sleep, 23,* Suppl 1, S23-S38.

Ashton. H. (1994). The effects of drugs on sleep. In R. Cooper (Ed.), *Sleep* (pp. 175–211). London: Chapman & Hall Medical.

Attarian, H. (2004). *Clinical Handbook of Insomnia.* Totowa, New Jersey: Human Press.

Becker, P. M. (1993). Insomnia: Use of a decision tree to assess and treat. *Postgraduate Medicine, 93,* 66–85.

Beydon, L., Rauss, A., Lofaso, F., Lui, N., Cherqui, D., Goldbenberg F., & Bonnet. F. (1994). Survey of the quality of sleep during the perioperative period. *Annals of French Anesthesia. 13,* 669–674.

Buysse. D. J. (1990). Insomnia. In M. J. Thorpe, *Handbook of Sleep Disorders* (pp. 375–433). New York, NY: Marcel Dekker.

Dement. W. C. (1999). *The Promise of Sleep.* New York: Delacorte Press.

Ford, D. E., & Kamerow, D. B. (1989). Epidemiologic study of sleep disturbances and psychiatric disorders: An opportunity for prevention? *JAMA, 262,* 1479–1484.

Gallop Organization for the National Sleep Foundation. (1995). *Sleep in America.* Princeton, NJ: National Sleep Foundation.

Hauri, P. J. (1998). Insomnia. *Clinical Chest Medicine, 19,* 157–108.

Leger, D. (2000). Public health and insomnia: Economic impact. *Sleep, 23*(suppl 3), S69–S76.

Mendelson, W. B., & Aikens, J. E. (1999). Insomnia: Exploring underlying processes and treatment [Monograph]. *Psychiatric Times.*

National Commission on Sleep Disorders Research. (1993). *Wake Up America: A National Sleep Alert.* Washington, DC: U.S. Government Printing Office, 2:114–149.

National Institutes of Health (NIH). (1998). *Insomnia: Assessment and Management in Primary Cure.* Washington, DC: NIH.

National Institutes of Health (NIH) Consensus Conference. (1984). Drugs and insomnia: The use of medications to promote sleep. *JAMA, 251,* 2410–2414.

National Sleep Foundation. (2005). Sleep in America Poll. Retrieved October 1. 2005. from http://www.sleepfoundation.org.

National Sleep Foundation (NSF). (2000). *Treating Insomnia in the Primary Care Setting.* Washington, DC: NSF.

Owens, J. F., & Matthews, K. A. (1998). Sleep disturbances in healthy middle-aged women. *Maturitas, 30,* 41–50.

Richardson, G. S. (2000). Managing insomnia in the primary care setting: Raising the issues. *Sleep, 23*(suppl 1). S9–S15.

Simon, G. E., & Vonkoff, M. (1997). Prevalence, burden, and treatment of insomnia in primary care. *American Journal of Psychiatry, 154,* 1417–1423.

Smolensky, M., & Lamberg, L. (2000). The body clock guide to better health: How to use our body's natural clock to light illness and achieve maximum health. New York: Henry Holt & Company.

Stimmel, G. L. (1999). Future directions in the drug treatment of insomnia [Monograph]. *Psychiatric Times.*

Yasuma, F., & Okada, T. (1989). Sleep disturbances complicated by surgical stress: a questionnaire survey of fifty patients. *Masaui, 38*(l), 66–70.

UNDERSTANDING DETAILS

1. Define insomnia in your own words. What is the difference between primary and secondary insomnia?
2. What are the most significant consequences of insomnia?
3. Describe the stages of a normal sleep cycle.
4. Explain the Circadian rhythm in your own words. What does it help us accomplish?

THINKING CRITICALLY

5. According to the author, why is sleep so important to a healthy life?
6. Why do we need different amounts of sleep at different times in our lives?
7. What role can nurses play in the treatment of insomnia? Is this an important part of the process in your opinion?
8. In what ways do you believe sleep should be a priority in our lives? Do you follow healthy sleep patterns?

DISCOVERING RHETORICAL STRATEGIES

9. Do the subheadings help guide you through the essay? Explain your answer.
10. What is the author's purpose in this article?
11. What rhetorical modes does Nadolski use to accomplish her purpose? Give an example of each strategy you find.
12. This essay demonstrates the American Psychological Association (APA) documentation style. How is this documentation style different from MLA?

MAKING CONNECTIONS

13. Compare and contrast the quality of research in the essays by Nadolski, Ehren-reich ("The Ecstasy of War"), and/or Edward Ayers ("The American Civil War, Emancipation, and Reconstruction on the World Stage"). Which essay do you find most convincing? Why?

14. Evaluate the use of medical data in essays by Nadolski, Jessica Mitford ("Behind the Formaldehyde Curtain"), Sucheng Chan ("You're Short, Besides!), and/or Michael Dorris ("The Broken Cord"). Which author uses this information most skillfully? Why?

15. Both Nadolski and Stephen Jay Gould ("Dorothy, It's Really Oz") use scien-tific information to convince their audience. How is the authors' purpose dif-ferent in each essay?

IDEAS FOR DISCUSSION/WRITING

Preparing to Write

Write freely about your health, both physical and mental: How do you feel on a daily basis? To what do you attribute this general feeling? How important is sleep to your physical and mental health? Are you generally able to follow a healthy diet? Do you exercise regularly? When you are rushed, where do you compromise? Does this compromise affect your health in any way? Do you think any of these health issues affect your performance in college? What could you do to take better care of yourself?

Choosing a Topic

1. You have been invited back to your high school to talk to the senior class about college: What is your best advice about performing well in college? Include academic issues, time management, and health concerns in your presentation. Prepare your ideas in the form of an essay before you deliver your talk.

2. Take an informal poll of ten to fifteen college students to determine their sleep habits; then write an essay that records your general observations and analyzes these observations. Do you notice any common occurrences? What do you make of the data you collected?

3. Write an essay that outlines and analyzes your formula for a healthy existence in college. Considering the extra pressures and erratic sleep that college students often experience, how do you keep yourself mentally and physically healthy?

4. Mick Winter has a personal Web site called "Insomnia? 41 Simple Tips to Help You Get to Sleep" (http://www.well.com/~mick/insomnia). Visit this Web site and scroll through the bulleted links. Click on several of the links to read his suggestions about what works and what doesn't work when people try to fight insomnia. With these in mind, create your own contrasting Web site entitled "13 Simple Tips for Staying Up All Night." Remember the importance of audi-ence and tone as you compose your suggestions.

Before beginning your essay, you might want to consult the checklists on page 560.

EDWARD AYERS   (1953–   )

The American Civil War, Emancipation, and Reconstruction on the World Stage

Edward Ayers, who is currently Dean of the College and Graduate School of Arts and Sciences at the University of Virginia, was educated at the University of Tennessee and later at Yale University, where he earned his Ph.D. in American Studies. He has written nine books, the most prominent of which is *The Promise of the New South: Life After Reconstruction,* which was a finalist for the National Book Award and the Pulitzer Prize and was named the best book on the history of American race relations and the South in 1992. Additional publications include *Vengeance and Justice: Crime and Punishment in the Nineteenth-Century American South* (1984), *All Over the Map: Rethinking American Regions* (1996), *In the Presence of Mine Enemies: War in the Heart of America* (2003), and *What Caused the Civil War* (2005). A brilliant and charismatic classroom instructor, Ayers has won many teaching prizes, most recently the 2003 Carnegie Foundation National Professor of the Year Award for Doctoral and Research Universities. Ayers lives in Charlottesville, Virginia, with his wife of nearly 32 years and his two college-age children. An avid basketball player, he participates in a game every Sunday that has been going on for fifteen years. His advice to students using *The Prose Reader* is "to imagine that every word you use costs you money. This will make you a better writer because you will write with greater force and clarity."

Preparing to Read

This article was first published in the *OAH Magazine of History*. In it, Edward Ayers tries to present the causes and effects of the Civil War to the general public.

Exploring Experience: As you prepare to read this essay, consider your perspective on the American Civil War: Who fought in this war? Why did they fight? What did the war accomplish? What are other alternatives to war? Were these options available in the 1850s? Why or why not? What else do you know about the Civil War? Was this a successful war in your view?

Learning Online: Spike Lee and Kevin Willmott directed a new mock-documentary called *The Confederate States of America,* which analyzes the United States as if the South had won the Civil War. Go to the movie Web site (http://www.csathemovie.com), and view the "Trailer" by clicking the link in the center of the page. Consider Lee's and Willmott's ideas about this fictional future as you read Edward Ayers's essay.

A mericans demanded the world's attention during their Civil War and   1
Reconstruction. Newspapers around the globe reported the latest
news from the United States as one vast battle followed another, as
the largest system of slavery in the world crashed into pieces, as American
democracy expanded to include people who had been enslaved only a few
years before.[1]

Both the North and the South appealed to the global audience. Abraham   2
Lincoln argued that his nation's Civil War "embraces more than the fate of
these United States. It presents to the whole family of man, the question,
whether a constitutional republic, or a democracy . . . can, or cannot, maintain its territorial integrity." The struggle, Lincoln said, was for "a vast future,"
a struggle to give all men "a fair chance in the race of life."[2] Confederates
claimed that they were also fighting for a cause of world-wide significance:
self-determination. Playing down the centrality of slavery to their new nation, white Southerners built their case for independence on the right of
free citizens to determine their political future.[3][2]

People in other nations could see that the massive struggle in the United   3
States embodied conflicts that had been appearing in different forms throughout the world. Defining nationhood, deciding the future of slavery, rein-
venting warfare for an industrial age, reconstructing a former slave society—all
these played out in the American Civil War.

By no means a major power, the United States was nevertheless woven into   4
the life of the world. The young nation touched, directly and indirectly, India
and Egypt, Hawaii and Japan, Russia and Canada, Mexico and Cuba, the
Caribbean and Brazil, Britain and France. The country was still very much
an experiment in 1860,[3] a representative government stretched over an
enormous space, held together by law rather than by memory, religion, or
monarch. The American Civil War, played out on the brightly lit stage of a
new country, would be a drama of world history. How that experiment fared
in its great crisis—regardless of what happened—would eventually matter to
people everywhere.

*****

More obviously than most nations, the United States was the product of   5
global history. Created from European ideas, involvement in Atlantic trade,
African slavery, conquest of land from American Indians and European powers, and massive migration from Europe, the United States took shape as the

---

Reading Critically

[1] According to Ayers, why did America demand the world's attention during the Civil War?

[2] Why did the South downplay their reliance on slavery in arguing for its independence?

[3] In what way was the United States "still very much an experiment in 1860"?

world watched. Long before the Civil War, the United States embodied the possibilities and contradictions of modern western history.

Slavery was the first, most powerful, and most widespread kind of glob-   6 alization in the first three centuries after Columbus. While colonies came and went, while economies boomed and crashed, slavery relentlessly grew—and nowhere more than in the United States. By the middle of the nineteenth century, the slave South had assumed a central role on the world stage. Cotton emerged as the great global commodity, driving factories in the most advanced economies of the world. The slaves of the South were worth more than all the railroads and factories of the North and South combined; slavery was good business and shrewd investment. ❹

While most other slave societies in the hemisphere gradually moved to-   7 ward freedom, the American South moved toward the permanence of slavery. Southerners and their Northern allies, eager to expand, led the United States in a war to seize large parts of Mexico and looked hungrily upon the Caribbean and Central America. Of all the slave powers—including the giants of Brazil and Cuba, which continued to import slaves legally long after the United States—only the South and its Confederacy fought a war to maintain bondage.[4]

Ideas of justice circulated in global intercourse just as commodities did and   8 those ideas made the American South increasingly anomalous as a modern society built on slavery. Demands for universal freedom came into conflict with ancient traditions of subordination. European nations, frightened by revolt in Haiti and elsewhere and confident of their empires' ability to prosper without slavery, dismantled slavery in their colonies in the western hemisphere while Russia dismantled serfdom.

Black and white abolitionists in the American North, though a tiny de-   9 spised minority, worked with British allies to fight the acceptance of slavery in the United States. A vision of the South as backward, cruel, and power-hungry gained credence in many places in the North and took political force in the Republican party. The global economy of commodities and ideology, demanding cotton while attacking slavery, put enormous and contradictory strains on the young American nation.[5] ❺

Meanwhile, a new urge to define national identity flowed through the   10 western world in the first half of the nineteenth century. That determination took quite different forms. While some people still spoke of the universal

---

Reading Critically

❹ Why did some people consider slavery "good business and shrewd investment"?

❺ How did the demand for cotton, coupled with the global attack on slavery, "put enormous and contradictory strains on the young American nation"?

dreams of the French and American Revolutions, of inalienable attributes of humankind, others spoke of historical grievance, ethnic unity, and economic self-interest. Many longed for new nations built around bonds of heritage, imagined and real.[6]

White Southerners, while building their case for secession with the language of constitutions and rights, presented themselves as a people profoundly different from white Northerners. They sought sanction for secession in the recent histories of Italy, Poland, Mexico, and Greece, where rebels rose up against central powers to declare their suppressed nationhood, where native elites led a "natural, necessary protest and revolt" against a "crushing, killing union with another nationality and form of society."[7]   11

As the South threatened to secede, the Republicans, a regional party themselves, emphasized the importance of Union for its own sake, the necessity of maintaining the integrity of a nation created by legal compact. It fell to the United States, the Republicans said, to show that large democracies could survive internal struggles and play a role in world affairs alongside monarchies and aristocracies.[8]   12

Once it became clear that war would come, the North and the South seized upon the latest war-making strategies and technologies. From the outset, both sides innovated at a rapid pace and imported ideas from abroad. Railroads and telegraphs extended supply lines, sped troop reinforcements, and permitted the mobilization of vast armies. ⑥ Observers from Europe and other nations watched carefully to see how the Americans would use these new possibilities. The results were mixed. Ironclad ships, hurriedly constructed, made a difference in some Southern ports and rivers, but were not seaworthy enough to play the role some had envisioned for them. Submarines and balloons proved disappointments, unable to deliver significant advantages. Military leaders, rather than being subordinated by anonymous machinery, as some expected, actually became more important than before, their decisions amplified by the size of their armies and the speed of communication and transport.[9]   13

The scale and drama of the Civil War that ravaged America for four years, across an area larger than the European continent, fascinated and appalled a jaded world. A proportion of the population equal to five million people today died and the South suffered casualties at a rate equal to those who would be decimated in Europe's mechanized wars of the twentieth century.   14

The size, innovation, and destructiveness of the American Civil War have led some, looking back, to describe it as the first total war, the first truly modern war. Despite new technologies and strategies, however, much of the   15

Reading Critically

⑥ How did railroads and telegraphs affect the Civil War?

Civil War remained old-fashioned. The armies in the American Civil War still moved vast distances on foot or with animals. The food soldiers ate and the medical care they received showed little advance over previous generations of armies. [7] The military history of the Civil War grew incrementally from world history and offered incremental changes to what would follow. Although, late in the war, continuous campaigning and extensive earthen entrenchments foreshadowed World War I, Europeans did not grasp the deadly lesson of the American Civil War: combining the tactics of Napoleon with rapid-fire weapons and trenches would culminate in horrors unanticipated at Shiloh and Antietam. [10]

Diplomacy proved challenging for all sides in the American crisis. The fragile balance of power on the Continent and in the empires centered there limited the range of movement of even the most powerful nations. The Confederacy's diplomatic strategy depended on gaining recognition from Great Britain and France, using cotton as a sort of blackmail, but European manufacturers had stockpiled large supplies of cotton in anticipation of the American war. British cartoonists, sympathetic to the Confederacy, ridiculed Abraham Lincoln at every opportunity, portraying him as an inept bumpkin—until his assassination, when Lincoln suddenly became sainted. [8] Overall, the North benefited from the inaction of the British and the French, who could have changed the outcome and consequences of the war by their involvement. [11] 16

Inside the United States, the change unleashed by the war was as profound as it was unexpected. Even those who hated slavery had not believed in 1861 that generations of captivity could be ended overnight and former slaves and former slaveholders left to live together. The role of slavery in sustaining the Confederacy through humbling victories over the Union created the conditions in which Abraham Lincoln felt driven and empowered to issue the Emancipation Proclamation. The Union, briefly and precariously balanced between despair and hope, between defeat and victory, was willing in 1862 to accept that bold decision as a strategy of war and to enlist volunteers from among black Americans. [12] [9] 17

The nearly 200,000 African Americans who came into the war as soldiers and sailors for the Union transformed the struggle. The addition of those men, greater in number than all the forces at Gettysburg, allowed the Union to build its advantage in manpower without pushing reluctant Northern whites into the draft. The enlistment of African Americans in the struggle for their own freedom ennobled the Union cause and promised to set a 18

Reading Critically

[7] In what ways was the war "old-fashioned"?

[8] How did the political cartoons of Lincoln change after his assassination?

[9] How did the Emancipation Proclamation help the North in the Civil War?

new global standard for the empowerment of formerly enslaved people. The world paid admiring attention to the brave and disciplined black troops in blue uniforms.[13]

The destruction of American slavery, a growing system of bondage of nearly four million people in one of the world's most powerful economies and most dynamic nation-states, was a consequence of world importance. Nowhere else besides Haiti did slavery end so suddenly, so completely, and with so little compensation for former slaveholders.[14] Had the United States failed to end slavery in the 1860s the world would have felt the difference. An independent Confederate States of America would certainly have put its enslaved population to effective use in coal mines, steel mills, and railroad building, since industrial slavery had been employed before secession and became more common during wartime. Though such a Confederacy might have found itself stigmatized, its survival would have meant the evolution of slavery into a new world of industrialization. The triumph of a major autonomous state built around slavery would have set a devastating example for the rest of the world, an encouragement to forces of reaction. It would have marked the repudiation of much that was liberating in Western thought and practice over the preceding two hundred years.[15] 🔟 20

Driven by the exigencies of war, Northern ideals of color-blind freedom and justice, so often latent and suppressed, suddenly if briefly bloomed in the mid-1860s. The Radical Republicans sought to create a black male American freedom based on the same basis as white male American freedom: property, citizenship, dignity, and equality before the law. They launched a bold Reconstruction to make those ideals a reality, their effort far surpassing those of emancipation anywhere else in the world. The white South resisted with vicious vehemence, however, and the Republicans, always ambivalent about black autonomy and eager to maintain their partisan power, lost heart after a decade of bitter, violent, and costly struggle in Reconstruction. Northern Democrats, opposing Reconstruction from the outset, hastened and celebrated its passing.[16]

If former slaves had been permitted to sustain the enduring political power they tried to build, if they had gone before juries and judges with a chance of fair treatment, if they had been granted homesteads to serve as a first step toward economic freedom, then Reconstruction could be hailed as a turning point in world history equal to any revolution. 🔟 Those things did not happen, however. The white South claimed the mantle of victim, of a

---

Reading Critically

🔟 What kind of an example would the South have set for the rest of the world if it had won the Civil War?

🔟 What modifications would Reconstruction have needed to be more successful?

people forced to endure an unjust and unnatural subordination. They won international sympathy for generations to follow in films such as Birth of a Nation (1915) and Gone With the Wind (1939), which viewed events through the eyes of sympathetic white Southerners. Reconstruction came to be seen around the world not as the culmination of freedom but as a mistake, a story of the dangers of unrealistic expectations and failed social engineering. Though former slaves in the American South quietly made more progress in landholding and general prosperity than former slaves elsewhere, the public failures of Reconstruction obscured the progress black Southerners wrenched from the postwar decades.[17]

When the South lost its global monopoly of cotton production during the Civil War, governments, agents, and merchants around the world responded quickly to take the South's place and to build an efficient global machinery to supply an ever-growing demand in the world market. As a result, generations of black and white sharecroppers would compete with Indian, Brazilian, and Egyptian counterparts in a glutted market in which hard work often brought impoverishment. The South adapted its economy after the war as well. By the 1880s, the South's rates of urban growth, manufacturing, and population movement kept pace with the North—a remarkable shift for only twenty years after losing slavery and the Civil War—but black Southerners were excluded from much of the new prosperity.[18] 12

The destruction of slavery, a major moral accomplishment of the United States Army, of Abraham Lincoln, and of the enslaved people themselves, would be overshadowed by the injustice and poverty that followed in the rapidly changing South, a mockery of American claims of moral leadership in the world. Black Southerners would struggle, largely on their own, for the next one hundred years. Their status, bound in an ever-tightening segregation, would stand as a rebuke to the United States in world opinion. The postwar South and its new system of segregation, in fact, became an explicit model for South Africa. That country created apartheid as it, like the American South, developed a more urban and industrial economy based on racial subordination.

Americans read about foreign affairs on the same pages that carried news of Reconstruction in the South. Even as the Southern states struggled to write new constitutions, Secretary of State William Henry Seward purchased Alaska in 1867 as a step toward the possible purchase of British Columbia. President Grant considered annexation of Santo Domingo, partly as a base for black Southern emigration; he won the support of black abolitionist Frederick Douglass, who wanted to help the Santo Domingans, but was opposed by Radical Republican Senator Charles Sumner.

22

23

24

Reading Critically

12 Why were black Southerners excluded from the South's prosperity after the war?

Americans paid close attention to Hawaii in these same years. Mark Twain   25
visited the islands in 1866, and Samuel Armstrong—the white founder of
Hampton Institute, where Booker T. Washington was educated—argued that
Hawaiians and former slaves in the South needed similar discipline to become
industrious. At the same time, Seward signed a treaty with China to help
supply laborers to the American West, a treaty that laid the foundation for a
large migration in the next few decades. In 1871, American forces intervened militarily in Korea, killing 250 Korean soldiers. The leaders of the
Americans admitted they knew little about their opponents, but brought the
same assumptions about race to the conflict that they brought to their dealings with all non-Europeans everywhere. Koreans—like Hawaiians, Chinese,
American Indians, and African Americans—needed to be disciplined, taught,
and controlled. **13**

No master plan guided Americans in their dealings with other peoples.   26
In all of these places, the interests of American businessmen, the distortions
of racial ideology, and hopes for partisan political advantage at home jostled
with one another. As a result, the consequences of these involvements were
often unclear and sometimes took generations to play out. Nevertheless,
they remind us that Americans paid close attention to what was happening
elsewhere, whether in the Franco-Prussian War (1870–1871), where the evolution of warfare continued to become more mechanized and lethal, or the
Paris Commune (1871), where some thought they saw the result of unbri-
dled democracy in chaos and violence—and wondered if Reconstruction did
not represent a similar path.

Some people around the world were surprised that the United States did   27
not use its enormous armies after the Civil War to seize Mexico from the
French, Canada from the English, or Cuba from the Spanish. Conflict among
the great powers on the European Continent certainly opened an opportunity and the United States had expanded relentlessly and opportunistically
throughout its history. Few Americans, though, had the stomach for new adventures in the wake of the Civil War. The fighting against the American Indians on the Plains proved warfare enough for most white Americans in the
1870s and 1880s.[19]

The United States focused its postwar energies instead on commerce. Con-   28
solidated under Northern control, the nation's economy proved more for-
midable than ever before. The United States, its economic might growing
with each passing year, its railroad network and financial systems consoli-
dated, its cities and towns booming, its population surging westward, its mines

---

Reading Critically

13 How did America's "assumptions about race" affect its relationships with non-Europeans
everywhere?

turning out massive amounts of coal and precious minerals, its farms remarkably productive, and its corporations adopting new means of expansion and administration, became a force throughout the world. American engineers oversaw projects in Asia, Africa, and Latin America. American investors bought stock in railroads, factories, and mines around the globe. American companies came to dominate the economies of nations in Latin America.[20]

Americans became famous as rich, energetic, and somewhat reckless players amid the complexity of the world. As the Civil War generation aged, younger men looked with longing on possible territorial acquisitions in their own hemisphere and farther afield. They talked openly of proving themselves, as their fathers and grandfathers had, on the battlefield. Some welcomed the fight against the Spanish and the Filipinos in 1898 as a test of American manhood and nationalism. The generation that came of age in 1900 built monuments to the heroes of the Civil War but seldom paused to listen to their stories of war's horror and costs.   29

*****

The American Civil War has carried a different meaning for every generation of Americans. In the 1920s and 1930s leading historians in a largely isolationist United States considered the Civil War a terrible mistake, the product of a "blundering generation." After the triumph of World War II and in the glow of the Cold War's end, leading historians interpreted the Civil War as a chapter in the relentless destruction of slavery and the spread of democracy by the forces of modernization over the forces of reaction. Recently, living through more confusing times, some historians have begun to question straightforward stories of the war, emphasizing its contradictory meanings, unfulfilled promises, and unintended outcomes.[21] 14   30

The story of the American Civil War changes as world history lurches in unanticipated directions and as people ask different questions of the past. Things that once seemed settled now seem less so. The massive ranks, fortified trenches, heavy machinery, and broadened targets of the American Civil War once seemed to mark a step toward the culmination of "total" war. But the wars of the twenty-first century, often fought without formal battles, are proving relentless and boundless, "total" in ways the disciplined armies of the Union and Confederacy never imagined.[22] Nations continue to come apart over ancient grievances and modern geopolitics, the example of the United States notwithstanding. Coerced labor did not end in the nineteenth century, but instead has mutated and adapted to changes in the global economy. "A fair chance in the race of life" has yet to arrive for much of the world.   31

Reading Critically

14 How have opinions about the Civil War changed over the years?

The great American trial of war, emancipation, and reconstruction mat-   32
tered to the world. It embodied struggles that would confront people on
every continent and it accelerated the emergence of a new global power. The
American crisis, it was true, might have altered the course of world history
more dramatically, in ways both worse and better, than what actually tran-
spired. The war could have brought forth a powerful and independent Confederacy based on slavery or it could have established with its Reconstruction
a new global standard of justice for people who had been enslaved. As it was,
the events of the 1860s and 1870s in the United States proved both powerful and contradictory in their meaning for world history. ◆15

Endnotes

1. For other portrayals of the Civil War in international context, see David
   M. Porter, "Civil War," in C. Vann Woodward, ed., <u>The Comparative Approach to American History</u> (New York: Basic Books, 1968), pp. 135–45;
   Carl N. Degler, <u>One Among Many: The Civil War in Comparative Per-
   spective</u>, 29th Annual Robert Fortenbaugh Memorial Lecture (Gettysburg, PA: Gettysburg College, 1990); Robert E. May, ed., <u>The Union, the
   Confederacy, and the Atlantic Rim</u> (West Lafayette, IN: Purdue University Press, 1995); Peter Kolchin, <u>A Sphinx on the American Land:
   The Nineteenth-Century South in Comparative Perspective</u> (Baton
   Rouge: Louisiana State University Press, 2003). My view of the workings of world history has been influenced by C. A. Bayly, <u>The Birth of
   the Modern World, 1780–1914: Global Connections and Comparisons</u>
   (Maiden, MA: Blackwell, 2004). Bayly emphasizes that "in the nineteenth century, nation-states and contending territorial empires took on
   sharper lineaments and became more antagonistic to each other at the
   very same time as the similarities, connections, and linkages between
   them proliferated." (p. 2). By showing the "complex interaction between
   political organization, political ideas, and economic activity," Bayly avoids
   the teleological models of modernization, nationalism, and liberalism
   that have dominated our understanding of the American Civil War.
2. Lincoln quoted in James M. McPherson, <u>Abraham Lincoln and the Second American Revolution</u>, reprint (New York: Oxford University Press:
   1992, 1991), p. 28.
3. The seminal work is Drew Gilpin Faust, <u>The Creation of Confederate
   Nationalism: Ideology and Identity in the Civil War South</u> (Baton

---

Reading Critically

◆15 How did the events of the Civil War prove "both powerful and contradictory" in world
history?

Rouge: Louisiana State University Press, 1988). For an excellent synthesis of the large literature on this topic, see Anne S. Rubin, <u>A Shattered Nation: The Rise and Fall of the Confederacy, 1861–1868</u> (Chapel Hill: University of North Carolina Press, 2005).

4. For a useful overview, see Robert W. Fogel, <u>Without Consent or Contract: The Rise and Fall of American Slavery</u> (New York: W. W. Norton, 1989).

5. David Brion Davis, <u>Slavery and Human Progress</u> (New York: Oxford University Press, 1984); Davis, <u>The Problem of Slavery in the Age of Revolution, 1770–1823</u> (Ithaca, NY: Cornell University Press, 1975), and Davis, <u>Inhuman Bondage: The Rise and Fall of Slavery in the New World</u> (Oxford University Press, 2006).

6. For helpful overviews of the global situation, see Steven Hahn, "Class and State in Postemancipation Societies: Southern Planters in Comparative Perspective," <u>American Historical Review</u> 95 (February 1990): 75–98, and Hahn, <u>A Nation Under Our Feet: Black Political Struggles in the Rural South From Slavery to the Great Migration</u> (Cambridge, MA: Belknap Press of Harvard University Press, 2003).

7. Quoted in Faust, <u>Creation of Confederate Nationalism</u>, p. 13.

8. There is a large literature on this subject, not surprisingly. A useful recent treatment is Susan-Mary Grant, <u>North Over South: Northern Nationalism and American Identity in the Antebellum Era</u> (Lawrence: University of Kansas Press, 2000). Peter Kolchin also offers penetrating comments on nationalism in <u>A Sphinx on the American Land</u>, 89–92.

9. Brian Holden Reid, <u>The American Civil War and the Wars of the Industrial Revolution</u> (London: Cassell, 1999), 211–13; John E. Clark Jr., <u>Railroads in the Civil War: The Impact of Management on Victory and Defeat</u> (Baton Rouge: Louisiana State University Press, 2001); Robert G. Angevine, <u>The Railroad and the State: War, Politics, and Technology in Nineteenth-Century America</u> (Stanford, CA: Stanford University Press, 2004).

10. For a range of interesting essays on this subject, see Stig Förster and Jörg Nagler, eds. <u>On the Road to Total War: The American Civil War and the German Wars of Unification, 1861–1871</u> (Washington, DC: The German Historical Institute, 1997).

11. See D. P. Crook, <u>The North, the South, and the Powers, 1861–1865</u> (New York: Wiley, 1974), R. J. M. Blackett, <u>Divided Hearts: Britain and the American Civil War</u> (Baton Rouge: Louisiana State University Press, 2001), James M. McPherson, <u>Crossroads of Freedom: Antietam</u> (Oxford: Oxford University Press, 2002), May, ed., <u>The Union, the Confederacy, and the Atlantic Rim</u>, and Charles M. Hubbard, <u>The Burden of Confederate Diplomacy</u> (Knoxville: University of Tennessee Press, 1998).

12. See Allen C. Guelzo, <u>Lincoln's Emancipation Proclamation: The End of Slavery in America</u> (New York: Simon and Schuster, 2004).

13. See Joseph T. Glatthaar, <u>Forged in Battle: The Civil War Alliance of Black Soldiers and White Officers</u> (New York: Free Press, 1990).

14. See Leon Litwack, <u>Been in the Storm So Long: The Aftermath of Slavery</u>, 1st Vintage ed. (New York: Vintage, 1980, 1979) and the major documentary collection edited by Ira Berlin, Leslie S. Rowland, and their colleagues, sampled in <u>Free At Last: A Documentary History of Slavery, Freedom, and the Civil War</u> (New York: The New Press, 1992).

15. See Davis, <u>Slavery and Human Progress</u>, for a sweeping perspective on this issue.

16. The classic history is Eric Foner, <u>Reconstruction: America's Unfinished Revolution, 1863–1877</u> (New York: Harper and Row, 1988). I have offered some thoughts on Reconstruction's legacy in "Exporting Reconstruction" in <u>What Caused the Civil War? Reflections on the South and Southern History</u> (New York: W. W. Norton, 2005).

17. On the legacy of Reconstruction, see David W. Blight, <u>Race and Reunion: The Civil War in American Memory</u> (Cambridge, MA: Belknap Press of Harvard University Press, 2001).

18. For a fascinating essay on the South's loss of the cotton monopoly, see Sven Beckert, "Emancipation and Empire: Reconstructing the Worldwide Web of Cotton Production in the Age of the American Civil War," <u>American Historical Review</u> 109 (December 2004): 1405–38. On South Africa: John W. Cell, <u>The Highest Stage of White Supremacy: The Origins of Segregation in South Africa and the American South</u> (Cambridge: Cambridge University Press, 1982) and George M. Fredrickson, <u>White Supremacy: A Comparative Study in American and South African History</u> (New York: Oxford University Press, 1981).

19. See the discussion in the essays by Robert E. May and James M. McPherson in May, ed., <u>The Union, the Confederacy, and the Atlantic Rim</u>.

20. For the larger context, see Eric J. Hobsbawm, <u>The Age of Empire, 1875–1914</u> (New York: Pantheon, 1987) and Bayly, <u>Birth of the Modern World</u>.

21. I have described this literature and offered some thoughts on it in the essay "Worrying About the Civil War" in my <u>What Caused the Civil War?</u>

22. Reid, <u>American Civil War</u>, p. 213.

Bibliography

Surprisingly, no one book covers the themes of this essay. To understand this era of American history in global context, we need to piece together accounts from a variety of books and articles. For recent overviews of different components of these years, see Jay Sexton, "Towards a Synthesis of Foreign Relations in the Civil War Era, 1848–1877," American Nineteenth-Century History 5 (Fall 2004): 50–73, and Amy Kaplan, The Anarchy of Empire in the Making of U. S. Culture (Cambridge, MA: Harvard University Press, 2002).

Robert E. May, in the introduction to the book he edited, The Union, the Confederacy, and the Atlantic Rim (West Lafayette, IN: Purdue University Press, 1995), provides a useful summary of the larger context of the war. Though it is older, the perspective of D. P. Crook, The North, the South, and the Powers, 1861–1865 (New York: Wiley, 1974) brings a welcome worldliness to the discussion. On the crucial debate in Britain, see Howard Jones, Union in Peril: The Crisis Over British Intervention in the Civil War (Chapel Hill: University of North Carolina Press, 1992) and R. J. M. Blackett, Divided Hearts: Britain and the American Civil War (Baton Rouge: Louisiana State University Press, 2001).

James M. McPherson offers characteristically insightful, and hopeful, analysis in several places. Perhaps the single best focused portrayal of the interplay between events in the United States and in the Atlantic World is in his Crossroads of Freedom: Antietam (Oxford: Oxford University Press, 2002). McPherson's essay, " 'The Whole Family of Man': Lincoln and the Last Best Hope Abroad," in May, ed., The Union, the Confederacy, and the Atlantic Rim, makes the fullest case for the larger significance of the war in encouraging liberal movements and belief around the world.

Peter Kokhirfs, A Sphinx on the American Land: The Nineteenth-Century South in Comparative Perspective (Baton Rouge: Louisiana State University Press, 2003), offers an elegant and up-to-date survey that puts the conflict in the larger context of emancipation movements. A useful overview appears in Steven Hahn, "Class and State in Postemancipation Societies: Southern Planters in Comparative Perspective," American Historical Review 95 (February 1990): 75–98.

Another pioneering work is Drew Gilpin Faust, The Creation of Confederate Nationalism: Ideology and Identity in the Civil War South (Baton Rouge: Louisiana State University Press, 1988). Faust changed historians' perspective on nationalism in the South, which had been considered largely fraudulent before her account. Building on Faust are two recent books that offer fresh interpretations: Anne S. Rubin, A Shattered Nation: The Rise and Fall of the Confederacy, 1861–1868 (Chapel Hill: University of North Carolina Press, 2005) and Susan-Mary Grant, North Over South: Northern Nationalism and American Identity in the Antebellum Era (Lawrence: University of Kansas Press, 2000).

On the much-debated issue of the relative modernity and totality of the Civil War, see Stig Förster and Jörg Nagler, eds., On the Road to Total War:

The American Civil War and the German Wars of Unification, 1861–1871 (Washington, DC: The German Historical Institute, 1997); the essays by Stanley L. Engerman and J. Matthew Gallman, Earl J. Hess, Michael Fellman, and Richard Current are especially helpful. Brian Holden Reid, in The American Civil War and the Wars of the Industrial Revolution (London: Cassell, 1999), offers a concise but insightful portrayal of the war in larger military context.

For a powerful representation of the role of slavery in this history, David Brion Davis's works are all helpful. His most recent account synthesizes a vast literature in an accessible way: Inhuman Bondage: The Rise and Fall of Slavery in the New World (Oxford University Press, 2006).

Excellent examples of what might be thought of as the new global history appear in Sven Beckert, "Emancipation and Empire: Reconstructing the Worldwide Web of Cotton Production in the Age of the American Civil War," American Historical Review 109 (December 2004): 1405–38; and Gordon H. Chang, "Whose 'Barbarism? Whose 'Treachery'? Race and Civilization in the Unknown United States-Korea War of 1871," Journal of American History 89 (March 2003): 1331–65.

UNDERSTANDING DETAILS

1. What were some of the main differences in ideology between the North and the South during the Civil War?
2. In what ways was the United States trying to carve out an identity for itself in this period of history?
3. How did the 200,000 African Americans who fought in the Civil War transform the struggle?
4. After the Reconstruction efforts, where did the United States focus its post-war energy?

THINKING CRITICALLY

5. What was Lincoln arguing for when he said he wanted to give all men "a fair chance in the race of life" (paragraph 2)?
6. Why was the Civil War so important in the history of the world?
7. How did U.S. slavery affect the world economy?
8. According to Ayers, why was the reconstruction effort after the Civil War a failure?

DISCOVERING RHETORICAL STRATEGIES

9. What is the author's purpose in this article?
10. This essay ends by suggesting that the Civil War was both "powerful and contradictory" (paragraph 32). In what ways is this an effective conclusion for the essay? Explain your answer.
11. What rhetorical modes does Ayers use to accomplish his purpose? Give an example of each strategy.

12. This essay demonstrates the Chicago Manual of Style (CMS) documentation style. How is this documentation style different from MLA and APA?

MAKING CONNECTIONS

13. Imagine that Ayers, Barbara Ehrenreich ("The Ecstasy of War"), and Bruce Catton ("Grant and Lee: A Study in Contrasts") were discussing the reasons why wars are fought. Briefly summarize each author's opinion on the subject; then explain your own opinion.

14. Compare and contrast Ayers's use of cause and effect with the same rhetorical technique in essays by Stephen King ("Why We Crave Horror Movies") and Michael Dorris ("The Broken Cord"). Which essay moves most skillfully from causes to effects? Why do you think this is so?

15. Contrast Ayers's use of research with that employed by Nancy Nadolski ("Getting a Good Night's Sleep"). Whose essay is most convincing? Why?

IDEAS FOR DISCUSSION/WRITING

Preparing to Write

Write freely about what we can learn from history: What can the past teach us? How can we learn these lessons? What do we have to look for to learn from history? Why would we want to learn from the past? How might this knowledge change our future? From your perspective, do you think we learn from history, or do we keep repeating the patterns of the past? Give examples to prove your point.

Choosing a Topic

1. Choose an important historical event, and, in the form of a coherent essay, analyze the lessons we learned from it. Did this event help us improve the quality of our lives in the United States? Or did we just ignore this lesson over time?

2. What event that occurred during your lifetime will teach future U.S. citizens how to live their lives effectively? Write an essay explaining what the U.S. citizens might learn from this event. How could they potentially use this knowledge? What might they do differently in the future because of this event?

3. Write a letter to someone your age in a country of your choice analyzing a specific event or ritual that characterizes some aspect of our culture in the United States. Explain the event or ritual, and suggest various lessons that someone in another culture might learn from it. What is the relationship between the ritual or event and the potential lessons to be learned?

4. Visit the Web site for *The Confederate States of America* movie (http://www.csathemovie.com), and click on the "Feedback" link. Scroll through the comments posted by other viewers, and consider your own opinions about this satirical movie. Write a one- to two-page response to the movie or to one of the comments posted by other viewers. Keep your remarks specific and your tone as academic as possible.

Before beginning your essay, you might want to consult the checklists on page 560.

Chapter Writing Assignments

Practicing Research Papers

1. In what ways can the Internet benefit college students? How could the Internet pose problems for students? Research this topic. Then, in an essay, explore the advantages and disadvantages of the Internet for students. Provide examples to illustrate your points.

2. Think of another health issue besides sleep that would have a broad appeal to readers; then, research that subject and other topics related to it. Next, write up your discoveries, taking a problem-solution approach to the issue you identified.

3. Find a story in the history of your home town that interests you. Research the past, present, and achievements of that aspect of your town. Then explain your view in a well-reasoned essay.

Exploring Ideas

4. In what ways is violence natural or unnatural to society? How does society promote or prohibit violence? Research this issue. Then write an essay presenting your view on the extent to which violence is or is not inherent in society.

5. Do you think the American government does a good job of protecting the health of its citizens? How involved in our health do you think our government should be? How could it improve its current role? Investigate the impact of our government on health issues over the past ten years. Then write an essay in which you review its history and discuss the role it should play in American health today.

6. What are the primary advantages and disadvantages of pursuing an online education or degree? After studying this option, write an essay discussing the reasons this type of education may benefit or hinder students and whether it is a worthwhile educational option.

Chapter 11

FURTHER THINKING, READING, AND WRITING
Combining Rhetorical Modes

In each of the preceding chapters, we have examined a single rhetorical mode to focus attention on how writers use that pattern to organize and present their thoughts. In this final chapter, we consider the topics of thinking, reading, and writing through the interrelated genres of essays, fiction, poetry, and drama as they creatively combine the various rhetorical modes we have previously studied.

Our primary purpose in this text has been to show how thinking, reading, and writing work together as fine machinery to help all of us function as intelligent and productive human beings. Our introduction discusses the relationship of thinking, reading, and writing; the text itself illustrates the crucial interdependence of these skills; and this last chapter concludes the book by presenting two essays, two short stories, three poems, and a brief play by some of America's best writers on such topics as why we feel the need to respond to others verbally, the morality of writing, the importance of reading, the secrets of communication, books, poetry, and the teaching of writing.

These different views of thinking, reading, and writing are intended for you to enjoy, letting your mind run freely through the material as you recall in a leisurely way what you have learned throughout this text. They bring together the theoretical framework of this book as they illustrate how thinking, reading, and writing inform each other and work interdependently to make meaning. They also integrate the rhetorical patterns in such a way that each entry in this final chapter is a complex blend of the various rhetorical modes discussed in the preceding chapters—a perfect summary of the topics and strategies you have been learning throughout this text.

ROGER ROSENBLATT   (1940–   )

"I Am Writing Blindly"

B esides the newsworthy revelation of Lieut. Captain Dimitri 1
Kolesnikov's dying message to his wife recovered from the husk of the
sunken submarine *Kursk*—that 23 of the 118 crewmen had survived
in an isolated chamber for a while, in contradiction to claims by Russian officials that all had perished within minutes of the accident—there was the
matter of writing the message in the first place.

In the first place, in the last place, that is what we people do—write mes- 2
sages to one another. We are a narrative species. We exist by storytelling—by
relating our situations—and the test of our evolution may lie in getting the
story right.

What Kolesnikov did in deciding to describe his position and entrap- 3
ment, others have also done—in states of repose or terror. When a JAL air-
liner went down in 1985, passengers used the long minutes of its terrible,
spiraling descent to write letters to loved ones. When the last occupants of
the Warsaw Ghetto had finally seen their families and companions die of
disease or starvation, or be carried off in trucks to extermination camps, and
there could be no doubt of their own fate, still they took scraps of paper on
which they wrote poems, thoughts, fragments of lives, rolled them into tight
scrolls, and slipped them into the crevices of the ghetto walls.

Why did they bother? With no countervailing news from the outside 4
world, they assumed the Nazis had inherited the earth; that if anyone discovered their writings, it would be their killers, who would snicker and toss
them away. They wrote because, like Kolesnikov, they had to. The impulse was
in them, like a biological fact.

So enduring is this storytelling need that it shapes nearly every human en- 5
deavor. Businesses depend on the stories told of past failures and successes and
on the myth of the mission of the company. In medicine, doctors increasingly
rely on a patient's narrative of the progress of an ailment, which is inevitably
more nuanced and useful than the data of machines. In law, the same thing.
Every court case is a competition of tales told by the prosecutor and defense attorney; the jury picks the one it likes best.

All these activities derive from essential places in us. Psychologist Jerome 6
Bruner says children acquire language in order to tell the stories that are already in them. We do our learning through storytelling processes. The man
who arrives at our door is thought to be a salesman because his predecessor
was a salesman. When the patternmaking faculties fail, the brain breaks down.
Schizophrenics suffer from a loss of story.

The deep proof of our need to spill, and keep on spilling, lies in reflex,   7
often in desperate circumstances. A number of years ago, Jean-Dominique
Bauby, the editor of *Elle* magazine in Paris, was felled by a stroke so destructive that the only part of his body that could move was his left eyelid.
Flicking that eyelid, he managed to signal the letters of the alphabet, and
proceeded to write his autobiography, *The Diving Bell and the Butterfly,* with
the last grand gesture of his life.

All this is of acute and consoling interest to writers, whose odd existences   8
are ordinarily strung between asking why we do it and doing it incessantly.
The explanation I've been able to come up with has to do with freedom.
You write a sentence, the basic unit of storytelling, and you are never sure
where it will lead. The readers will not know where it leads either. Your adventure becomes theirs, eternally recapitulated in tandem—one wild ride
together. Even when you come to the end of the sentence, that dot, it is still
strangely inconclusive. I sometimes think one writes to find God in every sentence. But God (the ironist) always lives in the next sentence.

It is this freedom of the message sender and receiver that connects them—   9
sailor to wife, the dying to the living. Writing has been so important in
America, I think, because communication is the soul and engine of democracy. To write is to live according to one's terms. If you ask me to be serious,
I will be frivolous. Magnanimous? Petty. Cynical? I will be a brazen believer
in all things. Whatever you demand I will not give you—unless it is with the
misty hope that what I give you is not what you ask for but what you want.

We use this freedom to break the silence, even of death, even when—in   10
the depths of our darkest loneliness—we have no clear idea of why we reach
out to one another with these frail, perishable chains of words. In the black
chamber of the submarine, Kolesnikov noted, "I am writing blindly." Like
everyone else.

RITA MAE BROWN   (1944–   )

Writing as a Moral Act

Language is decanted and shared. If only one person is left alive speak- 1
ing a language—the case with some American Indian languages—the
language is dead. Language takes two and their multiples.

Speaking is a social contract. You and I agree to exchange sounds whose 2
organized noises represent agreed-upon symbols. *Cat* means the same thing
to you as it does to me. It doesn't mean a thing to a Portuguese person. You
might think of a sleek tiger cat, and I might be thinking of a long-haired red
cat, but we are in sync about the species. If you want to get fancy you could
say feline (Latin again) but we're in the same ballpark.

Up to this point we are in agreement. We are cooperating as two indi- 3
viduals conceding to civilization. Literacy, or even simple speech, is the starting point of civilization. The unspoken truth is that we are unequal; we are
different. If you and I were exactly the same, a pair of identical strangers, we
wouldn't need to speak to one another or to write. You'd know what I was
thinking and vice versa. All communication rests upon inequality. That's the
sheer excitement of it. I don't know what you think. I can't wait to find out.
Language is the common thread by which we explore our differences and,
if we are both lucky and mature, the thread that will bring us to a form of
agreement or at least understanding.

Therefore it is imperative that people write and speak the truth. There can 4
be no community if a person is not as good as her/his word. How easy to
write that and how hard to put it in practice. You, my reader, whoever you
are, know things that will disturb others. You must tell. Camus said, "It is im-
moral not to tell."

Again we can split hairs. A dear friend of mine has put on ten pounds. Do 5
I say, "Gee, Frank, you're fat as a toad" (the truth) or "Frank, you look wonderful." It may be wonderful to see him, but he still looks fat. I'll choose to
make my friend feel better.

If Frank, involved in a sordid affair with the wife of another friend of 6
mine, asks my opinion, I'll tell him the truth. "Either she leaves him and goes
to you, or you leave her. Don't mess with married people."

Telling the truth should be simple. Writing the truth should be even eas- 7
ier because you don't have to look your listener/reader in the eye. Writing
the truth is far more treacherous. The act of putting words down on paper
gives them a glamour and permanence not associated with speech. Writing,
to most everyone, is a more serious act than speaking.

Every generation produces those people—writers, composers, plastic   8
artists, and even the re-creative artists—who shatter social convention and tell
the truth. They aren't saying "Here I am." They are saying "Here you are."
The "you" is both individual and plural. In the case of *Oedipus Rex* or *Crime
and Punishment,* this recognition can be horrifying. In the case of *The Birds*
or *School for Scandal* it can be deliciously funny.

If this is prevented from happening (as in Stalin's Soviet Union, Hitler's   9
Germany, Botha's South Africa) the civilization begins to die from the inside out. There may be a plethora of books in such nations but they aren't
upsetting. They merely entertain. Art must both entertain and provoke.

If people refrain from telling what they know, how long before they ac-   10
tively lie? Is there not a subtle and corrosive connection between withholding the truth and lying? You are as sick as you are secret.

If you don't believe that words will be followed by deeds, how can you   11
trust anyone? How can you form a community? When language no longer
corresponds to reality, any form of betrayal and misconduct are to be expected.

Writers are the moral purifiers of the culture. We may not be pure our-   12
selves, but we must tell the truth, which is a purifying act. Therefore it is impossible for a real fiction writer to be the mouthpiece for a political cause.
A writer should, as should any citizen, cherish his or her political beliefs but
that's not the same as being a propagandist.

By political beliefs I am not talking about the American two-party sys-   13
tem. The Republican party is a study in unlimited vandalism, and the
Democratic party presides over the cadaver of liberalism. The difference between Republicans and Democrats is the difference between syphilis and
gonorrhea. Political beliefs are stronger than that. The separation of church
and state is a political belief. Affirming or repudiating capital punishment is
a political belief. The desire for a state-controlled economy is not only a
political belief, in some nations it's a religion. You get the difference. Our
political parties skate over the political fashions that are current. Oppor-
tunism wears many masks.

Since politicians seek to conceal the truth in order to dupe the public,   14
every writer alive is critical of whatever political system s/he lives in. Not
everyone in politics is bad and politics is a necessary evil, *but* politics is never
ever about the truth. Politics seeks to conceal; Art, to reveal.

The severest blasts in Russia or in our own country are directed at peo-   15
ple the state considers expendable. First, writers get it because they are potentially dangerous. Scientists run into walls only if they become critical of
the uses of science by the government. If they shut up and continue as the
hired help, they're okay. In our country, we are too sophisticated to put writers in jail. It looks bad. Also, we are very fortunate in that most of our elected

officials are semi-illiterate, and therefore they don't even know what we're writing. Should a writer happen to become disturbing and powerful enough to come to the attention of our civic worthies, then the fur flies. A politician will cite the offending author and make a stink. His acolytes will press to have the subversive texts banned from the libraries. (Actually, the acolytes control the politician. S/he usually responds to their pressure.) Loathsome as it is, such talk does get into the newspapers, and once publicity attaches itself to a book, the sales shoot upward. Bless the narrow-minded! You can survive that. You'll know when you're really in Dutch when the IRS hounds you. You think a highly placed government official wouldn't stoop that low? You think the IRS is not a punitive instrument of whatever administration is current? You also believe in the tooth fairy, don't you?

Communist and fascist nations recognize the power of writers. They imprison them or drive them out of their homeland. The United States of America, no matter how absurd and contradictory our various administrations, has drawn the line here. When push comes to shove, we defend the First Amendment. By defending the First Amendment we are defending writers. Buried in the marrow of our collective bones is the recognition that we must know the truth about ourselves. Even the most bigoted American hates a liar. Despite our economic struggle, far better to be a writer here than elsewhere. 16

Morality is involved in issues other than lying or withholding information. What happens when the word is substituted for the deed? Some act of faith is always involved in the connection between theory and action. To write and talk and not produce the action is to destroy faith. Once again, community becomes impossible. 17

The best example I can think of for this phenomenon involves the protest movements of the late 1960s and early 1970s. While the Nazis committed unspeakable acts (I mean unspeakable—they had no word for what they were doing), the New Left and the Women's Movement spoke incessantly but committed few acts. This seems to be a hallmark of leftist politics: the substitution of the word for the deed. Yes, some things got accomplished, but compare it to the dedicated raising of money by the New Right and the intelligent daily application of those funds, and you quickly grasp the difference. 18

The New Right has few writers. The New Left was top-heavy with them. From the New Left true fiction writers emerged, leaving behind the restrictions of ideology and moving toward a wider embrace of human experience but, I hope, imbued with a belief in justice, equality, and innovation. To date, not one decent fiction writer has emerged from the New Right. 19

I was one of those people to emerge from the New Left. I recall the early days of the movement. The blind were leading the blind with great excitement 20 into walls, into ravines, into the waiting rifles at Jackson and Kent State. These anguished memories are then supplanted with pride; we did help to end a war which was ill-conceived. We wrested a few changes from the system for the nonwhite, and we created the conditions for the removal of a President who may have committed criminal acts. From this haunted terrain sprang a generation of scribblers. Perhaps the New Right will fool me yet and bring forth fiction writers capable of making us see ourselves as we really are. One thing is certain: That writer or those writers will get clobbered by their former associates. The Right suffers little dissent.

Some writers maintain that they are apolitical. A worm is apolitical; a   21 human being is not. If you live in a political system and do not seek to make it better, you are still a product of that system. Your lack of involvement is a political statement. All Art rests on a political foundation but it need not concern itself with politics.

Go back to *The Iliad*. Achilles has plopped his butt in his tent and won't   22 fight. Agamemnon took a damsel awarded to Achilles for his battle prowess. Briseis was her name, and Achilles, although in love with Patroclus, a man, wanted the girl. Why not eat your cake and have it too? The Greeks were not as ravaged by sexual definitions as we are. Agamemnon, as head of the armed forces (think of him as Eisenhower during World War II), could take this woman. He had the power but he didn't have the right. Achilles, by our standards, should set aside personal ego and fight for his people. Achilles, by Greek standards, is absolutely right. His first allegiance is to his honor. This conflict between the need of the individual to be sovereign and the need of the community to triumph/survive provides the context for the unfolding drama. *The Iliad* has a political basis but you can read it without giving politics a thought.

Even *Alice's Adventures in Wonderland* rests on a political foundation. It can   23 be read as a glorious fantasy, or it can be read as a comment on the powerlessness of a child, of children in society. You don't have to choose—you can read it on many levels, including reading it as a drug trip.

Both *The Iliad* and *Alice in Wonderland* ring true. People read them today   24 with as much pleasure as people derived from them when they were first written. A work lives like that if it is morally true.

You bring to a book your past, your system of beliefs. First, you read a book   25 and answer that book with those beliefs. If you are a student of literature, you will study the environment of the writer, and then you'll read the book again, setting aside your values. When you've finished the second reading you can engage the writer's beliefs with your own. Reading is an active moral and intellectual exchange. If you aren't reading books that challenge you, you're reading the wrong books.

If you aren't writing books that challenge you, keep writing. It takes years   26
to get there. I know the book I wanted to write, the challenging, lyrical
work I dreamed about. You know only the book I wrote. I am acutely aware
of the gap between desire and performance. Lash me though you might,
you'll never hit me as hard as I hit myself, for only I know the full extent of
my failure.

Morality shifts. Infanticide was acceptable to the Greeks. It isn't accept-   27
able to us. Your work will reflect your implied faiths and fears. Without your
being necessarily conscious of it, your work reflects your society. Here's an
example. Since *The Iliad,* Western writers have treated common experience
as comic relief. This attitude depends on a clear class structure in which the
superior classes, aristocrats, are assumed better than the inferior classes. When
the middle classes began to assert themselves, this shifted. Chaucer in *The
Canterbury Tales* presents sympathetic middle-class characters. Some are comic,
and some are not, but none of them is heroic. A great revolution took place
on the page. This accelerated over time. Shakespeare used all the classes, to
his and our great profit.

Eventually, middle-class people developed the leisure in which to write, and   28
what did they do? They wrote about themselves. As the Industrial Revolution wears on, their literature takes over. The middle-class character is not a
king or a landed aristocrat but a lawyer or a doctor perhaps. Chekhov comes
to my mind instantly. The tendency to present ordinary people (an assumption in itself—are there ordinary people?) as vaguely comic still exists but it
isn't as strict a literary convention as it was for a good two thousand years.

When you reject inferiority at the lowest level, you topple the whole   29
structure of dominance. The shift in literature, beginning with Chaucer, reflected real life and, in turn, had an impact upon real life. No longer were
kings and queens so important. They were replaced with parliaments or by
revolutions. They were replaced on the page. Morally, there's nothing wrong
with having a king for your form of government or for your literary hero,
but as an American I bet you don't write about one.

This struggle for literary representation bubbles over the decades. Today,   30
the lower classes, thanks to programs to get them into colleges, are producing literature. The class in control of the arts, the middle class, finds itself be-
sieged from below. Not only are the lower classes becoming literate, nonwhite
and non-Christians have acquired the skills to create English literature. Stick
around—the show is just beginning!

As Shakespeare arrived at a creative imbalance between the passing me-   31
dieval world and the coming modern world (Bacon, Newton, Descartes), so
we are at a similar overlap between the nation–state and global interdependence, between men and women, between whites and nonwhites, between

the Christian world and science, the Christian world and the non-Christian world, between spiritual concerns and material ones. Like Shakespeare we find ourselves in a time where the future, so thrilling to the nonrigid, terrifies the rigid. Every action has an equal and opposite reaction. Every cultural/social push forward is followed by people organizing to hold back the hands of time. Those men who were willing to kill you if you thought the earth revolved around the sun instead of believing Ptolemy are still here. Those people, like Elizabeth I, who killed their political enemies are here too. Like Shakespeare, you've got to try to make sense of it. You don't have to explain it. He didn't. You need to use it, use every bit of it. This overlap and straining of divergent world views is a gift. Don't ask to live in tranquil times. Literature doesn't grow there.

RICHARD WRIGHT   (1908–1960)

The Library Card

One morning I arrived early at work and went into the bank lobby   1
where the Negro porter was mopping. I stood at a counter and
picked up the Memphis *Commercial Appeal* and began my free reading of the press. I came finally to the editorial page and saw an article dealing with one H. L. Mencken. I knew by hearsay that he was the editor of the
American Mercury, but aside from that I knew nothing about him. The article was a furious denunciation of Mencken, concluding with one, hot, short
sentence: Mencken is a fool.

I wondered what on earth this Mencken had done to call down upon   2
him the scorn of the South. The only people I had ever heard denounced
in the South were Negroes, and this man was not a Negro. Then what ideas
did Mencken hold that made a newspaper like the *Commercial Appeal* casti-
gate him publicly? Undoubtedly he must be advocating ideas that the South
did not like. Were there, then, people other than Negroes who criticized the
South? I knew that during the Civil War the South had hated northern
whites, but I had not encountered such hate during my life. Knowing no
more of Mencken than I did at that moment, I felt a vague sympathy for him.
Had not the South, which had assigned me the role of a nonman, cast at
him its hardest words?

Now, how could I find out about this Mencken? There was a huge li-   3
brary near the riverfront, but I knew that Negroes were not allowed to pa-
tronize its shelves any more than they were the parks and playgrounds of
the city. I had gone into the library several times to get books for the white
men on the job. Which of them would now help me to get books? And how
could I read them without causing concern to the white men with whom
I worked? I had so far been successful in hiding my thoughts and feelings
from them, but I knew that I would create hostility if I went about the business of reading in a clumsy way.

I weighed the personalities of the men on the job. There was Don, a Jew;   4
but I distrusted him. His position was not much better than mine and I knew
that he was uneasy and insecure; he had always treated me in an offhand, ban-
tering way that barely concealed his contempt. I was afraid to ask him to help
me get books; his frantic desire to demonstrate a racial solidarity with the
whites against Negroes might make him betray me.

Then how about the boss? No, he was a Baptist and I had the suspicion   5
that he would not be quite able to comprehend why a black boy would

want to read Mencken. There were other white men on the job whose attitudes showed clearly that they were Kluxers or sympathizers, and they were out of the question.

There remained only one man whose attitude did not fit into an anti-Negro category, for I had heard the white men refer to him as a "Pope lover." He was an Irish Catholic and was hated by the white Southerners. I knew that he read books, because I had got him volumes from the library several times. Since he, too, was an object of hatred, I felt that he might refuse me but would hardly betray me. I hesitated, weighing and balancing the imponderable realities. 6

One morning I paused before the Catholic fellow's desk. 7

"I want to ask you a favor," I whispered to him. 8

"What is it?" 9

"I want to read. I can't get books from the library. I wonder if you'd let me use your card?" 10

He looked at me suspiciously. 11

"My card is full most of the time," he said. 12

"I see," I said and waited, posing my question silently. 13

"You're not trying to get me into trouble, are you, boy?" He asked, staring at me. 14

"Oh, no sir." 15

"What book do you want?" 16

"A book by H. L. Mencken." 17

"Which one?" 18

"I don't know. Has he written more than one?" 19

"He has written several." 20

"I didn't know that." 21

"What makes you want to read Mencken?" 22

"Oh, I just saw his name in the newspaper," I said. 23

"It's good of you to want to read," he said. "But you ought to read the right things." 24

I said nothing. Would he want to supervise my reading? 25

"Let me think," he said. "I'll figure out something." 26

I turned from him and he called me back. He stared at me quizzically. 27

"Richard, don't mention this to the other white men," he said. 28

"I understand," I said. "I won't say a word." 29

A few days later he called me to him. 30

"I've got a card in my wife's name," he said. "Here's mine." 31

"Thank you, sir." 32

"Do you think you can manage it?" 33

"I'll manage fine," I said. 34

"If they suspect you, you'll get in trouble," he said. 35

"I'll write the same kind of notes to the library that you wrote when you 36
sent me for books," I told him. "I'll sign your name."

He laughed. 37

"Go ahead. Let me see what you get," he said. 38

That afternoon I addressed myself to forging a note. Now, what were the 39
names of books written by H. L. Mencken? I did not know any of them. I
finally wrote what I thought would be a foolproof note: *Dear Madam: Will
you please let this nigger boy*—I used the word "nigger" to make the librarian
feel that I could not possibly be the author of the note—*have some books by
H. L. Mencken?* I forged the white man's name.

I entered the library as I had always done when on errands for whites, but 40
I felt that I would somehow slip up and betray myself. I doffed my hat, stood
a respectful distance from the desk, looked as unbookish as possible, and
waited for the white patrons to be taken care of. When the desk was clear
of people, I still waited. The white librarian looked at me.

"What do you want, boy?" 41

As though I did not possess the power of speech, I stepped forward and 42
simply handed her the forged note, not parting my lips.

"What books by Mencken does he want?" she asked. 43

"I don't know, ma'am," I said, avoiding her eyes. 44

"Who gave you this card?" 45

"Mr. Falk," I said. 46

"Where is he?" 47

"He's at work, at the M——— Optical Company," I said. "I've been in 48
here for him before."

"I remember," the woman said. "But he never wrote notes like this." 49

Oh, God, she's suspicious. Perhaps she would not let me have the books? 50
If she had turned her back at that moment, I would have ducked out the door
and never gone back. Then I thought of a bold idea.

"You can call him up, ma'am," I said, my heart pounding. 51

"You're not using these books, are you?" she asked pointedly. 52

"Oh, no, ma'am. I can't read." 53

"I don't know what he wants by Mencken," she said under her breath. 54

I knew now that I had won; she was thinking of other things and the race 55
question had gone out of her mind. She went to the shelves. Once or twice
she looked over her shoulder at me, as though she was still doubtful. Finally
she came foreward with two books in her hand.

"I'm sending him two books," she said. "But tell Mr. Falk to come in next 56
time, or send me the names of the books he wants. I don't know what he
wants to read."

I said nothing. She stamped the card and handed me the books. Not dar- 57
ing to glance at them, I went out of the library, fearing that the woman

would call me back for further questioning. A block away from the library I opened one of the books and read a title: *A Book of Prefaces.* I was nearing my nineteenth birthday and I did not know how to pronounce the word "preface." I thumbed the pages and saw strange words and strange names. I shook my head, disappointed. I looked at the other book; it was called *Prejudices.* I knew what that word meant; I had heard it all my life. And right off I was on guard against Mencken's books. Why would a man want to call a book *Prejudices?* The word was so stained with all my memories of racial hate that I could not conceive of anybody using it for a title. Perhaps I had made a mistake about Mencken? A man who had prejudices must be wrong.

When I showed the books to Mr. Falk, he looked at me and frowned.   58

"That librarian might telephone you," I warned him.   59

"That's all right," he said. "But when you're through reading those books, 60 I want you to tell me what you get out of them."

That night in my rented room, while letting the hot water run over my 61 can of pork and beans in the sink, I opened *A Book of Prefaces* and began to read. I was jarred and shocked by the style, the clear, clean, sweeping sentences. Why did he write like that? And how did one write like that? I pictured the man as a raging demon, slashing with his pen, consumed with hate, denouncing everything American, extolling everything European or German, laughing at the weaknesses of people, mocking God, authority. What was this? I stood up, trying to realize what reality lay behind the meaning of the words. . . . Yes, this man was fighting, fighting with words. He was using words as a weapon, using them as one would use a club. Could words be weapons? Well, yes, for here they were. Then, maybe, perhaps, I could use them as a weapon? No. It frightened me. I read on and what amazed me was not what he said, but how on earth anybody had the courage to say it.

Occasionally I glanced up to reassure myself that I was alone in the room. 62 Who were these men about whom Mencken was talking so passionately? Who was Anatole France? Joseph Conrad? Sinclair Lewis, Sherwood Anderson, Dostoevski, George Moore, Gustave Flaubert, Maupassant, Tolstoy, Frank Harris, Mark Twain, Thomas Hardy, Arnold Bennett, Stephen Crane, Zola, Norris, Gorky, Bergson, Ibsen, Balzac, Bernard Shaw, Dumas, Poe, Thomas Mann, O. Henry, Dreiser, H. G. Wells, Gogol, T. S. Eliot, Gide, Baudelaire, Edgar Lee Masters, Stendhal, Turgenev, Huneker, Nietzsche, and scores of others? Were these men real? Did they exist or had they existed? And how did one pronounce their names?

I ran across many words whose meanings I did not know, and I either 63 looked them up in a dictionary or, before I had a chance to do that, encountered the word in a context that made its meaning clear. But what strange world was this? I concluded the book with the conviction that I had somehow overlooked something terribly important in life. I had once tried to write, had once reveled in feeling, had let my crude imagination roam, but the impulse to dream had been slowly beaten out of me by experience. Now it surged up again and I hungered for books, new ways of looking and seeing. It was not a matter of believing or disbelieving what I read, but of feeling something new, of being affected by something that made the look of the world different.

As dawn broke I ate my pork and beans, feeling dopey, sleepy. I went to 64 work, but the mood of the book would not die; it lingered, coloring everything I saw, heard, did. I now felt that I knew what the white men were feeling. Merely because I had read a book that had spoken of how they lived and thought, I identified myself with that book. I felt vaguely guilty. Would I, filled with bookish notions, act in a manner that would make the whites dislike me?

I forged more notes and my trips to the library became frequent. Read- 65 ing grew into a passion. My first serious novel was Sinclair Lewis's *Main Street*. It made me see my boss, Mr. Gerald, and identify him as an American type. I would smile when I saw him lugging his golf bags into the office. I had always felt a vast distance separating me from the boss, and now I felt closer to him, though still distant. I felt now that I knew him, that I could feel the very limits of his narrow life. And this had happened because I had read a novel about a mythical man called George F. Babbitt.

The plots and stories in the novels did not interest me so much as the point 66 of view revealed. I gave myself over to each novel without reserve, without trying to criticize it; it was enough for me to see and feel something different. And for me, everything was something different. Reading was like a drug, a dope. The novels created moods in which I lived for days. But I could not conquer my sense of guilt, my feeling that the white men around me knew that I was changing, that I had begun to regard them differently.

Whenever I brought a book to the job, I wrapped it in newspaper—a 67 habit that was to persist for years in other cities and under other circumstances. But some of the white men pried into my packages when I was absent and they questioned me.

"Boy, what are you reading those books for?" 68

"Oh, I don't know, sir." 69

"That's deep stuff you're reading, boy." 70

"I'm just killing time, sir." 71

"You'll addle your brains if you don't watch out." 72

I read Dreiser's *Jennie Gerhardt* and *Sister Carrie* and they revived in me a 73 vivid sense of my mother's suffering; I was overwhelmed. I grew silent, wondering about the life around me. It would have been impossible for me to have told anyone what I derived from these novels, for it was nothing less than a sense of life itself. All my life had shaped me for the realism, the naturalism of the modern novel, and I could not read enough of them.

Steeped in new moods and ideas, I bought a ream of paper and tried to   74
write; but nothing would come, or what did come was flat beyond telling.
I discovered that more than desire and feeling were necessary to write and
I dropped the idea. Yet I still wondered how it was possible to know people sufficiently to write about them? Could I ever learn about life and people? To me, with my vast ignorance, my Jim Crow station in life, it seemed
a task impossible of achievement. I now knew what being a Negro meant.
I could endure the hunger; I had learned to live with hate. But to feel that
there were feelings denied me, that the very breath of life itself was beyond
my reach, that more than anything else hurt, wounded me. I had a new
hunger.

In buoying me up, reading also cast me down, made me see what was   75
possible, what I had missed. My tension returned, new, terrible, bitter, surging, almost too great to be contained. I no longer *felt* that the world about
me was hostile, killing; I *knew* it. A million times I asked myself what I could
do to save myself, and there were no answers. I seemed forever condemned,
ringed by walls.

I did not discuss my reading with Mr. Falk, who had lent me his library   76
card; it would have meant talking about myself and that would have been too
painful. I smiled each day, fighting desperately to maintain my old behavior,
to keep my disposition seemingly sunny. But some of the white men dis-
cerned that I had begun to brood.

"Wake up there, boy!" Mr. Olin said one day.   77
"Sir!" I answered for the lack of a better word.   78
"You act like you've stolen something," he said.   79
I laughed in the way I knew he expected me to laugh, but I resolved to   80
be more conscious of myself, to watch my every act, to guard and hide the
new knowledge that was dawning within me.

If I went north, would it be possible for me to build a new life then? But   81
how could a man build a life upon vague, unformed yearnings? I wanted to
write and I did not even know the English language. I bought English grammars and found them dull. I felt that I was getting a better sense of the language from novels than from grammars. I read hard, discarding a writer as
soon as I felt that I had grasped his point of view. At night the printed page
stood before my eyes in sleep.

Mrs. Moss, my landlady, asked me one Sunday morning: 82
"Son, what is this you keep on reading?"   83
"Oh, nothing. Just novels."   84
"What you get out of 'em?"   85
"I'm just killing time," I said.   86
"I hope you know your own mind," she said in a tone which implied   87
that she doubted if I had a mind.

I knew of no Negroes who read the books I liked and I wondered if any   88
Negroes ever thought of them. I knew that there were Negro doctors,
lawyers, newspapermen, but I never saw any of them. When I read a Negro
newspaper I never caught the faintest echo of my pre-occupation in its pages.
I felt trapped and occasionally, for a few days, I would stop reading. But a
vague hunger would come over me for books, books that opened up new
avenues of feeling and seeing, and again I would forge another note to the
white librarian. Again I would read and wonder as only the naïve and un-
lettered can read and wonder, feeling that I carried a secret, criminal burden
about with me each day.

That winter my mother and brother came and we set up housekeeping,   89
buying furniture on the installment plan, being cheated and yet knowing
no way to avoid it. I began to eat warm food and to my surprise found that
regular meals enabled me to read faster. I may have lived through many ill-
nesses and survived them, never suspecting that I was ill. My brother obtained a job and we began to save toward the trip north, plotting our time,
setting tentative dates for departure. I told none of the white men on the job
that I was planning to go north; I knew that the moment they felt I was
thinking of the North they would change toward me. It would have made
them feel that I did not like the life I was living, and because my life was completely conditioned by what they said or did, it would have been tantamount
to challenging them.

I could calculate my chances for life in the South as a Negro fairly clearly   90
now.

I could fight the southern whites by organizing with other Negroes, as my   91
grandfather had done. But I knew that I could never win that way; there
were many whites and there were but few blacks. They were strong and we
were weak. Outright black rebellion could never win. If I fought openly I
would die and I did not want to die. News of lynchings were frequent.

I could submit and live the life of a genial slave, but that was impossible.   92
All of my life had shaped me to live by my own feelings, and thoughts. I
could make up to Bess and marry her and inherit the house. But that, too,
would be the life of a slave; if I did that, I would crush to death something
within me, and I would hate myself as much as I knew the whites already
hated those who had submitted. Neither could I ever willingly present myself to be kicked, as Shorty had done. I would rather have died than do that.

I could drain off my restlessness by fighting with Shorty and Harrison. I   93
had seen many Negroes solve the problem of being black by transfering their
hatred of themselves to others with a black skin and fighting them. I would
have to be cold to do that, and I was not cold and I could never be.

I could, of course, forget what I had read, thrust the whites out of my   94
mind, forget them; and find release from anxiety and longing in sex and

alcohol. But the memory of how my father had conducted himself made that course repugnant. If I did not want others to violate my life, how could I voluntarily violate it myself?

I had no hope whatever of being a professional man. Not only had I been 95
so conditioned that I did not desire it, but the fulfillment of such an ambition was beyond my capabilities. Well-to-do Negroes lived in a world that was almost as alien to me as the world inhabited by whites.

What, then, was there? I held my life in my mind, in my consciousness each 96
day, feeling at times that I would stumble and drop it, spill it forever. My reading had created a vast sense of distance between me and the world in which I lived and tried to make a living, and that sense of distance was increasing each day. My days and nights were one long, quiet, continuously contained dream of terror, tension, and anxiety. I wondered how long I could bear it.

The Secrets of Bats

Alice Leung has discovered the secrets of bats: how they see without   1
seeing, how they own darkness, as we own light. She walks the halls
with a black headband across her eyes, keening a high C—*cheat cheat
cheat cheat cheat cheat*—never once veering off course, as if drawn by an invisible thread. Echolocation, she tells me, it's not as difficult as you might
think. Now she sees a light around objects when she looks at them, like halos
on her retinas from staring at the sun. In her journal she writes, *I had a dream
that was all in blackness. Tell me how to describe.*

It is January: my fifth month in Hong Kong.   2
In the margin I write, *I wish I knew.*   3

After six, when the custodians leave, the school becomes a perfect acoustic   4
chamber; she wanders from the basement laboratories to the basketball courts
like a trapped bird looking for a window. She finds my door completely
blind, she says, not counting flights or paces. Twisting her head from side to
side like Stevie Wonder, she announces her progress: another room mapped,
a door, a desk, a globe, detected and identified by its aura.

You'll hurt yourself, I tell her. I've had nightmares: her foot missing the   5
edge of a step, the dry crack of a leg breaking. Try it without the blindfold,
I say. That way you can check yourself.

Her mouth wrinkles. This not important, she says. This only practice.   6
Practice for what, I want to ask. All the more reason you have to be careful.   7
You keep saying, she says, grabbing a piece of chalk. E-x-p-e-r-i-m-e-n-t,   8
she writes on the blackboard, digging it in until it squeals.

That's right. Sometimes experiments fail.   9
Sometimes, she repeats. She eyes me suspiciously, as if I invented the word.   10
Go home, I tell her. She turns her pager off and leaves it in her locker;   11
sometimes police appear at the school gate, shouting her name. Somebody,
it seems, wants her back.

In the doorway she whirls, flipping her hair out of her eyes. Ten days more,   12
she says. You listen. Maybe then you see why.

The name of the school is Po Sing Uk: a five-story concrete block, cracked   13
and eroded by dirty rain, shoulder-to-shoulder with the tenements and gar-
ment factories of Cheung Sha Wan. No air conditioning and no heat; in
September I shouted to be heard over a giant fan, and now, in January, I
teach in a winter jacket. When it rains, mildew spiderwebs cross the ceiling

of my classroom. Schoolgirls in white jumpers crowd into the room forty at a time, falling asleep over their textbooks, making furtive calls on mobile phones, scribbling notes to each other on pink Hello Kitty paper. If I call on one who hasn't raised her hand, she folds her arms across her chest and stares at the floor, and the room falls silent, as if by a secret signal. There is nothing more terrifying, I've found, than the echo of your own voice: *Who are you?* it answers. *What are you doing here?*

I've come to see my life as a radiating circle of improbabilities that grow   14 from each other, like ripples in water around a dropped stone. That I became a high school English teacher, that I work in another country, that I live in Hong Kong. That a city can be a mirage, hovering above the ground: skyscrapers built on mountainsides, islands swallowed in fog for days. That a language can have no tenses or articles, with seven different ways of saying the same syllable. That my best student stares at the blackboard only when I erase it.

She stayed behind on the first day of class: a tall girl with a narrow face,   15 pinched around the mouth, her cheeks pitted with acne scars. Like most of my sixteen-year-olds, she looked twelve, in a baggy uniform that hung to her knees like a sack. The others streamed past her without looking up, as if she were a boulder in the current; she stared down at my desk with a fierce vacancy, as if looking itself was an act of will.

How do you think about bats?   16

Bats?   17

She joined her hands at the wrist and fluttered them at me.   18

People are afraid of them, I said. I think they're very interesting.   19

Why? she said. Why very interesting?   20

Because they live in the dark, I said. We think of them as being blind, but   21 they aren't blind. They have a way of seeing, with sound waves—just like we see with light.

Yes, she said. I know this. Her body swayed slightly, in an imaginary breeze.   22

Are you interested in bats?   23

I am interest, she said. I want to know how—she made a face I'd already   24 come to recognize: *I know how to say it in Chinese*—when one bat sees the other. The feeling.

You mean how one bat recognizes another?   25

Yes—recognize.   26

That's a good idea, I said. You can keep a journal about what you find.   27 Write something in it every day.

She nodded vehemently, as if she'd already thought of that.   28

There are books on bat behavior that will tell you—   29

Not in books. She covered her eyes with one hand and walked forward   30
until her hip brushed the side of my desk, then turned away, at a right angle.
Like this, she said. There is a sound, she said. I want to find the sound.

18 September   31
First hit tuning fork. Sing one octave higher: A B C. This is best way.
Drink water or lips get dry.
I must have eyes totally closed. No light!!! So some kind of black—like cloth—is good.

Start singing. First to the closest wall—sing and listen. Practice ten times, twenty times.   32
IMPORTANT: can not move until I HEAR the wall. Take step back, one time, two
time. Listen again. I have to hear DIFFERENCE first, then move.
Then take turn, ninety degrees left.
Then turn, one hundred eighty degrees left. Feel position with feet. Feet very impor-
tant—they are wings!!!

I don't know what this is, I told her the next day, opening the journal   33
and pushing it across the desk. Can you help me?

I tell you already, she said. She hunched her shoulders so that her   34
head seemed to rest on them, spreading her elbows to either side. It is like
a test.

A test?   35

In the courtyard rain crackled against the asphalt; a warm wind lifted   36
scraps of paper from the desk, somersaulting them through the air.

The sound, she said impatiently: I told you this.   37

I covered my mouth to hide a smile.   38

Alice, I said, humans can't do that. It isn't a learned behavior. It's some-   39
thing you study.

She pushed up the cover of the composition book and let it fall.   40

I think I can help you, I said. Can you tell me why you want to write this?   41

Why I want? She stared at me wide-eyed.   42

Why do you want to do this? What is the test for?   43

Her eyes lifted from my face to the blackboard behind me, moved to the   44
right, then the left, as if measuring the dimensions of the room.

Why you want come to Hong Kong?   45

Many reasons, I said. After college I wanted to go to another country, and   46
there was a special fellowship available here. And maybe someday I will be a
teacher.

You are teacher.   47

I'm just learning, I said. I am trying to be one.   48

Then why you have to leave America?   49

I don't, I said. The two things—I took off my glasses and rubbed my eyes.   50
All at once I was exhausted; the effort seemed useless, a pointless evasion.

When I looked up she was nodding, slowly, as if I'd just said something profound.

I think I will find the reason for being here only after some time, I said.   51
Do you know what I mean? There could be a purpose I don't know about.

So you don't know for good. Not sure.   52

You could say that.   53

Hai yat yeung, she said. This same. Maybe if you read you can tell me why.   54

This is what's so strange about her, I thought, studying her red-rimmed   55
eyes, the tiny veins standing out like wires on a circuit board. She doesn't look
down. I am fascinated by her, I thought. Is that fair?

You're different from the others, I said. You're not afraid of me. Why is that?   56

Maybe I have other things be afraid of   57

At first the fifth-floor bathroom was her echo chamber; she sat in one cor-   58
ner, on a stool taken from the physics room, and placed an object directly
opposite her: a basketball, a glass, a feather. Sound waves triangulate, she
told me, corners are best. Passing by at the end of the day, I stopped, closing my eyes, and listened for the difference. She sang without stopping for
five minutes, hardly taking a breath: almost a mechanical sound, as if someone had forgotten their mobile phone. Other teachers walked by in groups,
talking loudly. If they noticed me, or the sound, I was never aware of it, but
always, instinctively, I looked at my watch and followed them down the
stairs. As if I too had to rush home to cook for hungry children or boil
medicine for my mother-in-law. I never stayed long enough to see if anything changed.

Document everything, I told her, and she did; now I have two binders of   59
entries, forty-one in all. *Hallway. Chair. Notebook.* As if we were scientists
writing a grant proposal, as if there were something actual to show at the end
of it.

I don't keep a journal or take photographs, and my letters home are fac-   60
tual and sparse. No one in Larchmont would believe me—not even my parents—if I told them the truth. *It sounds like quite an experience you're having!
Don't get run over by a rickshaw.* And yet if I died tomorrow—why should I
ever think this way?—these binders would be the record of my days. Those
and Alice herself, who looks out of her window and with her eyes closed sees
ships passing in the harbor, men walking silently in the streets.

26 January   61
Sound of light bulb—low like bees hum. So hard to listen!

A week ago I dreamed of bodies breaking apart, arms and legs and tor-   62
sos, fragments of bone, bits of tissue. I woke up flailing in the sheets, and remembered her immediately; there was too long a moment before I believed

I was awake. *It has to stop,* I thought, *you have to say something.* Though I know that I can't.

Perhaps there was a time when I might have told her, *This is ridiculous,* or,   63
You're sixteen, find some friends. What will people think? But this is Hong Kong, of course, and I have no friends, no basis to judge. I leave the door open, always, and no one ever comes to check; we walk out of the gates together, late in the afternoon, past the watchman sleeping in his chair. For me she has a kind of professional courtesy, ignoring my whiteness politely, as if I had horns growing from my head. And she returns, at the end of each day, as a bat flies back to its cave at daybreak. All I have is time; who am I to pack my briefcase and turn away?

There was only once when I slipped up.   64

Pretend I've forgotten, I told her, one Monday in early October. The jour-   65
nal was open in front of us, the pages covered in red; she squinted down at it, as if instead of corrections I'd written hieroglyphics. I'm an English teacher, I thought, this is what I'm here for. We should start again at the beginning, I said. Tell me what it is that you want to do here. You don't have to tell me about the project—just about the writing. Whom are you writing these for? Whom do you want to read them?

She stretched, catlike, curling her fingers like claws.   66

Because I don't think I understand, I said. I think you might want to find   67
another teacher to help you. There could be something you have in mind in Chinese that doesn't come across.

Not in Chinese, she said, as if I should have known that already. In Chi-   68
nese cannot say like this.

But it isn't really English, either.   69

I know this. It is like both.   70

I can't teach that way, I said. You have to learn the rules before you can—   71

You are not teaching me.   72

Then what's the point?   73

She strode across the room to the window and leaned out, placing her   74
hands on the sill and bending at the waist. Come here, she said, look. I stood up and walked over to her.

She ducked her head down, like a gymnast on a bar, and tilted forward,   75
her feet lifting off the floor.

Alice!   76

I grabbed her shoulder and jerked her upright. She stumbled, falling back;   77
I caught her wrist, and she pulled it away, steadying herself. We stood there a moment staring at each other, breathing in short huffs that echoed in the hallway.

Maybe I hear something and forget, she said. You catch me then. Okay?   78

28 January   79
It is like photo negative, all the colors are the opposite. Black sky, white trees, this way.
But they are still shapes—I can see them.

I read standing at the window, in a last sliver of sunlight. Alice stands on   80
my desk, already well in shadow, turning around slowly as if trying to dizzy
herself for a party game. Her winter uniform cardigan is three sizes too large;
unopened, it falls behind her like a cape.

This is beautiful.   81

Quiet, she hisses, eyebrows bunched together above her headband. One   82
second. There—there.

What is it?   83

A man on the stairs.   84

I go out into the hallway and stand at the top of the stairwell, listening.   85
Five floors below, very faintly, I hear sandals skidding on the concrete, keys
jangling on the janitor's ring.

You heard him open the gate, I say. That's cheating.   86

She shakes her head. I hear heartbeat.   87

The next Monday, Principal Ho comes to see me during the lunch hour.   88
He stands at the opposite end of the classroom, as always: a tall, slightly chubby
man in a tailored shirt, gold-rimmed glasses, and Italian shoes, who blinks as
he reads the ESL posters I've tacked up on the wall. When he asks how my
classes are and I tell him that the girls are unmotivated, disengaged, he nods
quickly, as if to save me the embarrassment. How lucky he was, he tells me,
to go to boarding school in Australia, and then pronounces it with a flattened
a, Australhlia, so I have to laugh.

Principal Ho, I ask, do you know Alice Leung?   89

He turns his head toward me and blinks more rapidly. Leung Ka Yee, he   90
says. Of course. You have problem with her?

No sir. I need something to hold; my hands dart across the desk behind   91
me and find my red marking pen.

How does she perform?   92

She's very gifted. One of the best students in the class. Very creative.   93

He nods, scratches his nose, and turns away.   94

She likes to work alone, I say. The other girls don't pay much attention to   95
her. I don't think she has many friends.

It is very difficult for her, he says slowly, measuring every word. Her   96
mother is—her mother was a suicide.

In the courtyard, five stories down, someone drops a basketball and lets it   97
bounce against the pavement, little *pings* that trill and fade into the infinite.

In Yau Ma Tei, Ho says. He makes a little gliding motion with his hand. 98
Nowadays this is not so uncommon in Hong Kong. But still there are superstitions.

What kind of superstitions? 99

He frowns and shakes his head. Difficult to say in English. Maybe just that 100
she is unlucky girl. Chinese people, you understand—some are still afraid of
ghosts.

She isn't a ghost. 101

He gives a high-pitched, nervous laugh. No, no, he says. Not her. He puts 102
his hands into his pockets, searching for something. Difficult to explain. I'm
sorry.

Is there someone she can talk to? 103

He raises his eyebrows. *A counselor,* I am about to say, and explain what it 104
means, when my hand relaxes, and I realize I have been crushing the pen in
my palm. For a moment I am water-skiing again at Lake Patchogue: releas-
ing the handle, settling against the surface, enfolded in water. When I look
up, Ho glances at his watch.

If you have any problem, you can talk to me. 105

It's nothing, I say. Just curious, that's all. 106

*****

She wears the headband all the time now, I've noticed: pulling it over her 107
eyes whenever possible, in the halls between classes, in the courtyard at
lunchtime, sitting by herself. No one shoves her or calls her names; she passes
through the crowds unseen. If possible, I think, she's grown thinner, her skin
translucent, blue veins showing at the wrists. Occasionally I notice the other
teachers shadowing her, frowning, their arms crossed, but if our eyes meet they
stare through me, disinterested, and look away.

I have to talk to you about something. 108

She is sitting in a desk at the far end of the room, reading her chemistry 109
textbook, drinking from a can of soymilk with a straw. When the straw gur-
gles she bangs the can down, and we sit silently, the sound reverberating in
the hallway.

I give you another journal soon. Two more days. 110

Not about that. 111

She doesn't move: fixed, alert, waiting. I stand up and move down the 112
aisle toward her, sitting two desks away, and as I move her eyes grow slightly
rounder and her cheeks puff out slightly, as if she's holding her breath.

Alice, I say, can you tell me about your mother? 113

Her hands fall down on the desk, and the can clatters to the floor, white 114
drops spinning in the air.

Mother? Who tell you I have mother? 115

It's all right—   116

I reach over to touch one hand, and she snatches it back.   117

Who tell you?   118

It doesn't matter. You don't have to be angry.   119

You big mistake, she says, wild-eyed, taking long swallows of air and spit-   120
ting them out. Why you have to come here and mess everything?

I don't understand, I say. Alice, what did I do?   121

I trust you, she says, and pushes the heel of one palm against her cheek. I   122
write and you read. I *trust* you.

What did you expect? I ask, my jaw trembling. Did you think I would   123
never know?

Believe me. She looks at me pleadingly. Believe *me*.   124

Two days later she leaves her notebook on my desk, with a note stuck to   125
the top. *You keep.*

> 1 February   126
> Now I am finished
> It is out there I hear it

I call out to her after class, and she hesitates in the doorway for a moment   127
before turning, pushing her back against the wall.

Tell me what it was like, I say. Was it a voice? Did you hear someone   128
speaking?

Of course no voice. Not so close to me. It was a feeling.   129

How did it feel?   130

She reaches up and slides the headband over her eyes.   131

It is all finish, she says. You not worry about me anymore.   132

Too late, I say. I stand up from my chair and take a tentative step toward   133
her: weak-kneed, as if it were a staircase in the dark. You chose me, I say. Remember?

Go back to America. Then you forget all about this crazy girl.   134

This is my life too. Did you forget about that?   135

She raises her head and listens, and I know what she hears: a stranger's   136
voice, as surely as if someone else had entered the room. She nods. *Whom do
you see?* I wonder. *What will he do next?* I reach out, blindly, and my hand
misses the door; on the second try I close it.

I choose this, I say. I'm waiting. Tell me.   137

Her body sinks into a crouch; she hugs her knees and tilts her head back.   138

Warm. It was warm. It was—it was a body.   139

But not close to you?   140

Not close. Only little feeling, then no more.   141

Did it know you were there?   142

No.   143

How can you be sure?   144

When I look up to repeat the question, shiny tracks of tears have run out   145
from under the blindfold.

I am sorry, she says. She reaches into her backpack and splits open a packet   146
of tissues without looking down, her fingers nimble, almost autonomous.
You are my good friend, she says, and takes off the blindfold, turning her face
to the side and dabbing her eyes. Thank you for help me.

It isn't over, I say. How can it be over?   147

Like you say. Sometimes experiment fails.   148

No, I say, too loudly, startling us both. It isn't that easy. You have to prove 149
it to me.

Prove it you?   150

Show me how it works. I take a deep breath. I believe you. Will you catch   151
me?

Her eyes widen, and she does not look away; the world swims around her   152
irises. Tonight, she says, and writes something on a slip of paper, not looking
down. I see you then.

In a week it will be the New Year: all along the streets the shop fronts are   153
hung with firecrackers, red-and-gold character scrolls, pictures of grinning
cats, and the twin cherubs of good luck. Mothers lead little boys dressed in
red silk pajamas, girls with New Year's pigtails. The old woman sitting next
to me on the bus is busily stuffing twenty-dollar bills into red *lai see* pack-
ets: lucky money for the year to come. When I turn my head from the window, she holds one out to me, and I take it with both hands, automatically,
bowing my head. This will make you rich, she says to me in Cantonese. And
lots of children.

Thank you, I say. The same to you.   154

She laughs. Already happened. Jade bangles clink together as she holds   155
up her fingers. Thirteen grandchildren! she says. Six boys. All fat and good-
looking. You should say Live long life to me.

I'm sorry. My Chinese is terrible.   156

No, it's very good, she says. You were born in Hong Kong?   157

Outside, night is just falling, and Nathan Road has become a canyon of   158
light: blazing neon signs, brilliant shop windows, decorations blinking across
the fronts of half-finished tower blocks. I stare at myself a moment in the reflection, three red characters passing across my forehead, and look away. No,
I say. In America. I've lived here only since August.

Ah. Then what is America like?   159

Forgive me, aunt, I say. I forget.   160

Prosperous Garden no. 4. Tung Kun Street. Yau Ma Tei.   161

A scribble of Chinese characters.   162

Show this to doorman he let you in.   163

The building is on the far edge of Kowloon, next to the reclamation; a   164
low concrete barrier separates it from an elevated highway that thunders
continuously as cars pass. Four identical towers around a courtyard, long
poles draped with laundry jutting from every window, like spears hung with
old rotted flags.

Gong hei fat choi, I say to the doorman through the gate, and he smiles with   165
crooked teeth, but when I pass the note to him all expression leaves his face;
he presses the buzzer and turns away quickly. Twenty-three A-ah, he calls
out to the opposite wall. You understand?

Thank you.   166

When I step out into the hallway I breathe in boiled chicken, oyster sauce,   167
frying oil, the acrid steam of medicine, dried fish, Dettol. Two young boys
are crouched at the far end, sending a radio-controlled car zipping past me;
someone is arguing loudly over the telephone; a stereo plays loud Canto-pop
from a balcony somewhere below. All the apartment doors are open, I notice, walking by, and only the heavy sliding gates in front of them are closed.
Like a honeycomb, I can't help thinking, or an ant farm. But when I reach
23A the door behind the gate is shut, and no sound comes from behind it.
The bell rings several times before the locks begin to snap open.

You are early, Alice says, rubbing her eyes, as if she's been sleeping. Behind   168
her the apartment is dark; there is only a faint blue glow, as if from a TV
screen.

I'm sorry. You didn't say when to come. I look at my watch: eight-thirty.   169
I can come back, I say, another time, maybe another night—

She shakes her head and opens the gate.   170

When she turns on the light I draw a deep breath, involuntarily, and hide   171
it with a cough. The walls are covered with stacks of yellowed paper, file
boxes, brown envelopes, and ragged books; on opposite sides of the room are
two desks, each holding a computer with a flickering screen. I peer at the one
closest to the door. At the top of the screen there is a rotating globe and,
below it, a ribbon of letters and numbers, always changing. The other, I see,
is just the same: a head staring at its twin.

Come, Alice says. She has disappeared for a moment and re-emerged   172
dressed in a long dress, silver running shoes, a hooded sweatshirt.

Are these yours?   173

No. My father's.   174

Why does he need two? They're just the same.   175

Nysee, she says impatiently, pointing. Footsie. New York Stock Exchange.   176
London Stock Exchange.

Sau Yee, a hoarse voice calls from another room. Who is it?   177

It's my English teacher, she says loudly. Giving me a homework assignment.   178

Gwailo a?   179

Yes, she says. The white one.   180

Then call a taxi for him. He appears in the kitchen doorway: a stooped   181
old man, perhaps' five feet tall, in a dirty white T-shirt, shorts, and sandals. His
face is covered with liver spots, his eyes shrunken into their sockets. I sorry-
ah, he says to me. No speakee English.

It's all right, I say. There is a numbness growing behind my eyes: I want to   182
speak to him, but the words are all jumbled, and Alice's eyes burning on my
neck. Goodbye, I say, take care.

See later-ah.   183

Alice pulls the hood over her head and opens the door.   184

She leads me to the top of a dark stairwell, in front of a rusting door with   185
light pouring through its cracks. *Tin paang,* she says, reading the characters
stenciled on it in white. Roof. She hands me a black headband, identical to
her own.

Hold on, I say, gripping the railing with both hands. The numbness be-   186
hind my eyes is still there, and I feel my knees growing weak, as if there were
no building below me, only a framework of girders and air. Can you answer
me a question?

Maybe one.   187

Has he always been like that?   188

What like?   189

With the computers, I say. Does he do that all the time?   190

Always. Never turn them off.   191

In the darkness I can barely see her face: only the eyes, shining, daring me to   192
speak. *If I were in your place,* I say to myself, and the phrase dissolves, weightless.

Listen, I say. I'm not sure I'm ready.   193

She laughs. When you be sure?   194

Her fingers fall across my face, and I feel the elastic brushing over my   195
hair, and then the world is black: I open my eyes and close them, no difference.

We just go for a little walk, she says. You don't worry. Only listen.   196

I never realized, before, the weight of the air: at every step I feel the great   197
mass of it pressing against my face, saddled on my shoulders. I am breathing
huge quantities, as if my lungs were a giant recirculation machine, and sweat
is running down from my forehead and soaking the edge of the headband.
Alice takes normal-sized steps and grips my hand fiercely, so I can't let go.
Don't be afraid, she shouts. We still in the middle. Not near the edge.

What am I supposed to do?   198

Nothing, she says. Only wait. Maybe you see something.   199

I stare fiercely into blackness, into my own eyelids. There is the afterglow   200
of the hallway light, and the computer screens, very faint; or am I imagining it? What is there on a roof? I wonder, and try to picture it: television an-
tennas, heating ducts, clotheslines. Are there guardrails? I've never seen any
on a Hong Kong building. She turns, and I brush something metal with my
hand. Do you know where you're going? I shout.

Here, she says, and stops. I stumble into her, and she catches my shoulder.   201
Careful, she says. We wait here.

Wait for what?   202

Just listen, she says. I tell to you. Look to left side: there's a big building 203
there. Very tall white building, higher than us. Small windows.

All right. I can see that.   204

Right side is highway. Very bright. Many cars and trucks passing.   205

If I strain to listen I can hear a steady whooshing sound, and then the   206
high whine of a motorcycle, like a mosquito passing my ear. Okay, I say. Got
that.

In the middle is very dark. Small buildings. Only few lights on.   207

Not enough, I say.   208

One window close to us, she says. Two little children there. You see them?   209

No.   210

Lift your arm, she says, and I do. Put your hand up. See? They wave to you.   211

My God, I say. How do you do that?   212

She squeezes my hand.   213

You promise me something.   214

Of course. What is it?   215

You don't take it off, she says. No matter nothing. You promise me?   216

I do. I promise.   217

She lets go of my hand, and I hear running steps, soles skidding on   218
concrete.

Alice! I shout, rooted to the spot; I crouch down, and balance myself with   219
my hands. Alice! You don't—

Mama, she screams, ten feet away, and the sound carries, echoes; I can see   220
it slanting with the wind, bright as daylight, as if a roman candle had exploded
in my face. *Mama mama mama mama mama mama mama,* she sings, and I am
crawling toward her on hands and knees, feeling in front of me for the edge.

She is there, Alice shouts. You see? She is in the air.   221

I see her. Stay where you are.   222

You watch, she says. I follow her.   223

She doesn't want you, I shout. She doesn't want you there. Let her go.   224

There is a long silence, and I stay where I am, the damp concrete soak-   225
ing through to my knees. My ears are ringing, and the numbness has blos-
somed through my head; I feel faintly seasick.

Alice?   226

You can stand up, she says in a small voice, and I do.   227

You are shaking, she says. She puts her arms around me from behind and   228
clasps my chest, pressing her head against my back. I thank you, she says.

She unties the headband.   229

6 February   230
Man waves white hands at black sky
He says arent you happy be alive
arent you
He kneels and kisses floor

BILLY COLLINS   (1941–   )

Books

From the heart of this dark, evacuated campus   1
I can hear the library humming in the night,
a choir of authors murmuring inside their books
along the unlit, alphabetical shelves,
Giovanni Pontano next to Pope, Dumas next to his son,   5
each one stitched into his own private coat,
together forming a low, gigantic chord of language.

I picture a figure in the act of reading,
shoes on a desk, head tilted into the wind of a book,
a man in two worlds, holding the rope of his tie   10
as the suicide of lovers saturates a page,
or lighting a cigarette in the middle of a theorem.
He moves from paragraph to paragraph
as if touring a house of endless, paneled rooms.

I hear the voice of my mother reading to me   15
from a chair facing the bed, books about horses and dogs,
and inside her voice lie other distant sounds,
the horrors of a stable ablaze in the night,
a bark that is moving toward the brink of speech.

I watch myself building bookshelves in college,   20
walls within walls, as rain soaks New England,
or standing in a bookstore in a trench coat.

I see all of us reading ourselves away from ourselves,

straining in circles of light to find more light
until the line of words becomes a trail of crumbs   25
that we follow across a page of fresh snow;

when evening is shadowing the forest
and small birds flutter down to consume the crumbs,
we have to listen hard to hear the voices
of the boy and his sister receding into the woods.   30

ROBERT FRANCIS   (1901–1987)

Catch

Two boys uncoached are tossing a poem together,   1
Overhand, underhand, backhand, sleight of hand, every hand,
Teasing with attitudes, latitudes, interludes, altitudes,
High, make him fly off the ground for it, low, make him stoop,
Make him scoop it up, make him as-almost-as-possible miss it,   5
Fast, let him sting from it, now, now, fool him slowly,
Anything, everything tricky, risky, nonchalant,
Anything under the sun to outwit the prosy,
Over the tree and the long sweet cadence down,
Over his head, make him scramble to pick up the meaning,   10
And now, like a posy, a pretty one plump in his hands.

Glass

Words of a poem should be glass   1
But glass so simple-subtle its shape
Is nothing but the shape of what it holds.

A glass spun for itself is empty,
Brittle, at best Venetian trinket.   5
Embossed glass hides the poem or its absence.

Words should be looked through, should be windows.
The best words were invisible.
The poem is the thing the poet thinks.

If the possible were not,   10
And if the glass, only the glass,
Could be removed, the poem would remain.

NEENA BEBER   (1964–   )

Misreadings

(Lights up on SIMONE.)   1

SIMONE. It's important to dress right. I want to look slick. To look sleek.   2
To look like a fresh thing. I've got a message. I'm the message. Study me, baby,
because in ten minutes, I'm outta here.

(SIMONE lights a cigarette. Lights up on RUTH. A stack of blue exam composi-   3
tion books on her desk.)

RUTH. What are the issues for which you would kill? I like to ask my   4
students this on their first day of class. I assign novels where the hero or
heroine kills, or is killed. I try to bring it home. They tell me they would kill
to defend their family. They'd kill to defend their friends. I ask them if they
would kill for their country . . . for their freedom . . . what would it take?

SIMONE. I'd kill for a pair of Prada velvet platforms in deep plum. *Those*   5
are to die for.

RUTH. Simone. I didn't know what she was doing in my class. Neither   6
did she, apparently. (*To SIMONE.*) Nice segue, Simone; would we be willing to die for the same things we'd kill for? (*Out.*) She usually sat in the
back, rarely spoke, wore too much lipstick and some costume straight out of,
what, *Vogue.* When she did speak, it was always—disruptive.

SIMONE. I'd die for love except there ain't no Romeos, not that I've seen;   7
I'd take a bullet for my daddy but he's already dead; I'd die of boredom if it
were lethal, but I guess it isn't.

RUTH. If I couldn't inspire her, I wanted her gone. I'd asked her to come   8
to my office hours. I asked her several times. She was failing, obviously. I
would have let her drop the class, but it was too late for that. She never bothered to come see me. Not until the day before the final exam. She wanted
me to give her a passing grade. (*RUTH turns to SIMONE.*) How can I do
that, Simone? You haven't even read the material. Have you read any of the
material?

SIMONE. I don't find it relevant.   9

RUTH. If you haven't read it, how do you know? You may find yourself   10
surprised. *Anna Karenina* is wonderful.

SIMONE. It's long.   11

RUTH. Why not give it a shot?   12

SIMONE. The books you assign are depressing. I don't want to be de-   13
pressed. Why read stuff that brings you down? Kafka, Jesus Christ—I started
it, okay? The guy was f★★★ up.

RUTH. So you were moved at least.   14

SIMONE. Moved to shut the book and find something more interesting   15
to do.

RUTH. That's too bad; you might have found one of these books get-   16
ting under your skin, if you stuck with it. Haven't you ever read something
that's really moved you?

SIMONE. Nothing moves me, Dr. Ruth.   17

RUTH. I'm going to have to ask you to put out that cigarette.   18

SIMONE. Okay, ask. (*But she puts it out.*) See art or be art. I choose the   19
latter.

RUTH. Somebody must be paying for this education of yours. I imag- 20
ine they expect a certain return for their money.

SIMONE. How do you know I'm not the one paying for it?   21

RUTH. I don't believe someone who was spending their own money   22
would waste it so flagrantly.

SIMONE. Okay, Dad chips in.   23

RUTH. Would that be the same father you said was dead?   24

SIMONE. That was a joke or a lie, take your pick.   25

RUTH. You're frustrating the hell out of me, Simone.   26

SIMONE. I don't consider it a waste, you know. I like the socialization 27
part.

RUTH. If you fail out of this school, you won't be doing any more "so- 28
cialization."

SIMONE. You assume that I'm failing the others.   29

RUTH. So it's just this class, then? That you have a problem with?   30

SIMONE. (*Referring to her grammar.*) Dangling. (*Beat.*) Do you enjoy being 31
a teacher?

RUTH. Yes, I do.   32

SIMONE. So I'm paying for your enjoyment.   33

RUTH. It's not a sin to enjoy one's work, Simone.   34

SIMONE. I just don't think you should charge me, if it's more for your 35
pleasure than for mine.

RUTH. I didn't say that.   36

SIMONE. Did you ever want to teach at a real school, not some second- 37
rate institution like this?

RUTH. I like my job. You're not going to convince me otherwise.   38

SIMONE. Four-thousand two-hundred and ninety-eight.   39

RUTH. That is—?   40

SIMONE. Dollars. That's a lot of money. Do you think you're worth it? 41
Do you think *this class* is *worth* it? Because I figured it out: this is a four credit
class, I broke it down. Four-thousand two-hundred and ninety-eight. Big

ones. Well, do you think that what you have to teach me is worth that? Come on, start talking and we'll amortize for each word.

RUTH. You're clearly a bright girl. You can't expect an education to be broken down into monetary terms.   42

SIMONE. You just did. That's a lot of money, right? It's, like, food for a starving family in a fifth-world country for a year at least. It's a car. Well, a used one, anyway. Minus the insurance. Suddenly this number doesn't sound so huge. It's a couple of Armani suits at most. I don't even like Armani. So hey, come on, can't you even say "Yes, Simone, I am worth two Armani suits. I have that to offer you . . ."   43

RUTH. I can't say that, no.   44

SIMONE. No useful skills to be had here.   45

RUTH. The money doesn't go into my pocket, by the way.   46

SIMONE. I think it should. It would be more direct that way; you'd feel more of a responsibility. To me. Personally. Don't you think, Dr. Ruth?   47

RUTH. I'd prefer that you not call me that.   48

SIMONE. Wrong kind of doctor, man. All you're interested in is a bunch of books written a hundred years ago, and the books written about those books; you're probably writing a book about a book written about a book right now, am I right?   49

RUTH. If you don't see the connection between books and life, you aren't reading very well. I want you to try. Can you do that? Books might even show you a way to live.   50

SIMONE. I'm already living, Dr. Ruth. Are you? Because it looks like you haven't changed your hair style in twenty-five years.   51

RUTH. You weren't even born then, Simone.   52

SIMONE. Stuck in your best year? Because I see you in a close-cropped, spiky thing.   53

RUTH. That's enough.   54

SIMONE. P.S.: You might want to do something about the way you dress.   55

RUTH. Have you been in therapy?   56

SIMONE. Don't think that's an original suggestion.   57

RUTH. I'm not suggesting anything. I simply want to point out that this is not therapy. I am a teacher, not your therapist. You can't just waltz into my office and say whatever hateful thing you please.   58

SIMONE. I don't know how to waltz.   59

RUTH. I'm giving up here, Simone. You don't like my class, you don't like me, you want to fail out, I can't stop you. (*RUTH goes back to her work. SIMONE doesn't budge.*) What?   60

SIMONE. Drew Barrymore would move me.   61

RUTH. Who?   62

SIMONE. I think Drew would do it. Getting to meet Drew.   63

RUTH. Who is Drew Barrymore?   64

SIMONE. Damn, you really should know these things. She's extremely   65
famous. She's been famous since she was, like, born. I saw her on TV yesterday and she was so real. She connected. You know? You really might relate
to your students better if you got a little more up to date.

RUTH. You might be right. But you might not be so behind in class if   66
you spent a little less time watching television.

SIMONE. Drew is a *film* star, she's in *films*.   67

RUTH. You said you saw her on television.   68

SIMONE. Don't you even go to the movies? Probably only the ones that   69
are totally L-Seven. And I know you don't know what that means. (*She makes
an "L" and a "7" with her fingers.*) Square? Anyway, Drew was on TV because
she was being interviewed. They have these daytime talk shows nowadays?

RUTH. I've heard of them.   70

SIMONE. And this chick was in the audience and she started to cry. Be- 71
cause she couldn't believe she was there in the same room with Drew, who's
been famous forever, right? She was just, like, sitting there sobbing. And this
chick, she had her bleached blond hair pasted down real flat, and she was
wearing a rhinestone barrette just like Drew used to, but that whole look is
so old Drew, so ten-minutes-ago Drew. The new Drew is sleek and sophisticated and coiffed and this girl, this girl who wanted to be Drew so bad, she
wasn't even *current*.

RUTH. I don't think we're getting anywhere.   72

SIMONE. And that is so sad. Because the thing about Drew is, she's al- 73
ways changing. It's a constant thing with her, the change. And that is, like, what
you've got to do . . . keep moving or you die. Drew knows that. How to invent yourself again and again so you can keep being someone that you like,
the someone that you want to be. And once you're it, you've got to move
on. Now where was it you were hoping we'd get to?

RUTH. The exam is tomorrow morning at 9 AM. If you read the mate-   74
rial, any of the material, I might actually be able to give you a passing grade.
But right now I don't think we need to waste any more of each other's time.

SIMONE. (*Starts to go.*) You might have said that I go to the movies the 75
way you read books. I would have pointed that out, Dr. Ruth.

RUTH. Well, I suspect we don't think very much alike.   76

(*SIMONE turns back.*)   77

SIMONE. A wall between our souls? (*RUTH looks at her, about to say*   78
something, about to reach out.) I'm sorry if I've been rude. I'm sure a lot of
people like your class. Maybe I wasn't raised well. I'm sure somebody's to
blame.

(*SIMONE goes.*)   79

RUTH. The next day she showed up at nine on the dot. I felt a certain   80
pride that I had somehow managed to reach her, that she was finally going
to make a real effort, but she handed in her blue book after a matter of minutes. I was rather disgusted and let it sit there, until a pile formed on top of
it, a pile of blue books filled with the scrawling, down-to-the-last-second
pages of my other more eager, or at least more dutiful, students. Later I began
to read them straight through from the top, in the order they were stacked
in. I wasn't looking forward to Simone's.

In answering my essay question about how the novel *Anna Karenina* moves   81
inevitably toward Anna's final tragic act, my students were, for the most part,
thorough and precise. They cited all of the events that led to Anna's throwing herself in front of the train, touching on the many parallel plots and the
broader social context. I was satisfied. I felt I had taught well this last semester. My students had learned.

In the blue book she had written, "All happy people resemble one another,   82
but each unhappy person is unhappy in their own way." So I guess she had
read *Anna K;* the opening sentence, at least. My first instinct was to correct
the grammar of her little variation. There was nothing else on the page. I
flipped through the book; she'd written one more line on the last page: "Any
world that I'm welcome to is better than the one that I come from." I'm told
it's a rock lyric. Something from the seventies. Anna was written in the seventies, too, funnily enough, a century earlier.

I would have given Simone an F, but I noticed she had already marked   83
down the failing grade herself, on the back of the book. Or maybe the grade
was for me.

By the time I came to it, days had passed. I didn't leap to conclusions.   84
Come to think of it, Anna's suicide always takes me by surprise as well,
though I've read the novel many times and can map its inexorable progression.

(SIMONE, just as before . . .)   85

SIMONE. That's a lot of money. Do you think you're worth it? Do you   86
think *this class* is *worth* it?

(RUTH turns to her.)   87

RUTH. I live in worlds made by words. Worlds where the dead can speak,   88
and conversations can be replayed, altered past the moment of regret, held
over and over until they are bent into new possibilities.

(RUTH tries to reach out . . .)   89

SIMONE. Do you think I'm worth it? Am I? Am I? Am I?   90

RUTH. I live there, where death is as impermanent as an anesthesia, and   91
the moment of obliteration is only . . . a black-out.

(SIMONE lights a cigarette as lights black out.)   92

SIMONE. Ten minutes, time's up—told you I'd be gone by now, baby.   93

(The flame illuminates her for a moment, darkness again.)   94

THE END   95

Chapter Writing Assignments

Practicing Thinking, Reading, and Writing

1. In her essay, Rita Mae Brown claims, "Reading is an active moral and intellectual exchange." In what way is reading an "exchange." How does this notion make reading more interesting and worthwhile? Write an essay in which you explain how to engage in different types of reading material that a college student encounters. Anticipate questions that another student might ask.

2. Think about the details of your own writing process, and list all the activities, routines, rituals, and crises you go through to produce a good piece of writing. Then write a humorous essay that makes fun of your own writing process. Through satire, guide students to an understanding of the features of a good, functional writing process.

3. Discuss in an essay the differences between fiction, such as short stories and novels, and non-fiction, such as informational essays and excerpts from your college textbooks. How is each kind of reading important for a college student? What can we learn from each genre?

Exploring Ideas

4. In what ways do you believe television, video games, movies, computers, and other technology have affected reading? In an essay written to other college students, identify the ways technology has improved and/or decreased the reading skills of a particular group of people (for example, college students, children, people on the job).

5. If thought is at least partly language-based, how does our ability to use language influence our ability to think? Can we have a thought that we have no language to express? Write an essay that explores the effect language skills have on our ability to think.

6. Choose a word that has changed over a period of time. Think about what it meant originally and the connotations or meanings it has acquired over time. How do changes in our words reflect changes in our thinking? Write an essay that explores the way changes in language reflect changes in thought, using the initial word you chose as an example.

GLOSSARY
OF USEFUL TERMS

Numbers in parentheses indicate pages in the text where the term is defined and/or examples are given. Italicized terms within definitions are also defined in this glossary.

Abstract (141–142) nouns, such as *truth* or *beauty,* are words that are neither specific nor definite in meaning; they refer to general concepts, qualities, and conditions that summarize an entire category of experience. Conversely, *concrete* terms, such as *apple, crabgrass, computer,* and *French horn,* make precise appeals to our senses. The word *abstract* refers to the logical process of abstraction, through which our minds are able to group together and describe similar objects, ideas, or attitudes. Most good writers use *abstract* terms sparingly in their *essays,* preferring instead the vividness and clarity of *concrete* words and phrases.

Allusion is a reference to a well-known person, place, or event from life or literature. In "Summer Rituals," for example, Ray Bradbury alludes to Herman Melville's great novel *Moby Dick* when he describes an old man who walks on his front porch "like Ahab surveying the mild day" (46).

Analogy (300) is an extended *comparison* of two dissimilar objects or ideas.

Analysis (2–3, 14, 15, 188–189, 545–546) is examining and evaluating a topic by separating it into its basic parts and elements and studying it systematically.

Anecdote (91) is a brief account of a single incident.

Argumentation (446–461) is an appeal predominantly to *logic* and reason. It deals with complex issues that can be debated.

Attitude (95, 97) describes the narrator's personal feelings about a particular subject. In "Dorothy, It's Really Oz," Stephen Jay Gould shows his deep contempt for the expression of creationist views in a science classroom.

Audience (23, 32, 37–39, 194–195, 450–451, 453–456) refers to the person or group of people for whom an *essay* is written.

Cause and effect (398–410) is a form of *analysis* that examines the causes and consequences of events and ideas.

Characterization (98) is the creation of imaginary yet realistic persons in fiction, drama, and *narrative* poetry.

643

Chronological order (23, 93, 97, 147, 194) is a sequence of events arranged in the order in which they occurred. Brent Staples follows this natural time sequence in his *example* essay entitled "A Brother's Murder."

Classification (245–255) is the analytical process of grouping together similar subjects into a single category or class; *division* works in the opposite fashion, breaking down a subject into many different subgroups. In "The Truth About Lying," Judith Viorst classifies lies into several distinct categories.

Clichés are words or expressions that have lost their freshness and originality through continual use. For example, "busy as a bee," "pretty as a picture," and "hotter than hell" have become trite and dull because of overuse. Good writers avoid clichés through vivid and original phrasing.

Climactic order (147) refers to the *organization* of ideas from one extreme to another—for example, from least important to most important, from most destructive to least destructive, or from least promising to most promising.

Cognitive skills (2–4) are mental abilities that help us send and receive verbal messages.

Coherence (147) is the manner in which an essay "holds together" its main ideas. A coherent *theme* will demonstrate such a clear relationship between its *thesis* and its logical structure that readers can easily follow the argument.

Comparison (299–311) is an *expository* writing technique that examines the similarities between objects or ideas, whereas *contrast* focuses on differences.

Conclusions (30, 454) bring *essays* to a natural close by summarizing the argument, restating the *thesis,* calling for some specific action, or explaining the significance of the topic just discussed. If the *introduction* states your thesis in the form of a question to be answered or a problem to be solved, then your *conclusion* will be the final "answer" or "solution" provided in your paper. The *conclusion* should be approximately the same length as your *introduction* and should leave your reader satisfied that you have actually "concluded" your discussion rather than simply run out of ideas to discuss.

Concrete: See *abstract.*

Conflict is the struggle resulting from the opposition of two strong forces in the plot of a play, novel, or short story.

Connotation and Denotation (456) are two principal methods of describing the meanings of words. *Connotation* refers to the wide array of positive and negative associations that most words naturally carry with them, whereas *denotation* is the precise, literal *definition* of a word that might be found in a dictionary. See, for example, Amy Tan's description of the terms "broken" or "fractured" English in "Mother Tongue" (173).

Content and Form (25–26, 30) are the two main components of an *essay*. *Content* refers to the subject matter of an *essay*, whereas its *form* consists of the graphic symbols that communicate the subject matter (word choice, spelling, punctuation, paragraphing, etc.).

Contrast: See *comparison*.

Deduction (454) is a form of logical reasoning that begins with a *general* assertion and then presents specific details and *examples* in support of that *generalization*. *Induction* works in reverse by offering a number of *examples* and then concluding with a *general* truth or principle.

Definition (354–364) is a process whereby the meaning of a term is explained. Formal *definitions* require two distinct operations: (1) finding the *general* class to which the object belongs and (2) isolating the object within that class by describing how it differs from other elements in the same category. In "Grandma," for example, Erma Bombeck defines grandmothers as their grandchildren's mothers' mothers (366), and in "Beliefs About Families," Mary Pipher defines a family as "a collection of people who pool resources and help each other over the long haul" (378).

Denotation: See *connotation*.

Description (31–44) is a mode of writing or speaking that relates the sights, sounds, tastes, smells, or feelings of a particular experience to its readers or listeners. Good descriptive writers, such as those featured in Chapter 1, are particularly adept at receiving, selecting, and expressing sensory details from the world around them. Along with *persuasion, exposition,* and *narration, description* is one of the four dominant types of writing.

Development (23–25) concerns the manner in which a *paragraph* of an essay expands on its topic.

Dialect is a speech pattern typical of a certain regional location, race, or social group that exhibits itself through unique word choice, pronunciation, and/or grammatical *usage*. See John McPhee's "The Pines," in which Fred and Bill, two residents of a wilderness area in southern New Jersey, speak in a discernible *dialect*.

Dialogue is a conversation between two or more people, particularly within a novel, play, poem, short story, or other literary work.

Diction (23, 456) is word choice. If a vocabulary is a list of words available for use, then good *diction* is the careful selection of those words to communicate a particular subject to a specific *audience*. Different types of *diction* include *formal* (scholarly books and articles), *informal* (essays in popular magazines), *colloquial* (conversations between friends, including newly coined words and expressions), *slang* (language shared by certain social groups), *dialect* (language typical of a certain region, race, or social group), *technical* (words that make up the basic vocabulary of a specific area of study, such as medicine or law), and *obsolete* (words no longer in use).

Division: See *classification*.

Dominant impression (34, 36, 38) in *descriptive* writing is the principal effect the author wishes to create for the *audience*.

Editing (25–26, 30) is an important part of the *rewriting* process of an *essay* that requires writers to make certain their work observes the conventions of standard written English.

Effect: See *cause and effect*.

Emphasis (92, 452) is the stress given to certain words, phrases, sentences, and/or *paragraphs* within an *essay* by such methods as repeating important ideas; positioning thesis and *topic sentences* effectively; supplying additional details or *examples;* allocating more space to certain sections of an *essay;* choosing words carefully; selecting and arranging details judiciously; and using certain mechanical devices, such as italics, underlining, capitalization, and different colors of ink.

Essay is a relatively short prose composition on a limited topic. Most *essays* are five hundred to one thousand words long and focus on a clearly definable question to be answered or problem to be solved. *Formal essays,* such as bell hooks' "Justice: Childhood Love Lesson," are generally characterized by seriousness of *purpose,* logical organization, and dignity of language; *informal essays,* such as Garrison Keillor's "How the Crab Apple Grew," are generally brief, humorous, and more loosely structured. *Essays* in this textbook have been divided into nine traditional *rhetorical* types, each of which is discussed at length in its chapter introduction.

Etymology (359) is the study of the origin and development of words.

Evidence (447, 450, 453–454) is any material used to help support an *argument,* including details, facts, *examples,* opinions, and expert testimony. Just as a lawyer's case is won or lost in a court of law because of the strength of the *evidence* presented, so, too, does the effectiveness of a writer's essay depend on the evidence offered in support of its *thesis statement*.

Example (141–152) is an illustration of a *general* principle or *thesis statement*. Harold Krents's "Darkness at Noon," for instance, gives several different examples of prejudice against handicapped people.

Exposition is one of the four main *rhetorical* categories of writing (the others are *persuasion, narration,* and *description*). The principal purpose of expository prose is to "expose" ideas to your readers, to explain, define, and interpret information through one or more of the following modes of exposition: *example, process analysis, division/classification, comparison/contrast, definition,* and *cause/effect*.

Figurative language (39, 456) is writing or speaking that purposefully departs from the literal meanings of words to achieve a particularly vivid, expressive, and/or imaginative image. When, for example, Scott Russell Sanders in "Homeplace" says that a tornado "peeled off the roof, splintered the garage, and rustled two cows" (319), he is using *figurative language*. Other principal figures of speech include *metaphor, simile, hyperbole, allusion,* and *personification.*

Flashback (97) is a technique used mainly in *narrative* writing that enables the author to present scenes or conversations that took place prior to the beginning of the story.

Focus (21–24) is the concentration of a *topic* on one central point or issue.

Form: See *content.*

Formal essay: See *essay.*

Free association (19) is a process of generating ideas for writing through which one thought leads randomly to another.

General words (141–142) are those that employ expansive categories, such as *animals, sports, occupations,* and *clothing; specific* words are more limiting and restrictive, such as *koala, lacrosse, computer programmer,* and *bow tie.* Whether a word is *general* or *specific* depends at least somewhat on its context: *Bow tie* is more specific than *clothing,* yet less *specific* than "the pink and green striped bow tie Aunt Martha gave me last Christmas." See also *abstract.*

Generalization (141–142, 143, 454–455) is a broad statement or belief based on a limited number of facts, *examples,* or statistics. A product of inductive reasoning, generalizations should be used carefully and sparingly in *essays.*

Hyperbole, the opposite of *understatement,* is a type of *figurative language* that uses deliberate exaggeration for the sake of emphasis or comic effect (e.g., "hungry enough to eat 20 chocolate eclairs").

Hypothesis (403, 546) is a tentative theory that can be proved or disproved through further investigation and analysis.

Idiom refers to a grammatical construction unique to a certain people, region, or class that cannot be translated literally into another language.

Illustration (141–142) is the use of *examples* to support an idea or *generalization.*

Imagery (37–39) is *description* that appeals to one or more of our five senses. See, for example, Malcolm Cowley's description in "The View from 80" of one of the pleasures of old age: "simply sitting still, like a snake on a sun-warmed stone, with a delicious feeling of indolence that was seldom attained in earlier years" (77). Imagery is used to help bring clarity and vividness to descriptive writing.

Induction: See *deduction.*

Inference (454) is a *deduction* or *conclusion* derived from *specific* information.

Informal essay: See *essay.*

Introduction (25) refers to the beginning of an *essay.* It should identify the subject to be discussed, set the limits of that discussion, and clearly state the *thesis* or general *purpose* of the paper. In a brief (five-*paragraph*) *essay,* your *introduction* should be only one *paragraph;* for longer papers, you may want to provide longer introductory sections. A good *introduction* will generally catch the audience's attention by beginning with a quotation, a provocative statement, a personal *anecdote,* or a stimulating question that somehow involves its readers in the topic under consideration. See also *conclusion.*

Irony (156) is a figure of speech in which the literal, *denotative* meaning is the opposite of what is stated.

Jargon is the special language of a certain group or profession, such as psychological *jargon,* legal *jargon,* or medical *jargon.* When *jargon* is excerpted from its proper subject area, it generally becomes confusing or humorous, as in "I have a latency problem with my backhand" or "I hope we can interface tomorrow night after the dance."

Levels of thought (1–2) is a phrase that describes the three sequential stages at which people think, read, and write: literal, interpretive, and analytical.

Logic (447, 454) is the science of correct reasoning. Based principally on *inductive* or *deductive* processes, *logic* establishes a method by which we can examine *premises* and *conclusions,* construct *syllogisms,* and avoid faulty reasoning.

Logical fallacy (399–401, 454–455) is an incorrect conclusion derived from faulty reasoning. See also *post hoc, ergo propter hoc,* and *non sequitur.*

Metaphor (39, 456) is an implied *comparison* that brings together two dissimilar objects, persons, or ideas. Unlike a *simile,* which uses the words *like* or *as,* a *metaphor* directly identifies an obscure or difficult subject with another that is easier to understand. For example, when Ray Bradbury describes a piano as "yellow-toothed" (46), he is using a metaphor to explain how the piano keys are like stained human teeth.

Mood (97, 456) refers to the atmosphere or *tone* created in a piece of writing. The mood of Jessica Mitford's "Behind the Formaldehyde Curtain" is sarcastic and derisive, and of Mary Roach's "Meet the Bickersons," good-humored and sensible.

Narration (91–103) is storytelling: the recounting of a series of events, arranged in a particular order and delivered by a narrator to a specific *audience* with a clear *purpose* in mind. Along with *persuasion, exposition,* and *description,* it is one of the four principal types of writing.

Non sequitur from a Latin phrase meaning "it does not follow," refers to a *conclusion* that does not logically derive from its *premises.*

Objective (32, 36) writing is detached, impersonal, and factual; *subjective* writing reveals the author's personal feelings and attitudes. Judith Wallerstein and Sandra Blakeslee's "Second Chances for Children of Divorce" is an *example* of *objective* prose, whereas Amy Tan's "Mother Tongue" is essentially *subjective* in nature. Most good college-level *essays* are a careful mix of both approaches, with lab reports and technical writing toward the *objective* end of the scale and personal *essays* in composition courses at the *subjective* end.

Organization (23, 25–26, 91, 97–98, 146–148, 194–195, 453–454, 456–457) refers to the order in which a writer chooses to present his or her ideas to the reader. Five main types of *organization* may be used to develop *paragraphs* or *essays:* (1) *deductive* (moving from general to specific), (2) *inductive* (from specific to general), (3) *chronological* (according to time sequence), (4) *spatial* (according to physical relationship in space), and (5) *climactic* (from one extreme to another, such as least important to most important).

Paradox is a seemingly self-contradictory statement that contains an element of truth. In "The View from 80," Malcolm Cowley paradoxically declares that the Ojibwa Indians were "kind to their old people" by killing them when they became decrepit (72).

Paragraphs are groups of interrelated sentences that develop a central topic. Generally governed by a *topic sentence,* a *paragraph* has its own *unity* and *coherence* and is an integral part of the logical *development* of an *essay.*

Parallelism is a structural arrangement within sentences, *paragraphs,* or entire *essays* through which two or more separate elements are similarly phrased and developed. Look, for example, at the following sentences from Sherman Alexie's "The Joy of Reading and Writing: Superman and Me": "I began to think of everything in terms of paragraphs. Our reservation was a small paragraph within the United States. My family's house was a paragraph, distinct from the other paragraphs of the LeBrets to the north, the Fords to our south, and the Tribal School to the west. Inside our house, each family member existed as a separate paragraph but still had genetics and common experiences to link us" (424–425).

Paraphrase (549) is a restatement in your own words of someone else's ideas or observations.

Parody is making fun of a person, an event, or a work of literature through exaggerated imitation.

Person (38–39, 97) is a grammatical distinction identifying the speaker or writer in a particular context: first person (I or we), second person (you), and third person (he, she, it, or they). The *person* of an *essay* refers to the voice of the narrator. See also *point of view.*

Personification is *figurative language* that ascribes human characteristics to an abstraction, animal, idea, or inanimate object. Consider, for example, Robert Ramirez's description in "The Barrio" of the bakery that "sends its sweet messenger aroma down the dimly lit street, announcing the arrival of fresh, hot, sugary *pan dulce*" (372).

Persuasion (446–461) is one of the four chief forms of *rhetoric.* Its main purpose is to convince a reader (or listener) to think, act, or feel a certain way. It involves appealing to reason, to emotion, and/or to a sense of ethics. The other three main *rhetorical* categories are *exposition, narration,* and *description.*

Point of view (38–39, 97) is the perspective from which a writer tells a story, including *person, vantage point,* and *attitude.* Principal *narrative* voices are first-person, in which the writer relates the story from his or her own vantage point "I've often wondered if I would have been a different person had I not been physically handicapped" (349) from "You're Short, Besides!" (by Sucheng Chan); omniscient, a third-person technique in which the narrator knows everything and can even see into the minds of the various characters; and concealed, a third-person method in which the narrator can see and hear events but cannot look into the minds of the other characters.

Post hoc, ergo propter hoc (400), a Latin phrase meaning "after this, therefore because of this," is a *logical fallacy* confusing *cause and effect* with *chronology.* Just because Cheryl wakes up every morning before the sun rises doesn't mean that the sun rises *because* Cheryl wakes up.

Premise (454) is a proposition or statement that forms the foundation of an *argument* and helps support a *conclusion.* See also *logic* and *syllogism.*

Prereading (4–8, 29) is thoughtful concentration on a topic before reading an *essay.* Just as athletes warm up their physical muscles before competition, so, too, should students activate their "mental muscles" before reading or writing *essays.*

Prewriting (18–24, 25–26, 30), which is similar to *prereading,* is the initial stage in the composing process during which writers consider their topics, generate ideas, narrow and refine their *thesis statements,* organize their ideas, pursue any necessary research, and identify their *audiences.* Although prewriting occurs principally, as the name suggests, "before" an essay is started, writers usually return to this "invention" stage again and again during the course of the writing process.

Process analysis (188–199), one of the seven primary modes of *exposition,* either gives directions about how to do something (directive) or provides information on how something happened (informative).

Proofreading (25–26, 30), an essential part of *rewriting,* is a thorough, careful review of the final draft of an *essay* to ensure that all errors have been eliminated.

Purpose (23, 34–35, 37, 450–451, 456–457) in an *essay* refers to its overall aim or intention: to entertain, inform, or persuade a particular *audience* with reference to a specific topic (to persuade an audience, for example, that violence on television and in video games is psychologically damaging our children in Dave Grossman's "We Are Training Our Kids to Kill"). See also *dominant impression.*

Refutation is the process of discrediting the *arguments* that run counter to your *thesis statement.*

Research paper (545–560) is a library or term paper that integrates *paraphrases, summaries,* and *quotations* from secondary sources with the writer's own insights and conclusions. Such *essays* normally include bibliographic references within the paper and, at the end, a list of the books and articles cited.

Revision (25–26, 30), meaning "to see again," takes place during the entire writing process as you change words, rewrite sentences, and shift *paragraphs* from one location to another in your *essay.* It plays an especially vital role in the *rewriting* stage of the composing process.

Rewriting (25–26, 30) is a stage of the composing process that includes *revision, editing,* and *proofreading.*

Rhetoric is the art of using language effectively.

Rhetorical questions are intended to provoke thought rather than bring forth an answer. See, for example, Jay Weiner's opening rhetorical question in "Sports Centered": "How far back must we go to remember that sports matter?" (219).

Rhetorical strategy or mode is the plan or method whereby an *essay* is organized. Most writers choose from methods discussed in this book, such as *narration, example, comparison/contrast, definition,* and *cause/effect.*

Sarcasm is a form of *irony* that attacks a person or belief through harsh and bitter remarks that often mean the opposite of what they say. See, for example, Jessica Mitford's sarcastic praise of the funeral director in "Behind the Formaldehyde Curtain": "He has relieved the family of every detail, he has revamped the corpse to look like a living doll, he has arranged for it to nap for a few days in a slumber room, he has put on a well-oiled performance in which the concept of *death* has played no part whatsoever. . . . He has done everything in his power to make the funeral a real pleasure for everybody concerned" (215). See also *satire.*

Satire is a literary technique that attacks foolishness by making fun of it. Most good satires work through a "fiction" that is clearly transparent. Bill Cosby, for example, feigns amazement that anyone would ever want to have children in "The Baffling Question," yet he clearly loves kids and believes the opposite.

Setting refers to the immediate environment of a *narrative* or *descriptive* piece of writing: the place, time, and background established by the author.

Simile (39, 456) is a *comparison* between two dissimilar objects that uses the words *like* or *as*. See, for example, Ray Bradbury's description of the women in "Summer Rituals," who appear "like ghosts hovering momentarily behind the door screen" (49). See also *metaphor.*

Slang is casual conversation among friends; as such, it is inappropriate for use in formal and informal writing, unless it is placed in quotation marks and introduced for a specific rhetorical purpose: "Hey dude, what's up?"

Spatial order (92, 147) is a method of *description* that begins at one geographical point and moves onward in an orderly fashion. See, for example, the opening of John McPhee's "The Pines," which first describes the front yard of Fred Brown's house, then moves through the vestibule and into the kitchen, and finally settles on Fred himself, who is seated behind a porcelain-topped table in a room just beyond the kitchen (64).

Specific: See *general* words.

Style is the unique, individual way in which each author expresses his or her ideas. Often referred to as the "personality" of an *essay, style* is dependent on a writer's manipulation of *diction,* sentence structure, *figurative language, point of view, characterization, emphasis, mood, purpose, rhetorical strategy,* and all the other variables that govern written material.

Subjective: See *objective.*

Summary (549) is a condensed statement of someone else's thoughts or observations.

Syllogism (454) refers to a three-step *deductive argument* that moves logically from a major and a minor *premise* to a *conclusion.* A traditional example is "All men are mortal. Socrates is a man. Therefore, Socrates is mortal."

Symbol refers to an object or action in literature that metaphorically represents something more important than itself. In Malcolm X's "Learning to Read," books are a symbol of freedom for the imprisoned man.

Synonyms are terms with similar or identical *denotative* meanings, such as *aged, elderly, older person,* and *senior citizen.*

Syntax describes the order in which words are arranged in a sentence and the effect that this arrangement has on the creation of meaning.

Thesis statement or thesis (23) is the principal *focus* of an *essay.* It is usually phrased in the form of a question to be answered, a problem to be solved, or an assertion to be argued. The word *thesis* derives from a Greek term meaning "something set down," and most good writers find that "setting down" their thesis in writing helps them tremendously in defining and clarifying their topic before they begin to write an outline or a rough draft.

Tone (97, 456) is a writer's *attitude* or *point of view* toward his or her subject. See also *mood*.

Topic sentence is the central idea around which a *paragraph* develops. A *topic sentence* controls a *paragraph* in the same way a *thesis statement* unifies and governs an entire essay. See also *induction* and *deduction*.

Transition (97) is the linking together of sequential ideas in sentences, paragraphs, and essays. This linking is accomplished primarily through word repetition, pronouns, parallel constructions, and such transitional words and phrases as *therefore, as a result, consequently, moreover,* and *similarly.*

Understatement, the opposite of *hyperbole,* is a deliberate weakening of the truth for comic or emphatic purpose. Commenting, for example, on the great care funeral directors take to make corpses look lifelike for their funerals, Jessica Mitford explains in "Behind the Formaldehyde Curtain," "This is a rather large order, since few people die in the full bloom of health" (211).

Unity (147) exists in an *essay* when all ideas originate from and help support a central *thesis statement*.

Usage (25–26, 30) refers to the customary rules that govern written and spoken language.

Vantage point (38–39, 97) is the frame of reference of the narrator in a story: close to the action, far from the action, looking back on the past, or reporting on the present. See also *person* and *point of view.*

CREDITS

Index of Authors and Titles